GREAT AMERICAN TRIALS

Highlights

Great American Trials provides an abundance of information on the most significant and celebrated trials in U.S. history, from 1637 to the present. Included are brief and accurate summaries of trials known for their historic or legal significance, political controversy, public attention, legal ingenuity, or literary fame. *Great American Trials* covers a broad scope of trials, including:

- Salem Witchcraft Trials (1692)
- Dred Scott Trial (1856)
- Lizzie Borden Trial (1893)
- Triangle Shirtwaist Fire Trial (1911)
- Leopold and Loeb Trial (1924)
- Teapot Dome Trials (1926)
- Hollywood Ten Trials (1948–50)
- Trial of Julius and Ethel Rosenberg and Morton Sobell (1951)
- Brown v. Board of Education (1954)
- Charles Manson Trial (1970–71)
- Roe v. Wade (1973)
- Ted Bundy Trials (1976 & 1979)
- John Demjanjuk Denaturalization Trial (1981)
- Jim Bakker Trial (1989)
- Mike Tyson Trial (1992)
- O.J. Simpson Trials (1995–1997)
- Bill Clinton Impeachment (1998–99)
- 2000 Presidential Election Trials (2000)
- and many more—378 courtroom cases in all

Each trial begins with the facts—setting up the key players, the charges, and site of the trial, followed by a narrative that explains the circumstances that led to the trial, pre-trial maneuvers, the trial itself, the judgment, appeals (if any), and any subsequent implications of the trial.

Special features:

- Chronological arrangement of trials shows the developmental pattern of law: today's cases apply yesterday's precedents
- Most entries end with suggestions for further reading, enabling the user to easily continue research on a particular trial
- Three tables of contents—chronological, alphabetical, and categorical—provide easy access to any specific trial
- More than 240 subject-specific photographs and drawings
- Glossary defining legal terms
- Comprehensive index lists key figures, subjects, and areas of law

CONTENTS

In Chronological Order (by date of trial)

1800s

1970–1979

1990s

CONTENTS

In Alphabetical Order
(by name of trial)

A

B

C

D

H

I

J

K

L

M

Q

R

S

U

V

W

CONTENTS

In Subject Order (by the crime[s] charged)

Admiralty & Maritime Law

Assassinations & Assassination Attempts

Birth Control

Bribery

Civil Suits

Constitutional Issues

Fraud

Freedom of Speech & Press

Heresy

Libel

Mafia & Organized Crime

Medical

Murder, Manslaughter, & Homicide

Rape & Sex Crimes

Taxes & Tax Evasion

Treason & Sedition

Voting Rights

War Crimes

PREFACE

Great American Trials provides readers and researchers with brief, accurate, and readable summaries of the most significant and celebrated trials in U.S. history.

As with any encyclopedic undertaking, the selection process was a complex one and inevitably involved some subjectivity given space limitations. Since the settlement of Jamestown in 1607, literally millions of civil and criminal trials have been conducted in American courts. Many thousands of these had some historic or legal significance or attracted wide public attention for one reason or another. From these, I have selected the 378 I judged best met the following criteria:

Historic Significance: Did the trial have a major impact on the course of American history? Trials such as *Scott v. Sanford* (the Dred Scott case), which was a fateful step on the road to the Civil War, and the Boston Massacre Trial, which set the stage for the American Revolution, are included under this criterion.

Legal Significance: Did the trial result in an important legal precedent or a landmark Supreme Court decision? Examples of such trials include those of Dr. Sam Sheppard, which established a significant precedent concerning pre-trial publicity, *In Re Baby M,* which affected the validity of surrogate motherhood contracts, and *Gideon v. Wainwright,* which led the Supreme Court to rule that states had to provide free counsel to indigent defendants in criminal trials.

Political Controversy: Did the trial crystallize or generate a national political controversy? Among the trials included under this criterion are the Sacco–Vanzetti murder trial, which was tainted by hostility to radicals and immigrants; the Julius and Ethel Rosenberg treason trial; the trial of the Chicago Seven for instigating disruptive anti-Vietnam War demonstrations; and the Clinton impeachment trial which polarized American political life.

Public Attention: Because of the fame of the participants or the nature of the alleged crime, many trials in our history have been national sensations. The trial of Bruno Hauptmann for kidnapping the Lindbergh baby falls under this category, as do the trials of Daniel Sickles, Lizzie Borden, Harry Thaw, Jean Harris, Patty Hearst, and Charles Manson.

Legal Ingenuity: Some trials earned a place in this book because the courtroom skills demonstrated by one or more of participating lawyers have become legendary. Among the trials included under this criteria are *Martinez v. Del Valle,* the occasion of Joseph Choate's most famous cross-examination; the Leopold and Loeb murder trial, featuring Clarence Darrow for the defense; and the Triangle Shirtwaist Fire trial, where Max Steuer won an acquittal few thought possible.

Literary Fame: Trials have inspired novelists, playwrights, screen-writers, non-fiction writers, and even songwriters. Their works have often left a greater impression on the public than the original trial. Among the trials that have been immortalized in literature are the Chester Gillette murder trial, the Salem Witchcraft trials, Joe Hill's murder trial, the Scopes "Monkey" trial, and the Richard Hickok/Perry Smith murder trial.

In my selection process, I have intentionally applied these criteria more leniently to recent trials than to those from the more distant past. This was done to serve the needs of readers who, I suspect, are far more likely to need or desire information on recent trials.

Because the important decisions of the Supreme Court are adequately covered in a host of other standard reference works, I have intentionally minimized the number of such decisions in ***Great American Trials.*** Only those that resulted from an actual courtroom trial (*Buck v. Bell*), had an impact on the way trials are conducted in this country (the *Miranda* decision), or marked critical turning points in American history (*Roe v. Wade*) have been included.

While another editor might have included some trials that I have not or omitted some that I included, the vast majority of trials would make any editor's list of the most important trials in our history. Several precautions were taken to avoid oversights and omissions. The legal editors of this volume—Lisa Paddock and Stephen Christianson—assisted me in compiling and evaluating the list of trials as did several members of the editorial staff at The Gale Group. Although their assistance has been very helpful, the responsibility for any omissions is mine.

Each entry begins with a set of basic facts about the trial. This is followed by a narrative explaining the circumstances that led to the trial, pre-trial maneuvers, the trial itself, the judgment, and any subsequent appeals. We sought to entertain as well as inform. We have tried to provide the maximum amount of accurate information in the space available.

The extent of sources consulted varies considerably with the trial. Some trials, such as Lizzie Borden's and Sacco and Vanzetti's, have produced shelves of well-researched histories. Others are barely mentioned in secondary sources. Our contributors have dug as deep into the sources as necessary to establish the essential facts of each trial. However, for some 17th-, 18th-, and early 19th-century trials, the surviving records are sparse, failing even to note the full names of judges or lawyers.

All but a few entries end with suggestions for further readings. Contributors were asked to include their suggestions for further reading the most readily and widely available sources of additional information. As the intended audience for this book is general readers rather than legal researchers, we have excluded legal citations.

The trials are presented in chronological order. This was chosen as the most logical sequence for several reasons. First, the law evolves chronologically; today's cases apply yesterday's precedents. Second, many trials are emblematic of a particular historical period and are directly or indirectly connected (the various espionage and anti-Communist trials of the late 1940s and early 1950s, for example.) Third, there is no preferable alternative. Without a generally accepted convention for naming trials, an alphabetical arrangement would be of little benefit to readers. As ***Great American Trials*** contains three tables of contents—chronological, alphabetical, and category—plus a comprehensive index, readers will have little difficulty in locating any specific trial.

In editing this book, I have made a determined effort to translate legalese into plain English. Unfortunately, there are some legal terms that defy translation; the definition is so particular to the law that no plain English equivalent exists and any paraphrase would risk distorting the meaning. Such terms have been defined in the glossary found at the end of the volume.

For the revised edition, we have added 178 new trials and revised 17 trials from the first edition. The revisions were made either because additional information became available—for example, the opening of archives in the former Soviet Union produced new revelations about Alger Hiss and Julius and Ethel Rosenberg—or because there were new developments, such as the release from prison of Jean Harris.

Many people made vital contributions to the planning, writing, editing, and production of ***Great American Trials:***

Chris Nasso of Gale Research provided indispensable support, encouragement, and wise counsel when this book was in its formative stages. Charles A. Bayne and Alan Nichter deserve special recognition for their roles as advisors to the book.

Steve Christianson and Lisa Paddock, the book's legal editors, together scrutinized the manuscript and corrected many misinterpretations of trial procedures and misstatements about the intricacies of the American legal system.

The writers who contributed to ***Great American Trials***—Hendrik Booraem, John S. Bowman, Michael Burgan, Rodney Carlisle, Steven G. Christianson, Kathryn Cullen-DuPont, Teddi DiCanio, Colin Evans, Ronald J. Formica, Elizabeth Gwillim, Ronald Lansing, Buckner F. Melton, Jr., Carol Wilcox Melton, David I. Petts, Bernard Ryan, Jr., Thomas C. Smith, Mark A. Thorburn, William Weir, and B.J. Welborn—were dogged researchers, skilled word smiths, and astonishingly conscientious about meeting their tight deadlines. Larry Hand and Susan Paruch copyedited this book with exceptional skill and diligence.

Susan Brainard helped me manage this project day-in, day-out, over two years with unfailing good humor and care. Jil Nelson Kaplan tracked down the illustrations for the first edition, a task that proved far more difficult than either of us imagined when we began, and Vicki Hanlon developed the picture recommendations for the revised edition.

Finally I owe special thanks to my wife and partner, Elizabeth Frost Knappman, who has tolerated my foibles and helped me over the rough patches for 35 years, and to my daughter, Amanda, who brightens the days.

—Edward W. Knappman
August 2001

INTRODUCTION

Trials have been the ultimate means to resolve disputes in American society from Colonial times to the present. Many of the great turning points in the nation's history have occurred in courtrooms—from John Peter Zenger's trial for allegedly libeling the British governor of Colonial New York through *Roe v. Wade*, which barred states from prohibiting abortions in the early months of pregnancy.

Trials have been a prime source of popular entertainment, public ritual, and real-life human drama. In person and through the news media, Americans have flocked to courtrooms to be titillated, scandalized, uplifted, inspired, educated, and just plain amused. Before the age of mass communications, the local courthouse provided one of the few diversions available to a largely rural population. Indeed, judges, preachers, and editorial writers have so long and frequently denounced the "circus-like" atmosphere prevailing at many locally or nationally celebrated trials that the phrase has become a cliché of courtroom journalism. In more recent times, real and fictional trials have become a staple of movie producers and television programmers. Today, cable television's Court TV network enables trial junkies to perpetually indulge themselves without ever changing the channel.

As compelling as trials may be as drama, they fill a far more serious purpose in our society: they offer a mechanism for maintaining public order when one person, or other legal entity such as a corporation, violates the legally protected rights of another person or society at large. In this sense, a trial fulfills the human need for retribution, providing even the losing side with a sense that he or she at least has had an opportunity to air grievances, or has had his or her "day in court."

Trials, therefore, are the central focus of American jurisprudence. However, the process of resolving disputes through a trial of the facts—litigation—is only one area of legal practice. Only a fraction of those cases filed by litigators ever goes to trial. Indeed, most efforts of the vast majority of lawyers who are not litigators are devoted to avoiding trials by advising clients how to stay on the right side of the law and by drafting legal documents, such as contracts.

Fundamentals of the Law

To appreciate what made many of the trials described in ***Great American Trials*** "great" requires some familiarity with the branches of the law, the history and contours of the American system of jurisprudence, and the rules of procedure and evidence that govern the way trials are conducted. While the editors and contributors have attempted to translate legalese into plain English whenever possible, for some legal terms there is no common word or phrase with an identical meaning. Readers will find a glossary of such terms at the end of this book.

Perhaps the most important factor about a court is that it is a public body. In each case, a court must determine the facts, but in determining their legal significance, the court is performing a service not just to the litigants, but to the larger community as well. In deciding a particular controversy according to the law, courts provide guidance to others who may in the future confront similar issues, thereby ideally forestalling at least some potential litigation.

This evolutionary method of devising so-called judge-made law—as opposed to legislation—is a natural by-product of common-law systems of jurisprudence like ours, in which current cases are decided in accordance with precepts derived from earlier cases. This "common law" is a body of complex rules formulated out of thousands of decisions reached by generations of judges, beginning in England during the Middle Ages. As such, common law predates the creation of legislative bodies, whose primary function is drafting the rules interpreted and applied by modern courts to the cases tried before them.

"Civil law," by contrast, grew out of a written code of Roman laws and today is the system of laws prevailing in Western Europe (except for the United Kingdom, of course), as well as the state of Louisiana. Although today the number of statutes regulating both public, or criminal, law (in which the government has the most direct interest) and private, or civil, law (directly involving the interests of individuals) continues to grow, the common-law system predominates in the rest of our nation.

The Roots of the American Court System

The British judicial system was transplanted wholesale to the American colonies. In 17th-century America, lawmaking and judging were regarded as one and the same. As in England, Parliament was regarded as the highest court. The colonies, however, began to develop their own layered court systems. At the top of the hierarchy stood colonial legislatures, which served primarily as courts of appeals. Beneath them was a network of superior courts, which often included colonial governors among their presiding judges, and which mainly heard appeals in civil matters first tried in lower courts. Superior courts also tried criminal cases. The third level of local courts saw most of the trials in colonial America. These local courts performed governmental functions as well, such as levying and collecting taxes, and provided townspeople with an opportunity to socialize, conduct business, and discuss politics.

A modified version of this three-tier system remains the structure of the various state court systems today. Trials are held in the lowest level of courts; a level of appellate courts reviews all appeals from the trial courts; and a supreme court considers appeals on important issues of law.

As the population of the colonies grew, so did the length of court trial dockets. Courts dealt with increasing demand for their services largely by increasing the formality of their proceedings. When courts began to enforce procedural requirements, fewer cases were filed, and many of those were dismissed. This trend was reversed by the early 18th century with an increase in the number of trained lawyers.

Judges, by contrast, were often appointed lay persons unschooled in the law. This lack of a trained judiciary increased the importance of juries. At the trial of John Peter Zenger for seditious libel (1735), the jury found the defendant not guilty despite the clear import of the judge's instructions to the contrary. This helped establish the principle that juries could exercise considerable discretion in interpreting judicial instructions. Later in the 18th century, however, judges gained the power to order new trials in the face of verdicts that were, in their opinion, contrary to the weight of the evidence. Today, in trials conducted without a jury—so-called bench trials—judges settle questions of both law and fact. In jury trials the roles are apportioned so that jurors decide the facts of the case, while decisions about the law are left to judges.

The use of fictitious litigant names, a common practice by the time of *Roe v. Wade* (1973), first appeared in the late 1680s in a case involving "John Doe" and "Richard Roe." Obscuring the real names of the plaintiff and defendant meant the case would be decided on its specific merits rather than on the influence and connections of the contestants, which was a pattern that had encouraged many plaintiffs to hope that quick, rough justice would be administered in their favor.

The Courts under the Constitution

Article III of the United States Constitution, together with the first Judiciary Act (1789), established three types of federal courts, roughly modeled on the tripartite structure then operating in individual states. The two lower tiers, consisting of trial and appeals courts, are organized along regional lines, with the former vastly outnumbering the latter. District courts were and still are trial courts, each manned by a single district judge. Circuit courts, now federal appellate courts, employed three-judge panels then, as they do now. While circuit courts were then primarily trial courts, today the circuit courts of appeals are devoted to reviews of district court decisions. The Supreme Court was then mainly—and is now almost exclusively—devoted to reviewing decisions of lower appellate courts, both federal and state,[1] and consists of nine justices sitting *en banc,* or altogether.

The principles of Federalism recognized by the framers of the Constitution mandated that the states retain important rights. While the federal government concerned itself with national affairs, such as foreign relations and commerce among the states, states retained under their traditional police powers the right to govern matters of public health, safety, and morality.[2] Consequently, throughout the 19th century, development of many areas of the law was left to individual state legislatures and courts. To this day, important differences exist among states as to contract law, criminal law, and the law of torts, or non-criminal injuries.

In contrast, federal courts' jurisdiction, or power to hear and decide cases, was limited to hearing cases between citizens of different states, admiralty cases, and cases arising under federal law. This third area of empowerment led to the development of federal common-law doctrines and embraced the authority to interpret constitutional and statutory provisions, or even overturn them, as in *Marbury v. Madison* (1803), which established the principle of judicial review.[3] When federal courts hear cases between citizens of different states, known as diversity cases, they must apply the substantive law of whichever state has the strongest interest in the outcome.

Trial Procedures

Each state court system has its own set of procedural rules, but since 1938 and 1945, respectively, federal courts have followed their own rules of civil and criminal procedure, which often differ sharply from procedures observed by state courts.

Rules of procedure govern not just the trial itself, but also all the legally significant events leading up to it. They may, for example, govern the form in which the plaintiff in a civil case files his set of pleadings, customarily called a complaint, which initiates the lawsuit. These rules will ordinarily stipulate the time by which the defendant must respond to the plaintiff's charges in a formal answer. These rules are multitudinous and complex, as they must impose order on the vast array of legal weapons in a litigation attorney's arsenal, the majority of which are deployed before the trial ever begins. In fact, most litigators rarely see the inside of a courtroom. Instead, they spend their time negotiating with the opposing side (always, if that party is represented by counsel, through his or her attorney[4]) and drafting motion papers. Motions can pertain to such things as the pretrial testimony of potential witnesses and the exchange of documents and information that are a prelude to trial. Collectively, this is known as "discovery." Attempts to have an opponent's case dismissed on various grounds before trial also are made in the form of motions.

The purpose of discovery is to preserve evidence that might not be available at trial, such as the testimony of an infirm witness, to ascertain the issues actually in controversy, and to prevent either side from being taken off guard—by surprise evidence, for example. It seems fundamental that both sides should be in possession of all information relevant to the case before proceeding to trial, but the disclosure afforded by discovery is a relatively recent innovation. Discovery only became a vital part of the litigation process with the adoption of the Federal Rules of Civil Procedure. It has since become the focus of much of the debate about the delay and costs associated with modern-day litigation.

Once discovery is complete and rulings are made on motions by the two sides, more precautions are taken to ensure trials are conducted fairly. Both plaintiff's and defendant's counsels submit draft pretrial orders to the court. The pretrial order includes such items as lists of all witnesses the party intends to call and of all documentary evidence, or exhibits, the party intends to present at trial. The parties then proceed to select a jury if the trial is a criminal prosecution or if the plaintiff in a civil case has elected to have a jury trial. This selection process is called *voir dire* and, particularly in recent years, is a crucial stage of the trial, as each opposing counsel subtly maneuvers to get a trial (or *petit*) jury sympathetic to his or her case.

In some criminal prosecutions, a grand jury has already heard the case. Traditionally composed of 23 jurors (as opposed to the six- to 12-person juries used in trials), the grand jury's purpose is to determine whether the facts and accusations presented by the prosecutor warrant an indictment and eventual trial of the accused. Others accused of criminal acts can face other types of juries convened before trial to hear only prosecution testimony. For example, although because of her age she did not herself appear, Cheryl Christina Crane, the 14-year-old daughter of film star Lana Turner, was the subject of a 1958 inquest by a coroner's jury into the murder of her mother's lover. Because the coroner's jury returned a verdict of justifiable homicide, criminal proceedings against Crane were discontinued.

The Sixth Amendment to the Constitution guarantees the accused the right to a trial by a jury of his or her peers, a concept as old as common law itself. The Sixth Amendment also guarantees the accused the right to be tried by an impartial jury, thus making the process of jury selection even more stringent in criminal trials. While voir dire always permits the attorneys for either side to excuse potential jurors for cause or for no cause at all (called a peremptory challenge), the Sixth Amendment mandates that this process result in a jury that represents a fair cross-section of the community and does not discriminate against any class of potential jurors. Disputes about a potential jury's racial balance can be central to the trial strategy of either side, as it was for the defendant's attorney in the 1968 murder trial of Black Panther activist Huey P. Newton. If excessive publicity surrounds the case, the court may take additional measures to make sure the jury remains impartial: sequestering the jury, delaying the trial, even granting a change of venue, as in the 1967 trial of mass murderer Richard Speck.

Trials begin with opening arguments delivered by attorneys for both sides, beginning with plaintiff's counsel—which in the case of most criminal prosecutions will be the government's attorney, such as a district attorney. (A defendant may reserve the right to present an opening statement until after the plaintiff's presentation of its case is complete.) These arguments present the judge and jury with an overview of the evidence each side intends to present and of their respective theories of the case. Plaintiff's counsel then presents his or her case. That starts with direct examination of the plaintiff's designated witnesses, which can include so-called expert witnesses who do not testify about the facts of the case, but about matters requiring specialized knowledge. Documentary or concrete evidence is introduced in the course of direct examination. Each side is permitted to ask open questions only of its own witnesses, unless that witness proves to be hostile, in which case he or she may be asked leading questions and even be cross-examined.

Cross-examination is generally reserved for counsel for the opposing side, who can question each witness before he or she steps down. The purpose of cross-examination is to discredit the witness or cast testimony already given in a light more favorable to the party represented by the cross-examiner. If cross-examination elicits testimony damaging to the party presenting its case, that party may seek to rebut or clarify it through redirect examination of the witness.

When the plaintiff has presented all of its evidence, the defense presents its case using the same process. After both sides have made their cases to the judge, or to judge and jury, plaintiff's counsel, then defendant's, delivers a closing statement summarizing his or her client's case. If it is a jury trial, the judge will then instruct the jurors on the applicable law, including which side has the burden of proof and what the measure of that burden is. There are three standards for the measure of proof that the party bearing the burden must meet to win the case. Most civil cases use the "preponderance of the evidence" standard, which means that the fact finder must be convinced that the fact at issue is more probably true than not. Some civil cases, such as those involving fraud, require proof by clear and convincing evidence, i.e., that there is a high probability that the fact at issue exists. The highest standard applies to criminal prosecutions, in which the defendant's guilt must be established beyond a reasonable doubt.

Juries deliberate, sometimes for weeks on end. Judges acting as finders of both law and fact sometimes deliberate or sometimes rule immediately from the bench. If the trial is criminal in nature, the verdict must be unanimous. Its delivery often is followed by a long delay before the trial court pronounces judgment and holds a sentencing hearing.

Rules of Evidence

Formal rules govern the introduction of both testimonial and documentary evidence. While not all states have codified their evidentiary rules, the Federal Rules of Evidence, which became effective in 1975, govern civil and criminal cases in most federal courts. As might be expected, additional rules apply in criminal cases. For example, if the state wishes to introduce the confession of a defendant at a criminal trial, the court must conduct an examination outside the presence and hearing of the jury (also called *voir dire*). This is done to determine if the statements were voluntarily obtained in compliance with the defendant's Miranda rights,[5] and therefore constitutionally admissible.

Attorneys can attempt at trial to introduce whatever new evidence—largely witness testimony—they feel will help their clients' cases; it is their opponents' job to object to and thus prevent the evidence from being admitted. The most common of these objections are relevance, hearsay, and privilege.

Relevance pertains to the link between the proposed evidence and the proposition it is supposed to support. Relevant evidence, whether direct or circumstantial, must tend to prove a fact that is material to the issue. Even relevant evidence may be excluded if its probative value is outweighed by the danger of unfair prejudice, confusion of the issues, or misleading of the jury.[6] Certain categories of relevant evidence, such as proof that a person was insured against liability in a case where his or her negligence is an issue, are never admissible.

The rule against hearsay is probably the most important—certainly the most complex—exclusionary rule of evidence. The Federal Rules define hearsay as "a statement, other than one made by the declarant while testifying at the trial or hearing, offered in evidence to prove the truth of the matter asserted." In other words, a witness's testimony about what someone else said or wrote or communicated nonverbally is not considered credible evidence of the content of that communication. The reason for the hearsay rule is that the witness's credibility is key to determining the truthfulness of his or her testimony. Without the adverse party's ability to cross-examine the communicant and without the jury's ability to scrutinize his or her demeanor, there is no adequate basis on which to judge the accuracy of the statement. An additional question arises in criminal cases in that the Sixth Amendment grants the accused the right to confront and cross-examine all the witnesses against him or her.

There are numerous exceptions to the hearsay rule, generally based on how trustworthy the statement at issue is and the necessity of making the exception. A witness's recital of a dying individual's declarations, for example, is generally admissible on the theory that a dying person has nothing to gain by lying,[7] and because this is the only method whereby such statements can be admitted as evidence after the speaker dies. As might be expected, exceptions in criminal trials are usually narrower to provide the defendant—who may have his or her life or liberty at stake—with additional safeguards. This is not always the case, however. One state-law exception permits statements made by one conspirator to be admitted against co-conspirators even if the statements are made after all conspirators are in custody. This has been ruled constitutional even though the usual rule is that this co-conspirator exception does not apply to any post-custody utterances.

The third common ground for objecting to admissibility is privilege, which applies to communications taking place in the context of legal or other confidential relationships, such as that between husband and wife, priest and penitent, physician and patient.

There is also, of course, a person's right under the Fifth Amendment to the Constitution to refuse to testify against himself or herself, the privilege against self-incrimination.

Appeals Procedures

The time in which an appeal from the trial court's decision is permitted begins to run after the verdict has been reached and, in a criminal case, the sentence pronounced. In a criminal case, the decision or the sentence can be appealed. The executions of Julius and Ethel Rosenberg after their 1951 espionage trial were delayed for two years, while both the conduct of their trial and the severity of their sentences were appealed.

There are two potential stages of appeal in federal and in most state court systems: from the trial court to the intermediate appellate court, then to the supreme court. While losing parties customarily have an automatic right to appeal to the intermediate courts, in most superior courts of appeal, appeals are usually heard only at the discretion of the court. (Appeals almost always reach the U.S. Supreme Court after a petition has been filed for a writ of *certiorari.*)

In the early stages of development of common law, both in England and in America, courts were divided into two types: courts of law and courts of equity. Courts of law ruled according to accepted common-law principles, but when injuries occurred for which law courts had no ready remedy, equity courts were able to address these issues according to general principles of fairness. An appeal in equity subjected both facts and law to review and retrial. Now, however, the two types of courts have been merged. Appeals seek a reversal of the lower court's opinion or a retrial, based almost exclusively on some misapplication of the law—such as in the judge's instructions to the jury regarding the law pertinent to the case—or on procedural error.

Criminal and civil appeals generally follow similar courses. One significant area of difference, however, falls under the rubric of double jeopardy. The principle of double jeopardy, applicable only in criminal prosecutions, is fundamental to common law and finds its expression in the Fifth Amendment, which provides that "No person . . . shall . . . be subject for the same offense to be twice put in jeopardy of life and limb." This principle operates at the federal and state levels. It prevents a second trial unless the first ended in a mistrial—one declared void prior to verdict, usually because the jury is deadlocked—or the defendant appeals a conviction, as Claus von Bülow did after being found guilty in 1982 of attempting to murder his wife. Von Bülow was acquitted of all charges after his second trial in 1985. For defendants less fortunate than von Bülow, double jeopardy also prevents double punishment and even makes the imposition of any higher penalty on retrial subject to increased judicial scrutiny.[8]

Legal Skills

Few, if any, attorneys are so versatile that they are equally adept in all facets of legal practice. Appellate practice often requires a keener grasp of legal technicalities than is required of a trial attorney. Often, a trial attorney's skill rests instead on keen intuitions about human nature. In the Triangle Shirtwaist Trial (1911), for example, defense attorney Max Steuer was able to secure a not-guilty verdict in the face of enormous odds because he understood the psychology of the jury.

Two manufacturers were on trial for the deaths by fire of 146 of their workers, owing to the fact that the doors to the New York City sweatshop where they worked were locked on the defendants' orders. As unsympathetic as these defendants' case appeared, however, Steuer was able to overcome the jury's emotions by appealing to their intellect. Steuer had the principal prosecution witness, a young female survivor of the fire, repeat her testimony three times. The first two recitals were identical; in the third she changed one word. Steuer won the case by making sure that the jury recognized that the witness had been rehearsed.

Other trial attorneys—Daniel Webster immediately comes to mind—succeed not so much on the basis of their examination technique, but on the eloquence and persuasiveness of their oratory. When great trial skills are combined with great issues, memorable trials result. Although the issue at stake in the 1925 Scopes "Monkey Trial," the teaching of evolution, was of great social significance, what made the trial most unforgettable was Clarence Darrow's clever examination of Fundamentalist politician William Jennings Bryan, whom the defense called to the stand as an expert on the Bible—an unorthodox maneuver, given that Bryan was also acting as plaintiff's counsel.

The Scopes trial was memorialized in a play and subsequent film, both entitled *Inherit the Wind.* Other trials, like the 1943 Errol Flynn rape trial, are famous because they featured an irresistible combination of celebrities and scandal. Some trials become infamous because the public perceives them to be a miscarriage of justice, like the 1979 Dan White case, where the accused was convicted of voluntary manslaughter rather than murder—in part because of the success of the unconventional "Twinkies Defense," which argued that White's intake of junk food was the real culprit.

Some trials are celebrated, though, not because they feature notable parties, salacious facts, or incomparable trial tactics. As noted at the outset of this essay, what matters most about the American court system, ultimately, is its public nature. While spectacle certainly is one aspect of many great trials, perhaps the "greatest" one in American history, the one which arguably has had the most profound and lasting effect on our people, is *Brown v. Board of Education* (1954). *Brown v. Board of Education* was finally decided by the U.S. Supreme Court, and the attorney for the winning side, Thurgood Marshall, was himself later to become a Supreme Court justice. But the case revolved around a modest individual's attempt to gain recognition of his child's right to a good education. By overturning the "separate but equal" doctrine that had up to that time made ours a legally segregated society, *Brown v. Board of Education* fueled a social revolution that has changed the lives of every one of us.

—*Lisa Paddock, Esq.*

[1]The Supreme Court, however, has been known to give state sovereignty great deference. For example, in *Buck v. Bell* (1927), the Court upheld the constitutionality of a Virginia statute permitting the forced sterilization of 18-year-old Carrie Buck, whose mother had been feebleminded.

[2]With increased emphasis on civil rights in the latter half of this century, many of the states' attempts to regulate morality were overturned. In *Griswold v. Connecticut* (1964), for example, the Supreme Court found unconstitutional an 1879 state statute prohibiting the use or distribution of or advisory services concerning contraceptives. While the justices found no basis in the Bill of Rights for voiding the statute, they explained their decision in terms of a newly explored right, the right of privacy, which was further expanded in such cases as *Roe v. Wade.*

[3]The only other instance before the Civil War in which the Supreme Court struck down a federal law occurred in the more infamous *Scott v. Sanford* (1856), in which the Court found the Missouri Compromise unconstitutional and the plaintiff, a slave, consequently not a citizen.

[4]Parties in civil actions—and even in some criminal cases—can appear *pro se,* that is, represent themselves. In *Gideon v. Wainwright* (1963), however, the Supreme Court ruled that every defendant in a felony trial had a right to counsel, and that if the defendant could not afford to hire his or her own lawyer, the state had to provide one. This decision makes impossible situations such as that prevailing during the second treason trial of John Fries in 1800, in which Justice Samuel Chase acted from the bench—much to the defendant's detriment—as Fries' counsel after the defendant's attorneys withdrew in the face of Chase's open hostility toward their client.

[5]Such rights are named for the landmark case of *Miranda v. Arizona* (1967), which ruled that at the time of their arrests, suspected criminals had to be read their rights to remain silent, to know that anything they said could be used against them, and that if they were indigent the state would provide them with counsel.

[6]The persuasiveness and prejudicial possibilities of circumstantial evidence are well illustrated by the 1955 kidnapping and murder trial of Burton Abbott, who was sentenced to death in the gas chamber largely because the district attorney managed, despite the lack of any real foundation, to introduce the victim's unwashed undergarments and overwhelm the jury with their sight and smell.

[7]For an example of the questionableness of this rationale, one need turn no further than the Finch-Tregoff trial of 1960, in which one of the accused murderers was permitted to recite in open court his dying wife's apology for her own killing.

[8]Under the U.S. system of federalism, states and the national government are considered separate "sovereigns." Therefore, each can try a defendant for the same actions under different laws without violating the prohibition against double jeopardy. This principle permitted the federal government to prosecute four Los Angeles police officers in 1993 for violating the civil rights of Rodney King even though the defendants had been acquitted the prior year on state charges of using excessive force.

Anne Hutchinson Trials: 1637 and 1638

Defendant: Anne Hutchinson **Crimes Charged:** "Traducing the ministers and their ministry" and heresy **Chief Defense Lawyer:** None **Chief Prosecutors:** Civil trial: John Winthrop; religious trial: the Reverend John Davenport **Judges:** Civil trial: John Winthrop and the Magistrates of Massachusetts; religious trial: John Wilson and the ministers of the Church of Boston **Places:** Civil trial: Newtown (Cambridge); religious trial: Boston **Dates of trials:** Civil trial: November 7–8, 1637; Religious trial: March 22, 1638 **Verdicts:** Guilty **Sentences:** Banishment from the colony and excommunication from the Church of Boston

SIGNIFICANCE

Anne Hutchinson was the defendant in the most famous of the trials intended to squelch religious dissent in the Massachusetts Bay Colony.

The Massachusetts Bay Colony had been founded so that the Puritans might perfectly practice their own faith. Religious liberty for others—a concept Americans would later take for granted—was not part of the Puritans' plan. Instead, founding Governor John Winthrop envisioned a model "Citty [sic] upon a hill," an example of Christian unity and order. Not incidentally, women were expected to play a submissive and supporting role in this society.

Anne Hutchinson, a skilled midwife and herbal healer with her own interpretation of Puritan doctrine, challenged the leaders of this "wilderness theocracy," as Barbara Ritter Dailey describes it. She arrived in the colony in 1634 and began holding religious meetings in her home. She quickly drew crowds of 60 to 80 men and women on a weekly basis. An alarmed assembly of church elders agreed that "women might meet [some few together] to pray and edify one another" but, without naming Hutchinson, denounced "one woman . . . [who] took upon her the whole exercise . . . [as] disorderly, and without rule."

Hutchinson continued to outline her views. Puritan doctrine emphasized the performance of "good works," which might be interpreted as evidence, or justification, that an individual had been elected for salvation. Hutchinson's favorite minister, John Cotton, stressed a "covenant of grace"—the idea that one's own spiritual consciousness of God's election might also be justification.

Hutchinson expanded this idea to include an in-dwelling Holy Ghost whose guidance replaced the self-will of the saved. She then denounced all of the colony's ministers except Cotton and her brother-in-law, John Wheelwright, for preaching only the "Covenant of Works."

Anne Hutchinson preaching. (Courtesy, Library of Congress)

General Court Summons Hutchinson

The General Court summoned Hutchinson in November 1637. She was put on trial for her theological views and for stepping outside the bounds assigned to women. Governor John Winthrop, acting as prosecutor, outlined the charges: "Mrs. Hutchinson, you are called here as one of those that have troubled the peace . . . you have spoken of divers[e] things . . . very prejudicial to the honour of the churches and ministers thereof, and you have maintained a meeting . . . that hath been condemned . . . as a thing not tolerable nor comely in the sight of God nor fitting for your sex."

Hutchinson responded haughtily, "I am called here to answer before you, but I hear no things laid to my charge."

Winthrop said, "I have told you some already and more I can tell you."

Finally, exasperated by Hutchinson's "What have I said or done?" stance, Winthrop exclaimed, "Why for your doings, this you did harbour and countenance those that are parties in this faction that you have heard of." He was referring to the fact that Hutchinson had encouraged others to sign a petition in support of Wheelwright, who, found guilty of sedition and contempt, had been banished.

Hutchinson simply stated, "That's a matter of conscience, Sir."

Winthrop replied: "Your conscience you must keep or it must be kept for you."

He then denounced her support for Wheelwright and his sympathizers. "What breach of law is that, Sir?" Hutchinson inquired.

"Why dishonoring of parents," Winthrop immediately replied, placing the commonwealth's governor and magistrates in that role.

Hutchinson asked sarcastically, "But put the case Sir that I do fear the Lord and my parents, may I not entertain them that fear the Lord because my parents will not give me leave?"

After some further discussion of the theological point, Winthrop directed his line of questioning toward a woman's right to hold religious meetings.

Hutchinson demanded, "[C]an you find a warrant [permission] for yourself and condemn me for the same thing?" Denying that men had attended, she cited a "clear rule in Titus, that the elder women should instruct the younger."

Winthrop told her to "take it in this sense that elder women must instruct the younger about their business and to love their husbands and not make them to clash." When Hutchinson objected, saying "it is meant for some publick times," Winthrop criticized her for drawing her students away from their housework: "[I]t will not well stand with the commonwealth that families should be neglected for so many neighbours and dames and so much time spent, we see no rule of God for this . . . and so what hurt comes of this you will be guilty of and we for suffering you."

Seven ministers then testified in turn, as Winthrop summarized it, that Hutchinson "did say that they [the ministers] did preach a covenant of works and that they were not able ministers of the gospel." Shortly afterward, Hutchinson was ordered "to consider of it," and the court recessed until the following morning.

The next day, John Cotton's sympathetic testimony on theological points and the question of whether Hutchinson had "traduced the ministers" brought Hutchinson close to acquittal. Then, suddenly, she told the court that she knew through an immediate revelation from God that her inquisitors would be destroyed. This was proof enough of heresy, and Hutchinson was "banished from out of our jurisdiction as being a woman not fit for our society." The sentence was modified, however, to permit Hutchinson to remain "confined" in the colony until spring.

Church of Boston Enters Fray

Hutchinson continued to spread her views. Finally, as Winthrop recorded, "the Elders of Boston . . . declared their readinesse to deale with Mistris Hutchinson in a Church way."

At this trial, Cotton opposed Hutchinson and emphasized the dangers he thought a dissenting woman courted: "[T]hough I have not herd, nayther do I thinke, you have bine unfaythful to your Husband in his Marriage Covenant, yet that will follow upon it." He turned to the women present in the church and instructed them to ignore Hutchinson's teachings, saying "[Y]ou see she [Hutchinson] is but a Woman and many unsound and dayngerous principles are held by her."

The Reverend Thomas Shepard then testified that Hutchinson sought "to seduce and draw away many, Espetially simple Weomen of her owne sex." Her theological views were condemned, and the spiritual penalty of excommunication was then added to the earlier civil punishment of banishment. When the Reverend John Wilson ordered her "as a Leper to withdraw your selfe out of the Congregation," one woman—Mary Dyer—walked over to Hutchinson and joined hands with her. The two women walked together to the church door, where Hutchinson turned to deliver her own verdict to the ministers: "The Lord judgeth not as man judgeth, better to be cast out of the Church than to deny Christ."

The Aftermath: a Mixed Picture

Reaction to the trials was mixed. Hutchinson herself, as Winthrop recorded, "gloried in her sufferings, saying, that it [her excommunication] was the greatest happiness, next to Christ, that ever befel her." Hutchinson's husband William left the colony at her side; he later explained that "he was more nearly tied to his wife than to the church." Their son Francis later blasted the church as "a strumpet" and was excommunicated and fined 40 pounds. When he refused to pay the fine, he was jailed.

Finally, as Lyle Koehler points out, the church found it necessary to continue disciplining women for similar offenses, especially during the 18 months following Hutchinson's excommunication. Katherine Finch, for example, "spoke against the magistrates, against the Churches, and against the Elders" and was ordered whipped on October 10, 1638. Even after this punishment, Finch failed to conduct herself "dutifully to her husband." She was forced to make a public promise that she would, in the future, comply to his wishes. Phillip Hammond was excommunicated in 1639, in part for publicly declaring that "Mrs. Hutchinson neyther deserved the Censure which was putt upon her in the Church, nor in the Common Weale." In 1646, Sarah Keayne was excommunicated by the Boston church for holding her own mixed religious meetings and "irregular[ly] prophesying." Joan Hogg, found guilty of "disorderly singing and . . . saying she is commanded of Christ to do so," was also excommunicated.

To Hutchinson's detractors, however, the most stunning commentary on the controversy was when Mary Dyer and Anne Hutchinson became pregnant following Hutchinson's trials, and experienced what Boston clergy described as "monster births" and divine signs of guilt. (Hutchinson's modern diagnosis is of a hydatidiform mole.)

In 1643, when Hutchinson was killed by Indians in what would become New York state, the Reverend Peter Bulkeley delivered the ministers' final summation: "Let her damned heresies shee fell into . . . and the just vengeance of God, by which shee perished, terifie all her seduced followers from having any more to doe with her leaven."

—Kathryn Cullen-DuPont

Suggestions for Further Reading

Battis, Emery. "Anne Hutchinson," *Notable American Women, 1906–1950.* Edited by Edward T. James, Janet Wilson James, and Paul S. Boyer. Cambridge, Mass.: Belknap Press of Harvard University Press, 1971.

Dailey, Barbara Ritter. "Anne Hutchinson," *A Reader's Companion to American History.* Edited by Eric Foner and John A. Garraty. Boston: Houghton Mifflin, 1991.

Evans, Sara M. *Born for Liberty: A History of Women in America.* New York: The Free Press, A Division of Macmillan, Co. 1989.

Flexner, Eleanor. *Century of Struggle.* Cambridge, Mass.: Belknap Press of Harvard University Press, 1959.

Hutchinson, Thomas. *The History of the Colony and Province of Massachusetts Bay.* Edited from Hutchinson's copy of Vols. I and II and his manuscript of Vol. III by Lawrence Shaw Mayo, 1936. Volume II, Appendix II, pp. 366–391, reprint in Nancy Cott, ed. *Roots of Bitterness: Documents of the Social History of American Women.* New York: E. P. Dutton, 1972.

Koehler, Lyle. "The Case of the American Jezebels: Anne Hutchinson and Female Agitation during the Years of the Antinomian Turmoil, 1636–1640." *William and Mary Quarterly,* 3d ser., 31 (1974): 55–78, reprint in Linda K. Kerber and Jane DeHart Mathews, eds. *Women's America: Refocusing the Past.* New York: Oxford University Press, 1972.

Morgan, Edmund S. *The Puritan Dilemma: The Story of John Winthrop.* Boston: Little, Brown and Company, 1958.

Stanton, Elizabeth Cady, Susan B. Anthony, and Matilda Joslyn Gage, eds. *History of Woman Suffrage, 1881.* Reprint Salem, N.H.: Ayer Co., 1985.

Winthrop, John. *Winthrop's Journal, "History of New England," 1630–1649* (2 vols.). New York: Charles Scribner's Sons, 1908.

Dorothy Talbye Trial: 1638

Defendant: Dorothy Talbye **Crime Charged:** Murder
Chief Defense Lawyer: No Record **Chief Prosecutor:** No Record
Judge: Governor John Winthrop **Place:** Boston, Massachusetts Bay Colony
Date of Trial: October 4, 1638 **Verdict:** Guilty **Sentence:** Death by hanging

SIGNIFICANCE

The Talbye case demonstrated that early American society and its legal system did not fully understand or acknowledge the concept that someone could commit a crime and yet be judged not guilty by reason of insanity. There was no practical alternative to treating the insane as ordinary criminals. Although England's officials had a few institutions, such as the Hospital of St. Mary of Bethlehem (known as Bedlam), to which they could send people, the American colonies had none.

A defense of not guilty by reason of insanity is a comparatively recent innovation. However, by 1641, the Massachusetts Bay Colony's "Body of Liberties" did state that:

> Children, Idiots, Distracted persons . . . shall have such allowances and dispensations in any Cause whether Criminall or other as religion and reason require.

Even if these words had been written three years earlier in 1638, they still might not have saved the "distracted" Dorothy Talbye from the gallows, for such "allowances" were limited. The 17th-century society could do little to either aid or restrain the severely mentally ill.

Over time, Dorothy Talbye changed from a respected member of the community, "of good esteem for godliness," into a melancholy woman given to fits of violence. She fought with family and neighbors. She experienced what she believed to be divine revelations, sometimes on a daily basis.

Talbye's husband and children were often the targets of her madness. Her revelations told her to starve her family and herself. According to her husband John, she tried to kill him. Prayers and admonitions of ecclesiastical authorities were useless. Finally, she was expelled from the church.

The expulsion seemed to aggravate her emotional state. Eventually her actions twice brought her before civil authorities. The second time a magistrate ordered her to be whipped. For a time, Talbye seemed to improve. But her condition worsened again. Dorothy's revelations convinced her that the only way to "free" Difficult, her daughter, "from future misery" such as Dorothy herself had suffered, was to kill the child. She took the 3-year-old to a secluded spot and broke her neck. When apprehended, Talbye confessed freely.

Talbye was charged in the Court of Assistants. Although she had earlier confessed to what she had done, in court Talbye "stood mute for a space" and would not enter a plea until Governor John Winthrop threatened she would be pressed (have stones piled on her chest). She pleaded guilty. The record states:

> When she was to receive judgment, she would not uncover her face, nor stand up, but as she was forced, nor give any testimony of her repentance, either then or at her execution.

Talbye was no stalwart martyr. As she had cursed her excommunication, so did she fight her execution. Talbye was dragged to the gallows where she refused to stand. She grabbed at the ladder. She may have been willing to "free" her daughter from "misery" but she was unwilling to be freed herself.

—Teddi DiCanio

Suggestions for Further Reading

Powers, Edwin. *Crime and Punishment in Early Massachusetts, 1620-1692, A Documentary History.* Boston: Beacon Press, 1966.

Winthrop, John. *Winthrop's Journal,* Vol. I. New York: Charles Scribner's Sons, 1908.

Judith Catchpole Trial: 1656

Defendant: Judith Catchpole **Crimes Charged:** Infanticide and witchcraft
Chief Defense Lawyer: No Record **Chief Prosecutor:** No Record
Judges: Michael Brook, William Fuller, Edward Lloyd, John Pott, and Richard Preston **Place:** Patuxent County, Maryland **Date:** September 22, 1656
Verdict: Not Guilty

SIGNIFICANCE

While trying to adhere to common law, colonial judicial practices often arose from immediate practical needs, as had the common law itself. In this case, the practical need was for a woman's expertise, which led to an all-female jury.

Even after obtaining the vote with passage of the Nineteenth Amendment, for decades some states still prohibited women from serving on juries. Nevertheless, in 1656, an all-woman jury was impaneled to decide the case of Judith Catchpole. Although unusual, hers is not the only recorded case of a female jury.

Catchpole was an indentured servant, who had arrived in Maryland in January 1656 aboard the *Mary and Francis.* An unnamed fellow passenger, identified in court records only as the indentured servant of William Bramhall, told a bizarre story claiming Catchpole had given birth to a child that she subsequently murdered. The storyteller died before Catchpole could be tried, but not before telling his tale to other servants.

> Andrew Wilcox sworn and Examined Saith that William Bramhalls man Servant that dyed Said that when the Murther was done all the people and Seamen in the Ship were asleep and after it was done Judith Catchpole and the Said Servant of William Bramhall went up upon the Deck and walked a quarter of an hour afterward off they went to their lodging this being at Sea in the middle of the Night.

This trial was held eight months after Catchpole arrived. Others had not come forward to accuse her of infanticide. Nor was there any explanation of how Catchpole could hide a pregnancy and give birth aboard a cramped ship without anyone noticing.

According to additional hearsay evidence, the dead manservant also spoke of witchcraft. He claimed that she had "cut the Skinn of a maid's throat when She was a sleep," then sewn it up again without waking her. Catchpole was also supposed to have "prickt a Seaman in the back" with a knife the manservant had ground "Dutch fashion," following which she rubbed a little grease into the man's back "and he Stood up again." The manservant said that she was to kill several others.

In addition to weighing the evidence presented in testimony, the jury acted in an investigative capacity. The women examined Judith Catchpole for any physical signs of recent pregnancy and childbirth. They found none and gave an oath to that effect.

The court appeared to pay little attention to the charges of witchcraft. The decisions of the court seem to have hinged on the plausibility of the charges. Neither the judges nor the jury could give credence to the accusations made by the dead manservant. They declared Judith Catchpole's accuser to have been of unsound mind and released her.

—Teddi DiCanio

Suggestions for Further Reading

Browne, William Hand, ed. *Archives of Maryland.* Baltimore: Maryland Historical Society, 1883.

Rose, Lou. "A Memorable Trial in Seventeenth-Century Maryland." *Maryland Historical Magazine,* Vol. 83. (Winter 1988).

Semmes, Raphael. *Crime and Punishment in Early Maryland.* Montclair, N.J.: Patterson Smith, 1970. [Reprint from Johns Hopkins Press, 1938.]

Mary Dyer Trials: 1659 and 1660

Defendant: Mary Dyer **Crime Charged:** Quakerism
Chief Defense Lawyer: None **Chief Prosecutor:** No Record
Judge: Governor John Endecott **Place:** Boston, Massachusetts Bay Colony
Dates: October 19, 1659; May 31, 1660 **Verdicts:** Guilty
Sentences: First trial: death by hanging, commuted to banishment from the colony and hanging should she return; second trial: death by hanging

SIGNIFICANCE

Quaker Mary Dyer's conviction and execution for practicing her faith in a manner other than the one approved by Massachusetts' colonial government was indicative of the draconian measures the puritan leaders of the colony were prepared to use to insure total theological conformity.

In 1638, when Anne Hutchinson was excommunicated from the Church of Boston, Mary Dyer walked to Hutchinson's side and offered her hand in solidarity. Accounts of Hutchinson's trials in the Massachusetts Bay Colony appear in every child's first American history text, while Mary Dyer's own trials—22 years later and with far more drastic consequences for the accused—are rarely examined.

The Puritan officials of the Massachusetts Bay Colony had struggled since the colony's founding to eliminate dissenters. In 1658, they found Quakers, or members of the Society of Friends, particularly alarming: The *Records of the Governor* states emphatically that "The doctrine of this sect of people . . . tends to overthrow the whole gospell [sic] & the very vitalls [*sic*] of Christianitie . . ." On October 19, 1558, the colony passed a law banishing Quakers "on pajne [*sic*] of death."

Two Quakers, William Robinson and Marmaduke Stephenson, were imprisoned in Boston in 1659; that summer, Dyer visited them and was thrown into prison as well. All three were ordered banished and threatened with execution should they ever return to the colony. They were released on September 12, 1659, but returned within a few weeks to "look [the] bloody laws in the face."

The three were thrown into jail for, as the governor's records describe it, "theire rebellion, sedition, & presumptuous obtruding themselves upon us," and "as underminers of this government." They stood trial before the General

Court on October 19, 1659. "[B]rought to the barre," they "acknowledged themselves to be the persons banished" and earlier "convicted for Quakers." Governor John Endecott declared the sentence to each of them in turn, using the same words: "You shall go from hence to the place from whence you came [jail], & from thence to the place of execution, & there hang till you be dead."

When Dyer heard her sentence, she said, "The will of the Lord be done." Her husband, William Dyer, accepted the situation with less equanimity. On August 30, 1659, he had written to the "Court . . . assembled at Boston" to object to the restriction of his wife's religious liberty. He likened the members of the General Court to the "Popish inquisitors" of the 13th century, since they served as "a judge and accuser both." He complained bitterly that the Puritans, who had left England to escape persecution, now persecuted others: "[S]urely you or some of you, if ever you had the courage to looke a bishop in the face, cannot but remember that the 1. 2 or third word from them was, You are a Puritane are you not, & is it not so in N. England, the magistracy having . . . assumed a coercive power of conscience, the first or next word After appearance is You are a Quaker."

Statue of Mary Dyer in Boston. (Courtesy, Massachusetts Art Commission)

Governor Thomas Temple of Nova Scotia, Governor John Winthrop, Jr., of Connecticut, and Dyer's son William added their objections, and Dyer received a dramatic suspension of her sentence. With Robinson and Stephenson, she was escorted by drum-beating soldiers to "the place of execution, & there [made] to stand upon the gallowes, with a rope about her necke." Robinson and Stephenson were both hanged but Dyer, to her surprise, was granted "liberty for forty eight howers . . . to depart out of this jurisdiction, after which time, being found therein, she is forthwith to be executed."

She remained outside the colony for only seven months before returning. Before Governor Endecott and the General Court on May 31, 1660, "she acknowledged herself to be Mary Dyer, . . . denied our lawe, [and said she] came to bear witness against it." Then "The whole court mett together voted, that the said Mary Dyer, for her rebelliously returning to this jurisdiction . . . shall . . . according to the sentence of the General Court in October last, be put to death."

Mary Dyer was hanged on June 1, 1660. In 1959, the Massachusetts General Court ordered a seven-foot statue of Dyer— which bears the inscription "Witness for Religious Freedom"—to be placed on the lawn of the Boston State House.

—Kathryn Cullen-DuPont

Suggestions for Further Reading

Chu, Jonathan M. *Neighbors, Friends, or Madmen: The Puritan Adjustment to Quakerism in Seventeenth-Century Massachusetts Bay.* Westport, Conn.: Greenwood Press, 1985.

Dyer, William. *Mary Dyer, Quaker: Two Letters of William Dyer of Rhode Island, 1659–1660.* Printed for Worthington C. Ford by the University Press, Cambridge, U.S.A., n.d.

McHenry, Robert, ed. *Famous American Women: A Biographical Dictionary from Colonial Times to the Present.* New York: Dover Publications, 1983.

Shurtleff, Nathaniel B., ed. *Records of the Governor and Company of the Massachusetts Bay in New England.* Boston: From the Press of William White, Printer to the Commonwealth, 1854.

Tolles, Frederick B. "Mary Dyer," *Notable American Women, 1906–1950.* Edward T. James, Janet Wilson James, and Paul S. Boyer, eds. Cambridge, Mass.: Belknap Press of Harvard University Press, 1971.

Nicholas More Impeachment: 1685

Defendant: Nicholas More **Crimes Charged:** High crimes and misdemeanors **Chief Defense Lawyer:** None **Chief Prosecutor:** None **Place:** Philadelphia, Colony of Pennsylvania **Date of Indictment:** May 15, 1685 **Verdict:** None, although More was relieved of his judicial duties

SIGNIFICANCE

Like other early America impeachments, Pennsylvania's methods for impeaching a sitting judge were drawn from English precedents and from procedures improvised at the time due to immediate need. The Nicholas More case illustrated a potential area for conflict both between various branches of government and between the colonies and the distant mother country.

Most American colonies had no specific provision for impeachment in their charters. As needed, colonial legislatures appropriated to themselves the same right to impeach an official that England's House of Commons exercised. By the early 1700s, as American impeachments came to the attention of the Privy Council, crown lawyers repeatedly stated that colonial assemblies had no such right. Provincial legislators fashioned legal justifications for colonial impeachments during the decades-long quarrel between Mother England and her daughter colonies concerning parliamentary authority vs. colonial autonomy in local affairs.

William Penn, proprietor of the colony of Pennsylvania, appointed Nicholas More as chief justice in 1684. Like many of Penn's political appointments, More was a man of wealth. He had purchased 10,000 acres of land from Penn. Penn believed that men with a stake in the colony's future would serve Pennsylvania best, and he had faith in the abilities of men of business. Unfortunately, More, a physician with no legal training, was arrogant and contentious and thus temperamentally unsuited to the job.

Using a brief clause in Pennsylvania's Charter of Liberties, the Assembly impeached More. On May 15, 1685, an Assembly member introduced a formal complaint. More, a delegate that day, was asked to withdraw. After some discussion, the individual articles of impeachment were approved one by one. To name a few, the Assembly charged that More had: bullied a jury into rendering an unjust verdict; mistreated judges; harassed a witness; summoned juries unlawfully; altered a charge; and missed serving in several circuit courts. The articles were then presented to the colony's Council, which decided to hear evidence on the following day and ordered More to appear to answer the charges.

Furious, More refused to appear even when threatened with being "ejected as an unprofitable member of the House." Nor could the Assembly obtain records from the Provincial Court. The court's clerk, Patrick Robinson, made excuses for not turning over the records and continued to do so after his arrest on the Assembly's warrant.

After days of squabbling, the Assembly expelled More from the legislature and resolved that Robinson ought to be dismissed from his office. Even without court records, the Assembly presented enough evidence to the Council to substantiate several charges. John White, the Assembly's speaker, asked that both More and Robinson be removed from their offices.

The Council was inclined to do nothing. Although it finally deprived More of his bench, the Council avoided taking the impeachment matter further. Robinson remained in office one more year until impertinence to judges lost him his position.

After several months, the Assembly sent a petition to Penn. Penn's reaction was simply to appoint More to the five-member board that made up the Executive of the Province. More never served and he died in 1689.

—Teddi DiCanio

Suggestions for Further Reading:

Hoffer, Peter Charles, and N.E.H. Hull. *Impeachment in America, 1635–1805.* New Haven, Conn.: Yale University Press, 1984.

Lewis, Jr., Lawrence. "The Courts of Pennsylvania in the Seventeenth Century." *Pennsylvania Magazine of History and Biography,* Vol. V. Philadelphia: Historical Society of Pennsylvania, 1881.

Jacob Leisler Trial: 1691

Defendants: Jacob Leisler, Jacob Milborne, eight other men
Crimes Charged: The treasonable act of holding the king's fort by force against the royal governor, such action resulting in several deaths
Chief Defense Lawyer: None
Committee for Preparing the Prosecution: Nicholas Bayard, William Pinhorne, and Stephen Van Cortlandt **Chief Prosecutors:** James Emmott, George Farewell, and William Nichols
Judges for Court of Oyer and Terminer: Captain Isaac Arnold, Joseph Dudley, Captain Jasper Hickes, Major Richard Ingoldesby, Thomas Johnson, John Laurence, William Pinhorne, Sir Robert Robinson, William Smith and Colonel John Young **Place:** New York, N.Y. (Colony) **Dates of Trial:** April 10–27, 1691 **Verdict:** Leisler, Milborne, and six others: guilty; two others acquitted; all eventually pardoned except Leisler and Milborne
Sentence: Death by hanging, disembowelment, decapitation, and quartering

SIGNIFICANCE

The trial and the harsh sentence imposed reflected the extreme personal and political animosities that marked New York politics. The executions, applauded by many of the colony's Anglo-Dutch elite as an example to the Leislerians, exacerbated those animosities.

The American colonies were already restive when mother England created a Dominion of New England in an effort to obtain greater control of the region. Many measures adopted were disliked by colonists. Thus, when England's Glorious Revolution replaced Catholic James II with Protestant William and Mary (James' daughter) of Orange, the colonies overthrew some appointed royal officials, including the lieutenant governor for New York, Francis Nicholson.

On May 30, 1689, an argument between two officers at New York's Fort James sparked a rumor that Nicholson planned to burn the city. On May 31, a German immigrant merchant, Jacob Leisler, leading 500 men, seized the fort.

Two weeks later Nicholson sailed for England. He left his councillors in charge: Nicholas Bayard, Frederick Phillipse, and Stephen Van Cortlandt. They were unable to thwart Leisler's usurpation of civil authority, which was supported by members of the merchant, artisan, and laboring groups.

Leisler Assumes Control

In December 1689, John Riggs arrived from Britain bringing dispatches from the king for the lieutenant governor or "to such as for the time being take care to keep the peace and administer the laws of New York" in the governor's absence. The dispatches were clearly for the council, but Leisler interpreted the orders to declare himself lieutenant governor.

Some of Leisler's actions were laudable, such as strengthening the province's defenses. Others are subject to interpretation. Leisler held a convention of delegates from the counties and towns. (Not everyone came.) Later, based on writs he issued, an assembly was elected. Some historians praise this as the first representative body for the province. Others believe Leisler manipulated both convention and assembly, often by threat of arms.

In February 1691, Major Richard Ingoldesby arrived in New York, ahead of the new governor, Colonel Henry Sloughter. Ingoldesby demanded Leisler surrender. Leisler refused, saying Ingoldesby had no royal commission. Even when Sloughter arrived, Leisler delayed briefly before surrendering. His behavior gave his enemies justification for insisting on a criminal inquest, instead of the general inquiry ordered by the Crown.

Ten men were indicted. Leisler and Jacob Milborne, his son-in-law, refused to plead, insisting the judges must first rule on the legality of the authority by which they had held Fort James. That "authority" rested on the king's letter by which Leisler had declared himself lieutenant governor. After an unfavorable ruling, the two men still refused to plead. The jury acquitted two, but found Leisler, Milborne, and six others guilty. They were sentenced to death. In response to a petition, Sloughter wrote the king recommending a pardon for all except Leisler and Milborne.

A clamor arose to execute Leisler and Milborne without delay. Eventually Sloughter gave in. On May 16, 1691, from the scaffold, Leisler and Milborne insisted they had had no intent save "than to maintaine against popery or any Schism or heresy" in the interests of the Crown. They begged forgiveness for any offenses and prayed that all hate be buried with them. They were then executed. Several years later, their estates, which had been seized, were restored to their heirs.

—Teddi DiCanio

Suggestions for Further Reading

Andrews, Charles M. *Narratives of the Insurrections, 1675–1690.* New York: Barnes & Noble, 1915. Reprinted 1967.

Balmer, Randall. "Traitors and Papists: The Religious Dimensions of Leisler's Rebellion." *New York History* (1989). Vol. 70.

Reich, Jerome R. *Leisler's Rebellion: A Study of Democracy in New York, 1664–1720.* Chicago: University of Chicago Press, 1953.

Salem Witchcraft Trials: 1692

Defendants: 200 accused, including: Bridget Bishop, Reverend George Burroughs, Martha Carrier, Giles Corey, Martha Corey, Mary Easty, Sarah Good, Elizabeth How, George Jacobs, Susannah Martin, Rebecca Nurse, Alice Parker, Mary Parker, John Procter, Ann Pudeator, Wilmot Reed, Margaret Scott, Samuel Wardwell, Sarah Wild, and John Willard.
Crimes Charged: Witchcraft **Chief Examiners:** Jonathan Corwin and John Hathorne **Place:** Salem Village (now Danvers, Massachusetts)
Dates of Hearings: March 1, 1692 through the spring
Chief Defense Lawyers: None **Chief Prosecutors:** None
Judges for Court of Oyer and Terminer: Jonathan Corwin, Bartholomew Gedney, John Richards, Nathaniel Saltonstall, William Sergeant, Samuel Sewall, William Stoughton, and Wait Winthrop. **Place:** Salem Town (present-day Salem, Massachusetts) **Dates of Trials:** June 2, 1692–September 1692. The court was then suspended. A superior court, convened in January 1693, held trials in several cities. **Verdicts:** 29 found guilty
Sentences: 19 hanged; remaining convicted and accused released over a period of years

SIGNIFICANCE

America's only massive witch-hunt resembled those that occurred in Europe over the centuries in that it transpired during a period of political unrest, but it was atypical in that it was localized and comparatively brief. However, the American witch-hunt remains singular in the effect it has exerted on the American imagination as historian and nonhistorian try to fathom the reasons for this frightening example of the perils of hysteria.

In the 17th century there was an almost universal belief in the effective power of witchcraft. English courts were specifically interested in maleficia, the performance of malicious acts against one's neighbors. Many mishaps, major and minor, were attributed to the malice of witches. Yet prior to the Salem Witch Trials, Massachusetts records indicate only about 100 people had ever been formally accused of witchcraft, 15 of whom were executed. In 1692, 200 were accused in a matter of months.

Over the centuries, witch-hunts generally occurred during times of anxiety or social upheaval. From the time the settlers first landed, they had enjoyed a nearly autonomous form of self-government. But in 1684 Massachusetts lost its charter. England then created the Dominion of New England combining several unwilling colonies. Not only was political autonomy threatened, but the dominion's new governor, Sir Edmond Andros, had declared that the revocation of the charter invalidated land titles. During the wake of England's Glorious Revolution of 1688, James II was deposed and Andros was overthrown. The colony was drifting in a legal limbo.

During the winter of 1691–92, in the kitchen of the Reverend Samuel Parris, Tituba, a Carib Indian slave entertained 9-year-old Betty, the minister's daughter, and 11-year-old Abigail Williams, his niece, with fortune-telling and magic. Eventually, the girls invited in eight more girls, ranging in age from 12 to 20. Key among them was Ann Putnam, Jr., the brilliant daughter of an embittered woman.

To Puritan eyes there was nothing innocent about flirting with magic spells for amusement. Moreover, Puritanism was unrelenting in its admonitions that the grace of God was man's only rescue from deserved damnation—a grace seemingly measured in droplets. However exciting their games, the girls were tense from the strain of their secret misdeeds. By January 1692, tension turned into what would now be termed hysteria.

Betty Parris and Abigail Williams began exhibiting strange symptoms. They fell into trances and, if addressed, made noises and gestures. Abigail suffered convulsions and screamed as if in pain. Other girls soon exhibited similar symptoms. Panic seized the village.

In February, Reverend Parris called in Dr. William Griggs, who, after extensive examination and treatment, concluded they were bewitched. Several ministers came to pray over the girls to no avail. The ministers insisted the girls must name those bewitching them.

An accepted maxim was that the Devil had to work through one person to affect another; in other words, he had to persuade someone to act as his agent. The Devil could then appear to his victims in the shape of his agent and harm them. The spectral shape was thought to be visible only to the afflicted. Such "spectral evidence," criticized by some, was accepted by the court.

Pressed, the girls finally named Tituba, the slave, Sarah Good, a near derelict, and the unpopular Sarah Osburn. On February 29, 1692, warrants were issued and they were arrested.

Magistrates Hold a Hearing

On March 1, two magistrates, Jonathan Corwin and John Hathorne opened a public hearing in the packed meeting house of the village. The examiners conducted themselves more like prosecutors than investigators. Pregnant, dressed in rags, the haggard Sarah Good stood before the magistrates and flatly denied tormenting the children. The girls fell into fits and blamed Good for their pains. Before being removed, Good shifted any possible blame onto Sarah Osburn.

Osburn, dragged from a sick bed when arrested, also denied tormenting the children. The girls again performed. Osburn said she "more like to be bewitched than that she was a witch." She reported a dream in which she was visited by something "like an Indian all black, which did pinch her in her neck" and drag her toward her door. Osburn died in jail awaiting trial. Others met the same fate.

Tituba told the magistrates what they wanted to hear. After briefly denying she had "familiarity" with the Devil, she said:

> [T]here is four women and one man, they hurt the children, and then they lay all upon me; and they tell me, if I will not hurt the children, they will hurt me.

She named Good and Osburn, but claimed she could not identify the other two. Following the magistrates' lead, Tituba wove into her testimony elements of spectral evidence such as talking cats, riding on sticks, and a tall, unidentified man of Boston.

One of the next two accused, Martha Corey, was vulnerable because she had unequivocally disbelieved the girls' claims. But Rebecca Nurse, a frail, elderly, pious matriarch, had never questioned the girls' condition. Few had a harsh word to say about her, except, perhaps, those engaged in a long land dispute with her family. Her sisters were subsequently accused of witchcraft. In the course of their investigations, the magistrates unearthed and recorded many old arguments and suspicious activities. Both women had to testify amidst the girls' fits and visions. The examiners made even less pretense of impartiality than they had with Good, Osburn, and Tituba, but they could not shake the two women in their denials.

Jails Fill with Accused

By May, the jails of Salem Town and Boston were filled with people awaiting trial. More women than men, the accused ranged from Dorcas Good, 5-year-old daughter of Sarah, to the Reverend George Burroughs, formerly the pastor of Salem Village. Ann Putnam claimed Burroughs was responsible for the deaths of his first two wives and of soldiers fighting Indians along the border. Reverend Cotton Mather believed Burroughs was the witches' master conspirator.

Also by May, Massachusetts had a new charter and a new governor, Sir William Phips. Phips convened the General Court, which appointed a special court to try the witches. He then left to tackle more pressing matters of skirmishes along the borders.

The first tried was Sarah Bishop, a tavern keeper. According to Samuel Gray, Bishop's specter appeared over the cradle of his child, bringing about the child's illness and death. Bishop was convicted and, on June 10, hanged.

Next, the judges consulted several ministers for guidance on witchcraft evidence. The ministers warned against heavy reliance on spectral evidence, saying the "demon may assume the shape of the innocent."

The court reconvened June 28. Of the five tried, one was briefly acquitted. The jury was impressed by Rebecca Nurse's demeanor and by a petition testifying to her character. Her daughter, Sarah Nurse, submitted a deposition:

> I saw Goody [term of address] Bibber pull pins out of her close [*sic*] and held them between her fingers and clasped her hands round her knees and then she cried out and said Goody Nurse Pinched her. This I can testify.

Nineteenth-century depiction of a witch trial. (Courtesy, Library of Congress)

After the verdict was read, the girls fell into howling fits, and Justice William Stoughton addressed the jury foreman:

> I will not impose on the jury, but I must ask you if you considered one statement made by the prisoner. When Deliverance Hobbs was brought into court to testify, the prisoner, turning her head to her said, "What, do you bring her? She is one of us.' Has the jury weighed the implications of this statement?

Asked for an explanation, the half-deaf woman did not answer. After reconsideration, Rebecca Nurse was found guilty.

On July 19, the five women were hanged. Urged to confess by Reverend Nicholas Noyes, because "she knew she was a witch," Good retorted:

> You're a liar. I am no more a witch than you are a wizard. If you take my life away, God will give you blood to drink.

Reports are that Noyes died bleeding from the mouth.

Six more were convicted in August. The execution of Elizabeth Proctor was delayed because she was pregnant. The delay saved her life. Her husband, John Proctor, an outspoken critic of the girls' visions, was hanged. His servant girl, Mary Warren, had tried to recant. Away from magistrates and the other girls, Warren would slowly return to a rational state of mind. Faced by them, she would dissolve into hysteria. Sarah Churchill, who also briefly recanted, said in private:

> If I told Mr. Noyes but once I had set my hand to the Book [witches book] he would believe me, but if I told him one hundred times I had not he would not believe me.

In September, 15 were convicted. Eight were hanged. These would be the last hangings. Trials were suspended and further executions postponed by Phips. Phips soon released into the custody of their families those against whom there was only spectral evidence.

Evidence Questioned

An independent opinion from New York clergy criticized almost every type of evidence accepted by the Massachusetts court. When the next court convened, spectral evidence was eliminated as a basis for conviction. Only three were convicted. Eventually Phips reprieved all the condemned.

But the reprieved still had legal and financial problems caused by the trials. The simplest was that jail residents had to pay their prison (lodging) fees before they were released.

As the emotional temper of the colony quieted, qualms about the witch trials grew. In January 1697, the General Court ordered a day of prayer and fasting. In 1703 and 1710, in response to petitions, the legislature reversed most of the convictions and voted compensation to the convicted or their families. Even Ann Putnam eventually repented in church. The convictions of seven, for whom no one submitted petitions, remain on record.

—Teddi DiCanio

Suggestions for Further Reading

Gragg, Larry. "Under an Evil Hand." *American History Illustrated* (March–April 1992): 54–59.

Starkey, Marion L. *The Devil in Massachusetts, A Modern Enquiry into the Salem Witch Trials.* Garden City, N.Y.: Doubleday & Co. 1949.

Upham, Charles W. *Salem Witchcraft.* Williamstown, Mass.: Corner House Publishers, 1971.

John Peter Zenger Trial: 1735

Name of Defendant: John Peter Zenger **Crime Charged:** Seditious libel
Chief Defense Lawyers: Andrew Hamilton and John Chambers
Chief Prosecutor: Richard Bradley **Judge:** James De Lancey **Place:** New York, New York **Date of Trial:** August 1735 **Verdict:** Not guilty

SIGNIFICANCE

By accepting truth as a legitimate defense in a libel case brought against a newspaper editor by a public official, the jury laid the foundations of freedom of the press in America later codified in the Bill of Rights.

Arguably the single most significant political trial ever held in an American courtroom took place in New York City in 1735, well before the colonies fought for and gained independence. The defendant was a printer charged with the crime of seditious libel for publishing items in the *New York Weekly Journal* that skewered and taunted the greedy royal governor of the colony of New York and his judicial appointees. John Peter Zenger's acquittal deeply and firmly planted the roots of freedom of the press in American soil by overthrowing the orthodox legal view that the publication of stinging criticism or ridicule of public officials was, at the very least, a threat to law and order and, at the worst, treason, and thus worthy of severe punishment as "seditious libel."

Fifty years later, American statesman and diplomat Gouverneur Morris described the verdict in this case as "the morning star of liberty which subsequently revolutionized America." Embedded in the Declaration of Independence and in the Bill of Rights of the U. S. Constitution, which Morris helped write, are the basic freedoms for which Zenger and his allies fought.

Zenger's Attack on the Royal Governor

Zenger hardly seemed destined to play a pivotal role in American history. He appeared an ordinary enough man, his career a struggling and undistinguished one until he reached his middle years. Born in the German Palatinate, Zenger emigrated to America in 1710 as a boy of 13. The following year he was accepted as an apprentice by William Bradford, the British colony's royal printer, who enjoyed a monopoly on government printing. By 1725, he became Bradford's partner in the colony's official newspaper, *New York Gazette,* but that year he decided to go into business for himself. Zenger eked out a living until 1733 printing religious pamphlets, supplementing his income by playing an organ in church.

What set Zenger's fate in motion was the arrival in New York from England of a new royal governor, William Cosby. While it is not certain that Cosby was a thief, he was unquestionably a grasping and tactless man who demanded huge sums in payment from the New York colonial council for his services. He even attempted to force the prior interim governor, Rip Van Dam, to turn over half the salary he had been paid. When Van Dam refused, Cosby instituted a claim against Van Dam, to whose cause rallied a sizable number of the colony's wealthier gentlemen.

To propagandize their contempt for Cosby—a sentiment as prevalent among the masses as among the rich—and knowing they could expect no help from Bradford's *Gazette* (not if Bradford wanted to continue to be royal printer), Cosby's enemies turned to Zenger, offering to finance a newspaper for which Zenger would act as editor-publisher. Zenger's *Weekly Journal* made its first appearance November 5, 1733, and, unlike the Bradford paper, was hardly dry reading. With many of the scorching editorials written by a Van Dam ally, attorney James Alexander, the *Journal* quickly got attention, particularly for its mock advertisements. In one of them, Francis Harrison, a Cosby lackey, was described as "a large Spaniel, of about 5 feet 5 inches high . . . lately strayed from his kennel with his mouth full of fulsome panegyrics," or lavish praise for his master. The sheriff found himself described as a "monkey . . . lately broke from his chain and run into the country." Song sheets stronger in their invective than their meter or rhyme followed. ("The petty-fogging knaves deny us rights as Englishmen. We'll make the scoundrel raskals fly, and ne'er return again.")

None of this set well with Cosby and his friends—one of whom threatened Alexander's wife—and, on November 2, 1734, Cosby ordered that four issues of Zenger's paper be burned by the common hangman. The hangman refused. The sheriff then "delivered the papers into the Hands of his own Negroe" who set the bonfire.

Cosby Strikes Back

Fifteen days later, Zenger was arrested, charged with "presenting and publishing several seditious libels . . . influencing [the people's] Minds with Contempt of his Majesty's Government." Zenger was confined to the dungeon of the old city hall, which housed the courts, on 400 pounds bail, an amount easily two or three times Zenger's annual revenue from the newspaper. (It was the bail placed on Zenger that later influenced the writing of the Eighth Amendment of the U.S. Constitution, forbidding excessive bails and fines.)

Cosby's next step was to disbar Zenger's lawyers, William Smith and James Alexander, when they argued against the bail and challenged the commission of Chief Justice James De Lancey, a Cosby appointee. Appointed to defend Zenger—who missed producing only one issue of his newspaper while in prison, dictating editorials to his wife through the dungeon door—was John Chambers, a conscientious enough fellow but one who belonged to the Cosby party.

Despite jury lists that seemed rigged in Cosby's favor, eventually a panel was obtained that contained seven New Yorkers of Dutch descent, among whom anti-British feeling was strong. Even so, the prosecution was confident of victory. Most legal opinion of the time held that defamatory words equaled libel, regardless of the truth or falsity of the words. Under the law, as interpreted by Cosby's attorney general, Richard Bradley, it was solely up to the judge, a Cosby appointee and crony, to decide if the articles were seditious and defamatory. The jury's role was limited to determining if Zenger was "guilty" of publishing the articles in question. Since the printer never denied this, the jury's verdict seemed a foregone conclusion.

Unknown to the Cosby forces, Zenger's friends had not been idle. As a result of their endeavors, a 59-year-old man was sitting in the audience as the trial began. Now he arose, and to the dismay of the judge and prosecutor, identified himself as Andrew Hamilton of Philadelphia, the most famous trial lawyer in the colonies. It was Hamilton's role in the Zenger trial that inspired the phrase, "When in trouble, get a Philadelphia lawyer."

Defense attorney Chambers, in a difficult spot, gladly deferred to Hamilton. From the start, Hamilton admitted Zenger had printed the papers, but observed that for a libel to be proved it must be both false and malicious. "It is a right," said Hamilton, "which all freemen claim, and are entitled to, to complain when they are hurt; they have a right publicly to remonstrate against abuses of power in the strongest terms, to put their neighbors upon their guard against the craft or open violence of men in authority"—a function for a newspaper to perform—"and to assert with courage the sense they have of the blessings of liberty."

Prosecutor Bradley vigorously contested Hamilton's argument, insisting on defining libel as words that were "scandalous, seditious, and tend to disquiet the people." To no one's surprise, Judge De Lancey sided with Bradley, declaring, "You cannot be admitted, Mr. Hamilton, to give the truth of a libel in evidence." Challenged by Hamilton, the chief justice, testily quoting from a British court ruling, declared, "The greater appearance there is of truth in any malicious invective, so much the more provoking it is." Although Hamilton quickly pointed out that the quote came from one of the notorious secret trials of religious dissenters held by the Star Chamber (a former oppressive English court), De Lancey was unmoved and the ruling stood, barring Hamilton from calling witnesses who would testify to the truth of the *Weekly Journal*'s articles, testimony that Royal Governor Cosby very much wanted to avoid.

Hamilton's Appeal for Press Freedom

Since he was unable to present his evidence, Hamilton's only chance to acquit his client was through his summation to the jury. He began by pointing out that "the suppression of evidence ought always to be taken for the strongest

On November 2, 1734, Royal Governor Cosby ordered four issues of Zenger's *Weekly Journal* burned. (Courtesy, Library of Congress)

evidence." Warming to his subject, he denounced the inequities of "corrupt and wicked magistrates," the evils of the Star Chamber and its forbiddance of trial by jury. Liberty, he declared, is our "only bulwark against lawless power." Closing his argument, Hamilton declared:

> I am truly very unequal to such an undertaking on many accounts. And you see I labor under the weight of many years, and am borne down with great infirmities of body; yet old and weak as I am, I should think it my duty, if required, to go to the utmost part of the land where my service could be of any use in assisting to quench the flame of persecutions upon informations set on foot by the government to deprive a people of the right of remonstrating of the arbitrary attempts of men in power. Men who injure and oppress the people under their administration provoke them to cry out and complain; and then make that very complaint the foundation for new oppressions and prosecutions. . . . Gentlemen of the jury, . . . it is not the cause of a poor printer, nor of New York alone, which you are now trying. No! It may in its consequences affect every freeman that lives under a British government on the main of America. It is the best cause. It is the cause of liberty; and I make no doubt but your upright conduct this day will not only entitle you to the love and esteem of your fellow citizens, but every man who prefers freedom to a life of slavery will bless you and honor you, as men who have baffled the attempt of tyranny.

This spellbinding summation, one of the most famous and memorable in legal history, emboldened jurymen and spectators alike. As Zenger himself later noted: "The jury withdrew, and in a small time returned, being asked by the clerk whether they were agreed of their verdict, and whether John Peter Zenger was guilty of printing and publishing the libels in the information aforementioned, they answered by Thomas Hunt, their foreman: Not Guilty. Upon which there were three huzzas in the hall, which was crowded with people and the next day I was discharged from imprisonment."

Zenger Verdict's Legal Impact

Zenger quickly published the transcript of the trial, and his and other printings—one by Benjamin Franklin—soon spread the story of the trial throughout the American colonies and to England. While cheered by many people on both sides of the Atlantic, legal authorities and public officials were slow to accept the verdict as a binding legal precedent. It took the British Parliament until 1792, with the passage of the Fox Libel Act, to formally give juries the right to consider truth, not just publication, in seditious libel cases.

Although freedom of the press was enshrined in the American Bill of Rights, the bitter political battle between Federalists and Republicans after independence was won from Britain sparked seditious libel cases against newspapers in several states. In the 1803 prosecution of a scurrilous Federalist editor, Harry Croswell, for libeling President Thomas Jefferson, a devoutly Republican Justice Morgan Lewis ordered the jury to rule strictly on the fact of publication and banned evidence on the truth of the libel. Another Hamilton—Alexander—appealed to the New York Supreme Court to overturn the jury's guilty verdict and order a new trial, basing his argument on the Zenger case. Although the court split two-and-two on the issue, thus in effect denying the appeal, the eloquence of Hamilton's argument won over public opinion, and the prosecution dropped the proceedings against Croswell. The legal principles enunciated by Hamilton and repeated in the written opinion of Supreme Court Justice James Kent were incorporated into the New York Constitution of 1821.

Through the powerful oratory of both Hamiltons and the courage of Zenger's jurors, the right to free speech—to a free press—was established, and the importance of the right to trial by jury as a safeguard against oppressive government recognized.

—Edward W. Knappman

Suggestions for Further Reading

Buranelli, Vincent. *The Trial of John Peter Zenger.* Westport, Conn.: Greenwood Press, 1975.

Fleming, Thomas J. "A scandalous, malicious and seditious libel." *American Heritage* (December 1967): 22–7, 100–06.

Goebel, Julius and T.R. Naughton, *Law Enforcement in Colonial New York.* New York: Commonwealth Fund, 1944.

Hopkins, W. Wat. "John Peter Zenger." In *A Biographical Dictionary of American Journalism,* edited by Joseph P. McKerns. Westport, Conn.: Greenwood Press, 1989.

Konkle, B.A. *The Life of Andrew Hamilton, 1676–1741.* Philadelphia: National Publishing Co., 1941.

Morris, Richard. *Fair Trial.* New York: Alfred A. Knopf, 1952.

Rutherford, Livington. *John Peter Zenger, His Press, His Trial, and a Bibliography of Zenger Imprints.* New York: Arno Press, 1904.

Schuyler, L.R. *Liberty of The Press in The American Colonies Before The Revolutionary War.* New York: T. Whittaker, 1905.

John Wesley Trial: 1737

Defendant: John Wesley **Plaintiff's Claim:** Defamation of Character
Defense Lawyer: No Record **Lawyer for Plaintiff:** No Record
Judge: Thomas Causton **Place:** Savannah, Georgia **Date of Trial:** August 27–September 1, 1737 **Verdict:** Indicted on 10 charges, 2 relating to the original charge of defamation and 8 relating to alleged ecclesiastical errors
Sentence: Never formally sentenced

SIGNIFICANCE

Because these proceedings took place in a then isolated and obscure colony, they had no effect on the legal system, but this incident does confirm how intolerant of deviant religious beliefs the early colonies were. Also, the fact that John Wesley fled from and never returned to America may well have influenced the development of Methodism: Had Wesley stayed in the colonies, Methodism might have become both a more radical and more regional sect.

In 1729, two brothers, John and Charles Wesley, were at Oxford University in England, John as a teacher and Charles as a student. Sons of a clergyman in the Church of England, John was already an ordained priest and Charles was on his way to becoming one, but during the next few years, both began to express serious doubts about the teachings and activities of Britain's established church. In particular, they felt that the Church of England was too remote and passive in its rituals and teachings. They advocated a Christianity that was both more responsive to and demanding of the religious impulses of the common folk. They gathered around them a small circle of like-minded young tutors and students, and sometime during the early 1730s, these devout young men became known around Oxford as "Methodists," in reference to the more disciplined and demanding way they practiced Christianity.

A Fateful Move

In 1735 John and Charles were in London, where they were introduced to James Edward Oglethorpe, who in 1733 had started a colony in America named Georgia. Oglethorpe encouraged the brothers to go to Georgia to preach to the many Christians as well as to the "heathen" Indians, and in December 1735 the brothers set sail with Oglethorpe himself. When their group arrived in Savannah in February 1736, they brought the total colonists to about 650, spread among six settlements. Charles Wesley did not find conditions to his liking and returned to England in July, but John stayed on and tried to impart his more robust form of Christianity to the colonists.

One of the first he seems to have tried to convert was a young woman, Sophia Christina Hopkey. Very soon the two seemed to have moved beyond the roles of priest and parishioner; he began to tutor her in French and she tended him when he became ill at one point. As rumors of their relationship spread, one of Wesley's friends asked him if he was intending to marry Sophia. It was reported that, for some reason, he then consulted a group of German Protestants who had their own settlement in Georgia and they—again, for an unknown reason—advised him not to marry her.

Painting of John Wesley. (Courtesy, Library of Congress)

Whatever the full story, in March 1737, Sophia married another young colonist, William Williamson. Eight days later, Williamson forbade Sophia to attend the services of Wesley and even to speak with him, but by July at least she did attend a service. Wesley chose to rebuke her in public for several things wrong in her behavior and then early in August actually refused to let her take Communion.

The very next day, Wesley was brought before a bailiff in Savannah to answer to a complaint by William Williamson that his wife Sophia had been defamed. The hearing was set for August 22. The presiding judge was the chief magistrate of the colony, Thomas Causton, but not only was Causton known as an ill-tempered, virtually despotic man, his wife was an aunt of Sophia Williamson. During these days, Causton openly sided with his niece, at one point even calling on Wesley and demanding that he explain in writing why he had refused Sophia the right to take Communion. Moreover, Causton was alleged to have tried to influence at least some of the members of the grand jury by offering them extra food and provisions.

The Case Against Wesley

The proceedings were much like a formal trial, although it was technically a grand jury hearing, with 44 people sitting to consider the charge against Wesley. Allegedly many of them were known to have personal quarrels with Wesley or at least to disapprove of his form of Christianity. Causton opened with a long speech warning the jury "to oppose the new, illegal authority which was usurped over their consciences." He then had read aloud an affidavit by Sophia Williamson in which she claimed that not only had Wesley once proposed to her, he had tried to get her to say she was marrying Williamson under pressure from her family.

At this point, the proceedings against Wesley took a dramatic new turn, for in addition to facing a claim of defamation of one person's character, Wesley found himself facing a whole series of charges accusing him virtually of heretical behavior. Magistrate Causton, hardly a disinterested judge up to this point, now read out to the jury "A List of Grievances" that he himself had drawn up to show that Wesley "deviates from the principles and regulations of the Established Church." They included such charges as: changing the liturgy; altering passages of the psalms; introducing hymns "not inspected or authorized;" baptizing infants by total immersion, denying Communion, confessions, and other sacraments to those "who will not conform to a grievous set of penances, confessions, [and] mortifications;" administering the sacraments to "boys ignorant and unqualified;" "venting sundry uncharitable expressions of all who differ from him;" "teaching wives and servants that they ought absolutely to follow the course of mortifications, fastings, and diets;" "refusing the Office of the Dead" to certain individuals; "searching into and meddling with the affairs of private families."

Sophia Williamson was then called and testified that, in fact, she had no objection to Wesley's behavior before her marriage. Thomas Causton and his wife testified that, in fact, they would not have objected to Wesley marrying Sophia. Ten other witnesses gave testimony, some supporting the charges, others contradicting them. Finally several of Wesley's letters to Sophia were read, convincing some of the propriety of his dealings with her and others of his inappropriate behavior.

The jury spent several days considering the evidence and then, on September 1, presented their findings. A majority of 32 found Wesley guilty of 10 charges, including "forcing his conversation to Sophia Williamson" and refusing Communion to her "much to the great disgrace and hurt of her character." The 12 dissenters also reported their findings; for the most part, they agreed on the facts but they found reasonable justification for Wesley's actions. Most importantly, they stated that "they were thoroughly persuaded that the charges against Mr. Wesley were an artifice of Mr. Causton's, designed rather to blacken the character of Mr. Wesley than to free the colony from religious tyranny, as he had alleged."

Wesley then spoke before the court and argued that 9 of the 10 indictments were "matters of an ecclesiastical nature" and so the court had no jurisdiction. On the "secular" charge that he behaved improperly with Sophia Williamson, he agreed to proceed to a regular trial. Magistrate Causton said that such a trial would have to wait for the next regular session.

Threats, Flight, and a New Church

In the weeks that followed, Wesley showed up at seven different court sessions, but no one moved for his trial. Meanwhile, Wesley was removed from the church in Savannah and assigned to a smaller settlement, but this did not stop his evangelical preaching and praying. Then on November 22, Magistrate Causton sent for him and produced an affidavit in which he, Causton, accused Wesley of "calling him a liar, villain, and so forth."

He continued to preach but he also let it be known that he was considering returning to England. At that, William Williamson issued a notice that he had brought an action asking for £1,000 damages and that anyone assisting in Wesley's escape from the colony would be prosecuted. On December 2, the court sent for Wesley and warned him not to leave; when the bailiff insisted on his posting a bond, Wesley refused and left the premises. The court immediately published an order requiring all officers and guards in the colony to prevent Wesley from leaving.

That evening, Wesley and four other men left under cover of darkness and made their way by boat some 20 miles along the river from Savannah. From there they walked overland to Port Royal, South Carolina, which they reached on December 7. There he took a ship to Charles Town, and on December 22, 1737, he sailed for England. Wesley's "crimes" went largely unknown until an English merchant, Robert Williams, returned from Georgia in 1739 and published an attack on Wesley's behavior there; this prompted Wesley to publish (in 1740) the first volume of his journals in which he gave his own version of events. The episode soon faded from the public's awareness in both Britain and America, and although Wesley would never return to North America, the Methodist Church he founded in England would eventually flourish in the United States.

—John S. Bowman

Suggestions for Further Reading

Stephens, William. *A Journal of the Proceedings in Georgia.* 1742 Reprint, Atlanta, Ga.: Franklin, 1906.

Tyerman, L. *The Life and Times of the Rev. John Wesley, M.A., Founder of the Methodists.* Vol. 1. New York: Harper & Brothers, 1872.

Wesley, John. *The Works of John Wesley.* Vol. 18. Nashville: Abingdon Press, 1984.

The "Great Negro Plot" Trial: 1741

Defendants: More than 170 people, including: Caesar and Prince; John and Sarah Hughson, Sarah Hughson (daughter); Margaret Sorubiero, alias Kerry; Quack; Cuffee; and John Ury. **Crimes Charged:** Entering, theft (Caesar, Prince); receiving stolen goods, conspiracy to commit arson (John and Sarah Hughson, Sorubiero); conspiracy to commit arson (Sarah Hughson, daughter); arson, conspiracy to murder inhabitants of New York (Quack, Cuffee); conspiracy to commit arson and being a Catholic ecclesiastic (Ury) **Chief Defense Lawyer:** None **Chief Prosecutors:** James Alexander, Richard Bradley, John Chambers, Abraham Lodge, Joseph Murray, Richard Nicolls, and William Smith **Judges:** James De Lancey, Daniel Horsmanden, and Frederick Philipse **Dates of Trials:** 1741: May 1, (Caesar, Prince); May 6, (John and Sarah Hughson, and Sorubiero for receiving stolen goods); May 29, (Quack, Cuffee); June 4, (John and Sarah Hughson, Sarah Hughson, daughter, and Sorubiero, for conspiracy with Quack and Cuffee); July 29, (Ury). **Place of Trials:** New York, Colony of New York **Verdicts:** Guilty **Sentences:** 70 blacks, 7 whites banished from British North America; 16 blacks, four whites hanged; 13 blacks burned at the stake. Of the defendants named above: Hanging (Caesar, Prince, John and Sarah Hughson, Margaret Sorubiero, Ury); hanging, but pardoned in exchange for testimony, particularly against Ury (Sarah Hughson, daughter); burning at the stake (Quack, Cuffee)

SIGNIFICANCE

This series of cases served as a brutal example of the consequences of panic when legal procedures become dispensable.

The panic over the "Great Negro Plot" has been likened to the hysteria of the Salem Witchcraft Trials. The "plot" was thought to be a conspiracy to stage an uprising among slaves who would burn New York and murder the white citizens. A conspiracy is defined as an agreement to commit a crime. The crime of conspiracy exists separately from the crime or crimes agreed upon. The key question of the "Great Negro Plot" is the kind of conspiracy that existed, if any. That a few people conspired to burn and loot some buildings appears to be true.

That some slaves occasionally indulged in talk about revolt is plausible. Beyond that, the conspiracy was a delusion bred of fear.

In February 1741, Robert Hogg's tobacco shop was burglarized. An investigation led to the arrest of two slaves, Caesar and Prince, who frequented a tavern owned by John Hughson. Following the arrests, Mary Burton, a 16-year-old indentured servant in Hughson's tavern, dropped hints about the burglary. When questioned, Burton claimed that the Hughson family dealt in stolen property, assisted by a woman living at the tavern, Margaret (Peggy) Kelly or Sorubiero. (Caesar was rumored to be the father of her child.) Constables found the goods, arrested Hughson, and held the other three as accomplices.

Soon after the arrests, New York suffered several mysterious fires, starting with the city's fortress, Fort George. Subsequent fires, accompanied by theft, suggested arson. Indications that slaves were involved helped spark the conspiracy theories. Soon two slaves, Quack and Cuffee, were in custody.

They denied everything, even when convicted. Faced with the stake, they tried to save themselves with confessions. But the sheriff could not fight the mob that came to see them die.

By the time Mary Burton testified to the grand jury, the story she told was that John Hughson led a conspiracy that included Caesar, Prince, and Cuffee. They met at Hughson's to plan the fires and the massacre of the white population.

> Caesar should be governor, and Hughson . . . king . . . that she has seen twenty or thirty negroes at one time in her master's house . . . the three aforesaid negroes . . . were generally present . . . that the other negroes durst not refuse to do what they commanded them . . . That she never saw any white person . . . when they talked of burning the town, but her master, her mistress, and Peggy.

Mary Burton's testimony became wilder as the number of people she accused grew. Prosecutor Richard Bradley used the legally inadmissible testimony of convicted thief Arthur Price, who swore that several of the accused made damning admissions to him while in jail—admissions denied by defendants. Bradley also used hearsay evidence and testimony of frightened defendants trying to obtain mercy or to direct suspicion elsewhere. The court permitted Bradley's legal violations. Since no lawyer in New York would agree to defend any of the accused, no one objected. Next, Governor James Oglethorpe of Georgia wrote authorities in other colonies, warning them to beware of Spanish plots and spies. This led New York authorities to link this conspiracy to Spain and English schoolmaster John Ury.

Ury, skilled in Latin and theology, faced the flimsiest testimony "proving" he was a Catholic priest and the real head of the conspiracy. This contradicted earlier claims that Hughson was the leader. Ury produced witnesses to attest to his whereabouts during alleged plotting sessions. Nevertheless, he was hanged.

There were no more grand jury indictments, but Judge Daniel Horsmanden's obsession with the conspiracy led to one last death, a slave named Tom.

—Teddi DiCanio

Suggestions for Further Reading

Davis, T.J. *A Rumor of Revolt.* New York: The Free Press, 1985.

Horsmanden, Daniel. *The New York Conspiracy.* Boston: Beacon Press, 1971 [reprint].

Writits Of Assistance Trial: 1761

Petitioner for the Writ: James Cockle, a deputy customs official of Salem **Petitioners against the Writs:** Merchants of Salem and Boston, Massachusetts Bay Colony **Attorney for the Customs Officials:** Jeremiah Gridley **Attorneys for the Merchants:** James Otis and Oxenbridge Thacher **Chief Judge:** Thomas Hutchinson **Place:** Boston, Massachusetts Bay Colony **Date:** February 24, 1761 **Verdict:** Deferred until a legal opinion could be obtained from England

SIGNIFICANCE

The case was the first major judicial confrontation over the extent and limits of English authority over colonial affairs. The argument highlighted the growing American notion of fundamental "constitutional" laws that included inalienable rights. The case helped lay the ideological foundations for the American Revolution and the Fourth Amendment of the Bill of Rights, which banned abusive search and seizure.

Under England's navigation laws, which governed the British Empire's commerce, the American colonies faced prohibitions and restrictions on trading and manufacturing certain goods within and without the empire. The British West Indies could not produce the amount of molasses needed by the colonists to make rum, a major product, and New England merchants were troubled by the substantial duty on molasses purchased from outside Britain's island colonies. Need, as well as greed, contributed to colonial smuggling.

During the French and Indian War, some smugglers continued to trade with French territories, supplying the enemy with essential goods. The smugglers faced weak opposition. Customs officials seldom bothered to search ships while they lay at anchor. Many customs appointees lived in England and assigned their duties to poorly paid colonial deputies, who often did not do the work. Great Britain spent an average of 8,000 pounds to collect 2,000 pounds in duties.

As the French and Indian War wound down, England moved to combat illegal trade. Merchants feared the crackdown would rely heavily on writs of assistance. Such writs had been issued in the past in the colonies, but they were seldom used. Writs of assistance were essentially general search warrants of tremendous scope.

The writs offered more latitude than ordinary search warrants. Usually a search warrant was based on a sworn statement of legitimate suspicion and permitted officials to examine a specific place for specific goods. Writs of assistance permitted customs officers (or anyone holding the writ), to search shops, ships, homes, and warehouses at will during the day. Once issued, they could be used again and again.

Writs of assistance expired within six months after the death of a reigning monarch. When George II died, a battle arose in Massachusetts over the legality of issuing new writs. Colonial merchants, represented by James Otis and Oxenbridge Thacher, petitioned Superior Court to refuse applications by customs officials for new writs. Otis had been the king's advocate general of Boston's Vice-Admiralty Court and had resigned rather than argue for customs officials.

Writs Versus Rights

The case turned on interpretation of the legal basis for the writs. Jeremiah Gridley, acting for the customs officials, maintained that necessities of state justified limitations on traditional English rights:

> It is true the common privileges of Englishmen are taken away in this Case, but even their privileges are not so in case of Crime and fine. 'Tis the necessity of the Case and the benefit of the Revenue that justifies this Writ. Is not the Revenue the sole support of Fleets & Armies abroad, & Ministers at home? without which the Nation could neither be preserved from the Invasion of her foes, nor the Tumults of her own Subjects. Is not this I say infinitely more important, that the imprisonment of Thieves, or even Murderers? yet in these Cases 'tis agreed Houses may be broken open.

Gridley included in his argument references to statutory precedents.

In rebuttal, Oxenbridge Thacher also referred to precedents. The colonial Superior Court's power was in the case of the writs being held comparable to that of the Court of Exchequer in England. Thacher reasoned there was no justification for such a comparison. He also criticized the longevity of the writs, stressing how their power could be abused by repeated use.

Following Thacher, James Otis spoke like "a flame of fire," according to John Adams. He, too, spoke of precedent. He built an elaborate argument that began with an individual's God-given natural rights and the birth of societal compacts. He continued through old Saxon laws, Magna Carta, and actions taken over time to secure and confirm rights and principals of England's unwritten constitution.

Otis repeatedly attacked the writs as directly contrary to basic English liberties:

> It appears to me the worst instrument of arbitrary power, the most destructive of English liberty and the fundamental principles of law, that ever was found in an English law book.

Otis preferred "special warrants" which specified name, place, what was suspected, and by whom. Complaining of the unaccountability of those armed with writs of assistance, Otis said:

> Every one with this writ may be a tyrant in a legal manner . . . Now one of the most essential branches of English liberty is the freedom of one's house. A man's house is his castle; and whilst he is quiet, he is as well guarded as a prince in his castle. This writ, if it should be declared legal, would totally annihilate this privilege.

Otis repeated a well-known story. A man named Ware held a writ which had been endorsed to him by a customs official. Ware was brought to court for swearing on the Sabbath. He took revenge on the judge and the constable who had arrested him. He used his writ to ransack their homes looking for smuggled goods.

Otis spoke for four hours. John Adams wrote:

> Every man of an immense crowded audience appeared to me to go away as I did, ready to take arms against Writs of Assistance. . . . Then and there, the child Independence was born. In fifteen years, i.e. in 1776, he grew up to manhood and declared himself free.

The court did not immediately issue the writs, although it was known that Chief Justice Thomas Hutchinson favored them:

> The Court has considered the subject of writs of assistance, and can see no foundation for such a writ; but as the practice in England is not known, it has been thought best to continue the question to the next term, that in the mean time opportunity may be given to know the result.

The query was sent to the colonial agent for Massachusetts in England. Legal authority to issue the writs was upheld and the court quietly did so. But apparently no customs official had the temerity to use them.

—Teddi DiCanio

Suggestions for Further Reading

Adams, John. Charles Francis Adams, ed. *Works*. Boston: 1856.

Gipson, Lawrence Henry. *The Coming of the Revolution, 1763–1775*. New York: Harper & Row, 1954.

Hart, Albert B. and Edward Channing, eds. *American History Leaflets*. New York: Simmons, 1892–1911.

Langguth, A.J. *Patriots, The Men Who Started the American Revolution*. New York: Simon & Schuster, 1988.

The Parsons' Cause Trial: 1763

Plaintiff: Reverend James Maury **Defendants:** The collectors of the tax for Louisa County, Colony of Virginia **Plaintiff Claim:** 300 Pounds in back pay **Chief Defense Lawyer:** Patrick Henry, taking over from John Lewis **Chief Lawyer for Plaintiff:** Peter Lyons **Judge:** John Henry **Place:** Hanover County, Colony of Virginia **Date of Hearing:** December 1, 1763 **Verdict:** Damages awarded, one penny

SIGNIFICANCE

The case provided a forum for challenging the limits of England's power to control American colonial affairs.

The Parsons' Cause began as an argument over a piece of financial legislation and ended with an impassioned speech on a theory of government. That speech was one of the first signs of the schism occurring between England and her American colonies.

Because the Anglican Church was the established church of the colony of Virginia, its clergy were supported by taxes. By a 1748 statute, the salary of a parson was set at 16,000 pounds of tobacco a year. (Tobacco was a common form of tender during the colonial period.) In 1755 and again in 1758, due to shortages of tobacco brought on by drought, laws were enacted allowing tobacco obligations to be fulfilled with Virginia's paper money. Paper money, which generally depreciated in value, was blessed by debtors and loathed by creditors.

The 1758 law, the Two Penny Act, a temporary, one-year measure, allowed the ministers' salaries to be paid in currency at a fixed rate of twopence per pound of tobacco. The prevailing inflated market rate at the time was running at fourpence to sixpence per pound. Once depreciation was factored in, a clergyman was receiving about one-third of his normal, stipulated salary. The colony's council approved and, with the House of Burgesses, convinced Francis Fauquier, the royal governor, to allow the act to go into effect.

Virginia's revenue measures were supposed to be approved by the Privy Council back in London before being implemented. But Fauquier, in a letter to Great Britain's Board of Trade, argued that, given the economic need and the short-term duration of the measure, suspending the act until the Council could review was tantamount to rejecting it and, thus, eliminating all economic relief. Such a decision would repudiate the almost unanimous economic wisdom of experienced local legislators and to ignore the 1755 precedent for which the previous governor "incurred no Censure for having pass'd it."

The clergy objected. They argued that they should reap the benefit of high tobacco prices since they had had to accept whatever their tobacco would sell for when the price was low. But the Privy Council would probably have let the measure stand had it not been for the persistence of the Reverend John Camm of York County. Camm led a group of Anglican ministers determined to see the Two Penny Act nullified. When a war of pamphlets and lawsuits availed them nothing, Camm sailed for England.

Patrick Henry, above, served as counsel for the defense in the Parson's Cause Trial, despite the fact that his father was the presiding judge. (Courtesy, The National Portrait Gallery)

In England he enlisted the help of the Archbishop of Canterbury and the Bishop of London. Camm argued that the Two Penny Act was a manifestation of the deliberate erosion of royal and Anglican authority in Virginia. Camm's narrow-minded focus on his own list of grievances ignored the act's purpose as a financial relief measure. (Some historians have questioned the need for the act and there were those in Virginia who were happy to see the ministers take a financial blow. But there is little evidence that the House of Burgesses deliberately set out to penalize the clergy.) The king and his council, on the recommendation of the Board of Trade, disallowed the measure and its predecessors.

Since the Two Penny Act of 1758 already had expired, the repeal of the law would have been moot had not several clergymen sued for back pay. Two cases were rejected on the grounds that the act was valid until it was actually disallowed by the Privy Council. One court awarded a parson double his salary in damages. But it was the case filed by Reverend James Maury of Louisa County that turned out to be the most significant.

The Suit

Maury filed suit, in neighboring Hanover County to avoid the politically hostile climate in his home county. In November of 1763, the presiding judge, Colonel John Henry, ruled that the Two Penny Act had been rendered null from its beginning, contrary to the rulings in the earlier cases. Next came a hearing for damages in which the jury would determine what was due Maury.

At this point, the judge's son, young Patrick Henry, was requested to take over council for the defense. (Such conflicts of interest were common in colonial America.) On December 1, the hearing commenced and the Reverend Maury protested at the prospective jurors offered by the sheriff. Later, in a letter, Maury described them as "the vulgar herd." Maury had some justification for his protest. Three jurors were religious dissenters, and a fourth was a cousin of Patrick Henry's. Henry countered, "They were honest men, and, therefore, unexceptionable, they were immediately called to the book and sworn."

Next, Maury's gifted lawyer, Peter Lyons, rose, summed up the verdict of the previous month and called two tobacco dealers. They testified that the market price of tobacco averaged 50 shillings per 100 pounds in 1759. At 16,000 pounds of tobacco a year as salary, Lyons computed that Maury had been due 450 British pounds in cash, rather than the approximately 150 pounds he had received under the Two Penny Act. Thus Lyons, after praising the Anglican clergy at some length, asked the jury to award Maury 300 British pounds.

Patrick Henry rose. After a faltering start, the great oratorical gift that was to make him famous surfaced. Henry based his argument on an idea called the compact theory of government. According to Maury's letter, Henry stated:

> [The] act of 1758 had every characteristic of a good law, that it was a law of general utility, and could not, consistently with what he called the original compact between King and people, stipulating protection on the one hand and obedience on the other, be annuled.

Henry argued that by disallowing good laws, a king forfeited his right to the obedience of his subjects. Instead of being a father to his people, he "degenerates into a Tyrant." Lyons cried out that Henry had "spoken treason," a sentiment echoed by a few others in the courtroom.

Henry also attacked the Anglican clergy, accusing them of greed:

> Do they feed the hungry and clothe the naked? Oh, no, gentlemen! These rapacious harpies would, were their power equal to their will, snatch from the hearth of their honest parishioner his last hoe-cake, from the widow and her orphan children her last mich cow! the last bed-nay, the last blanket-from the lying-in woman!"

In conclusion, Patrick Henry suggested Reverend Maury be awarded one farthing. After five minutes of deliberation, the jury awarded four times that amount: one penny. This decision effectively put an end to any more suits.

Henry's spectacular performance gained him fame, good will, clients, and an entre into the political arena. More important, arguments over the compact theory of government and the limitations of royal and parliamentary authority would arise repeatedly as America pulled away from "Mother England." Indeed, its fullest and most eloquent expression would appear 13 years later in the Declaration of Independence.

—Teddi DiCanio

Suggestions for Further Reading

Beeman, Richard R. *Patrick Henry, A Biography.* New York: McGraw-Hill Book Co., 1974.

Langhuth, A.J. *Patriots: The Men Who Started the American Revolution,* New York: Simon & Schuster, 1988.

McCants, David A., "The Authenticity of James Maury's Account of Patrick Henry's Speech in the Parsons' Cause." *Southern Speech Communication Journal,* Vol. 42 (1976).

Nettels, Curtis P., *The Roots of American Civilization, A History of American Colonial Life.* New York: Appleton-Century Crofts, 1938.

Boston Massacre Trials: 1770

Defendants: Captain Thomas Preston; Corporal William Wemms; Privates Hugh White, John Carroll, William Warren, and Matthew Killroy, William McCauley, James Hartegan, and Hugh Montgomery
Crimes Charged: Murder and accessories to murder
Chief Defense Lawyers: Both trials: John Adams, Josiah Quincy, Jr.; First trial: Robert Auchmuty; Second trial: Sampson Salter Blowers
Chief Prosecutors (Attorneys for the Crown): Samuel Quincy and Robert Treat Paine **Judges:** John Cushing, Peter Oliver, Benjamin Lynd, and Edmund Trowbridge **Place:** Boston, Massachusetts Bay Colony
Dates of Trials: *Rex v. Preston:* October 24–30, 1770; *Rex v. Wemms et al.:* November 27–December 5, 1770 **Verdicts:** First trial: Captain Robert Preston, Not guilty; Second trial: Corporal Wemms, Privates White, Carroll, Warren, McCauley, and Hartegan, Not guilty; Privates Killroy and Montgomery, Not guilty of murder but guilty of manslaughter **Sentences:** Branding on the thumbs for Killroy and Montgomery

SIGNIFICANCE

This case was a landmark on the road to the American Revolution. Despite a politically hostile atmosphere, two reasonably fair trials were conducted and the concept of the right of self-defense was upheld.

On the night of March 5, 1770, three men lay dead and two more were dying, following shots fired by British troops into an angry crowd outside of the Custom House in Boston, Massachusetts. This scene, known as the Boston Massacre, came after months of feuding between Bostonians and the soldiers sent to the city to protect newly appointed Customs commissioners. The British king and his cabinet viewed Boston as a hotbed of dissent in the colonies, where ill will blossomed in the years following the French and Indian War. Quarrels arose over Indian and frontier affairs, over customs regulations, over taxes, and particularly over how extensive was Parliament's right to tax the colonies. Boston, with its unusually stormy Stamp Act riots, seemed to be the focal point of the American political ferment.

Although some British troops had remained in the colonies following the war, the stationing of a large number of troops in a colonial city was a new and unwelcome phenomenon. In the 18th century, British citizens and colonists viewed the maintenance of a standing army in peace time as an abomination, much as Americans would regard a secret police force today. The ever-present troops in Boston seemed proof of the erosion of the colonists' rights as individuals and the usurpation of the powers of their cherished political institutions.

In such an atmosphere, trouble was inevitable. Snubs, shoving matches, loud arguments, and occasional fistfights occurred between Boston residents and the soldiers almost from the day the first contingent landed in the fall of 1768.

Snowballs, then Musket Balls Fly

The series of events that led to the confrontation on March 5, 1770, apparently began with a nasty exchange between Private Patrick Walker of the 29th Regiment and William Green, a local rope-maker.

Soldiers of low rank routinely augmented their meager salaries with odd jobs. As Walker passed Green on March 2, the rope-maker asked the soldier if he wanted work. When Walker said yes, Green replied, "Well, then go and clean my shithouse." Insulted, Walker swore revenge. He walked away and, in a few minutes, returned with several other soldiers.

A fight ensued between the soldiers and the rope-makers, who had rallied around Green. Clubs and sticks were used, as well as fists. The rope-makers routed the soldiers.

But the lull in the fighting was brief. Skirmishes popped up over the next two days. Rumors flew and tensions mounted. The commander of the 29th Regiment, Lieutenant Colonel Maurice Carr, wrote to Acting Governor Thomas Hutchinson to complain of the abuse his men were forced to endure from the citizens of Boston. On March 5, Hutchinson put the letter before the Governor's Council. The unanimous reply was that the people of the town would not be satisfied until the troops were removed.

The evening of the fifth was cold, and a foot of snow lay on the ground. When a wig-maker's apprentice named Edward Garrick insulted Private Hugh White, who was stationed at a sentry box near the Main Guard, the army's headquarters, White struck Garrick on the head with a musket. Nevertheless, other apprentices continued to bait White and throw snowballs at him.

Periodically, cries of "fire" could be heard in the streets, although no buildings were burning that night. Soldiers passed up and down Brattle Street carrying clubs, bayonets, and other weapons. In Boylston's Alley, a battle of snowballs and insults was quelled by a passing officer, who led the troops to nearby Murray's barracks and told their junior officers to confine them. Outside the barracks, a few more words were exchanged before Richard Palmes, a Boston merchant, persuaded many members of the crowd to go home. But some of the crowd shouted that they should go "away to the Main Guard."

At about the same time, some 200 people gathered in an area called Dock Square. More people joined them as groups flowed in from Boston's North End. Some came carrying cudgels. Others picked up whatever weapons they could find in the square. The crowd eventually gathered around a tall man whose words evidently sent the crowd to the Main Guard.

Meanwhile, Private Hugh White retreated from his sentry box near the Main Guard to the steps of the Custom House. From there, he threatened to fire on the approaching crowd and called for the assistance of other soldiers.

When word of the sentry's predicament reached Captain Thomas Preston, he led a small contingent from the 29th Regiment to White's rescue. With bayonets affixed, two columns of men managed to reach the beleaguered Private White. When the soldiers prepared to retrace their route, the prospect of retreating through the menacing crowd appeared more daunting. The soldiers positioned themselves in a rough semicircle, facing the crowd with their captain just in front of them. Their muskets were loaded. Some in the crowd flung angry words and taunts to fire. Finally, someone hurled a club, knocking down soldier Hugh Montgomery. He got to his feet, and a cry was heard to fire. Montgomery fired one shot. No one seemed to be hit and the crowd pulled away a little from the troops. There was a pause during which Captain Preston might have given an order to cease firing. The pause between the first and the subsequent shots could have been as little as six seconds or as much as two minutes, according to witnesses' accounts.

However long the pause, the troops commenced firing. Confusion ensued. Most people in the crowd believed the soldiers were firing only powder, not bullets. But two men were hit almost immediately. Samuel Gray fell with a hole in his head. A tall, burly sailor known as Michael Johnson (true name Crispus Attucks), variously described as black, mulatto, or Indian, took two bullets in the chest. As some members of the crowd surged forward to prevent further firing, another sailor, James Caldwell, was hit.

A ricocheting bullet struck 17-year-old Samuel Maverick as he ran toward the Town House. He died several hours later at his mother's boarding house. The fifth fatality was Patrick Carr. Struck in the hip by a bullet that "tore away part of the backbone," he lingered until the 14th of March. Carr's dying testimony later helped bolster the defense attorneys' claim that the soldiers fired in self-defense.

Captain Preston yelled at his men, demanding to know why they had fired. The reply was they thought he ordered them to shoot when they had heard the word "fire." As the crowd, which had fallen back, began to help those who had fallen, the troops again raised their muskets. Preston commanded them to cease fire and went down the line pushing up their musket barrels. The crowd dispersed, carrying the wounded, the dying, and the dead. Captain Preston and his men marched back to the Main Guard. The Boston Massacre was over. Although the city did not quiet, there were no more deadly altercations.

Following a brusque interview with Captain Preston, Royal Governor Hutchinson made his way to the council room of the town hall. Addressing the crowd from a balcony, Hutchinson promised a full inquiry and asked the townspeople to go home. He said, "The law shall have its course; I will live and die by the law." Thus, the Crown undertook an investigation into the Boston Massacre.

The Redcoats are Indicted

That very night, two justices of the peace went to the council chamber and spent the next several hours calling witnesses to be examined. By morning, Captain Preston and his eight men had been incarcerated. A week later, a grand jury was sworn in, and, at the request of Attorney General Jonathan Sewall, indictments were promptly handed down.

But Sewall, a loyalist, busied himself with legal affairs out of town, leaving the prosecution of the soldiers to whomever the royal court appointed. The disappointing choice was another loyalist, Samuel Quincy, the colony's solicitor general. To strengthen the prosecution, at a town meeting, radicals led by Samuel Adams, persuaded Boston selectmen and citizens to pay prosecution expenses, bringing in the very successful lawyer Robert Treat Paine.

The choice of loyalist Robert Auchmuty to serve as the senior counsel for Captain Preston was no surprise, but the other two attorneys who agreed to act for the defense were: Josiah Quincy, Jr. (brother of the prosecutor Samuel Quincy), a fiery radical; John Adams, the cousin of Samuel Adams and just as offended as he by the presence of the king's troops in Boston. Both Quincy and Adams had participated in the funeral procession for four of the men the soldiers were accused of killing. For the trial of the soldiers, Auchmuty dropped out, and Adams became senior counsel, with Samuel Salter Blowers as junior counsel.

The trials were delayed more than once, providing a long period for tempers to cool. The radicals, thwarted in their efforts to obtain an immediate trial, tried to convict the troops in the press.

The decision on whether to hold one trial or two was not announced until the last minute. The troops wanted to be tried *with* Captain Preston. They believed separate trials would lessen their chances of acquittal, particularly if Preston were tried first and found not guilty, which would indicate that his men bore the responsibility for firing without orders.

Additionally, if the Captain and his men were tried together, the prosecution would have a difficult case in proving that a bullet from one specific gun, fired by one specific soldier had hit one specific victim. Furthermore, the troops knew that if the Crown *could* prove that Preston had given the order to fire, the greater share of responsibility and guilt would be his.

Probably to the disappointment of the troops, it was decided there would be two separate trials: the first for Captain Preston, the second for the troops.

Captain Preston's Trial

If a transcript of the trial of Captain Preston ever existed, it has disappeared. Summaries and notes of the testimony were made by various, sometimes partisan, individuals. The reconstruction from the available evidence is as follows.

The captain's trial began October 24, 1770, and was over October 30, 1770. It was the first criminal trial in Massachusetts to last longer than a day.

Samuel Quincy opened for the prosecution and called as its first witness Edward Garrick, the apprentice wig-maker whose taunts had ended with his being struck by Private Hugh White. After describing this incident, Garrick testified that he had seen soldiers in the streets carrying swords before Preston had led his men to the Custom House. The next witness, Thomas Marshall, supported that statement and added that Preston most certainly did have time to order his men to cease fire between the first and subsequent shots.

A fanciful engraving of the Boston Massacre. (Courtesy, Library of Congress)

Witnesses that followed also gave damning testimony. Peter Cunningham said that Preston had ordered his men to prime and load their muskets. Later, he qualified his statement by saying that the man who had ordered the troops to fire was definitely an officer by reason of the way he was dressed. Witnesses William Wyatt and John Cox both insisted that Preston had given the order to fire.

But on the following day, the Crown's testimony floundered. Witness Theodore Bliss said Preston had been standing in front of the guns. Bliss heard someone shouting "Fire" but did not think it was the captain. Henry Knox testified that the crowd was shouting, "Fire, damn your blood, fire." And Benjamin Burdick said he heard the word "Fire" come from behind the men.

The Crown regained some ground with witness Daniel Calef, who unequivocally stated that he had "looked the officer in the face when he gave the word" to fire. The next witness, Robert Goddard, also stated firmly that Preston, standing behind his men, had given the order to fire.

Samuel Quincy did not close the Crown's case with a summation of the evidence. Instead, he quoted from a few legal treatises:

> Not such killing only as proceeds from premeditated hatred or revenge against the person killed, but also in many other cases, such as is accompanied with those circumstances that shew the heart to be perversely wicked, is adjudged to be of malice prepense, and consequently murder.

The first three witnesses for the defense testified to the threats uttered against the soldiers by those in the street. According to one, Edward Hill, after the firing, he saw Preston push up a musket and say, "Fire no more. You have done mischief enough."

On the following day, a string of witnesses vividly described the confusion and anger that reigned March 5. The first witness for the defense, John Edwards, stated firmly that it was the corporal, William Wemms, who had given the men the order to prime and load their muskets. Another, Joseph Hilyer, said, "The soldiers seemed to act from pure nature, . . . I mean they acted and fired by themselves."

Reasonable Doubt

Richard Palmes testified that he had had his hand on Preston's shoulder just as the order to fire was given. At the time, the two men were in front of the troops. Even at that distance, Palmes could not be sure whether Preston or someone else had given the order. Palmes' testimony, even with its measure of ambiguity, threw a strong element of "reasonable doubt" on the Crown's case.

Another major witness for the defense was Andrew (no last name recorded). He was a slave, but he was always referred to as the "Negro servant" of merchant Oliver Wendell, a Son of Liberty, who testified emphatically to Andrew's integrity. In meticulous, coherent detail, Andrew described the explosive scene on March 5—the taunts, the threats, the objects thrown (mostly snowballs), the clash of stick against bayonet. Andrew also testified that the voice that gave the order to fire was different from the other voices calling out and he was sure the voice had come from beyond Preston.

When John Gillespie took the stand, he testified about an event that occurred at least two hours before the Massacre. He spoke of seeing a group of townspeople carrying swords, sticks, and clubs, coming from the South End. The tone of Gillespie's testimony implied a "plot" to expel the troops from Boston. Adams was opposed to such testimony and was angry with Josiah Quincy, who had prepared the witnesses. He feared attacking Boston's reputation would backfire on the defendant, angering a jury to a guilty verdict or inciting a mob to lynching. Adams threatened to withdraw from the case if any further evidence of that nature was introduced.

In making closing arguments, defense attorney Adams spoke first. He said, "Self-defence [*sic*] is the primary canon of the law of nature," and he explained how a homicide was justifiable under common law when an assaulted man had nowhere to retreat. Carefully reviewing the evidence, Adams ruthlessly demolished the Crown's weakly presented case. Instead of attacking the Crown's witnesses, he deftly wove parts of their testimony into his arguments and dismissed as honest mistakes those that he couldn't use.

In his summation for the prosecution, Paine, in an effort to dismiss the notion of self-defense introduced by Adams, pointed out that defense witness Palmes was standing in front of the soldiers' muskets. "Would he place himself before a party of soldiers and risque his life at the muzzles of their guns," Paine reasoned, "when he thought them under a necessity of firing to defend their life?"

In the judges' charge to the jury, the main points the jurors had to consider were: Whether the soldiers' party constituted an unlawful assembly? Whether that party was assaulted? Whether the crowd constituted an unlawful assembly? Whether Preston ordered the loading of the muskets and, if so, why? Was this a defensive action? And, most important, did Preston give the order to fire? Finally, in a move that favored the defense, the judges reminded the jury that self-defense was a law of nature.

The court adjourned at 5:00 P.M. on Monday. By 8:00 A.M. on Tuesday, the jury had reached a verdict. Preston was found not guilty.

The Soldiers' Trial

One month later in the trial of the soldiers, the Crown's first witnesses testified about the behavior of soldiers—who may or may not have been among those on trial—in the hours before the Massacre. Prosecution witnesses spoke of off-duty officers, armed with cutlasses, running through the streets and randomly assaulting citizens.

Apparently the prosecution wanted to broaden the court's scope of inquiry, a questionable move since testimony about other soldiers was irrelevant. The defense had little objection so long as it could introduce equally irrelevant testimony concerning the actions of citizens prior to the crucial events. The court permitted the lawyers to have their way.

Of the Crown's first witnesses, only one made a major point. The town watchman, Edward Langford, described the death of a citizen, John Gray. According to Langford, Gray had definitely been shot by Private Matthew Killroy.

The following day the Crown's witnesses faltered. James Brewer, who consistently denied that the crowd had uttered any threats against the soldiers, admitted that people all around were calling "Fire." Asked if he had thought the cry referred to a fire or if it was bidding the soldiers to fire, Brewer answered he could not "tell now what I thought then."

Another witness, James Bailey, was quite clear on the fact that boys in the street had pelted the soldiers with pieces of ice large enough to do injury. Bailey also stated that Private Montgomery had been knocked down and that he had seen Crispus Attucks (one of the men killed) carrying "a large cord-wood stick."

One of the prosecution's most effective witnesses was Samuel Hemmingway, who testified that Private Killroy had said, "He would never miss an opportunity, when he had one, to fire on the inhabitants, and that he had wanted to have an opportunity ever since he landed."

In his opening remarks for the defense, Josiah Quincy spoke about the widespread notion "that the life of a soldier was of very little value; of much less value, than others of the community. The law, gentlemen, knows no such distinction. . . . What will justify and mitigate the action of one, will do the same to the other." He dwelt on the bad feeling between the citizens and the soldiers and the fears of citizens that their liberties were threatened.

Like those for the prosecution, the first defense witnesses spoke of extreme behavior throughout the town. A picture emerged of a possible riot in the making. The testimony of William Hunter, an auctioneer who had seen the tall man addressing the crowd in Dock Square, suggested some of the crowd's activities may have been organized rather than spontaneous. But for the same reasons he had cited during the first trial, John Adams put a stop to further testimony of this sort. And again he threatened to withdraw from the case.

For two days, the defense presented solid evidence that the soldiers at the Custom House were jeopardized by a dangerous crowd. A stream of 40 witnesses appeared. One of the last witnesses was Dr. John Jeffries, who had cared for Patrick Carr, the fifth victim, as he lay dying. Jeffries said,

> I asked him if he thought the soldiers would have been hurt, if they had not fired. He said he really thought they would, for he heard many voices cry out, kill them. I asked him then, meaning to close all, whether he thought they fired in self-defense, or on purpose to destroy the people. He said he really thought they did fire to defend themselves; that he did not blame the man whoever he was, that shot him.

In his closing remarks, Quincy pointed out that even a "moderate" person might impulsively seek to exact vengeance from the soldiers at the Custom House for the actions of soldiers elsewhere in the town that night. But the law did not permit this. The evidence demonstrated that the troops had acted in self-defense.

In his closing summation, a brilliant blend of law and politics, John Adams argued self-defense. He portrayed the wrath of the crowd, while subtly exonerating the city of Boston from blame and placing much of the blame on "Mother England." He pointed out, "At certain critical seasons, even in the mildest government, the people are liable to run into riots and tumults." The possibility of such events "is in direct proportion to the despotism of the government."

Adams turned his attention to a description of the crowd. "And why we should scruple to call such a set of people a mob? . . . Soldiers quartered in a populous town, will always occasion two mobs, where they prevent one. They are wretched conservators of the peace."

After 2 and one-half hours of deliberation, the jury acquitted Corporal William Wemms, and Privates White, Warren, Carroll, McCauley, and Hartegan. Privates Killroy and Montgomery were found not guilty of murder but guilty of manslaughter. Sufficient evidence had shown that these two men had definitely shot their weapons. There was not enough evidence to prove which of the other soldiers had or had not fired.

On December 14, 1770, Killroy and Montgomery returned to court for sentencing. They pleaded "benefit of clergy." This legal technicality dated back centuries to a time when a member of a religious order could only be tried in an ecclesiastical court. By the 18th century, benefit of clergy had become a legal oddity, extended to those who could read and write, which enabled them to obtain a reduced sentence. The court granted the request to Killroy and Montgomery who were branded on the thumbs and released from custody.

The mystery of who actually gave the order to fire was solved after the trials. Shortly before he left Boston, Private Montgomery admitted to his lawyers that it was he who cried "Fire" after he had been knocked down by a thrown stick.

The massacre and the subsequent trials persuaded the British that troops quartered in Boston were more likely to spark than quench the flames of rebellion. Although British troops were soon withdrawn from Boston, patriots continued to use the massacre as evidence of British perfidy and to goad their fellow colonists toward insurrection.

—Teddi DiCanio

Suggestions for Further Reading

Adams, John. *The Adams Papers: The Legal Papers of John Adams*, 3 vols. Edited by L. Kinvin Wroth and Hiller B. Zobel. Cambridge, Mass.: Harvard University Press, 1965.

Calhoon, Robert McCluer. *The Loyalists in Revolutionary, America, 1760–1781.* New York : Harcourt Brace Jovanovich, 1973

Fleming, Thomas J. "The Boston Massacre." *American Heritage.* (December 1969): 6–11, 102–111.

Hansen, Harry. *The Boston Massacre: An Episode of Dissent and Violence.* New York: Hastings House, 1970.

Kidder, Frederic. *History of the Boston Massacre.* Albany, N.Y.: Munsell, 1870

Middlekauff, Robert. *The Glorious Cause, The American Revolution, 1763–1789.* New York: Oxford University Press, 1982.

Quincy, Josiah, Jr. *Reports of Cases Argued and Adjudged in the Superior Court of Judicature of the Province of Massachusetts Bay, between 1761 and 1772.* Edited by Samuel M. Quincy. Boston: 1885.

Zobel, Hiller B. *The Boston Massacre.* New York: W.W. Norton & Company, 1970.

Sergeant Thomas Hickey Court-Martial: 1776

Defendant: Sergeant Thomas Hickey **Crimes Charged:** Mutiny and sedition
Chief Defense Lawyer: None **Chief Prosecutor:** None
Court-Martial Board: Colonel Samuel Parsons, presiding officer
Place: Richmond Hill, New York **Date of Court-Martial:** June 26, 1776
Verdict: Guilty **Sentence:** Death by hanging

SIGNIFICANCE

The case reflected the uncertain, ill-defined state of American governmental affairs, particularly the chaotic state of the courts. Because New York's courts were "as yet held by authority derived from the Crown," the Provincial Congress handed soldiers accused of treasonous activities over to General George Washington, whose authority derived from the Continental Congress, the country's one unifying quasi-legal institution. The status of 13 civilian conspirators, although charged, seemed unsure. They were sent to Connecticut temporarily.

Expecting the British army to attack New York, George Washington's Revolutionary army prepared for battle in a city uneasily divided in its loyalties. In June 1776, a Tory conspiracy was discovered. Wild stories circulated. One said Washington was to be murdered. Stripped of exaggeration, the basic "plot" was to stage a combined uprising of Loyalists and secret turncoats in Washington's army timed to coincide with the landing of British forces.

William Collier, an alert waiter, notified a city official of a conspiracy involving Gilbert Forbes, a gunsmith, Royal Governor William Tryon, hiding in a warship anchored offshore, and David Mathews, the mayor. A businessman informed authorities that a former employee, James Mason, had said he was receiving money from the British. Mason, when questioned, implicated several soldiers, including members of Washington's guard. One of those named was Sergeant Thomas Hickey, then under arrest on suspicion of counterfeiting.

In jail, Hickey spoke too freely. According to fellow prisoner Israel Young, Hickey and prisoner Michael Lynch said they would never again fight for the American cause and boasted that "there were near seven hundred men inlisted [*sic*] for the King." Another prisoner, Isaac Ketchum, testified Hickey had tried to enlist him and that Hickey and Lynch had bragged of their involvement in a conspiracy against Washington.

A secret committee investigated the charges, then issued warrants for the arrest of several people, including the mayor. The soldiers involved were turned over to General Washington, who ordered a court-martial for Hickey.

William Greene, a soldier named by Mason, testified before the court-martial that he had bribed Hickey to enlist in the king's service after having himself been bribed by the mayor. Greene said that both his and Hickey's names were on a list in Tryon's possession. The gunsmith, Forbes, corroborated Greene's testimony, adding that Mayor Mathews had given him 100 pounds, supplied by Tryon, with which to bribe Continental soldiers. Ketchum reported Hickey had said American soldiers were ready to fire on their compatriots once British forces landed.

Hickey, pleading not guilty, defended his actions, saying he:

> engaged in the scheme at first for the sake of cheating the Tories, and getting some money from them, and afterwards consented to have his name sent on board the man-of-war, in order that, if the enemy should arrive and defeat the army here, and he should be taken prisoner, he might be safe.

Hickey, an Irishman, had deserted from the British army several years earlier.

Hickey was found guilty and sentenced to hang. Washington ordered that all men not on duty be present at Hickey's execution in the hopes that Hickey's "unhappy fate" would "be a warning to" all. On June 28, 20,000 people watched as Hickey, minus stripes and buttons, having refused a chaplain (he claimed clergy were all cutthroats), mounted the scaffold and died. The following day, British warships sailed into New York Harbor.

Hickey was the only conspirator executed. The 13 sent to Connecticut were never tried. Several conspirators, including Mayor Mathews, escaped. By fall the British had taken New York. The secret investigative committee had accused one man, James Clayford, of plotting to kidnap George Washington. But there seems to be no surviving record of what eventually happened to him.

—*Teddi DiCanio*

Suggestions for Further Reading

Fenwick, Ben C. "The Plot to Kill Washington." *American History Illustrated* (February 1987): 8–12.

Hughes, Rupert. *George Washington, The Rebel and the Patriot.* New York: William Morrow & Co., 1927.

Smith, Page. *A New Age Now Begins,* Vol. 1. New York: McGraw-Hill, 1976.

Van Doren, Carl. *The Secret History of the American Revolution.* New York: Augustus M. Kelley, 1973.

Wightman, William. *Minutes of a Conspiracy Against the Liberties of America.* New York: Arno Press, 1969.

Penhallow v. The *Lusanna*: 1777

Libelants: John Penhallow and Jacob Treadwell, representing 15 Portsmouth merchants who owned the privateer *McClary,* and George Wentworth, acting as agent for the ship's crew **Claimants:** Elisha Doane, owner of the *Lusanna,* Isaiah Doane (son), and James Shepherd
Lawyer for the Libelants: Sewall (no other name listed)
Lawyers for the Claimants: John Adams, John Lowell, and Oliver Whipple
Dates of Trial: Circa December 16–20, 1777 **Place of Trial:** Portsmouth, New Hampshire **Judge of Admiralty:** Dr. Joshua Brackett **Verdict:** For the libelants

SIGNIFICANCE

Throughout its 18-year history, this case highlighted the controversy of federal vs. state jurisdiction.

Privateering was a kind of legal piracy by which warring countries preyed on each other's shipping. An authorized ship of Country A would capture a ship belonging to Country B, tow it to a port, then petition a court to "libel" the seized ship. If granted, the ship and cargo were auctioned and the proceeds divided, depriving Country A of resources.

When British authorities closed Boston's port, merchant Elisha Doane, with whale oil to sell and credits due him being held in London, moved to safeguard his financial affairs. Doane sent his son-in-law Shearjashub Bourne to England with the oil. Due to the volatile state of political affairs, Bourne had great discretion in making whatever decisions seemed necessary. Actions, taken to safeguard investors' interests, would be used in court as evidence of loyalist sympathies.

En route, Doane's ship, the *Lusanna,* was damaged by a storm. While in Halifax for repairs, the ship was seized twice by British authorities, then released. The second release was on condition the *Lusanna* be re-registered in Halifax. Later in London, Bourne would re-register the ship in his own name and sail for Gibraltar.

Upon returning to London, Bourne tried to reclaim a cargo of Doane's seized from the brigantine *Industry.* Bourne, in the guise of a loyal subject, submitted a memorial to the Treasury of England. His request was rejected when a former member of the Massachusetts Bar, Daniel Leonard, insisted Bourne had no true interest in the cargo and the owners probably planned to take military supplies to the rebels. The memorial, but not Leonard's refutation, would be used as evidence in the *Lusanna* trial.

Heading for Halifax on her return trip, the *Lusanna* was captured by the American privateer *McClary* on October 30, 1777. At Portsmouth, New Hampshire, the *Lusanna* was "libeled" in the state's Court Maritime on November 11. On December 1, attorney John Lowell filed claims on behalf of the owners to recover the ship and her cargo.

The libelants claimed that the ship and cargo belonged to inhabitants or subjects of Great Britain and the *Lusanna* was carrying supplies to the enemy's "Fleet or Army" in Halifax. The libelants also tried to claim:

> Cause of Condemnation viz. that the Brig made a Voyage to Gibralter with King's Stores in the Year 1776, tho this Cause is not set forth in the Libel.

Based on depositions, invoices, and the ship's register, the libelants maintained Bourne was a loyalist, and that Bourne, not Elisha Doane, owned the ship and much of the cargo. Records showed that government, possibly military, stores were part of *Lusanna*'s cargo to Gibralter. However, witnesses testified Bourne had refused to let the ship to the military transport service.

The claimants, too, had documents and depositions contradicting various allegations. But Bourne's testimony was needed. Under 18th-century rules of evidence, "interested" witnesses could not testify. Bourne conveyed to Isaiah Doane any interests he had in the cargo. His testimony was still barred.

It fell to the claimants' lawyers to argue that Bourne's actions were reasonable. John Adams pointed out that unless contradicted by law, a man could transport his property by whatever methods he chose. Moreover, a ship's registration did not convey property and the practice of altering registrations to protect property was common. Adams also insisted:

> there was no Law or Resolution of Congress that prohibited a Voyage to Gibralter, the Troops and Fleet not coming within the Meaning of the Law ie, Enemies acting against the United States of America.

Furthermore, Bourne would not have been cleared to leave London unless headed for a British, rather than an American, port.

The jury found for the libelants. The court decreed the *Lusanna* and her cargo forfeit. An appeal to Congress was denied on grounds the appeal could only be heard by the state's superior court. In September 1778, the claimants lost their appeal although they had amassed much evidence to justify Bourne's actions. This court, too, refused an appeal to Congress and on September 18, 1778, the *Lusanna* and her cargo were auctioned.

Elisha Doane petitioned Congress to review the case. Congress' Court of Congressional Commissioners of Appeals had recently reversed a decree of the Pennsylvania Admiralty Court. The Philadelphia court had refused to obey the reversal and suspended activities. After pondering the controversy, on March 6, 1779, Congress resolved that: its war powers enabled it to try prize appeals based on questions of fact and law; right of appeal could not be denied by state law;

and the commissioners could make the final decree. New Hampshire voted for the resolution.

In June 1779, the commissioners ruled they had jurisdiction in the *Lusanna* affair, then delayed continuing the case until New Hampshire could react to Congress' March resolution. The case was heard September 11–13, 1783. (Elisha Doane was dead.) In 1780, the Congress had established a Court of Appeals in Cases of Capture which, on September 17, 1783, reversed the lower courts and ordered the claimants' property restored.

The libelants petitioned Congress, insisting the commissioners lacked jurisdiction. A congressional committee agreed. The Congress as a whole did not.

To have the court of appeals decree enforced, the claimants filed in Massachusetts where eventually its Supreme Judicial Court decided the court of appeals had no jurisdiction and declared the New Hampshire decree to be final. In March 1786, the claimants filed suit in Philadelphia's Court of Common Pleas to attach a ship belonging to a libelant. In 1787, that court decided it lacked jurisdiction in admiralty cases and discontinued the attachment.

The case languished until the Constitution was ratified and a federal court system established. In March 1792, administrators for Doane's estate asked the U.S. District Court in New Hampshire to execute the decree. Because the judge had once acted for the libelants, the case was moved to Circuit Court. There, Justice John Blair found for the administrators and asked for a report ascertaining damages. The report was submitted a year later. On October 24, 1794, Judge William Cushing awarded the claimants $38,518.69.

In 1795, the *McClary*'s owners appealed to the U.S. Supreme Court, on writ of error, to no avail. However, adjustments were made about damages.

—Teddi DiCanio

Suggestions for Further Reading

Adams, John. *Diary and Autobiography of John Adams.* Lyman H. Butterfield, ed., Cambridge, Mass.: Howard University Press, 1961.

——. *The Legal Papers of John Adams,* Vol. 2, L. Kinvin Roth & Hiller Zobel, eds. Cambridge, Mass.: Belknap Press, 1965.

Daniel Boone Court-Martial: 1778

Defendant: Daniel Boone **Crime Charged:** Treason
Chief Defense Lawyer: No record **Chief Prosecutor:** No record
Judges: A panel of Kentucky Militia officers, the names of whom were not recorded **Place:** Fort Logan, Kentucky **Date of Trial:** 1778 (the exact date is unknown) **Verdict:** Not guilty

SIGNIFICANCE

The trial showed the fluid nature not only of the early American frontier, but the difficulty of drawing lines in the West between races, ideologies, and loyalties. It also showed that Americans were willing to forget, explain away, and even whitewash the reputation of its early popular heroes.

Daniel Boone is one of America's great frontier legends, remembered for being a frontiersman, a land agent, an Indian fighter, and one of Kentucky's earliest settlers. The legend often overshadows the man who stands behind it, and it has helped to obscure the darkest episode of his life—his court-martial for treason.

Neither Patriot nor Loyalist

As a backwoodsman, and a founder and citizen of the Kentucky Boonesborough settlement, Daniel Boone was not much concerned with politics. Like many other Westerners, he was no strong supporter of the Whigs or the American Revolution. He was no Loyalist either, but his wife's family, the Bryans, were. Boone himself was proud of the captain's commission he had received from Lord Dunmore, Virginia's royal governor, in 1774. His willingness to act sometimes with the Whigs while keeping a royal commission was the cause of some controversy, and it may have been partly responsible for what happened to him in 1778.

In 1774, Lord Dunmore's War against the Indians began on the Virginia frontier. For the next 20 years the Ohio River Valley, the "Dark and Bloody Ground," was a place of constant violence as white settlers challenged and fought the Shawnee, Wyandot, and other tribes for control of Indian lands. Boone was one of the ablest fighters, but sometimes he seemed to condemn white settlers' actions, describing them as a "war of intrusion" against the tribes designed to "dispossess them of their desirable habitations." Then the Revolutionary War moved west, and the British forces headquartered in Detroit began to supply and support Indian raids along the frontier. During this time Boone would act in ways that caused people to question his loyalty not only to the revolutionary cause, but to the white campaign.

In early 1777, Indians began to make attacks on Boonesborough. By the end of the year, supplies, especially salt stores, were running low. Boone agreed to head an expedition to the Blue Lakes, a salt-rich area several miles from the settlement, to replenish supplies, and in February of 1778, a group of about 30 men set out for the salt lick. Meanwhile an Indian offensive was underway. Winter campaigns were rare, but British governor Henry Hamilton of Detroit had recently dispatched more than a dozen war parties to demoralize white settlers. The Shawnee were especially militant at this point over the western whites' recent unjustified murder of three of their chiefs, whom the whites had taken captive at Fort Randolph.

Boone "Adopted" by the Shawnee

In February 1778, while Boone was out hunting to supply the salt expedition, a large Shawnee war party captured him. He recognized its leader as Chief Blackfish, whom he had met 20 years earlier while serving in General Braddock's army. Blackfish, although very friendly and hospitable towards Boone, told him that he intended to destroy Boonesborough to avenge the recent deaths of the Shawnee chiefs. Boone, who knew that the winter raid would catch Boonesborough by surprise, offered to go with the war party and order the settlement to surrender—if the Shawnee would wait until spring, when the whites would be able to march to the Shawnee lands to the North of the Ohio River. When Blackfish announced that he intended to kill everyone in the salt expedition, Boone offered to surrender all of those men immediately, and to let them go north with the Indians. The Shawnee agreed.

When Boone approached the salt licks, the men realized that he had Shawnee with him. As someone raised the alarm, Boone called out. "Don't fire!" he shouted. "If you do all will be massacred." He asked for his men to trust him, and he ordered them to stack arms and surrender, which they did. But a few men escaped and returned to warn Boonesborough.

Meanwhile Boone and the men marched north with their captors. At first the Shawnee debated whether or not to kill all the whites, but after an impassioned speech from Boone, they agreed to let them live, although they made Boone run the gauntlet. Afterward they complimented him on his skill as a warrior, and once they arrived at the Shawnee town of Chillicothe, they even adopted Boone and some of the others into the tribe, making Boone the son of Chief Blackfish himself.

Boone seemed content with his new life. Rumors later surfaced that he had taken a Shawnee wife, although he was already married to Rebecca Bryan. A month after Boone's capture, Blackfish took him to Detroit, where he met with Governor Hamilton. Boone reportedly showed Hamilton his captain's commission from Lord Dunmore, and Hamilton tried to ransom Boone from the Shawnee, but they refused.

Boone's Return Met with Suspicion

After four months in Shawnee captivity, Boone escaped suddenly during a wild turkey hunt. He covered the 160 miles to Boonesborough in four days. When he arrived at the settlement, he was met with suspicion. He looked like an Indian, and the men who had escaped from the Shawnee had told of his cooperation with the Shawnee. Nevertheless, he regained the settlers' trust, and he began to prepare Boonesborough for a siege. By August he suggested that the whites strike first by raiding a Shawnee town on Paint Creek just across the Ohio. Others pointed out that such a raid would draw off many of Boonesborough's defenders. But Boone convinced 30 men to come with him, although a third returned to Boonesborough the following day. After a brief skirmish with a small Shawnee war party, Boone and his group found the Indian town abandoned. This meant, they knew, that the Shawnee were all headed for Boonesborough, to which Boone and his men returned.

Daniel Boone. (Courtesy, Library of Congress)

Facing nearly 500 warriors, Boone took a group beyond the settlement's walls and negotiated with Chief Blackfish. After a few days, Boone and his men agreed with the Shawnee that the Ohio River would be the boundary between white and Indian lands. Boone, suspecting treachery, had ordered sharpshooters to take aim secretly at the negotiators. As the Indians and whites began to shake hands on the deal, suddenly the Indians tried to grab the white leaders. The sharpshooters opened fire, the whites retreated into the settlement, and the Boonesborough siege began. After 11 days the Indians broke off the siege and retreated.

Boone Tried by Military Officers

Shortly after the siege, two militia officers, Richard Callaway and Benjamin Logan, charged Boone with treason. Callaway had earlier objected to Boone's plan to attack Paint Creek, and he saw treasonous designs in Boone's behavior. The charge consisted of four particulars: That Boone had voluntarily surrendered the salt lick expedition; that he had consorted with the British at Detroit, engaging with them to capture Boonesborough's population; that he had weakened Boonesborough's defenses by staging the raid on Paint Creek; and that he had taken Boonesborough leaders beyond range of the settlement's guns when negotiating with Chief Blackfish.

The trial took place at a fort named Logan's Station, and large numbers of people attended. Kentucky militia officers served as his judges and jurors, taking testimony from Callaway, some of the escaped captives, and Boone himself. "Boone was in favor of the British government," declared Callaway. "All of his conduct proved it. . . . He ought to be broak of his commission." In response Boone told the story he had told all along: outmanned and outgunned, he had decided to "use some stratagem" and deceive the Shawnee and the British, telling them "tales to fool them," and trying to stop the Shawnee from attacking a weakened Boonesborough. To his wife, Rebecca, Boone spoke more bluntly. "God damn them," he said of the British. "They had set the Indians on us."

The court-martial quickly acquitted Boone, and it even promoted him from captain to major to show its approval of him. Nevertheless, the accusations crushed Boone and clouded his reputation. The trial details are sketchy, since the Boone family rarely talked of it; the official records of the court-martial vanished; and the public chose to overlook the blemish on Boone's career.

—Buckner F. Melton, Jr.

Suggestions for Further Reading

Bakeless, John. *Daniel Boone: Master of the Wilderness.* New York: William Morrow and Co., 1939.

Eckert, Allan W. *That Dark and Bloody River.* New York: Bantam Books, 1995.

Faragher, John Mack. *Daniel Boone: The Life and Legend of an American Pioneer.* New York: Henry Holt and Co., 1992.

Lofaro, Michael A. *The Life and Adventures of Daniel Boone.* Lexington: University Press of Kentucky, 1978.

Trial of Bathsheba Spooner, et al.: 1778

Names of Defendants: Bathsheba Ruggles Spooner, William Brooks, James Buchanan, Ezra Ross. **Crimes Charged:** Murder, accomplice before the fact. **Chief Defense Lawyer:** Levi Lincoln **Chief Prosecutor:** Robert Treat Paine **Judges:** William Cushing, Jedediah Foster, Nathaniel Peaslee Sargeant, David Sewall, James Sullivan **Place:** Worcester, Massachusetts **Date of Trial:** April 24, 1778 **Verdict:** Guilty **Sentence:** Execution by hanging.

SIGNIFICANCE

Set against the background of the social disruption of the American Revolutionary War, this murder was sensational in its day, and has continued to intrigue historians and writers because of several unresolved elements in the characters and motivations of Bathsheba Spooner and her accomplices.

At a time when class distinctions were important and social status was determined by family lineage, both Bathsheba Ruggles Spooner and her husband, Joshua Spooner, were scions of prominent families of the colonial aristocracy, raised to a life of wealth and privilege. The Declaration of Independence and the ensuing war, however, caused family rifts and animosities that quite possibly affected the course of events that culminated in Bathsheba's execution. Her father, Brigadier General Timothy Ruggles, a lawyer, and himself chief justice of the Court of Common Pleas in Worcester, Massachusetts, from 1762 to 1764, remained a Loyalist, and the hatred generated by this extended to members of his family. Joshua Spooner's father, John Spooner, had immigrated from England and became a wealthy Boston commodities merchant. Although the bulk of his estate was inherited by his eldest son John, Joshua Spooner, the third son, was a wealthy and well-connected young man when he married.

Joshua Spooner was born in 1741; Bathsheba Ruggles in February 1746. They were married on January 15, 1766, and had their first child in April 1767. Three more children were born between 1770 and 1775, although the second son, John, died a few weeks after his birth. In these years immediately before the Revolution they were living in what was considered an elegant two-story house in Brookfield, Massachusetts, and were considered wealthy by their neighbors. However, it was becoming common knowledge that the marriage was not happy, and that Bathsheba had developed what she was to characterize as an "utter aversion" towards her husband. The reasons for the rift are not fully known, but records indicate that Joshua Spooner was frequently drunk and sometimes physically abusive of his wife, and was also a weak manager of his household and affairs. Bathsheba, on the other hand was independent, strong-willed, and impetuous.

Bathsheba Plots to Kill Her Husband

In March 1777 Ezra Ross came to Brookfield. He was only 16, but had already served for a year in the Revolutionary War in a regiment under George Washington. He was making his way home, on foot, to Linebrook, Massachusetts, a distance of some 240 miles from Washington's encampment. Disease was rampant among the troops and it was a severe winter. Ross was ill, and Bathsheba Spooner took him into her household for several weeks and nursed him back to health. He then continued on his way home. He visited the Spooner household again in July 1777 when on his way back to rejoin the army, and he came back to Brookfield in December after participating in the four-month campaign that culminated with the surrender of the British under General Burgoyne at Saratoga.

During the following two months Ezra Ross came to be on good terms with Joshua Spooner, and began to accompany him on short business trips. He also became Bathsheba's lover, and she apparently began to urge him to poison her husband. In early February when Ezra Ross left with Joshua Spooner on an extended trip to Princeton, he had with him a bottle of nitric acid for that purpose; but he did not use it. Instead of coming back to Brookfield at the conclusion of business in Princeton, he returned home to Linebrook.

From subsequent events it has been inferred that it must have been around the end of January 1778, that Bathsheba Spooner realized she was pregnant, and her behavior became increasingly irrational. It has been generally assumed that Ezra Ross was the father, but this cannot be known with certainty; there are suggestions in the records that she may have had other lovers. In the months following the British surrender, there were many displaced British soldiers at large in the Massachusetts countryside. In mid-February, while her husband and Ezra Ross were in Princeton, Bathsheba invited two, Sergeant James Buchanan (spelled "Buchannon" in some records) and William Brooks, into her house, and according to servants and neighbors, entertained them lavishly. According to their subsequent confessions, Bathsheba discussed her plans for killing her husband with them, and, when he returned, not having been poisoned by Ezra, she began to try to recruit them to assist her. She also wrote to Ezra informing him of these developments, and he returned quickly to Brookfield, arriving on Saturday February 28, the same day that Bathsheba returned from spending two days in Worcester. In the late evening of the following day the three men waited at the house for Joshua Spooner to return home from an evening spent drinking with friends. As he entered the garden William Brooks attacked, beat, and strangled him. When he was either dead or unconscious Buchanan and Ross helped to push him, head down, into the well.

The Soldiers Are Arrested and Confess

Brooks, Buchanan, and Ross were arrested the next day in Worcester. They apparently had made no plans for escaping, and had called attention to themselves by, in the case of Brooks and Buchanan, getting very drunk, and being in possession of Joshua Spooner's silver shoe buckles, and in the case of Ezra Ross, trying to hide himself in the attic of the tavern. They immediately confessed, implicating Bathsheba and two servants in the household, Sarah Stratton and Alexander Cummings. On April 21 a grand jury returned an indictment charging Brooks with assaulting Joshua Spooner and inflicting the wounds from which he died, Buchanan and Ross with aiding and abetting in the murder, and Bathsheba Spooner with inciting, abetting, and procuring the manner and form of the murder. They were arraigned and pleaded not guilty. Twelve male freeholders of Worcester were impaneled as jurors and the trial was set for the following Friday, April 24, before a panel of five judges, Jedediah Foster, Nathaniel Peaslee Sargeant, David Sewall, James Sullivan, and Chief Justice William Cushing. The trial was held in the Old South meeting house, before a packed courtroom. It lasted only one day, but began at 8:00 A.M. and ended at midnight.

The prosecution presented many neighbors and acquaintances who testified both to the family relationships between Joshua Spooner and his wife, and to events on the night of the murder. Sarah Stratton and Alexander Cummings, who, it is thought, must have been aware of the plan, and may have assisted in it, testified for the prosecution, presumably in return for a grant of immunity. Levi Lincoln, a young Worcester attorney who would later become U.S. attorney general under Thomas Jefferson, was assigned to defend the four accused. He had a difficult task, as the three men had signed written confessions. He apparently presented no witnesses. There was little he could do for Brooks or Buchanan, but he was more eloquent on behalf of Ezra Ross and Bathsheba Spooner. Ross, he tried to persuade the jury, had had no design to harm Joshua Spooner, and was unaware of the plan until a few hours before it was carried out. He had not physically assisted in the murder, and had appeared to favor it in order "to keep on terms" with his lover. Of Bathsheba he said that, "There is the best evidence of a disordered mind that the nature of the thing will admit of." Many of her actions before and after the murder were irrational. No plan had been formed for the murder itself, or to conceal it, or for the perpetrators to escape.

The following day the jury returned a verdict of guilty for all four prisoners and they were sentenced to death by hanging. The execution was set for June 4, but in May it was postponed. Bathsheba petitioned for delay on the grounds of her pregnancy. Common law generally protected the life of a fetus which had "quickened"—that is, begun to move independently. Before that stage its existence was not recognized in the law. A panel of 12 women examined

Bathsheba on June 11, and they all signed a sworn statement that they did not find her "quick with child." Bathsheba protested the finding, and a second examination was made on June 27. This time four of the examiners supported Bathsheba's claim, but no action was taken on this finding. Ezra Ross's parents submitted a long and eloquent petition for clemency for their young son, but this also was ineffective. On July 2 all four were executed by hanging in Worcester before a crowd estimated at five thousand. Bathsheba Spooner never signed a confession or indicated remorse, but went calmly and peacefully to her death.

A post-mortem autopsy, which Bathsheba had requested, showed that she was carrying a well-formed male fetus of approximately five months. Historians have therefore questioned the veracity and motivations of the examiners who found her not to be quick with child, as well as the motivation of the Council of Massachusetts in its intransigence over the execution. It has been argued that she bore the brunt of the community's hostility towards her father for his devotion to the Loyalist cause. In her book *Murdered by His Wife,* Deborah Navas points out that the deputy secretary of the Council of Massachusetts, who signed the final warrant for the execution, was not only Joshua Spooner's stepbrother, but also a member of a small group of patriots who all pursued a vendetta against Brigadier General Timothy Ruggles. Also unresolved are the issues of Bathsheba's personality and motivation. It can probably never be known whether she was a cold-blooded murderer or whether circumstances not fully understood caused her to become mentally deranged. Nor is it known how she was able to persuade others to assist her in such a foolish and doomed scheme.

—David I. Petts

Suggestions for Further Reading

Bullock, Chandler. *The Bathsheba Spooner Murder Case.* Worcester, Mass: American Antiquarian Society, 1939.

Chandler, Peleg W. "Trial of Mrs. Spooner and Others." In *American Criminal Trials.* Vol. 2. Boston: T. H. Carter, 1844.

Navas, Deborah. *Murdered by His Wife.* Amherst: University of Massachusetts Press, 1999.

Charles Lee Court-Martial: 1778

Defendant: Charles Lee **Crimes Charged:** Disobedience of orders; misbehavior before the enemy; disrespect to the commander in chief
Chief Defense Lawyer: No Record **Presiding Officer:** Lord Stirling
Chief Prosecutor: No Record **Court:** No Record **Place:** Brunswick, New Jersey **Date of Trial:** July 4–August 12, 1778 **Verdict:** Guilty
Sentence: Suspension from the army for one year

SIGNIFICANCE

The court martial of George Washington's second-in-command at a crucial stage in the War of Independence was the culmination of a tense relationship between the two men and ended General Charles Lee's military career.

Charles Lee was born in Cheshire, England, in 1731 and followed his father in embarking on a military career. He was with British troops on the North American continent as a young officer and was badly wounded at Fort Ticonderoga in 1758. In the 1760s he was a member of several expeditionary forces in Europe. He returned to America in 1773 with the British army, but soon sided with the patriots, resigned his commission, and enthusiastically embraced the causes of liberty and independence. Lee remains a perplexing figure, and the question of his ultimate loyalty is still controversial. To some of his contemporaries he appeared highly educated, clever, and a brilliant military strategist; to others he seemed boorish, slovenly, and possibly a charlatan. What is beyond dispute is that he was eccentric, ambitious, fiercely independent, and intemperate.

In June 1775 Charles Lee was one of three former British officers appointed to the rank of major general by the Continental Congress, at the same time that, for political rather than military reasons, it appointed George Washington to be commander in chief. Washington's relative lack of military experience was well known, particularly in fighting the kind of warfare that was anticipated against British troops. Lee was considered the foremost military expert serving in the American army, and he made no secret of his contempt for Washington's military abilities. General Lee acquitted himself well during 1775 and 1776, at the seige of Boston, the defense of New York, and particularly in his supervision of the defense of South Carolina and Georgia, but he became more outspokenly critical of Washington. In December 1776, possibly due to his own recklessness and a desire for female companionship, and after failing to comply with an order from Washington to withdraw, he was captured by the British at Basking Ridge, New Jersey. He was held in close confinement for more than a year before Washington arranged for his release in a prisoner exchange. Lee immediately rejoined the army at Valley Forge in May 1778.

Lee's Retreat at Monmouth

The events which led to General Lee's court-martial occurred the following month. Lee continued to be critical of Washington's tactics, arguing that the American soldiers lacked the discipline and experience to successfully engage the British in conventional warfare, and that they should therefore rely on what would now be called guerilla operations. On June 26, 1778, Washington decided to send an advance guard to attack the rear of the British forces under Sir Henry Clinton at Monmouth, New Jersey. Lee disagreed with the plan and at first declined the command, but then changed his mind. He advanced with his detachment across rough terrain that had not been reconnoitered and made contact with the British rear, but Clinton reacted quickly and enveloped the American right flank. Lee then ordered a retreat. When this news was brought to George Washington, some five miles away, he rode quickly to Lee's detachment and accosted General Lee angrily. An altercation occurred between the two men. There is no entirely reliable account of what exactly was said, but this has been reported to be the only occasion on which Washington was heard to swear in public, and he is said to have called Lee a "damned poltroon" (a craven coward, or worthless wretch). After this Washington took command of the battlefield, regrouped the troops and counterattacked the British. The fighting continued until dark, and the next morning the British troops were found to have retreated out of reach.

General Charles Lee. (Courtesy, National Archives)

Lee Goads Washington

There are indications that Washington had no intention of taking any further action over the incident, but Lee forced the issue by writing a note to Washington, using language considered by the standards of the day to be inappropriate, and demanding an apology for the language Washington had used in addressing him during their encounter the previous day. Washington replied, politely but firmly indicating his displeasure. This further enraged General Lee, who wrote a second note demanding a court of inquiry. Washington's patience was exhausted, and he responded by having General Lee arrested and court-martialled.

Lee's Trial

The presiding officer of the court was Lord Stirling, and the court sat from time to time over several weeks between July 4 and August 12 as the Continental army continued to march. Three charges were specified against General Lee as violations of the Articles of War (the precursor of the current Uniform Code of Military Justice):

1. Disobedience of orders in not attacking the enemy, despite repeated instructions to do so.

2. Misbehavior before the enemy, in making an unnecessary, disorderly, and "shameful" retreat.

3. Disrespect to the commander in chief in two letters written after the action.

General Lee presented his own spirited defense, characterized by at least one contemporary observer as "masterly," in which he attempted to demonstrate that any other action than the retreat he ordered would have put the British at a great advantage and thus risked the destruction of the entire army. He was supported by some of his officers, with whom he was apparently a popular commander. The court-martial, however, returned a verdict of guilty on all charges, except that in returning the verdict they omitted the word "shameful" from the second count. The sentence was that he be suspended from his command for a period of one year. Some have noted that, given the seriousness of the charges, the penalty was relatively light. Lee was by no means alone in his critical assessment of George Washington as a military strategist, contrary to the image that popular history has bestowed upon him. In view of the light sentence, there has been speculation that Lee might have been acquitted on the first two counts, or that they would not have been brought at all, were it not for the provocation that Lee himself presented through his letters.

Lee became a recluse, living in squalor with his dogs—poodles, which had accompanied him on his campaigns. He continued to write abusive letters to the Congress about George Washington. As a result, he was challenged by a friend of Washington to a duel, in which he was wounded, and in 1780 the Continental Congress dismissed him from the army. He died of tuberculosis in Philadelphia in 1782.

Some 80 years after Lee's death, papers were discovered showing that while he was held prisoner by the British between December 1776 and early 1778 he had discussed military plans to defeat the patriots with General Howe, then the commander of the British forces. To some this has seemed to be proof that Lee was, in fact, a traitor. To others it only demonstrates that he was an eccentric soldier of fortune, fascinated with military strategy as an intellectual exercise. In any case, this was not a factor in his court-martial, and the most widely held view is that he ruined his own career by his unwillingness or inability to temper his criticism of his commander in chief, and not because of disloyalty or military incompetence.

—David I. Petts

Suggestions for Further Reading

Sparks, Jared. *Lives of Charles Lee and Joseph Reed.* Boston: Little Brown, 1846.

Stryker, W. S. *The Battle of Monmouth.* Princeton, N.J.: Princeton University Press, 1927.

Abraham Carlisle and John Roberts Trials: 1778

Defendants: Abraham Carlisle, John Roberts **Crime Charged:** Treason
Chief Defense Lawyers: George Ross, James Wilson, William Lewis, Elias Boudinot **Chief Prosecutor:** Jonathan Dickinson Sergeant
Judges: Thomas McKean, William Atlee, and John Evans, justices of the Pennsylvania Supreme Court **Place:** Philadelphia, Pennsylvania
Date of Trials: Carlisle: September 25, 1778; Roberts: September 30, 1778
Verdict: Guilty **Sentence:** Death by hanging

SIGNIFICANCE

John Roberts and Abraham Carlisle were victims of a politically motivated sentence for treason. The judiciary of Pennsylvania wanted to show its toughness toward collaborators with the enemy. Though guilty, they were no more so than other collaborators who escaped death.

The Revolutionary War was still in progress in late June of 1778, when the British army, because of a change in its strategy, abandoned Philadelphia and marched to New York. In British America's largest city, Philadelphia, they left a residue of property damage and hard feelings among American patriots toward those Philadelphians who had collaborated with the British during the year that they controlled the city.

Collaborators

As early as mid-July this resentment took political form. Citizens' organizations were formed in Philadelphia to gather evidence against collaborators with the British during the occupation and bring them to justice. In addition, there were threats of extralegal activity, physical attacks, and harassment against persons accused of having supplied the British with information or goods, or having cooperated with them in any way. Newspapers printed the names of suspects.

Thomas McKean, chief justice of the Pennsylvania Supreme Court, anxious to avoid the possibility of vigilante justice against collaborators, set the court system in motion as quickly as possible to handle their cases. Through August and September, he and his two fellow justices sat in the city hall collecting evidence and interviewing accused persons. McKean, who believed that moderation toward dissidents was good policy in wartime, released all the accused on bond, commenting that no credible evidence had yet been produced against them. The Philadelphia grand jury, however, after hearing the evidence, brought in 33 indictments for the September court, most of them for treason—collaboration with the enemy—which was punishable by death under state law.

Abraham Carlisle was one of the first defendants brought to trial. A prosperous, elderly carpenter, he had guarded the city gates under the British rule, and was therefore charged with having accepted a commission from them. Several witnesses testified to his service as a guard, but his defense lawyers argued that he could not be convicted of treason, since no written commission was produced. The jury deliberated 24 hours and found him guilty. His conviction was appealed to the Pennsylvania Supreme Court and was upheld. The State Executive Council, which had the power to commute Carlisle's sentence, turned down numerous appeals to do so, including one from Justice McKean, who had originally pronounced it.

A few days after Carlisle's conviction, and after several other defendants had been acquitted of charges of treason, the case of John Roberts came up. Roberts, like Carlisle, was a prosperous older citizen, in this case a miller. He was charged with recruiting men to join the British army. Testimony showed that he had in fact attempted to persuade men to enlist in the British forces, but his defense lawyers argued that his efforts were unsuccessful and that he could not be convicted unless the prosecution showed that someone had actually enlisted as a result of Roberts's persuasion. They also objected to the introduction of his confession, which could not, they said, be used as evidence in a trial for treason. These arguments failed to convince the jury, which found Roberts guilty as charged. His case, like Carlisle's, was appealed to the Supreme Court and the State Executive Council, and the sentence affirmed by both authorities. Carlisle and Roberts were hanged on November 4, 1778.

Chosen as Examples

There is little doubt that both men received fair trials. They had first-rate counsel— James Wilson, a lawyer for both, was a signer of both the Declaration of Independence and the Constitution, and one of the best lawyers in America. But on the basis of the evidence presented, both men were guilty of treason under Pennsylvania law. The question about their trials relates to the comparative fairness of their sentences. Several other defendants, shown to have committed equally serious offenses, were acquitted on technicalities or given much lighter punishment by the same court. It seems clear that Carlisle and Roberts were singled out for harsh treatment on the basis of something other than their acts.

That basis was political necessity. McKean was convinced that it was essential for the courts to take control of the punishment of collaborators, and for them to show that they were prepared to be severe, in order to head off the danger of private revenge and mob violence in a wartime situation. In other words, a few defendants had to be sentenced to death to show that the courts meant business. McKean, not a bloodthirsty man, hoped that the sentence could be reversed at a higher level—hence his petition to the State Executive Council.

Carlisle and Roberts were selected because their guilt was clear and because they were older men of some prominence in the community. McKean, in an earlier case not involving treason, had commented that it did little good to execute a poor, obscure defendant, since his death would have less effect on people's behavior than that of a defendant who was of high status and widely known. By sending the two men to be hanged, the courts showed that wealth and prominence were no protection against strict justice.

Carlisle and Roberts were both Quakers. There were suggestions at the time, which have been repeated since, that their deaths were part of a persecution of Quakers by the Pennsylvania authorities, who resented the Quakers' refusal to fight on the American side because of their peace testimony. In fact, the pro-British actions of both men were inconsistent with the peace testimony of the Society of Friends. They were disowned by the Philadelphia Meeting, which refused to seek a pardon for either man, although it deplored the severity of their sentences. No other Quakers were put to death.

Other collaborators who stayed in Philadelphia suffered no private violence or vigilante justice in the years after 1778. After the war ended, most of them were accepted by their neighbors. The executions of Carlisle and Roberts may or may not have been related to this outcome.

—Hendrik Booraem V

Suggestions for Further Reading

Oosterhout, Anne M. "A State Divided: Opposition in Pennsylvania to the American Revolution." *Contributions in American History,* no. 123. New York: Greenwood Press, 1987.

Rowe, G. S. *Embattled Bench: The Pennsylvania Supreme Court and the Forging of a Democratic Society, 1684–1809.* Newark: University of Delaware Press, 1994.

Major John Andre Trial: 1780

Defendant: Major John Andre **Crime Charged:** Espionage
Board of Enquiry: 14 generals of George Washington's staff headed by Major General Nathanael Greene. **Place:** Tappan, New York
Date of Trial: September 29, 1780 **Verdict:** Guilty **Sentence:** Death by hanging

SIGNIFICANCE

Major John Andre's trial for espionage sent shock waves through the American colonies by revealing the depth of a treason plot by General Benedict Arnold to hand over the American stronghold at West Point to the British. Had Andre not been captured and the conspiracy foiled, the American Revolution might well have been crushed.

On October 2, 1780, Major John Andre, a British officer, was hanged for espionage. His executioners would have preferred to hang the man with whom Andre consorted: the traitor, General Benedict Arnold.

Arnold was a talented field commander and one of that circle of men who were surrogate sons to General George Washington. Yet he was adept at making enemies. Appointed by Washington to command military forces in Philadelphia while he recovered from war wounds, Arnold's relentless ambition and greed eventually led to complaints to Congress that he was abusing his powers. Documents would later surface indicating Arnold was much more dishonest than local authorities ever suspected—documents unavailable when they lodged their complaints. After a list of eight charges wound its way first through Congress and then a haphazard court-martial (it was interrupted by wartime events), it was decided enough evidence existed to uphold two of the accusations. Arnold was found guilty of having used public wagons for private purposes and of having improperly issued a pass allowing a ship, the *Charming Nancy*, to leave port when all other vessels were quarantined. Arnold was sentenced to "receive a reprimand" from General Washington.

Arnold himself had asked—or more accurately, maneuvered—for a trial. "I ask only for justice," he wrote to Washington, complaining of his countrymen's treatment of him after all his sacrifices. He added, "I wish your Excellency for your long and eminent services, may not be paid in the same coin."

But, in the fall of 1779, at the same time he was trying to enlist Washington's help, Arnold opened a secret correspondence with Major John Andre, head of British intelligence. Arnold offered to either immediately enlist or "cooperate on some concealed plan with Sir Henry Clinton." Arnold sought at least 10,000 pounds for his "services." Negotiations were protracted and at one point the correspondence lapsed.

Eventually the persistent Arnold obtained command of the fort at West Point, on the Hudson River in New York, and the surrounding area. He agreed to deliver West Point to Clinton for the extraordinary sum of 20,000 pounds if the venture were completely successful and 10,000 pounds if it were not.

To plan the details of the surrender, Arnold and Andre wanted a meeting. Clinton reluctantly agreed but ordered that Andre: not go behind enemy lines; not carry any compromising papers; and never wear a disguise—he was to remain in uniform. If he were to be captured, this would protect Andre from any charge of spying (and execution).

On September 20, 1780, Joshua Smith, a loyalist friend of Arnold's, fetched Andre from the H.M.S. *Vulture.* The terms of the passes Smith carried allowed only one man to come. Thus, Colonel Beverly Robinson, who was to accompany Andre, was left behind.

Rather than going to Smith's house as originally planned, Andre and Arnold met six miles up river, at the foot of Long Clove Mountain. A British contingent was to attack West Point. The moves of the opposing forces had to be plotted in advance. Each order Arnold gave to his men had to appear reasonable at the time, yet still lead ultimately to the loss of the fort.

The two farmers who had been pressed into rowing the boat that had brought Andre, refused to take him back when he and Arnold were finished. As daylight broke, Arnold and Andre, his uniform covered by a cloak, rode to Smith's home on the Hudson River within sight of the *Vulture.* They passed an American sentry, which placed Andre behind American lines.

Several hours later, any hope of slipping Andre back aboard ship was blasted away by an American colonel at nearby Dobbs Ferry. Colonel James Livingston, with a small artillery battery, peppered the frigate, damaging her hull and driving her two miles away.

The simplest and safest action for Andre to have taken would have been to ride out in uniform carrying a flag of truce. Such actions were common as both sides made attempts to negotiate the exchange of prisoners. But Andre, a romantic who enjoyed amateur theatrics, yielded to Smith's insistence that he switch to civilian attire. Worse still, Andre carried a map and other incriminating documents, the contents of which he could have memorized.

Before leaving for West Point, Arnold wrote out three passes, one of which allowed Smith to transport Andre across the Hudson. But Smith was unwilling to venture again upon the water. Instead, the two rode toward White Plains. A day and a half later, as Andre entered a no-man's-land area, Smith left him.

Andre's Capture

A few miles later Andre encountered three Patriot "skinners." Andre mistook them for Loyalists and introduced himself as a British officer "on business of importance." He soon realized his mistake and showed them Arnold's pass made out to John Anderson, the name Andre had used in his correspondence. Andre tried to bluff them with threats that Arnold would be displeased if Andre were detained, implying that his first statement had been a ruse to protect himself from Loyalist "cow boys." Skinners and cow boys often relieved their respective enemies of worldly goods.

An etching of Major John Andre from an English textbook. (Courtesy, Library of Congress)

The men, John Paulding, David Williams, and Isaac Van Wert, of the New York militia, stripped and searched Andre. They found papers between his stocking and his English boot. Only Paulding could read. He realized Andre was a spy. After a brief conversation about the possibility of delivering Andre to British hands, for a consideration, the men took Andre to Lieutenant Colonel John Jameson at North Castle.

Jameson had received orders several days earlier to permit a John Anderson to pass through to West Point to visit Arnold. But this Anderson was headed in the wrong direction. The handwriting on all the papers, including the pass, was the same. However, Jameson was unfamiliar with Arnold's handwriting. Andre insisted he be taken to Arnold. Jameson reluctantly agreed. However, unbeknownst to Andre, Jameson sent the documents to General Washington.

Shortly after Andre left, under guard, Major Benjamin Tallmadge, the able head of Washington's secret service, arrived. Tallmadge convinced Jameson to recall this "John Anderson" but failed to convince him to recall the messenger sent to inform Arnold of Anderson's detention. Arnold escaped to the *Vulture* shortly before Washington reached West Point. The incriminating documents caught up with Washington there and he sent men in pursuit of Arnold. But it was too late.

Andre realized he could no longer carry on the pretense of being John Anderson. He wrote to Washington. "What I have as yet said concerning myself was in the justifiable attempt to be extricated." Without naming Arnold, Andre stated that he had come, in uniform, "to meet, upon ground not within posts of either army, a person who was to give me intelligence.'' Andre insisted that his presence behind American lines was unplanned and undesired. Andre's argument was that he was, in effect, a prisoner of war and as such had a right to attempt escape in civilian clothes. This would be his defense at his trial.

Washington also received a letter from Arnold:

> I have ever acted from a principle of love to my country, since the commencement of the present unhappy contest between Great Britain and the colonies. The same principle of love to my country actuates my present conduct, however it may appear inconsistent to the world, who very seldom judge right of any man's actions.

He exonerated his wife (who had plotted with him) of any complicity and asked Washington to protect her.

Andre's Trial

At Washington's order, on September 29, 1780, a board was convened to examine and try Major John Andre. Andre's testimony conflicted on a major, damning point with evidence presented in letters from Arnold, Clinton, and Robinson. They all claimed that Andre had traveled to Arnold under a flag of truce. When asked the question directly, Andre, unaware of the letters, said:

> that it was impossible for him to suppose he had come on shore under that sanction; and added that, if he had come ashore under that sanction, he might certainly have returned under it.

The board could not take seriously Andre's arguments about being made a prisoner of war, subject to Arnold's orders. Historian James Flexner pointed out, "Had Andre been acting legally, he would have had no need for an assumed name. An officer is not obligated to obey an enemy's orders.'' Flexner also wrote, "Flags do not cover suborning of treason.'' However, a flag would have given the board a semblance of an excuse to avoid a judgment of espionage, which it would have preferred to do. Andre's conduct brought him respect and sympathy. However, the evidence was overwhelming and the decision of the board was unanimous:

> Major Andre, Adjutant General of the British Army, ought to be considered a spy from the enemy, and that, agreeable to the law and usage of nations, it is their opinion he ought to suffer death.

The next day Washington confirmed the verdict and ordered that Andre's execution take place the following day.

Sir Henry Clinton, under a flag of truce, sent a delegation to present arguments that Andre was not a spy, thus giving Washington an excuse to delay the execution. The British produced another letter from Arnold in which he took all blame upon himself. There were veiled threats that if Andre were executed, there might be a retaliation against American prisoners of war.

Hints reached Clinton that Andre could be exchanged for Arnold. Although Clinton despised Arnold, and Andre was his favorite aide, he rejected the idea; as members of the same side could not be exchanged as if prisoners of opposing sides. Moreover, returning Arnold to Washington would hardly encourage further defections from the revolutionary cause.

Eventually all negotiations fell through. Washington again set an execution date for Andre. He rejected an appeal from Andre for a soldier's death by firing squad over what was considered the less honorable mode of execution "on the gibbet." In the 18th century, spies were always hanged. To deviate from this practice would have thrown doubt on Andre's guilt. If Andre was not a spy, then he was a prisoner of war and should not be executed at all.

Until he saw the gallows, Andre was unaware that Washington had denied his request. He blanched briefly. Asked if he had any last words, Andre requested that those present "bear me witness that I meet my fate as a brave man." He, himself, adjusted his noose and the handkerchief over his eyes. He supplied the handkerchief with which his arms were tied. Andre, in uniform, was hanged about noon. As he died, many of those watching wept.

— *Teddi DiCanio*

Suggestions for Further Reading

Brown, Richard C. "Three Forgotten Heroes," *American Heritage* (August 1975): 25.

Flexner, James Thomas. *The Traitor And The Spy.* Boston: Little, Brown & Co., 1953.

Ford, Corey. *A Peculiar Service.* Boston: Little, Brown & Co., 1965.

Hatch, Robert McConnell and Don Higginbotham. *Major John Andre: A Gallant in Spy's Clothing.* Boston: Houghton Mifflin, 1986.

Smith, Page. *A New Age Now Begins,* Vol. II. New York: McGraw-Hill Book Co., 1976.

The Quock Walker Trials: 1781–83

Case 1: *Jennison v. Caldwell,* civil suit and appeal **Case 2:** *Walker v. Jennison,* civil suit and appeal **Case 3:** *Commonwealth v. Jennison,* criminal indictment **Plaintiffs:** Nathaniel Jennison, (1); Quock Walker, (2) **Defendants:** Nathaniel Jennison, (2,3); John and Seth Caldwell (2) **Charge:** Assault and battery (1,3); deprivation of the benefit of his servant, Walker (2) **Chief Prosecutor:** Robert Treat Paine (3) **Lawyers for Walker and the Caldwells:** Levi Lincoln, Caleb Strong **Lawyers for Jennison:** John Sprague, William Stearns **Judges:** Moses Gill, Samuel Baker, Joseph Dorr, and Moses Gill (1,2); In appeals, Nathaniel P. Sargent, presiding, David Sewall, James Sullivan (1,2); Chief Justice William Cushing, Nathaniel Sargent, David Sewall, and Increase Sumner (3) **Dates of Trials:** Circa June 12–16, 1781 (1); June 12–19, 1781 (2); September 1781 (both appeals); April 20, 1783 (3) **Place of Trials:** Worcester, Massachusetts **Verdict:** For the plaintiff, (1) reversed on appeal; For the plaintiff (2), appeal dismissed; guilty (3) **Sentence:** 25 pounds (1); 50 pounds (2); 40 shillings (3)

SIGNIFICANCE

These were the most famous cases concerning the abolition of slavery in Massachusetts.

The exact point at which slavery ceased to exist in Massachusetts is unclear. Furthermore, whether slavery existed "legally" in Massachusetts is also questionable. The colony's *Body of Liberties* expressly forbade slavery except for war captives, indentured servants, and as punishment for a crime.

Slaves in colonial Massachusetts, from time to time, filed "freedom suits." Sketchy records are unclear as to whether slaves who succeeded were freed on legal or moral principles or because defects existed in masters' titles.

Massachusetts courts shut down during the Revolution. When they reopened in 1781, a brand-new state constitution stated:

> All men are born free and equal, and have certain natural, essential, and unalienable rights; among which may be reckoned the right of enjoying and defending their lives and liberty;

This clause would be invoked in court. In 1754, James Caldwell purchased a slave couple and their infant, Quock Walker. Caldwell died when Quock was 10. Caldwell's widow, who had inherited Quock, eventually married Nathaniel Jennison and ownership of Quock passed to him. Or did it? Quock Walker maintained Caldwell had promised he would be free at age 25 and Mrs. Caldwell had amended that promise to age 21. Isabell Caldwell Jennison died in 1773, when Walker was about 19.

Jennison would not set him free. At age 28, Walker ran away. Jennison found him working for John and Seth Caldwell, brothers of James. With help, Jennison beat Walker, dragged him back to his own farm, then locked Walker in a barn.

Quock Walker filed a civil suit against Nathaniel Jennison for assault and battery. Jennison filed suit against the Caldwell brothers for unlawfully enticing his servant—the word slave was not used—Walker "from the business & service of the said Nathaniel." Jennison asked for damages of 1,000 pounds.

Both cases came before Worcester County Court of Common Pleas on June 12, 1781. The *Jennison v. Caldwell* case appears to have been heard first. Jennison won and was awarded 25 pounds.

In *Walker v. Jennison*, Jennison's attorneys produced the bill of sale for Walker's purchase. Walker insisted his former master had promised him his freedom, while attorney Levi Lincoln attacked slavery on moral grounds. The jury found Quock Walker to be a free man and awarded him 50 pounds.

Both cases were appealed. In September 1781, the Massachusetts Supreme Judicial Court dismissed Jennison's appeal of *Walker v. Jennison* because his lawyers failed to submit the court records. In the Caldwell appeal, Lincoln insisted slavery was contrary to the law of God and to the Massachusetts Constitution's Declaration of Rights. Again, a jury decided Walker was a free man. As such, the Caldwells were within their rights to employ him.

In January 1782, Jennison asked the legislature that he be permitted to reenter his Walker appeal because he had "lost his law" through attorney negligence. In June 1782, he submitted a memorial claiming "he was deprived of ten Negro Servants" due to the court's interpretation of the Declaration of Rights clause, and claiming he should also be relieved of any obligation to support them. No final decision was made on either petition.

In April 1783, two years after a criminal indictment had been brought against Jennison, he was tried for assault, found guilty, and fined 40 shillings. A notion arose that this particular case abolished slavery in Massachusetts. The notion was born of the charge given to the jury by Chief Justice William Cushing, critical of "the right of Christians to hold Africans in perpetual servitude, and sell and treat them as we do horses and cattle," and voicing the opinion that slavery was inconsistent with the state constitution.

Actually, slavery was abolished by erosion. Each slave case won encouraged another. In the 1790 census, Massachusetts reported (probably erroneously) that it had no more slaves.

—Teddi DiCanio

Suggestions for Further Reading

Moore, George H., *Notes on the History of Slavery in Massachusetts*. New York: Negro Universities Press, 1968 [reprint].

O'Brien, S.J., William, "Did the Jennison Case Outlaw Slavery in Massachusetts?" *The William and Mary Quarterly*, Vol. XVII (April 1960).

Spector, Robert M., "The Quock Walker Cases (1781–83): The Abolition of Slavery and Negro Citizenship in Early Massachusetts." *The Journal of Negro History*, Vol. LIII (April 1968).

Paul Revere Court-Martial: 1782

Defendant: Paul Revere **Crimes Charged:** Disobedience of an order; leaving the Penobscot River without orders from his commanding officer
Chief Defense Lawyer: No record **Presiding Officer:** No Record
Chief Prosecutor: No Record **Court:** No Record **Place:** Boston, Massachusetts **Date of Trial:** February 1782 **Verdict:** Acquitted on both counts

SIGNIFICANCE

The reputation of Paul Revere as a patriotic hero of the American Revolution was tarnished by the accusations made against him after the disastrous Penobscot expedition in 1779. A court-martial was eventually held, at Revere's insistence, in 1782, and he was acquitted.

Paul Revere has become an icon in the mythology of the American Revolution largely as a result of the historically inaccurate account of his famous "midnight ride" given in Henry Wadsworth Longfellow's popular poem. Revere was born in 1735, the son of a Boston silversmith. He took up his father's craft and excelled in it. His contributions to the design and manufacture of fine silverware justify his place in history perhaps as much as his patriotic and military exploits.

The Penobscot Expedition

The legendary night ride to warn the patriots of the advance of British troops took place in April 1775. Paul Revere was captured by the British, but released without his horse. As the Revolutionary War progressed he was given command of a garrison at Castle Island in Boston Harbor, with the rank of lieutenant colonel. Then, in 1779 he was made commander of the land artillery on the Penobscot Expedition, notorious for turning into one of the worst naval disasters in American military history. The commander of the expedition was Dudley Saltonstall, commodore of the fleet; the purpose was to drive the British out of what is now Castine, Maine (then known as Maja Bagwaduce, with various alternate spellings), where they had begun the construction of a fort. The American expedition, which left Boston on July 19 and reached Penobscot Bay six days later, consisted of 900 men with 21 armed ships and 24 unarmed transport vessels. Construction of the British fort, in fact, had hardly begun, and it had only three guns, but Commodore Saltonstall refused to believe reports to this effect and did not attack. British land reinforcements arrived, but the Americans, though still having the advantage, did not attack. On August 14 four British warships arrived, and the American fleet fled up the Penobscot River, where the ships were trapped. The Americans burned at least 17 of their own fleet rather than let the British capture them, and they fled overland.

Initial Allegations Against Revere

The charges brought against Paul Revere were a consequence of the confusing events that ended this ignominious expedition. The major blame for the disaster lay clearly with Commodore Saltonstall, and he was court-martialled and dismissed from the service. Other factors at work, however, resulted in the charges against Revere. There was bad feeling and rivalry between the different branches of the military forces—friction and argument between the naval command and the artillery and marines. In his diary Revere commented on the undisciplined nature of his forces—raw recruits, old men and boys, undisciplined and difficult to work with. There was also personal animosity between Revere and certain other officers with whom he had clashed while commanding the garrison at Castle Island.

As soon as he returned overland to Boston, Revere attempted to resume command of his garrison, but was asked to resign and await the results of an inquiry into the Penobscot expedition to be conducted by a committee of the Massachusetts General Court. Captain Thomas Jenners Carnes, who had commanded the marines on board the *General Putnam*, charged Revere with disobedience, unsoldierlike behavior, and cowardice. Revere was also criticized by General Peleg Wadsworth, particularly in regard to his refusal to give up a boat that he was using during the flight.

Paul Revere on his legendary "midnight ride." (Courtesy, National Archives)

Revere conducted his own defense before the inquiry very vigorously, depicting the charges as motivated only by a desire for personal revenge, and bringing several officers to testify that he was a diligent officer. In support of this he introduced as part of his deposition sections of the diary he had kept throughout the operation. However, he had a relatively weak defense against the specific charges of insubordination.

The report of the inquiry came out on October 7. It found that the principal reason for the disaster was "the want of proper spirit and energy on the part of the Commodore;" the inquiry recommended a court-martial, and it was quickly done, resulting in his dismissal from the service on October 25. Revere, however, was extremely distressed to find that the report made no mention whatever of his activities or the charges made against him. Anxious to vindicate himself and insisting that it was unsatisfactory to be neither condemned nor acquitted, he asked for a court-martial under the direction of an artillery officer. He was to file six such petitions before getting his wish. In response to his petition, a second committee of inquiry met in November 1779, but Revere was even more dissatisfied with its report. The committee criticized his conduct, though in rather ambiguous terms, declaring him to have been blameworthy for "disputing the orders of Brigadier-General Wadsworth" and holding that his leaving the Penobscot River with his men without specific orders to do so was "not wholly justifiable."

Revere Court-Martialled at His Own Insistence

Several months after all hostilities in the Revolutionary War had ceased and only after several more petitions, Revere was reluctantly granted the court-martial he wanted. By this time, all references to cowardice had disappeared from the charges, and the allegations had been reduced to two:

1. "For his refusal to deliver a certain Boat to the order of General Wadsworth when upon the Retreat up Penobscot River, from Major Bagwaduce."
2. "For his leaving Penobscot River without Orders from his Commanding Officer."

The court, consisting of one general and 12 captains, met in February 1782. Its ruling, though late and not entirely without qualification, provided Revere with the vindication of his character that he sought:

> The Court finds the first charge against Lieu't Col Paul Revere to be supported (to wit) his refusing to deliver a certain Boat to the Order of General Wadsworth when upon the Retreat up Penobscot River from Major Bagwaduce: but the Court taking into consideration the suddenness of the refusal, and more especially that the same Boat was in fact employed by Lieu't Colo Paul Revere to effect the Purpose ordered by the General as appears by the General's Deposition, are of the Opinion that Lieu't Colo Paul Revere be acquitted of this Charge . . . On the second charge, the Court considers that the whole army was in great Confusion and so scattered and dispersed, that no regular Orders were or could be given, are of the Opinion, that Lieu't Colo Paul Revere, be acquitted with equal Honor as the other Officers in the same Expedition.

Revere accepted this as a vindication of his character, in spite of its ambiguous wording; some have thought there was a particular sting in its tail, since no officers seemed to have come away from Penobscot with much honor.

Revere lived for almost 40 years after the war, becoming renowned as a craftsman. Pioneering in a number of areas, he designed and printed the first issue of Continental paper currency, cast cannons and bells in bronze, and built the first copper-rolling mill in America. Ironically, he even engaged in a successful trading venture with Dudley Saltonstall. While his conduct as a military officer was perhaps less than exemplary, the circumstances were unusual and neither he nor his forces were professional military men.

—David I. Petts

Suggestions for Further Reading

Flood, Charles Bracelen. *Rise, and Fight Again.* New York: Dodd, Mead, 1976.

Forbes, Esther. *Paul Revere and the World He Lived In.* Boston: Houghton Miflin, 1942.

Triber, Jayne E. *A True Republican: The Life of Paul Revere.* Amherst, Mass: University of Massachusetts Press, 1998.

Nancy Randolph and Richard Randolph Trial: 1793

Defendants: Richard Randolph, Anne Cary (Nancy) Randolph
Crimes Charged: Murder **Chief Defense Lawyers:** John Marshall, Patrick Henry **Chief Prosecutors:** No record **Judge:** A Panel of 16 justices; there are no surviving records of their names **Place:** Cumberland County, Virginia
Date of Trial: April 1793 **Verdict:** Acquittal

SIGNIFICANCE

When two young members of one of colonial Virginia's oldest aristocratic families were engulfed in scandalous allegations of criminal behavior, they called upon two of the nascent nation's most famous leaders and lawyers, John Marshall and Patrick Henry, to defend them.

On Christmas Day 1789 Richard Randolph married his distant cousin, Judith Randolph. He was 19, she 17; both were descended from William Randolph of Turkey Island, who, in the middle of the seventeenth century, had founded what was to become one of the great extended dynastic families of late colonial Virginia, holders of great estates, wealth, and many slaves. In the fall of 1790 the young couple set up house on a family plantation called Bizarre. Soon after that Judith's younger sister, named Anne Cary after her mother, but known as Nancy, joined their household, apparently because of differences with her new stepmother, Gabriela, who was a woman not much older than she. By all accounts Nancy was an attractive and lively young woman, who at the age of 16 already had several socially eligible suitors, among them Richard's younger brother, Theodorick. Many years later Nancy would claim that she had been engaged to marry Theodorick, but no announcement was ever made, and in February 1792 Theodorick died after a long and wasting illness.

On Monday, October 1, 1792, Richard Randolph, his wife, and Nancy arrived at the home of a cousin, Randolph Harrison, and his wife, Mary, on their estate at Glenlyvar in southern Virginia. The Harrisons would later testify to what they saw and heard during the night that followed. They were awakened by screams coming from Nancy's bedroom, which was above theirs, and then a servant came to say that Nancy was sick, and to ask Mrs. Harrison to take up some laudanum. When Mary Harrison went upstairs she had to go through

Richard and Judith's bedroom to get to the room occupied by Nancy. Judith Randolph was sitting up in bed, but Richard was in Nancy's room, and had to open the door, which was bolted from the inside. Mary Harrison was not allowed to take a candle into the room, but stayed a few minutes with Nancy, before returning to her own room. Later that night the Harrisons heard footsteps, which they believed to be Richard's, going down the stairs and then returning. The next day Nancy remained in her room. Mary Harrison observed bloodstains on the stairs, and on Nancy's pillowcase. She also noticed that the bed had neither sheets nor quilt, though it had had both the day before. At the end of the week the three Randolphs left Glenlyvar.

Rumors Began Circulating

Within a short time rumors, apparently originating among the slaves of the Harrison household, began to circulate around southern Virginia. Nancy Randolph, it was said, had given birth during the night of October 1, the baby being the result of an adulterous affair with her sister's husband, Richard Randolph. The baby had been killed and its body disposed of. One of the Harrison slaves took Randolph Harrison to a pile of old shingles and there Harrison saw bloodstains; the slave claimed that this was where the body had been left. But no body was ever found. As the stories spread and were embellished, the honor and reputation of the Randolph family became an issue. Richard Randolph sought the advice of his stepfather, Henry St. George Tucker, a prominent lawyer. His initial advice was to do nothing; these were scurrilous tales spread among the lower classes and should not be dignified with a response. They would soon fade away. However, this did not happen, and it soon became apparent to Richard Randolph that he was suspected by members of his own social class. He, therefore, took the unusual step of issuing a challenge in the form of an open letter, dated March 29, 1793, and subsequently published in the *Virginia Gazette.* It referred to the circulation of calumnies against him, and declaring that he would present himself at the next session of the Cumberland Court, ready to answer any charges that might be brought against him. True to his word, Richard Randolph came to the Cumberland Court in the third week of April, apparently expecting that this bold defiance would put an end to the rumor mongering. Instead he was arrested by the high sheriff and put in jail, charged with "feloniously murdering a child said to be born of Nancy Randolph."

A Skillful Defense

Richard Randolph retained John Marshall, then 37 years old, and destined less than a decade later to begin his tenure as the most celebrated of all chief justices of the U.S. Supreme Court, as his counsel. Marshall was distant kin of the Randolphs and a close friend of St. George Tucker. It was also decided to enlist the help of the legendary leader of the revolution and former diplomat, Patrick Henry. As the well known story goes, when initially offered a fee of 250 guineas, Henry declined the case on the grounds of ill health, but when the offer was doubled, he decided he was well enough to travel. As an attorney, Henry was known for his skill in cross-examining witnesses. Marshall already had a reputation for his ability to analyze evidence and to present forceful logical arguments for whatever position he was defending.

There are no extant official records of the trial; the proceedings have been reconstructed from notes taken, particularly the "Notes of Evidence" in the papers of John Marshall. The trial was held before a panel of 16 "gentlemen justices," but not all necessarily sympathetic to the Randolphs—among them were members of other prominent Virginia families with whom the Randolphs had long-standing feuds. Under Virginia law Richard and Nancy Randolph could not be required to testify, nor could slaves appear as witnesses, although Mary Harrison had seen two young female slaves in Nancy's bedroom when she had taken in the laudanum. Randolph and Mary Harrison testified to their involvement on the night of October 1–2 and the events they were aware of. But under cross-examination by Patrick Henry, Randolph Harrison asserted that he had not entertained "any suspicion of criminal correspondence" between his guests. Mary Harrison told the court that she had no suspicions of Nancy until after she heard the rumors, and even then she considered the probability of a birth or miscarriage having occurred to be low.

An incident in Patrick Henry's cross-examination of an aunt, Mary Page, has been frequently retold as an example of his skill in undermining what might have been strong evidence. Mary Page had apparently suspected that Nancy was pregnant for some time before the night in question. Henry asked her to describe the circumstances which had caused this suspicion, eventually bringing her to the point of describing how she had found the opportunity to observe Nancy, undressed, through a crack in a locked door, and had concluded that she looked pregnant. Henry is then said to have leaned toward the witness and asked, "Madam, which eye did you peep with?" As laughter erupted in the crowded courtroom Henry turned to the panel of justices and boomed, "Great God, deliver us from eavesdroppers!"

John Marshall delivered the closing statement for the defense. He did not attempt to dispute any of the facts presented by the witnesses. He pointed out that there had been no proof that a baby had been born that night, much less that it had been killed. All of the other circumstances were open to an innocent interpretation. If relatives had observed expressions of fondness between Richard and Nancy, was this not quite natural? She was his wife's sister, she had been obliged to leave her own home, and her suitor, Theodorick, had died. If the two had been engaged in an adulterous relationship, would they not have been careful *not* to appear fond of each other before other family members? If Mary Page had observed a change in Nancy's size that was due to pregnancy as early as May, would it not have been obvious to all that she was pregnant by the end of September? Nancy had procured a medication believed to have the possible side effect of inducing an abortion, but if the other testimony is correct, this was at a time when she was near delivery, so there would have been no point to using it for that purpose. Marshall concluded that although "the friends of Miss Randolph cannot deny that there is some foundation on which suspicion may build," at the same time her enemies could not deny that "every circumstance may be accounted for, without imputing guilt to her. In this situation candor will not condemn or exclude from society a person who may be only unfortunate." The justices accepted this argument. There was insufficient evidence for a conviction and the pair were freed, apparently to the jubilation of the community which had been so ready to condemn them.

Only three years, later Richard Randolph was suddenly taken ill with a high fever, became delirious, and died. Nancy continued to live with her sister for some years, but in 1809 she married one of America's Founding Fathers, Gouverneur Morris. Among his many distinctions, he had been personally responsible for the drafting of large parts of the American Constitution, as a member of the constitutional convention in Philadelphia in 1787. It was a happy marriage and they had a son in 1813. The following year John Randolph of Roanoke, known as Jack, the younger brother of Richard and Theodorick, who after a distinguished political career had become embittered and rancorous, chose to revive the old accusations against Nancy, along with others, in a letter addressed to her, but intended for her husband. Nancy chose to reply, and in a letter that she was careful to circulate to Jack Randolph's political enemies, she said that she had indeed given birth that October night in 1792 at Glenlyvar, but the baby had not been killed; it was born dead. The father, she said, was not Richard, but Theodorick, whom she had intended to marry, and whom she considered as her husband "in the presence of . . . God. . . ." The baby had been conceived, she indicated delicately, just a few days before Theodorick's death. Her claim, however, has not been universally accepted as true, and there are still those who believe it is more likely that the original allegations were well-founded.

—David I. Petts

Suggestions for Further Reading

Baker, Leonard. *John Marshall: A Life in the Law.* New York: Macmillan Publishing, 1974.

Biddle, Francis. "Scandal at Bizarre," *American Heritage,* Aug.1961, 10.

Crawford, Alan Pell. *Unwise Passions.* New York: Simon and Schuster, 2000.

"Notes on Evidence." In *The Papers of John Marshall, Correspondence and Papers.* Vol. 2, July 1788–December 1795. Edited by Charles T. Cullen and Herbert A. Johnson. Chapel Hill: University of North Carolina Press, 1977.

Alien and Sedition Acts: 1798

Defendants: 24 people, including: James Thompson Callender, Thomas Cooper, William Duane, Anthony Haswell, and Matthew Lyon. **Crime Charged:** Seditious libel **Chief Defense Lawyers:** Lyon acted for himself, advised by Israel Smith; David Fay and Israel Smith (Haswell); Thomas Cooper and Alexander Dallas, (Duane); Cooper acted for himself; and William B. Giles, George Hay and Philip Nicholas (Callender) **Chief Prosecutors:** Charles Marsh (Lyon, Haswell); William Rawle (Duane, Cooper); and Thomas Nelson (Callender) **Judges:** William Paterson and Samuel Hitchcock (Lyon, Haswell); Samuel Chase, and Richard Peters (Cooper); Bushrod Washington and Peters (Duane); and Samuel Chase (Callender) **Dates of Trials:** October 8, 1799 (Lyon); May 5, 1800 (Haswell) April 16, 1800 (Cooper); June 3, 1800 (Callender); June 11, 1800 (Duane court appearance) **Place:** Rutland, Vermont (Lyon); Windsor, Vermont (Haswell); Norristown, Pennsylvania (Duane); Philadelphia, Pennsylvania (Cooper); and Richmond, Virginia (Callender) **Verdict:** Guilty (Lyon, Haswell, Cooper, and Callender) **Sentences:** $1,000 fine, $60.96 court costs, 4 months in jail (Lyon); $200 fine, 2 months in jail (Haswell); $400 fine, 6 months in prison, a $2,000 surety bond upon leaving prison (Cooper); and $200 fine, 9 months in prison, a $1,200 bond for good behavior (Callender)

SIGNIFICANCE

On paper only, the terms of the Sedition Act were an improvement over traditional common law. But the fact that the federal government would enact a sedition law was a blow to freedom of the press.

Partisan politics contributed to the creation of the Alien and Sedition Acts. However, American perceptions and worries about European affairs, particularly realistic fears of a possible war with France, also contributed to their enactment. American attempts to maintain neutrality pleased no one at home or abroad.

The Naturalization and Alien Acts, which increased residency requirements for citizenship and gave extraordinary powers over aliens to the president, passed into oblivion unused. However, there were several prosecutions under the Sedition Act. The act's most pertinent provision allowed prosecutions against persons publishing "any false, scandalous and malicious writing" that brought the federal government, the Congress, or the president into disrepute.

Under common law, liberty of the press generally meant no prior restraint on publications. However, the publisher was responsible for what he (or she) wrote. If a court deemed the material to be libelous, the writer could be punished. Libel was a published statement that damaged a person's reputation, or in the case of seditious libel, the government or a government official. Truth was not a defense, nor did there need to be proof of malicious intent. Despite First Amendment prohibitions, most states had their own libel and sedition acts.

Satiric portrayal of the first fight in Congress—between Matthew Lyon and Roger Griswold. Lyon was later prosecuted under the Sedition Act. (Courtesy, Library of Congress)

The federal Sedition Act tried to strike a compromise between common law and new American freedoms. Truth was a defense under the new federal statute, proof of malicious intent was required, and the jury would decide whether a libel existed. Under common law, the judge decided if material was libelous and he was free to determine any sentence. The Sedition Act stipulated that those convicted could be fined not more than $2,000 and imprisoned for no more than two years.

In practice these changes availed nothing to those prosecuted. Federalist courts insisted on turning the truth-as-a-defense clause into a presumptive-guilt clause. The plaintiff, the government, did not have to prove that the statements made were false. The defendant had to prove they were true. And such attempts often were thwarted by the judge.

Benjamin Franklin Bache, the vitriolic publisher of the *Aurora,* spurred passage of the Sedition Act when he obtained and published a copy of a letter from France's foreign minister, Tallyrand. This action convinced many Federalists that connections existed between Republicans and the French government. Before the Sedition Act could be passed, Bache's intemperate remarks earned him a common law indictment for libeling President John Adams and his administration. Bache died of yellow fever before he could be tried.

The first man actually indicted under the new Sedition Act was a member of Congress, Matthew Lyon. Charges stemmed from publication of two letters. One, Lyon wrote to a newspaper in reply to an attack on him.

> When I shall see the efforts of that power bent on the promotion of the comfort . . . of the people, that executive shall have my zealous and uniform support: but whenever I shall . . . see . . . the public welfare swallowed up in a continual grasp for power . . . behold men of real merit daily turned out of office . . . men of meanness preferred for the ease with which they take up and advocate opinions . . . when I shall see the sacred name of religion employed as a state engine to make mankind hate . . . I shall not be their humble advocate.

The other letter, published by Lyon, was written by Joel Barlow. Commenting on a speech of Adams', Barlow wondered why Congress had not sent the president "to a mad house."

Lyon tried to defend himself on the grounds that the Sedition Law was unconstitutional. The court did not look kindly on this defense. Found guilty, Lyon wrote, published, and was re-elected from his cell.

Anthony Haswell, a supporter of Lyon's, was indicted because an advertisement to raise funds for Lyon's fine, described "the oppressive hand of usurped power" Lyon suffered and "the indignities . . . heaped upon him by a hard-hearted savage" [the jailer]. Also, reprinted from the *Aurora* was a charge Tories were holding government office. Haswell tried, unsuccessfully, to obtain testimony from the Secretary of War to prove the Tory charges. His lawyers argued just as unsuccessfully that the "oppressive hand of power" referred only to the marshal and the jailer.

The most elusive Republican was William Duane, who had married Bache's widow and taken over the *Aurora.* Duane charged that the British wielded great influence over administration politics and had spent a fortune in bribes. He claimed there was a secret alliance between England and America against France.

Duane appeared for trial, only to have the trial suspended for several months. A procedural reason was given, but the true reason rested with a letter Duane had obtained from Tench Coxe, one-time assistant to Alexander Hamilton in the Treasury. The letter, written years earlier to Coxe by John Adams, claimed the Pinckneys from South Carolina were enlisting help from the British to obtain federal appointments. Although this letter did not prove Duane's extravagant allegations, it showed some evidence of British influence.

While awaiting the new trial, Duane aggravated the Senate. He criticized a proposed, unpublished bill, to settle disputed presidential and vice presidential elections. Then, when summoned to answer questions, he refused to go because his lawyers refused to appear. They believed Senate rules precluded mounting an effective defense. Duane was arrested on a contempt warrant signed by Thomas Jefferson, president of the Senate.

Not until after the Congress adjourned did the administration indict Duane for libeling the Senate. When Jefferson became president, he dismissed that suit. To preserve the Senate's rights, Jefferson ordered a new suit instituted. The grand jury refused to indict.

Because he was one of Duane's lawyers, Thomas Cooper was indicted for a handbill published months prior to Duane's summons from the Senate. Prosecutor William Rawles treated the handbill as inflammatory:

> Error leads to discontent, discontent to a fancied idea of oppression, and that to insurrection.

Cooper maintained that his statements were true, he held no malicious motives, and had attributed none to Adams. The judge, Samuel Chase, blocked Cooper's defense at every turn.

When James Thompson Callender faced Judge Chase after being indicted for his savage writings about Adams, like met like. Callender had no regard for truth or decency. Chase had little regard for truth or law. Chase struck down every reasonable defense request made, harassing the defense lawyers until they withdrew from the case.

Callender's sentence expired the day the Act expired. The new Jefferson administration did not seek to renew the Sedition Act, although libel actions did continue under common law.

—*Teddi DiCanio*

Suggestions for Further Reading

Miller, John C. *Crisis in Freedom.* Boston: Little, Brown & Co., 1951.

Smith, James Morton. *Freedom's Fetters, The Alien and Sedition Laws and American Civil Liberties.* Ithaca, N.Y.: Cornell University Press, 1956.

John Fries Trials: 1799

Defendant: John Fries **Crime Charged:** Treason
Chief Defense Lawyers: First trial: Alexander Dallas, James Ewing, and William Lewis; second trial: none **Chief Prosecutors:** First trial: William Rawle and Samuel Sitgreaves; second trial: Jared Ingersoll and Rawle
Judges: First trial: James Iredell and Richard Peters; second trial: Samuel Chase and Peters **Dates of Trials:** First trial: April 30–May 9, 1799; second trial: April 24–25, 1800 **Place:** Philadelphia, Pennsylvania
Verdict: Guilty, both trials **Sentence:** Hanging. However, President John Adams pardoned Fries.

SIGNIFICANCE

John Fries' fate hinged on the interpretation of his actions, whether they constituted riot or levying war, i.e., treason.

In 1798, the U.S. Congress, anticipating a possible war with France, passed a tax to be laid according to assessed values on slaves, lands, and houses. The legislation, well publicized in urban areas, was little known or understood in some rural areas. This lack of understanding, particularly in northeastern Pennsylvania where many residents knew only German, led to confrontations with excise officers as they tried to examine property. One series of incidents led to a charge of treason after a band of armed men from Bucks County, led by John Fries, a former Continental Army officer, forced U.S. Marshal William Nichols to release 23 men being held on charges of insurrection. No one was hurt.

As comprehension about the tax legislation grew and affairs quieted down in Bucks and neighboring Northampton counties, rumors grew in Washington that the disturbances constituted a "plot." Members of both the Federalist and Republican "parties" fantasized reasons as to why the other group would create trouble. President John Adams dispatched troops to the area.

Upon their arrival were no disturbances to quell. Instead the military sought the ringleaders of the "insurrection." At an auction, troops grabbed John Fries and others who did not scramble away quickly enough. Of these, 15, including Fries, were charged with treason and taken to Philadelphia. The only ones tried were Fries, Anthony Stahler, and Frederic Hearny.

At Fries' first trial, prosecutor William Rawle stated that an action taken to prevent the execution of a public officer's duties was "an act of levying war," i.e., treason. Fries' fears about his rights and property were insufficient reasons to justify resistance. The defense argued that Fries' action constituted riot, which was a high misdemeanor, rather than treason. Alexander Dallas spent hours weaving points of English common law into an argument that the jury had the power to decide whether actions taken constituted treason as well as whether the defendant had committed said actions. Moreover, Fries' inability to read English had left him ignorant of the excise officers' purposes. But, in his charge to the jury, Judge James Iredell made it clear that armed resistance constituted treason.

The jury found Fries guilty. However, the judges agreed to a request for a new trial since apparently one juror had formed an opinion before the trial.

But the second trial promised to be worse than the first when Judge Samuel Chase issued a written opinion prior to the trial. It was this action which brought the trial so much attention. Chase maintained English common law had no bearing on the case and that:

> Any insurrection . . . for the purpose of resisting or preventing by force . . . the execution of any statute of the United States . . . is levying war against the United States, within the . . . true meaning of the Constitution.

Although prosecutor Rawle persuaded Chase to withdraw his opinion, the defense lawyers withdrew from the case. Given the mind of the court, it would be impossible to mount an adequate defense. Fries declined to obtain other counsel, and the judge advised the defendant throughout the trial, which was an old common law practice. Fries was found guilty and sentenced to hang. He appealed to President Adams for a pardon, a step he also had taken after the first trial.

THE
TWO TRIALS
OF
JOHN FRIES,
on an Indictment for
TREASON;
TOGETHER WITH A BRIEF REPORT OF THE TRIALS OF SEVERAL OTHER PERSONS, FOR
Treason and Insurrection,
In the Counties of Bucks, Northampton and Montgomery,
IN THE *CIRCUIT COURT* OF THE *UNITED STATES*,
Begun at the City of Philadelphia, April 11, 1799; continued at Norristown, October 11, 1799;—and concluded at Philadelphia, April 11, 1800; before the Hon. Judges, IREDELL, PETERS, WASHINGTON and CHASE.
TO WHICH IS ADDED,
A copious Appendix, containing the evidences and arguments of the counsel on both sides, on the motion for a new trial; the arguments on the motion for removing the case to the county where the crime was committed, and the arguments against holding the jurisdiction at Norristown.
TAKEN IN SHORT HAND BY THOMAS CARPENTER.
[*COPY-RIGHT SECURED.*]
PHILADELPHIA:
Printed and sold by WILLIAM W. WOODWARD, No. 17 Chesnut, near Front street.
1800.

A facsimile of a published account of the trial of John Fries. (Courtesy, The Library Company of Philadelphia)

Adams sent his son Thomas to ask the defense lawyers for their briefs. He did not ask for the judges' notes—an unusual move. After consulting his cabinet members, who were opposed to much leniency, Adams first granted amnesty to all those awaiting trial, then pardoned those already convicted: Fries, Stahler, and Hearny.

—Teddi DiCanio

Suggestions for Further Reading

Davis, W.W.H. *The Fries Rebellion, 1798–99.* Doylestown, Pa.: 1899.

Dos Passos, John. *The Men Who Made the Nation.* Garden City, N.Y.: Doubleday & Co., 1957.

Elsmere, Jane Shaffer. "The Trials of John Fries." *The Pennsylvania Magazine of History and Biography* (October, 1979): Vol. CIII, No.4.

Wharton, Francis. *State Trials of the United States.* Philadelphia: 1849.

Levi Weeks Trial: 1800

Defendant: Levi Weeks **Crime Charged:** Murder
Chief Defense Lawyers: Aaron Burr, Alexander Hamilton, Brockholst Livingston **Chief Prosecutor:** Cadwallader D. Colden **Judges:** John Lansing, Richard Harrison, Richard Varick **Place:** New York, New York
Date of Trial: March 1800 **Verdict:** Not guilty

SIGNIFICANCE

The Levi Weeks trial revolved around one of the nation's first "murder mysteries," sparked a public outcry, and showcased some of the finest legal talent in the United States.

New York, like many other large cities, has a reputation for crime and violence. Even in earlier days, when the city was much smaller than now, it still had its share of criminal activity. In 1800 it was the scene of one of the nation's first great murder mysteries, which culminated in a famous trial.

A Less than Discreet Affair

Gulielma Sands—Elma to her family and friends—was a vivacious 22-year-old who lived with her cousin Catherine Ring on Greenwich Street. Catherine and her husband, Elias Ring, were Quakers who ran a boarding house, and in July 1799, a young carpenter named Levi Weeks moved in. His arrival was unfortunate, for the Rings and their other boarders soon noticed that Weeks was paying excessive attention to Sands. The two spent a great amount of time together, a lot of it in Sands's bedroom, the door of which they sometimes locked. The hours at which Weeks came and went, the piles of clothes that Sands left in odd places, and even the sounds from her bedroom told the story that the two were sexually involved. Because this was inappropriate behavior for an unmarried couple, everyone suspected that Sands and Weeks must be planning on getting married: only that step could make their behavior somewhat less scandalous.

But Sands's life was less than happy. She was often ill, and in the fall of 1799 she seemed depressed, sometimes telling her cousin and others that she wished she were dead and toying with the idea of taking an overdose of laudanum. Weeks, too, had emotional outbursts and run-ins with other boarders.

Nobody ever knew for sure, but the circumstances suggest that Sands, herself an illegitimate child, might have been pregnant.

Eventually, though, Sands grew much happier, confiding to her cousin Catherine that she and Weeks were in fact getting married. The wedding, she said, was set for Sunday evening, December 22. For a day or two beforehand, she seemed in good spirits as she and her cousins prepared for the nuptials. Finally Sunday evening arrived. This would be the last time anyone would see her alive.

Nobody actually witnessed Sands and Weeks leave the Rings' house together, but nearly everyone thought that that was what happened. Sands was upstairs dressing, and Weeks was by the front door. People heard someone come down the stairs, and then they heard whispers by the door, which opened and closed. Shortly thereafter, a friend saw Sands in a crowd on Greenwich Street and went to speak with her. But someone—the friend did not notice who—told Sands, "Let's go," and Sands said good-night and moved on. She was never seen again. But a half hour later, a woman's cries of "Murder!" and "Lord help me!" were heard coming from the vicinity of the Manhattan Well, near Greene and Spring Streets, and people saw a one-horse sleigh, with a dark horse and no bells, traveling away from the area. The description of this vehicle matched the appearance of one belonging to Ezra Weeks, Levi's wealthy brother. Witnesses would later swear that they saw Ezra's sleigh leaving his premises that evening, and others would say that they saw a sleigh in the vicinity of the well containing two men and a woman, all of whom were laughing loudly. No positive identification of these persons was ever made. The entire scenario involving the sleigh has a macabre resemblance to the song "Jingle Bells," except that no bells were involved, and the ride ended in cries of "murder," which no one bothered to investigate.

Late that evening, Weeks returned to the Rings' house alone, asking where Sands was. This made Catherine Ring suspicious, and a few days later, with Sands still missing, she told Weeks so. She also told him that Weeks had mentioned the planned wedding to her. The revelation that people knew of the secret engagement seemed to upset Weeks greatly.

Weeks Indicted for Murder

A few days after Elma Sands vanished, a boy drawing water from the Manhattan Well found the muff she had been wearing. But not until nearly a week after this, inexplicably, did Elias Ring and some others sound the well with poles and find Sands's body. She had apparently been beaten savagely before being thrown, dead or alive, into the well. The body was put on public display for a few days, not only in the Ringses' boarding house, but in the street in front of it, which stirred up public outrage at what had happened to Sands. Within a week or so of the body's discovery, a grand jury indicted Weeks for the murder of Elma Sands.

Weeks promptly lined up some of the city's, and the nation's, best legal talent to defend him. His three attorneys were Brockholst Livingston, whom

Thomas Jefferson would later appoint to the U.S. Supreme Court; Alexander Hamilton, former Secretary of the Treasury and New York's Federalist leader; and Aaron Burr, former U.S. senator and future vice president. Hamilton and Burr were especially strong talents, being without question the best attorneys anywhere in the state. Despite their strong political and personal rivalries—Burr would kill Hamilton in a famous duel four years later—the two men often worked together. Their talents did not come cheaply, though; possibly Ezra Weeks helped pay for their services. Both Hamilton and Burr had reputations for womanizing, and both of their names were linked with stories of sexual scandal. Perhaps these facts had something to do with their decisions to take Levi Weeks's case.

A Two-Day Trial

The trial took two days, lasting until late at night, an unusual length and schedule for the time. During the proceedings, an angry mob could be heard outside the courthouse chanting, "Crucify him! Crucify him!" The prosecutor, future New York mayor and congressman Cadwallader Colden, had to rely on circumstantial evidence to try to prove that Weeks had had means, motive, and opportunity to murder Sands. He put on witnesses to show that Weeks and Sands had had a sexual relationship; that he had promised to marry her; that he had left the boarding house with her the night she was killed; and that his brother's sleigh had been identified at the crime scene. But he could not produce any direct evidence in support of any of these things.

The defense, on the other hand, claimed that the public outcry surrounding the crime had prejudiced the case. Weeks's attorneys took pains to show that one of the prosecution's star witnesses, boarder Richard David Croucher, had had run-ins with Weeks and was perhaps envious of Sands's affection for the young carpenter. Croucher had been one of Levi's most outspoken persecutors both before and after the discovery of Weeks's body. The defense team also found witnesses who swore that Levi had spent the whole evening with Ezra and others, and that he thus could not have been at the well. Still other witnesses testified that Ezra's sleigh had never gone out that night.

The testimony ended at two in the morning. Chief Judge John Lansing—who was himself to disappear mysteriously from the New York streets one night 30 years later, never to be seen again—instructed the jury that the case against Levi Weeks was purely circumstantial, but he did not direct a verdict. As things turned out, he did not need to: the jurors took only five minutes to acquit Weeks.

The Weeks case stirred up a storm of controversy that continued to swirl for decades, and Lansing drew strong criticism for his jury instructions. The case was a cause celébre of the day, especially since it was a key election year and Hamilton and Burr were engaged in a major political battle with each other. But in a larger sense the Weeks trial, with its sexual scandal and grisly murder, set the stage for chronic urban violence that would only come to full flower in America more than a century later.

—Buckner F. Melton, Jr.

Suggestions for Further Reading

John D. Lawson, ed. *American State Trials*. Vol. 1. St. Louis: F. H. Thomas Law book Co., 1914.

Liva Baker, "The Defense of Levi Weeks." *American Bar Association Journal*, 63 (June 1977): 818.

Marbury v. Madison: 1803

Plaintiffs: William Marbury, William Harper, Robert R. Hooe, and Dennis Ramsay **Defendant:** Secretary of State James Madison **Plaintiff Claim:** That Madison had illegally refused to deliver judicial commissions to their rightful recipients **Chief Defense Lawyer:** U.S. Attorney General Levi Lincoln **Chief Lawyer for Plaintiffs:** Charles Lee **Justices:** Samuel Chase, William Cushing, John Marshall, Alfred Moore, William Paterson, and Bushrod Washington **Place:** Washington, D.C. **Dates of Trial:** February 10–11, 1803 **Verdict:** Plaintiffs could not force Madison to deliver the commissions, because the Judiciary Act of 1789 was unconstitutional.

SIGNIFICANCE

Marbury v. Madison may be the most important case in American history, because it established the principle of judicial review.

In the late 18th century and early 19th century, the two parties dominating the American political scene were the Federalists and the Democratic-Republicans. In the presidential election of 1800, the Electoral College had a tie vote, and it fell to the House of Representatives to decide the outcome. After a bitter battle and 36 ballots, the House voted February 17, 1801 for Democratic-Republican candidate Thomas Jefferson.

The outgoing president, Federalist John Adams, had as his secretary of state the distinguished lawyer John Marshall. In January 1801, Adams secured Marshall's nomination as chief justice of the United States. Marshall was sworn in February 4 but continued to serve as Adams' secretary of state until March 3, when Adams' term ended. Meanwhile, Adams and the Federalists in Congress had been moving to pack the federal judiciary with as many new Federalist judges as possible before the Jefferson administration took power.

As part of the Federalists' efforts to preserve their control over the judiciary, on February 27, 1801, Congress gave Adams the power to appoint justices of the peace for the District of Columbia. On March 2, one day before the end of his term, Adams appointed 42 justices of the peace, and Congress approved their appointments the next day. As secretary of state, Marshall signed and sealed the necessary judicial commissions, but the commissions were not delivered by the end of March 3. Thomas Jefferson's term began March 4, and he ordered his new secretary of state, James Madison, not to deliver the commissions. Jefferson decided to view the commissions as invalid unless delivered.

Portrait of Secretary of State James Madison, defendant in *Marbury v. Madison*, which established the principle of judicial review. (by Gilbert Stuart, Courtesy of National Archives and Records Administration)

Marbury Goes to Court

Having demonstrated his power, Jefferson ultimately allowed most of the Adams appointees to take their offices. One of the appointees that Jefferson did not allow to take office, William Marbury, filed a petition with the Supreme Court December 16, 1801 requesting that the Supreme Court order Madison to deliver Marbury's commission. Marbury was joined by three other disappointed appointees, William Harper, Robert R. Hooe, and Dennis Ramsay. Of course, by now Marshall had been the chief justice for over nine months. Under the Judiciary Act of 1789, the Supreme Court had the power to issue the order Marbury requested, called a "writ of mandamus."

On December 18, 1801, Marshall ordered a hearing on Marbury's petition, to take place at the Court's next session, the February Term of 1803. The hearing began February 10, 1803. Charles Lee, a Federalist and former attorney general, represented Marbury and the others. Jefferson's attorney general, Levi Lincoln was present in court as a witness, but not as Madison's lawyer.

Lee argued that Madison, as secretary of state, was not only an official of the executive branch, bound to obey the president, but a public servant obligated to perform his duty and deliver Marbury's lawful commission. Therefore, the Court must exercise its authority under the Judiciary Act to issue a writ of mandamus against Madison. Attorney General Lincoln said practically nothing, except that the issue of the commissions was purely political and thus not subject to the judiciary.

Marshall Proclaims the Doctrine of Judicial Review

On February 24, 1803, Chief Justice Marshall issued the Court's opinion. He proceeded in three steps.

First, he reviewed the facts of the case. He stated that Marbury had the right to receive his commission:

> To withhold his commission, therefore, is an act deemed by the court not warranted by law, but violative of a vested right.

Second, Marshall analyzed Marbury's legal remedies. He concluded that the Judiciary Act clearly entitled Marbury to the writ of mandamus he requested.

Marshall's third and final question, therefore, was whether the writ of mandamus could be issued by the Supreme Court. Although the Judiciary Act would allow the Court to issue the writ, Marshall was concerned about the Court's authority under Article III, Section 2, Paragraph 2 of the U.S. Constitution, which states:

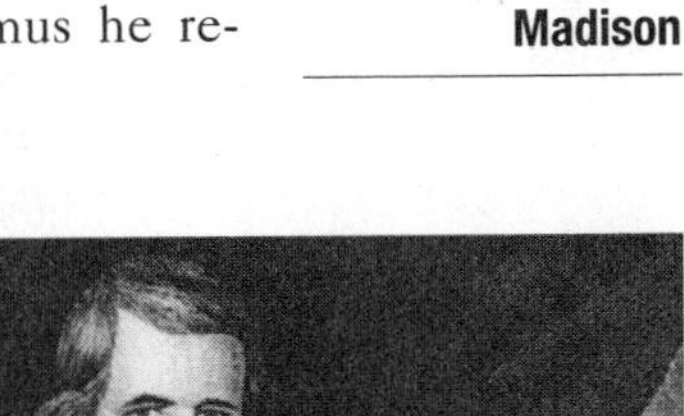

Engraving of Chief Justice John Marshall with Supreme Court building in the distance. (by Alonzo Chappell, Courtesy, Supreme Court of the United States).

> In all cases affecting ambassadors, other public ministers and consuls, and those in which a State shall be a Party, the Supreme Court shall have original jurisdiction. In all other cases . . . Supreme Court shall have appellate jurisdiction. . . .

If the Court didn't have original jurisdiction—the responsibility for hearing the evidence and making an initial decision—then under the Constitution, Marbury couldn't go directly to it to get his requested writ of mandamus. He would have to go to a federal District Court, and only if he lost there could he then appeal to the Supreme Court under its *appellate* jurisdiction. As Marshall stated:

> To enable this court, then, to issue a mandamus, it must be shown to be an exercise of appellate jurisdiction. . . .

Marshall now addressed the critical question: Would the court use the authority that the Judiciary Act granted it, but that the Constitution denied it, to issue Marbury's writ of mandamus?

Marshall said no, it would not. No act of Congress, including the Judiciary Act, could do something forbidden by the Constitution:

> Certainly all those who have framed written constitutions contemplate them as forming the fundamental and paramount law of the nation, and consequently, the theory of every such government must be, that an act of the legislature, repugnant to the constitution, is void.

Therefore, because the Judiciary Act violated the Constitution, it was unenforceable. Marbury and the others could not get their writ of mandamus from the Court because their petition had been sent to the Court directly, not on appeal. In declaring the Judiciary Act unconstitutional, Marshall set forth for the first time the doctrine of judicial review. Judicial review means that the federal courts, above all the Supreme Court, have the power to declare laws unenforceable if they violate the Constitution:

> It is emphatically the province and duty of the judicial department to say what the law is. Those who apply the rule to particular cases must of necessity expound and interpret the rule. If two laws conflict with each other, the courts must decide on the operation of each.

Marshall's decision meant that the Court would not give his fellow Federalist Marbury the writ of mandamus. Nevertheless, it was a brilliant move. In refusing to confront Jefferson, Marshall had asserted a new and potent power for the judiciary, namely the doctrine of judicial review. Despite various issues, such as whether Marshall should have removed himself from the case because of his role as Adams' secretary of state, *Marbury v. Madison* permanently established the principle of judicial review. This power to overturn unconstitutional laws is the basis for the courts' power today to prevent such evils as civil rights violations.

—*Stephen G. Christianson*

Suggestions for Further Reading

Baker, Leonard. *John Marshall: A Life in Law.* New York: Macmillan Co., 1974.

Berger, Raoul. *Congress v. the Supreme Court.* Cambridge: Harvard University Press, 1969.

Beveridge, Albert J. *The Life of John Marshall.* Marietta, Ga.: Cherokee Publishing, 1990.

Bickel, Alexander M. *The Least Dangerous Branch: the Supreme Court at the Bar of Politics.* New Haven: Yale University Press, 1986.

Cusack, Michael. "America's Greatest Justice?" *Scholastic Update* (January 1990): 11.

Ellis, Richard E. *The Jeffersonian Crisis: Courts and Politics in the Young Republic.* New York: Oxford University Press, 1971.

Levy, Leonard Williams. *Judicial Review and the Supreme Court.* New York: Harper & Row, 1967.

McHugh, Clare. "The Story of the Constitution: Conflict and Promise." *Scholastic Update* (September 1987): 8–11.

Warren, Charles. *The Supreme Court in United States History.* Littleton, Colo.: F.B. Rothman, 1987.

Samuel Chase Impeachment: 1805

Defendant: Associate Supreme Court Justice Samuel Chase
Crime Charged: "High Crimes and Misdemeanors" within the meaning of Article II, Section 4 of the Constitution **Chief Defense Lawyers:** Robert Goodloe Harper, Joseph Hopkinson, and Luther Martin
Chief Prosecutor: Trial Managers John Randolph and Caesar Rodney
Judges: The U.S. Senate, with Vice President Aaron Burr presiding
Place: Washington, D.C. **Dates of Trial:** February 4–March 1, 1805
Verdict: Not guilty

SIGNIFICANCE

Congress for the first and only time exercised its constitutional prerogative to try a justice of the U.S. Supreme Court.

Samuel Chase was born in Somerset County, Maryland in April of 1741. During the next 70 years, until his death in 1811, he would become one of America's most famous and controversial founding fathers.

Chase was active in politics from an early age and was elected to colonial Maryland's Assembly on the strength of his anti-English platform. He was Maryland's delegate to the Continental Congress of 1774 in Philadelphia, Pennsylvania and was one of the signers of the 1776 Declaration of Independence. After fighting in the Revolutionary War, during which he became friends with George Washington, Chase returned to Maryland. Chase used his influence in the Federalist Party to further his judicial career, and he swiftly rose through a succession of ever more prestigious posts. Chase was appointed presiding justice of the Baltimore Criminal Court, then in 1791 he was appointed chief justice of the Maryland Court of Appeals, and finally in 1796 he was appointed to the U.S. Supreme Court. Chase's Supreme Court nomination had Washington's personal backing.

From the Maryland courts to the Supreme Court, Chase was an openly Federalist judge, and he never hid his political loyalties. He zealously enforced the Federalist-sponsored Alien and Sedition Acts, and he supported the strict prosecution of persons involved in antigovernment demonstrations and allegedly treasonous activities. Chase presided at several trials involving supporters of his fellow founding father and presidential contender Thomas Jefferson.

Jefferson was the candidate of the opposition Democratic-Republican Party and won the hotly contested election of 1800.

Jefferson had a series of political struggles with the Federalists, whose supporters such as Chase and Supreme Court Chief Justice John Marshall dominated the federal judiciary. For several years, Jefferson's energies were focused on the legal issues in *Marbury v. Madison* (see separate entry), which ended on February 24, 1803 with Marshall's famous opinion proclaiming the doctrine of judicial review.

Painting of Samuel Chase. (Courtesy, National Historical Park Collection)

Congress Impeaches Chase

After *Marbury*, Jefferson adopted a different tactic in attacking the Federalist judiciary. He decided to exploit his party's domination of the Senate, where 25 of the 34 senators were Democratic-Republicans and only nine were Federalists. Under Article II, Section 4 of the Constitution, federal judges can be impeached for "High Crimes and Misdemeanors," and under Article I, Section 3, the trial must be conducted before the Senate. Jefferson's allies in the House of Representatives passed Articles of Impeachment against Chase, which were duly received by the Senate.

The Senate's High Court of Impeachment, presided over by Vice President Aaron Burr, opened on February 4, 1805. The "trial managers," or prosecutors, were John Randolph and Caesar Rodney. Chase's lawyers were Robert Goodloe Harper, Joseph Hopkinson, and Luther Martin. There were eight Articles, or charges, which named a variety of Democratic-Republican grievances against Chase concerning the trials over which he had presided. The charges ranged from giving a false legal definition of treason during the trial of one John Fries (see separate entry) in Article One to making very political comments to a Baltimore grand jury in Article Eight.

There was certainly plenty of evidence that Chase was a highly opinionated Federalist judge, who had perhaps acted with little regard for courtroom niceties, but there was very little proof that his actions were serious enough to be deemed constitutional violations. Even the Democratic-Republican senators felt uncomfortable. Trial manager Rodney in his closing argument lamely begged the Senate:

> Remember, if this honorable court acquit the defendant, they declare in the most solemn manner, . . . that he has . . . behaved himself well, in a manner becoming the character of a judge worthy of his situation.

On March 1, 1805, the Senate voted on Chase's impeachment. On each of the eight Articles, enough Democratic-Republican senators joined the Federalists in voting "not guilty" so that Chase was acquitted of all the charges against him. Chase continued to serve on the Supreme Court until he died in June 1811.

Samuel Chase's acquittal was a defeat for Thomas Jefferson, who may have planned to impeach Chief Justice John Marshall if Chase had been found guilty. The Samuel Chase impeachment was the first and only time Congress impeached a justice of the U.S. Supreme Court.

—Stephen G. Christianson

Suggestions for Further Reading

Elsmere, Jane Shaffer. *Justice Samuel Chase.* Muncie, Ind.: Janevar Publishing, 1980.

Haw, James. *Stormy Patriot: the Life of Samuel Chase.* Baltimore: Maryland Historical Society, 1980.

Rehnquist, William H. *Grand Inquests: the Historic Impeachments of Justice Samuel Chase and President Andrew Johnson.* New York: William Morrow & Co., 1992.

Philadelphia Cordwainers Trial: 1806

Defendants: Underl Barnes, John Dubois, John Harket, John Hepburn, George Keimer, Peter Pollen, George Pullis, George Snyder
Crime Charged: Conspiracy to raise their wages
Chief Defense Lawyers: Caesar A. Rodney, Walter Franklin
Chief Prosecutors: Jared Ingersol, Joseph Hopkinson **Judges:** John Innskep, Mayor of Philadelphia, *ex officio;* Moses Levy, recorder, presiding; Andrew Pettit, Abraham Shoemaker, Philip Wager, aldermen, jury.
Place: Philadelphia, Pennsylvania **Date of Trial:** January 2, March 26, 28–29, 1806 **Verdict:** Guilty **Sentence:** Each defendant fined $8 plus the costs of the suit

SIGNIFICANCE

The history of the American labor movement can be traced through a series of trials that, stage by stage, mark its struggle to gain the right to organize. The earliest of these trials happened to involve shoe- and bootmakers. Of all these early trials, the one in 1806 of the Philadelphia Cordwainers is regarded as perhaps the most crucial.

From the earliest days of the European colonies in North America, shoe- and bootmakers played a special role in society. Everyone, poor or rich, needed footwear, so such craftsmen were found everywhere. Making durable and/or stylish leather footwear led to pride in one's craft, which in fact required intelligence, discipline, and special skills. Yet it was the widespread need for and nature of this product that exposed it to ongoing changes in both industrial and commercial practices—mass production in the former case, retail competition in the latter case.

The Shoemaking Trade in Philadelphia

By the late 1700s, there had been major developments in the nature of the footwear trade. During the first decades in America, almost all leather shoes and boots were custom-made, and the men who made them were also the men who sold them. Gradually, though, some master craftsmen began to expand their business and came to employ journeymen craftsmen to fulfill orders. By the end of the eighteenth-century, some of these employers were expanding their business—selling a standardized line of wares in public markets and exporting on a wholesale-volume level to even distant cities. The nature of these new markets meant that the employers needed to produce a cheaper line of footwear; for this they wanted to pay slightly lower wages to the journeymen "cordwainers."

This name for shoe- and bootmakers has a curious etymology. It is a word that appeared in England in the Middle Ages and came from an anglicized pronunciation of a French word, *cordoan,* which referred to Cordovan leather; that in turn referred to Cordoba, Spain, whose fine-grained leather was regarded as the finest in Europe. Thus "cordwainers" were the men who worked with leather.

In 1794, numerous journeymen shoemakers in Philadelphia formed the Federal Society of Journeymen Cordwainers with the goal of protecting their wages. During the next several years, they called several "turn-outs," what we today would call strikes, during which the society's members tried to prevent all journeymen from working for less than standard wages. Those journeymen who defied the society's request were known as "scabs," the same term still used today. Then in November 1805, the society called another major turn-out. Because of the alleged tactics used by some members against cordwainers who either had refused to join the society or who continued working as "scabs," eight of the leaders of the society were brought to trial in January 1806.

If the Shoe Fits. . . .

The trial, officially known as *The Commonwealth v. George Pullis, et al.,* was conducted during two days before a so-called Mayor's Court; although a criminal action, it explicitly sided with the employers. The eight defendants were charged with several serious offenses, including resorting to "threats, menaces, and other unlawful means" to advance their "conspiracy" to maintain higher wages.

The society had hired two prestigious lawyers, Caesar A. Rodney, nephew of a signer of the Declaration of Independence, and Walter Franklin, a distinguished lawyer. The prosecution was conducted by two equally distinguished lawyers. The jury was composed of 12 men, nine of whom we would regard as employers—innkeepers, merchants, etc.—and three who were craftsmen—a hatter, tailor, and watchmaker. It was, in fact, an early showdown between capitalists and labor.

The prosecution conducted its case by calling as witnesses 13 journeymen shoemakers or shopowners, who, one by one, testified that the society put strong pressure on all established journeymen to join, forced all new journeymen shoemakers in town to join, fined members who were found to have worked as scabs, withdrew their members from employers if they hired any scab workers, fined members who failed to attend meetings held virtually every night, and sent a "tramping committee" around town to make sure all journeymen belonged to the society.

But the witnesses made even more serious charges, claiming that the society's members constantly harassed those who did not join or who worked as scabs, even going as far as physically roughing them up. John Bedford, an employer and shop owner, testified: "Once they broke the window with potatoes, which had pieces of broken shoemakers' tacks in them, at least the one had which they aimed at my person and was near hitting me in the face." Anthony Bennett, a journeyman, even testified that he had been forced to join the society and that if he had not, "they have threatened to [kill me]. Not to my face, but according to what I have understood."

When it came to the defendants' case, their lawyers called 10 witnesses, seven new ones and three of the prosecution's. Walter Franklin, the defense lawyer, opened by claiming that much of the testimony actually described events that had taken place many years previously: "Indeed all the circumstances which have been so long dwelt upon, and which were so nicely calculated to touch your feelings and excite your sensibility, happened long before any of the defendants, except one, had any concern in the association."

He then resorted to sarcasm when he admitted that the defendants had indeed formed an association to "promote the [members'] happiness": "But, unfortunately for these poor and ignorant men, they went a step beyond this! They mistook their privilege! They thought they had a right to determine for themselves the value of their own labor! And among other acts of their association, committed the unpardonable sin of settling and ascertaining the price of their own work!"

The journeymen who testified on behalf of the defendants naturally portrayed the society, its members, its rules, its procedures, as nothing but reasonable and restrained. Their lawyers, meanwhile, especially stressed that the prices and wages these journeymen sought were completely in line with those in such cities as Albany, Baltimore, and New York, and in fact lower than in some other American cities.

A moment of humor came when an employer testified that he sometimes sold his fancy boots for several dollars more per pair than was considered standard. He went on to say: "If any gentleman is disposed not to credit me, as I can see by the expression of some countenances, I can refer them to my customers by name"—and then proceeded to name two such. At that, the prosecutor cracked, "Then these are the gentlemen who have more money than wit?" The witness shot back: "They are gentlemen who have a right to indulge their fancy."

The summations were long and predictable, each of the four lawyers highlighting the elements that supported his position. What is to be noted, though, is that both sides said virtually nothing about the alleged acts of harassment but focused entirely on the issues of the "combination and conspiracy"—what we today might call "collusion" and "a closed shop." The prosecution described a conspiracy to impose membership and pay; the defense described a lawful association to obtain a fair wage.

Equally notable is that the defense lawyers, although themselves from the highest socioeconomic class in Philadelphia, often employed a populist, almost socialist rhetoric, employing the term "masters" to suggest that the avaricious employers were out to exploit the journeymen. Thus Caesar A. Rodney claimed that masters "who employ twenty-four journeymen, must make near $15,000 dollars a year, when the best journeyman receives about six hundred, a sum scarcely adequate to the frugal maintenance of himself and his family in this city, though living on the simplest and cheapest fare which the market affords."

Verdict and Aftermath

The jury retired at 9 P.M. and apparently reached a verdict fairly quickly, but were not asked to return it until the next morning. They found all eight guilty "of a conspiracy to raise their wages." The punishment was that each of the eight defendants was fined $8 and forced to pay all the costs of the trial. The fine itself was a little less than what the average journeyman could make in a week; paying the fees of those four Philadelphia lawyers must have come to far more than that. Presumably the society of journeymen cordwainers paid all costs.

Nothing more is heard of these individuals or their activities. But in the years that followed, trial after trial throughout the United States would gradually establish the right of laboring people to form associations to seek better wages. In effect, these Philadelphia cordwainers had taken the first step toward forming unions.

—John S. Bowman

Suggestions for Further Reading

Commons, John R. et al. eds. *A Documentary History of American Industrial Society*. Vol. 3, *Labor Conspiracy Cases*. Cleveland, Ohio: Arthur H. Clark Co., 1910.

Cox, Archibald et al. eds. *Cases and Materials in Labor Law*. 12th ed. Westbury, N.Y.: Foundation Press, 1996.

Tomlins, Christopher. *Law, Labor and Ideology in the Early American Republic*. New York: Cambridge University Press, 1993.

Dominic Daley and James Halligan Trial: 1806

Defendants: Dominic Daley, James Halligan **Crime:** Murder
Chief Defense Lawyers: Francis Blake, Thomas Gould, Edward Upham, Jabez Urham **Chief Prosecutors:** James Sullivan, John Hooker
Judges: Theodore Sedgwick, Samuel Sewall **Place:** Northampton, Massachusetts **Date of Trial:** April 24, 1806 **Verdict:** Guilty
Sentence: Death by hanging

SIGNIFICANCE

This otherwise obscure trial—rightly or wrongly—later came to be seen as epitomizing the anti-Irish bias that was widespread in New England during the early nineteenth century.

As the new American republic moved into the nineteenth century, most New Englanders were still of British stock and Protestant persuasion. Many of these Americans made no secret of their detestation of all Roman Catholics. Most especially, although they had just finished a war to break away from Great Britain, many New Englanders kept alive their English relatives' deep-seated prejudice against the Irish. It is against this background that an otherwise routine trial in a corner of Massachusetts has come to be judged by later generations.

The Crime

It was on November 10, 1805, that the body of a young man—his head bludgeoned and with a bullet hole in his chest—was discovered in a stream near Springfield, Massachusetts, after his horse had been found wandering in a nearby field on the afternoon of November 9. Two pistols were found near the scene of the murder. Letters in the horse's saddlebags identified the victim as Marcus Lyon, who turned out to be a young farmer from Connecticut making his way home from upstate New York.

Several local men and a young boy quickly came forward with reports of two strangers seen walking along the turnpike in that vicinity on November 9.

On Monday, November 11, a sheriff's posse set out and, by asking everywhere along the road, were able to catch up on Tuesday with two such men in Cobscrossing, Connecticut (near Rye, New York). They were Dominic Daley and James Halligan, two fairly recent Irish immigrants, and they admitted that they had come along that turnpike while walking from Boston en route to New York City. Although both men denied having any knowledge of the murder, they were arrested and brought back to Massachusetts to await trial. For some reason, Daley was singled out as having performed the actual act of murder while Halligan was accused of "aiding and abetting."

The Trial

On Thursday, April 24, 1806, the courtroom in Northampton, a county seat in western Massachusetts, was so packed that the trial was moved to the town's meeting house. Each defendant had been assigned two lawyers, but they had been given barely 48 hours to prepare a defense. The presiding judges were two of the most distinguished jurists in Massachusetts; a jury of 12 had been agreed upon. In the weeks before the trial, rumors had surfaced throughout the region promising that there would be no end of evidence linking these two to the murder. But in the end, the prosecution's case rested for the most part on a series of witnesses who could at best claim they recognized one or both of the defendants as having been walking along the turnpike near the murder scene on November 9.

There was also a gun dealer from Boston who testified that he had sold two pistols like the presumed murder weapons to a man who "talked like an Irishman"; otherwise he could not identify either of the two defendants as the purchaser. The owner of the inn where Lyon had spent some months in upstate New York testified that Lyon, the night before he had set out on his journey, had shown him some banknotes, two of which were exactly like those found on the person of Daley. Although the judge would instruct the jury to regard the testimony about the guns and the money as "circumstances too remote to bear upon the present case," the fact is the jury had been allowed to hear this. A 13-year-old boy, Laertes Fuller, gave the most damaging testimony. He alone connected the two men to the very locale of the murder and to the horse at about midday on November 9, although even he did not claim to have had a good look at Halligan.

When the prosecution rested its case, Daley and Halligan's lawyers offered no witnesses and the defendants, due to the law then in effect in Massachusetts, could not take the stand. Instead, one of Daley's lawyers, Francis Blake, delivered a long speech attacking the prosecution's case. Occasionally legalistic, sometimes eloquent, occasionally irrelevant, sometimes right-on point, Blake proceeded to argue that in fact there was no proof that Lyon had even been murdered on November 9, the day that Daley and Halligan were said to have been walking along that stretch of highway. The pistols were two of thousands in use at that time. (He said nothing about the banknotes, and the prosecution itself chose to drop that testimony—possibly because it appeared too "neat" to be true.) The case effectively rested on the testimony of the 13-year-old boy. Blake argued that the murder could not possibly have taken place during the brief 15 minutes when the boy said he first saw the two men on foot and then with the horse—during which brief period, moreover, the boy said he heard no gunshot.

No, said Blake, the real reason these two men were being charged was because they were Irishmen. After referring to the Boston gun dealer's identification as that of a "mind infected, in common with others, with that national prejudice which would lead him to prejudge the prisoners because they are Irishmen," Blake rose to even more rhetorical heights:

> Pronounce then a verdict against them! Condemn them to a gibbet! Hold out an awful warning of the wretched fugitives from that oppressed and persecuted nation! . . . That the name of an Irishman is, among us, but another name for a robber and an assassin; that everyman's hand is lifted against him; that when a crime of unexampled atrocity is perpetrated among us, we look around for an Irishman.

But it was to no avail. The trial ended about 11 that evening, and the jurors returned with their verdict about midnight. Both men were found guilty, and the next day they were sentenced to hang.

An Execution and an Exoneration

In the days before their execution, the Reverend Jean Louis Cheverus, a Roman Catholic priest, came out from Boston and heard their confession. The two were hanged before a crowd estimated as 15,000 on June 5, 1806. Father Cheverus explained to the many Protestant questioners that "the doctrine of the Church" forbade him ever to reveal what the men had confessed. Inevitably rumors about this crime continued to surface but it was not until 1879 that there first appeared in print the claim that a man had confessed on his deathbed to being the true murderer. In later years, this claim was enhanced by such details as the confessor's having been the uncle of the young Laertes Fuller. But there was no corroborating evidence for either the confession or the uncle's ties to the crime, and eventually most people of western Massachusetts forgot about Daley and Halligan. However, as the Irish-American community became both more integrated and confident, individuals eventually succeeded in gaining a reconsideration of the case, and in March 1984 Massachusetts Governor Michael Dukakis proclaimed the innocence of Daley and Halligan.

The Issue of Bias

The now-accepted version is that Daley and Halligan were totally innocent and were persecuted only because of their being Irish and Catholic. But has this been proven? There is no denying that Roman Catholics in general, and Irish immigrants in particular, had to endure great discrimination and injustices at the time of the trial. Most people would agree that the case against Daley and Halligan was weak, even unacceptable by today's standards. In those days, there were no tests for fingerprints, ballistics, "crime scene," or other investigations for evidence. But still unclear to some is whether Daley and Halligan were found guilty solely because of their ethnic and religious ties. In fact, they were the men seen traveling along that road, and the posse that set out after them had no notion that they were Irish Catholics. The only overt reference to their being Irish on the part of the prosecution was the Boston gundealer's allusion to the speech. Nothing else said by the prosecution or judges referred to their being Irish or Catholics.

The issue of their guilt by dint of being Irish, in fact, seems to have been raised—and exploited—entirely by the defense lawyer. Daley and Halligan may well have been innocent, but the claim that they were convicted solely because of their being Irish Catholics seems unproved—and probably forever unprovable.

—*John S. Bowman*

Suggestions for Further Reading

Camposeo, James M. "Anti-Catholic Prejudice in Early new England: The Daley-Halligan Murder Trial." *Historical Journal of Western Masachusetts*, 6 (Spring 1978).

Garvey, Richard C. "The Hanging of Daley and Halligan." In *The Northampton Book: Chapters from 300 Years in the Life of a New England Town*. Northampton, Mass.: Tercentary Committee, 1954.

Member of the Bar. *Report of the Trial of Dominic Daley and James Halligan for the Murder of Marcus Lyon Before the Supreme Judicial Court*. Northampton, Mass.: S. & E. Butler, 1806.

Sullivan, Robert. "The Murder Trial of Halligan and Daley—Northampton, Mass., 1806." *Massachusetts Law Quarterly*, 49 (September 1964): 211–24.

William S. Smith and Samuel G. Ogden Trials: 1806

Defendants: William S. Smith, Samuel G. Ogden **Crime Charged:** Violating the Neutrality Act of 1794 **Chief Defense Lawyers:** Thomas A. Emmet, Cadwallader D. Colden, Josiah Ogden Hoffman, Washington Morton, and Richard Harison (Note: the transcript of the trial, as reproduced by Thomas Lloyd who was the stenographer at the trial, states that the last attorney's surname was Harison, with one "R") **Chief Prosecutors:** Nathan Sanford, Pierpont Edwards **Judges:** William Paterson, Matthias B. Talmadge **Place:** New York, New York **Date of Trial:** July 14–26, 1806 **Verdict:** Not guilty

SIGNIFICANCE

The 1806 prosecution of William Smith and Samuel Ogden for their role in helping Francisco de Miranda fight Spanish rule in Latin America was a nearly forgotten trial that involved mercenaries, a potential war, allegations of government persecution, and a president's decision not to allow federal officials to testify in court.

Between 1783 and 1805, Francisco de Miranda traveled across Europe and the United States to win support for independence for his native Venezuela and the other Spanish colonies in the Western Hemisphere. During this time, he met virtually every major American leader. Most politely ignored Miranda, but many supported his cause; some because they wanted to help free the colonists from Spanish tyranny, others because of the profit they could gain from such an adventure.

Miranda Dines at the White House

In November 1805, Miranda arrived in New York City from England carrying a letter addressed to Rufus King. (King had been America's top diplomat in London from 1796 to 1803.) The correspondence, written by a member of Parliament, indicated that the British government was dropping its support for Miranda despite its war with Spain. King forwarded the letter to Secretary of State James Madison. After reviewing its contents, Madison and President

Thomas Jefferson decided to meet with Miranda to get a better understanding of Britain's new policy concerning Spain's colonies. (At this time, Spanish-American relations were poor. The United States had designs on Spain's possessions in Texas and Florida, and Madrid was angered when France sold Louisiana to the Americans. For a short time in late 1805, it appeared that a war might start.)

The president and Madison met Miranda over dinner. What was said is still a matter of debate. Madison claimed that Miranda discussed his plans for revolution in "very general terms" and said that it would help if the United States declared war on Spain, but was rebuffed when told that America intended to remain at peace with that country. In contrast, Miranda said that Madison hinted "whatever might be done should be discreetly done" and that "although the [American] Government would not sanction, it would wink" at a military expedition launched from the United States. Publicly, the president said nothing, but privately he denied sanctioning any action by Miranda.

Rebel Vessel Sails from New York

Whatever was said at that dinner, by the end of the month a prominent federal official in New York, Colonel William Stephens Smith, was using his influence to obtain men, money, and war material for Miranda. A Revolutionary War hero, former diplomat, and, since 1800, surveyor of customs for the Port of New York, Smith had known Miranda for over 20 years and had once toured with him across Europe. In addition, Smith had impeccable connections: his father-in-law was former President John Adams and his brother-in-law was U.S. Senator (and future president) John Quincy Adams.

On February 2, 1806, Miranda sailed from New York City for Venezuela on an American-owned vessel, the *Leander*, with 180 men (mostly Americans) and weapons. Among the adventurers was Colonel Smith's 19-year-old son, William Steuben Smith. However, the *Leander* was soon captured by the Spanish. Miranda escaped, but the young Smith and the others did not. (William Steuben Smith later eluded his captors and made his way home.)

After the *Leander's* seizure became public, Colonel Smith and the ship's owner, Samuel Ogden, were arrested for violating the Neutrality Act of 1794. That law made it illegal to "set on foot directly or indirectly within the United States any military expedition or enterprise to be carried on against the territory of a foreign . . . state with whom the United States is at peace."

On March 1, Judge Matthias Talmadge of the U.S. District Court in New York, questioned Smith and Ogden and they signed incriminating statements outlining their roles in the affair. (These statements were later introduced into evidence at Smith's and Ogden's trials.)

Smith and Ogden were formally indicted on April 7. If convicted, they each faced up to three years in prison. In the meantime, the president dismissed Smith from his post.

President's Role at Issue

While Smith and Ogden were awaiting trial, Jefferson's political adversaries did everything they could to exploit the situation. Opposition newspapers had a field day charging the government with persecuting Smith and Ogden while attempting to hide its own misdeeds. Petitions were even submitted to Congress on behalf of the defendants to seek whatever relief that body might give, but after a bitter debate, the requests were denied.

Smith and Ogden were tried separately. Smith's trial began on July 14, 1806. Since his arrest, Smith and his wife had lived in a small cottage within the prison in New York City. His defense team consisted of five eminent lawyers including the city's former prosecuting attorney, Cadwallader D. Colden, and the famous Irish patriot turned American lawyer, Thomas A. Emmet.

Presiding at Smith's trial were two judges. Besides Talmadge, who had taken Smith's and Ogden's depositions, the other jurist was William Paterson, an associate justice of the United States Supreme Court. (At this time, between court sessions, associate justices presided over major federal trials.) It is possible that Paterson may have felt some animosity towards Smith. Although the judge was, like Smith's father-in-law, a member of the Federalist Party and a political opponent of President Jefferson's, he was also a member of the Federalist faction that opposed President Adams' reelection in 1800. Also in 1800, Paterson was passed over by Adams for promotion when Chief Justice Oliver Ellsworth resigned.

Smith's defense was that he was acting under direct orders from Jefferson and Madison and that he was being made a scapegoat so the White House could appease the Spanish and pretend that it disapproved of Miranda's expedition. It was also argued that while the power to declare war rests with Congress, it is up to the president to decide if an actual state of war exists when Congress has not yet acted. (Thus, if Jefferson approved or ordered Smith's actions, then that would be strong evidence that the United States was, in fact, at war with Spain and the Neutrality Act did not apply.)

A major problem for the defense, however, was that most of the witnesses who could speak about the president's role were unavailable to testify. Madison, as well as three other members of Jefferson's cabinet and various State Department officials, were named as defense witnesses and subpoenaed to appear. They all, however, refused because the president deemed it more important that they remain in Washington to do their jobs. Specifically:

> . . . the president of the United States, taking into view the state of our public affairs, has specially signified to us that our official duties cannot, consistently therewith, be at this juncture dispensed with.

Instead, it was suggested that the testimony of Madison and the others be taken by interrogatories (written answers to questions submitted by the prosecution and defense) or by other means. This suggested alternative, however, was not acceptable to Smith's lawyers, who argued that their client had the right to compel these witnesses to testify at his trial. Therefore, the defense sought a continuance as well as a court order forcing Madison and the others to appear.

The prosecution countered that, even if Jefferson knew or ordered Smith to help Miranda, the president's actions did not justify Smith's violation of the law. Only the Congress can declare war and any argument to the contrary: . . . proceeds altogether upon the idea that the executive may dispense with the laws at pleasure; a supposition as false in theory as it would be dangerous and destructive to the constitution in practice.

Therefore, since whatever the president did was not a defense, then anything Madison or the others had to say on the matter was irrelevant to Smith's guilt or innocence.

After three days of argument, Judge Paterson ruled on July 17 that nothing Jefferson did could justify Smith's actions. "The president of the United States cannot . . . authorize [sic] a person to do what the law forbids." The court also held that, until Congress declared war, the United States and Spain were at peace. Therefore, any testimony regarding the president's participation in the *Leander* affair was immaterial in determining Smith's guilt and both the motion for a continuance and the motion to compel the presence of Madison and the others were denied. (Severely ill, Paterson took no further part in either Smith's or Ogden's trial after this ruling. He died seven weeks later.)

During the next five days, several prosecution witnesses testified, but the government had difficulty proving that Smith was fully apprised of Miranda's plans. In contrast, most of the defense witnesses who were at the trial were there only to speak about Jefferson's role in the affair. Therefore, few were permitted to testify because, according to Judge Paterson, what they had to say was irrelevant. Still, although no evidence was allowed about Jefferson's role, Smith's lawyers were allowed to concentrate on that very issue during their concluding remarks to the jury. As one of his attorneys said:

> No gentlemen, he [i.e., Smith] has not wilfully [sic] and knowingly infracted the statute—his mind has perpetrated no crime, for he acted under the conviction, that his proceedings were legally sanctioned by the chief magistrate of the union . . . Did the president of the United States and the secretary of state approve of and countenance this expedition? The man who can doubt it, after hearing this trial, must be obstinate indeed in prejudice.

Plotters Acquitted

The defense lawyers were also permitted in their closing statements to discuss whether Smith was being made a fall guy by the government and whether the United States and Spain were actually at peace or war. The prosecution countered that the jury should not lightly disregard the court's rulings that peace existed between the two countries and that the government's role in the *Leander* affair was irrelevant to Smith's guilt or innocence. But it was to no avail; after considering their decision for two hours, the jury returned with a verdict of "not guilty."

Almost immediately, on July 25, Ogden's trial began. The entire proceeding was a virtual repeat of the Smith trial; same judge, same lawyers, same witnesses, and the same issues—only the jury was different. The trial lasted a mere two days and Ogden, too, was acquitted of the charge facing him.

After the trials were over, Jefferson indicated that he was not dissatisfied with the juries' decisions. "I had no wish to see Smith imprisoned. He has been a man of integrity and honor, led astray by distress." Still, the president fired the U.S. marshal in New York City because he believed the marshal, who was also a friend of Smith's, had packed the jury panel with so many die-hard Federalists that an impartial jury could not be chosen at the trial.

Although Smith was acquitted, his career was now in shambles and he quietly retired to his farm in upstate New York. However, Smith briefly returned to public life in 1812 when he was elected to Congress.

—Mark Thorburn

Suggestions for Further Reading

Lloyd, Thomas. *The Trials of William S. Smith and Samuel G. Ogden for Misdemeanours, Had in the Circuit Court of the United States for the New York District, in July 1806.* New York: I. Riley and Company, 1974.

Nagel, Paul C. *Descent from Glory: Four Generations of the John Adams Family.* New York: Oxford University Press, 1983.

Raymond, Marcius D. "Colonel William Stephens Smith." *New York Genealogical and Historical Record* 25, 4 (1894): 153–61.

Roof, Katharine Metcalf. *Colonel William Smith and Lady: The Romance of Washington's Aide and Young Abigail Adams.* Boston: Houghton Mifflin, 1929.

Withey, Lynne. *Dearest Friend: A Life of Abigail Adams.* New York: The Free Press, 1981.

George Sweeney Trial: 1806

Defendant: George Wythe Sweeney **Crime Charged:** Murder
Chief Defense Lawyers: Edmund Randolph and William Wirt
Chief Prosecutor: Philip Norborne Nicholas **Judges:** Joseph Prentes and John Tyler, Sr. **Place:** Richmond, Virginia **Dates of Trial:** September 2–8, 1806 **Verdict:** Not guilty

SIGNIFICANCE

Because the law forbade blacks from testifying in the criminal trial of a white man, George Wythe Sweeney was acquitted of the murder of his distinguished granduncle, George Wythe.

George Wythe was born in 1726 in Elizabeth City County, Virginia. He had a long and distinguished career as one of America's founding fathers. Wythe was admitted to practice law before the bar of Virginia's General Court at the early age of 20. In addition to becoming one of Virginia's preeminent lawyers, Wythe was a successful politician. He was elected to Virginia's House of Burgesses several times before the American Revolution and was a member of the 1775 Continental Congress. In 1776, he signed the Declaration of Independence on behalf of the Commonwealth of Virginia.

After the Revolution, Wythe served as a judge on Virginia's High Court of Chancery and as the first professor of law at the College of William and Mary. In 1789 he moved to Richmond to live out his final years. Wythe continued to serve on the High Court of Chancery after the turn of the 19th century and was strong and healthy until the age of 80, well past the average life expectancy of the times.

Unfortunately for Wythe, his young grandnephew, George Wythe Sweeney, came to live with him in Richmond. Sweeney had inherited none of Wythe's character. Sweeney lived off Wythe's fortune, and he lost considerable sums of money drinking and gambling. In 1805, Sweeney stole some books from Wythe's personal library and tried to sell them at a public auction. In April 1806, Sweeney forged Wythe's name on six bank checks. The next month, Sweeney became afraid that the forgeries would be discovered. Further, Sweeney knew that he was a beneficiary in Wythe's will, and he was too greedy for his inheritance to let Wythe die naturally. Therefore, Sweeney decided to murder Wythe.

Sweeney Poisons Wythe and is Tried for Murder

In late May 1806, Sweeney bought a large quantity of yellow arsenic. Early in the morning of Sunday, May 25, Sweeney laced the household's kitchen coffee pot with some of the poison. Wythe and a servant, a free black servant boy named Michael Brown, drank some of the coffee. After days of slow, agonizing illness, Brown died on June 1 and Wythe on June 8. Wythe's last words were typical of the way he had lived his life: "Let me die righteous."

Suspicion immediately fell on Sweeney, and on June 18 he was arrested. Prosecutor Philip Norborne Nicholas charged Sweeney with murdering Wythe and Brown. The judges were Joseph Prentes and John Tyler, Sr. Sweeney was represented by Edmund Randolph and William Wirt. The trial began September 2, 1806 in the District Court of Richmond.

Lydia Broadnax, a free black woman who had been Wythe's cook for several decades, testified that suspicious circumstances indicated Sweeney put something into the coffee on the morning of May 25. Broadnax had drunk some of the coffee, but not enough to die:

> He went to the fire, and took the coffee-pot to the table, while I was toasting the bread. He poured out a cupful for himself and then set the pot down. I saw him throw a little white paper in the fire. . . . I didn't think there was anything wrong then.

Broadnax's suspicions became aroused, however, when she, Wythe, and Michael Brown fell ill after drinking the coffee:

> I gave Michael as much coffee as he wanted, and then I drank a cup myself. After that, with the hot water in the kettle I washed the plates, emptied the coffee-grounds out and scrubbed the coffee-pot bright, and by that time I became so sick I could hardly see, and had a violent cramp. Michael was sick, too; and old master [Wythe] was as sick as he could be. He told me to send for the doctor. All these things makes [*sic*] me think Mass [*sic*] George must have put something in the coffee-pot.

Judges Prentes and Tyler, however, refused to allow Broadnax's testimony, and that of other black servants who had seen suspicious behavior by Sweeney, into evidence. The judges were bound by a principle of law that prevented blacks from testifying against whites in criminal trials: "It was gleaned from negroes, which is not permitted by our laws to go against a white man."

Therefore, prosecutor Nicholas was forced to rely on such white witnesses as he could produce. Nicholas did his best under the circumstances and was able to come up with some evidence. William Rose, the Richmond city jail warden, testified that Sweeney was not searched after he was arrested and soon thereafter a packet of arsenic was found in the prison yard, as if thrown from Sweeney's cell window. Samuel McCraw, a friend of Wythe's, testified that when he visited Wythe on his deathbed, Wythe asked McCraw to search Sweeney's room. McCraw stated that he found arsenic in a glass container in Sweeney's room.

In addition to these witnesses, there was the fact that Wythe amended his will before he died to exclude Sweeney from any inheritance. On June 1, 1806 Wythe executed a codicil to his will which revoked:

> The said will and codicils in all the devises and legacies in them or either of them, contained, relating to, or in any manner concerning George Wythe Sweeney, the grandson of my sister: but I confirm the said will and codicils in all other parts except as to the devise and bequest to Michael Brown, . . . who, I am told, died this morning.

Nicholas' witnesses, however, could give only hearsay testimony. Under the law, this wasn't enough to convict Sweeney. On September 8, 1806, the jury returned a verdict of not guilty after deliberating for only a few minutes.

Sweeney was acquitted because traditional legal principles prevented blacks from testifying against whites in criminal trials. This rule of law was not changed in Virginia until 1867. As for Sweeney, there are only rumors about what happened to him after his acquittal. According to the most reliable accounts, however, he went to Tennessee, where he was eventually arrested and convicted for stealing horses.

—*Stephen G. Christianson*

Suggestions for Further Reading

Blackburn, Joyce. *George Wythe of Williamsburg.* New York: Harper & Row, 1975.

Boyd, Julian P. *The Murder of George Wythe.* Philadelphia: Philobiblon Club, 1949.

Brown, Imogene E. *American Aristides: a Biography of George Wythe.* Rutherford, N.J.: Fairleigh Dickinson University Press, 1981.

Clarkin, William. *Serene Patriot: a Life of George Wythe.* Albany N.Y.: Alan Publications, 1970.

Kirtland, Robert B. *George Wythe: Lawyer, Revolutionary, Judge.* New York: Garland, 1986.

Aaron Burr Trial: 1807

Defendant: Former Vice President Aaron Burr **Crime Charged:** "Treason" within the meaning of Article III, Section 3 of the U.S. Constitution **Chief Defense Lawyers:** Benjamin Botts, Luther Martin, Edmund Randolph, and John Wickham. **Chief Prosecutors:** George Hay, Gordon MacRae, and William Wirt **Judges:** Cyrus Griffin and John Marshall **Place:** Richmond, Virginia **Dates of Trial:** August 3–September 1, 1807 **Verdict:** Not guilty

SIGNIFICANCE

The Aaron Burr treason trial was the only time in American history that a court tried such a high-level official of the United States for treason. Although Burr was acquitted, his political career was destroyed.

With the exception of scholars of American history, most people are oblivious to how unstable the political situation in the United States was in the early decades of the 1800s. In the years immediately following the Revolutionary War, the country suffered under the disastrous Articles of Confederation of 1781 until the states adopted the Constitution in 1789. However, even after the Constitutional Convention, there were serious differences among the political elite. The two main political camps were the Federalists and the Democratic-Republicans, and they had fundamentally different notions over what direction the new United States should take in its foreign policy.

The Federalists believed that, since the United States had been shaped by the cultural and economic influence of Great Britain, the Revolutionary War should not prevent the reestablishment of ties with the "Mother Country." The Democratic-Republicans believed that the United States should ally itself with France instead. Not only had France provided critical assistance to the colonies during the Revolutionary War, but the French Revolution had installed a government in France that professed belief in democratic ideals. Further, an alliance with France, a European great power, represented the only viable opportunity for the fledgling United States to oppose the might of the British Empire. Aaron Burr's political career put him squarely in the center of this schism.

Aaron Burr's Roller-Coaster Career

Burr's impeccable credentials as an American patriot made him an unlikely candidate to be charged with treason. Born in Newark, New Jersey, and educated at what became Princeton University, he was commissioned as an officer in the American army during the Revolutionary War. Burr distinguished himself in combat, and by the end of the war had risen to the rank of lieutenant colonel. After the war, Burr turned his energies to the legal profession. He did not graduate from a law school but instead studied law under an attorney's supervision, a practice which today is permitted by only one state (Virginia) but was then common. Burr was successful in his studies, and in 1782 was admitted to the New York state bar.

Burr capitalized on his successful career and entered into politics. He joined the pro-French Democratic-Republicans and became their candidate for vice president in the elections of 1800. At the time, members of the electoral college cast two votes each: one for the presidential candidate and one for the vice presidential candidate. Each Democratic-Republican elector had cast a vote for Burr and a vote for the party's presidential candidate, Thomas Jefferson. The result was a tie, and it fell to the House of Representatives to decide the outcome of the election. After a bitter battle and 36 ballots, the House voted for Jefferson, and Burr became vice president. Understandably, Jefferson suspected Burr of disloyalty and in 1804 managed to arrange his rejection by the Democratic-Republicans for a second vice presidential nomination.

Aaron Burr's political career was destroyed by his "imperial ambitions." (Courtesy, Library of Congress)

Burr and Alexander Hamilton, one of the principal Federalists, became intense adversaries and quarreled at every opportunity. In 1804, with Burr seeking the governorship of New York, Hamilton publicly denounced him and expressed his opinion that Burr was unfit for public office. Furious, Burr challenged Hamilton to a duel. Hamilton accepted. On July 11, 1804, at Weehawken, New Jersey, Burr shot Hamilton in the chest. Hamilton died soon thereafter.

Although he won the duel, Burr lost in the ensuing political uproar. State authorities in both New York and New Jersey sought to prosecute Burr for Hamilton's death, and Hamilton's supporters made Burr a political outcast in Washington.

In March 1805, Burr left the increasingly hostile capital for the frontier lands of the recently acquired Louisiana Purchase. Burr abandoned his allegiance to the Democratic-Republicans, and concocted a grandiose plan to lead a revolt with British assistance in these western lands. Burr hoped to establish a "Western Empire" with himself as ruler.

Burr's imperial ambitions were supported by Anthony Merry, the British envoy to the United States. Burr had other powerful allies for his scheme. Senator Jonathan Dayton of New Jersey and a wealthy Ohioan named Harman Blennerhassett joined Burr and extended financial support for the planned revolt. Finally, Burr had the support of General-in-Chief of the Army James Wilkinson, who was also one of the joint commissioners for the Territory of Louisiana.

The conspirators' procrastination, however, proved to be their undoing. By the fall of 1806, still they had not moved. Great Britain's new foreign minister, Charles James Fox, recalled Anthony Merry and terminated British support for Burr's plan. Wilkinson grew nervous, and went to President Jefferson with the details of Burr's conspiracy. When Burr finally decided to act in November 1806, he used Blennerhassett's Ohio estates and private island as the base of operations for the revolt. Jefferson arranged for Ohio Governor Edward Tiffin to send in the local militia and the conspiracy was crushed. Burr went into hiding but was arrested within a few months.

Burr Tried Before Chief Justice Marshall

On March 26, 1807, Burr was taken by his captors to Richmond, Virginia, for trial before the federal court. Normally, Judge Cyrus Griffin of the District of Virginia would have presided over the trial. At the time, however, Supreme Court Chief Justice John Marshall was present in Richmond to hear appeals from the circuit that encompassed Virginia. Griffin soon found himself playing second fiddle to the eminent Marshall, who took control over the widely publicized trial.

The principal charge against Burr was treason against the United States. The prosecutors also made a related charge of "high misdemeanors" against Burr. George Hay, William Wirt, and Gordon MacRae formed the team of prosecutors for the government. Hay was a prominent attorney, thanks largely to his political connections as James Monroe's son-in-law. Wirt, a tall blond man, had a reputation for having an excellent courtroom presence. MacRae was primarily a politician and, in addition to being a prosecutor, was also Virginia's lieutenant governor.

Burr's defense attorneys were Edmund Randolph, John Wickham, Luther Martin, and Benjamin Botts. The distinguished Randolph was not only a former attorney general, but had served as George Washington's Secretary of State and as Governor of Virginia as well. Wickham, Martin and Botts were also widely respected and prominent attorneys.

Their task was also much easier than that of the prosecution, due to the particular requirements of Article III, Section 3 of the Constitution.

Article III, Section 3 states:

> Treason against the United States, shall consist only in levying War against them, or in adhering to their Enemies, giving them Aid and Comfort. No Person shall be convicted of Treason unless on the Testimony of two Witnesses to the same overt Act, or on Confession in open Court.

Thus, the prosecution not only had to produce two witnesses, but those witnesses had to have seen some overt act by Burr in "levying war" or leading the planned revolt against the United States. Luckily for Burr, he had not been present in Ohio when Governor Tiffin's militia stormed Blennerhassett's island compound. As Burr himself stated, Jefferson's prompt action based on General Wilkinson's confession led to the destruction of the plot before the procrastinating Burr had taken much action: "Mr. Wilkinson alarmed the President and the President alarmed the people of Ohio."

Marshall's concern over whether the prosecution could bear the heavy burden of proof demanded by the Constitution caused the trial to be delayed until August 3, 1807. In the interim, the prosecution presented a series of witnesses, including General Wilkinson. These witnesses testified as to treasonous statements made by Burr and on the military preparations made on Blennerhassett's island. The evidence presented convinced a grand jury that Burr should be tried on the charges filed against him, and Marshall finally opened the trial.

The prosecution, led by Wirt, argued that Burr's involvement in the conspiracy made him "constructively present" on the island and thus involved in an overt act. Referring to the mercenaries arrested during the Blennerhassett raid, Wirt said:

> What must be the guilt of [Burr], to that of the poor ignorant man who was enlisted into his services with some prospect of benefitting himself and family?

Definition of an Overt Act Debated

Burr's defense counsel countered Wirt's impressive oratory by keeping the focus of attention on the prosecution's strained interpretation on what constituted an "overt act." After all, the only act of the revolt remotely "overt" had been the preparations at Blennerhassett's island during which Burr had not been present. Therefore, Botts retorted:

> Acts on the island were not acts of war; no war could be found in Mississippi or Kentucky. There was no bloody battle. There was no bloody war. The energy of . . . [the] government prevented that tragical consequence.

On August 31, Marshall made a lengthy ruling on the arguments presented by both sides, later turning the tide in favor of Burr. Marshall held that if the prosecution had proven with two witnesses that Burr had "procured" or caused the men and material to assemble on the island to launch a revolt, then the necessary overt act could be established. The prosecution had not done this, however. All they had presented at trial was testimony that would "confirm" or "corroborate" such eyewitnesses, but not any eyewitnesses themselves. Therefore, the prosecution's evidence was inadmissible and the jury had to ignore it.

Faced with Marshall's ruling, the jury had no choice. On September 1, the jury acquitted Burr when it gave its somewhat left-handed verdict: "We of the jury say that Aaron Burr is not proved to be guilty under this indictment by any evidence submitted to us."

Although he was acquitted, the press and public still considered Burr a traitor, and his political career was ruined. Burr went to Europe for several years, staying one step ahead of money lenders who financed his lifestyle, and finally returned to the United States in 1812. He lived out the rest of his life in obscurity, dying a broken man in 1836.

—Stephen G. Christianson

Suggestions for Further Reading

Burr, Aaron. *Reports of the Trials of Colonel Aaron Burr*. New York: Da Capo Press., 1969 (repr. of 1808 ed.).

Lomask, Milton. *Aaron Burr*, Vols. 1 and 2. New York: Farrar, Straus & Giroux, 1979 and 1982.

Nolan, Charles J., Jr. *Aaron Burr and the American Literary Imagination*. Westport, Conn.: Greenwood Press, 1980.

Parmet, Herbert S. and Marie B. Hecht. *Aaron Burr: Portrait of an Ambitious Man*. New York: Macmillan Co., 1967.

Wilson, R.J. "The Founding Father." *New Republic* (June 1983): 25–31.

James Barron Court-Martial: 1808

Defendant: Commodore James Barron **Crimes Charged:** "Negligently performing the duty assigned him; neglecting, on the probability of an engagement, to clear ship for action; failing to encourage in his own person his inferior officers and men to fight courageously; not doing his utmost to take or destroy the *Leopard,* which vessel it was his duty to encounter."
Defense Lawyer: Robert B. Taylor **Prosecutor:** Lyttleton W. Tazewell, Judge Advocate **Senior Presiding Officer:** John Rodgers **Court:** William Bainbridge, Hugh G. Campbell, Stephen Decatur, Jr., John Shaw, John Smith, David Porter, Jacob Jones, James Lawrence, Charles Ludlow, Joseph Tarbell
Place: On board the USS *Chesapeake,* Norfolk, Virginia
Date of Trial: January 9–February 8, 1808 **Verdict:** Guilty on second charge **Sentence:** Suspension from command for five years with loss of pay

SIGNIFICANCE

This was one of the most extraordinary court-martials in American history, occasioned as it was primarily by a clear need to find a scapegoat for a humiliating incident. It also exemplifies the incredible infighting that then afflicted the American navy. The punishment meted out was relatively mild, but it led to the most tragic of encounters, James Barron's duel with a major American hero, Stephen Decatur.

James Barron belonged to a Virginia family with a seafaring tradition. Enlisting in the navy as a youth, by 1799 he was serving as captain of the *USS United States* (which included in the crew a young midshipman, Stephen Decatur, Jr.). In 1806, Barron was promoted to commodore and in 1807 was assigned to command the *USS Chesapeake.* Although it had an inexperienced crew and poorly prepared equipment, it was hastily ordered by the navy to head for the Mediterranean on June 22, 1807.

The *Chesapeake-Leopard* Incident

At this time Britain was at war with France and it was engaging in the practice known as "impressment"—stopping American ships at sea to search for men it regarded as deserters from its own navy. The *Chesapeake* was barely 10 miles offshore that day when a British warship, the *HMS Leopard*, sailed up to her and demanded the right to look for British citizens. Barron refused and suddenly the *Leopard* fired three broadsides into the Chesapeake, killing three crewmen and wounding 18 (including Barron). Barron had one shot fired but, recognizing that further resistance was futile—for one thing, the *Leopard* had 50 guns to his own 36—had his flag lowered in surrender. The British then boarded and took away four men. (One was hanged, another died in captivity, and the other two were eventually returned to U.S. Navy service.) The *Chesapeake* limped back to Norfolk, Virginia.

As word quickly spread from Virginia throughout the American states, there was a tremendous outcry and even a call for war. President Thomas Jefferson himself stated, "Never since the battle of Lexington, have I seen this country in such a state of exasperation." But above all, there was a call for some assignment of responsibility, and inevitably the finger pointed at Commodore James Barron. The indignation was fanned by six of the junior officers, who wishing to free themselves from blame, quickly submitted a letter casting all responsibility on Barron.

In October, the secretary of the navy convened a court of inquiry composed of three naval officers to look into the incident and Barron's role. In November, the panel reported that Barron should be held responsible and called for a general court martial.

The Court-Martial

The court that met in January 1808 in Barron's own quarters on the *Chesapeake* was composed of some of the most distinguished officers in the U.S. Navy at that time. Barron's relations with several of them were at best ambiguous, most especially with Captain John Rodgers, the presiding officer. Not much more than a year before, Rodgers had challenged Barron to a duel over allegedly "slanderous rumors," and only the intervention of other officers had led them to a formal if cool reconciliation. Meanwhile, Stephen Decatur, who was befriended by Barron at the outset of his naval service, had for some reason taken the lead in criticizing him for what happened with the *Leopard.*

In addition to Barron, two officers and one chief gunner were also standing trial, but it was quite clear that Barron was the major target. In fact, Master Commandant Charles Gordon, one of those charged with negligence, was also the chief witness for the prosecution against Barron. Gordon's role was important, because it was he who had actually been responsible for assembling the crew and supplies and readying the ship before Barron took command only two days before sailing. To the extent that the crew was not properly prepared, the decks were obstructed with supplies, and the ship's guns were not battle ready, Gordon was as responsible as Barron.

Yet, the prosecution allowed Gordon to evade answering crucial questions. For instance, a letter was produced in which Gordon on June 19 assured Barron: "We are . . . ready for weighing the first fair wind. . . . The guns are all charged and if possible we have an exercise this evening." Yet the examination of the witness went thus:

Judge Advocate: Were your guns exercised on the evening of [June 19]?

Gordon: I decline answering that question.

Judge Advocate: Had they been exercised before?

Gordon: I decline answering that question.

For his defense, Barron did not take the stand but submitted a long letter responding to all the charges. In general, he argued that it was the navy's practice to hold a man in Gordon's position responsible for assuring that a ship was seaworthy; that the Navy Department knew that the four disputed men were aboard and that the British had their ships offshore; that he was under clear orders to avoid "whatever may have a tendency to bring us into collision with any other power"; that had he done anything to initiate hostilities against the *Leopard*, "to what censure would I not have exposed myself?"; and finally, that the decision to surrender was based on his seasoned judgment that resistance was futile.

After four days of deliberation, the court appeared with its verdict. It started with exonerating Barron of the third and fourth charges that impugned his courage and his judgment in the face of the *Leopard's* overwhelming advantages. They also found him not guilty of the first charge, general negligence. But they did find him guilty of the second charge, "neglecting, on the probability of an engagement, to clear his ship for action." The sentence: to be suspended from all command and pay for five years. Gordon and the other officer were both found guilty of negligence but were let off with a reprimand; the gunner was also found guilty of failing to perform his duties and was dismissed from the navy.

A Fatal Backfire

Few verdicts would have such profound repercussions. Although his family and close friends stood by Barron, in general, his fellow naval officers shunned him. In 1812 he was hired to command a merchant vessel to transport materials to Portugal; from there he sailed to Sweden and then in July to Copenhagen. Before he could set sail for home, the United States had declared war on Britain. Although he made several attempts to return home, Barron had to be especially careful as he was technically still an officer of the U.S. Navy, and so he was stranded in Copenhagen throughout the war. After the war, Barron stayed on in an effort to promote some of his inventions such as machinery to improve a ship's windlass, windmills, rope-making, and cork-cutting, finally returning home in 1818.

He found no support in Washington in his efforts to regain active duty assignment. Instead, he began to hear that Stephen Decatur, his former protege and a leader in the move to court-martial him, was making what he considered libelous and derogatory remarks. In 1820, Barron challenged him to a duel, and although both wounded each other, Barron survived and Decatur died. Barron did in fact regain an active duty assignment with the navy in 1824, but it was his fate to go down in American history as "the man who killed Decatur."

—John S. Bowman

Suggestions for Further Reading

Proceedings of the General Court Martial Convened for the Trial of Commodore James Barron . . . January 1808. Washington, D.C.: James Gideon, Jr., 1808.

Stevens, William Oliver. *An Affair of Honor: The Biography of Commodore James Barron, U.S.N.* Chesapeake, Va.: Norfolk Historical Society, 1969.

Watson, Paul Barron. *The Tragic Career of Commodore James Barron, U.S. Navy.* New York: Coward-McCann, 1942.

General William Hull Court-Martial: 1814

Defendant: William Hull **Crimes Charged:** Treason, cowardice, neglect of duty, unofficer-like conduct **Chief Defense Lawyers:** William Hull (representing himself) assisted by Robert Tillotson, Cadwallader D. Colden **Chief Prosecutors:** Martin Van Buren, Philip S. Parker **Judges:** Henry Dearborn, Joseph Bloomfield, Peter Little, William N. Irvine, James House, William Scott, William Stewart, J. R. Fenwick, Robert Bogardus, Richard Dennis, Samuel S. Conner, S. B. Davis, John W. Livingston, James G. Forbes (Forbes was a Supernumerary Member of the Court and, as such, did not participate in the court's reaching its verdict) **Place:** Albany, New York **Date of Trial:** January 3–March 28, 1814 **Verdict:** Court had no jurisdiction to hear the treason charge; guilty of all other charges **Sentence:** Death (President James Madison later remitted the sentence); also, Hull was dishonorably discharged and his name was stricken from the rolls of the army

SIGNIFICANCE

Although his sentence was later remitted, General William Hull is the only U.S. general to be sentenced to death by an American court-martial.

When the United States declared war on Great Britain on June 19, 1812, largely arrogant and politically ambitious men who had little or no military experience commanded its small and unequipped army. In addition, there was no carefully prepared strategy or plan for prosecuting the war. Disaster was waiting to strike and it did on August 16, 1812, when General William Hull surrendered Detroit to the British without a fight. When news of the capitulation reached the rest of the country, Hull's superiors, as well as the public, did not take time to consider the many factors that were beyond the general's control. Instead, he was immediately branded as a coward and a traitor. A year and a half later, Hull became the only American general in history to be sentenced to death by a court-martial of the U.S. Army.

An Army of State Militiamen and Inexperienced Officers

When the War of 1812 began, the army consisted of only 6,750 officers and men. There were between 500,000 and 700,000 state militiamen who could be called into federal service, but most of them were untrained, unorganized, and unarmed and many refused to fight beyond their own state's borders. Furthermore, most officers in both the regular army and the militias had little training or experience and owed their jobs to political influence rather than to any skill or merit.

One of the army's politician-officers was William Hull. Revolutionary War hero, lawyer, Massachusetts legislator, state judge, and a major general in the Bay State's militia, he was appointed governor of the Michigan Territory in 1805. (In 1810, Michigan had a population, not counting the Indians, of only 4,762, about 800 of whom resided in the village near Fort Detroit. The military garrison at the fort, the largest in the territory, had 94 men.) As war clouds loomed, Hull sought a military command even though he was 58 years old and had not seen combat in more than 25 years. Still, he had more experience than most of the men who would be his superior officers. In April 1812, he was commissioned a brigadier general and was placed in command of what was called the North Western Army.

General William Hull, engraving by David Hull after a painting by Gilbert Stuart. (Bettmann/Corbis)

In anticipation of hostilities, Hull's orders were to muster his army at Urbana, Ohio, move north to Detroit, and then await further instructions. His force consisted of 1,200 Ohio militiamen and 800 regular soldiers from the Fourth U.S. Infantry. Immediately, there was bickering between the regular soldiers and the militiamen, a mutiny by some Ohioans who refused to leave Urbana until they got paid, and a lack of cooperation (if not downright insubordination) from the three Ohio militia colonels.

Hull Ordered to Invade Canada

To expedite the trip to Detroit, Hull chartered a schooner, the *Cayauga,* and sent it ahead loaded with his instructions from the War Department and other military papers as well as his army's muster rolls, medical supplies, tools, and uniforms. He reached Detroit on July 5. In the meantime, war was declared, but because no one in Washington, D.C., was in any hurry to tell him, Hull did not hear the news until July 2. In contrast, the British at Fort Malden (a few miles from Detroit) received word days earlier and had captured Hull's schooner with its valuable cargo.

On July 9, Hull received orders to invade Canada if he believed his army "equal to the enterprise." Three days later, he led his men across the Detroit River and occupied the town of Sandwich. Despite this initial success, Hull did not attempt to seize either Fort Malden or the British naval base at nearby Amherstburg because he was convinced that he did not have the strength to capture those installations.

While in Canada, Hull's communication lines were cut by Britain's Indian allies, thereby severing his supply and intelligence links with the United States, and the two detachments he sent to reopen them were thrown back. There were also reports of approaching British reinforcements. Then, on August 3, Hull learned about the surrender of the American fort on Mackinac Island (located in the strait between Lake Huron and Lake Michigan). Fearing that the latest news meant that an onslaught of hostile Indians from Michigan's interior would soon be upon him, he retreated back to Detroit on August 8.

To make matters worse, on August 9, contrary to repeated orders to attack the British forces along the Niagara River (near Buffalo, New York) and in Kingston (across the St. Lawrence River from upstate New York where the river meets Lake Ontario), the American commander for those areas, Major General Henry Dearborn, entered into a truce with his British counterparts. The truce was to extend to Hull's theater of operations if Hull concurred, but Dearborn sent word to Hull only by regular mail. The cessation of hostilities in the east allowed the British to send to Fort Malden the troops that would have otherwise fought Dearborn. Those troops arrived at Fort Malden on August 13.

On August 15, the British crossed the border three miles south of Detroit and demanded Hull's surrender. Even though Hull's fort could have repulsed an initial assault, his garrison would not have survived a long siege. In addition, the British commander stated that once an attack began, the conduct of his Indian allies would be beyond his control. Hull had a number of noncombatants inside his fort, including women and children. He also knew firsthand the savagery of Indian warfare and the disregard the Natives had for the lives of civilians and prisoners of war. Believing his cause to be hopeless and not wanting to needlessly shed blood, Hull surrendered Detroit on August 16 without firing a shot. Ironically, his nephew, Captain Isaac Hull of the U.S. Navy, defeated the *H.M.S. Guerrieré* three days later—the first American naval victory of the war—while in command of the *U.S.S. Constitution.*

Hull Viewed as a Coward

News of Hull's surrender hit the United States like a shock wave. Everyone wanted his head and even former president Thomas Jefferson demanded that Hull be hanged or shot. Almost immediately, there were hints that the government would make Hull the scapegoat for the fall of Detroit.

Hull and almost 600 of his men were taken to Canada as prisoners while the rest of his command were left to find their way back to Ohio. A few months later, Hull was paroled (a common practice of the time whereby a prisoner of war is released upon his promise not to fight again). Returning to the United States, the disgraced general requested an investigation into his conduct and a court-martial was scheduled for early 1813, but President James Madison cancelled it. A second court-martial was convened on January 3, 1814.

Hull faced three charges of treason, four counts of cowardice, and seven counts of neglect of duty and unofficer-like conduct. The entire proceeding was stacked against him. The presiding officer on the 13-member court was General Dearborn, the very person whose truce with the British allowed the enemy to send reinforcements to Fort Malden. The prosecution included the young New York state senator (and future U.S. President) Martin Van Buren. While Hull was allowed to consult with lawyers (including Colonel Cadwallader Colden, the former district attorney of New York City), he had to conduct his own defense because his lawyers were not allowed to examine or cross-examine any witnesses or to address the court.

Documents that Hull needed to defend himself were denied to him. His own copies of his orders, military correspondence, and other records had either been captured with the *Cayauga* or were taken by the British when they seized Fort Detroit. Permission for Hull to examine the files of the War Department to locate and copy what he needed was refused. While the government would allow its clerks to make copies of whatever Hull wished, many of the documents the general requested were nowhere to be found. (Years later, Hull was permitted to examine the government's files, and he found what had earlier been "missing.")

In addition, possibly as a reward for the statements they were to give in court, all of the officers who served under Hull and who were now going to testify against him had been promoted. For example, Lewis Cass and Duncan McArthur, two of the Ohio militia colonels who gave Hull so much trouble, were now brigadier generals. Hull said: "My expedition was more prolific of promotion than any other unsuccessful military enterprise I ever heard of."

Despite Hull's objections, witnesses were permitted to give their statements in court in each other's presence. (To insure that they do not change their stories to match what others might say, witnesses are usually not allowed to hear one another's testimony.) Statements about charges not covered in the allegations were allowed into evidence without any warning to Hull that the testimony was going to be offered. Finally, opinions, as opposed to statements of fact about what had occurred at Detroit, were permitted to be heard.

The court met 38 times over the span of nearly three months. Sometimes, adjournments of up to two weeks would occur. Then, on March 25, 1814, the judges announced their verdict. As to the charge of treason, the court ruled that it did not have any jurisdiction to try Hull for that crime, but from the evidence submitted the judges did not believe that he was guilty. However, the general was found guilty of all the other charges. The following day, with two-thirds of the court concurring, Hull was sentenced to be shot. In recognition of his

Revolutionary War service and his age, the judges recommended to the president that Hull be shown mercy. The decision of the court was finalized on March 28. One month later, on April 25, President Madison signed a one-line document which stated that "the sentence of the court is approved and the execution of it remitted." That same day, Hull was dishonorably discharged from the army.

Hull's life was spared, but he lived the rest of his life in disgrace. Continually trying to clear his name, Hull succeeded in part with the publication of his memoirs in 1824. He died the following year.

—*Mark Thorburn*

Suggestions for Further Reading

Elting, John R. *Amateurs, to Arms!: A Military History of the War of 1812.* Chapel Hill, N.C.: Algonquin Books of Chapel Hill, 1991.

Forbes, James G. *Report of the Trial of Brig. General William Hull; Commanding the North Western Army of the United States by a Court Martial . . .* New York: Eastburn, Kirk, and Company, 1814.

Hull, William. *Memoirs of the Campaign of the North Western Army of the United States in the Year 1812: Addressed to the People of the United States.* Boston: True and Greene, 1824.

Quaife, M. M. "General William Hull and His Critics." *Ohio State Archaeological and Historical Quarterly,* 47 (April 1948): 168–82.

Scott, Leonard H. "The Surrender of Detroit." *American History Illustrated* (June 1977): 28–36.

Van Deusen, John G. "Court Martial of General William Hull." *Michigan History Magazine* (Autumn 1928): 668–94.

Denmark Vesey Trial: 1822

Defendant: Denmark Vesey et al. **Crime Charged:** Conspiracy to commit insurrection and murder **Chief Defense Lawyers:** Vesey defended himself with assistance from George Warren Cross
Chief Prosecutors and Judges: Lionel Kennedy, Thomas Parker, William Drayton, Nathan Heyward, James Legare, James R. Pringle, Robert J. Turnbull **Place:** Charleston, South Carolina **Date of Trial:** June 23–28, 1822 **Verdict:** Guilty **Sentence:** Death

SIGNIFICANCE

Along with the later Nat Turner uprising, the Vesey conspiracy prompted new legislation that made it more difficult to free slaves and placed more severe restrictions on free blacks.

In 1822, Denmark Vesey, a 60-year-old former slave who had bought his freedom with the winnings from a lottery ticket, planned what would have been the most extensive slave rebellion in American history. He plotted to seize Charleston, South Carolina, recruiting thousands of slaves to help him and writing to the president of the black Haitian Republic, asking for Haitian military assistance. On the night of the uprising, his coconspirators, the house servants of prominent Charlestonians, were to assassinate the governor and other officials while they slept. Afterwards, six infantry and cavalry companies of armed slaves would move through Charleston and murder the entire white population. The only whites to be left alive were ships' captains, who would carry Vesey and his revolutionaries to Haiti. Before leaving South Carolina, he planned to burn Charleston to the ground.

A Long Brewing Plot

Vesey's plot developed over a five-year period. In 1817 he seized upon Charleston's African Methodist Episcopal (AME) Church as a means of organizing the insurrection. The church had over 4,000 members, both free black and slave, and it was remarkably free of white supervision. The literate Vesey taught Bible there. At his trial one witness testified that Vesey "studied the Bible a great deal, and tried to prove from it that slavery and bondage is against the Bible." Another slave described how Vesey "read to us from the Bible, how the children of Israel were delivered out of Egypt from bondage." Once, when a listener objected to Vesey's call for violence and genocide to redress the evil of slavery, he replied simply, "The Lord commanded it."

Vesey also appealed to non-Christian blacks with the help of slave Jack Pritchard. "Gullah Jack," as he was known in Charleston, had been born in Angola and was an Obeah-man or conjure man. Many in the black community believed he had the power to create charms that could protect the wearer against bullets. Gullah Jack was key in recruiting help for the plot among the Gullah population of Charleston and the neighboring islands.

By December 1821 Vesey had four main lieutenants. One was Ned Bennett, the trusted slave of South Carolina governor Thomas Bennett. Another was Rolla Bennett, who routinely took charge of the governor's household during his absences. Although Rolla later testified that "the governor treats me like a son," he was willing to murder the governor and his family. The third man, Monday Gell, "enjoyed all the substantial comforts of a free man." His master allowed him to keep a goodly portion of his earnings as a harness maker. The fourth lieutenant, Peter Poyas, was a ship's carpenter, who believed that "we are obliged to revolt."

By mid-1822, Ned Bennett was spreading the word in the country that Sunday, June 14 had been chosen for the uprising. Peter Poyas, Rolla Bennett, and Monday Gell were collecting and organizing armed companies among the AME congregation, and Gullah Jack alerted the islanders to prepare their boats and weapons for an attack on Charleston. The date was well chosen. Blacks were permitted to gather at the city market on Sundays with little supervision, and by mid-July many of the city's elite and militia members had left town to escape the heat.

The Secret Plot is Revealed

Vesey had managed to keep his conspiracy secret for a remarkably long time considering the number of persons involved. He had warned that any traitor would be "put to instant death." He had also largely avoided involving mulattos and house slaves, whom he considered a security risk. But three weeks before the appointed day, Peter Prioleau, a house servant of Colonel John Prioleau, was approached by a strange black man while he was on an errand down by the wharves. "We are determined to shake off our bondage," the stranger told Peter. "Many have joined, and if you go with me, I will show you the man, who has a list of names, who will take yours down." Stunned, Peter Prioleau left quickly. Eventually, he told his master about the encounter.

Surprisingly little happened at first. Colonel Prioleau rushed to tell Charleston's mayor, Intendent James Hamilton. Peter told his story to the governor and the city council, all of whom initially refused to believe that anything serious was afoot. Colonel Prioleau, acting on his own initiative, arrested William Paul, the man who had approached Peter. After a week of solitary confinement and physical abuse, Paul revealed the outline of Vesey's plan and the identity of all of Vesey's main lieutenants. Still the authorities did little. The governor claimed, upon learning that his slave Ned was involved, that Ned's "attachment and fidelity" to him were beyond question. Several other conspirators were questioned and released. But Vesey himself was neither named nor suspected, and all the while he was working to move up the date of the revolt before the white population could learn more about it.

Meanwhile, Major John Wilson, who was more suspicious than the governor, arranged for his mulatto servant George to make undercover inquiries. On June 14 George confirmed that the plot was real and that midnight of Sunday June 16 was the appointed time. This convinced Hamilton, who summoned the state militia to reinforce the city guard, but he raised no public alarm.

Vesey and Others Finally Arrested

By Sunday June 16, Vesey noticed the influx of armed troops into the city and canceled the insurrection. Soon most of the ringleaders had been arrested, except for Vesey. Interrogators remarked later that he "enjoyed so much confidence of the whites, that when he was accused, the charge was not only discredited, but he was not even arrested for several days after, and not until proof of his guilt had become too strong to be doubted."

On June 18, Hamilton summoned seven prominent merchants and lawyers to convene as a *pro tempore* court for all blacks arrested for insurrection. This special court had no jury and its sentences could not be appealed. The seven judges both heard cases and prosecuted them. This practice was legal under the state Negro Act of 1740, which was still in force and allowed for special courts for blacks, "severe" physical interrogation, and capital punishment. The defendants did have the right to counsel, to know the identity of hostile witnesses and to cross-examine other slaves, and to challenge hearsay evidence.

Of the four witnesses called against Vesey, only one specifically testified that Vesey urged slaves to seize weapons and fight for freedom. The only other evidence came from an unidentified white barber, who claimed that Vesey had hired him to make wigs from Caucasian hair. (Vesey had hoped that wigs and white paint would deceive the city guard in the dark sufficiently to let slaves near enough to them to kill them,) Vesey denied knowing the man, but when Hamilton produced one of the wigs, Vesey remarked "Good God!" and confessed he knew the hairdresser and said he had had the wig made for his own use.

Vesey himself did not take the stand, and from jail he urged other defendants to die like men and say nothing. He was allowed to cross-examine witnesses and to act as his own counsel. In the end, however, Judge Lionel Kennedy pronounced him guilty and sentenced him to death. "It is difficult to imagine what *infatuation* could have prompted you to attempt an enterprise so wild and visionary," Kennedy remarked. "From your age and experience you *ought* to have known that success was impracticable." On July 2, 1822, Vesey and five of his main conspirators were hanged. By the end of August an additional further 131 blacks were arrested and 35 hanged.

The conspiracy had two long-term results. First, the city of Charleston established the Citadel to help protect its citizens against "an enemy in the bosom of the state." Second, Secretary of War John C. Calhoun ordered U.S. military forces to take up indefinite duty in Charleston to help "in quelling the disturbances" there, and established a military presence that would last until, and ultimately trigger, the Civil War.

—*Carol Willcox Melton*

Suggestions for Further Reading

Lofton, John. *Denmark Vesey's Revolt: The Slave Plot That Lit the Fuse to Fort Sumter.* Kent, Ohio: Kent State University Press, 1964.

Pearson, Edward A., ed. *Designs against Charleston: The Trial Record of the Denmark Vesey Slave Conspiracy of 1822.* Chapel Hill, N.C.: University of North Carolina Press, 1999.

Robertson, David. *Denmark Vesey.* New York: Alfred A. Knopf, 1999.

State v. Mann: 1829

Defendant: John Mann **Crime Charged:** Assault and battery
Chief Defense Lawyer: No record **Chief Prosecutor:** No record
Judge: Thomas Ruffin **Place:** North Carolina
Date of Decision: December 1829 **Verdict:** Judgment reversed, and judgment entered for the defendant

SIGNIFICANCE

A Southern judge with little sympathy for slavery rendered a powerful and logical pro-slavery opinion, further entrenching Southern slavery, while opening it to Northern attack.

North Carolina had fewer slaves than most other states in the future Confederacy. But in the two decades leading up to the Civil War, that state's Supreme Court produced one of the most notorious pro-slavery opinions in American history.

In 1829 Elizabeth Jones, who owned a slave named Lydia, hired her out for a year to John Mann of Chowan County. Lydia was unhappy with the arrangement, and at one point Mann decided to punish her, possibly by whipping her. But Lydia escaped during the punishment, and began to run away. Mann shouted to her, ordering her to stop, but Lydia continued to run. Mann then shot and wounded her. Such, at least, was Mann's story.

The circumstances were so odd, however, that a local grand jury took the unusual step of indicting Mann for assault and battery against a slave. During the trial, the judge told the jury that if it believed that the punishment Mann inflicted was "cruel and unwarrantable, and disproportionate to the offense committed by the slave that, in the law the Defendant was guilty," particularly since he was not even her owner. This is obviously exactly what the jury thought, for it found Mann guilty. Mann then appealed to the Supreme Court of North Carolina.

Thomas Ruffin was the chief justice of that court, and the appeal put him in a very bad position. He disliked the idea of slavery, and he was horrified that a white man had used such violence against a black woman. On the other hand, he could not escape the fact that slavery was perfectly legal in North Carolina. Torn between his sense of justice and his sense of duty to the law, he penned a startling opinion.

"A Judge cannot but lament, when such cases as the present are brought into court," he began. "The struggle . . . in the Judge's own breast between the feelings of the man, and the duty of the magistrate, is a severe test." But despite his veiled denouncement of the evils of slavery, Ruffin then proceeded to side with the law. "It is criminal in a Court to avoid any responsibility which the laws impose. With whatever reluctance therefore it is done, the Court is compelled to express an opinion upon the extent of the dominion of the master over the slave in North Carolina."

In Defense of Slavery

The rest of Ruffin's opinion, in fact, was one of the most readable, logical, and capable defenses of slavery that a Southerner ever wrote. Ruffin observed that although Mann did not own Lydia, and that Elizabeth Jones might well be able to sue him for damaging her property, Mann still had the right to use as much force to control Lydia as Jones herself would have had, since Lydia was legally under his control. The question, then, was how much force a master could use against his slave.

Ruffin's conclusion was blunt. Slavery was designed for the good of the master, and not for the good of the slave, he wrote. In order for the master to have the full benefit of the slave, he had to be able to break the slave's will, to make the slave obey him. "Such obedience," wrote Ruffin, "is the consequence only of uncontrolled authority over the body. There is nothing else which can operate to produce the effect." The court could not interfere with the master's power over his slave, continued Ruffin. "The slave, to remain a slave, must be made sensible, that there is no appeal from the master." In short, Ruffin held, the law gave the master absolute power over the slave. He recognized that this was unjust, but clearly it was the law.

The *Mann* opinion came down just as abolitionism was gaining ground in the North. It highlighted the tension between law and justice, and the fact that more and more people were coming to see that slavery was wrong, even though it was both legal and constitutional. In 1856 Harriet Beecher Stowe, author of *Uncle Tom's Cabin*, wrote *Dred: A Tale of the Great Dismal Swamp*. In this new antislavery book she modeled the character of Judge Clayton after Thomas Ruffin, and she had Clayton deliver an opinion that strongly resembled the one in *State v. Mann*. The case, as well as Stowe's fictionalized treatment of it, helped widen the breach between North and South and gave the abolitionists further ammunition to use against the legal system and the judges who protected the morally evil institution of slavery.

—*Buckner F. Melton, Jr.*

Suggestions for Further Reading

Cover, Robert M. *Justice Accused: Anti-Slavery and the Judicial Process*. New Haven, Conn.: Yale University Press, 1975.

Stowe, Harriet Beecher. *Dred: A Tale of the Great Dismal Swamp*. New York: Penguin Books, 2000.

John Francis Knapp and Joseph Jenkins Knapp Trials: 1830

Defendants: John Francis Knapp and Joseph Jenkins Knapp
Crimes Charged: Accessories to murder **Chief Defense Lawyers:** F. Dexter and W.H. Gardiner **Chief Prosecutor:** Daniel Webster
Judges: Marcus Morton, Samuel Putnam, and Samuel S. Wilde
Place: Salem, Massachusetts **Dates of Trials:** July Term, 1830 for John Francis Knapp; November Term, 1830 for Joseph Jenkins Knapp
Verdicts: Guilty, both trials **Sentences:** Death by hanging, both trials

SIGNIFICANCE

In this prosecution of the Knapps by the famous lawyer Daniel Webster, the actual murderer was a hired assassin named Richard Crowninshield, who committed suicide before the Knapps went to trial. Due to Webster's eloquence, this became one of the first cases in which accessories to murder were tried, convicted and executed even though the actual murderer was never convicted.

Brothers John Francis Knapp (who went by his middle name) and Joseph Jenkins Knapp had a wealthy uncle, Captain Joseph White, who lived in Salem, Massachusetts. Captain White was 82 years old, an extraordinary age for that time, but the Knapps were impatient to receive their anticipated inheritance and decided that they couldn't wait for the old man to die naturally. The Knapps hired a hit man, 28-year-old Richard Crowninshield, to murder Captain White.

On the night of April 6, 1830, Crowninshield quietly broke into Captain White's house and went into the bedroom where the old man was asleep. While Francis and Joseph Knapp waited in the street outside, approximately 300 feet away, Crowninshield clubbed and stabbed Captain White to death. With the Knapp brothers' help, Crowninshield fled the house without being seen.

For a while it seemed as if the Knapps' scheme had succeeded. The citizens of Salem were outraged by the brutal murder of the prominent Captain White and formed a Committee of Vigilance to search for the killer. After two months of searching, however, the Committee had gotten nowhere. Then, the police in New Bedford arrested a pickpocket, who testified before a grand jury that he was a friend of Crowninshield and that Crowninshield had told him that he killed Captain White.

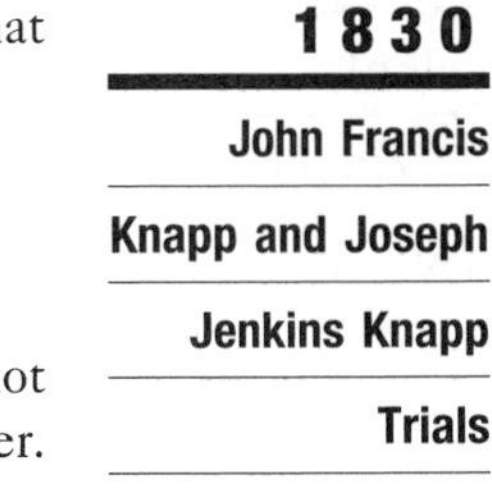

Trail Leads to Knapps

Crowninshield was promptly arrested, but he kept quiet since he could not implicate Francis or Joseph Knapp without confessing to his role in the murder. Unfortunately, Crowninshield had told another one of his criminal acquaintances, John Palmer, about the Knapps' involvement. Palmer wrote a blackmail letter to the Knapps, but it was received instead by the Knapps' father. The elder Knapp turned the letter over to the police, who arrested the Knapp brothers. After Joseph Knapp confessed, Crowninshield realized that no hope was left and hung himself in his prison cell.

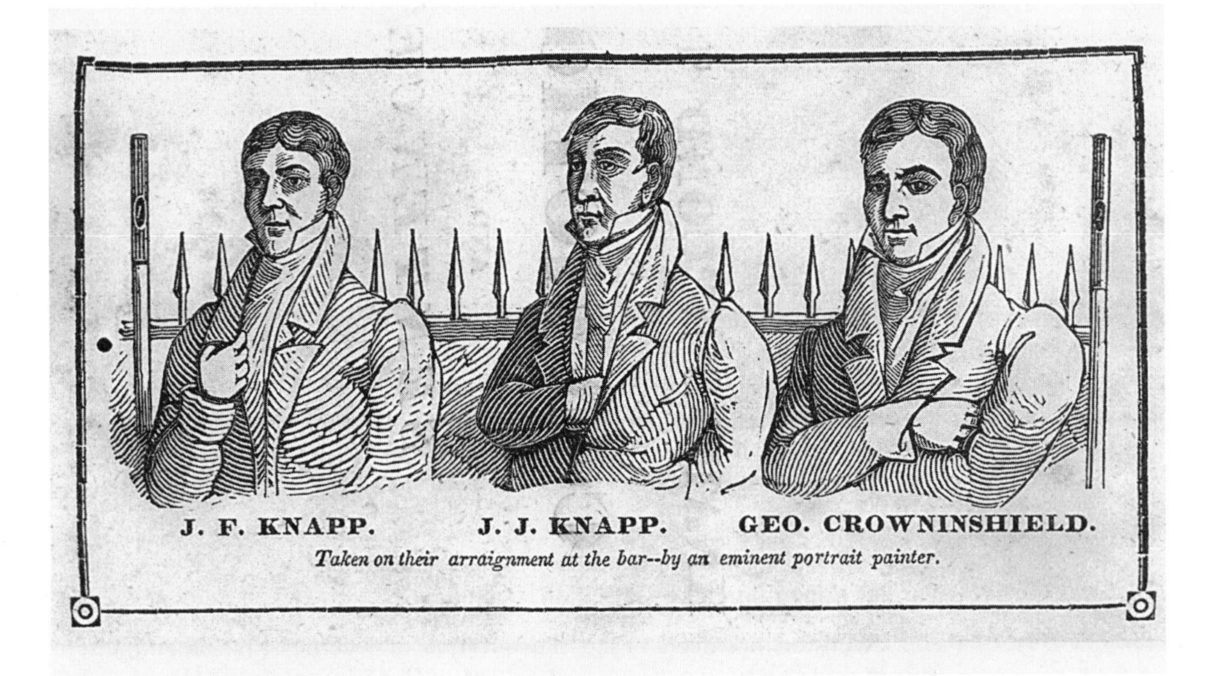

The Knapp brothers and Richard Crowninshield at their arraignment. (Courtesy, Essex Institute Historical Collections)

To prosecute the Knapps, the Massachusetts attorney general used the distinguished Daniel Webster. Born in 1782, Webster had practiced law in New Hampshire for a while before coming to Boston, which he would eventually leave for service in the federal government. Like many attorneys in private practice at the time, Webster occasionally worked for the state as a prosecutor.

The Knapps were charged with being accessories to murder. Both Francis and Joseph Knapp were to be tried before the Salem division of the Massachusetts Supreme Judicial Court. The judges were Marcus Morton, Samuel Putnam, and Samuel S. Wilde. For their defense, the Knapps were represented by F. Dexter and W.H. Gardiner. Francis Knapp was to be tried first, and the most important issues would be addressed in his trial.

Francis Knapp's trial was set for the court's 1830 July Term. Webster knew that his biggest difficulty lay in the fact that Richard Crowninshield, the actual murderer, had committed suicide before he could be tried and convicted. Under the ancient common law of England, which was the primary influence on the legal principles of all American states, accessories to murder could not be convicted unless (1) the actual murderer had been convicted, or (2) the accessories had been present at the time of the murder. Crowninshield was dead, and the Knapps had been 300 feet away in the street at the time of the murder.

Like every good prosecutor, Webster laid the foundation for his case by appealing to the jury's emotions. He described Captain White, who had gone to sleep on the night of the murder unaware of his nephews' plot:

> A healthful old man to whom sleep was sweet, the first sound slumbers of the night held him in their strong embrace.

Webster went on to portray Crowninshield's stolen entry into White's home:

> With noiseless feet he paces the lonely hall half lighted by the moon; he winds up the ascent of the stairs . . . beholds his victim before him . . . the moon resting on the grey locks of this aged victim shows him where to strike.

As to Crowninshield's suicide, Webster assured the jury that divine justice was punishing Crowninshield's soul:

> A vulture is devouring it. . . . It can ask no sympathy from Heaven or Earth.

Dexter and Gardiner tried to keep the focus of the trial on the fact that Webster had not satisfied the legal requirements for conviction:

> Upon this evidence the prisoner cannot be convicted as a principal in the murder. A principal in the second degree, according to the law of England, is by our statutes an accessory before the fact, and cannot be tried until there has been a conviction of the principal.

Verdict Hangs on Legal Definition

Webster, however, raised the question of whether Francis and Joseph Knapp could be legally considered as "present" during the murder so that they could be convicted. True, the Knapps had been 300 feet away in the street, but they had been there to help Crowninshield:

> To constitute a presence, it is sufficient if the accomplice is in a place, either where he may render aid to the perpetrator of the felony, or where the perpetrator supposes he may render aid. If they selected the place to afford assistance, whether it was well or ill chosen for that purpose is immaterial. The perpetrator would derive courage and confidence from the knowledge that his associate was in the place appointed.

Webster's definition of presence would include Francis Knapp and, by implication, ultimately anyone involved in a murder who had come near enough to the scene of the crime to be considered "aiding and abetting" the actual murderer. Dexter argued strenuously for a conservative approach, that only physical presence at a murder could mean legal presence. According to Dexter, Francis Knapp would have to have been in Captain White's bedroom with Crowninshield to be considered present and found guilty:

> To make a man a principal by aiding and abetting in a felony, he must be in such a situation at the moment when the crime is committed, that he can render actual and immediate assistance to the perpetrator; and that he must be there by agreement, and with the intent to render such assistance.

Faced with these powerful but opposing legal arguments, the jury at first could not reach a verdict, but ultimately it found Francis Knapp guilty by the close of the July Term. Knapp was going to hang, and now it was his brother Joseph's turn to be tried.

Joseph Knapp's trial took place during the Court's November Term of 1830. Joseph Knapp had testified against Crowninshield at the arraignment, but he refused to testify against his brother Francis at his trial. Therefore, the state dropped its earlier promise to give Joseph Knapp immunity and put him before Webster to be prosecuted. Dexter and Gardiner had lost the debate over the legal definition of presence at Francis Knapp's trial, so in Joseph Knapp's trial, they shifted their attack to whether the Knapps had been close enough to aid and abet Crowninshield. The trial record states:

> The prisoner's counsel now offered evidence in regard to the place at which the principal . . . was stationed during the perpetration of the murder, their object being to show that in that situation it was impossible for him to aid and abet the person who was actually striking the blow.

The jury rejected Dexter and Gardiner's last-ditch attempt to save Joseph Knapp, however, and by the close of the November Term found him guilty.

Francis and Joseph Knapp went to the gallows. Having successfully convicted them of murder, the state of Massachusetts also tried and convicted George Crowninshield, a brother of Richard's who had a minor role in the whole affair, of aiding and abetting Captain White's murder.

The whole Francis and Joseph Knapp affair would have gone down in history as a typical sordid murder if it had not been for Daniel Webster's eloquence. Webster persuaded the judges and the jury to expand the boundaries of an accessory's liability for murder. Once thus expanded, the old common law restrictions that would have prevented guilty men such as Francis and Joseph Knapp from being brought to justice were, over time, eventually swept away.

—*Stephen G. Christianson*

Suggestions for Further Reading

A Biographical Sketch of the Celebrated Salem Murderer. Boston: Unknown publisher, 1830.

Bartlett, Irving H. *Daniel Webster*. New York: W.W. Norton & Co., 1978.

Wilson, Colin. *Encyclopedia of Murder.* New York: G.P. Putnam's Sons, 1962.

Wiltse, Charles M. and Harold D. Moser, editors. *The Papers of Daniel Webster.* Hanover, Mass.: Published for Dartmouth College by the University Press of New England, 1974–1989.

Cherokee Nation v. Georgia: 1831

Plaintiffs: Cherokee Indian Nation **Defendant:** State of Georgia
Plaintiffs Claim: That under the Supreme Court's power to resolve disputes between states and foreign nations, the Court could forbid Georgia from unlawfully attempting to move the Cherokees from their lands
Chief Defense Lawyer: None **Chief Lawyer for Plaintiffs:** William Wirt
Justices: Henry Baldwin, Gabriel Duvalt, William Johnson, John Marshall, John McLean, Joseph Story, and Smith Thompson **Place:** Washington, D.C.
Date of Decision: March 5, 1831 **Decision:** That the Court had no power to hear the dispute, because Indian tribes are not foreign nations

SIGNIFICANCE

By refusing to help the Cherokees, the U.S. Supreme Court left the Indians at the mercy of land-hungry settlers. The Cherokees ultimately were forced to move to Oklahoma along the famous "Trail of Tears."

The Cherokee Indians originally inhabited much of America's southeastern seaboard. In the 17th and 18th centuries, European settlers pushed the Cherokees from many of their lands. Unlike most Indians, however, the Cherokees were able to resist white encroachment by adapting to white ways. After the American Revolution, the Cherokees copied white farming methods and other aspects of the white economy. The Cherokees sent some of their children to American schools and permitted mixed marriages. Further, they signed a series of treaties with the federal government that seemed to protect what remained of their lands.

The Cherokee presence was particularly strong in Georgia, where they prospered under the new ways. Cherokee plantations even had Negro slaves. However, in 1828, prospectors discovered gold in Cherokee territory. Georgia wanted to give the land to whites, and enacted laws to force the Cherokees to leave. The Cherokees fought back, hiring white lawyers to represent them.

The Cherokees' chief lawyer was William Wirt. He went directly to the Supreme Court and asked for an injunction forbidding Georgia from removing the Cherokees. Because Article III, Section 2 of the U.S. Constitution gives the Court original jurisdiction in cases to which a state is a party, Wirt didn't have to go through the Georgia state courts and couldn't go through the lower federal courts. Unfortunately, Article III, Section 2 generally limits the Court's jurisdiction to cases involving American citizens, and Indians were not yet recognized as citizens. The only arguable basis for jurisdiction was the Court's power to hear disputes "between a State, or the Citizens thereof, and foreign States, Citizens or Subjects."

Associate Justice Story did not vote with the majority in the 1831 *Cherokee Nation v. Georgia* decision that led to the "Trail of Tears." (Courtesy, Library of Congress)

Therefore, Wirt had to convince the Court that the Cherokees were a foreign nation or the Court would refuse to act. On March 5, 1831, in Washington, D.C., he pleaded the Cherokees' case before Supreme Court Justices Henry Baldwin, Gabriel Duvalt, William Johnson, John Marshall, John McLean, Joseph Story, and Smith Thompson. Georgia, an ardent supporter of states' rights, denied that the federal courts had jurisdiction and refused to send a defense lawyer.

Wirt reminded the Court that the Cherokees had uncontestable rights to the lands in Georgia:

> The boundaries were fixed by treaty, and what was within them was acknowledged to be the land of the Cherokees. This was the scope of all the treaties.

Next, Wirt begged the Court to prevent what was about to happen to the Cherokees:

> The legislation of Georgia proposes to annihilate them, as its very end and aim. . . . If those laws be fully executed, there will be no Cherokee boundary, no Cherokee nation, no Cherokee lands, no Cherokee treaties. . . . They will all be swept out of existence together, leaving nothing but the monuments in our history of the enormous injustice that has been practised towards a friendly nation.

That same day, the Supreme Court denied Wirt's petition, holding that the Cherokees and other Indian tribes were only "domestic dependent nations," not foreign nations, and thus the Court had no authority to help them. A year later, in the 1832 case of *Worcester v. Georgia,* the Court freed some missionaries who were sympathetic to the Cherokee cause and had been arrested by Georgia authorities, but only because the missionaries were white citizens.

Powerless to resist, the Cherokees were stripped of all their lands by 1838. In that year, over 7,000 soldiers forced the Cherokees to leave what was left of their territory for relocation in Oklahoma. Over 4,000 Cherokees died during the journey of thousands of miles to the west, which became known as the Trail of Tears.

—*Stephen G. Christianson*

Suggestions for Further Reading

Guttmann, Allen. *States' Rights and Indian Removal: the Cherokee Nation v. the State of Georgia*. Boston: D.C. Heath, 1965.

Lumpkin, Wilson. *The Removal of the Cherokee Indians from Georgia*. New York: Arno Press, 1969.

Peck, Ira. "Worcester v. Georgia: the Campaign to Move the Cherokee Nation." *Senior Scholastic* (November 1982): 17–20.

Warren, Mary Bondurant. *Whites Among the Cherokees*. Danielsville, Ga.: Heritage Papers, 1987.

Wilkins, Thurman. *Cherokee Tragedy*. Norman: University of Oklahoma Press, 1986.

Ephraim Avery Trial: 1833

Defendant: Ephraim Avery **Crime Charged:** Murder
Chief Defense Lawyers: Jeremiah Mason, Richard Randolf, George Turner, Henry Cranston, Joseph Hathaway, Joseph Blake (Nathaniel Bullock assisted with pretrial matters) **Chief Prosecutors:** Albert C. Greene, Dutee J. Pearce (William Staples assisted with pretrial matters) **Judges:** Samuel Eddy, Charles Brayton, Job Durfee **Place:** Newport, Rhode Island
Date of Trial: May 6–June 2, 1833 **Verdict:** Not guilty

SIGNIFICANCE

The "moral character" of the victim was as much on trial as the man accused of her murder. Because the man was a Methodist minister with a wife and children, the long trial also garnered the attention of New England Puritans suspicious of the relatively new religion of Methodism.

On the bitterly cold morning of Friday, December 21, 1832, John Durfee made a horrifying discovery on his father's farm in Tiverton, Rhode Island. Hanging by the neck from a cord lashed to a five-foot haystack post was the frozen body of 30-year-old Sarah Maria Cornell. At first, it was believed that the young lady had committed suicide, but then a note, in her handwriting and dated the day of her death, was found among her effects. It said, "If I should be missing, enquire of the Rev. Mr. Avery of Bristol, he will know where I am." Other incriminating letters were found, suspicions were aroused, and an autopsy was performed, which uncovered that the unmarried woman was four months pregnant when she died. Thus began an affair that received national attention and led to one of the longest murder trials in Rhode Island's history.

A Victim of Questionable Morals?

The victim had lived in Fall River, Massachusetts, just one-half mile away from where her body was found. Raised in a small, rural Connecticut community by her mother as a member of the Congregational Church, Sarah Cornell wanted more out of life than what her surroundings gave her, so she left home at age 18 and worked as a weaver and loom-operator in a number of mill towns across New England. Also while a teenager, Cornell converted to Methodism.

The person suspected in her death, the Reverend Ephraim Avery, was a 33-year-old Methodist minister with a wife and children who resided 16 miles away in Bristol, Rhode Island. He and Cornell had known each other since July 1830, when Avery was assigned to a church in Lowell, Massachusetts, and Cornell was a member of his congregation. (The pastor was reassigned to Bristol, and she moved to Fall River, in 1832.) For a brief time, Cornell lived in the pastor's home as a servant, but was cast out when the minister's son reported to his mother that "Pa kissed Maria." In October 1830, Avery excommunicated Cornell when she was accused of, and confessed to, numerous sexual affairs.

The Methodist Church was the center of Cornell's life, so she moved to other towns and joined other congregations, but the Reverend Avery always found out and forced her to leave those parishes as well. Realizing that she needed Avery's approval to rejoin the church, Cornell met him at a Methodist camp meeting in August 1832. Cornell later told her sister that it was there the pastor had his way with her and she became pregnant.

Cornell's murder, however, was more than just the alleged attempt by a married man to hide the fact that a single woman was carrying his child. Several major social changes were also going on at the same time that caused Avery's trial to receive national attention.

A Crime in a Changing New England

New England in the 1820s and 1830s was going through a tremendous transformation. The Industrial Revolution had begun and thousands of people were moving from the farms into the cities. For the first time, young women could leave home and obtain some degree of independence by working in the cotton mills that sprang up across the region. A religious "second awakening" was also occurring. For centuries, the Congregationalists with their strict morals and dull church services were predominant in New England, but now the new Methodist Church, with its joyful singing, shouting, and clapping of hands and with its outdoor meetings (that were as much unchaperoned social events as spiritual gatherings), was attracting thousands of youthful followers.

Many looked upon these developments with great disfavor. To them, the Industrial Age meant the loosening of family ties and the exposure of the young to the evils of the city. Likewise, the new religion was not a legitimate faith, but a cult that attracted the naïve and simple-minded. And while the idea that a girl like Sarah Cornell could leave the home and church of her parents to work in a factory and join the Methodist Church was terrible enough, the fact that a man of the cloth (even a Methodist) could be tied to her pregnancy and death was proof that the world was going mad.

Other people also had an interest in the case. There were the industrialists whose mills depended upon the labor of women like Cornell. For years, they asserted that the girls were just as safe under their care as they were at their parents' farms. Thus, it was in their interest to champion Cornell's cause, to keep her name from being dragged through the mud, and to find her killer. The

Methodist Church, on the other hand, was trying hard to win both respectability and converts and it could not afford to have one of its ministers found guilty of scandal and murder. As a result, both groups contributed great amounts of time, money, and manpower to the prosecution (or defense) of the Reverend Avery and helped find many of the witnesses who would later testify at his trial.

Suicide or Murder?

The initial coroners' jury in Tiverton, which met before the autopsy of Cornell's body, concluded that she had "committed suicide by hanging herself upon a stake . . . and was influenced to commit said crime by the wicked conduct of a married man." After the post-mortem, however, a second coroners' jury in Bristol accused Avery of being the "principal or accessory" in her death. Avery was arrested for murder, but was quickly released on his own recognizance.

The residents of Fall River were shocked by Cornell's death. When she was buried on Christmas Eve, a large, angry crowd attended her funeral. That evening, at a mass meeting in Fall River, funds were pledged and two committees selected "to aid the inhabitants of Tiverton" in the investigation of the crime. On Christmas Day (the holiday was not celebrated in Puritan-dominated New England), one hundred men from Fall River chartered a steamer, sailed to Bristol, and marched to Avery's home. Once there, they demanded that the reverend show himself, but he stayed upstairs while a friend confronted the crowd. There might have been a lynching if the steamer had not rung its bell announcing its return to Fall River.

An inquest was then held in Bristol. In the end, the two justices of the peace concluded that there was not enough evidence to try Avery for murder. The residents of Fall River were outraged and rumors flew that at least one of the judges was a Methodist who wanted to protect the reputation of the church. Harvey Harnden, Fall River's deputy sheriff, then got a warrant for Avery's arrest from a Rhode Island Superior Court judge, but the minister had fled before a Rhode Island sheriff could serve it.

Avery supposedly ran on the advice of a friend after being told that his life was in danger. He was found by Harnden in Rindge, New Hampshire, on January 20, 1833, and was promptly returned to Rhode Island, where he was committed to the Newport jail. On March 8, the pastor was indicted for murder by the Newport County grand jury and he pleaded "not guilty."

High-powered Attorneys for the Defense and Prosecution

The trial before the state's three-member Supreme Judicial Council (Rhode Island's highest court, now called the Supreme Court) began on May 6. The prosecutors were Albert Greene, the attorney general of Rhode Island, and one of Greene's predecessors, Dutee Pearce. Jeremiah Mason, a former U.S. Senator and one of the greatest lawyers in the country, led the six-man defense team, hired by the Methodist Church.

The trial lasted 27 days, during which 500 spectators crowded every day into the courtroom in the old Colony House. During the proceeding, Avery did not speak for himself because, under Rhode Island law at that time, defendants in a capital case were not allowed to testify in their own defense. Still, the jury had plenty of other witnesses to listen to. In all, the prosecution called 68 people to the witness stand while the defense called 128. As was the practice of the day, the members of the jury were not allowed to take notes and they may have been confused by the enormous amount of testimony that was given.

Defense Raises the Issue of the Victim's Moral Character

Mason and his colleagues argued that the pastor was not present when the murder happened. However, the largest and most controversial part of Avery's defense was its attack on the victim's moral character. Sarah Cornell was described by one of the reverend's attorneys as "utterly abandoned, unprincipled, profligate." It was brought up that Cornell had been expelled from the Methodist Church for fornication. Numerous witnesses testified that she was promiscuous, that she had once been treated for venereal disease, that she had often threatened suicide, and that she frequently acted in a deranged manner.

Medical experts also debated whether Cornell's unborn baby was conceived in August, 1832, or at an earlier date. Topics such as Cornell's menstrual cycles and female anatomy were discussed in detail. Still, due to the Puritan standards of modesty that existed then in Rhode Island, it was sometimes difficult for the lawyers to get the testimony they needed. For example, when one of the women who examined Cornell's body was asked about the condition of the corpse, she refused to answer and angrily replied, "I never heard such questions asked of nobody." Indeed, some testimony embarrassed one of the court reporters to such an extent that he simply omitted it from his version of the transcript.

On Sunday, June 2, 1833, after considering the evidence for 16 hours, the jury found Ephraim Avery "Not Guilty." The minister was promptly released and he returned to his pastoral duties, but the public was convinced that a great injustice had been done. Contempt and hatred followed him wherever he went. At more than one location Avery was hanged or burned in effigy and once, when a mob in Boston recognized him, he was almost lynched. Many people were also angry at the Methodist Church, so to calm the unrest, the church's New England Conference conducted its own trial. Avery was acquitted in that proceeding as well, but that did not lessen the controversy.

To escape the public's eye, the Reverend Ephraim Avery finally left the ministry and went to Ohio with his family in 1836, where he lived out the last 33 years of his life as a farmer. In contrast, Cornell's grave was visited for many years by hundreds as if it were a shrine, but as time has passed, the crowds dwindled until most forgot about the woman from Fall River and the significance her murder had in the social history of the United States.

—*Mark Thorburn*

Suggestions for Further Reading

Cable, Mary. *Avery's Knot.* New York: G. P. Putnam's Sons, 1981.

Howe, George. "The Minister and the Mill Girl." *American Heritage Magazine* (October 1961): 34–7, 82–8.

Kasserman, David Richard. *Fall River Outrage: Life, Murder, and Justice in Early Industrial New England.* Philadelphia: University of Pennsylvania Press, 1986.

McLoughlin, William G. "Untangling the Tiverton Tragedy: The Social Meaning of the Terrible Haystack Murder of 1833." *Journal of American Culture,* 7 (Winter 1984): 75–84.

Paul, Raymond. *The Tragedy at Tiverton.* New York: Viking Press, 1984.

Williams, Catherine Read. *Fall River, An Authentic Narrative.* Edited by Patricia Caldwell. New York: Oxford University Press, 1993.

Commonwealth v. Aves: 1836

Name of Respondent: Thomas Aves **Cause of Action:** Writ of habeas corpus for a slave girl, Med **Commonwealth Attorneys:** Ellis Gray Loring, Rufus Choate, Samuel Sewall **Respondent's Counsel:** Benjamin Robbins Curtis, C. P. Curtis **Judge:** Lemuel Shaw **Place:** Massachusetts **Date of Decision:** 1836 **Verdict:** Med was freed, becoming a ward of the court

SIGNIFICANCE

Shaw's opinion in the *Aves* case established a precedent in law that slavery was local and liberty general. This precedent was widely appealed to by antislavery forces in their future litigation.

In 1836 New Orleans resident Mary Slater went to visit her father Thomas Aves in Boston, bringing with her a young slave girl about six years of age named Med. While in Boston Slater fell ill, and asked her father to take care of Med until she recovered. During Slater's illness, the Boston Female Anti-Slavery Society, antislavery sympathizer Levin H. Harris, and others sought a writ of habeas corpus against Aves, asking by what right he was holding Med. Aves answered that he was acting as his daughter's agent. This reply brought the case before the Massachusetts Supreme Court and its famous chief justice, Lemuel Shaw.

What followed turned into a judicial inquiry into slavery's legality in Massachusetts, although at first the question was narrower. While some cases had already held that a slave became free when the master took him or her permanently into a free state, no court had ever addressed the question of a slave who left the slave states temporarily with his or her master. In that regard the *Aves* case foreshadowed the U.S. Supreme Court's infamous *Dred Scott* decision of 1857. Lawyers for the commonwealth included Ellis Gray Loring, a prominent member of the Massachusetts Anti-Slavery Society, while Aves was represented by Benjamin Robbins Curtis, who would serve as an associate justice of the *Dred Scott* Court.

Slave or Free?

The Massachusetts court heard the case in a single, long day, from nine in the morning until seven at night, with practically no recesses. During the elaborate arguments, Loring and the other antislavery lawyers argued that slavery could not exist in Massachusetts unless the commonwealth expressly allowed it. Curtis and his co-counsel disagreed sharply. The federal Constitution clearly required the return of fugitive slaves who escaped to free states, they pointed out; thus a slave did not become free merely because he breathed the air of a free state. He told Shaw and his fellow jurists that what they thought, whether "as men or as moralists," was not at issue; only what the law said was moral mattered, and American law recognized slavery.

A unanimous court ruled against Aves a week later. Shaw first decided that Massachusetts had clearly abolished slavery, although he had great trouble pointing to exactly when and how it had done so. He proclaimed that "by the general and now well established law of this Commonwealth, bond slavery cannot exist, because it is contrary to natural right, and repugnant to numerous provisions of the constitution and laws." He then asked how far Massachusetts must go in respecting a slaveholder's property rights. Citing large numbers of English and American cases and commentators, he found that although the federal Constitution required a state to return a runaway slave to his or her owner, Med was not a runaway. Mary Slater had willingly brought her to Boston. Since Massachusetts was a free state, Shaw concluded, Slater could not exercise her property rights in a slave while there. He found that "all persons coming within the limits of a state, become subject to all its municipal laws, civil and criminal, and entitled to the privileges which those laws confer; . . . this rule applies as well to blacks as whites." The court thus barred Slater from taking Med back to Louisiana, ordering that Med be put into a guardian's custody instead. She was later adopted by Isaac Knapp, the publisher of the leading abolitionist newspaper *The Liberator*. Antislave forces had won an important battle.

Shaw's opinion in *Commonwealth v. Aves* stands in sharp contrast to Thomas Ruffin's opinion in *State v. Mann*. The *Mann* opinion was short, clear, logical, and well-crafted. It also led to a result that hindsight reveals as immoral. In contrast, Shaw's *Aves* opinion was long and rambling, relying on hyper-technical legal discussion and poor logic, but it reached a more morally acceptable result, although Southern slaveholders disagreed. Together the two cases showed a widening gap in the courts and the constitutional system between what was legal and what was right, a gap that eventually became a civil war.

—*Buckner F. Melton, Jr.*

Suggestions for Further Reading

Cover, Robert M. *Justice Accused: Anti-Slavery and the Judicial Process*. New Haven, Conn.: Yale University Press, 1975.

Levy, Leonard W. *The Law of the Commonwealth and Chief Justice Shaw*. Cambridge, Mass.: Harvard University Press, 1957.

Richard Parmelee Robinson Trial: 1836

Defendant: Richard Parmelee Robinson **Crime Charged:** Murder
Chief Defense Lawyers: Ogden Hoffman, Hugh Maxwell, William Price
Chief Prosecutors: Thomas Phoenix, Robert H. Morris **Judge:** Ogden Edwards **Place:** New York, New York **Date of Trial:** June 2–7, 1836
Verdict: Not guilty

SIGNIFICANCE

Perhaps the first of the sex-sin-and-mayhem cases that have come to dominate much of the daily news, the Helen Jewett murder gives us insight into the intimate side of life among young men and women some 125 years before the sexual revolution.

At 3:00 A.M. on Sunday, April 10, 1838, at a prosperous brothel on Thomas Street in lower Manhattan, a highly paid prostitute known as Helen Jewett, whose clientele included numbers of the city's gentry, was found dead in her bed. The bedclothes had been set afire and still smoldered. Blood had poured from three deep gashes in her head.

New York City then had almost no professional police force. "Watchmen" at sentry posts a few blocks apart, most of them laborers moonlighting for small pay, were alert for fires and robberies, while a few worked full-time as officers. Two such, watchman George Noble and constable Dennis Brink, raced to the whorehouse and ordered watchmen to search for clues. A long cloak was found in a rear yard nearby. In the brothel's backyard, a hatchet caked with wet earth turned up.

Bill Easy and Frank Rivers

Brink and Noble questioned brothel proprietor Rosina Townsend, her "girls," and their Saturday night "guests." Most Saturday evenings, they learned, 23-year-old Helen Jewett entertained a man known as Bill Easy. But on April 9 she had told Townsend not to send Easy to her. Instead, between nine and ten o'clock, another young gent who was also a frequent visitor, Frank Rivers, had been admitted. An hour later, when Townsend delivered a bottle of champagne ordered by Jewett, she saw the back of Rivers's head as he relaxed in Jewett's bed. No other man had called to see Jewett. No one had seen Rivers depart. Townsend had discovered the fire, and the body, after a late-arriving customer knocked at the street door.

Brink and Noble soon learned Rivers's business address and his real name: Richard Parmelee Robinson. The 19-year-old son of a Connecticut landowner and state legislator, he was living in a crowded boardinghouse while clerking in a big-city store to learn business. The investigators also learned that Bill Easy was really another young clerk, George P. Marston, whose father was a lawyer and judge in Massachusetts.

At the boardinghouse, Brink and Noble awakened Robinson and his roommate, James Tew. The watchmen escorted both to the crime scene, which Robinson viewed with, they thought, surprising composure. The roommates said they had gone together to Townsend's the night before. Tew said he lingered there briefly, then went home and to bed, leaving Robinson, who insisted he had returned home by eleven thirty.

A coroner's jury quickly concluded that ". . . Helen Jewett came to her death by a blow or blows inflicted on the head, with a hatchett [sic] by the hand of Richard P. Robinson." The accused was jailed.

". . . Well Known to Every Pedestrian . . ."

The Jewett murder rapidly became one of the era's most sensational crimes. Prominent *New York Herald* editor James Gordon Bennett himself examined and reported on the crime scene, noting that "Jewett was well known to every pedestrian in Broadway." Another visitor, New York City Mayor Cornelius W. Lawrence, made his distress clear: New York, a city of 270,000, had seen only seven official homicides the year before. The crime immediately boosted the circulation figures of a dozen or more New York newspapers, all of which vociferously argued the likelihood of Robinson's guilt.

Research by editor Bennett disclosed that Helen Jewett was a Maine native named Dorcas Doyen. She had wended her way to Massachusetts as an apprenticed servant girl, learning "gentle manners" and an appreciation of the arts and literature. Seduced at 16, she had taken the first of four assumed names as she moved into brothel life in Portland, Maine, then in Boston. She had worked in New York for three years.

Joseph Hoxie, proprietor of the store where Robinson clerked, hired a prominent lawyer, Ogden Hoffman, to defend him. As the trial opened on Thursday, June 2, some 6,000 would-be spectators thronged the city hall courtroom and corridors. Twenty reporters strained to catch the testimony (no official transcripts were made) as Judge Ogden Edwards repeatedly demanded quiet. Next day, the judge summoned 50 extra marshalls to maintain order. When only 21 of 59 called jurymen appeared and only seven were seated, the judge ordered the drafting of "talesmen"—individuals rounded up from streets and stores nearby. All but one were established businessmen.

Opening for the prosecution, District Attorney Thomas Phoenix called on Rosina Townsend. She testified that Robinson had visited Jewett frequently in recent weeks but that George Marston, known as Bill Easy, was Jewett's usual Saturday-night client. Cross-examination by defense lawyer Hugh Maxwell failed to shake her story of admitting Robinson, seeing him in Jewett's room, and discovering the murder and fire.

Hatchet, Cloak, and Tassel

Constable Brink testified on Robinson's denying ownership of a cloth cloak that later witnesses said he did own. Other witnesses ascribed string found on the hatchet to a tassel on the cloak. A porter from Hoxie's store identified the hatchet as one used to open crates.

The defense produced differing testimony. Had the tassel been added to the hatchet and the cloak *after* the crime by brothel-mates determined to frame Robinson? Might the jurors consider jealousies among the "girls" as motives for the murder? One, Elizabeth Salters, testified that she had been intimate with Robinson for some weeks before Jewett moved into the house. Servant Sarah Dunscombe said she dusted a miniature portrait of Robinson in Jewett's room on Friday-the same miniature found in Robinson's room when he was arrested on Sunday.

A police witness described the impecunious Robinson's wallet as fat with bills of exchange (equivalent to today's bank checks) made out to his employer Hoxie—a tantalizing implication of embezzlement. Prosector Phoenix failed to pursue the subject.

Seeking evidence that clerk Robinson obtained the hatchet from the store on Saturday evening, Phoenix could not get proprietor Hoxie to say the accused had a store key. Next, Phoenix failed to link Robinson's handwriting to letters that could tie him to murderous threats. A defense objection to Phoenix's reading the letters aloud led to the prosecution's resting its case—leaving the jury to wonder whether the letters might have revealed a motive.

Now the defense introduced a surprise witness, Robert Furlong, owner of a small grocery store. He testified that on Saturday evening Robinson bought a bunch of cigars, smoked one while sitting on a barrel and reading a newspaper, checked his pocket watch when the store clock struck ten, and departed at 10:15 saying, "I believe I'll go home, I am tired." Cross-examined, Furlong provided details of the coat, not cloak, Robinson wore.

James Tew testified that Robinson was in bed at home before 2:00 A.M. Fellow boarder Rodman Moulton, while testifying that he had seen Robinson wearing a cloak with tassels, could not identify the cloak in evidence. The defense rested.

Jurors Knew Star Witness

During rebuttals, one juror, allowed (in the legal convention of the time) to question a witness, revealed that he and other jurors knew witness Furlong personally and held him in high regard. Judge Edwards permitted prosecutor

Phoenix to read a letter from Robinson to Jewett entreating her to break off their relationship and return the prized miniature of him, which witness Dunscombe had dusted in Jewett's room on April 8 and police had found in Robinson's quarters on April 10.

Following closing arguments that consumed ten and a half hours, the jury began deliberations at half-past midnight. Less than 15 minutes later, Robinson was acquitted. No one else was ever brought to trial.

Within a year, under the name Richard Parmalee, Robinson opened a saloon and billiard room in Nacogdoches, Texas. Using the business acuity learned in Hoxie's store, he built a trade in clothing and personal items. He bought a farm, married in 1845, and died of an unidentifiable fever in 1855 during an Ohio River steamboat trip.

—Bernard Ryan, Jr.

Suggestions for Further Reading

Cohen, Patricia Cline. *The Murder of Helen Jewett: The Life and Death of a Prostitute in Nineteenth-Century New York.* New York: Knopf, 1998.

Halttunen, Karen. *Murder Most Foul: The Killer and the American Gothic Imagination.* Cambridge, Mass.: Harvard University Press, 1998.

Isenberg, Nancy. *Sex and Citizenship in Antebellum America.* Chapel Hill: University of North Carolina Press, 1998.

Paul, Raymond. *The Thomas Street Horror: An Historical Novel of Murder.* New York: Viking, 1992.

Srebnick, Amy Gilman. *The Mysterious Death of Mary Rogers: Sex and Culture in Nineteenth-Century New York.* New York: Oxford University Press, 1997.

James Fenimore Cooper Libel Trials: 1839–45

Defendants: Andrew M. Barber, Park Benjamin, Theodore S. Gold, Horace Greeley, Thomas McElrath, Elius Pellet, William Leete Stone, James Watson Webb, Thurlow Weed **Plaintiff Claim:** Libel
Chief Defense Lawyers: Joshua Spencer (for Barber) Peter Clark (for Greeley); Willis Hall, R. G. Wheaton, L.S. Chatfield (for Weed); L.J. Walworth and Ambrose Jordan (for Webb); A. B. Conger, William H. Seward (for Greeley) **Chief Lawyer for Plaintiff:** Richard Cooper **Judges:** Philo Gridley, John Willard **Places:** Cooperstown, Utica, Fonda, Ballston, and Albany, New York **Dates of Trials:** Intermittently from February 1839 to December 1845. In addition to the actual trials, there were numerous pretrial hearings and appeals. **Decisions:** Of the 18 legal suits brought by Cooper, he won 11 of them and was awarded damages totaling $3,060. One resulted in a verdict of not guilty (for Webb); one suit was settled by arbitration (but in Cooper's favor); three suits were dropped when the editors printed retractions; one was reversed on appeal; and one was set aside by an appeals court.

SIGNIFICANCE

The Cooper libel trials and related legal proceedings both darkened his own final years and placed him in a bad light with the American public. Beyond that, the issues raised by the disposition of these cases influenced the move to redefine the libel law in New York State so that suits like Cooper's would have little success in the future.

When James Fenimore Cooper set sail with his family for Europe in 1826, he was at the height of his reputation with critics and of popularity with his readers. His novels such as *The Spy*, *The Pioneers*, and *The Last of the Mohicans* were also selling so well that he could afford to travel and reside in Europe for the next several years. During that time, however, he published certain works that seemed to Americans to be unfairly critical of his homeland, so that when he arrived back in New York in 1832 he was already becoming regarded as an anti-democratic, pseudo-aristocratic scold.

The First Trespassers

The next step toward confrontation was taken when Cooper decided to settle back in the upstate New York town founded by his father, Cooperstown. In taking over the estate of his recently deceased father, Cooper discovered that the townspeople had long been accustomed to making use of a small promontory on Lake Otsego that actually belonged to his family. On July 22, 1837, Cooper placed a formal notice in the local newspaper warning the public to cease trespassing on this land, known as Three Mile Point.

That very evening, the angry villagers held a meeting at which they drew up resolutions contesting Cooper's claims to ownership of Three Mile Point. They also voted to recommend that the trustees of the library remove "all books of which Cooper is the author." In August, several upstate New York newspapers chose to report these proceedings along with comments by the editors highly critical of Cooper's position. In September Cooper commenced libel suits against three of the editors—Andrew Barber, Theodore Gold, and Elius Pellet—but during the next year no action was taken.

James Fenimore Cooper. (Courtesy, National Portrait Gallery)

Instead, Cooper spent that year writing several new works including *Home As Found,* published in November 1838. In this novel, the leading character, Edward Effingham, appears to be a not-very-thinly disguised version of Cooper himself; in particular, one plot line deals with Effingham's disputes with his fellow villagers that exactly parallel Cooper's own. Several newspapers printed reviews that not only pilloried the novel but said some undeniably disparaging things about him. (One review printed extracts said to exhibit Cooper's "insane vanity and his foolish pretension to be high-born.")

The Legal Suits

At this point, Cooper launched what became one of the most bizarre if now forgotten series of legal battles in American literary history. He revived his earlier suits against the three editors who had commented on the Three Mile Point dispute; he started libel suits against the editors of newspapers that printed the disparaging reviews of *Home As Found;* he sued an editor for a negative review of another of his books, *History of the Navy of the United States;* he initiated still new suits when the editors reported or commented on the previous suits; and he then sued the editors when they reported on their own trials.

One by one, between February 1839 and December 1845, these suits came before grand juries, judges, trial juries, arbitrators, or appeals courts. Although on occasion Cooper spoke in court on his own behalf, he relied throughout the proceedings on his lawyer-nephew, Richard Cooper. The defendants hired their own lawyers. The trials were held in various upstate New York county courts; the appeals were held in Albany. All the juried trials were presided over by either Justice John Willard or Justice Philo Gridley, who from the outset would allow the defendants to enter little extenuating evidence. Rather, the judges consistently ruled that all the juries had to consider was whether they regarded the editors' articles as having gone beyond criticism of the author's works to become libels on Cooper the man.

Sideshows and Footnotes

In the course of the various trials and legal actions, there were all kinds of incidents that would seem absurd if they weren't so unsettling. One of the most extraordinary episodes involved the trials of James Watson Webb for his review of *Home As Found.* In the first trial, Justice Willard allowed the entire novel (along with its companion work, *Homeward Bound*) to be read aloud in the court—it took 11 hours—and it is reported that "Mr. Cooper absented himself from the courtroom during the reading." When that trial ended with a hung jury, Webb was brought to trial for a second time (again, a hung jury) and then a third time (this time found not guilty), but Justice Willard would not allow the novel to be read aloud at either of the latter two trials. The flavor of court trials in this era is conveyed in the following exchange:

> Mr. Jordan [Webb's lawyer]: Of course I have no other alternative than to submit and except to this ruling of your honor. I would now ask, with all due deference to the court, why it has now been decided differently from its decision in 1841. . . .
>
> Judge Willard [agitated and pale]: This argument must cease here. You have my decision, the Books are ruled out, and if unjustly, you have your remedy by going to the Supreme Court.
>
> Mr. Jordan: At great expense and trouble, which amounts to a denial of justice; but I bow to the mandate of the court. Of course I am at liberty to read to the Jury the extracts from [Home As Bound] and published in [Webb's newspaper] containing the review.
>
> Judge Willard: Certainly.

Twice certain editors proposed to start "defense funds" to which all interested parties would contribute to cover the expenses of those to be sued. (Nothing seems to have come of this.) To collect from one of his libelers, Andrew Barber, Cooper got a sheriff to go to Barber's home and force him to open a chest to come up with the money. When William Stone died before paying Cooper the full sum due, Cooper actually tried to get his widow to pay it. (Cooper seems to have eventually given up this pursuit.) Cooper continually wrote letters to newspaper after newspaper, always trying to argue the justice of his cause and the falsity of claims against him, but the more he wrote, the more obsessive and cranky he sounded. Supporters of Cooper, however, insisted that much of the motivation for the attacks was political, launched by Whig Party sympathizers opposed to Cooper and his Democratic Party allies (and some scholars have since supported this charge).

In any case, the various editors never ceased their attacks. Throughout the years, and even in the trials, they sarcastically referred to Cooper as "the handsome Mr. Effingham" or "the amiable Mr. Effingham." These epithets from the novel were intended both to ridicule Cooper's vanity and to enforce their claim that, since he had gone public with his own case against the people of Cooperstown, he had to expect attacks on himself. They also argued that many of Cooper's works in fact libeled his fellow Americans.

Early on, Horace Greeley, the noted editor of the *New York Tribune,* aligned himself and his paper on the side of the editors. After being sued for libel and losing, he wrote a mocking article in his paper that included an account of how Cooper had refused to accept the excuse of Thurlow Weed that he could not get to court because his wife and daughter were seriously ill. After a delay, Cooper demanded a judgment and was awarded damages of $400. Of Cooper's behavior, Greeley said that "however it may have sounded to others, it did seem to us rather inhu—Hallo there! We had like to put our foot right into it again. . . ." and then went on to say, "It seemed to us, considering the present relations of the parties, most ungen—There we go again!" But Greeley's attempts at humor were not appreciated by Cooper, who instantly sued him once more for libel, citing these two obvious uncompleted words. This case never came to trial.

Settling Up

With the final decision in December 1845 of a New York State Superior Court that Greeley could not be brought to trial for Greeley's words of innuendo, both sides backed off. Each side could claim victory of sorts. Cooper had won most of his suits, and the $3,060 in settlements was worth a great deal in an age when laborers earned about $500 a year. Cooper had returned to writing novels and regained some of his critical reputation, but he never fully recovered his status in the eyes of his fellow Americans. The editors, meanwhile, had gained a wide public for their opinions of Cooper and his works and had made him look at least quarrelsome. Perhaps the major impact of these suits was the influence they had on the developments of libel law in New York and to some extent in the country as a whole, by establishing the right of libel defendants to present evidence supporting their claims as to the truth of their statements.

—John S. Bowman

Suggestions for Further Reading

Adams, Charles H. *The Guardian of the Law": Authority and Identity in James Fenimore Cooper.* University Park: Penn State University Press, 1999.

Cooper, James Fenimore. *The Letters and Journals of James Fenimore Cooper.* Edited by James F. Beard.Volomes 3 and 4 (of 6 volumes). Cambridge, Mass.: Harvard University Press, 1960–68.

Outland, Ethel R. "The 'Effingham' Libels on Cooper: A Documentary History of the Libel Suits of James Fenimore Cooper . . ." *University of Wisconsin Studies in Language and Literature,* no. 28 (1929).

Waples, Dorothy. The Whig Myth of James Fenimore Cooper. New Haven, Conn.: Yale University Press, 1938.

U.S. v. Cinque: 1839

Defendants: Joseph Cinque and others **Crimes Charged:** Murder and piracy **Chief Defense Lawyers:** John Quincy Adams, Roger S. Baldwin, Joshua Leavitt, and Seth Staples **Chief Prosecutor:** William S. Holabird **Judges:** Andrew T. Judson and Smith Thompson **Place:** New Haven, Connecticut **Dates of Trial:** November 19, 1839–January 13, 1840 **Verdict:** Not guilty

SIGNIFICANCE

When the courts refused to convict slaves from the schooner *Amistad* after they killed their captors to free themselves, the decision was widely hailed as a victory for the cause of abolition.

By the 1830s, many countries were beginning to take steps to limit the age-old institution of slavery. Although slavery was still legal in the United States, it was illegal to bring new slaves into the country. Further, the abolitionist movement, which sought to do away with slavery altogether, was gaining more and more support. Great Britain was strongly in favor of abolition, and had used its naval power to pressure Spain, whose colonies were dominated by slave owners, to also make it illegal to bring new slaves into any Spanish possessions.

Spanish power in the New World was declining, however, and the government in Madrid lacked the power to enforce its will. The wealthy landowners in Cuba and elsewhere throughout the Spanish New World needed slaves to work their estates, and obeying the import restriction meant waiting for the children of existing slaves to mature. With slave owner demand strong and central authority weak, a flourishing illegal slave trade soon emerged. Slavers went to the west coast of Africa, captured healthy young black men and women, and brought them back to Cuba for sale. The colonial authorities did nothing to stop this trade. In 1839, slavers brought back a cargo of slaves from what is now Sierra Leone. Among the slaves was a young man they named Joseph Cinque.

In June of 1839, Jose Ruiz and Pedro Montes purchased 49 captured Africans, including Cinque, in Havana for their estates in the Cuban town of Puerto Principe. Ruiz and Montes put the slaves aboard the schooner *Amistad,* intending to sail from Havana up the Cuban coast to Puerto Principe. The Spanish crew taunted the ignorant slaves, telling them wild stories, such as that their new owners intended to kill and eat them when they arrived. On the night of July 1, Cinque led the blacks in a successful rebellion and seized control of the ship. The blacks killed several members of the crew in the struggle, but let Ruiz and Montes live. Cinque ordered Ruiz and Montes to take the ship to Sierra Leone so the blacks could go home.

The Spaniards sailed east for Africa by day, but secretly reversed course by night. For nearly two months, the *Amistad* meandered back and forth, but eventually winds and currents drove it north to the coast of the United States. On August 26, the U.S.S. *Washington* spotted the *Amistad* off the coast of New York, seized the ship, and brought it into New London, Connecticut.

It was ruled that Joseph Cinque, leader of the *Amistad* rebellion, and his comrades "were born free, and . . . of right are free and not slaves." (Courtesy, Library of Congress)

Cinque Goes on Trial

In New London, Ruiz and Montes described the slave rebellion to the American authorities, and pressed their claim for the return of the *Amistad* with its cargo of slaves. Despite the slaves' illegal capture, the Spanish government backed Ruiz's and Montes' claim. With the blessing of President Martin Van Buren's administration, District Attorney William S. Holabird charged Cinque and the other blacks with committing murder and piracy aboard the *Amistad.*

The trial was held in the U.S. District Court for Connecticut. The judge was District Court Judge Andrew T. Judson, assisted by Associate Supreme Court Justice Smith Thompson. The abolitionists hired a team of defense lawyers to represent the blacks, comprised of Roger S. Baldwin, Joshua Leavitt, Seth Staples, and an ex-president of the United States, John Quincy Adams.

The trial began November 19, 1839. The defense lawyers asserted that the blacks had the right to free themselves from the horrible conditions of slavery. In support of their position, they introduced Dr. Richard R. Madden, who had traveled extensively in Cuba and was an expert on slave conditions:

> [S]o terrible were these atrocities, so murderous the system of slavery, so transcendent the evils I witnessed, over all I have ever heard or seen of the rigour of slavery elsewhere, that at first I could hardly believe the evidence of my senses.

Further, as the testimony of Madden and various witnesses made clear, returning Cinque and the others to Cuba meant certain death at the hands of the pro-slavery colonial authorities. In addition, since the blacks had originally been captured in Africa in violation of Spanish law, the abolitionists argued that the blacks were not legally slaves and therefore were not "property" belonging to Ruiz and Montes.

Despite pressure from the Van Buren administration, which wanted to avoid diplomatic tension with Spain, on January 13, 1840, Judge Judson ruled in favor of the blacks. Although the *Amistad* with its goods would be returned to Ruiz and Montes, subject to salvage costs, Cinque and the others:

> were born free, and ever since have been and still of right are free and not slaves.

Further, because they had been illegally enslaved, the blacks were innocent of murder and piracy since they had only acted to free themselves.

The prosecution appealed Judson's decision to the Supreme Court. The abolitionists had anticipated this move, since five Supreme Court justices, including Chief Justice Roger B. Taney, were Southerners and had owned slaves. The defense relied on John Quincy Adams to present its case, banking on his prestige as much as on his legal ability. On February 22, 1840, the Supreme Court heard both sides' arguments, and on March 9 issued its opinion. The Court upheld Judson's decision, and so the blacks were finally free. Cinque and the other blacks were returned to Africa.

Technically, the *Amistad* decision did not condemn slavery, it only held that blacks not legally slaves were also not property. Still, the courts could have just as easily turned the blacks over to Spanish authorities or returned them to Cuba if they wished. The case was seen as a victory for the abolitionist cause, and was a milestone in the movement's quest for the total elimination of slavery.

In the late 1990s, the story of the *Amistad* returned to the public's attention. Several new books were published recounting the trial of Cinque, and a film directed by Steven Spielberg was released in 1997.

—*Stephen G. Christianson*

Suggestions for Further Reading

Adams, John Quincy. *Argument in the Case of U.S. v. Cinque.* New York: Arno Press, 1969.

Cable, Mary. *Black Odyssey: the Case of the Slave Ship Amistad.* New York: Penguin Books, 1977.

"Cinque." *Jet* (March 1984): 21.

Jones, Howard. *Mutiny on the Amistad: The Saga of a Slave Revolt and its Impact on American Abolition, Law, and Diplomacy.* New York: Oxford University Press, 1987.

Owens, William A. *Slave Mutiny: the Revolt on the Schooner Amistad.* New York: J. Day Co., 1953.

Pate, Alexis D., David Franzoni, and Steven Zaillian. *Amistad: A Novel.* New York: Signet, 1997.

Pesci, David. *Amistad: The Thunder of Freedom.* New York: Marlow & Co., 1997.

John Colt Trial: 1842

Defendant: John C. Colt **Crime Charged:** Murder
Chief Defense Lawyers: Dudley Selden, John Morrill, Robert Emmett
Chief Prosecutor: James Whiting **Judge:** William Kent **Place:** New York, New York **Date of Trial:** January 19–31, 1842 **Verdict:** Guilty
Sentence: Death by hanging

SIGNIFICANCE

The murder trial of John Colt, brother of repeating arms inventor Samuel Colt, began as a missing persons case and culminated with one of nineteenth century New York's most sensational suicides.

On September 17, 1841, printer Samuel Adams went to collect a debt from John Colt, a bookkeeping teacher for whom Adams had manufactured textbooks. The printer was never seen alive again. Adams had been missing for a week when his body was found in the hold of a ship about to leave New York. His decomposing corpse had been jammed into a packing crate addressed to St. Louis via New Orleans. Colt, who denied paying a man to deliver the box to the ship, was charged with murder. For over a year, Colt's case would captivate New York with increasingly astonishing turns.

The Colt Family's Black Sheep

Colt's past was distinguished by a reputation for gambling, forgery, burglary, and notorious romantic affairs, but he was well-connected socially. His brother Samuel was the inventor of the revolving rifle and pistol, while another brother, James, was a St. Louis attorney. The Colt family's connections allowed them to hire expert lawyers. From the moment he was arrested during the search for Adams' body, however, Colt's case became a scandal. Investigators found that he was living with a pregnant woman posing as his wife, Caroline Henshaw. They also found Adams' pocketwatch hidden at Colt's home.

Colt's trial began on January 19, 1842. The prosecution's first witness was Asa Wheeler, a bookkeeping teacher whose room was next door to Colt's office. On the afternoon of September 17, Wheeler and one of his students heard a loud noise, followed by what sounded like the rattle of fencing foils and a body falling on the floor. Wheeler went next door to investigate and peered through the keyhole. He saw a man stooped over something, but the man faced away from the door. Wheeler went to find the landlord, but returned alone. By then, Colt's keyhole cover was closed and no one answered knocks upon the door. Wheeler opened Colt's door the following morning with a borrowed key and peered inside. He noted that the floor was freshly scrubbed, a large box was now missing, and there were splashes of fresh ink and oil on the walls. When Colt arrived at the building later, Wheeler asked about the noise. At first Colt denied being in the building at all, but then told Wheeler that he had upset his writing table and ink bottles.

The building's janitor recalled seeing Colt wiggle a large crate down the stairs. A cartman testified that Colt paid him to take the same box to the packet *Kalamazoo.* Witnesses who found Adams' body in the *Kalamazoo's* hold recalled opening the crate and freeing a stench so horrific that most onlookers fled to the upper decks. The box and canvas in which the body was packed were brought into court, flooding the room with a smell lessened little by the four months since the murder. Other physical evidence included Adams' watch and a small hatchet, which Colt's indictment cited as the murder weapon.

Confusion Over Murder Weapons

Halfway through the trial, the prosecution introduced a new theory that Adams might have been killed by a Colt revolver. Colt's lawyers anticipated the move and objected immediately. Defense attorney Dudley Selden read the entire indictment, which stated that Adams was killed by blows from the confiscated hatchet. If the prosecution wished to establish that firearms killed Adams, Selden argued, then prosecutor James Whiting's indictment of Colt was improperly drawn, allowing the defense no preparation for refuting the new theory. Whiting replied furiously that he had only learned over the weekend that a pistol like the one invented by Colt's brother might be the murder weapon.

Over Selden's objections, Judge William Kent allowed the prosecution to propose that the slight clashing noise described by Asa Wheeler and his student might have been made by a revolver bullet propelled by a percussion cap. The defense responded by demonstrating how feeble a bullet without a noisy charge of gunpowder would be. Gun inventor Samuel Colt was called to demonstrate one of his pistols to the jury. Colt fired the chambers of a revolver primed only with caps and caught all five bullets in his hand. When Colt emptied the weapon again at a law book, the balls only penetrated the first nine leaves, about the same number marred when Selden asked Colt to throw the bullets at the tome.

The prosecution returned to its original theory, providing more theatrics. Adams' body was disinterred and his severed skull was displayed in court, so that doctors could declare that the hole in its side had been made by a hatchet, not a bullet or packing nail. The next day's tumult was provided by the appearance of Caroline Henshaw. The young woman recalled Colt coming home with black bruises on his neck on the fateful night. Henshaw characterized Colt as a mild-mannered man. Numerous witnesses echoed her depiction of Colt as even-tempered, in contrast to others who recalled Adams as being irritable whenever money was involved.

A Strange "Confession"

The final courtroom commotion began when defense attorney Robert Emmett read aloud a long, detailed statement written by Colt. According to this "confession," Adams had come to Colt's office, where a dispute erupted over a bill. The two men came to blows when Adams called Colt a liar. When Adams began choking him, Colt grabbed what he thought was a hammer and hit Adams on the head. The implement turned out to be the hatchet, which inflicted a fatal wound. After cleaning up a substantial amount of blood, Colt tried to clear his mind with a walk in a nearby park. To avoid the disgrace of a public trial, he packed the corpse, disposed of his bloody clothing in a privy, and went home.

Emmett argued that the marks on Colt's neck confirmed that Adams had tried to strangle Colt. If so, this was a case of justifiable homicide, not a planned murder. Emmett added that the efficiency with which Colt had disposed of the body should not be held against him as evidence of premeditation. Prosecutors accused Colt of killing Adams in the office for the isolation it provided and questioned why an innocent man would deliberate for hours over how to dispose of a dead body. Prosecutor Whiting testily defended his handling of the indictment, denying defense implications that he was pressing the case for political gain.

In his charge, Judge Kent told the jury that both victim and prisoner were men of good character, although "excitable." The judge asked the jury to weigh evidence of a motive or premeditation. The "confession" read by Robert Emmett was hypothetical and not evidence, instructed the judge. As such, it was irrelevant to final deliberations. On January 31, thousands of people waiting outside the courthouse learned the verdict was guilty. When the New York State Supreme Court denied Colt's final appeal on September 28, Judge Kent sentenced him to hang.

At noon on November 18, 1842, the day of his scheduled execution, Colt and Caroline Henshaw were married in his cell, surrounded by Samuel Colt and a few friends. Jailers returned at 3:55 to take the condemned man to the scaffold. They found Colt's bloody corpse on his bed. One of his final visitors had apparently slipped him a pocketknife, with which he had stabbed himself in the heart. A fire broke out in the jail at the same moment the body was found. The suspicious flames fueled abundant rumors that Colt's prominent friends had been plotting his escape.

Colt's suicide was not the final chapter in the case. Many observers surmised that Caroline Henshaw had been Samuel Colt's mistress and that the son she bore was Samuel's, not John's, child. The irony that John Colt had taken in his brother's spurned pregnant mistress as an act of kindness was yet one more indication to Colt's supporters that Adams' death had been a tragic accident for which a flawed but basically good man had been condemned.

—*Tom Smith*

Suggestions for Further Reading

"Colt Case." *New York Herald* (January 28, 1842): 1.

Grant, Ellsworth J. *The Colt Legacy.* Providence, R.I.: Mowbray Company, 1982.

Tucher, Andie. *Froth & Scum.* Chapel Hill: University of North Carolina Press, 1994.

Alexander Holmes Trial: 1842

Defendant: Alexander William Holmes **Crime Charged:** Manslaughter
Chief Defense Lawyer: David Paul Brown **Chief Prosecutor:** William M. Meredith **Judge:** Baldwin (historical records do not indicate his first name)
Place: Philadelphia, Pennsylvania **Dates of Trial:** April 13–23, 1842
Verdict: Guilty **Sentence:** 6 months in prison and a $20 fine

SIGNIFICANCE

In the Alexander Holmes trial, the court held that self-preservation was not always a defense to homicide.

On March 13, 1841, an American ship, the *William Brown*, left Liverpool, England for Philadelphia, Pennsylvania. In addition to her cargo, she carried 17 crewmen and 65 passengers, who were mostly Scots and Irish emigrants. On the night of April 19, 250 miles from Newfoundland, the *William Brown* struck an iceberg and began to sink rapidly. There were two lifeboats, one small and one large. The captain and most of the crew took the small lifeboat, and the passengers crowded aboard the large lifeboat. There was not enough space on the large lifeboat for all the passengers, and 31 died on board the *William Brown* when it sank.

First Mate Francis Rhodes, Alexander William Holmes, and another seaman commanded the large lifeboat. The passengers were still dressed in their night clothes and suffered terribly in the cold Atlantic weather, which was made worse by a pelting rain. The two lifeboats stayed together through the night but separated the morning of the 20th because the captain, George L. Harris, thought there was a better chance of rescue if the two boats took different directions. Rhodes said that his boat was overcrowded and that some people would have to be thrown overboard to keep it from capsizing. Captain Harris said, "I know what you'll have to do. Don't speak of that now. Let it be the last resort." Throughout the day of the 20th and into the night, the rain and the waves worsened. The boat began to leak and fill with water, despite constant bailing. Around ten o'clock that night, Rhodes cried out in despair, "This work won't do. Help me, God. Men, go to work." Holmes and the other seaman began throwing people overboard. They threw 14 men and two women into the freezing water. They chose single men only, spared the married men on board, and threw the two women overboard only because they were sisters of a man already thus ejected and had demanded to be sacrificed with their kin. None of the crew was thrown out.

Holmes Tried for Manslaughter

The next day, on the morning of the 21st, Holmes' lifeboat was spotted by a ship and rescued. Captain Harris' lifeboat was rescued by another ship six days later. Upon reaching Philadelphia, the news of the fate of the *William Brown* was an instant sensation, generating a great deal of public outrage against the crew. U.S. District Attorney William M. Meredith charged Holmes and Rhodes with manslaughter, which is a lesser degree of homicide than murder because it means killing without malice. Rhodes fled the city, never to be found, so Holmes was tried alone.

Holmes' chief defense lawyer was David Paul Brown, and the trial began on April 13, 1842. One of Meredith's assistants, Mr. Dallas (historical records do not indicate his first name) opened for the prosecution:

> [Holmes'] defense is that the homicide was necessary to self-preservation. First, then, we ask: was the homicide thus necessary? That is to say, was the danger instant, overwhelming, leaving no choice or means, no moment for deliberation? For, unless the danger were of this sort, the prisoner, under any admission, had no right, without notice or consultation, or lot, to sacrifice the lives of 16 fellow beings.

Holmes' defense lawyers countered that, in the dangerous circumstances Holmes was placed in, he was not required to wait until the last second to act in self-preservation:

> In other words, he need not wait until the certainty of the danger has been proved, past doubt, by its result. Yet this is the doctrine of the prosecution. They ask us to wait until the boat has sunk. . . . They tell us to wait until all are drowned.

After the prosecution and the defense had rested, Judge Baldwin (historical records do not indicate his first name) gave his instructions to the jury. Although he recognized the principle that self-preservation was a defense to homicide, he stated that there were some important exceptions. One of these exceptions was when someone had accepted a duty to others that implied that he or she would put his or her life at risk before risking the lives of the others. Judge Baldwin held that seamen like Holmes had accepted such a duty, and that therefore self-preservation was not an adequate defense to the charge of manslaughter:

> [W]e must look, not only to the jeopardy in which the parties are, but also to the relations in which they stand. The slayer must be under no obligation to make his own safety secondary to the safety of others. . . . Such . . . is the relation which exists on shipboard. The passenger stands in a position different from that of the officers and seamen. . . . The sailor . . . is bound to set a greater value on the life of others than on his own.

After 16 hours of deliberation, the jury found Holmes guilty on April 23, 1842. As the official court report notes, the verdict was given "with some difficulty," and was accompanied by the jury's recommendation for mercy. Judge Baldwin sentenced Holmes to six months in prison and a $20 fine. There was some public sympathy for Holmes, but a movement by the Seamen's Friend Society for a presidential pardon came to nothing.

The Alexander Holmes trial dictated that seamen have a duty to their passengers that is superior even to their own lives. Further, it held that the ancient defense of self-preservation was not always adequate in a homicide prosecution if the accused was under a special obligation to the deceased.

—Stephen G. Christianson

Suggestions for Further Reading

Duke, Thomas Samuel. *Celebrated Criminal Cases of America*. San Francisco: James H. Barry Co., 1910.

Hicks, Frederick Charles. *Human Jettison: a Sea Tale From the Law*. St. Paul, Minn.: West Publishing Co., 1927.

Mackenzie Court-Martial: 1843

Defendant: Commander Alexander Slidell Mackenzie **Crimes Charged:** 5 criminal offenses, including murder, for having executed 3 seamen suspected of mutiny **Chief Defense Lawyer:** None **Chief Prosecutor:** Judge Advocate William H. Norris **Judges:** Captains William C. Bolton, John Downes, John Gwinn, Isaac McKeever, Benjamin Page, George C. Read, John D. Sloat, Joseph Smith, George W. Storer, Daniel Turner, and Thomas W. Wyman, and Commanders Henry W. Ogden and Irvine Shubrick **Place:** New York, New York **Dates of Trial:** January 28–March 31, 1843 **Verdict:** Not guilty

SIGNIFICANCE

The alleged mutiny aboard Commander Alexander Slidell Mackenzie's ship, the U.S.S. *Somers,* was the first such incident in the history of the U.S. Navy. It was also the inspiration behind Herman Melville's novel *Billy Budd.*

On December 14, 1842, a warship of the U.S. Navy, the brig U.S.S. *Somers*, came into New York City harbor after a voyage to the African coast. The captain, Commander Alexander Slidell Mackenzie, reported to the astonished naval authorities that the vessel contained the bodies of three men hung for mutiny, the first such instance in American naval history.

The dead men were Samuel Cromwell, Elisha Small, and Philip Spencer. According to Mackenzie, they had been the ringleaders behind a plot to mutiny, murder Mackenzie and take the ship for themselves. Then, they would use the ship for piracy, preying on Atlantic shipping. Supposedly, two-thirds of the crew were prepared to join the mutiny, so Mackenzie was forced to act quickly by eliminating the leaders. Cromwell and Small were common sailors, but Spencer was the son of John C. Spencer, the powerful secretary of war for President John Tyler.

Mackenzie requested a court-martial to clear his name. It is probable that Secretary Spencer would have demanded a court-martial anyway: In addition to losing his son, he wanted to investigate America's first naval mutiny. The prosecutor, Judge Advocate William H. Norris, charged Mackenzie with five criminal offenses, the most significant of which was murdering the three seamen. Mackenzie had no lawyer; he represented himself. The judges were

Captains William C. Bolton, John Downes, John Gwinn, Isaac McKeever, Benjamin Page, George C. Read, John D. Sloat, Joseph Smith, George W. Storer, Daniel Turner, and Thomas W. Wyman, and Commanders Henry W. Ogden and Irvine Shubrick.

The trial began January 28, 1843. Under Norris' questioning, Mackenzie steadfastly maintained that imminent mutiny among the ship's crew made it imperative that he execute the three ringleaders. Apparently Mackenzie made this decision when quite a few disloyal sailors were discovered and a shipboard investigation was begun:

The USS *Somers* with the bodies of three alleged mutineers hanging from the yardarm. (Courtesy, Rear Admiral Elliot Snow, USN, U.S. Naval Historical Center)

> Question: When did you first suppose it would be necessary to execute Mr. Spencer, Cromwell, and Small, for the safety of the vessel, officers, and crew?
>
> Answer: When we made more prisoners [from the crew] than we had the force to take care of, and I was more fully convinced after the examination in the wardroom before the council of officers.

Norris introduced other personnel from the *Somers* as witnesses, but their testimony failed to contradict Mackenzie's tale. On March 31, the judges pronounced Mackenzie innocent:

> The court . . . do acquit Commander Alexander Slidell Mackenzie of the charges and specifications preferred by the secretary of the navy against him.

There is no direct evidence that Secretary Spencer had attempted to influence the proceedings. Still, the judges must certainly have been aware of Spencer's reputation as a vindictive man, and of his unsuccessful effort to bring Mackenzie to trial in the civil courts as well. The court's verdict had been made without the customary statement of confidence in the accused's innocence, probably to placate Spencer:

> As these charges involved the life of the accused, and as the finding is in his favor, he is entitled to the benefit of it, as in the analogous case of a verdict before a civil court; and there is no power which can constitutionally deprive him of that benefit. The finding, therefore, is simply confirmed and carried into effect, without any expression of approbation.

Mackenzie labored under the left-handed acquittal until he died in 1848. Meanwhile, the story of America's first naval mutiny had captured national attention in the press, and was the inspiration for Herman Melville's novel about struggle and life at sea, *Billy Budd.*

It also led to more concern within the U.S. Navy for the proper training and military discipline of American seamen, concerns vital to the emergence of the United States as a naval power in future years. For example, the *Somers* incident was the primary reason for the founding of the United States Naval Academy at Annapolis, Maryland in 1845.

—*Stephen G. Christianson*

Suggestions for Further Reading

Hayford, Harrison. *The Somers Mutiny Affair.* Englewood Cliffs, N.J.: Prentice Hall, 1959.

McFarland, Philip James. *Sea Dangers: the Affair of the Somers.* New York: Schocken Books, 1985.

Melville, Herman. *Billy Budd.* New York: F. Watts, 1968.

Van de Water, Frederic F. *The Captain Called it Mutiny.* New York: Washburn, 1954.

Thomas Wilson Dorr Trial: 1844

Defendant: Thomas Wilson Dorr **Crime Charged:** Treason
Chief Defense Lawyers: Thomas W. Dorr, representing himself, assisted by Samuel Y. Atwell, George Turner, Walter S. Burges
Chief Prosecutors: Joseph W. Blake, Alfred Bosworth **Judges:** Job Durfee, Levi Haile, William R. Staples, and George A. Brayton **Place:** Newport, Rhode Island **Date of Trial:** April 26–May 7, 1844 **Verdict:** Guilty
Sentence: Life imprisonment "at hard labor in separate confinement"

SIGNIFICANCE

Today, the right to vote is often taken for granted. Indeed, less than 50 percent of all voters cast their ballots in a typical election. However, in 1842, a local civil war almost broke out in Rhode Island over the issue of who would have access to the ballot and one man was sent to prison for it.

After the American Revolution, not everyone was allowed to vote. Women and ethnic minorities were denied the ballot, but so were men who had no property or wealth. In some states, for example, a person had to pay a poll tax before he could vote. In others, only those who owned large amounts of land were allowed to participate in the electoral process.

By 1840, many of these restrictions had been abolished in the United States, but not in Rhode Island. There, the charter granted in 1663 by England's King Charles II was still serving as the state constitution, and it gave only landowners and their eldest sons the right to vote. As a result, more than half of the adult males in the state were denied voting privileges.

Reformers Draft a "People's Constitution"

In October 1841, a convention led by a 35-year-old lawyer and former state legislator, Thomas Dorr, drafted a "People's Constitution" that guaranteed free suffrage to all adult white males. Two months later, the document was overwhelmingly approved in a referendum that was held in defiance of the state government; even the majority of those who were already entitled to vote backed it. In the meantime, the state authorities and their supporters drafted another constitution that extended the franchise but still did not give the vote to every adult white male. This second constitution was defeated in March 1842, when it was presented in a referendum limited to those who could vote under the 1663 charter.

In April 1842, both the state government and the supporters of the People's Constitution conducted their own elections for governor, the state legislature, and a variety of other offices. In addition, the charter government passed a statute declaring the reformers' election to be illegal. Known as the "Algerine Law," the ordinance also made it a crime to run for office in the reformers' election and made it treason against the state of Rhode Island, punishable by life imprisonment, for anyone to assume a statewide office under the People's Constitution. All trials arising under the Algerine Law were to come before the state's highest court, the Supreme Judicial Council, whose members had already declared themselves in favor of the old government. Finally, although a jury trial was provided for, the alleged crimes could be tried anywhere in the state, thereby assuring that the state government could prosecute the defendants wherever juries could be found that were likely to convict.

On April 18, 1842, the supporters of the People's Constitution elected Dorr as governor. Two days later, the backers of the charter government reelected Governor Samuel King. In early May, both governors, as well as rival state legislatures and other officials, were sworn in. There were now two governments in Rhode Island, with the reformers in control of the northern part of the state.

Reformers Attempt to Seize State Arsenal

Both Dorr and King appealed to President John Tyler for help. Tyler urged reconciliation, but he later indicated that federal troops would intervene, if necessary, to support the charter government. In the meantime, arrests began under the Algerine Law. To revive the seemingly waning fortunes of the reformers and to assert his authority as governor, Dorr led over 200 men on May 18 in an attempt to seize the state arsenal in Providence.

The attack failed and, within a short time, martial law was declared by Governor King, the state militia was called out, and more arrests were made. (The arrests would continue until July.) The reformers' government quickly collapsed and Dorr fled the state with a bounty on his head. On August 25, 1842, Dorr was indicted in absentia in state court for treason against Rhode Island.

Despite Dorr's exile and the brutal treatment by the police of those accused of breaking the Algerine Law, there was still a lot of sympathy in Rhode Island for the reformers' cause. To placate this dissent, the charter government adopted in April 1843, a new constitution that granted the right to vote to all American-born adult males (including free blacks) who did not own land provided, they had been residents of the state for at least two years. This was good enough for most reformers, but not for Dorr (who was still a wanted man). Believing that his trial and conviction would be appealed to the U.S. Supreme Court and, in the process, gain national support to his cause, Dorr returned to Rhode Island on October 31, 1843, and was immediately arrested.

Dorr's Treason Trial

Dorr sat in the Providence, Rhode Island, city jail for five months before he was arraigned. On March 5, 1844, he pled "not guilty" and trial was set for April 26. Bail denied, Dorr remained in jail during the interim.

The trial was held before the judges of the Rhode Island Supreme Court (the former Supreme Judicial Council) at the courthouse in Newport, the center of pro-charter support where the prosecution had no trouble finding a jury that was sure to convict.

Assisted by three attorneys, Dorr represented himself and primarily relied on two lines of defense. First, he argued that since treason is defined by the U.S. Constitution, it is a crime that can only be committed against the United States and not against any individual state. Therefore, he could not be charged with treason against Rhode Island. Dorr also argued that, during the 1842 crisis, he was the legitimate governor of the state and the Algerine Law was invalid. After all, before the statute was adopted by the charter government, the People's Constitution had been overwhelmingly approved by the voters. Furthermore, pursuant to that constitution, Dorr had been elected governor and, after his inauguration, the reformers' government had repealed the law.

As anticipated, the court rejected these arguments and did not allow them to be presented to the jury. First, according to the judges, "wherever allegiance is due, there treason may be committed. Allegiance is due to a State, and [therefore] treason may be committed against a State of this Union." Second, only the state legislature that was elected in 1843, and not any judge or jury, had the power to decide which government or constitution was legitimate in 1842. All that the jury could do was to consider the facts of the case (of which Dorr made no attempt to deny) and accept the court's interpretation of the law.

The jury retired at 11 P.M. on Monday, May 6, 1844, to consider their decision. After waiting for the crowd to disperse, it returned a verdict of "guilty" three hours later. Motions were made for a new trial, but they were denied. On June 20, 1844, Dorr was sentenced to be imprisoned "for the term of his natural life, and there kept at hard labor in separate confinement." He was taken to the state prison in Providence two days later.

For one year, the sentence of solitary confinement was strictly enforced. Dorr was forbidden to speak or write to anyone outside the prison except for his lawyer; even his parents were denied access to him. His requests to take daily strolls in the prison's corridors and to have books to read were refused. Dorr's health deteriorated while in the damp, poorly ventilated prison. Still, Dorr was determined to fight on and when the state legislature offered an amnesty provided he swore allegiance to the 1843 constitution, Dorr refused.

Dorr Gains Sympathy

Sympathy for Dorr grew and his imprisonment became the key issue in the gubernatorial election of 1845. The "liberationists" won both the governorship and a majority in the state legislature that year and, on June 27, 1845, a law was passed unconditionally discharging Dorr from prison. This was not a pardon, however, and Dorr's civil and political rights were not restored until his uncle, Philip Allen, became governor in 1851.

During his imprisonment, Dorr worked on his appeal to the U.S. Supreme Court, but he was released before the case reached the court's docket. The matter was continually postponed until Dorr withdrew the appeal in 1849.

After his release, Dorr continued his interest in politics and served as an advisor to his uncle. However, Dorr's health further declined and, by 1854, his imminent death was obvious to everyone. That year, the state legislature passed a bill that annulled Dorr's conviction, but his opponents promptly went to the state supreme court and obtained a ruling that the legislation was unconstitutional. Dorr died a few months later on December 27, 1854, unrepentant to the end.

—*Mark Thorburn*

Suggestions for Further Reading

Dennison, George M. *The Dorr War: Republicanism on Trial, 1831–1861.* Lexington, Ky.: The University Press of Kentucky, 1976.

Gettleman, Marvin E. *The Dorr Rebellion: A Study in American Radicalism, 1833–1849.* New York, N.Y.: Random House, 1973.

Mowry, Arthur May. *The Dorr War.* Providence, R.I.: Preston and Rounds Company, 1901. Reprint: New York, N.Y.: Johnson Reprint Corporation, 1968.

U.S. Congress. House. "Interference of the Executive in Affairs of Rhode Island" (commonly referred to as "Burke's Report"). Report No. 546, 28 Cong., 1 sess., 1844.

Albert Tirrell Trial: 1846

Defendant: Albert J. Tirrell **Crime Charged:** Murder
Chief Defense Lawyer: Rufus Choate **Chief Prosecutor:** Samuel D. Parker
Judges: Dewey, Hubbard, and Wilde (No record of first names)
Place: Boston, Massachusetts **Dates of Trial:** March 26–30, 1846
Verdict: Not guilty

SIGNIFICANCE
Albert Tirrell's trial was the first time in American history that sleepwalking was successfully used as a defense to a murder prosecution.

Not much is known about Albert Tirrell's life prior to his sensational murder trial. He came from a moderately prosperous family and had a wife and two children in Weymouth, Massachusetts. Tirrell had a reputation for wild and reckless behavior; he left his family in 1845 for a young prostitute named Maria Ann Bickford.

Bickford was very beautiful and lived in a Boston brothel, where she catered only to the richest customers. Tirrell had met her and fallen in love. He moved to Boston to be near her, and apparently she returned his affections but did not give up her profession. Bickford's patrons enabled her to live well; she had a maid and an expensive wardrobe.

The details are sketchy, but apparently on October 27, 1845, Tirrell came into Bickford's bedroom after she had spent an evening with a customer. Tirrell cut her throat from ear to ear with a razor and set three fires in the brothel before leaving. Brothel owner Joel Lawrence lived in the building and woke up in time to put out the fires. He discovered Bickford's body and alerted the police. Several people had seen Tirrell enter and leave the brothel, and the police began a search for him.

Tirrell fled Boston in the early hours of October 28. He took a carriage back to Weymouth, then went on to New York and finally New Orleans, Louisiana. The authorities caught up with Tirrell December 6, arrested him, and returned him to Boston for trial.

Rufus Choate Defends Tirrell

The state prosecutor was Samuel D. Parker and the judges assigned to oversee the trial were Justices Dewey, Hubbard, and Wilde (no record survives of the judges' first names). Tirrell's parents hired a famous lawyer, Rufus Choate, to defend him. Choate had a reputation for successfully using unusual legal defenses to acquit his clients. Tirrell's trial opened March 26, 1846.

Although Parker had plenty of witnesses as to Tirrell's affair with Bickford and his presence in the brothel on the night of Bickford's murder, no one had actually seen Tirrell kill her. No matter how overwhelming, the evidence was circumstantial. Choate argued to the jury that Tirrell had no motive to kill the woman he loved:

> [Tirrell] was fascinated by the wiles of the unhappy female whose death was so awful; he loved her with the love of forty thousand brothers, though alas, it was not as pure as it was passionate.

Choate laid two possible alternatives before the jury. First, Bickford could have committed suicide:

> What proof is there that she did not rise from her bed, set fire to the house, and in the frenzy of the moment, with giant strength, let out the stream of life. . . . Suicide is the natural death of the prostitute.

This was not a strong argument, however, for Choate knew that it was very hard to imagine Bickford cutting her own throat so savagely that her head was nearly severed from her body. Therefore, Choate relied more on his second alternative, namely that Tirrell was a habitual sleepwalker and thus must have murdered Bickford while in an unconscious trance or under the influence of a nightmare. In the 1840s, doctors could only guess at the causes of sleepwalking, and they differed over whether it was caused by disease, mental disorders, or insanity. Whatever the cause, however, Tirrell's sleepwalking gave Choate a means to influence the jury. Choate read descriptions of violence attributed to sleepwalking from popular treatises:

> This I mention as a proof that nothing hinders us, even from being assassins of others or murderers of ourselves, amid the mad follies of sleep, only the protecting care of our Heavenly Father!

Having thus introduced some doubt to the jury as to the prosecutions case against Tirrell, Choate cleverly reminded them that their guilty verdict meant certain execution for Tirrell. If Tirrell was executed while there was even the remotest chance that the crime had been committed by someone else, the jurors would be responsible:

> Every juror when he puts into the urn the verdict of Guilty, writes upon it also, "Let him die!" . . . Under the iron law of Rome, it was the custom to bestow a civic wreath upon him who should save the life of a citizen. Do your duty this day, gentlemen, and you too may deserve the civic crown.

Choates oratory was impressive, but it was far from certain that he would win. Not only had the Boston papers turned Bickford's murder into a popular sensation with the public being firmly convinced of Tirrell's guilt, but Choate had been criticized before for actions on behalf of clients that bordered on the unethical. Choate himself had admitted that the murder was particularly horrible—"murder and arson committed in a low brothel." While there was widespread respect for Choate's legal ability, there were also critics who said:

> [T]he lightnings of his genius were brandished with little regard to consequences, and that it was comparatively a matter of indifference to the great actor of the scene whether they purified the moral atmosphere by vindicating the cause of truth and justice, or struck down the fair fabrics of public virtue and public integrity.

The Jury Acquits Tirrell

On March 30, 1846, the jury announced its verdict after less than two hours of deliberation. The jurors pronounced Albert Tirrell innocent. Despite the questions about his conduct and the evidence against his client, Rufus Choate had successfully defended Tirrell on the grounds that Tirrell could have killed Bickford while sleepwalking and was thus not responsible for his behavior. Tirrell left the courtroom a free man, but it was not long before he was in trouble again.

In January 1847, the prosecution initiated new charges against Tirrell, this time charging him with arson relating to the fires he set in Bickford's brothel on the night of her murder. Choate represented Tirrell again. This time, the trial was presided over by Massachusetts Chief Justice and distinguished jurist Lemuel Shaw. The prosecution presented essentially the same witnesses as in the first trial concerning Tirrell's presence in the brothel on the night the fires were set. Once again, Choate was able to attack the prosecution's case for its reliance on solely circumstantial evidence.

The jury found Tirrell not guilty, and for the second and final time, he left the courtroom a free man. In addition to Choate's expertise, Tirrell was assisted by Judge Shaw's instructions to the jury. Shaw's instructions criticized the prosecution's witnesses, saying that they were of "disreputable character" and pointing out discrepancies in their testimony.

Tirrell had little gratitude for Choate's extraordinary accomplishments. In fact, Tirrell even demanded that Choate refund half his legal fees since Tirrell's innocence had been so "obvious" in two trials. Of course, Choate refused. Tirrell spent the rest of his life in obscurity, but his trials became famous for Choate's successful use of a sleepwalking defense to charges of murder and arson.

—Stephen G. Christianson

Suggestions for Further Reading

Bickford, James. *The Authentic Life of Mrs. Mary Ann Bickford.* Boston: The Compiler, 1846.

Brown, Samuel Gilman. *The Life of Rufus Choate.* Boston: Little, Brown & Co., 1898.

Fuess, Claude Moore. *Rufus Choate, the Wizard of the Law.* Hamden, Conn.: Archon Books, 1970.

"A Lady of Weymouth." *Eccentricities & Anecdotes of Albert John Tirrell.* Boston: Unknown publisher, 1846.

Matthews, Jean V. *Rufus Choate, the Law and Civic Virtue.* Philadelphia: Temple University Press, 1980.

Neilson, Joseph. *Memories of Rufus Choate.* Littleton, Colo.: F.B. Rothman, 1985.

John Charles Frémont Court-Martial: 1847–48

Defendant: John Charles Frémont **Crime:** Mutiny, disobedience, conduct prejudicing good order and military discipline
Chief Defense Lawyers: Thomas H. Benton, William Carey Jones
Chief Prosecutor: John Fitzgerald Lee, Judge Advocate
Presiding Officer: G. M. Brooke **Court:** De Russey, T. F. Hunt
Place: District of Columbia (Washington Arsenal) **Date of Trial:** November 2, 1847–January 31, 1848 **Verdict:** Guilty of all charges
Sentence: Dismissal from the army and loss of all privileges

SIGNIFICANCE

In one of the most tainted court-martials in American history, a man who would be a candidate for president in less than 10 years was charged with the most serious crimes an officer might commit. The trial itself was highly irregular and the sentence was never carried out, but the reputation of the principals would forever remain tarnished.

When Captain John Charles Frémont set off from St. Louis, Missouri in the summer of 1845, he was commanding his third major western expedition for the U.S. Army Topographical Corps and was already something of a national celebrity. By March 1846 he was in northern California and challenging the Spanish who owned this land. When war broke out between the United States and Mexico in April, Frémont moved quickly to provide military support to the American settlers who raised the Bear Flag in revolt in June and declared an independent republic. By January 1847, now a lieutenant colonel, Frémont was accepting the surrender of the last of the Spanish forces in California. He seemed to be at the peak of his career, but his troubles were just beginning.

The Showdown

Commodore Robert F. Stockton had arrived in California in 1846 as commander of a U.S. Navy squadron and then proceeded to take the lead in the fight to oust the Mexicans. With the end of the fighting, Stockton regarded himself as in charge of California and appointed Frémont as its military governor. In several of the final battles in December 1846 and January 1847, however, the American army forces were led by the newly arrived General Stephen Kearny, who was soon asserting that his orders placed him in command of all the civil and military forces in California. Frémont not unnaturally sided with Stockton. By March, however, Kearny had established that he was the real commander and, when Frémont continued to resist his orders, Kearny had Frémont arrested in August 1847 and ordered him to return to Washington to face a court-martial.

Portrait of Captain John Frémont. (Courtesy, Library of Congress)

The Trial

By the time the court-martial commenced at the Washington Arsenal in the District of Columbia, it had become a national scandal. Frémont, after all, had for some years been hailed as the explorer of the American West and more recently as a hero in helping to acquire California. Now he was being accused of mutiny in what most close observers regarded as a petty squabble between General Kearny and Commodore Stockton. Further adding to the drama was that Frémont's defense lawyers were Thomas Hart Benton, the flamboyant senator from Missouri and Frémont's own father-in-law, and William Carey Jones, Frémont's brother-in-law. Because the rules of court-martial restricted civilian lawyers to serve only as advisors, Frémont would conduct his own defense, although he was allowed to consult at all times with his lawyers.

The major witness against Frémont was the very man who had brought the charges, Brigadier-General Stephen Kearny. With preliminaries out of the way, Frémont began his cross-examination on November 4. Although Kearny was only 53 (Frémont was 34), he was soon made to appear almost befuddled, as he could not recall detail after detail. He could not remember exactly when he decided to arrest Frémont. He could not explain why he had waited so long to do so—if, as he claimed, he had the orders from Washington that put him in charge from the day he arrived there? And why, after the decisive battles that ended the fighting with the Mexicans, had Kearny submitted a casualty list addressed to "His Excellency R. F. Stockton, Governor of California"? He first denied that Frémont had offered to resign from the U.S. Army when his role was questioned, then he said he remembered that he had refused to accept it. Although Frémont was constantly asking questions that the court would not allow, when Kearny stepped down after two weeks of such relentless probing, he appeared to be both incompetent and untrustworthy.

The prosecution called several other witnesses who attempted to support Kearny's case; again, Frémont's questioning cast doubt on most of their assertions. Then on December 6, the first crucial witness for Frémont's defense took the stand—Commodore Stockton. Although he was about the same age as Kearny, he was a more attractive figure and was expected to clinch the case for Frémont. Instead much of his testimony proved to be irrelevant and inconsistent and the judge advocate managed to dilute his value. Other defense witnesses, however, clearly and decisively supported Frémont's case.

Kearny returned to the stand on January 5, 1848, and again insisted that he had never regarded Commodore Stockton as holding rank above him. Then, just before stepping down, he addressed the court with an extraordinary claim: "On my last appearance before this court . . . the senior counsel of the accused, Thomas H. Benton of Missouri, sat in his place making mouths and grimaces at me, which I considered were intended to offend, to insult, and to overawe me. I ask of this court no action on it . . . I am fully capable of taking care of my own honor."

In the code understood by all present, Kearny was suggesting that he would be challenging Benton to a duel. But Benton, never one to shrink from a quarrel, was allowed to address the court. He claimed that he had been watching Kearny's stares at Frémont during the trial and was determined to avenge his son-in-law. "And the look of today," said Benton, "was the consequence of the looks in this court before. I did today look at General Kearny when he looked at Colonel Frémont, and I looked at him till his eyes fell—till they fell upon the floor." In the code of the day, Benton had intimidated Kearny!

Frémont was allowed to present his defense summary, which took three days. The officers retired for three days of deliberations, and then reconvened on January 31. All the spectators and the nation's press were convinced that Frémont would be found innocent, but the presiding judge read the verdict: guilty of all charges and specifications. But then, in total contradiction to the gravity of the offenses, six of the twelve members of the court, issued a "Remarks by the Court:"

> Under the circumstances in which Lieutenant Colonel Frémont was placed between two officers of superior ranks, each claiming to command-in-chief in California—circumstances in their nature calculated to embarrass the mind and excite the doubts of officers of greater experience than the accused—and in consideration of the important professional services rendered by him previous to the occurrence of those acts for which he has been tried, the undersigned members of the court respectfully recommend Lieutenant Colonel Frémont to the lenient consideration of the President of the United States."

On February 16, President James K. Polk did set aside the first charge of mutiny but approved the other verdicts; however, he then set aside the sentence and concluded, "Lieutenant Colonel Frémont will accordingly be released from arrest, will resume his sword [rank], and report for duty." Frémont felt too hurt to accept this and instead resigned from the army. Stockton also resigned from the navy in 1850. Kearny was assigned as the military governor of newly defeated Mexican cities but within a year was dead from a disease he caught there. By 1856, Frémont was the brand-new Republican Party's first candidate for president of the United States.

—John S. Bowman

Suggestions for Further Reading

Dellenbaugh, Frederick S. *Frémont and '49.* New York: G. P. Putnam's Sons, 1914.

Egan, Ferol. *Frémont Explorer for a Restless Nation.* Garden City, N.Y.: Doubleday, 1977.

U.S. Adjutant-General's Office. *Proceedings of the General Court-Martial in the Case of Lieutenant-Colonel Frémont, 1847.* Washington: Senate Executive Document No. 33, 30th Cong., 1st sess., 1848.

Roberts v. City of Boston: 1848–49

Plaintiffs: Sarah Roberts, Benjamin F. Roberts **Defendant:** Boston, Massachusetts **Plaintiff's Lawyer:** Charles Sumner **Defendant's Lawyer:** Peleg Chandler **Judge:** Lemuel Shaw **Place:** Boston, Massachusetts **Date of Trial:** 1848–1849 **Decision:** The court nonsuited the plaintiff, in effect dismissing the case

SIGNIFICANCE

The Roberts case established the principle of "separate but equal" and validated segregation in public schools, providing the basis and rationale for the United States Supreme Court's infamous *Plessy v. Ferguson* decision nearly 50 years later.

When most people think of segregated schooling, they think of the American South during the first half of the twentieth century. But one of the earliest court rulings to uphold separate schools for African-American children came a hundred years earlier in Boston, Massachusetts.

The schools themselves had their origins in the late 1700s, when Boston's black community asked the city to establish them, since black children who attended white schools were subjected to hostility and prejudice. At first the request was refused; later, white philanthropic efforts helped create such a school, and in 1820, Boston made it a part of the public school system. A second black school was established in 1831.

White public schools, meanwhile, flourished in Boston. By the 1840s, the city had more than 150 primary schools for white children. Together with the two black schools, they were under the control of a General School Committee, which state law empowered to operate the educational system and distribute the students at its sole discretion. But the black schools' facilities were in much worse condition than those of their white counterparts; at the same time, anti-segregationist sentiment had started to grow in Boston's black community, which had reversed its earlier views on having separate schools. In 1846 black residents petitioned the General School Committee to end the segregation, but the committee denied the request.

Suit Challenges Segregated Schools

Although the General School Committee had nearly unfettered power to run the school system as it saw fit, state law did give every child a right, through his parents, to sue the city for damages if it unlawfully denied him or her admission to school. This was the provision that Benjamin F. Roberts and his five-year-old daughter Sarah used in 1848 when Sarah tried to attend a white school.

Charles Sumner, leading attorney in *Roberts v. City of Boston* argued this case which validated segregation in the public schools. (Courtesy, National Archives)

Sarah lived nearly half a mile from the closer of the two black schools. On the way to that school, she passed no fewer than five white schools. Attendance at one of these would have been much more convenient for her, so on February 15, 1848, she entered the white school closest to her home, but the teacher forced her to leave. Sarah's father tried to enroll her in a white school a total of four times; each time the General School Committee refused to allow the enrollment, simply because Sarah was black. After these repeated rebuffs, Roberts sued the city.

The Robertses' leading attorney was 38-year-old Charles Sumner, an erudite antislavery sympathizer who would soon be a U.S. senator. Sumner made a long and impassioned argument before the state's Supreme Court to show that segregation was not only illegal, but wrong. The Massachusetts Constitution and Massachusetts case law, Sumner declared, both required the equal treatment of all citizens. Thirteen years earlier, in 1836, the Massachusetts Supreme Court's *Aves* decision had abolished slavery in the commonwealth; since that time, Sumner argued, all were equal, and thus entitled to equal treatment.

The black schools were not actually equal, Sumner continued. What was more, he stated, they could never be legally equal, since by their existence they created a caste system. This sort of stereotyping, Sumner proclaimed, denied an individual's equality under the law. "He may be poor, weak, humble, or black," he argued, "he may be of Caucasian, Jewish, Indian, or Ethiopian Race . . . but before the Constitution of Massachusetts all these distinctions disappear . . . he is a MAN, the equal of all his fellow men." Against this onslaught, city solicitor Peleg W. Chandler could only argue that state law gave the General School Committee the power to run the school system in any way it chose. He also hinted that segregation, far from being unreasonable, served all of the children's best interest.

Court Backs Segregation

Hearing the case was a bench headed by Chief Justice Lemuel Shaw, one of the nation's best-known and most influential judges. Shaw was hostile to slavery, and in fact he was the judge who had handed down the *Aves* decision on which Sumner was relying. But now, inexplicably, Shaw wrote an opinion that upheld both segregation and the General School Committee's decision.

He began by citing the same clauses in the Massachusetts Declaration of Rights that Sumner had quoted, and that he himself had used in the *Aves* opinion to strike down slavery. It was true, he now wrote, that all persons were equal before the law. But that did not mean, he continued, that the law actually treated everyone equally, regardless of circumstance. He observed that men and women had different legal status; so, too, did adults and children. To these, Shaw added the third category of whites and blacks.

The General School Committee, Shaw held for a unanimous court, had plenary power to administer the school system as it wished, and the court should not interfere. In this instance, he found, the committee had decided "that the good of both classes of schools will be best promoted" by a segregated system, which was a reasonable decision. To Sumner's claim that this created a caste system, Shaw replied that the true source of that system was actually prejudice. "This prejudice," wrote Shaw, "is not created by law, and probably cannot be changed by law." If prejudice existed, the chief justice concluded, then forcing white and black children to associate in integrated schools would do nothing to eliminate it.

Shaw even discounted the Robertses' objection to the extra distance that Sarah had to walk as utterly trivial. "In Boston," he pointed out, "more than one hundred thousand inhabitants live within a space so small . . . it would be scarcely an inconvenience to require a boy of good health to traverse daily the whole extent of it." In light of this, he concluded, the extra distance that Sarah had to walk did nothing to make the committee's decision "unreasonable, still less illegal." With that, the court dismissed the Robertses' case.

Six years later, the Massachusetts legislature abolished segregated schooling, but the damage had already been done. Throughout the rest of the nineteenth century, courts in other states, both North and South, cited the *Roberts* opinion to show that separate white and black school systems did not violate principles of equality before the law. In the infamous 1896 case of *Plessy v. Ferguson,* the U.S. Supreme Court cited Shaw's opinion, helping itself to many of his findings wholesale and giving the "separate but equal" doctrine federal constitutional sanction. Not until 1954, in *Brown v. Board of Education,* did the Court change its mind, incorporating in that later opinion many of the same arguments that Charles Sumner had made in the Roberts case.

—*Buckner F. Melton, Jr.*

Suggestions for Further Reading

Baltimore, Roderick T., and Robert F. Williams. "The State Constitutional Roots of the 'Separate but Equal' Doctrine: *Roberts v. City of Boston.*" *Rutgers Law Journal* 17 (1986): 537

Levy, Leonard W. *The Law of the Commonwealth and Chief Justice Shaw.* New York: Harper Torchbooks, 1957.

Levy, Leonard W., and Douglas L. Jones, eds. *Jim Crow in Boston: The Origin of the Separate but Equal Doctrine.* New York: Da Capo Press, 1974.

Hansley v. Hansley: 1849

Plaintiff: Ruthey Ann Hansley **Defendant:** Samuel G. Hansley
Plaintiff's Claim: Seeking divorce **Chief Lawyer for Plaintiff:** Robert Strange **Chief Defense Lawyer:** William Henry Haywood, Jr.
Judges: Thomas Ruffin, Frederic Nash, Richmond M. Pearson
Place: Raleigh, North Carolina **Date of Decision:** December 1849
Verdict: Divorce Denied

SIGNIFICANCE

This case showed just how difficult it was for a woman to get a divorce, especially in an antebellum southern state.

America's earliest divorce statutes had their origins in English law. Due to the influence of Christianity, marriage in England was transformed during the Middle Ages from a private institution over which there was little regulation to a religious one that was governed by the Roman Catholic Church. As a result, marriages could legally be dissolved only by death or by an annulment granted by the Church. Then, in 1533, King Henry VIII wanted to divorce his wife. Denied an annulment by the Pope, Henry declared the Catholic Church in England independent of Rome, renamed the local Church, and proclaimed himself the head of the "Church of England." (The Episcopal Church in the United States is descended from that Church.)

After King Henry's actions, there were two types of divorce in England. An absolute divorce, or divorce *a vinculo matrimonii* (which would be regarded today as a regular divorce), was very difficult to get because every time a couple wanted their marriage dissolved a special law dissolving their marital bonds had to be passed by the English Parliament. A divorce from bed and board, or divorce a *mensa et thoro* (which today is called a legal separation), was also available, but it did not permit the parties to remarry. Furthermore, such divorces were regulated by special courts run by the Church of England and were granted only when one of the parties was guilty of adultery, cruelty, or unnatural practices. This system continued in Great Britain until 1857.

North American Colonies and Divorce Laws

As North America was settled, every English colony established its own laws regarding divorce. In New England (which was primarily inhabited by Puritans who rejected the teachings of the Church of England), absolute divorces could be granted by regular courts for such reasons as adultery, bigamy, and desertion. In other colonies, couples had to go to the colonial legislatures or to a special court that had exclusive jurisdiction over family law matters. But in the South, where most people were members of the Church of England, no absolute divorces were allowed at all.

After the American Revolution, the divorce laws in the southern states changed very slowly. Eventually, under limited circumstances, a couple could obtain an absolute divorce from the state legislature. Later, because so many petitions for divorce were filed with the state legislatures, laws were passed allowing the courts to end marriages. Still, many southern judges clung to old ideas about the undesirability of divorce and had serious misgivings about exercising their new powers. As a result, divorce laws were often strictly interpreted by the courts in order to prevent a divorce from being granted.

This was the situation faced by Ruthey Ann Hansley of New Hanover County, North Carolina, in 1849. Mrs. Hansley and her husband, Samuel, were married in 1836 and lived together until August 1844, when Mrs. Hansley left to reside with her brother. The following March, she filed for an absolute divorce. The allegations in her petition describe a living hell.

Mr. Hansley's Sudden Change

According to Mrs. Hansley, the couple was happily married for many years. Then, for reasons unknown to her, Mr. Hansley took to drink and would sometimes be intoxicated for up to a month. He also began to beat her and "absent himself from the petitioner [Mrs. Hansley] during the whole night." Mrs. Hansley later learned that her husband was sleeping with one of his slaves named Lucy. Still, Mrs. Hansley "tried to endure, as long as it was reasonable for any wife to endure, the conduct of her husband" before Mr. Hansley entirely abandoned his wife's bed for Lucy's.

Mr. Hansley then moved Lucy into the home, "deprived the petitioner of the control of all those domestic duties and privilege connected with the house which belong to a wife," and gave to Lucy "the full possession and enjoyment of those privileges and duties." Mr. Hansley also repeatedly ordered his wife to give her place to Lucy and encouraged Lucy to treat Mrs. Hansley with disdain and disrespect. Afterward, "not satisfied with the treatment as above set forth," Mr. Hansley would starve his wife for two or three days at a time and lock her outside the house overnight without any protection from the elements. Worst of all, Mr. Hansley often forced his wife to sleep in the same bed with him and Lucy while he had sex with the other woman.

Jury Agrees with Mrs. Hansley

As required by North Carolina law at that time, a jury trial was held in 1848 before the Superior Court for New Hanover County during which Mr. Hansley denied all of his wife's allegations. At the trial, evidence was submitted about the "acts of familiarity" between Mr. Hansley and Lucy as well as about Lucy acting "as a sort of manager of his house." Testimony was also given that Lucy had a child, that Mr. Hansley twice admitted that the child was his, and that Mr. Hansley, when approached by his brother-in-law about a possible reconciliation between him and his wife, said that "he [Mr. Hansley] would part with all the property he had before he would [part] with the said Lucy and his child."

The jury found Mrs. Hansley's allegations to be true and an absolute divorce was granted. In addition, an inquiry was ordered to determine a financial settlement between the parties. Possibly trying to avoid any payments to his wife, Mr. Hansley appealed.

State Supreme Court Sides with Husband

The case went before the Supreme Court of North Carolina. Presiding as chief justice was Thomas Ruffin, the most influential judge in the pre-Civil War South. The lawyers for both Mr. and Mrs. Hansley were distinguished attorneys and former U.S. Senators.

After hearing the arguments of each side and considering the legal authorities cited by the lawyers, the Supreme Court unanimously decided to overturn the trial court's decision and deny the divorce sought by Mrs. Hansley.

The court first ruled that testimony about anything Mr. Hansley said concerning Lucy's child was inadmissible unless there was also evidence about how he treated the child; otherwise, the comments may have been part of a secret plan by the Hansleys to get around North Carolina's tough requirements for getting a divorce.

More importantly, North Carolina's divorce statute permitted the granting of absolute divorces only when "either party has separated him or herself from the other and is living in adultery." However, Mrs. Hansley's petition did not allege that her husband continued his adulterous ways after she had left him. As a result, the Supreme Court ruled that no evidence about any adultery by Mr. Hansley after his wife moved out was admissible. As indicated by the court, the requirement that the offending party still live in adultery was to make sure no divorce was given until reconciliation was beyond all hope. As stated in Judge Ruffin's decision:

> . . . the law does not mean to dissolve the bonds of matrimony and exclude one of the parties from marriage until there is no just ground to hope for a reconciliation . . .
>
> . . . even when there is a separation, if the offending party should reform forthwith and lead a pure life afterwards, the law does not look upon it as hopeless, that reconciliation may in time follow the reformation. It may not be a case, indeed, in which the law will permit the husband to insist on a

> restoration of the conjugal rights of society and cohabitation, by compelling the wife's return. But, on the other hand, it is not a case in which it is past hope, that the wife may not, upon the strength of ancient affections, and a sense of duty and interest, be willing of herself, at some time, to partake of the society and share in the fate of her reformed husband.

Therefore, the North Carolina Supreme Court concluded that even though there were sufficient grounds to give Mrs. Hansley a legal separation or a divorce a *mensa et thoro,* no absolute divorce could be granted. The superior court's ruling was overturned and the divorce was denied.

—*Mark Thorburn*

Suggestions for Further Reading

Bardaglio, Peter W. *Reconstructing the Household: Families, Sex, and the Law in the Nineteenth-Century South.* Chapel Hill, N.C.: The University of North Carolina Press, 1995.

Eisler, Riane Tennenhaus. *Dissolution: No-Fault Divorce, Marriage, and the Future of Women.* New York: McGraw-Hill Book Company, 1977.

Griswold, Robert L. "Sexual Cruelty and the Case for Divorce in Victorian America." *Signs* 11 (1986): 529–41.

Iredell, James. *North Carolina Reports: Cases at Law Argued and Determined in the Supreme Court of North Carolina.* Vol. 32. Raleigh, N.C.: Turner and Hughes, 1850. Reprint, Raleigh, N.C.: E. M. Uzzell and Company, State Printers and Binders, 1909.

Dr. John Webster Trial: 1850

Defendant: Harvard Professor Dr. John Webster **Crime Charged:** Murder
Chief Defense Lawyers: Pliny Merrick and Edward D. Sohier
Chief Prosecutors: George Bemis and John H. Clifford **Judges:** Lemuel Shaw, Charles A. Dewey, Thomas Metcalf, and Samuel Wilde
Place: Boston, Massachusetts **Dates of Trial:** March 19–April 1, 1850
Verdict: Guilty **Sentence:** Death by hanging

SIGNIFICANCE

Because Dr. John Webster had dismembered his victim's body and disposed of most of the parts, the prosecution had to try Webster without showing the *corpus delicti,* or proof of the murder, namely the body. Webster's trial was one of the first murder convictions based on the testimony of the medical experts and other evidence produced by the prosecution that established guilt beyond a reasonable doubt.

By the 1840s Boston, one of America's oldest cities, had become home to many wealthy families with preeminent positions in American society, business, and politics. This East Coast elite were often referred to as "blue bloods." They were active in charitable and social causes, including supporting leading educational institutions such as the venerable Harvard University in nearby Cambridge.

Dr. John Webster, a professor of chemistry and mineralogy at Harvard's Medical College, had also earned his medical degree from Harvard. His fellow professors included Oliver Wendell Holmes, Sr. Webster, an educated and intelligent man, soon established a place for himself in Boston society. He socialized with some of America's great cultural and literary figures, including poet Henry Wadsworth Longfellow. However, Webster found his new social prominence expensive to support.

Webster lacked personal wealth. Unlike his peers, he had not inherited a family fortune. Nor did his modest Harvard salary allow for lavish entertaining. He could support his social ambitions only by going into debt. One of his many creditors included Dr. George Parkman, whose family was one of Boston's most prominent. Webster borrowed more than $400 from Parkman, which in the

1840s was a sizable sum. Webster could not repay the debt, and in the fall of 1849 Parkman began to hound Webster to repay him.

Webster Kills Dr. Parkman

Shortly before Thanksgiving Day, 1849, Parkman confronted Webster in person at Webster's laboratory on the Harvard Medical College grounds. Parkman demanded that Webster pay his debt and threatened to use his influence to have Webster removed from the faculty. What must have gone through Webster's mind is still an open question and is colored by his post-trial confession that suggests temporary insanity. Whether Webster developed an uncontrollable temper or was carrying out a plan of premeditated murder, the fact remains that he savagely struck Parkman on the head with a piece of firewood from the nearby fireplace.

The blow fractured Parkman's skull, and he fell to the floor. Webster's homicidal fury subsided, and he unsuccessfully attempted to revive Parkman. When this effort failed, Webster bolted his lab door shut and used his medical instruments to dismember Parkman's body. He burnt most of Parkman's body in the lab furnace, but the process went slowly.

Ephraim Littlefield, the Medical College's janitor, had seen an earlier confrontation between Webster and Parkman. Littlefield became suspicious when on the day of Parkman's fatal visit to Webster, Littlefield found the lab door bolted shut and the wall by the furnace red-hot. Several days later, the Parkman family began advertising rewards for information leading to the whereabouts of the missing doctor. Littlefield's suspicions deepened, and he took it upon himself to break into Webster's laboratory by patiently chiseling his way through one of the lab's brick walls. After a couple of days Littlefield broke through, and to his horror saw the partial remains of a human body, including portions of the legs and pelvis of a man.

Littlefield quickly informed the police, who searched Webster's lab and found more remains, charred and half-destroyed, in the furnace. The police arrested Webster, who unsuccessfully tried to commit suicide by swallowing a poison pill. The authorities charged Webster with Parkman's murder, to which he pleaded not guilty. Webster's well-heeled friends attempted to hire counsel on his behalf, but they were unable to find lawyers willing to represent someone who seemed guilty of a heinous crime. Webster was forced to rely on two court-appointed attorneys, Pliny Merrick and Edward D. Sohier, for his defense.

Webster's Trial Rocks Boston Society

The trial opened March 19, 1850. The principal judge was state Supreme Judicial Court Chief Justice Lemuel Shaw. Associate Justices Charles A. Dewey, Thomas Metcalf, and Samuel Wilde also sat on the bench. The state's case was handled by Attorney General John H. Clifford, with the assistance of George Bemis. The prosecution, aware of the problem of the missing *corpus delicti*, wasted no time in bringing forward a series of medical experts to testify that the remains discovered in Webster's lab were those of Dr. Parkman.

The prosecution's medical experts included Dr. Nathan C. Keep, Parkman's dentist. Keep testified that he recognized certain false teeth found among the human remains in Webster's lab as the very ones that Keep had made for Parkman years before. To establish the necessary connection between the experts' identification of Parkman's remains and their presence in Webster's lab, the prosecutors brought in Littlefield.

By this time, the spectators' gallery was packed. By the end of the trial, more than 50,000 people had been present at one time or another. The prosecution knew that Littlefield would make or break their case, and they brought out his testimony slowly but surely, leading eventually to Littlefield's climactic discovery of Parkman's remains in Webster's lab:

> I took the crowbar and knocked the bigness of a hole right through. . . . There are five courses of brick in the wall. I had trouble with my light, as the air drew strongly through the hole. I managed to get the light and my head into the hole, and then I was not disturbed with the draft. I held my light forward. The first thing which I saw was the pelvis of a man and two parts of a leg. The water was running down on these remains from the sink.

Littlefield's next comment was an understatement, to say the least:

> I knew that it was no place for these things.

Clifford had put on an excellent case, and Webster's attorneys were hard-pressed. They tried to attack the janitor Littlefield's testimony by questioning his motives, including his desire to collect the reward offered by Parkman's family. Unable to succeed with this tack, Merrick and Sohier then presented a series of character witnesses. Although the retinue of socialites who testified on Webster's behalf was impressive, they could not shake the facts set forth by Littlefield's and the medical experts' testimony.

Corpus Delicti Issue Decides Webster's Fate

Webster's lawyers still had one ace in the hole, however. The law required that the prosecutors prove the existence of a crime, or the *corpus delicti.* In a murder case, this had always been assumed to mean that the prosecutors must physically produce the corpse of the person allegedly murdered. Therefore, Merrick's closing argument for the defense rested on the assertion that, in the eyes of the law, the state had not proven that the remains found in the lab were Parkman's. Even if the remains were Parkman's, Merrick continued, the state hadn't shown how he was killed.

After the lawyers made their closing arguments, Judge Shaw spoke to the jury on the issue of whether circumstantial evidence could establish the existence of a crime. If so, then the prosecution's evidence would be enough to prove the *corpus delicti* and convict Webster of murder. Shaw's ruling destroyed the defense's chances for victory:

> It has sometimes been said by judges that a jury never ought to convict in a capital case unless the dead body is found. That, as a general proposition, is true. It sometimes happens, however, that it cannot be found, where the proof of death is clear. Sometimes, in a case of murder at sea, the body is thrown overboard on a stormy night. Because the body is not found, can anybody deny that the author of that crime is a murderer?

Therefore, Shaw made it possible for the jury to conclude from the overwhelming evidence presented by the prosecution that Webster had murdered Parkman. The jury took less than three hours of deliberation to find Webster guilty. On April 1, 1850, Shaw sentenced Webster to death by hanging. After an unsuccessful appeal and an equally fruitless petition for leniency from the governor, Webster confessed. Webster admitted that Parkman had visited him in his lab and that when Parkman pressed him for payment of his debts he had killed him, dismembered his body, and attempted to destroy the parts.

Webster's version of the events was that Parkman had provoked him to the point of blind fury, thus causing him to kill Parkman. After seeing what he had done, Webster said he panicked and butchered Parkman's body to conceal the evidence. Webster's confession, if made at trial and believed by the jury, could have led to his receiving a lighter sentence based on a plea of temporary insanity.

But it was too late for Webster to escape the hangman. His confession did not persuade the governor to commute his sentence. On August 30, Webster was executed. Webster's hanging put an end to one of the most sensational scandals to rock Boston society and Victorian America.

—*Stephen G. Christianson*

Suggestions for Further Reading

Cozzens, James Gould. *A Rope for Dr. Webster.* Columbia, S.C.: Bruccoli Clark, 1976.

Morris, Richard. *Fair Trial.* New York: Alfred A. Knopf, 1952.

Schama, Simon. *Dead Certainties.* New York: Alfred A. Knopf, 1991.

Sullivan, Robert. *The Disappearance of Dr. Parkman.* Boston: Little, Brown, & Co. 1971.

Thomson, Helen. *Murder at Harvard.* Boston: Houghton Mifflin, 1971.

The Whitman Massacre Trial: 1850

Defendants: Telokite, Tomahas, Kiamasumkin, Isiaasheluckas, Clokomas **Crime Charged:** Murder **Chief Defense Lawyer:** Kintzing Pritchette **Chief Prosecutor:** Amory Holbrook **Judge:** Orville C. Pratt **Place:** Oregon City, Oregon Territory **Dates of Trial:** May 21–24, 1850 **Verdict:** Guilty **Sentence:** Death by hanging

SIGNIFICANCE

This trial was the foremost attempt by the newly created Oregon Territory to move away from makeshift, frontier justice and to conduct a disciplined trial following formal court procedures such as: a written summary of proceedings, appointment of defense counsel, pretrial motions, organized selection of jurors, provision for interpreters, right of cross-examination, and observance of other decorum and safeguards. In spite of these protocols, former folkways surfaced and the trial reflected just the beginnings of a new order yet to be fully embraced. The trial also foreshadowed the degree to which U.S. courts would go in prosecuting Indians for crimes committed against U.S. citizens on Indian lands.

On November 29, 1847, deep in the wilds of the so-called "Oregon Country," 13 missionaries and white settlers were brutally murdered at a mission located off the Oregon Trail and near the Waiilatpu Camp of the Cayuse Indian nation. Eight months later, Congress and President Polk made Oregon a U.S. territory and sent officials (including Governor Joe Lane, Secretary Kintzing Pritchette, U.S. Attorney Amory Holbrook, Judge Orville C. Pratt, U.S. Marshall Joe Meek and a mounted rifle regiment) to bring U.S. government to the Pacific northwest and more specifically to try and punish the murderers.

Five Cayuse Braves Arrested

Two more years passed before U.S. troopers arrested Chief Telokite and four other Cayuse braves and brought them over two hundred miles to Oregon City to be tried for the murder of Dr. Marcus Whitman, his wife Narcissa, and the other victims. On Tuesday, May 21, 1850, Judge Pratt appointed three defense counsel (Secretary Pritchette and two calvary officers) to represent the five prisoners, who remained in chains throughout the trial. Two interpreters were also there to assist the defense.

On Wednesday, defense counsel presented three separate motions to the court. The first pleaded for a dismissal because the United States had no jurisdiction over an alleged crime that occurred eight months prior to U.S. takeover and that was committed on lands of the Cayuse nation. Judge Pratt denied the motion. The second motion asked that the trial be moved because townsfolk in Oregon City were hostile and sought vengeance against the prisoners. The motion was denied. The third motion sought a postponement of the trial in order to gain time for a defense witness (over two hundred miles away in Waiilatpu) to get to Oregon City. The judge denied the motion and ordered that the trial begin the next morning.

The Trial Begins

On Thursday morning, in selecting a jury, prosecutor Holbrook dismissed two of the 24 summoned prospects and the defense eliminated 20. So, Marshall Meek had to collar more prospects from the spectators. Although Cayuse tribesmen were in the audience, all of the 12 jurors chosen were white men, as was required by law.

The prosecutor called four witnesses: all former white residents at the mission and survivors of the massacre and a month of captivity. The purpose of their testimonies was to identify the five defendants as being tribesmen involved in the violence of that tragic day.

The defense called three witnesses: John McLoughlin, head of the Hudson's Bay trading company in Oregon; Reverend Henry Spalding, a fellow missionary of the Whitmans; and Stickus, a Cayuse Indian chief. McLoughlin testified that for years prior to the incident he had warned Whitman to leave the mission because the Cayuse were increasingly angered by his inability to cure them of the white man's diseases and by the shifting of his attention and care away from the tribe and toward the growing number of his fellow countrymen who brought those diseases along the ever-invasive Oregon Trail. Spalding testified that he and Whitman (visiting down the Columbia River) were warned on the day prior to the killings not to return to Cayuse country. Chief Stickus would have testified about the Cayuse custom of killing medicine men when their cures proved ineffective. But Judge Pratt refused to allow Cayuse law to be injected in a case tried under U.S. law. None of the defendants testified.

Passionate Closing Arguments

The closing arguments to the jury took over three hours. The defense counsel used the greatest amount of time. Indeed, one of the army officers took up half the time and broke two water tumblers in the process. In an era of fiery oratory, so-called "summations" typically took longer than the testimony.

On Friday morning, Judge Pratt took 70 minutes to instruct the jurymen as to the law. He told them that is was proper to infer guilt of each defendant from the fact that it was the tribe who had surrendered them to be tried—the tribe "knowing best who the murderers were." It was an immensely devastating and blatantly illicit bit of hearsay about a fact never proven at trial. The tribe had made the surrender in order to call off the pursuit of the troopers, who had hounded them for the last two years. Chief Telokite had told his captors, "Your Christ died to save his people? So die we to save our people."

During the jury deliberations, one of the jurymen, Jacob Hunsaker, felt that defendant Kiamasumkin was innocent because no witness had ever testified to seeing him do harm. So, the jury returned into court with their problem. Thereupon, Judge Pratt told them that there was evidence that all of the defendants were seen "armed" at the mission that day and that fact alone would be enough to satisfy a finding of Kiamasumkin's guilt.

The jury deliberated for 75 minutes and finally reached a verdict of guilty as to each defendant. Defense counsel moved for "an arrest of judgment," then for a new trial, and then for an appeal to the territorial supreme court. Judge Pratt denied all three motions.

The Sentence Is Death

On Friday afternoon, Judge Pratt pronounced the sentence: On June 3, 1850 ". . . you are . . . to be taken by the Marshall . . . to the gallows . . . to be erected in Oregon City and there . . . be hung by the neck until you are dead."

During the 10 days between the trial and the execution date, defense counsel Pritchette had one last card to play on behalf of the prisoners. Governor Lane had left Oregon City for California immediately after the trial. The territorial law stated that the secretary of the territory was to assume the governorship whenever the governor was out of the territory. Pritchette figured that he now had the power to pardon convicts. So, he ordered Marshal Meek to cancel the hanging and release the prisoners.

But Meek went to Judge Pratt and told him of the conflicting orders—one from the executive branch and the other from the judicial branch. Was he supposed to free the prisoners or hang them? Pratt ruled that Pritchette was not the acting governor until Lane had crossed the Oregon-California border three hundred miles away; and as of yet there was no evidence that Lane's journey (at best a 10-day horseback ride) had reached that crossing.

And so, on June 3, the marshal led the five Cayuse to a gallows erected in the dirt streets of Oregon City, placed hoods over their heads, five nooses around their necks, and hanged them en masse before a crowd of spectators. The last of them died after 15 minutes on the end of the rope. Before the trapdoor was sprung, one of the prisoners had called out to the crowd, "*Wawko sixto wah! Wawko sixto wah!*" Translated loosely, it meant *now we can be friends.*

—*Ronald B. Lansing*

Suggestions for Further Reading

Lansing, Ronald B. *Juggernaut: The Whitman Massacre Trial—1850.* Pasadena, Calif.: Ninth Judicial Circuit Historical Society, 1993.

Castner Hanway Treason Trial: 1851

Defendant: Castner Hanway **Crime Charged:** Treason
Chief Defense Lawyers: John M. Read, Joseph J. Lewis, Theodore Cuyler, Thaddeus Stevens, W. Arthur Jackson (David Paul Brown, an attorney for a defendant who was indicted with Hanway, also sat at the defense table)
Chief Prosecutors: For the United States: John W. Ashmead, George L. Ashmead, James R. Ludlow; for the State of Maryland: Robert J. Brent, Z. Collins Lee; for the Gorsch family: James Cooper, R. M. Lee
Judges: Robert C. Grier, John K. Kane **Place:** Philadelphia, Pennsylvania
Dates of Trial: November 24–December 11, 1851 **Verdict:** Not Guilty

SIGNIFICANCE

To show the country that it would strictly enforce the Fugitive Slave Act, the U.S. government put a Pennsylvanian on trial for treason after he refused to help a posse search for a runaway slave.

By 1840, an informal and secret network of hiding places existed to help runaway slaves escape from the South into northern states and Canada. Between 1830 and 1860, an estimated 50,000 blacks, aided by thousands of abolitionists, Quakers, and escaped slaves, used this "Underground Railroad" to find freedom. In 1851, in an attempt to halt this exodus, the federal government accused one man of treason.

To cut down on the number of runaway slaves, the federal government adopted the Fugitive Slave Act in 1850. This law provided, among other things, for the appointment of special commissioners who were authorized to issue and order U.S. marshals to execute warrants for the arrest of escaped slaves. An affidavit from the slave owner was all that was needed to prove ownership, and a black who claimed that he was free was denied the right to testify on his own behalf in any later court proceeding. Furthermore, the commissioners were entitled to call upon bystanders and to organize posses for help when deemed necessary to recover a runaway slave. Finally, people convicted of hiding or otherwise preventing the arrest of a fugitive slave were subject to a $1,000 fine and six months imprisonment.

Slave Master Killed Chasing Fugitive

In 1849, four slaves escaped from the Monkton, Maryland farm of Edward Gorsch. Two years later, Gorsch learned that the four were in Christiana, Pennsylvania. After receiving a warrant for their arrest, Gorsch, his son, deputy U.S. marshal Henry Kline, and six others, all heavily armed, went to Christiana. On September 11, 1851, the nine approached the house of William Parker, an escaped slave who was reported to be hiding the runaways.

Parker refused to hand over his guests, an argument ensued, and shots were fired. Mrs. Parker blew a horn to signal the local black community that help was needed. Other blacks (estimates vary from 30 to over 100) soon began to arrive with guns, scythes, and stones. Also arriving on a horse was a white man, Castner Hanway, who lived at the home closest to the Parker residence. Hanway was neither an abolitionist nor a Quaker, but he felt duty bound to prevent any disturbances in his neighborhood.

When the Gorsch party saw Hanway, they automatically assumed that he was an abolitionist protecting the runaways. Kline handed Hanway the warrant for the arrest of the four slaves. In the meantime, another white, Elijah Lewis, showed up. Hanway advised the deputy marshal that "the colored people have a right to defend themselves. You had better leave or there will be bloodshed." The deputy told Hanway and Lewis that he was holding them responsible for the Gorsch slaves and ordered a retreat. Hanway and Lewis, realizing that there was nothing they could do to alter the increasingly dangerous situation, also left. Suddenly, Gorsch turned to face the blacks and shouted, "I won't leave without my slaves. I'll have my property or go to hell." The crowd surged and during a short but fierce battle, Edward Gorsch was shot and then hacked to death with a corn cutter while his son was severely wounded. At least two blacks were wounded in the melee. It is not certain who shot or killed Gorsch.

The local district attorney, based on Kline's statements, issued warrants for the arrest of suspects for murder and riot. Since he did not know the names of those who gathered at the Parker home, Kline insisted on the apprehension of everyone, black and white, who could possibly have been involved. Hanway and Lewis turned themselves in once they learned that they were going to be charged. Parker and the four runaway slaves fled before they could be arrested. Then, the federal government decided to intervene.

Politics Dictates Treason Charge

News of Gorsch's death quickly spread across the country. People in the South (especially in Maryland) were demanding blood. Southern newspapers made the incident sound like a planned rebellion. President Millard Fillmore, along with his secretary of state, Daniel Webster, and his attorney general, John Crittenden, knew that something had to be done or the South would regard the whole affair as proof of the federal government's inability to enforce the Fugitive Slave Act. Therefore, it was decided to charge all the participants in the riot with treason. Even if there were no convictions, the government reasoned, the trials alone would dampen northern opposition to the enforcement of the fugitive slave law.

Treason is defined by the Constitution as levying war against the United States. The government's argument was that any action to prevent, by force, the enforcement of any federal law was treasonous. Furthermore, anyone who advocated such action, even if he or she did not actually participate in the violence, was also guilty of treason. Eventually, 41 people, including Hanway and Lewis, were indicted. (Parker and the four runaway slaves were among those charged with treason, but since they had escaped arrest, they would be tried *in absentia.*)

The trial was held in Independence Hall in Philadelphia. Assisted by W. Arthur Jackson, Hanway's defense lawyers were four of the most prominent attorneys in Pennsylvania and included the fiery orator and congressman Thaddeus Stevens as well as Theodore Cuyler, Joseph Lewis, and John Read.

The U.S. Attorney for eastern Pennsylvania, John Ashmead, was initially in charge of the prosecution. Urged by Daniel Webster himself to make as strong a case as possible, Ashmead was assisted by his cousin, George Ashmead, and by Philadelphia lawyer James Ludlow. However, there was a strong suspicion in Maryland that the entire judicial system in Pennsylvania was biased against southern slaveowners. Maryland attorney general Robert Brent advised Ashmead that he expected to play a prominent role in Hanway's prosecution, along with two lawyers hired by the Gorsch family. At first, Ashmead refused, but when the governor of Maryland complained to the White House, Ashmead was instructed to accommodate Brent and the others. One of the Gorsch family's attorneys, James Cooper, eventually became the prosecution's "leading counsel." Baltimore District Attorney Z. Collins Lee was later added to the team. Still, each group of prosecutors had different strategies that often lead to the submission of conflicting evidence.

Hanway Tried in Test Case

Presided over by Robert C. Grier, an associate justice of the United States Supreme Court, and by U.S. District Judge John K. Kane, the trial began on Monday, November 24, 1851. The prosecution decided to try Hanway first and if a conviction was reached, then the other defendants would be tried separately.

Hanway was charged with five counts of treason. Specifically, it was alleged that he, with "force and arms," did:

> assemble with others to "oppose and prevent, by means of intimidation and violence," the execution of the Fugitive Slave Act;
>
> prevent U.S. Deputy Marshall Kline's execution of the warrants for the arrest of the four runaway slaves;
>
> assault Kline and rescue Gorsch's slaves;
>
> conspire before the riot with "persons . . . as yet unknown" to resist the execution of the Fugitive Slave Act; and

prepare and distribute books, pamphlets, letters, and other writings urging people to resist the Fugitive Slave Act.

The prosecution did its best to prove that Hanway had led and incited the blacks at William Parker's house. For example, Kline claimed that Hanway had said something to the crowd after which the blacks attacked. However, the prosecution's other witnesses cast doubt on his story. It was also claimed that, upon Hanway's appearance, the blacks who were gathered at the Parker house suddenly became "inspired." Mrs. Parker's blowing of the horn and the rapid response by the Parkers' neighbors were even cited as evidence of a previously arranged plan. Still, after 14 witnesses and three days of testimony, all that the prosecution conclusively proved was that Hanway had refused to help Kline arrest Gorsch's runaway slaves.

After testimony was completed and all the lawyers offered their summations, Judge Grier instructed the jury that:

> Two questions present themselves for your inquiry—
>
> 1st, Was the defendant . . . a participant in the offenses proved to have been committed? Did he aid, abet, or assist the negroes in this transaction?
>
> 2nd . . . if he did, was the offense treason against the United States?

The first question was purely a factual one for the jury to decide. However, the second was a mixture of fact and law: it was up to the judge to define treason, but it was for the jury to decide if Hanway's actions met that definition.

Grier ruled that, for treason to exist:

> The conspiracy and the insurrection connected with it must be to effect [sic] something of a public nature, to overthrow the government, or to nullify some law of the United States, and totally hinder its execution, or compel its repeal.

However, Grier also stated that:

> A number of fugitive slaves may infest a neighborhood, and may be encouraged by the neighbors in combining to resist the capture of any of their number; they may resist with force and arms . . . [but] their insurrection is for a private object, and connected with no public purpose.
>
> . . . when the object of an insurrection is of a local or private nature, not having a direct tendency to destroy all property and all government, by numbers and armed force, it will not amount to treason.

So instructed, it took the jury 15 minutes to find Hanway "not guilty." After three months in jail, Hanway was now a free man.

If the other defendants came to trial, Judge Grier's definition of treason would certainly be applied in their cases as well. As a result, on December 17, 1851, six days after Hanway's acquittal, U.S. Attorney John Ashmead announced that the indictments against the others for treason would be dismissed. However, most of the remaining defendants still faced state charges of murder and riot. They remained in custody for another month until Deputy Marshal Henry Kline was himself indicted for lying at the defendants' pretrial hearing.

After the trial, many northerners felt that Hanway and the other defendants were entitled to honor and public sympathy. Southerners, however, were outraged and regarded Hanway's trial as a farce. Maryland's governor pleaded for calm, but warned that when "treason stalks unpunished, through the halls of Justice; the Nation can judge of the probable remoteness" of the violent breakup of the country. Indeed, some historians have called the Christiana Riot the first battle of the Civil War.

—*Mark Thorburn*

Suggestions for Further Reading

Bacon, Margaret Hope. *Rebellion at Christiana.* New York: Crown Publishers, 1975.

Hensel, W. U. *The Christiana Riot and the Treason Trials of 1851: An Historical Sketch.* 2nd rev. ed. Lancaster, Penn.: New Era Printing, 1911. Reprint, Miami, Fla.: Mnemosyne Publishing, 1969.

Katz, Jonathan. *Resistance at Christiana: The Fugitive Slave Rebellion, Christiana, Pennsylvania, September 11, 1851: A Documentary Account.* New York: Thomas Y. Crowell, 1974.

Robbins, James J. *Report of the Trial of Castner Hanway for Treason.* Philadelphia: King and Baird, 1852. Reprint, Westport, Conn.: Negro Universities Press, 1970.

United States v. Don Pedro Leon Lujan et al.: 1851–52

Defendants: Don Pedro Lujan **Crimes Charged:** Violation of the Trade and Intercourse Act of 1834, libel and indebtedness to the United States
Chief Defense Lawyers: George A. Smith (chief counsel), Josiah Slayton, William Pickett **Chief Prosecutor:** Seth M. Blair **Judge:** Zerubbabel Snow
Place: Great Salt Lake City, Utah **Dates of Trials:** December 30, 1851–January 1, 1852; January 15–17, 1852 **Verdict:** Guilty

SIGNIFICANCE

The trial was an opportunity for the newly formed Utah Territory to assert its control over the Indian slave trade.

In December 1851, authorities from Manti, Utah, arrested eight Spanish traders. Their leader was 57-year-old Don Pedro Leon Lujan of Abiquiu, New Mexico. The men were accused of violating the laws that regulated trade with the Indian tribes under the federal Trade and Intercourse Act of 1834. The New Mexicans allegedly had traded with the Ute Indians for nine slaves—one woman and eight children. Before leaving for Utah, Lujan had gone to James Calhoun, the governor and superintendent of Indian affairs for the New Mexico Territory, to get a license to trade with the Ute. He had posted a $1,000 bond and promised to follow "all the rules and regulations, adopted or that may be adopted" by the United States regulating commerce with the Indians in Utah. He received a license on August 14, 1851, which was valid until November 14, to trade with the "Utah Nation of Indians . . . in their own localities." Although the Ute lived mainly inside the Utah Territory and not in New Mexico, Calhoun seemed unaware of the actual extent of his jurisdiction or the fact that he could not issue licenses to govern Lujan's conduct outside of New Mexico.

A Well-Established Slave Trade

New Mexico had been a part of Mexico until 1848, and it had a well-established tradition of peonage, or debt labor. Employers kept their employees in perpetual debt through loans that could only be repaid with labor. These debts often passed on to a peon's heirs, who also had to repay them with their own labor. As there was a labor shortage in the Southwest, an active Indian slave trade developed. Every year in the spring, Mexican traders took cheap goods to exchange with the Navajo and Ute for broken-down horses and mules, which they took to Utah and bartered along with weapons and ammunition for Indian women and children. They in turn were taken to California and sold. The traders then bought more horses for the return trip. The horses were traded for more Indian captives, who were taken to Mexico.

When Mormon settlers came to Utah in 1847, slave trafficking was well-established between the Ute and Mexican traders along the Old Spanish Trail. From the beginning the Mormons found the slave trade morally repugnant, and they also saw that it was a potential threat to their settlements, because Ute slave raiding stirred up other tribes' hostility. Mormon settlers were then caught between warring tribes, all of whom were supplied with arms by Mexican traders. Nonetheless, the Mormons soon found themselves buying Indian children from slavers and poor Indian families alike. They eventually legalized the practice, justifying it as necessary for the children's spiritual redemption and physical safety. As in Mexico, their practice resembled indentured servitude more than slavery. Purchase became a form of manumission, with the Indian slaves' labor repaying their buyers' cost and eventually buying their freedom. Another justification was the fact that the Indian slavers often threatened to kill the captives if no one bought them as slaves. The abusive treatment of Indian captives was still further reason for the Mormon settlers to purchase the children.

Lujan Ordered Not to Trade with Indians

In 1848 New Mexico became part of the United States, and as a result, the status of Mexican traders was about to change dramatically. Events leading up to Lujan's arrest began with his peaceful request to Brigham Young, Utah's governor and ex officio superintendent of Indian affairs, for the extension or renewal of his trading license. In order to do this, Lujan had to find Young, who in the fall of 1851 was somewhere in Utah's Sanpete Valley. His purpose was to show Young his New Mexico license and find out "if it was good to trade with the Whites and Indians also, and if the license was not good, to endeavor to get one from the Governor." On November 3 he finally found Young. Instead of getting a license, Lujan got a lecture on the evils of Indian slavery. Young "pointedly forbade" the Mexicans to trade anything with the Indians. Lujan agreed to abide by the Mormon's decision and leave the territory after procuring supplies for the return trip.

But the Indians, accustomed to the traditional trade with Mexican traders, had other ideas. They stole livestock from Lujan's party, and the Ute slavers forced nine captives on to the New Mexicans. Shortly afterward, the Mormon authorities arrested Lujan and his associates for trading without a valid license with Indian captives in their possession. They were taken first to court in Manti and later to the First District Court of Utah Territory in Great Salt Lake City. The main issue in the trial was the trading in Indian slaves. Slavery itself was not illegal in Utah, so Lujan and the others were charged with violating the Trade and Intercourse Act of 1834, which prohibited trading with the Indians without a valid license.

In 1851 the Utah civil judiciary came under the control of a federally appointed supreme court, which presided over the territory's three judicial districts. The district courts were to hear non-Mormon and criminal cases. The federal judges immediately came into conflict with the Mormon leadership, and by mid-September most of the non-Mormon judges had returned to Washington, leaving the Mormon, Zerubbabel Snow, the only district judge in Utah. He was authorized to serve all three districts until new judges were appointed. But this still left the territory without a Supreme Court, so district cases could not be appealed.

Traders Brought to Trial

In December, prosecutor Seth Blair filed a libel action and a declaration of debt against the property confiscated by the authorities in Manti. He also filed a petition in debt for a $500 fine for violation of the Trade and Intercourse Act, for which all the traders' confiscated merchandise and property would be forfeit. On December 30, 1851, the prosecution began presenting its case. Its principal witnesses were Brigham Young and an Indian slave trader named Arapeen. Josiah Slayton, assistant counsel for the defense, objected to Arapeen's testimony since he was a party to the transaction. Slayton felt that Arapeen had told an extremely self-serving version of events and that the prosecution had coached him. But the court overruled his objection.

Prosecutor Blair argued that there was prima facie evidence of a crime because the traders had Indian captives in their possession. Naturally Lujan's attorneys asserted the legality of Lujan's New Mexico license; they also argued that regardless of its validity, the Indians had forced the New Mexicans into trading. The court scotched the first argument, finding that the New Mexico license was invalid in Utah. The court instructed the jury that if it determined that the defendants had brought horses and mules into the "usual hunting ranges" of the Indians without a valid license with the intent to trade with them, they were guilty, but if the defendants had the intention of obtaining a license first and then trading, or if the trading was coerced by the Indians, they were not guilty. The jury chose to believe that Lujan's story was "a device to evade the law," finding the defendants guilty of illegal trading with the Indians, and thus indebted to the United States.

Two weeks later, at a separate trial of the cases of libel and indebtedness, the defense attorneys filed motions to recover some of their clients' property citing irregularities in procedure and technicalities of the law. They also filed two motions for retrial on the basis of new information and irregularities in the first proceeding, and they filed a writ of *habeas corpus* on behalf of the Indian captives. Prosecutor Blair wanted to sell the Indians, along with the traders' other possessions, to help defray the court costs. But Judge Snow decided that Utah had never passed a law allowing Indian slavery, and he ordered the release of the captives. In fact the children were placed in Mormon homes, causing Lujan to complain of Mormon hypocrisy, observing that the captives had been "sold to the Mormons as servants, by the Mormon authorities." But within a month the Utah territorial legislature outlawed Indian, but not Negro, slavery, and laid out a procedure for purchasing Indian children as indentured servants for a period not to exceed 20 years. It was a longer period of servitude than tradition demanded for Indians sold in New Mexico.

—*Carol Willcox Melton*

Suggestions for Further Reading

Bancroft, Hubert Howe. *History of Utah.* San Francisco: History Co., 1890.

Jones, Sondra. *The Trial of Don Pedro Leon Lujan: the Attack against Indian Slavery and Mexican Traders in Utah.* Salt Lake City: University of Utah Press, 2000.

Rendition Hearing of Anthony Burns: 1854

Defendant: Anthony Burns **Crime Charged:** Being a fugitive slave **Claimant:** Charles Suttle **Chief Defense Lawyers:** Richard Henry Dana, Jr., Charles Mayo Ellis **Claimant's Lawyer:** Seth J. Thomas **Judge:** Edward Greeley Loring **Place:** Boston, Massachusetts **Dates of Hearing:** May 25–June 2, 1854 **Decision:** Anthony Burns was the property of Charles Suttle and was returned to him.

SIGNIFICANCE

The Anthony Burns hearing highlighted the strains that the issue of slavery had placed on the nation, tested the government's willingness to enforce the Fugitive Slave Law, and became a rallying point for the abolitionist movement.

On June 2, 1854, Boston became an armed camp during the rendition hearing of Anthony Burns, a fugitive slave from Virginia. Burns's owner, Charles Suttle, was demanding Burns's return under the Fugitive Slave Act of 1850. Abolitionist agitation was so great that the army, the marines, the militia, the police, and 120 newly deputized federal marshals had to guard the courthouse during the proceedings, while 50,000 Bostonians lined the streets in protest.

The story began in Virginia in 1852, when Suttle sent Burns to Richmond to work under William Brent. Burns was literate and skilled at a variety of jobs. He persuaded Brent to let him hire his own time and keep a percentage of the money. This was illegal in Virginia, but it was common in larger Southern cities. The arrangement was mutually beneficial since Brent would not have to pay to feed and clothe Burns, and Burns would have some autonomy. Burns made his payments to Brent while he began saving money and seeking friends among Northern seamen. In early 1854 he saw his chance to escape, stowing away on a Boston-bound ship. Once there he posed as a free man and began working in a clothing store belonging to Coffin Pitts, a well-known figure in the black community.

Tracked Down in Boston

Burns soon wrote his brother a letter, which he had mailed from Canada to conceal his location. But the letter was delivered to Suttle instead. Burns had been indiscreet enough to suggest that he was in Boston, and Suttle and Brent immediately set out to reclaim him. On May 24 they had him arrested on the spurious charge of robbing a jewelry store. Only when Burns was taken to the federal courthouse rather than the city jail did he realize that he had actually been seized as a fugitive slave.

At the jail Suttle asked Burns why he had run away. Burns replied that he had fallen asleep aboard the ship on which he was working. "Before I woke up, she set sail and carried me off," he claimed. Suttle asked Burns if he had not always treated him well. Burns made no reply, and Suttle continued. "Haven't I always given you money when you needed?" Burns countered "You have always given me 12 1/2 cents a year." This proved that Suttle and Burns knew each other, but not that Suttle owned Burns. For the rest of the night the marshal held Burns in the courthouse, while raucous guards tried to prod Burns into admitting that Suttle owned him.

The next morning U.S. Commissioner Edward Greeley Loring began a rendition hearing. The 1850 Fugitive Slave Act required special federal commissioners to hold summary hearings on the status of seized negroes, grant certificates of removal, and order federal marshals to hunt down alleged fugitives. The accused had no right to trial and the standard of proof needed to return a Negro to slavery was very low. Fugitives could not testify on their own behalves, and they had no right to counsel or public trial. The commissioner's job was to decide whether the slave described in the affidavit was the person standing before him. The commissioner's decision was final; the fugitive could not even seek a writ of *habeas corpus.* The restrictive nature of these hearings had enraged abolitionists since 1850.

Dana for the Defense

No doubt Burns would have been returned quickly to Suttle and Virginia except for the intervention of the famous abolitionist lawyer Richard Henry Dana, Jr., best remembered for his book, *Two Years before the Mast.* Dana forced his way into the courtroom and offered to represent Burns. Burns refused, saying, "It is of no use, they have got me. . . . I shall fare worse if I resist." But Dana asked Loring for a delay so that Burns could have time to consider whether or not to accept his offer. He argued that Burns was in no state to decide anything at that moment. Loring asked Burns directly what his wishes were. Burns made no answer. Loring then asked him if he wanted time to consider his situation. Burns, still unsure of what answer to give, said nothing. Loring then answered for him, saying, "Anthony, I understood you to say you would?" Burns agreed and Loring adjourned the hearing for two days.

A rendition hearing was supposed to be a summary proceeding, but the case took on many of the aspects of a full-blown trial. Although Dana had delayed the hearing, he still did not officially represent Burns. Hesitant to approach him directly, Dana sent two black men, the Reverend Leonard A. Grimes and Coffin Pitts, and the white abolitionist Wendell Phillips, to talk to him. When a marshal blocked their entry, Loring ordered him to let Burns see "a few friends." Once the three were admitted they persuaded Burns to accept Dana as counsel. Meanwhile, Dana was seeking co-counsel. After approaching several established lawyers in vain, he accepted the services of Charles Mayo Ellis, a young attorney, who volunteered his help.

Anthony Burns was declared to be the property of Charles Suttle and was returned to him. (Courtesy, Library of Congress)

When Burns met with Dana, he again said that he feared severe punishment, such as being sold on the New Orleans slave market or beaten, if he resisted return. Still the attorneys pressed him, hoping, despite the odds, to convince Loring not to remand Burns to slavery. But even if Burns were returned, a long hearing would provide useful propaganda for the abolitionists by showing the Fugitive Slave Act's blatant unfairness. Regardless of the outcome for Burns, other fugitives might benefit.

Abolitionists Mobilize

While Dana and Ellis were preparing for the hearing, other abolitionists called a mass meeting at Faneuil Hall. During the meeting, Thomas Wentworth Higginson led an unsuccessful attempt to rescue Burns, during which a deputy was killed. As a result, by early the next day, soldiers, militia, and emergency deputies had Boston under what appeared to be martial law. Loring postponed Burns's hearing until Monday.

Meanwhile, Suttle offered to sell Burns for $1,200. Burns's supporters quickly raised the money and Loring himself drew up a bill of sale. But at the last minute, the pro-slavery U.S. district attorney, Benjamin F. Hallett, announced that a slave could not be sold in Massachusetts. He then threatened to bill Suttle for all the government's expenses if he sold Burns before the hearing was over. The discussion continued until midnight, when Hallett announced it was now Sunday and that no sale could take place on the Sabbath.

The hearing commenced on Monday and lasted until Thursday. All the while the courtroom was filled with a U.S. marshal's guard of about 120 men drawn from the dregs of society. To reach the courtroom the parties had to duck under the heavy anchor chains that were draped around the building and pass through four or five cordons of police and armed soldiers.

Judge's Rulings Favor Master

During the hearing, Loring denied all Dana's motions and decided all questions of law and procedure in Suttle's favor. His most important decision was to let William Brent, Burns's former employer, testify to what Burns said to Suttle immediately after his arrest. But Loring forbade Burns from testifying about the same conversation.

Brent also testified that there was some doubt about who owned Burns under Virginia law. Suttle could not produce a deed or title and Brent hinted that the actual title was questionable. Brent also apparently lied about the timing of Burns's escape to avoid having to reimburse Suttle for the costs of retrieving him. Brent claimed to have seen Burns on March 20 and insisted that he escaped on March 24. In fact, Burns had left Virginia in February. To discredit Brent, Dana and Ellis called Boston witnesses who contradicted him.

Nevertheless, on June 2, Judge Loring ruled against Burns, citing Brent's testimony that Burns had recognized both Suttle and Brent. Dana was furious. Burns, he said, was "convicted on an *ex parte* record, against the actual evidence, [and] on his own admissions made at the moment of arrest to his alleged Master!"

That afternoon Burns was marched to the wharf to board a ship for Virginia. Once he was back in the South, Suttle confined him to jail for four months, where he was manacled and fettered, and frequently ill. After Burns's Boston subscribers declined to pay $1,500 for him, Suttle sold him to a North Carolina trader, but six months later the trader sold him to members of Boston's black community, and Burns returned to the North. Judge Loring's reputation did not survive his part in the matter. For the next four years he was the focus of vilification and agitation. Ultimately he lost both his positions as instructor at Harvard Law School and on the Suffolk County Probate Court.

The Burns hearing emphasized the growing strength of the abolitionist in the wake of the Fugitive Slave Act of 1850, and the government's determination to enforce an increasingly unpopular law.

—*Carol Willcox Melton*

Suggestions for Further Reading

Finkelman, Paul, ed. *Fugitive Slaves and American Courts: The Pamphlet Literature.* 4 vols. New York: Garland, 1988.

Pease, Jane H. and William H. *The Fugitive Slave Law and Anthony Burns: A Problem in Law Enforcement.* Philadelphia: J. B. Lippincott, 1975.

Von Frank, Albert J. *The Trials of Anthony Burns: Freedom and Slavery in Emerson's Boston.* Cambridge, Mass.: Harvard University Press, 1998.

Charity Lamb Trial: 1854

Defendant: Charity Lamb **Crime Charged:** Murder
Chief Defense Lawyers: James K. Kelly, Milton Elliot
Chief Prosecutor: Noah Huber **Judge:** Cyrus Olney **Place:** Oregon City, Oregon Territory **Date of Trial:** September 11–16, 1854 **Verdict:** Guilty of second-degree murder **Sentence:** Life imprisonment

SIGNIFICANCE

Charity Lamb was the Pacific Northwest's first convicted murderess. Her case represents one of the earliest known self-defense arguments predicated on what today would be called the spousal abuse syndrome. Then, as now, that defense ran against the traditional notion that in order for self-defense to be justified, the threat defended against had to be imminent and not merely inevitable.

On a Saturday evening, May 13, 1854, in a lonely pioneer cabin deep in the woods and hills of the Oregon frontier, a settler family was seated around the supper table. Four young sons and a teenage daughter, Mary Ann, were listening to their father, Nathaniel's, yarn about the bear he had shot at that day's hunt. A baby was cradled nearby. The woman of the house left the table, went to a woodpile, got an axe, came behind her husband's chair and drove the axe blade into the back of his head two times. Her name was Charity Lamb. Her actions betrayed that name, for in that moment she was neither charitable nor a lamb.

Settlers Shocked by Murder

Settlers throughout the Willamette Valley reacted with horror. Newspapers called it "revolting . . . cold-blooded . . . inhuman" and named the culprit a "monster." When her first trial date was postponed, those anxious for speedy justice labeled the delay a "farce." The *Oregon Spectator* said:

> Think of it ladies! If any of you feel disposed to walk up behind your husbands or fathers and chop their heads open, why, just pitch in—you are safe in doing so!

On September 11, her trial began in Oregon City in the U.S. District Court for the Oregon Territory. The prisoner stood before the presiding judge, Cyrus Olney. Carrying an infant in her arms, according to the *Oregon Spectator* she was:

> pale and sallow . . . emaciated as a skeleton, apparently fifty years of age . . . Her clothing was thin and scanty, and much worn and torn, and far from clean . . . She had a sad, abstracted and downcast look.

Lamb's court-appointed lawyers pled her "not guilty." In selecting the jury, the prosecutor sought to know whether the panelists had any hesitation about hanging a woman. A woman had never before been sentenced to die on the frontier or anywhere in the federal judicial system. The 12 jurors eventually selected were all men. The law did not allow women to serve on juries—not even in the trial of one of their peers.

Defendant's Children Testify

The trial began when the coroner established that the victim died in his bed one week after the infliction of two cuts that went through the top of the skull and into the brain.

Identification of Lamb as the culprit was easy. She implied her involvement by fleeing the scene. Furthermore, she told the doctor and the constable that she "did not mean to kill the critter, . . . only intended to stun him" and "she was sorry she had not struck him a little harder." Then too, her dying husband asked his wife, "My dear, why did you kill me for?" But the saddest evidence came from her own children. Son Thomas testified that he "saw her strike him one blow on the head with the axe." Son Abram testified that his father "fell over and scrambled about a little."

Finally the prosecutor had to show premeditation. Here, motive was the gate and a man named Collins was the key. The doctor testified that:

> there was a love affair between Collins and Mary Ann [the daughter]; that she [Charity] favored the suit, and Lamb opposed it; that she was mortified and vexed about it, for Collins was so nice a man.

That dispute blossomed into rage when, one week prior to the killing, Charity helped Mary Ann compose a love letter to Collins. Before it could be sent, Nathaniel discovered it, destroyed the letter, and threatened to kill Collins.

An axe in the back of the head was further proof of premeditation. It showed a planned selection of time, place, and weapon. Then too, she showed no sign of remorse. After the killing she was found smoking her pipe at fireside in a distant neighbor's cabin, her only concern being whether Nathaniel could come find her.

The Defense: Insanity

The first line of defense was insanity. Lamb's lawyers called her a "monomaniac." While the doctor described her as "very much excited . . . looked wild-like out of her eyes," he nevertheless "thought she was pretending." Although her mind may have been deranged, there was not enough to show *moral* ignorance, the traditional test of legal insanity.

As a second defense, her lawyers argued that she did not intend to kill her victim; "she only meant to stun him until she could get away." But that defense beggared reason: a blow with an axe blade instead of its butt was hardly the choice for stunning.

Finally, Lamb's lawyers urged that she killed to save herself from being killed. Throughout her marriage, Nathaniel had physically abused her. The children testified that once he threw a hammer at her and put a gash in her forehead. On several occasions when Lamb was sick in bed, Nathaniel threatened her with violence and ordered her to get up and work. One winter, "he knocked her down with his fists and kicked her over several times in the snow." Lamb told others that her husband also tried to poison her.

The children testified that their parents quarreled "lots of times." The quarrels sometimes ended with Lamb fleeing the encounter but having to turn back when her pursuing husband threatened to shoot her. Nathaniel had threatened to kill his wife and children if ever they told of his thefts of a horse and an ox. There was also evidence of Nathaniel's intemperate use of alcohol.

The final straw was the rage that followed the conflict over the love letter to Collins. Nathaniel had promised to kill Lamb, take the boys, and desert to California. One week before the killing, he told his wife that she "would not live on his expense longer than a week; that he was going to kill her next Saturday night"—May 13. The threat was now keyed to a specific time. During that week he sold his mare to make ready for the trip. When Saturday came, before he went off on his bear hunt, the children saw him fire a shot toward their mother.

In summation to the jury, Lamb's counsel did not emphasize self-defense. Instead they chose to rampage against the sins of capital punishment and to focus on the notion that Charity's mind was incapable of rational judgment.

Oddly enough, it was Judge Olney who stressed self-defense in his charge to the jury. He bent the law of self-defense toward a leniency not today and not then legally warranted. He instructed that she must be found innocent if she "acted out of a genuine belief in self-preservation," even if that "belief was a delusion of a disordered mind."

The Verdict

The jury was out more than one half a day when they returned to court with a question. They had boiled the matter down to the dregs of self-defense. What still simmered was: "What was meant by imminent danger, such as would justify killing?" They were apparently convinced that Nathaniel was a threat to her life but not at the very moment he was killed. How immediate did the danger have to be?

Reluctantly, Judge Olney had to tell the jurymen that a justifiable killing should be at that instant unavoidable: "If she saw that danger, before he returned home, it was her duty to have gone away."

The jury retired and had their verdict swiftly: "Charity Lamb is guilty of the killing purposely and maliciously . . . but without . . . premeditation and do recommend her to the mercy of the Court."

The next day Lamb stood before the bench with her baby in her arms. Judge Olney asked her if she had anything to say before sentencing. She had not testified at trial. She spoke for the first time and the only time in the record: "Well I don't know that I murdered him. He was alive when I saw him last . . . I knew he was going to kill me."

The judge said, "The jury thinks you ought to have gone away, in his absence."

To that, Lamb offered: "Well. He told me not to go, and if I went that he would follow me, and find me somewhere, and he was a mighty good shot . . . I did it to save my life."

Judge Olney may have been hard put to utter the sentence mandated by law for second-degree murder:

> The jury . . . recommended you to mercy. But the law gives the court no discretion . . . The sentence therefore is, that you be conveyed to the penitentiary of this territory and there imprisoned, and kept at hard labor, so long as you shall live.

Lamb wept and was led from the courtroom still carrying her baby, which would soon be taken from her.

She was taken to the prison in Portland, where she was confined with six other male inmates. Five years later she was still jailed there, doing the wash for the warden's family. Missionaries inspecting the prison noted that "she is not of sound mind." In 1862, she was transferred to the Hawthorne Insane Asylum.

The law took no account of her predicament—a choice between waiting for menacing immediacy or fleeing into a wild frontier without her children, without provender, without barter, without refuge, shelter, or whatever else it takes to survive while pioneering in a rugged and paternalistic society. Her judge, jury, lawyers, witnesses, and jailers had all been men. The media too were male reporters who, throughout her ordeal, were printing sermons such as:

> There must be a man born in the world for every woman—one whom, to see would be to love, to reverence, to adore . . . that she would recognize him at once her true lord.

True to the sentence mandated, she was kept behind walls so long as she lived. She died in the asylum in 1879—her family gone—her gravesite unattended—forgiveness never given.

—*Ronald B. Lansing*

Suggestions for Further Reading

Lansing, Ronald B. "The Tragedy of Charity Lamb, Oregon's First Convicted Murderess." *Oregon Historical Quarterly* 40 (Spring 2000).

State of Missouri v. Celia, a Slave: 1855

Defendant: Celia, a Slave **Charge:** Murder
Chief Defense Lawyers: Isaac M. Boulware, John Jameson, and Nathan Chapman Kouns **Chief Prosecutor:** Robert Prewitt **Judge:** William Hall
Place: Calloway County, Missouri **Dates of Trial:** October 9–10, 1855
Verdict: Guilty **Sentence:** Hanging

SIGNIFICANCE

This case graphically illustrates that enslaved women had no legal recourse when raped by their masters. Although the second article of Section 29 of the Missouri statutes of 1845 forbade anyone "to take any woman unlawfully against her will and by force, menace or duress, compel her to be defiled," Judge William Hall refused to instruct the jury that the enslaved Celia fell within the meaning of "any woman"—giving the jury no latitude to consider Celia's murder of her sexually abusive master a justifiable act of self-defense.

In 1850, the recently widowed Robert Newsom purchased the 14-year-old Celia, ostensibly to help his daughters with the housework. En route from Audrain County, the site of the transaction, to his own home in neighboring Calloway County, Missouri, Newsom raped the young girl. Back at his farm, Newsom ensconced her in a small cabin 150 feet from his home. Between 1850 and 1855, Celia bore two of Newsom's children, both of whom became her master's property. She also began a relationship with a fellow slave named George. When she became pregnant in 1855, she was unsure which of the men was the father. At that point, George told Celia that "he would have nothing more to do with her if she did not quit the old man."

Celia first asked Newsom's daughters to intercede. She told Mary (19 years old, as was Celia in 1855) and Virginia (36 and returned to her father's home with her own three children) that her pregnancy was making her feel unwell and that she wished Robert Newsom to respect her condition and leave her alone. There is no indication that either Newsom daughter challenged her father.

Celia herself pleaded with Newsom on June 23, but he brushed aside her objections and said "he was coming to her cabin that night." That afternoon, Celia brought a heavy stick, "about as large as the upper part of a Windsor chair, but not so long," into her cabin. When Newsom arrived and refused to back off, she killed him with two blows to the head. She spent the night burning his corpse in her fireplace. As morning approached, she ground the smaller bones into pieces with a rock; the larger bones, she hid "under the hearth, and under the floor between a sleeper and the fireplace." Later that day, she gave Newsom's unwitting grandson, Virginia's son Coffee Waynescot, "two dozen walnuts [to] carry the ashes out." Coffee disposed of his grandfather's remains on the ground beside "a beat down like" path on the property.

Celia Speaks

By Sunday, June 24, Newsom's family and neighbors had become concerned. They first questioned George, who quickly implicated Celia. (George afterward ran away.) Harry and David Newsom, Robert's sons, had come from their own homes to investigate; with Robert's neighbor William Powell, they demanded a confession from Celia. She at first denied any involvement. Then, afraid of Harry's and David's reactions, she told Powell she would confess if he would "send the two men out of the room." They left, and Celia told her story to Powell. Powell and the Newsom family then examined the fireplace, where Virginia located "buttons my sister [Mary] sewed on my father's breeches a few days before his death," and various splinters of bone. Newsom's larger bones were then recovered from the hiding space beneath the hearth.

On June 25, David Newsom delivered his affidavit to two local justices of the peace, D.M. Whyte and Isaac P. Howe. The affidavit stated that David Newsom "has cause to suspect and believe that one Negro woman named Celia a Slave of the said Robert Newsom did at the county aforesaid feloniously, willfully, and with malice aforethought with a club or some other weapon strike and mortally wound the said Robert Newsom, of which wound or wounds the said Robert Newsom instantly died." Celia was arrested and "deliver[ed] . . . forthwith to the keeper of the common jail of said County to await her trial."

Because white Calloway County residents were afraid Celia might have had help from another slave or slaves still at large, county Sheriff William T. Snell permitted two men, Thomas Shoatman and Jefferson Jones, to interrogate Celia. All of the above information about Celia's life on the Newsom farm comes from her interviews with William Powell, Jefferson Jones, and Thomas Shoatman. It does not come from Celia's trial testimony because she gave none. In the 19th century, blacks generally were not allowed to testify in criminal trials.

The Trial Begins

Celia's trial began on October 9, 1855. Her court-appointed attorneys, Isaac M. Boulware, John Jameson, and Nathan Chapman Kouns, seem to have given the most vigorous defense possible. On her behalf, they pleaded not guilty and described Celia as one who was "ready for trial, and prayed herself upon her God and her Country."

On October 10, prosecutor Robert Prewitt called Jefferson Jones to the stand. Jones recited for the court the account that Celia had given to him several months earlier. He said that Celia said she "had been having sexual intercourse" with her master and that George had threatened to leave her if these relations continued. When Jameson cross-examined Jones about Celia's account of the rape on the day of Newsom's purchase, Newsom's sexual demands during the following five years, and the birth of her two children fathered by Newsom, Jones said that he couldn't "say positively whether Celia said the accused had forced her on the way home" and couldn't "know with certainty whether she told me so."

Robert Newsom's daughter, Virginia Waynescot, was called by the prosecutor, and she described the discovery of some of her father's remains. Jameson then cross-examined her and tried tactfully and not very successfully to examine the relationship between her father and the enslaved Celia. Asked where her father customarily slept, Virginia replied: "[I] did not notice the [Newsom's] bed. Sister made the bed up." Virginia did, however, disclose that Celia "took sick in February. Had been sick ever since." Virginia's son, Coffee Waynescot, then testified about his disposal of his grandfather's ashes. On cross-examination, Jameson tried—again, with tact and with little success—to elicit information about the sexual relationship between Newsom and Celia.

William Powell was the next witness. For the prosecution, he related Celia's detailed confession that she had killed Newsom. During his cross-examination of Powell, Jameson abandoned the reticence he had shown to Newsom's daughter and grandson. Powell testified that Celia had told him of Newsom's misconduct and of her pleas to Newsom's daughters for intercession. He also testified that Celia had claimed to act only from a desperate wish to end Newsom's sexual demands.

Jameson called Dr. James M. Martin, a Fulton doctor, to testify. All of Jameson's questions to Dr. Martin concerning how long it would take to burn an adult human body brought objections from the prosecutor, which were sustained by Judge William Hall. Thomas Shoatman then testified for the defense, saying "the reason she gave for striking him the second blow was that he threw up his hands to catch her" and "only to hurt him, to keep him from having sexual intercourse with her." Judge Hall ordered both of these statements stricken from the record.

Jameson had valiantly tried to bring Celia's motives before the jury, and the prosecutor had fought to keep her motives from consideration. Slaves had the legal right to preserve their lives, even if the use of deadly force was required. Moreover, according Missouri law, it was a crime "to take any woman unlawfully against her will and by force, menace, or duress, compel her to be defiled." A homicide committed while warding off such a crime against one's person was justifiable. Therefore, when it was time for both the prosecuting and defending attorneys to present Judge Hall with proposed instructions for the jury, Jameson asked that the jury be instructed that "if they . . . believe from the testimony, that the said Newsom at the time of said killing, attempted to compel her against her will to sexual intercourse with him, they will not find her guilty of murder in the first degree." He also asked that "the words 'any woman' " in the Missouri rape statute quoted above, "embrace slave women, as well as free white women."

Jameson's proposed instructions challenged Missouri slave law, which held that since the owned woman was *property*, what we would view as the rape of an enslaved woman by someone other than her master was actually considered *trespass*. And, as Melton McLaurin summarizes the legal quandary posed by this definition, "an owner could hardly be charged with trespassing upon his own property."

Judge Hall refused to present Jameson's self-defense arguments to the jury. On October 10, 1855, Celia was found guilty and ordered "hanged by the neck until dead on the sixteenth day of November 1855." In the meantime, either during or shortly after her trial, Celia's pregnancy ended in a stillbirth.

On to the Missouri Supreme Court

Jameson appealed to the Missouri Supreme Court. He asked for, and expected, a stay of execution until such time as that court ruled.

The court agreed to hear the case but refused a stay of execution. Some unidentified but presumably outraged Calloway County residents "kidnapped" Celia from jail just before her scheduled execution and returned her once the date had passed. Jameson wrote a personal letter to one of the three Missouri Supreme Court justices. Two of the justices sitting in 1855—Judge William Scott and John F. Ryland—had participated in issuing the infamous, proslavery *Dred Scott* decision, which would be upheld by the U.S. Supreme Court in 1857. Jameson wrote to the third justice, Judge Abiel Leonard, saying Judge Hall had "cut out all means of defense," begging for a stay of execution, and pleading with the justices to "please give the matter your earliest attention."

The Supreme Court rendered its decision on December 14, 1855:

> Upon an examination of the record and proceedings of the Circuit Court of Calloway County in the above case, it is thought proper to refuse the prayer of the petitioner—there being seen upon inspection of the record aforesaid no probable cause for such appeal; nor so much doubt as to render it expedient to take the judgment of the Supreme Court thereon. It is thereby ordered by the Court, that an order for the stay of the execution in this case be refused.

Celia was interviewed by a *Fulton Telegraph* reporter on December 20. She said, "As soon as I struck him the Devil got into me, and I struck him with the stick until he was dead, and then rolled him in the fire and burnt him up." She was hanged on December 21, 1855.

—*Kathryn Cullen-DuPont*

Suggestions for Further Reading

Brownmiller, Susan. *Against Our Will: Men, Women, and Rape.* New York: Simon & Schuster, 1975.

Fox-Genovese, Elizabeth. *Within the Plantation Household: Black and White Women of the Old South.* Chapel Hill, N.C.: University of North Carolina Press, 1988.

McLaurin, Melton A. *Celia: A Slave: A true story of violence and retribution in antebellum Missouri.* Athens, Ga.: University of Georgia Press, 1991.

Sterling, Dorothy. *We Are Your Sisters: Black Women in the Nineteenth Century.* New York: W.W. Norton & Co., 1984.

Dred Scott Decision: 1856

Appellant: Dred Scott **Defendant:** John F.A. Sanford
Plaintiff Claim: That Scott, who was a slave, had become a free man when his owner had taken him to a state designated as "free" under the 1820 Missouri Compromise **Chief Defense Lawyers:** Hugh A. Garland, H.S. Geyer, George W. Goode, Reverdy Johnson, and Lyman D Norris
Chief Lawyers for Appellant: Samuel M. Bay, Montgomery Blair, George Ticknor Curtis, Alexander P. Field, Roswell M. Field, and David N. Hall
Justices: John A. Campbell, John Catron, Benjamin R. Curtis, Peter Daniel, Robert Cooper Grier, John McLean, Samuel Nelson, Roger B. Taney, and James M. Wayne. **Place:** Washington, D.C. **Date of Decision:** 1856 December Term **Decision:** That Dred Scott was still a slave, regardless of where his owner took him.

SIGNIFICANCE

The Dred Scott decision effectively ended the Missouri Compromise, hardening the political rivalry between North and South and paving the way for the Civil War.

Dred Scott was born in Virginia sometime in the late 1790s, although historical records concerning the exact time and place are incomplete. Because Scott was black and born into slavery, no one at the time would have taken much interest in such details, other than to note the arrival of another piece of property.

Scott's owner was Peter Blow, who owned a reasonably successful plantation. In 1819, Blow took his family and several slaves, including Scott, to Alabama to start a new plantation. Blow grew tired of farming, and in 1830 moved to St. Louis, Missouri. St. Louis was then a booming frontier town, and Blow opened a hotel. Both Blow and his wife became seriously ill, and were dead by 1832.

Scott's travels westward in a sense mirrored the expansion of the United States during this time period. From the original 13 states on the Atlantic Seaboard, American colonists had pushed to the Mississippi River and beyond. This expansion gave rise to serious political problems, however. Southern states wanted to bring slavery and the plantation lifestyle into the new territories, whereas the Northern states wanted to keep the territories free. Both sides were afraid that, when portions of the territories were eventually admitted as states, the other side would gain political supremacy in Congress owing to the new states' senators and representatives. In 1820, the North and the South struck a deal called the Missouri Compromise. Missouri was admitted to the union as a slave state and Maine was admitted as a free state, preserving the political balance in Congress. Further, slavery was forbidden in any territory north of, but permitted in any territory south of, Missouri's northern border at approximately 36 degrees latitude north.

After the Blows' deaths, their estate sold Scott to an army doctor named John Emerson. Emerson took Scott with him during tours of duty in Illinois and in that part of the Wisconsin and Iowa Territories which would become Minnesota. Both Illinois and Minnesota were within the free territory of the Missouri Compromise. Emerson returned to St. Louis and died December 29, 1843. He left everything, including Scott, to his wife and appointed as executor his wife's brother, John F.A. Sanford.

Scott Sues for Freedom

Tired of a lifetime of slavery, Scott tried to buy his freedom from the widow Emerson, without success. Scott had acquired more education than most slaves and realized that his travels into free territory might give him a claim to freedom. Represented by former Missouri Attorney General Samuel M. Bay, on April 6, 1846, Scott sued for his freedom in the Missouri Circuit Court for the City of St. Louis. Sanford and the widow Emerson were represented by George W. Goode. Because Sanford was the estate executor for Scott's former master, the official reports bear his name as the primary defendant, misspelled to read "*Scott v. Sandford.*"

Legally, Scott's suit was for assault and false imprisonment. A slave could be punished and kept as property, but a free person could not, so the legal charges were in fact window dressing for the issue of Scott's freedom. On June 30, 1847 the case came to trial before Judge Alexander Hamilton. Bay committed a technical error in presenting the plaintiff's evidence, and the jury returned a verdict that same day in Emerson and Sanford's favor. Hamilton granted Bay's motion for a new trial, which was held on January 12, 1850, again before Judge Hamilton. This time, Scott's lawyers were Alexander P. Field and David N. Hall. Sanford had by this time completely taken over the widow Emerson's affairs and retained Hugh A. Garland and Lyman D. Norris for the defense.

At the second trial, the jury held that Scott was a free man, based on certain Missouri state court precedents that held that even though Missouri was a slave state, residence in a free state or territory resulted in a slave's emancipation. Scott's freedom was short-lived, however.

Sanford appealed to the Missouri Supreme Court. After more than two years, Judge William Scott announced that court's decision on March 22, 1852.

Scott reversed the jury verdict of the second trial, stating that Dred Scott was still a slave. Although Judge Scott's decision was couched in legal terms concerning states' rights and the legality of slavery within Missouri's borders, in fact the real basis for the decision was the rise to power of pro-slavery Democrats on the court. Judge Scott justified the court's decision to reverse those legal precedents that supported Dred Scott's freedom by stating that blacks were destined to be slaves:

> We are almost persuaded that the introduction of slavery amongst [Americans] was, in the providence of God, who makes the evil passions of men subservient to His own glory, a means of placing that unhappy race within the pale of civilized nations.

Scott Tries Federal Courts

Following the Missouri Supreme Court's decision, the case was sent back to Judge Hamilton in St. Louis, who was supposed to issue the final order dismissing the case and returning Scott to slavery. Hamilton procrastinated, however, which gave Scott time to hire a new lawyer and get his case into the federal courts. Scott replaced Field and Hall. His new lawyer was Roswell M. Field, who was unrelated to the previous Field. The new Field realized that Sanford had moved to New York City, and was therefore no longer a resident of Missouri. Therefore, Field initiated new proceedings on November 2, 1853, in federal court, under legal provisions that give federal courts jurisdiction over cases between citizens of different states. This principle is called "diversity jurisdiction," and is still valid today. Diversity jurisdiction enabled Scott, as a citizen of Missouri, to sue Sanford, as a citizen of New York, in federal court. The issue of Scott's freedom was now before Judge Robert W. Wells of the U.S. Court for the District of Missouri, located in St. Louis.

The Supreme Court held that Dred Scott, above, was his owner's property and the only "rights" at issue were those of the owner. (Courtesy, Library of Congress)

At the circuit court's 1854 April Term, Wells held that Scott was a Missouri "citizen" for diversity jurisdiction purposes, despite the fact of Scott's slavery. The case then went to trial, which was held on May 15, 1854. In this, Scott's third freedom trial, the jury ruled in Sanford's favor and held that Scott was still a slave. This was despite the fact that Wells, who was a Southerner, was sympathetic to Scott's cause. Field promptly appealed to the U.S. Supreme Court in Washington, D.C. He convinced the distinguished lawyer Montgomery Blair to represent Scott before the Supreme Court, although Scott was virtually penniless.

Blair, who also was originally from Missouri, had successfully pursued political and legal ambitions in Washington. His residence was the now-famous Blair House on Pennsylvania Avenue. Blair was assisted by George Ticknor Curtis. With the assistance of Southern pro-slavery interests, who recognized the potential importance of the Scott case, Sanford also retained some very eminent lawyers. Sanford was represented before the Supreme Court by former Senator Henry S. Geyer, who like Blair had come from Missouri and made a name for himself as a Washington lawyer. Geyer was assisted by former Senator and U.S. Attorney General Reverdy Johnson, who was a personal friend of Chief Justice Roger B. Taney.

Victory for Slavery, Defeat for Scott

The Scott case was filed with the Supreme Court on December 30, 1854, and set for oral argument on the Court's February 1856 Term before Justices John A. Campbell, John Catron, Benjamin R. Curtis, Peter Daniel, Robert Cooper Grier, John McLean, Samuel Nelson, Roger Brooke Taney, and James M. Wayne.

The political makeup of the Court would weigh heavily in its eventual decision. Southern and pro-slavery justices had a clear majority. Campbell was from Alabama. Catron was from Tennessee. Curtis was from Massachusetts, but was sympathetic to the South. Daniel was from Virginia. Grier was from Pennsylvania, but he was a conservative states' rights advocate. McLean, from Ohio, was the only openly anti-slavery justice on the Court. Nelson was from New York, but like Grier he was a defender of states' rights and lukewarm to the anti-slavery cause. Taney, the chief justice, was from Maryland and the leader of the Court's Southern majority. Finally, Wayne was from Georgia. The justices also were conscious of the fact that 1856 was an election year, and that the Scott decision would have important political consequences.

During the 1856 February Term, the justices listened to the parties' arguments for three days. Scott's attorneys presented the "free soil" argument, one favored by Northern abolitionists: once a slave stepped into a free state or territory, he or she was emancipated, or else the power to prohibit slavery was meaningless. Sanford's attorneys presented the states' rights argument, which favored the institution of slavery: Scott had been a slave in Missouri, he had returned to Missouri, and had subjected himself to the jurisdiction of Missouri law and Missouri courts. Therefore, Missouri was entitled to declare Scott a slave, and ignore the fact that Scott would not be a slave elsewhere.

Not surprisingly, most of the justices were in favor of rejecting Scott's freedom plea. However, they could not agree on the proper legal grounds. Some justices wanted to hold that a slave couldn't sue in federal court, other justices wanted to discuss congressional power to prohibit slavery in the territories and the constitutionality of the Missouri Compromise. The justices decided to postpone their decision until after the presidential election and ordered Scott's and Sanford's lawyers to re-argue the case during the Court's 1856 December Term.

In November 1856, Democrat James Buchanan was elected president. Buchanan, indifferent to the slavery issue, would sit idly by over the next four years while the country was split into North and South and headed toward civil war. After the second round of oral argument in December, during which the parties reiterated the same basic positions, Chief Justice Taney announced the decision of the majority of the Court. Taney and six other justices voted to hold that Scott was still a slave. Taney refused to recognize any rights for blacks as citizens under the U.S. Constitution:

> We think they are not, and that they are not included, and were not intended to be included, under the word "citizens" in the Constitution, and can therefore claim none of the rights and privileges which that instrument provides for and secures to citizens of the United States. On the contrary, they were at that time considered as a subordinate and inferior class of beings, who had been subjugated by the dominant race, and, whether emancipated or not, yet remained subject to their authority, and had no rights or privileges but such as those who held the power and the Government might choose to grant them.

From this holding, Taney went on to state that Scott was a slave wherever he went, and could be reclaimed at any time by his lawful owner under that provision of the Constitution that forbids Congress from depriving Americans of life, liberty, and property without due process of law. Taney held that Scott was "property" and therefore the Missouri Compromise was unconstitutional:

> An Act of Congress which deprives a citizen of the United States of his property, merely because he came himself or brought his property into a particular Territory of the United States, and who had committed no offense against the laws, could hardly be dignified with the name of due process of law.

Scott was a slave once again, and the South had won an important victory. The Missouri Compromise, which had preserved the political status quo for nearly 40 years, was swept away. The North would eventually prevail and abolish slavery, but it would do so only after many battles of a much different and bloodier nature during the Civil War.

—Stephen G. Christianson

Suggestions for Further Reading

Ehrlich, Walter. *They Have No Rights: Dred Scott's Struggle for Freedom.* Westport, Conn.: Greenwood Press, 1979.

Fehrenbacher, Don Edward. *Slavery, Law, and Politics: The Dred Scott Case in Historical Perspective.* New York: Oxford University Press, 1981.

Kutler, Stanley I. *The Dred Scott Decision: Law or Politics?* Boston: Houghton Mifflin, 1967.

McGinty, Brian. "Dred Scott's Fight for Freedom Brought Him a Heap O' Trouble." *American History Illustrated* (May 1981): 34–39.

Sudo, Phil. "Five Little People Who Changed U.S. History." *Scholastic Update* (January 26, 1990): 8–10.

Emma Cunningham Trial: 1857

Defendant: Emma Augusta Cunningham **Crime Charged:** Murder
Chief Defense Lawyer: Henry L. Clinton **Chief Prosecutor:** A. Oakley Hall
Judge: Recorder Smith (historical records do not indicate first name)
Place: New York, New York **Dates of Trial:** May 6–May 9, 1857
Verdict: Not guilty

SIGNIFICANCE

Emma Augusta Cunningham was acquitted of Dr. Harvey Burdell's murder, and nearly succeeded in her attempt to collect Burdell's estate on the basis of a forged marriage certificate and a fake pregnancy. Victorian attitudes toward women prevented the authorities from bringing Cunningham to justice.

Emma Augusta Hempstead was born in New York City in 1816. She grew up to be an attractive and intelligent woman. She was also ambitious to make her fortune, and did so through one of the few means open to women of that era: by marrying wealthy men.

She became Emma Cunningham in 1835 when she married George Cunningham, whose life insurance policy left her with $10,000 (a sizable amount in those days) when he died in 1852. Cunningham was a widow but still attractive and only in her 30s when she met Dr. Harvey Burdell, a New York dentist.

Burdell was born in Herkimer, New York, in 1811. He learned dentistry and moved to New York City, where his practice prospered and he accumulated a personal fortune estimated to exceed $100,000. Despite his wealth and professional standing, however, Burdell was far from being a pillar of the community. He was constantly being accused by his creditors of reneging on debts. In 1835, Burdell caused a scandal when on his wedding day he demanded $20,000 from the wealthy father of the bride-to-be to go through with the marriage. Furious, the bride's father refused, threw Burdell out of his house, and canceled the wedding.

In the early 1850s, Cunningham met Burdell, and in 1855 rented a suite of rooms at Burdell's 31 Bond Street mansion. Burdell's mansion was so large that Burdell not only lived there, he also ran his dental practice there, in addition to keeping several tenants such as Cunningham. Cunningham soon developed an intimate relationship not only with Burdell, but also with another tenant, John J. Eckel.

On the night of January 30, 1857, a neighbor heard a scream from Burdell's house that sounded like, "Murder!" The next morning, one of Burdell's servants discovered the doctor's body in his office, covered with multiple stab wounds. Police medical experts examined the body, and determined that Burdell had been stabbed 15 times with a knife wielded by a left-handed assailant. The police suspected that Cunningham, who was left-handed, had murdered Burdell with Eckel's help. The police arrested Cunningham for Burdell's murder, and she was imprisoned until trial.

The crowded courtroom where the jury returned a verdict of not guilty. (*Harper's Weekly*)

Cunningham Makes Startling Announcement

From her prison cell Cunningham announced that she had been Burdell's wife and revealed a marriage certificate, which stated that the marriage took place on October 28, 1856. Eckel's physical appearance resembled Burdell's, however, and the police suspected that Cunningham had had Eckel impersonate Burdell to obtain the certificate. Further, Cunningham said she was pregnant with Burdell's baby. If Cunningham was Burdell's wife and the mother of his child, not only would it be harder for the prosecution to show motive for the murder but, if acquitted, Cunningham would be entitled to all of Burdell's $100,000 estate.

Cunningham's trial began May 6, 1857. Her lawyer was Henry L. Clinton. The prosecutor was District Attorney A. Oakley Hall and the judge was Recorder Smith. Very little of the actual trial testimony has survived, but according to several accounts, Cunningham testified that her marriage with Burdell was a happy one and she denied murdering her supposed husband. One of Burdell's maids, however, testified that Cunningham had once stated that Burdell was "not fit to live" and that it was time he "was out of this world." Further, according to the maid, Cunningham had called Burdell "a bad man."

Prosecutor Hall also introduced Mary Crane, an old friend of Dr. Burdell's, as a witness. Crane testified that shortly before his death Burdell told her "that he had let his house to a lady and that she was the most horrible woman he ever met." Further, according to Crane, Burdell suspected that Cunningham was involved with Eckel and had claimed that the two were "prowling about" at night.

Unfortunately for Hall, Burdell's own reputation made it difficult to make anything stick against Cunningham. Further, Clinton introduced witnesses such as Dr. Roberts, (no first name available) a colleague of Burdell's who testified that the relationship between Burdell and Cunningham had been to all appearances peaceful and loving. Finally, Cunningham's alleged pregnancy was now well advanced, and her abdomen was appropriately swollen whenever she appeared in public. On May 9, 1857, the jury returned a verdict of not guilty. Cunningham left the courtroom a free woman.

Victorian morality prevented doctors from examining Emma Cunningham and proving her pregnancy false. (*Harper's Weekly*)

The affair was not over yet, however. Dr. Uhl, (no first name available) who was attending to Cunningham during her supposed pregnancy, went to Hall and stated that he was suspicious. Uhl thought that Cunningham was simply stuffing her dress with cushions. Unfortunately, Cunningham had refused to let Uhl physically examine her, and Uhl's treatment had been limited to minor matters such as prescribing bed rest in response to Cunningham's verbal descriptions of her symptoms. At the time, however, it was not unusual for a woman to refuse physical examination during pregnancy on the grounds that it was immoral for any man not her husband to touch her.

Further, Victorian morality made it impossible for Hall to order Cunningham to submit to a proper medical examination. However, Hall ordered a stakeout of 31 Bond Street, where Cunningham still lived. On July 27, 1857, the police stopped a nun who was bringing a basket to the door. The basket contained a baby, which Cunningham had paid $1,000 to adopt.

Caught red-handed, Cunningham dropped her claims to Burdell's estate, thus implicitly admitting that she had never been married to Burdell nor been pregnant with his child. Hall didn't have any medical evidence to prove that Cunningham had faked her pregnancy, however, and since she had already been acquitted of Burdell's murder, the legal obstacles to bringing her to justice were practically insurmountable. Therefore, Hall was forced to let Cunningham go. Cunningham was smart enough to realize that she would always be under a cloud of suspicion in New York City, and she moved to California. Apparently she spent her final years running a moderately prosperous vineyard.

No one was ever convicted of Burdell's murder. If he had been able to get the proper medical evidence, Hall might have been able to prove that Cunningham was guilty. Victorian morality, however, prevented this. The real mother of the "market-basket" baby Cunningham had tried to purchase for $1,000 stayed in New York City, and rented her baby to P.T. Barnum's circus for $25 a week for the public to view.

—*Stephen G. Christianson*

Suggestions for Further Reading

Clinton, Henry Lauren. *Celebrated Trials.* New York: Harper & Brothers, 1897.

Duke, Thomas Samuel. *Celebrated Criminal Cases of America.* San Francisco: James H. Barry Co., 1910.

Lewis, Alfred Henry. *Nation-Famous New York Murders.* New York: G.W. Dillingham Co., 1914.

Paul, Raymond. *The Bond Street Burlesque: a Historical Novel of Murder.* New York: W.W. Norton & Co., 1987.

Pearson, Edmund Lester. *Murder at Smutty Nose, and Other Murders.* Garden City, N.Y.: Dolphin Books, 1965.

"Duff" Armstrong Trial: 1858

Defendant: William Armstrong **Crime Charged:** Murder
Chief Defense Lawyer: Abraham Lincoln **Chief Prosecutors:** Hugh Fullerton and J. Henry Shaw **Judge:** James Harriot **Place:** Beardstown, Illinois **Date of Trial:** May 8, 1858 **Verdict:** Not guilty

SIGNIFICANCE

William Armstrong's trial is considered to be Lincoln's most famous case. By introducing an almanac into evidence, Lincoln proved that the witness who swore that he saw Armstrong kill a man at night under a full moon was lying.

When he was nothing more than a young backwoods man struggling to make his way in the world, Abraham Lincoln lived for a while in the little town of New Salem, Illinois. He studied law while working in the local grocery store. One day, a local bully named Jack Armstrong challenged Lincoln to a wrestling match. Lincoln won the match, and earned Armstrong's respect. Soon, Lincoln was a close friend of Armstrong and his wife Hannah. When the Armstrongs had a baby, William, Lincoln used to rock the infant to sleep whenever he paid a visit.

Lincoln eventually left New Salem for Springfield, Illinois and an eminently successful career in law and politics. Over 20 years later, in 1857, Lincoln learned that William Armstrong, nicknamed "Duff" and now a grown man, had been charged with murder. According to the authorities, an intoxicated "Duff" Armstrong murdered James Preston Metzker on the night of August 29, 1857. Jack Armstrong, the father, was dead, and Hannah Armstrong was a widow. Lincoln wrote Mrs. Armstrong and asked to defend her son:

> I have just heard of your deep affliction, and the arrest of your son for murder. I can hardly believe that he can be capable of the crime alleged against him. It does not seem possible. I am anxious that he should be given a fair trial at any rate; and the gratitude for your long continued kindness to me in adverse circumstances prompts me to offer my humble service gratuitously in his behalf.

Lincoln went to the town of Beardstown, Illinois, where Armstrong was being tried. The trial was held May 8, 1858. Lincoln was the defense lawyer, and the prosecutors were Hugh Fullerton and J. Henry Shaw. The judge was James Harriot.

The prosecution's case rested on the testimony of key witness Charles Allen, who said that on the night of the murder he saw "Duff" Armstrong strike Metzker under the light of a full moon. According to the notes of an eyewitness, Lincoln was calm, almost bored while the prosecution made its case:

> Lincoln sat with his head thrown back, his steady gaze apparently fixed upon one spot of the blank ceiling, entirely oblivious to what was happening about him, and without a single variation of feature or noticeable movement. . . .

When it was his turn to cross-examine Allen, Lincoln asked Allen about the precise details of the night in question. Allen testified that on the night of August 29, 1857, there was a full moon and that from a distance of about 150 feet he saw Armstrong kill Metzker. Allen further stated that the incident occurred about 11:00 o'clock.

With dramatic suddenness, Lincoln dropped his bored veneer and asked Judge Harriot for permission to enter an 1857 almanac into evidence. Judge Harriot granted Lincoln's motion, and Lincoln had Allen read the almanac entry for August 29, 1857. There was no full moon that night; in fact, there had been no moon at all by 11:00 o'clock. Therefore, it would have been impossible for Allen to see anything from a distance of 150 feet. Allen had obviously lied under oath.

Armstrong's trial closed by the end of the day. Judge Harriot had allowed the jury to look at the almanac and confirm their opinion that Allen had perjured himself. After a passionate plea to the jury for Armstrong's freedom, Lincoln rested the defense. While the jury deliberated, Lincoln confidently predicted that they would acquit Armstrong by sunset. He was right: after only one ballot, the jury's verdict was not guilty.

Lincoln won Duff's acquittal by convincing Judge Harriot to allow into evidence scientific data in the form of the almanac as to what the actual lunar conditions had been. This procedure is called judicial notice, and is a common occurrence today. In the 1850s, however, it was a novelty because the judicial system relied almost entirely on witness testimony.

For what eventually would be regarded as his most famous case, Lincoln didn't charge "Duff" or Hannah Armstrong one cent. Illinois' most famous lawyer, and ultimately one of America's greatest presidents, did the case for free.

—Stephen G. Christianson

Suggestions for Further Reading

Fleming, Thomas. "Lincoln's Favorite Case." *Boys' Life* (September 1985): 20.

Frank, John Paul. *Lincoln as a Lawyer.* Urbana: University of Illinois Press, 1961.

Hill, Frederick Trevor. *Lincoln, the Lawyer.* New York: Century Co., 1906.

Whitney, Henry Clay. *Life on the Circuit with Lincoln.* Caldwell, Idaho: Caxton Printers, 1940.

Woldman, Albert A. *Lawyer Lincoln.* Boston & New York: Houghton Mifflin Co., 1936.

Daniel Sickles Trial: 1859

Defendant: Daniel Sickles **Crime Charged:** Murder
Chief Defense Lawyers: James T. Brady, John Graham, and Edwin M. Stanton **Chief Prosecutor:** Robert Ould **Judge:** Crawford (First name unavailable) **Place:** Washington, D.C. **Dates of Trial:** April 4–26, 1859
Verdict: Not guilty

SIGNIFICANCE

The first use of a plea of temporary insanity by a criminal defendant and the unabashed appeal to the "unwritten law" to justify homicide made the Daniel Sickles case noteworthy in American legal history. It was equally significant for the irreparable damage done to Sickles' promising career as a leader of the Democratic Party.

Daniel Sickles' murder of Philip Barton Key was the kind of crime that piques the interest of all but the most austere newspaper editors. The lurid trial captivated the nation's press.

The menu for the trial was perfect: glamorous celebrities, political intrigue, spellbinding lawyers, the plot of an Italian opera, and an adulterous affair. The accused, Dan Sickles, was a prominent and well-connected 39-year-old Congressman from New York with a hair-trigger temper and a reputation as a ladies' man; the victim, Barton Key, was not only a close friend of his killer, whose political clout with President James Buchanan had secured Key's appointment as Washington's district attorney, but he also was the son of Francis Scott Key, author of "The Star Spangled Banner". He was described as "the handsomest man in all Washington society" by the city's most prominent hostess and biggest gossip, Mrs. Clement Clay.

The very time and scene of the crime commanded the public's attention and sparked courtroom and editorial fireworks. Not even the most highbrowed Victorian could ignore a killing that occurred in broad daylight on a Sunday afternoon on the sidewalk surrounding Lafayette Park, literally so near the White House it could have been witnessed from its front windows.

But it was the motive that added the most spice to the story. Sickles gunned Key down after discovering that he and the beautiful 22-year-old Mrs. Sickles had been having an affair, at times carrying on in the front library of the Sickles home.

By the time Sickles was tipped off by an anonymous letter, dated February 24, 1859, the relationship between Teresa Sickles and Key was certainly the primary topic of conversation in the family's servant quarters and had started tongues wagging in Washington society. Confronting his wife with the evidence that he and a close friend collected, Dan Sickles extracted a detailed written confession from her and then, in state of near hysteria, called two of his political cronies to his home to ask for their advice.

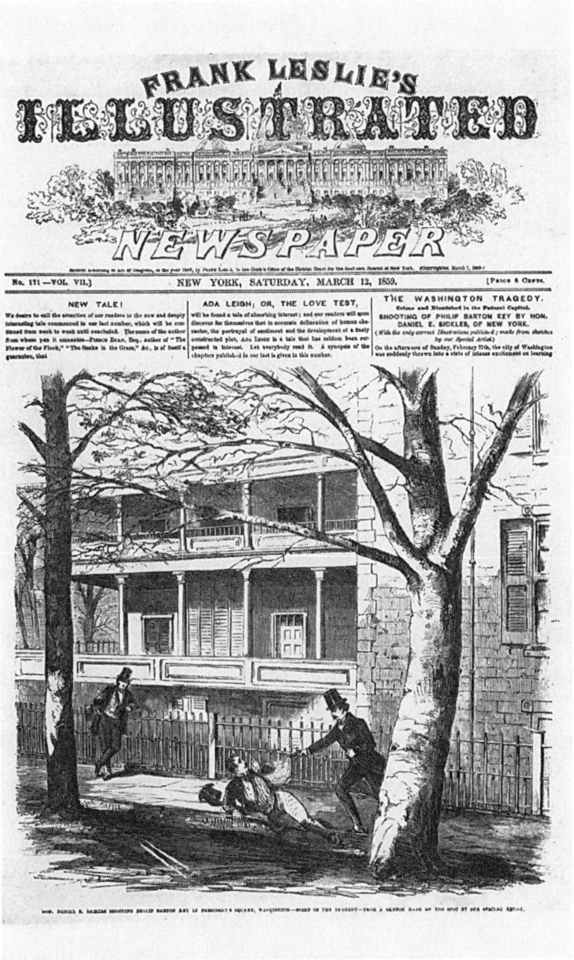
FRANK LESLIE'S ILLUSTRATED NEWSPAPER

No. 171—VOL. VII.] NEW YORK, SATURDAY, MARCH 12, 1859. [Price 6 Cents.

NEW TALE!

We desire to call the attention of our readers to the new and deeply interesting tale commenced in our last number, which will be continued from week to week until concluded. The name of the author from whose pen it emanates—Pierce Egan, Esq., author of "The Flower of the Flock," "The Snake in the Grass," &c., is of itself a guarantee, that

ADA LEIGH; OR, THE LOVE TEST,

will be found a tale of absorbing interest; and our readers will soon discover for themselves that in accurate delineation of human character, the portrayal of sentiment and the development of a finely constructed plot, Ada Leigh is a tale that has seldom been surpassed in interest. Let everybody read it. A synopsis of the chapters published in our last is given in this number.

THE WASHINGTON TRAGEDY.

Crime and Bloodshed in the Federal Capital.

SHOOTING OF PHILIP BARTON KEY BY HON. DANIEL E. SICKLES, OF NEW YORK.

(With the only correct Illustrations published; made from sketches by our Special Artist.)

On the afternoon of Sunday, February 27th, the city of Washington was suddenly thrown into a state of intense excitement on learning

Congressman Daniel Sickles' promising political future was doomed after he shot his friend Barton Key. (Courtesy, Library of Congress)

Meanwhile, upset because he had not heard from Teresa Sickles for several days, Key rented a front room in the Cosmos Club across Lafayette Park from the Sickles home. From there, peering through his opera glasses, he tried to spot a signal from Mrs. Sickles. Impatient and unaware that her husband knew all, Key twice passed in front of the Sickles' home on February 27, brazenly signaling Teresa Sickles with his white pocket handkerchief.

At home and pacing the floor, Dan Sickles abruptly stopped, looked out a front window, and cried out, "That villain is out there now making signs." One of the advisors consoling him, the Tammany politician Samuel F. Butterworth, agreed to go across the park to check whether Key had a room at the club. A few moments later, Butterworth recollected, Sickles stormed out of the house, whereupon he saw Key mingling with the Sunday afternoon strollers promenading around Lafayette Park.

Pounding up to Key, Sickles raged, "Key, you scoundrel, you have dishonored my house—you must die!"

Sickles pulled out a pistol and fired. The two men grappled momentarily before Sickles pulled himself away and fired again. Hurling his opera glasses at his attacker, the wounded Key ducked behind a tree where Sickles' next bullet lodged. Ignoring Key's cries for mercy, Sickles shot again and Key staggered and fell into the gutter. Standing over Key, Sickles aimed at his head, but the gun misfired. Finally, a passerby became involved, pinning Sickles' arms and subduing him.

While Key was dying inside the club, Sickles took a carriage to the home of Attorney General Jeremiah S. Black and surrendered.

Mobilizing the Defense

Refusing bail, Sickles awaited trial in Washington's vermin-infested jail as the press, fed juicy tidbits by the defense, rehashed the details of the case daily until the editors, bored with facts, filled their columns with malicious gossip and preposterous speculation, including a rumor that Teresa Sickles was pregnant with Key's child.

Washington and the nation anticipated a hugely entertaining trial. A reinforced police contingent barely contained the mobs demanding admission to the old City Hall where the court convened on April 4, 1859 to select a jury.

Inside the cramped courtroom, eight renowned lawyers assembled to defend Sickles. Led by the suave James T. Brady, a New York criminal lawyer famed for his ability to manipulate witnesses, the team included Edwin M. Stanton, a Constitutional expert and an emotional orator of unsurpassed decibel power, and John Graham, a defense lawyer famed for his ability to draw tears from the most hard-hearted juror. The prosecution was badly out-classed. U.S. District Attorney Robert Ould, Key's meek and untalented former assistant, had little heart for his arduous and unpopular task. Ould inspired so little confidence in Key's relatives that they insisted he take on James Carlisle as assistant counsel, paying his fee out of their own pockets.

If Ould and Carlisle had any illusions about their prospects, these were quickly dispelled during the three days it took to select a jury. Of the first 75 potential jurors called, 72 openly sympathized with Sickles. Some 200 were excused for pro-Sickles bias before a jury of tradesmen and farmers could be impaneled.

Cold-Blooded Murder or Justifiable Homicide?

Ould opened with a sarcastic attack on Sickles' desecration of the Sabbath by a "deed of blood" against an "unarmed and defenseless victim." Noting that Sickles "bravely" and "fully prepared" himself with three guns, Ould portrayed the slaying as deliberate, premeditated, and merciless—a clear case of murder "no matter what may be the antecedent provocations in the case." Of course, it was precisely these "antecedent provocations," or Teresa Sickles' adultery, that everyone, including the jurors, were most interested in and exactly what the defense planned to spotlight in its case.

The defense's version of the slaying was distilled to its essence in John Graham's opening statement: "The injured husband and father rushes upon" the "confirmed and habitual" adulterer "in the moment of his guilt, and under the influence of a frenzy executes upon him a judgment which was as just as it was summary." Generously sprinkling his statement with Biblical quotations,

Graham described Sickles' action as no less than the execution of "the will of Heaven."

Just in case the jury didn't accept Dan Sickles as one of the Lord's avenging angels, defense attorney Graham argued with equal fervor that the provocation had so unbalanced the defendant's mind that he could not be held accountable for his actions: "If he was in a state of white heat, was that too great a state of passion for a man to be in who saw before him the hardened, the unrelenting seducer of his wife?"

By the end of Graham's three-day statement, it was obvious Key would be the real defendant in the trial. Sickles' lawyers clearly planned to paint the victim as a lecher who richly deserved his fate at the hands of the accused. Despite this unveiling of the defense strategy, Ould did nothing to expose the hypocrisy of Sickles, who himself was vulnerable as a notorious philanderer. Instead, Ould contented himself with calling a series of eyewitnesses to the slaying who merely repeated the same tale in slightly different words.

The defense called numerous witnesses who attested to Sickles' mental anguish at the time of the slaying. Former Secretary of the Treasury Robert J. Walker declared Sickles was in "an agony of despair, the most terrible thing I ever saw in my life. . . . I feared if it continued he would become permanently insane." Sickles was so racked with sobs during Walker's testimony that he had to be ushered from the courtroom to compose himself. As he left, many in the audience wept.

When the defense attempted to introduce Teresa Sickles' confession into evidence, Ould leapt to his feet objecting that it was inadmissible as both hearsay and a privileged communication between husband and wife. Judge Crawford sustained him on the common law principle that putting such a document into the public record might do irreparable harm to the marriage. Judge Crawford's instruction to the jury to ignore the confession was so much wasted breath. The confession was reproduced in full on the front page of the April 23, 1859 issue of *Harper's Weekly.*

Time and again as the defense tried to introduce evidence of the adultery, prosecutor Ould furiously objected and Stanton responded with withering sarcasm. Trapped by the precedent of his own ruling in a similar case, Judge Crawford was forced in the end to permit the defense to present some evidence proving the adultery. However, the real damage was done in the uneven exchanges between Ould and Stanton, who skillfully maneuvered the prosecutor into seeming to conceal, if not excuse, infidelity and debauchery.

Assistant prosecutor Carlisle did his best to refute the defense claims of justifiable homicide and/or temporary insanity in his final statement before the jury. But, he couldn't compete with defense attorney Stanton's soaring and thunderous expression of indignation over the sanctity of the American family and the rights of the betrayed American husband. Wrapping himself and his client in the cloak of virtue, Stanton declaimed that a "higher law" than those enacted by human legislators "was written in the heart of man in the Garden of Eden" and that this law and even the laws of self-preservation set death as the penalty for seducing another man's wife. Inevitably, Stanton proclaimed, once a wife has "surrendered to the adulterer, she longs for the death of her husband, whose life is often sacrificed by the cup of the poisoner or the dagger or pistol of the assassin."

Before the case went to the jury April 26, Judge Crawford pointedly instructed the jurors that, in the eyes of earthly law, any delay between becoming aware of an adultery and the slaying of the adulterer by an enraged husband made the killing deliberate murder, or at the very least manslaughter.

Sickles' defense team successfully portrayed their client as temporarily insane. The jury returned a verdict of "not guilty" in less than one hour. (Courtesy, Library of Congress)

When the jury returned in a little over an hour and, to no one's surprise, delivered a verdict of "Not Guilty," it was greeted by three cheers and sparked a spirited celebration among spectators and the defense team. The usually dour Stanton performed a jig on the spot. That evening 1,500 people joined Sickles in a victory party.

Public Opinion Turns Against Sickles

Some segments of society and the legal profession were sickened by the verdict and even more by the way the defense had secured it. The mud thrown at the deceased's name, the public humiliation of Teresa Sickles, the manipulation of the press and, perhaps most of all, the cynical appeal to Old Testament morality in defense of a notorious Don Juan made the trial a farce and a travesty of justice in the eyes of many.

What little social standing and political aspirations Sickles retained were utterly destroyed when he and Teresa effected a public reconciliation only three months after the acquittal. The move flabbergasted his political cronies, scandalized society, and called down upon the couple the wrath and ridicule of the press.

Although Sickles partially redeemed his reputation in 1863 by losing a leg to a Confederate cannonball at the Battle of Gettysburg, public distrust was too deep for his political career to regain its early momentum. When Sickles died in 1914, he was remembered as the first accused murderer to escape punishment by pleading temporary insanity.

—Edward W. Knappman

Suggestions for Further Reading

Balderston, Thomas. "The Shattered Life of Teresa Sickles." *American History Illustrated* (September 1982): 41–45.

Cooney, Charles F. "The General's Badge of Honor." *American History Illustrated* (April 1985): 16–17.

Morris, Richard B. *Fair Trial.* New York: Alfred A. Knopf, 1952.

Pinchon, Edgcumb. *Dan Sickles, Hero of Gettysburg and "Yankee King of Spain."* Garden City, N.Y.: Doubleday & Co., 1945.

Swanburg, W.A. *Sickles the Incredible.* New York: Charles Scribner's Sons, 1956.

John Brown Trial: 1859

Defendant: John Brown **Crime Charged:** Insurrection and murder
Chief Defense Lawyers: Lawson Botts, Thomas C. Green, Samuel Chilton, and Hiram Griswold **Chief Prosecutor:** Andrew Hunter **Judge:** Richard Parker **Place:** Charles Town, Virginia **Dates of Trial:** October 27–November 2, 1859 **Verdict:** Guilty **Sentence:** Death by hanging

SIGNIFICANCE

Tried for leading a famous but unsuccessful raid on the federal arsenal in Harpers Ferry, Virginia, with the object of arming Southern slaves, John Brown's trial and execution by the Commonwealth of Virginia made him a martyr to Northerners determined to abolish slavery.

"A house divided cannot stand." These five words have been used by statesmen and historians alike to describe the condition of the United States in the years leading up to the Civil War. The tension between the Southern slave states and the Northern free states, which had never been resolved by the founding fathers, grew steadily worse after 1800 as the economic importance of cotton and slavery to the South increased. Despite repeated attempts at compromise, no satisfactory political formula could be found to reconcile North and South.

The schism widened as the newly settled territories of the West applied for admission to the Union in the early and middle decades of the 19th Century. Northerners wanted new states to be Free, and thus off limits to slavery. Southerners wanted new states to be Slave, and thus potential areas of expansion for the plantation economy of the South. Both sides wanted to have the votes of the representatives that a new state would send to Washington, particularly in the U.S. Senate, where every state, large or small, has two votes. As pro-slavery and anti-slavery forces from inside and outside the territories contested bitterly for control of these soon-to-be states, they turned to violence to resolve the issue.

Brown Raises Sword of Abolition

Sometimes great events thrust ordinary and obscure people into the limelight. Certainly this was true of John Brown, born in 1800 to Yankee farmers

Owen Brown and Ruth Mills Brown. The Browns made a modest living from the family farm near Torrington, Connecticut, enough to permit their son to enter school for training as a minister. John Brown was a poor student, however, and shortly returned to the family farm after failing his classes. This failure was to be the first of many. John Brown went on to try and fail at earning a living as a farmer, surveyor, real estate investor, postmaster, teacher, racehorse breeder, tanner, and wool merchant.

Unsuccessful in business throughout his life, Brown was already past 50 when he took up the cause of abolition. Some wealthy east coast businessmen and philanthropists gave Brown the support and financing necessary to set up a farm in North Elba, New York, where runaway slaves would be taught how to become independent farmers. Brown soon lost interest in the project, however, and set out for the "front lines" of the abolitionist struggle. In the mid-1850s, Brown took his wife and some of his many sons to the little hamlet of Osawatomie, Kansas.

Kansas at the time was a battleground, known as "Bleeding Kansas" for the undeclared war raging then between the Free and Slave state forces. Brown lost no time in joining the fray. From Osawatomie, Brown led his sons and several followers in a raid on the neighboring pro-slavery settlement of Pottawatomie that left five dead. After this massacre, Brown and his followers became fugitives, engaging in hit-and-run raids against pro-slavery forces in Kansas and elsewhere.

Despite his unabashed use of violence, Brown continued to attract wealthy and influential backers. Of his backers, the most important were the "Secret Six": Gerrit Smith, heir to a large fortune who had financed temperance and prison reform movements before turning to abolition; Franklin B. Sanborn, a young Massachusetts patrician with a Harvard education; George Luther Stearns, who financed Brown's activities with the profits from Stearns' thriving business; Samuel Gridley Howe, a prominent abolitionist who preached violence in the cause of ending slavery and looked to Brown to practice it; Thomas Wentworth Higginson, a liberal minister; and Ralph Waldo Emerson, the famous poet. In 1859, Brown obtained support from these men for a proposed raid on the federal arsenal at Harpers Ferry, Virginia. The plan was to seize the arsenal, arm the hordes of slaves who would supposedly flock to Brown's cause, and march on Southern state capitals to end slavery forever.

On October 16, 1859, Brown and 21 raiders succeeded in seizing the Harpers Ferry arsenal by surprise. Instead of attracting black followers, however, the raid only succeeded in bringing out the armed and angry local white residents, who surrounded the arsenal until federal troops arrived. Ironically, the soldiers sent to protect federal property were commanded by Colonel Robert E. Lee, the famous general of the Confederacy during the Civil War. After a brief siege, the arsenal was stormed. Brown, together with his few surviving followers, was captured and taken under guard to nearby Charles Town, Virginia. (Harpers Ferry and Charles Town later became part of West Virginia.)

Virginia Tries Brown for Treason

When news of Harpers Ferry reached Richmond, Henry A. Wise, the politically ambitious governor, had an important decision to make. Under the division of power that existed between state and federal governments before the Civil War, it was Wise's prerogative to decide whether Brown would be tried in a Virginia court for violating the laws of the commonwealth or turned over to the national authorities for prosecution in the federal courts. The Virginia court at Charles Town, where a grand jury was already in session, would be quicker. A federal court, however, would not be as open to charges of Southern bias. Whether out of fear that a mob would lynch Brown if he were not tried quickly, or out of a desire to score political prestige for himself and Virginia, Governor Wise decided to proceed with a state trial.

It fell to Andrew Hunter, the district attorney for Charles Town, to be the prosecutor. Hunter shared Governor Wise's desire to prosecute Brown quickly. To defend Brown, a magistrate appointed Lawson Botts, a local Virginia attorney, and Thomas C. Green, an attorney who was also the mayor of Charles Town. From his prison cell, Brown wrote his abolitionist allies for outside legal counsel.

Judge Richard Parker, justice of the circuit court for the town of Charles Town, was also an advocate of speedy justice. Judge Parker's grand jury returned an indictment against Brown within 24 hours. Further, Judge Parker denied Botts' and Green's request that the trial be delayed until Brown could recover from injuries sustained when the troops stormed the arsenal. As a result, when Brown's trial began on October 27, he attended the proceedings lying in a cot, nursing his wounds.

Brown's Lawyers Search for a Defense

Brown's attorneys had to put together a defense in the face of opposition not only from Judge Parker and prosecutor Hunter, but from Brown himself. When the trial began, Botts made a critical motion to Judge Parker. Botts asked him to declare Brown insane, using a telegram from a certain A.H. Lewis of Akron, Ohio, to support this plea. Lewis, who apparently had known Brown from when the family lived in Akron, wrote, "Insanity is hereditary in that family. . . . These facts can be conclusively proven by witnesses residing here, who will doubtless attend the trial if desired."

A successful insanity defense could have saved Brown from the gallows, leaving him to live out his life in an asylum. Brown himself, however, closed the door on the issue. Protesting from his cot, he said angrily: "I look upon this as a miserable pretext of those who ought to take a different course in regard to me, if they took any at all. . . . I am perfectly unconscious of insanity, and I reject, so far as I am capable, any attempt to interfere on my behalf on that score." This outburst effectively destroyed the chances for any insanity defense, despite some later attempts to revive the issue.

Despite their Virginia roots and the weight of Southern opinion, Botts and Green had gone out on a limb for Brown by asserting "hereditary insanity" and were soon out of the case. They were replaced by Hiram Griswold, a lawyer from Cleveland, Ohio, and Samuel Chilton, a lawyer from Washington, D.C. Judge Parker would not permit the momentum of Hunter's prosecution to slacken for one instant, however, and refused to give Griswold and Chilton any extra time to organize their defense. Hunter had more than enough witnesses ready to testify. To support the charge of murder, witnesses described the killings by Brown and his men during the Harpers Ferry raid. The charge of insurrection was supported by the testimony of witnesses who had overheard Brown talk of arming runaway slaves to fight their masters.

John Brown's photograph was taken shortly before his death. (Courtesy, Library of Congress)

Despite the disadvantages he labored under, Griswold put together an aggressive closing statement. He attacked the charge of insurrection, claiming that as a non-Virginian Brown didn't owe the commonwealth any duty of loyalty. This last line of defense fared no better than the insanity argument. After less than an hour of deliberation, the jury returned a guilty verdict. Judge Parker then held the trial in recess for a few days while one of Brown's fellow raiders was tried in the same courtroom. On November 2, the trial was reconvened and Judge Parker sentenced Brown to hang on December 2, 1859.

Brown's Martyrdom Secures Victory in Death

When he stood before Judge Parker on November 2, 1859, to receive his sentence, John Brown must have known he faced certain execution. Affirmation of the sentence by the Virginia Court of Appeals would be a formality. Brown used the occasion, however, to make a stirring statement that would galvanize Northern public opinion against slavery and the South:

> This court acknowledges, as I suppose, the validity of the law of God. I see a book kissed here which I suppose to be the Bible, or at least the New Testament. That teaches me that all things whatsoever I would that men should do to me, I should do even so to them. It teaches me, further, to "remember them that are in bonds, as bound with them." I endeavored to act up to that instruction. I say, I am yet too young to understand that God is any respecter of persons. I believe that to have interfered as I have done—in behalf of His despised poor, was not wrong, but right. Now, if it is deemed necessary that I should forfeit my life for the furtherance of the ends of justice, and mingle my blood further with the blood of my children and with

> the blood of millions in this slave country whose rights are disregarded by wicked, cruel, and unjust enactments, I submit, so let it be done!

In the month following Brown's sentencing, Governor Wise received thousands of letters and petitions pleading for mercy. Some came from astute Southerners, who realized that Brown's execution would rally anti-slavery forces. Nevertheless, Wise let the sentence stand. On December 2, 1859, before he went to the gallows, Brown delivered his final message to North and South alike, one that predicted and sealed in the minds of many Americans the inevitability of the Civil War:

> I John Brown am now quite certain that the crimes of this guilty land will never be purged away but with Blood. I had, as I now think, vainly flattered myself that without very much bloodshed it might be done.

—*Stephen G. Chrisrianson*

Suggestions for Further Reading

Ansley, Delight. *The Sword and the Spirit: A Life of John Brown.* New York: Thomas Y. Crowell Co., 1955.

Emerson, Ralph Waldo. "John Brown," *Emerson's Complete Works.* Boston and New York: Houghton Mifflin, 1878 and 1883.

"The Ghost at Harpers Ferry." *American Heritage* (November 1988): 30–31.

McGlone, Robert E. "Rescripting a Troubled Past: John Brown's Family and the Harpers Ferry Conspiracy." *Journal of American History* (March 1989): 1179–1200.

Oates, Stephen B. *To Purge This Land With Blood: A Biography of John Brown.* New York: Harper & Row, 1970.

Ruchames, Louis. *John Brown: The Making of a Revolutionary.* New York: Grossett & Dunlap, 1969.

Sanborn, Franklin B. *The Life and Letters of John Brown.* Boston: Roberts Brothers, 1885.

Dakota Conflict Trials: 1862

Defendants: 393 Dakota Sioux Indians and people of mixed racial background **Crimes Charged:** Murder and "other outrages" against citizens of the United States **Chief Defense Lawyer:** None **Chief Prosecutor:** None **Judges:** Military Commission Officers Lieutenant Rollin Olin (judge advocate), Colonel William Crooks, Colonel William Marshall, Captain Hiram Grant, Captain Hiram Bailey, and Major George Bradley (replaced Colonel Marshall after the first 29 cases) **Places:** Camp Release, Minnesota and Lower Agency, Minnesota **Dates of Trials:** September 28–November 3, 1862 **Verdicts:** 323 defendants: Guilty; 70 defendants: Not guilty **Sentences:** 303 defendants: Death by hanging (38 later hanged); 90 defendants: Imprisonment

SIGNIFICANCE

The trials satisfied the vengeance demands of outraged white settlers for the Dakota Conflict (also known as the "Sioux Uprising"), which took the lives of nearly 500 Minnesota residents. The trials and harsh sentences bred resentment among the Dakota Indians, and American-Sioux conflicts continued for nearly 30 years, finally ending with the massacre at Wounded Knee, South Dakota, on December 29, 1890.

In August 1862, about 7,000 Dakota Sioux lived on reservation lands on the Minnesota frontier. Many faced starvation because of failed crops. Annuity payments due to them for recent (and disputed) land cessions did not arrive on time, and Indian representatives pleaded with traders to distribute provisions held in agency warehouses on credit until the annuity payments finally arrived from Washington. Traders resisted the Sioux's pleas at an August 15 meeting. Andrew Myrick summarized his position in the bluntest possible manner: "So far as I am concerned, if they are hungry, let them eat grass."

Unbeknownst to the traders or the Indians, the long-delayed annuity payments—in the form of a barrel containing $71,000 worth of gold coins—were already on their way to southwestern Minnesota. The gold reached St. Paul the next day, then was sent to Fort Ridgely for distribution to the Sioux. The payments, however, arrived a few hours too late to prevent an unprecedented outbreak of violence that left nearly 500 settlers and an undetermined number of Dakota Sioux dead.

Two days after the meeting, four Indians from a breakaway band of young malcontents while on a hunting trip came across some eggs along the fence line of a settler's homestead. One of the four grabbed the eggs, while another warned him that the eggs belonged to a white man. The first young man became angry, dashed the eggs to the ground, and accused the other of being afraid of white men, even though being half-starved. Apparently to disprove the accusation of cowardice, the other Sioux said that to show he was not afraid of white men he would go the house and shoot the owner; he challenged the others to join him. Minutes later the occupants—three men, a woman, and a 15-year-old girl—lay dead.

Big Eagle, a Dakota Sioux chief, recounted what happened after the young men reached Chief Shakopee's camp late on that night:

> The tale told by the young men created the greatest excitement. Everybody was waked up and heard it. Shakopee took the young men to [Chief] Little Crow's, and he sat up in bed and listened to their story. He said war was now declared. Blood had been shed, the payment would be stopped, and the whites would take a dreadful vengeance because women had been killed. Wabasha, Wacouta, myself and others still talked for peace, but nobody would listen to us, and soon the cry was "Kill the whites and kill all these cut-hairs who will not join us." A council was held and war was declared. Parties formed and dashed away in the darkness to kill settlers. The women began to run bullets and the men to clean their guns. . . .

The Dakota Conflict, or "Sioux Uprising," began with an attack on the Lower Agency along the Minnesota River. One of the first casualties was trader Andrew Myrick, who was discovered dead, his mouth stuffed full of grass. Over the next few days nearly 200 settlers were killed, as the Sioux massacred farm families and attacked frontier fortifications. Southwestern Minnesota was largely depopulated, as refugees set off in wagons and on foot for larger towns to the east. Governor Alexander Ramsey mobilized the state's military forces to suppress the uprising. On September 6, Governor Ramsey sent a telegram to President Lincoln pleading for federal help: "It is a national war. . . . Answer me at once. More than 500 whites have been murdered by the Indians."

Lincoln dispatched General John Pope, the general having recently lost the second battle of Bull Run, to be the commander of the new Military Department of the Northwest. Six weeks after the fighting began, the military effort by the United States—assisted by "friendlies" (Sioux opposed to the war)—succeeded in quelling the uprising. The end of heavy fighting left 1,250 Dakota Sioux warriors as prisoners of the U.S. government.

Military Commission Appointed to Try Dakota Warriors

On September 28, 1862, Colonel Henry Sibley, field commander of American forces, appointed a five-member military commission to "try summarily" Dakota Sioux and mixed-bloods for "murder and other outrages" committed against Americans. Whether Sibley had authority to appoint such a commission is a matter of substantial dispute. The commission was convened immediately, meeting near Camp Release along the Minnesota River in western Minnesota.

Reverend Stephen Riggs, a man who spoke the Dakota Sioux language and knew many of the Indians as a result of years of missionary work in the area, undertook the job of gathering evidence and witnesses. Isaac Heard, recorder for the trials and the leading historian on the war, wrote that Riggs "was, in effect, the grand jury of the court." He assembled half-breeds and white survivors in a tent and interrogated them concerning the suspects. Charges were written and names of witnesses were appended to each charge.

The commission conducted 16 trials the first day it met, convicting and sentencing to death 10 prisoners and acquitting another 6. Over the six weeks that followed, the military court would try a total of 393 people, convicting 323 and sentencing 303 to death by hanging. According to the trial recorder, the defendants that were found guilty ranged from boys of about 15 to "old men scarcely able to walk or speak." The only Sioux woman tried by the commission was acquitted.

The trials were quick affairs, becoming shorter as they progressed. The commission heard nearly 40 cases on November 3, the last day it met. The commission believed that mere participation in a battle justified a death sentence; therefore, in the many cases—perhaps two-thirds of the total—where the prisoner admitted firing any shots at all, it proceeded to a guilty verdict in a matter of a few minutes. Trials in which the charge was the murder or rape of settlers usually required more deliberation because in those cases admissions were rare.

Under the procedures adopted by the commission, the trials opened with a reading of the charges, or "specifications." The defendant then gave whatever response he cared to make to the charge. Prosecution followed. When prosecution witnesses contradicted the testimony of the defendant, the commission almost invariably found the prisoner to be guilty.

The best witnesses for the prosecution turned out to be some of the accused. Convicted in the commission's first trial, Joseph Godfrey, or Otakle, a mulatto married to a Dakota Sioux woman, gave evidence in 55 cases. Recorder Isaac Heard described Godfrey as "the greatest institution of the commission." According to Heard, when a defendant proclaimed his innocence and Godfrey knew him to be guilty, Godfrey "would drop his head upon his breast, and convulse in a fit of musical laughter." With his "melodious voice" and "remarkable memory" he seemed to Heard "specifically designed as an instrument of justice." In return for his testimony for the prosecution, Godfrey's death sentence was commuted to 10 years in prison.

Some of the prisoners found guilty had committed horrific crimes, while others had simply been one of hundreds who had only participated in the battles. The most notorious of the convicted—a Dakota Sioux called "Cut-Nose" by the trial recorder—was found to have tomahawked to death 11 women and children as they huddled in wagons near the Beaver Creek settlement. Cut-Nose also, according to prosecution witnesses, snatched an infant from its mother's arms and riveted the small child to a fence, leaving it to die, "writhing in agony."

Henry Whipple, an Episcopal bishop who had worked among the Indians, criticized the commission for its refusal to distinguish between degrees of guilt. "There is a broad distinction," Whipple wrote, between those "committing fiendish violence" and the "guilt of timid men who under threat of death engaged in some one battle."

Were the Trials Fair?

Then and ever since, the fairness of the trials has been questioned. In addition to concerns about the sufficiency of the evidence supporting the convictions; the rapidity of the trials; and the denial of legal counsel, commission members have been suspected of being prejudiced against the defendants. At the very least there appeared to be conflicts of interest. The commission members—though believed to be men of integrity—were also military men whose troops had recently been under attack by the very men whose cases they were judging.

Critics of the trials believe that the commission wrongly treated the defendants as common criminals rather than as the legitimate belligerents of a sovereign power. They also contend that the trials should have been conducted in state courts using normal rules of criminal procedure rather than by military commission. Finally, many critics point out that the unsophisticated prisoners often did not understand the nature of the proceedings and, as a result, made damaging statements that sealed their convictions.

Colonel Sibley viewed summary trials by a commission as necessary to avoid vigilante justice by angry mobs of Minnesotans. Even with the swiftness of the trials, mob violence was a real concern: Angry white settlers attacked the 303 condemned prisoners in the southwestern Minnesota town of New Ulm as they were being transported to a prison camp after their trials to await execution. A month later, soldiers guarding the prisoners foiled a planned attack of the prison camp by several hundred armed local citizens.

President Lincoln Reviews the Dakota Cases

The final decision on whether to go ahead with the planned mass execution of the 303 Dakota and mixed-bloods rested with President Lincoln. General John Pope campaigned by telegraph for the speedy execution of all the condemned. Virtually all of the editorial writers, politicians, and citizens of Minnesota agreed with Pope. One of the few who did not was Henry Whipple, the Episcopal bishop of Minnesota. Whipple traveled to Washington to meet with Lincoln and discuss the causes of the Dakota Conflict. Lincoln later wrote of Whipple's visit, "He came here the other day and talked with me about the rascality of this Indian business until I felt it down to my boots. If we get through this war, and I live, *this Indian system shall be reformed!*"

Lincoln knew full well that the lust for Indian blood could not be ignored; to prevent any executions from going forward might well have condemned all

303 to death at mob hands. Lincoln asked two clerks to go through the commission's trial records and identify those prisoners convicted of raping women or children. They found only two such cases. Lincoln then asked his clerks to search the records a second time and identify those convicted of participating in the massacres of settlers. This time the clerks came up with 39 names that were later included in Lincoln's handwritten order of execution written on December 6, 1862.

Largest Mass Execution in U.S. History

In Mankato, Minnesota, at 10 A.M. on the morning of December 26, soldiers led 38 prisoners (one person was reprieved between the date of Lincoln's order and the execution), wearing white muslin coverings and singing Dakota Sioux death songs, to gallows arranged on a circular scaffold. The warriors took the places assigned to them on the platform; ropes were placed around each neck. At the signal of three drumbeats, a single blow from an ax cut the rope that held the platform and 37 people fell to their deaths. One prisoner's rope broke and he consequently had to be rehung, prolonging whatever agony he may have felt before dying. A loud cheer went up from the thousands of spectators gathered to witness the event. The bodies were buried in a mass grave on the edge of town. Soon area physicians, including one named Mayo, arrived to collect cadavers for their medical research.

The hanging stands as the largest mass execution in American history.

The Aftermath

In April 1863, Congress enacted a law providing for the forcible removal from Minnesota of all Sioux. Most of the captured, after suffering through a harsh winter at an encampment near St. Paul, were removed to South Dakota. Convicted prisoners who were reprieved from execution were transported on the steamboat *Favorite* down the Mississippi to Camp McClellan, near Davenport, Iowa. After President Andrew Johnson ordered the release of the 177 surviving prisoners on March 22, 1866, they were moved to the Santee Reservation near Niobrara, Nebraska.

The acknowledged leader of the Dakota Uprising, Chief Little Crow, was not among the Sioux tried by the military commission. He, along with 150 or so of his followers, fled after the war to present-day North Dakota and Canada. In June 1863, Little Crow returned to Minnesota on a horse-stealing foray. On July 3, Little Crow was shot by a farmer while picking berries with his son in western Minnesota. The farmer received a $500 reward from the state.

The Sioux wars continued for many years. A military expedition carried the fighting into the Dakota Territory in 1863 and 1864. As the frontier moved westward, new fighting erupted. Finally, in 1890 at Wounded Knee, the generation of warfare that began in Minnesota in August of 1862 came to a final and tragic end.

—Douglas O. Linder

Suggestions for Further Reading

Anderson, Gary Clayton and Alan R. Woolworth, eds. *Through Dakota Eyes: Narrative Accounts of the Minnesota Indian War of 1862.* Minnesota Historical Society Press, 1988.

Board of Commissioners. *Minnesota in the Civil and Indian Wars, 1861-1865* (Two Volumes). Minn.:1890, 1893.

Carley, Kenneth, *The Sioux Uprising of 1862.* Minnesota Historical Society Press, 1976.

Folwell, William Watts. *A History of Minnesota.* Vol. II. Minnesota Historical Society Press, 1961.

Linder, Douglas O. *The Dakota Conflict Trials.* http://law.umkc.edu/faculty/projects/ftrials/dakota.htm.

Fitz-John Porter Court-Martial: 1862–63

Defendant: Fitz-John Porter **Crimes Charged:** Disobedience of orders in violation of the Ninth Article of War; misbehavior before the enemy by shamefully retreating, in violation of the Fifty-second Article of War
Presiding Officer: D. Hunter **Court:** E. A. Hitchcock; Rufus King; M. Prentiss; James B. Ricketts; Silas Casey; James A. Garfield; N. B. Buford; J. P. Slough. **Chief Prosecutor:** J. Holt, Judge-Advocate-General
Place: Washington, D.C. **Date of Trial:** November 1862–January 1863
Verdict: Guilty **Sentence:** Cashiered and dismissed from the army and disqualified from holding any office of trust or profit under the government of the United States

SIGNIFICANCE

Following the defeat of Union forces at the Battle of Second Manassas (Bull Run) in August 1862 Major General John Pope, the commanding officer, attempted to place blame on Major General Fitz-John Porter. The ensuing court-martial was politically motivated and the verdict is widely believed to have been a great injustice.

Fitz-John Porter was a New Hampshire native, born in 1822, and a career military officer. He graduated from West Point in 1845, and was appointed to the artillery. He fought in the Mexican campaign under General Zachary Taylor in 1847, and was wounded at Chapultepec. He returned to West Point as an instructor from 1849 to 1855, and then went back to service in the adjutant general's department as a captain, and participated in the campaign against the Mormons. Following the outbreak of the Civil War he proved a very successful leader and was rapidly promoted, becoming a colonel in the 15th Infantry in May 1861, and then a brigadier general of the United States Volunteers in August 1861. He commanded a division of the Army of the Potomac from the fall of 1861 to the spring of 1862, and in July of that year achieved the rank of major general in the volunteers. During his service with the Army of the Potomac he became a close friend of General George Brinton McClellan, an alliance which proved damaging to him in the political climate that ensued.

Porter's Retreat at Second Manassas

Porter's court-martial followed the defeat of Union forces by Confederate troops at the Battle of Second Manassas (Bull Run) in August 1862. Porter had been given command of a provisional corps created by McClellan when the latter was general in chief of all armies, a position from which he was removed by President Lincoln in March 1862 because the president believed that McClellan was not moving rapidly enough against Confederate troops. Fitz-John Porter's command was ordered to northern Virginia to reinforce the troops of General John Pope.

On August 29 General Pope transmitted orders to General Porter stressing the importance of driving the enemy from Manassas, and in successive orders instructed Porter to begin a march at 1 A.M. in order to make contact with the Confederate forces after daylight. Pope's order stated that Porter's line of march would bring him upon the right flank of Stonewall Jackson's troops and that he was to attack their rear and flank. However, Pope's understanding of the military situation was inaccurate: he did not know that on August 29, 10,000 Confederate troops under General James Longstreet had linked up with the rear of Jackson's forces, making it impossible for Porter to attack the flank and rear of Jackson's troops. Instead, Longstreet launched an attack on the Federal flank, Porter was forced to retreat, and General Pope's forces were defeated.

Court-Martial Follows Lincoln—Pope Meeting

General Pope met with Fitz-John Porter on September 2. Porter explained the situation that had confronted him, and Pope told him that he fully accepted the explanation and had no intention of taking any proceedings against his subordinate. However, Pope's reputation was tarnished by the defeat, and McClellan became commander of all troops in the Washington area. On September 17 the bloodiest battle of the war was fought at Antietam, with 12,500 casualties on the Union side and 11,000 Confederate soldiers killed or wounded. General McClellan forced the Confederate army to retreat, but enraged President Lincoln by not pursuing it into Virginia. Shortly before Antietam, General Pope had had a meeting with President Lincoln which, as he subsequently testified, had "opened my eyes to many matters which I had before been loth to believe. . . ." In November Fitz-John Porter was relieved of his command and ordered court-martialled, although the charges were not brought by General Pope, but by Brigadier General B. S. Roberts, the inspector-general of Pope's Army of Virginia. In November General McClellan's military career also came to an end when President Lincoln replaced him with General Ambrose Burnside.

There were two charges against Fitz-John Porter. The first was that of a violation of the Ninth Article of War, by disobedience of orders. There were five specifications. The first related to Porter's not marching at 1 A.M. as ordered, but deciding to delay his start until 3 A.M. The others related to his failure to attack the rear and flank of Jackson's troops. The second charge was a violation of the Fifty-second Article of War, misbehavior before the enemy, the misbehavior being his retreat following the attack by General Longstreet. There were four specifications, although the last was immediately withdrawn.

Porter Found Guilty on Key Charges

The court-martial met continuously for 45 days. A large number of officers testified, including General Pope, both against Porter and on his behalf. At the end of the session General Porter submitted a lengthy statement summarizing his defense. The core of his argument was that it is well established in military law and practice that an order does not require passive obedience unless the commander and the officer ordered are physically together; in this case General Pope was 11 miles away from Porter, and the orders took several hours to reach him. Pope was not aware of the military situation that Porter confronted when he received the orders, and therefore he (Porter) used "judicious discretion" in attempting to carry them out. He did not dispute that he had delayed the start of his march until 3 A.M., but argued that his men were exhausted from the previous day's march and needed rest. Also it was extraordinarily difficult to move wagons and artillery pieces on muddy roads on a very dark night. To the more serious charge of failing to attack the enemy's rear and flank, Porter emphasized that when he sent the order General Pope did not know that Longstreet's line had linked up with Jackson's. Porter's march did not bring him upon the rear and right flank of Jackson's forces, but upon the front of Longstreet's, making it impossible to carry out the order. To have attempted an attack upon the combined forces would have risked the destruction of his, and a worse defeat for the entire Union army under General Pope.

Major General Fitz-John Porter, court-martialed after the defeat of the Union troops at the Battle of Bull Run. (Courtesy, National Archives)

The court delivered its verdict on January 10, 1863. Although found "Not Guilty" on the 4 and 5 specifications of the first charge, which pertained to allowing one of his brigades to march to Centreville on August 30, Porter was declared "Guilty" of the major charges of disobedience and misbehavior. The sentence of the court was that he "be cashiered . . . and forever disqualified from holding any office of trust or profit under the Government of the United States." The proceedings, findings, and sentence were transmitted to President Lincoln, who approved and confirmed them on January 21.

In his defense General Porter indicated the political nature of the proceedings by referring to General Pope's change of mind after his meeting with the president. Historians have also pointed out that the officers for the court were carefully selected by Secretary of War Edwin Stanton, and many received promotions after reaching their verdict. Fitz-John Porter immediately set out to clear his name, a task which he pursued assiduously for years. In 1878 a board of general officers reviewed the case and reported in Fitz-John Porter's favor, agreeing with his argument that to have attempted an attack would have been wrong. In 1881 Chester Arthur succeeded to the presidency following the assassination of James A. Garfield, who, as a young brigadier, had served on Fitz-John Porter's court-martial. In 1882 President Arthur remitted that part of Porter's sentence which disqualified him from holding office under the United States. In 1886, by a special act of Congress, he was recommissioned as a colonel in the artillery, to date from May 14, 1861. Although back pay was denied, Porter considered this a vindication, and retired at his own request two days later.

—David I. Petts

Suggestions for Further Reading

Hattaway, Herman, and Archer Jones. *How the North Won: A Military History of the Civil War.* Champagne, Ill.: University of Illinois Press, 1983.

Official Records, Series I, Volume XII, Part II, Supplement (Eisenschiml, Otto, *The Celbrated Case of Fitz-John Porter*)

Clement L. Vallandigham Court-Martial: 1863

Defendant: Clement L. Vallandigham **Crime Charged:** Publicly opposing the federal government's prosecution of the war while supporting the enemies of the Union **Chief Defense Lawyers** Edward A. Ferguson, George H. Pendleton, George E. Pugh **Chief Prosecutor:** James M. Cutts, Judge Advocate **Senior Presiding Officer:** Robert B. Potter **Court:** J.F. DeCourcy, E. R. Goodrich, J. L. Van Buren, J. M. Brown, A. H. Fitch, P. M. Lydig **Place:** Cincinnati, Ohio **Date of Trial:** May 6–7, 1863 **Verdict:** Guilty of all but one specification **Sentence:** Confinement in a military prison for the duration of the war

SIGNIFICANCE

This was the most publicized and controversial of several trials of civilians by Union court-martials. Although Supreme Court Chief Justice Roger B. Taney, in *Ex Parte Merryman* (1861), had stated that the military did not have the right to deny a private citizen his right to a civil trial, other Union judges chose to back the military trials. This procedure, however, would not be allowed after the Civil War.

The federal government's war against the Confederacy was by no means supported by everyone in the North, and the most outspoken opponents of the war, especially those Democrats in the midwestern states, came to be known as "Copperheads," a direct allusion to the poisonous snake species. The most zealous of the Copperheads was Clement L. Vallandigham, a native Ohioan who had served in the House of Representatives from 1858 to 1863. An ardent anti-abolitionist as well as a supporter of states' rights, from the day the Civil War broke out, Vallandigham took a vehement stand against it—in Congress, in newspaper articles, and in public gatherings.

Conflicting Orders

Containing such opposition was a major concern of Abraham Lincoln's administration. Particularly as the war dragged on, month after month, and the Union forces experienced defeat after defeat, the fiery words of Vallandigham came to seem ever more dangerous to those Union leaders charged with pursuing the war. One such was Major General Ambrose E. Burnside, who after his terrible defeat at Fredericksburg, Virginia, in December 1862, was assigned to be Commander of the Department of the Ohio. Infuriated by the antiwar sentiments expressed by Vallandigham and others like him, on April 13, 1863, entirely on his own, Burnside issued "General Orders, No. 38," which stated that the "habit of declaring sympathy for the enemy" would not be tolerated, and that those "committing such offenses" would be arrested and subject to military procedures, not civil courts. This simply served to incite Vallandigham to speak out still more strongly, and on May 1, while addressing a rally in Mount Vernon, Ohio, he deliberately taunted Burnside and said that his right to criticize was based on " 'General Orders No. 1'—the Constitution of the United States, signed by General George Washington."

Clement L. Vallandigham, a civilian court-martialed by a military court. (Courtesy, Library of Congress)

When Burnside was informed of Vallandigham's provocative speech, he sent a company of soldiers to arrest him at his home in Dayton, Ohio. Brought by train to Cincinnati in the early hours of May 5, Vallandigham was at first detained in an army barracks, but later in the morning was moved to a suite in the finest hotel in Cincinnati. Controversy over the merits of Burnside's arresting Vallandigham quickly spread around Ohio—a mob of Vallandigham supporters set fire to a newspaper that supported the war—but Burnside felt there was no turning back. Still without any authorization from his superiors in Washington, and realizing full well that delay might allow his decision to be countermanded from above, he chose a panel of eight officers from his staff and convened a court-martial for the next day.

The Court Martial

Vallandigham was led by a squad of soldiers into a room in the Newport barracks to face the panel—none of whom, as it happened, was a citizen of Ohio. Vallandigham could not have known that, but at his first opportunity to speak he protested that such a military tribunal had no authority to be trying him, a civilian. The presiding officer ignored this, and the judge advocate read the charges: "Publicly expressing, in violation of 'General Orders, No. 38' . . . sympathies for those in arms against the Government of the United States, declaring disloyal sentiments and opinions, with the object and purpose of weakening the power of the Government in its effort to suppress the unlawful rebellion." Asked to enter a plea, Vallandigham—who was himself a lawyer—repeated that he did not recognize the authority of this court. For that reason, too, he declined to have his lawyers at his side during the trial.

The only witnesses called against Vallandigham were two army officers who had been sent by Burnside in civilian clothes to attend the rally where he had spoken so defiantly. Vallandigham acted as his own counsel in cross-examining them, but they both had made notes and there was little that Vallandigham wanted to deny except minor details. Thus he corrected the witness who testified that Vallandigham had said Lincoln's administration had "insolently rejected" an appeal by France to mediate a settlement of the war: "The word used was 'instantly,' not 'insolently.' "

On the second day, Vallandigham called his only witness, Ohio congressman Samuel S. Cox; although a Democrat like Vallandigham, he supported the federal decision to go to war and was regarded as a moderate. Cox, who had also been present at the rally, testified that Vallandigham had not attacked Burnside personally; that he had not specifically attacked "General Orders, No. 38"; that he had not advocated resisting any laws; and that all Vallandigham wanted was peace and reunion. Vallandigham's examination of Cox allowed him to emphasize several of his other favorite arguments:

> Vallandigham: Do you remember his comments on the change of the policy in the war?
>
> Cox: He did refer to the change in the policy of the war, and devoted some time to showing that it was now carried on for the abolition of slavery; that it has been perverted from a war for the preservation of the Union to one for the abolition of slavery. . . .
>
> Vallandigham: Did he counsel any other mode in that speech of resisting usurpation of arbitrary power, except by free discussion and the ballot box?
>
> Cox: He did not.

The trial concluded with Vallandigham's own summation, in which he continued to challenge the right of the military court to be trying him, continued to assert the right of all citizens to criticize, and continued to deny that he had ever advocated disobedience to the laws of the land.

The room was then cleared so that the panel could deliberate, but since the "jury" was composed of officers handpicked by General Burnside, there was little doubt about their verdict. After three hours, Vallandigham was called back in and informed of the verdict. He was found guilty of the charge and all its specifications except one. The sentence was that he be "placed in close confinement in some fortress of the United States, to be designated by the commanding officer of the Department, there to be kept during the continuance of the war."

An Anti-Climactic End

Vallandigham's lawyers naturally appealed to a federal court on the issue of the right of a military court to try a civilian, but the presiding judge upheld the authority of the court-martial. Burnside had already announced that Vallandigham was to be held at Fort Warren in Boston Harbor, but now President Lincoln faced a dilemma. He had come to detest Vallandigham, but he also was reluctant to restrict freedom of speech; furthermore, he and others in authority in Washington felt that Burnside had overstepped his authority in issuing the "General Orders, No. 38" and then in conducting the court-martial. At a cabinet meeting on May 19, Lincoln was easily persuaded by some members that imprisoning Vallandigham would only make him a martyr, and when it was proposed instead to turn him over to the Confederacy, Lincoln readily agreed. Orders were given, and on May 25, Vallandigham was handed over to a Confederate officer near Shelbyville, Tennessee. Vallandigham soon made his way to Bermuda, and then moved on to Canada; by late August, he settled in Windsor, Ontario, across from Detroit, and was already the Democratic Party's candidate for the governor of Ohio. He lost that election, and in February 1864, he also lost his appeal to the U.S. Supreme Court. On June 14, 1864, however, Vallandigham made his way in disguise back to Ohio, and although there was some call for his re-arrest, Lincoln chose to ignore him. After the war, Vallandigham supported President Andrew Johnson's effort at moderate reconstruction policies. Failing to revive his political career, he returned to the practice of law, and in 1871, intending to demonstrate how a man had accidentally shot himself, he used a pistol he thought was unloaded and killed himself.

—*John S. Bowman*

Suggestions for Further Reading

Klement, Frank. L. *The Limits of Dissent: Clement L. Vallandigham and the Civil War*. Lexington, Ky.: University of Kentucky Press, 1970.

"Proceedings of a Military Commission Convened in Cincinnati, May 6, 1863." Roll 273, National Archives Microfilm Publication M345, Union Provost Marshal's File, One Name Papers RE: Citizens.

Vallandigham, Clement L. *Record of Hon. C. L. Vallandigham on Abolition, the Union and the Civil War*. Columbus, Ohio: J. Walters & Co., 1863.

Vallandigham, James. *A Life of Clement L. Vallandigham*. Baltimore: Turnbull Brothers, 1872.

Packard v. Packard: 1864

Plaintiff: Reverend Theophilus Packard, Jr. **Defendant:** Elizabeth Parsons Ware Packard **Plaintiff Claim:** That his wife was insane and that he was therefore entitled to confine her at home **Chief Defense Lawyers:** Stephen Moore and John W. Orr **Chief Lawyer for Plaintiff:** No record **Judge:** Charles R. Starr **Place:** Kankakee, Illinois **Dates of Trial:** January 13–18, 1864 **Verdict:** Elizabeth Packard declared sane and restored to liberty

SIGNIFICANCE

In 1864, Illinois law permitted a man to institutionalize his wife "without the evidence of insanity required in other cases." After her own court-ordered release, Elizabeth Packard campaigned to change the law in Illinois and similar laws in 30 other states; during her lifetime, four states revised their laws.

Near the end of 1863, the Reverend Theophilus Packard locked his wife Elizabeth in the nursery and nailed the windows shut. Earlier, he had committed her for three years to the Illinois State Hospital for the Insane, based only on his own observation that she was "slightly insane," a condition he attributed to "excessive application of body and mind." In many states in the 19th century, it was a husband's legal prerogative to so institutionalize his wife, and Elizabeth Packard had no recourse against that earlier confinement. Now, however, she had a valid argument: the law did not permit a husband to "put away" a wife *in her own home.* Elizabeth Packard dropped a letter of complaint out her window, which was delivered to her friend, Sarah Haslett. Haslett immediately appealed to Judge Charles R. Starr.

Judge Starr issued a writ of *habeas corpus* and ordered Reverend Packard to bring Elizabeth to his chambers on January 12, 1864. Packard produced Elizabeth and a written statement explaining that she "was discharged from [the Illinois State] Asylum without being cured and is incurably insane . . . [and] the undersigned has allowed her all the liberty compatible with her welfare and safety." Unimpressed, the judge scheduled a jury trial to determine whether Elizabeth Packard was insane.

Reverend Packard Presents his Case

Reverend Packard was a Calvinist minister with an austere interpretation of his faith, and he claimed his wife's religious views had convinced him of her insanity. Dr. Christopher Knott, who had spoken with Elizabeth prior to her commitment to Illinois State, testified, "Her mind appeared to be excited on the subject of religion. On all other subjects she was perfectly rational. . . . I take her to be a lady of fine mental abilities. . . . I would say she was insane," he concluded, "the same as I would say Henry Ward Beecher, Spurgeon, Horace Greeley, and like persons are insane."

Lithograph of Elizabeth Parsons Ware Packard. (Courtesy of Illinois State Historical Society)

Dr. J.W. Brown had been falsely introduced to Elizabeth as a sewing machine salesman several weeks before, and had surreptitiously interviewed her during what she thought was a sales pitch. She had described her husband, Dr. Brown testified, as wishing that "the despotism of man may prevail over the wife," but it was during their discussion of religion that he "had not the slightest difficulty in concluding that she was hopelessly insane." Elizabeth Packard, Dr. Brown said, had claimed to be "the personification of the Ghost." Moreover, "She found fault that Mr. Packard would not discuss their points of difference in religion in an open manly way instead of going around and denouncing her as crazy to her friends and to the church. She had a great aversion to being called insane. Before I got through the conversation she exhibited a great dislike to me."

Abijah Dole, the husband of Reverend Packard's sister Sybil, testified that he knew Elizabeth had become disoriented because she told him that she no longer wished to live with Reverend Packard. Dole also testified that Elizabeth had requested a letter terminating her membership in her husband's church. "Was that an indication of insanity?" Elizabeth's lawyer, John W. Orr, inquired. Dole replied: "She would not leave the church unless she was insane."

Sybil Dole also testified against Elizabeth, stating, "She accused Dr. Packard very strangely of depriving her of her rights of conscience—that he would not allow her to think for herself on religious questions because they differed on these topics."

Sarah Rumsey, a young woman who had briefly served as a mother's helper for the Packards, also gave evidence of what she considered Elizabeth Packard's insanity: "She wanted the flower beds in the front yard cleaned out and tried to get Mr. Packard to do it. He would not. She put on an old dress and went to work and cleaned out the weeds . . . until she was almost melted down with the heat. . . . Then she went to her room and took a bath and dressed herself and lay down exhausted. . . . She was angry and excited and showed ill-will."

Finally, a certificate concerning Elizabeth's discharge from the Illinois State Hospital, issued by the superintendent, Dr. Andrew McFarland, was read. It said that Elizabeth Packard was discharged because she could not be cured. Reverend Packard's lawyers rested their case.

Elizabeth Packard Defends her Sanity

Elizabeth Packard's lawyers, Stephen Moore and J.W. Orr, asked her to read aloud an essay which she had written for a Bible class. It contained statements such as ". . . the Christian farmer has no more reason to expect success in his farming operations than the impenitent sinner." Then Mr. and Mrs. Blessing, Methodist neighbors of the Packards, testified in turn as to Mrs. Packard's sanity.

Sarah Haslett described Elizabeth's housekeeping efforts after her release from the Illinois State Hospital: "I called to see her a few days after she returned from Jacksonville. She was in the yard cleaning feather beds. . . . The house needed cleaning. And when I called again it looked as if the mistress of the house was *home*." Haslett then testified about her friend's in-home confinement and described the sealed window, "fastened with nails on the inside and two screws passing through the lower part of the upper sash and the upper part of the lower sash from the outside."

The last person to testify on Mrs. Packard's behalf was a Dr. Duncanson, who was both a physician and theologian. He testified that he had conversed with Mrs. Packard for three hours, and he disagreed with Dr. Brown's understanding of Mrs. Packard's thoughts concerning her relationship to the Holy Ghost. Mrs. Packard later wrote, "A spiritual woman is a living temple of the Holy Ghost." At her trial, Dr. Duncanson located this belief in a neglected 16th century doctrine expounded by Socinus of Italy. "I did not agree with . . . her on many things," Duncanson testified, "but I do not call people insane because they differ with me. . . . You might with as much propriety call Christ insane . . . or Luther, or Robert Fuller. . . . I pronounce her a sane woman and wish we had a nation of such women."

Verdict Takes Seven Minutes

On January 18, the jury reached its verdict in seven minutes. "We, the undersigned, Jurors in the case of Mrs. Elizabeth P.W. Packard, alleged to be insane, having heard the evidence . . . are satisfied that [she] is sane." Judge Starr ordered "that Mrs. Elizabeth P.W. Packard be relieved of all restraints incompatible with her condition as a sane woman." Neither the judge nor jury addressed the question of whether, had Mrs. Packard been found insane, Mr. Packard had the right to confine her at home rather than in an asylum.

The Packards remained married but estranged for the remainder of their lives. Elizabeth Packard wrote, lectured, and lobbied on behalf of the rights of women and those alleged to be insane; she was instrumental in changing the commitment laws in four states and in passing a married women's property law in Illinois.

—Kathryn Cullen-DuPont

Suggestions for Further Reading

Burnham, John Chynoweth. "Elizabeth Parsons Ware Packard," in *Notable American Women, 1906–1950.* Edward T. James, Janet Wilson James and Paul S. Boyer, eds. Cambridge, Mass.: Belknap Press of Harvard University Press, 1971.

Packard, Elizabeth Parsons Ware. *Great Disclosure of Spiritual Wickedness!! in high places. With an appeal to the government to protect the inalienable rights of married women.* Written under the inspection of Dr. M'Farland, Superintendent of Insane Asylum, Jacksonville, Illinois, 4th ed. Boston: Published by the authoress, 1865.

——. *Marital Power Exemplified in Mrs. Packard's Trial and self-defense from the charge of insanity, or, Three years imprisonment for religious belief, by the arbitrary will of a husband, with an appeal to the government to so change the laws as to afford legal protection to married women.* Hartford, Conn.: Case, Lockwood & Co., 1866.

——. *The Mystic Key; or, The Asylum Secret Unlocked.* Hartford, Conn.: Case, Lockwood & Brainard Co., 1886.

——. *The prisoners' hidden life, or Insane asylums unveiled: as demonstrated by the Report of the Investigating Committee of the Legislature of Illinois, together with Mrs. Packard's coadjustors' testimony.* Chicago: The Author; A. B. Case, Printer, 1868.

Sapinsley, Barbara. *The Private War of Mrs. Packard.* New York: Paragon House, 1991.

Dr. Samuel Mudd Trial: 1865

Defendant: Dr. Samuel A. Mudd **Crimes Charged:** Treason and conspiracy
Chief Defense Lawyer: General Thomas Ewing **Chief Prosecutor:** Judge Advocate Joseph Holt **Judges:** Military commission officers Lieutenant Colonel David Clendenim, Brevet Brigadier General James Ekin, Brigadier General Robert Foster, Brigadier General T. M. Harris, Major General David Hunter, Brigadier General Alvin Howe, Brevet Major General August Kautz, Brevet Colonel C. H. Tompkins, and Major General Lew Wallace
Place: Washington, D.C. **Dates of Trial:** May 9–June 30, 1865
Verdict: Guilty **Sentence:** Life imprisonment, pardoned in 1868

SIGNIFICANCE

During his flight after assassinating President Abraham Lincoln, John Wilkes Booth visited Dr. Samuel A. Mudd for treatment of his broken ankle. Although there was little evidence linking him to Booth's crime, Mudd was convicted by a military commission interested more in vengeance than justice. The military's assertion of its authority over that of civilian courts represented the post-Civil War Union's thirst for retribution at the expense of justice.

By spring 1865, the Civil War was all but over. General Robert E. Lee surrendered his army at Appomattox, Virginia, effectively ending the Confederacy. Although the North resounded with triumph, Southerners and their sympathizers were bitter and resentful. Particularly bitter was a minor actor from Maryland named John Wilkes Booth.

After Appomattox, Booth, long a Confederate sympathizer, vowed to kill President Abraham Lincoln. On April 14, 1865, Booth had his chance. Lincoln went to see the play *Our American Cousin* at Ford's Theater in Washington D.C. The lone security guard assigned to protect Lincoln had gone to a nearby bar for a drink. Unimpeded, Booth sneaked into the theater. From behind the presidential party's box seats, Booth pulled out his pistol and shot Lincoln in the head. Booth leapt from the box to the stage, 12 feet below, breaking his left ankle in the process. After shouting "Sic Semper Tyrannis!" ("thus shall it ever be for tyrants," the state motto of Virginia), Booth ran from the theater and fled Washington on horseback.

Troops Search for Booth and his Co-Conspirators

Lincoln died within hours. On the same night, two of Booth's accomplices, David Herold and Lewis Payne, tried unsuccessfully to assassinate Secretary of State William H. Seward. Payne was arrested at the boarding house where he lived, as was Mary Surratt, the owner of the house. Herold was able to join Booth across the Anacostia River in Maryland and the two rode south. Meanwhile, the authorities continued to round up others suspected of assisting Booth.

As Booth rode through southern Maryland, his ankle worsened. On April 15, shortly before dawn, he stopped at Dr. Samuel Mudd's house outside Bryantown and asked for help. Mudd did what he could for Booth's ankle, provided Booth with crutches, and collected $25 as his fee. Booth then continued to ride south, eventually crossing into Virginia and eluding the authorities. On April 26, federal troops caught up with Booth outside the town of Port Royal, Virginia. A soldier shot Booth, who had barricaded himself in a barn.

Secretary of War Edwin M. Stanton had anyone suspected of conspiring with Booth arrested. In addition to Herold, Payne, and Surratt, the authorities arrested Samuel Arnold, George A. Atzerodt, Michael O'Loughlin, Edward Spangler, and the unfortunate Dr. Mudd. Each of the first four men had had some degree of contact with Booth. Although there was no proof that Mudd was involved in the conspiracy, he had met Booth at least once before the assassination.

Mudd and Conspirators Tried

Nine officers—Major General David Hunter, Major General Lew Wallace, Brevet Major General August Kautz, Brigadier General Alvin Howe, Brigadier General T. M. Harris, Brigadier General Robert Foster, Brevet Brigadier General James Ekin, Brevet Colonel C.H. Tompkins, and Lieutenant Colonel David Clendenim—comprised the military commission formed to try Dr. Mudd and the others. The trial began May 9, 1865, with Judge Advocate Joseph Holt as prosecutor and General Thomas Ewing as Mudd's defense counsel.

From May 9 until June 30, the military commission listened to the evidence Holt presented. Although Mudd was entitled to a presumption of innocence until proven guilty, the trial was conducted under military jurisdiction, making the rules of the game favor the prosecution. Further, the public was clamoring for convictions. Nevertheless, Ewing showed with remorseless logic how the prosecution had failed to prove that Mudd was guilty of treason in tending to Booth's broken ankle:

> I will show, first, that Dr. Mudd is not, and cannot possibly be, guilty of any offense known to the law.
>
> One. Not of treason. The overt act attempted to be alleged is the murder of the President. The proof is conclusive, that at the time the tragedy was enacted Dr. Mudd was at his residence in the country, thirty miles from the place of the crime. Those who committed it are shown to have acted for themselves, not as the instruments of Dr. Mudd. He, therefore, cannot be

charged, according to law, and upon the evidence, with the commission of this overt act. There are not two witnesses to prove that he did commit it, but abundant evidence to show negatively that he did not.

Ewing went on to show that, since the prosecution had not proven that Mudd was a member of Booth's conspiracy, Mudd could not be convicted of being an "accessory after the fact" in tending to Booth's ankle. Under the law, Mudd could only be convicted of being an accessory after the fact if the prosecution proved that he knew Booth was trying to escape the authorities because of Lincoln's murder:

> If a man receives, harbors, or otherwise assists to elude justice, one whom he knows to be guilty of felony, he becomes thereby an accessory after the fact in the felony. . . . Now, let us apply the facts to the law, and see whether Dr. Mudd falls within the rule. On the morning after the assassination, about daybreak, Booth arrived at his house. He did not find the Doctor on watch for him, as a guilty accomplice, expecting his arrival, would have been, but he and all his household were in profound sleep. . . . The Doctor rose from his bed, assisted Booth into the house, laid him upon a sofa, took him up stairs to a bed, set the fractured bone. . . . But he did not know, and had no reason to suspect, that his patient was a fugitive murderer.

Despite Ewing's eloquence, the military commission focused on any circumstance that tended to implicate Mudd, including the fact that Mudd had met Booth on at least one occasion prior to Lincoln's assassination. On June 30, 1865, the commission pronounced Mudd guilty and sentenced him to life imprisonment. Of the other defendants, Atzerodt, Herold, Payne, and Surratt were sentenced to death by hanging. Arnold and O'Loughlin were also given life sentences, and Spangler was sentenced to imprisonment for six years.

Was Mudd Really Guilty?

The government first sent Mudd to serve his sentence in an Albany, New York penitentiary. Later the government sent Mudd to a prison on Dry Tortugas Island in Florida. Poor prison conditions, low 19th-century standards of hygiene, and the tropical climate led to an epidemic of disease on the island. Mudd used his professional training to save the lives of many fellow inmates. President Andrew Johnson pardoned Mudd for his humanitarian work in 1868.

Although Mudd was a free man after 1868, he was tainted by the military commission's guilty verdict until he died in 1883. While there were certainly some guilty individuals among the convicted conspirators, Mudd's involvement seemed so innocent that many historians as well as Mudd's descendants have challenged the commission's guilty verdict as being politically motivated. These believers in Mudd's innocence kept his cause alive. In the late 1970s, President Jimmy Carter wrote Mudd's descendants to express his belief in Mudd's innocence and effectively extended Johnson's pardon to cover any implication that Mudd had been involved in Booth's conspiracy.

—*Stephen G. Christianson*

Suggestions for Further Reading

Carter, Samuel. *The Riddle of Dr. Mudd.* New York: Putnam, 1974.

Herold, David E. *The Assassination of President Lincoln and the Trial of the Conspirators.* Westport, Conn.: Greenwood Press, 1974.

———. *The Conspiracy Trial for the Murder of the President.* New York: Arno Press, 1972.

Mudd, Samuel Alexander. *The Life of Dr. Samuel A. Mudd.* Linden, Tenn.: Continental Book Co., 1975.

Weckesser, Elden C. *His Name Was Mudd.* Jefferson, N.C.: McFarland & Co., 1991.

Henry Wirz Trial: 1865

Defendant: Captain Henry Wirz **Crimes Charged:** 13 counts of murder, assault, battery, torture and other offenses against Union prisoners
Chief Defense Lawyer: Louis Schade **Chief Prosecutor:** Judge Advocate Colonel N. P. Chipman **Judges:** Military Commission officers Brevet Colonel T. Allcock, Brevet Brigadier General John F. Ballior, Brigadier General A. S. Bragg, Brigadier General Francis Fessenden, Brevet Major General G. Mott, Lieutenant Colonel J. H. Stibbs, Brevet Major General L. Thomas, and Major General Lew Wallace **Place:** Washington, D.C. **Dates of Trial:** August 23–October 18, 1865 **Verdict:** Guilty **Sentence:** Death by hanging

SIGNIFICANCE

After the Civil War, the Union tried Confederate Captain Henry Wirz for war crimes resulting from his command of a prison camp for Union captives at Andersonville, Georgia. Henry Wirz's trial was the first war-crimes trial in U.S. history and the only trial for war crimes of a Confederate after the Civil War.

Toward the end of the Civil War, General William T. Sherman launched his famous March to the Sea through Georgia. Sherman's troops stripped the land of food and destroyed every plantation, railroad track, and other things of military importance in their path. As they cut a swath 60 miles wide through the heart of the crumbling Confederacy, Sherman's troops encountered some men, nearly starved to death and in tattered clothing, who claimed that they had escaped from a Confederate prison camp at Andersonville, Georgia, where thousands more like them were still captive. When Union troops took Andersonville, they found these reports were true.

Like the Allied troops in 1945 advancing deep into the Nazi heartland and coming upon Auschwitz or Treblinka decades later, Union soldiers saw how in modern warfare a civilized country could treat its enemies with barbarism. In the middle of some of the South's richest farm land, Union prisoners starved to death. Captain Henry Wirz kept them under heavy guard on a small patch of land, through which a little creek flowed and provided the only source of drinking water and sanitation. The creek was soon fouled with excrement, causing disease to spread like wildfire among the prisoners penned up in

Andersonville. Wirz did nothing to ensure that adequate food, clothing, or medical care reached the men under his care.

In his Andersonville diary, John Ransom wrote that in particularly bad months, one-third to one-half of the prisoners in Andersonville died from the terrible conditions there. Although these tragedies were taking place every month, Andersonville's population continued to swell due to fresh battles and Confederate captures of Union troops. For example, in August 1864, there were nearly 40,000 men in Andersonville, which was designed to hold only 10,000.

Captain Wirz, reclining, the only person tried by the Union for war crimes following the Civil War. (Courtesy, Library of Congress)

After Union troops arrived, the liberated prisoners spoke of atrocities Wirz personally committed. According to the prisoners, Wirz had on several occasions shot, tortured, and otherwise mistreated Union prisoners for no reason.

Wirz Tried for War Crimes

General James H. Wilson arrested Wirz and kept him imprisoned at Wilson's headquarters. In May 1865 Wirz was taken under heavy guard to Washington, D.C., for trial. The escort was not so much to prevent Wirz from escaping, but to protect him from being killed en route by his ex-prisoners. To try Wirz, the military authorities in Washington formed a commission, comprised of Major General Lew Wallace, Brevet Major General L. Thomas, Brevet Major General G. Mott, Brigadier General Francis Fessenden, Brigadier General A. S. Bragg, Brevet Brigadier General John F. Ballior, Brevet Colonel T. Allcock, and Lieutenant Colonel J. H. Stibbs. The prosecutor was Judge Advocate Colonel N. P. Chipman.

Wirz's trial began August 23, 1865. His chief defense lawyer was Louis Schade. The prosecution opened the case with witnesses on Wirz's authority as commandant of Andersonville. Ex-Confederate officers' testimony quickly established that Confederate authorities had given Wirz supreme authority over the prison camp. The prosecution could now make its case that, having had the power to alleviate conditions at the prison camp, by not doing so Wirz was responsible for the prisoners' suffering.

Union Prisoners' Testimony Destroys Wirz

First, witnesses testified that Wirz had established a "Dead Line," or boundary about the prison camp, which prisoners could not cross without being shot by guards or attacked by vicious dogs. Then, the prosecution introduced as witnesses several Confederate doctors stationed in Andersonville, such as Chief Surgeon Dr. R. Randolph Stevenson. Stevenson testified to the abysmal medical and psychological condition of the prisoners:

> The mental condition connected with long confinement, with the most miserable surroundings, and with no hope for the future, also depressed all the nervous and vital actions, and was especially active in destroying the appetite. The effects of mental depression, and of defective nutrition, were manifested not only in the slow, feeble motions of the wasted, skeleton-like forms, but also in such lethargy, listlessness, and torpor of the mental faculties as rendered these unfortunate men oblivious and indifferent to their afflicted condition.

One of the prosecution's charges was that Wirz and General John H. Winder, one-time commander of Confederate prisons, had conspired to kill as many Union prisoners as possible. Perhaps the prosecution suspected that Wirz and Winder hoped to weaken Union armies by reducing the number of men returned in any prisoner exchange between the Union and the Confederacy. There was testimony that Wirz had boasted he was killing more Union soldiers than the Confederate armies in the field. At any rate, the prosecution went on to argue that not only had Wirz been responsible for the prisoners' suffering in general, but that he had inflicted suffering and death on individual prisoners. Of the Union soldiers' testimony, the following was typical:

> On the 8th of July I arrived at Andersonville, with 300 or 400 other prisoners, most of them sick and wounded. We were brought up to Captain Wirz' headquarters; were drawn up in line, four ranks deep, and kept there for a considerable length of time, without any business being transacted. The guards had orders to let none of us go to the water. One of the prisoners was attacked with epilepsy or fits; he fell down; some of his friends or neighbors standing near him ran down to the creek after water.
>
> Question by the prosecution: By permission of the guard?

> I don't know; I suppose so; because the guard was tied up by the thumbs for permitting them to do so. First I heard a shot fired, without seeing who fired it. After hearing that shot fired, I looked down to the left, and I saw Captain Wirz fire two more shots, wounding two men. . . .
>
> He asked the lieutenant of the guard, "Where is the guard who allowed this [Union prisoner] to fall out of ranks?" The guard was pointed out, and Captain Wirz ordered him to be tied up by the thumbs for two hours. After this, Captain Wirz pointed out [the Union prisoner], and said, "That is the way I get rid of you damned sons of bitches."

More than 100 witnesses testified at Wirz's trial, and the trial record ran into thousands of pages. In addition to testimony such as the above, Union soldiers related how any prisoner who went near or beyond the Dead Line was either immediately shot or cruelly ripped apart by guard dogs. Given the prosecution's parade of witnesses, defense counsel Louis Schade never really had a chance, despite his various pleas that Wirz should be tried before a civil court and that Wirz was immune from prosecution under the terms of surrender given to former Confederates.

On October 18, 1865, the prosecution ended its case. The military commission declared Henry Wirz guilty and sentenced him to death by hanging. President Andrew Johnson approved Wirz's sentence, and on November 10, 1865, Wirz went to the scaffold. Wirz was the only person tried by the Union for war crimes after the Civil War, and he has the dubious distinction of being the first person in history to be judged a war criminal.

—Stephen G. Christianson

Suggestions for Further Reading

The Andersonville Diary & Memoirs of Charles Hopkins. Kearny, N.J.: Belle Grove Publishing Co., 1988.

Foote, Shelby. *The Civil War: A Narrative.* New York: Vintage Books, 1986.

Hopkins, Charles. "Hell and the Survivor." *American Heritage* (October–November 1982): 78–93 (a portion of the book listed below).

McElroy, John. *This Was Andersonville.* New York: McDowell, Obolensky, 1957.

Ransom, John L. *John Ransom's Andersonville Diary.* Middlebury, Vt.: Paul S. Eriksson, 1986.

Rutherford, Mildred Lewis. *Andersonville Prison and Captain Henry Wirz' Trial.* Plains, Ga.: United Daughters of the Confederacy, 1983.

Stearns, Amos Edward. *The Civil War Diary of Amos E. Stearns, a Prisoner at Andersonville.* London: Associated University Presses, 1981.

George Armstrong Custer Court-Martial: 1867

Defendant: George Armstrong Custer **Crimes Charged:** Absence without leave from his command; conduct prejudicial to good order and military discipline. In addition to three formal charges, there were eight detailed specifications. **Defense Lawyer:** Charles C. Parsons **Prosecutor:** Captain Robert Chandler, Judge Advocate **Presiding Officer:** William Hoffman **Court:** Benjamin Grierson, Pitcain Morrison, Michael Morgan, Franklin Callender, Thomas English, Henry Asbury, Stephen Lyford **Place:** Fort Leavenworth, Kansas **Date of Trial:** September 15–October 11, 1867 **Verdict:** Guilty of five of the 11 charges and specifications. **Sentence:** Suspended from rank and command for one year and forfeit of pay for the same period.

SIGNIFICANCE

This court-martial was not untypical of the way the U.S. military held its officers to account in that era, but it was also typical of the way internal and personal motives could play a role in who was singled out for discipline. Many observers then and since have felt that George Armstrong Custer was being used as a scapegoat for the failure of the costly 1867 expedition against the Kansas Indians. On the other hand, Custer's treatment of the deserters seems highly questionable, and in retrospect his actions portend the rash behavior that led to the disaster at Little Bighorn in 1876.

There were many heroes from both the Union and Confederate forces who emerged from the Civil War but among the most dashing was George Armstrong Custer. As a young graduate from West Point's Class of 1861, he participated as a cavalry officer in virtually all the battles of the Army of the Potomac from the first to the last. By April 1865, his bold actions had earned him a temporary promotion to major general at the age of 25.

At the end of the war, Custer reverted to his permanent rank of captain; in 1866 he was promoted to lieutenant colonel and assigned to command the Seventh Cavalry Regiment based at Fort Riley in eastern Kansas. At this time, the Indians across the West were increasing their attacks on all forms of white people's encroachments—forts and supply outposts, the new railroads, overland wagon trains, and settlers. General William T. Sherman, commander of the military forces in the vast western region, assigned Major General Winfield S. Hancock to take charge of a campaign to commence in the spring of 1867. Custer's Seventh Cavalry was assigned a major role.

George Armstrong Custer whose actions during the expedition against the Kansas Indians may have led to his rash behavior at Little Big Horn. (Courtesy, Library of Congress)

As the weeks passed, Hancock's campaign was increasingly regarded as ineffectual until in June it was decided to pursue the Indians more aggressively. Encounters between the Indians and the U.S. troops accelerated in frequency, violence, and casualties; desertions in the U.S. forces were also increasing. Fort Wallace, the westernmost military post in Kansas, was effectively under siege by Indians when Custer arrived there on July 13. Finding its beleaguered forces short of food, medical supplies, and ammunition, and with men dying from cholera almost daily, Custer decided on his own to lead about 75 of his troops to Fort Harker, some 225 miles to the east, to obtain vital supplies to take back to Fort Wallace.

He set off on July 15 and arrived at Fort Harker on July 19. By July 21, Commander, Colonel Andrew J. Smith placed him under arrest. On August 7, General in Chief of the U.S. Army Ulysses S. Grant ordered a general court-martial to try Custer at Fort Leavenworth, Kansas, in September. What had Custer done wrong?

The Court-Martial

On September 16, the charges with the specifications were read aloud in the court. Under the charge of "absence without leave from his command," it was specified that he left Fort Wallace for Fort Harker without proper authority from his superiors. Many of the other specifications fell under the charge of "conduct prejudicial to good order and military discipline." Two of these specifications claimed that he had marched some of his men "upon private business" and that he had used two ambulances and four mules to travel the last leg of the journey to Fort Harker. Behind these charges, however, lay the larger accusation that Custer should have been devoting his time and energy and forces and resources to pursuing Indians.

These might be considered almost administrative issues, but the remaining specifications were more serious. One claimed that on the trip from Fort Wallace to Fort Harker, after receiving a report that two of his men had been killed by Indians who had attacked a detachment, Custer neglected to pursue the Indians or to recover and bury the bodies. Another claimed that, on his long trip to Fort Wallace earlier in July, he ordered some of his men to pursue and shoot three known deserters, without conducting any trial; that after these wounded men were hauled 18 miles in a wagon to Custer's encampment, he refused to allow the doctor to treat them; and that one of these wounded men, Charles Johnson, subsequently died because of Custer's orders.

Custer pleaded not guilty to all charges and the trial proceeded. The prosecution called witness after witness, and although not all were antagonistic to Custer, their testimony tended to support the general outlines of the charges. Numerous differences involving distances and dates and other details inevitably emerged, and some testimony actually aided Custer. Although Custer's own brother, Lt. Thomas Custer, a member of his staff, testified that George had said, "I want you to get on your horse and go after those deserters and shoot them down," the officers who first fired at three deserters claimed they had done so in self-defense. The doctor who treated the three wounded men testified that Custer had only forced him to wait about a half hour and that Custer had in fact quietly told him to give the men proper medical treatment.

When it came time for Custer to mount his defense, in addition to several witnesses who offered testimony in his support, he submitted a series of official military orders showing that other U.S. Army officers—including his superior, Major General Hancock—had authorized killing deserters. He also offered an elaborate table showing the high numbers of desertions from the Seventh Cavalry.

Custer himself never took the stand but he submitted a long report in which he justified his action against the deserters by stating that, after these three men were shot, "Not a single desertion took place from that time so long as I remained with command." Aside from that, he presented what he regarded as more than reasonable explanations for all the charges against himself.

On October 11, the court went into deliberation and within hours returned to announce they had found Custer guilty on five of the charges and specifications. He was immediately sentenced to be suspended from his rank and command for one year and to forfeit his pay for the same period.

The Aftermath

From the outset of his indictment, Custer had been supported by many fellow officers and he had hopes that the verdict would be set aside on appeal by some of his old colleagues in the Union army. Instead, Lieutenant General William Sherman issued a statement saying that the findings "are approved by General Grant." It was also reported that General Grant "is convinced that the Court, in awarding so lenient a sentence for the offenses of which the accused is found guilty, must have taken into consideration his previous record." But if he could not get his sentence set aside, Custer did not suffer that much. Major General Philip Sheridan lent Custer and his wife the use of his suite of rooms at Fort Leavenworth, and there they lived in some comfort.

There was one surprising development, though, when on January 2, 1868, Custer was served with a warrant from the state court of Kansas and charged with the murder of Charles Johnson, the deserter who had died. At first the case was dismissed on the grounds that the court had no jurisdiction. A second warrant, however, led to several days of examination and testimony, but on January 18 the judge found that the evidence did not support the charge. That spring, Custer and his wife moved to a home in Michigan, where he was free to boat, fish, and hunt. Then in August, reports began to come through of a new round of attacks by Indians in Kansas. General Philip Sheridan was ordered to head a campaign, and on September 24 he telegraphed Custer: "Generals Sherman, Sully and myself, and nearly all the officers of your regiment, have asked for you . . . Can you come at once?" Custer took a train the very next day and on September 30 he was back with the Seventh Cavalry and ready to start fighting Indians. He would not stop until June 25, 1876, when he was killed at the battle of Little Bighorn.

—*John Bowman*

Suggestions for Further Reading

Frost, Lawrence A. *The Court-Martial of General George Amstrong Custer*. Norman: University of Oklahoma Press, 1968.

Monaghan, Jay. *The Life of General George Armstrong Custer*. Boston: Little, Brown, 1959.

Whittaker, Frederick. *A Complete Life of Gen. George A. Custer*. New York: Sheldon & Company, 1876.

President Andrew Johnson Impeachment Trial: 1868

Defendant: President Andrew Johnson **Crime Charged:** "High Crimes and Misdemeanors" within the meaning of Article II, Section 4 of the Constitution
Chief Defense Lawyers: William Maxwell Evarts and Benjamin R. Curtis
Chief Prosecutors: Seven "trial managers" from the House of Representatives **Judges:** U.S. Senate, with Chief Justice Salmon P. Chase presiding **Place:** Washington, D.C. **Dates of Trial:** March 30–May 26, 1868 **Verdict:** No impeachment

SIGNIFICANCE

The U.S. Congress for the first time exercised its Constitutional prerogative to try a president of the United States for impeachable offenses. Johnson survived the Senate impeachment trial by one vote, but his hopes for re-election in 1868 were destroyed. Johnson was succeeded by the corrupt administration of Ulysses S. Grant.

After five years of bloody Civil War, the Union emerged victorious. President Abraham Lincoln and his Republican administration were vindicated. On April 14, 1865, to the shock and horror of the Union, while attending a performance at Ford's Theatre, Lincoln was assassinated by John Wilkes Booth. The next day, Vice President Andrew Johnson was sworn in as president of the United States. Ironically, the man who would lead the United States into the Reconstruction era was a Southerner.

Born in North Carolina and raised in Tennessee, Johnson entered into politics and had enjoyed a successful career with the Democratic Party. He was chosen to represent Tennessee in the U.S. Senate. When the Southern states left the Union to form the Confederacy, Johnson was widely admired in the North for being the only Southern senator to remain loyal while his state seceded.

Johnson's loyalty and newfound fame caught the attention of President Abraham Lincoln. First, Lincoln appointed Johnson the Union's military governor of Tennessee. When Lincoln was up for re-election in 1864 against General George McClellan, Lincoln chose Johnson as his running mate. As a Southern

Democrat and loyalist, Johnson would attract moderate voters in addition to the abolitionist and radical Republican forces already in Lincoln's camp.

Lincoln won the election of 1864. Although his assassination makes it impossible to know for certain how his Reconstruction administration would have proceeded, he had chosen Johnson as vice-president and had used the phrase "with malice toward none, with charity for all" in advocating leniency toward the South. Thus, many historians have concluded that Lincoln would have pursued a moderate and conciliatory approach toward the reunited Confederate states.

Johnson Becomes an Unpopular President

Johnson lacked the stature that Lincoln had gained as the president who held the Union together. Although Lincoln would probably have approved of Johnson's moderate policies toward Reconstruction, Johnson did not have the prestige necessary to convince Congress or the American people that he was suited to the job. The electorate of the victorious Union, having undergone the bloodiest war in American history, sent mostly Republicans to Congress because the Republicans had been Lincoln's party. Within Congress, the Republican majority became Johnson's enemy.

The political antagonism between Johnson and Congress was further aggravated by Johnson's opposition to the Fourteenth Amendment, which expanded Constitutional protection of basic civil liberties, and such Congressional initiatives as establishment of the Freedmen's Bureau to assist freed slaves. Johnson went on a nationwide speaking tour, known as the "Swing Around the Circle," in which he made a series of abrasive and blunt speeches full of accusations against his political enemies in Congress. The Swing Around the Circle only served to erode further Johnson's public support.

Sensing vulnerability, Congress moved against Johnson by passing the Tenure of Office Act, which limited Johnson's ability to remove cabinet officials without Congressional approval. Predictably, Johnson fought the act, particularly because he wished to rid his cabinet of Secretary of War Edwin M. Stanton, who was now allied with the opposition. When Johnson attempted to fire Stanton, Congress retaliated. Thaddeus Stevens, a Representative from Pennsylvania who spoke for radical Republicans in favor of harsh treatment for the South as "conquered territory," led the House of Representatives to a 126–47 vote in favor of a short but historic resolution: "Resolved, that Andrew Johnson, President of the United States, be impeached of high crimes and misdemeanors in office."

Senate Tries President Johnson

Although the House of Representatives had adopted the resolution to impeach Johnson, Article I, Section 3 of the Constitution mandates that the Senate must conduct the impeachment trial. This provision further states that at least two-thirds of the Senate must vote in favor of impeachment and, because a presidential impeachment was at issue, that Chief Justice Salmon P. Chase of the Supreme Court must preside.

Therefore, the House appointed seven congressmen as "trial managers," or prosecutors for the impeachment. These congressmen were John A. Bingham, George Boutwell, Benjamin F. Butler, John A. Logan, Thaddeus Stevens, Thomas Williams and James F. Wilson. Although Stevens had been the House leader, illness forced him to relinquish most of his authority to Benjamin Butler.

The Senate impeachment trial of President Andrew Johnson. (Courtesy, Library of Congress)

Butler was a colorful character. A general in the Union army during the Civil War, he was the military governor of New Orleans after the city was taken. During his governorship, he tolerated no pro-Southern dissent. One day when Butler perceived that he had been slighted by a group of New Orleans women, he issued an order that any woman showing "contempt for a United States officer" should be considered a "woman of the town plying her avocation" and thus implicitly subject to prosecution for prostitution. After the war, Butler returned to Massachusetts and was elected to the House. Butler lost no time in launching the House's case against Johnson. From the beginning, however, it was clear that the proceedings would be dominated by the political struggle between Johnson and Butler. Legal niceties were secondary.

Under Butler's direction, the trial managers presented the House's articles of impeachment. These eleven articles consisted of various nonspecific charges of "high crimes and misdemeanors" against Johnson. For example, Johnson was accused of making "intemperate, inflammatory, and scandalous harangues" against Congress during the Swing Around the Circle. Johnson's response to these vague charges was quick and furious:

> Impeach me for violating the Constitution! Damn them! I have been struggling and working ever since I have been in this chair to uphold the Constitution they trample underfoot! I don't care what becomes of me, but I'll fight them until they rot! I shall not allow the Constitution of the United States to be destroyed by evil men who are trying to ruin this government and this nation!

The trial began March 30, 1868. After some initial confusion, the trial managers decided to pursue a two-pronged attack. They would attempt to prove that Johnson's opposition to the Tenure of Office Act was unconstitutional and that Johnson had flagrantly abused his office with his comments about Congress. The testimony of witnesses the trial managers produced was not limited to these issues, however. There was testimony on practically any matter that could serve to discredit Johnson, such as Johnson's alleged excessive drinking habits.

Johnson's defense rested with William Maxwell Evarts, a New York attorney highly regarded throughout the North, and Benjamin R. Curtis, a former Supreme Court justice. Other lawyers, such as former Attorney General Henry Stanbery, assisted with the defense. All of Johnson's counsel felt strongly enough about the importance of the case that they worked free of charge.

Senate Republicans Thwart Johnson's Defense

Johnson's lawyers attempted to introduce evidence showing that Johnson's opposition to the Tenure of Office Act was no more than a legitimate desire to test the constitutional validity of the act in the federal courts. The defense offered to produce witnesses who could testify that Johnson's opposition to the act on constitutional grounds had long preceded his quarrel with Secretary of War Stanton. Chief Justice Chase ruled that this evidence was admissible. Although a two-thirds vote of the Senate was necessary for a conviction of impeachment, it took only a simple majority vote to decide procedural matters. Therefore, despite Chase's rulings, the Senate repeatedly voted to prevent the defense from producing its witnesses concerning Johnson's legitimate opposition to the act.

The second prong of the trial managers' attack concerned Johnson's public statements. But the defense argued that the Senate could hardly impeach Johnson for exercising the right of freedom of speech that the Constitution gave to every American. Butler's retort made little legal sense but was good rhetoric and played well with the anti-Johnson public of the North:

> Is it, indeed, to be seriously argued here that there is a constitutional right in the President of the United States, who, during his official life, can never lay aside his official life, can never lay aside his official character, to denounce, malign, abuse, ridicule, and condemn, openly and publicly, the Congress of the United States: a coordinate branch of the government?

Consciences of Seven Republicans Save Johnson

Throughout the two-month-long trial, Johnson's defense lawyers repeatedly saw their sound legal arguments thwarted by purely political forces. However, seven Republican senators were disturbed by how the proceedings had been manipulated to permit a one-sided presentation of the evidence. Senators William Pitt Fessenden, Joseph S. Fowler, James W. Grimes, John B. Henderson, Edmund G. Ross, Lyman Trumbull, and Peter G. Van Winkle defied their party and public opinion and voted against impeachment.

The Senate met on May 26, 1868, for the final vote. The shift by the seven Republicans proved critical: the tally was 35 to 19 in favor of impeachment, one vote short of the two-thirds majority necessary to impeach Johnson. Johnson was acquitted. But his political career never recovered. Later in 1868 the war hero General Ulysses S. Grant was elected the next president of the United States.

—*Stephen G. Christianson*

Suggestions for Further Reading

Aymar, Brandt and Edward Sagarin. *Laws and Trials That Created History.* New York: Crown Publishers, 1974.

Dorris, Jonathan Truman. *Pardon and Amnesty Under Lincoln and Johnson.* Chapel Hill: University of North Carolina Press, 1953.

Gerson, Noel B. *The Trial of Andrew Johnson.* Nashville and New York: Thomas Nelson, 1977.

Paul, M. "Was Andrew Johnson Right?" *Senior Scholastic* (Teachers' Edition). (November 1982): 26.

Simpson, Brooks D., Leroy F. Graf, and John Muldowny. *Advice After Appomattox: Letters to Andrew Johnson.* Knoxville: University of Tennessee Press, 1987.

Smith, Gene. *High Crimes & Misdemeanors: The Impeachment and Trial of Andrew Johnson.* New York: William Morrow & Co., 1977.

Strong, George Templeton. *Diary.* New York: Macmillan Co., 1952.

Trefousse, Hans L. *Andrew Johnson, a Biography.* New York and London: W.W. Norton & Co., 1989.

Hester Vaughan Trial: 1868

Defendant: Hester Vaughan **Crime Charged:** First-degree murder
Chief Defense Lawyer: Guforth (No first name listed.)
Chief Prosecutor: No record. **Judge:** Ludlow (No first name listed)
Place: Philadelphia, Pennsylvania **Dates of Trial:** June 10–July 2, 1868
Verdict: Guilty **Sentence:** Death

SIGNIFICANCE

When the teenaged Hester Vaughan allegedly murdered her newborn infant, she was prosecuted by a male district attorney, defended by a male attorney, found guilty by an all-male jury and sentenced to death by a male judge. Women's rights leaders, protesting that Vaughan had not had "a trial by a jury of her peers," promptly organized their followers. The women's outcry gained much attention in the press and persuaded Pennsylvania Governor John Geary to exile Vaughan to her native England rather than sign her death warrant.

According to Hester Vaughan's report to her female sympathizers, she had traveled to the United States from her native England to marry her American fiancé. After one and a half years—and upon Vaughan's discovery that her "husband" had another wife and family—Vaughan was deserted. Too ashamed to return home, she accepted a housekeeper's position in Philadelphia, Pennsylvania. She was raped by a member of her employer's household and became pregnant. She left that household, rented a small room, and took in odd sewing jobs while awaiting her baby's birth.

The press and other historical accounts of the trial are sketchy and riddled with gaps. It is clear that on February 8 or 9, 1868, Hester Vaughan, malnourished and living alone in an unheated room at 703 Girard Avenue, Philadelphia, gave birth. Two days later, she asked another resident of the building for a box in which to place a dead baby. She also asked that the matter be kept secret.

Instead, the police were notified. Vaughan was arrested and brought to trial on murder charges on June 30, 1868. The prosecution presented several witnesses, whose testimony was summarized by the *Philadelphia Inquirer*:

> [Vaughan] explained [to the resident from whom she had requested a box] that she had been frightened by a lady going into the room with a cup of coffee, and fallen back upon her child, thus killing it. . . . Dr. Shapleigh [of

> the Coroner's office], who examined the body, found several fractures of the skull, made apparently with some blunt instrument, and also clots of blood between the brain and skull. The lady who took the coffee to the prisoner heard the child give one or two faint cries.

The commonwealth rested its case, and Judge Ludlow ordered Vaughan's lawyer, a Mr. Guforth, to present the defense's witnesses the next morning. According to reports later published by women's rights leaders Elizabeth Cady Stanton and Susan B. Anthony, Vaughan had paid Guforth her last few dollars to retain him as her lawyer, but Guforth, after taking her money, never saw her again until the first day of trial.

On the morning of July 1, Guforth presented a witness or witnesses who testified as to Vaughan's good character. He then offered his own arguments against her conviction: First, "the prisoner should not be convicted of murder in the first degree, because in the agony and pain she must have suffered, she may have been bereft of all reason," and second, "the death may have been caused by accident, for the prisoner was the only human being who saw the death, and her lips were sealed by law." Presumably, this latter argument may have referred to the 19th-century belief that women were incompetent witnesses.

Sentenced to Die

Vaughan was found guilty and sentenced to die. Susan A. Smith, M.D., one of the country's first women doctors, learned of the case and visited Vaughan in Moyamensing prison. Upon medical examination and after repeated interviews, Dr. Smith wrote to Pennsylvania Governor John W. Geary concerning the circumstances of Vaughan's pregnancy, labor and delivery:

> [Vaughan] rented a third story room . . . from a family who understood very little English. She furnished this room, found herself in food and fuel for three months on twenty dollars. She was taken sick in this room at midnight on the 6th of February and lingered until Saturday morning, the eighth, when her child was born, she told me she was nearly frozen and fainted or went to sleep for a long time.
>
> You will please remember, sir, throughout this period of agony she was alone, without nourishment or fire, with her door unfastened.
>
> My professional opinion in Hester Vaughan's case is that cold and want of attention produced painful and protracted labor—that the mother, in endeavoring to assist herself, injured the head of her child in its birth—that she either fainted or had a convulsion, and was insensible for a long time.

Despite court testimony that the baby had cried, Dr. Smith and another woman doctor, Clemence Lozier, later questioned whether the child had even been born alive.

When Governor Geary failed to respond to Dr. Smith's request for Hester Vaughan's pardon, the case was brought to the attention of Elizabeth Cady Stanton, Susan B. Anthony, and other members of the Working Women's National Association. They promptly scheduled a protest meeting in New York City's Cooper Institute. Cady Stanton and Anthony decried what they called

Vaughan's "condemn[ation] on insufficient evidence and with inadequate defense." However, their protest was based primarily on 19th-century women's exclusion from the ballot and jury boxes. The crowd in attendance voted unanimously to petition Governor Geary for either a new trial or an unconditional pardon for Hester Vaughan. They sent the governor—and several major newspapers—the following resolution:

> Whereas, The right of trial by a jury of one's peers is recognized by the governments of all civilized nations as the great palladium of rights, of justice, and equality to the citizen: therefore, Resolved, That this [Working Women's National] Association demand that in all civil and criminal cases, woman shall be tried by a jury of her peers; shall have a voice in making the law, in electing the judge who pronounces her sentence, and the sheriff who, in case of execution, performs for her that last dread act.

In their travels across the country and in their own newspaper, the *Revolution*, Cady Stanton and Anthony kept up a campaign of condemnation against a male dominated society that would sentence to death a "young, artless, and inexperienced girl." Women, exhorted by Cady Stanton and Anthony to view the case with a "sense of . . . responsibility in making and executing the laws under which [our] daughters are to live or perish," responded: they continued to petition the governor and even wrote poems about the case of Hester Vaughan.

Finally, in the summer of 1869, Governor Geary pardoned Vaughan—but with the condition that private funds be raised to pay her passage back to England. Cady Stanton and Anthony raised the money and triumphantly published Vaughan's thank-you letter in the *Revolution* on August 19, 1869.

—*Kathryn Cullen-DuPont*

Suggestions for Further Reading

Barry, Kathleen. *Susan B. Anthony.* New York: New York University Press, 1988.

Harper, Ida Husted. *Life and Work of Susan B. Anthony,* Vol. 1. 1898, reprint, Salem, NH: Ayer Co., Publishers, 1983.

New York Times, December 4, 1868.

Philadelphia Inquirer, July 1–2 and December 3–4, 1868.

Revolution, December 10, 1868–August 19, 1869.

Ex Parte McCardle: 1868

Defendant: William H. McCardle **Crimes Charged:** Inciting insurrection and impeding post-Civil War Reconstruction **Chief Defense Lawyers:** Jeremiah S. Black, David Dudley Field, Charles O'Conor, W. L. Sharkey, and Robert J. Walker **Chief Prosecutors:** Mathew H. Carpenter and Lyman Trumbull **Justices:** Salmon P. Chase, Nathan Clifford, David Davis, Robert Cooper Grier, Stephen, J. Field, Samuel F. Miller, Samuel Nelson, and Noah H. Swayne. **Place:** Washington, D.C. **Date of Decision:** 1868 December Term **Decision:** That the Supreme Court was without jurisdiction to render a decision, because Congress had repealed certain appeals legislation

SIGNIFICANCE

For the first and only time in American history, Congress exercised its authority to prevent the Supreme Court from hearing certain types of politically sensitive cases.

After the Civil War, the victorious Union army occupied the defeated Confederacy and the period known as Reconstruction began. On March 2, 1867, Congress passed a law entitled "An Act to Provide for the More Efficient Government of the Rebel States," which officially provided for the military administration of the South. The act abolished the legal existence of the Southern states, and divided the Confederacy into a series of military districts, each commanded by a General who possessed extensive powers to suppress any act of defiance.

In the city of Vicksburg, Mississippi, public resentment against the Union was particularly high. The city was strategically located on the Mississippi River and had fallen to the Union after a long and bloody siege by General Ulysses S. Grant. After the Civil War, the Fourth of July was not celebrated in Vicksburg for 75 years.

William H. McCardle was the editor of a local newspaper, the *Vicksburg Times*. McCardle published various articles criticizing Reconstruction in general and Major General Edward O.C. Ord in particular. Ord was the Commanding General of the Fourth Military District, which included Vicksburg. General Ord was not amused. He had McCardle arrested in November 1867 for various offenses relating to inciting insurrection and impeding Reconstruction. On November 11, 1867, McCardle sent a petition to the Circuit Court of the United States for the Southern District of Mississippi, asking for a writ of *habeas corpus*, meaning a court order to free McCardle from illegal imprisonment. The circuit court refused McCardle's request, and McCardle appealed to the Supreme Court.

Congress Denies McCardle Access to Supreme Court

The Supreme Court is the only federal court specifically provided for by the Constitution. Under Article III, Section 2, the Supreme Court has original jurisdiction, meaning sole authority, only in "Cases affecting Ambassadors, other public Ministers and Consuls, and those in which a State shall be Party." In all other cases, the Supreme Court has jurisdiction only on appeal from such federal courts as Congress may decide to create and from state supreme courts. This appellate jurisdiction is expressly subject to "such Exceptions, and under such Regulations as the Congress shall make."

On September 24, 1789 Congress passed the Judiciary Act, which is the basis for the federal court system and gave the Supreme Court various appellate powers. On February 5, 1867 Congress amended the Judiciary Act to enable the Supreme Court to hear appeals in *habeas corpus* cases. It was precisely this amendment, called the Habeas Corpus Act of 1867, that enabled the Court to hear the McCardle case.

The Radical Republicans who controlled Congress feared that the McCardle case would give the Court an excuse to overturn Reconstruction legislation and end martial law in the South. Therefore, on March 27, 1868, Congress passed a law repealing the appeal provisions of the Habeas Corpus Act of 1867:

> And be it further enacted, That so much of the act approved February 5, 1867, entitled 'An act to amend an act to establish the judicial courts of the United States, approved September 24, 1789,' as authorized an appeal from the judgment of the Circuit Court to the Supreme Court of the United States, or the exercise of any such jurisdiction by said Supreme Court, on appeals which have been, or may hereafter be taken, be, and the same is hereby repealed.

The case came before the Supreme Court during the 1868 December Term. McCardle was represented by Jeremiah S. Black, David Dudley Field, Charles O'Conor, W.L. Sharkey and Robert J. Walker. The government was represented by Mathew H. Carpenter and Lyman Trumbull.

The hearing focused on the effect of Congress' repeal of the Court's jurisdiction. If the Court didn't have jurisdiction, the validity or invalidity of McCardle's imprisonment was irrelevant. Sharkey argued that Congress' action was unconstitutional because it was designed solely to affect the McCardle case:

> Its language is general, but, as was universally known, its purpose was specific. If Congress had specifically enacted 'that the Supreme Court of the United States shall never publicly give judgment in the case of McCardle, already argued, and on which we anticipate that it will soon deliver judgment, contrary to the views of the majority in Congress, of what it ought to decide,' its purpose to interfere specifically with and prevent the judgment in this very case would not have been more real or, as a fact, more universally known.

Congress Could not be Denied

Carpenter and Trumbull responded by citing the plain language of Article III, Section 2 of the Constitution, under which Congress' authority to restrict the Court's appellate jurisdiction could not be denied. Further, Carpenter Trumbull pointed out that the language of Congress' repeal of the Court's authority "embraces all cases in all time." Although Sharkey was certainly accurate in describing Congress' real motivations, Carpenter and Trumbull correctly pointed out that legally, any assumption that the repeal was aimed specifically at McCardle couldn't be proven and therefore was "gratuitous and unwarrantable."

Chief Justiice Salmon Chase (center) announced the Court's unanimous decision in *Ex parte McCardle.* (Bettmann/Corbis)

By the end of the 1868 December Term, Chief Justice Salmon P. Chase announced the Court's unanimous decision. Chase held that McCardle's appeal was dismissed for lack of jurisdiction, because of Congress' repeal of the Court's authority. Chase stated in blunt terms that Congress had undeniably exercised its power to create exceptions to the Court's authority:

> The provision of the act of 1867 affirming the appellate jurisdiction of this court in cases of *habeas corpus* is expressly repealed. It is hardly possible to imagine a plainer instance of positive exception.

The McCardle case is the only time in American history that Congress used its power under the Constitution to prevent the Supreme Court from hearing certain types of politically sensitive cases. There have been periodic movements in Congress to restrict the Court's authority to hear school desegregation cases, school prayer cases, abortion cases and other politically sensitive cases, but nothing has ever happened. However the Court did not completely surrender to Congress actions. Only one year later, in 1869, the Court agreed to hear a case very similar to McCardle's called Ex Parte Yerger, and side-stepped Congress' repeal of the Court's authority. Yerger was released from custody before the Court could hear the case and get into any confrontation with Congress. As more than one legal commentator has opined, given the need for the different branches of government to work peacefully with each other, it may be politically healthy that the limits of congressional power under the Constitution have never been completely clarified.

—*Stephen G. Christianson*

Suggestions for Further Reading

Franklin, John Hope. *Reconstruction: After the Civil War*. Chicago: University of Chicago Press, 1961.

Morris, Richard B. *Encyclopedia of American History*. New York: Harper & Row, 1982.

Tortora, Anthony. "Ex parte McCardle." *National Review* (September 19, 1980): 1140–1141, 1157.

Trefousse, Hans L. *Historical Dictionary of Reconstruction*. Westport, Conn: Greenwood Press, 1991.

Daniel McFarland Trial: 1870

Defendant: Daniel McFarland **Crime Charged:** Murder
Chief Defense Lawyers: Elbridge T. Gerry, John Graham, Charles Spencer
Chief Prosecutors: Noah Davis, Samuel Garvin **Judge:** (No record of first name) Hackett **Place:** New York, New York **Date of Trial:** April 4–May 10, 1870 **Verdict:** Not guilty

SIGNIFICANCE

This trial underscores several points that seem just as relevant today as they were more than 13 decades ago: that skillful lawyering can acquit a clearly guilty murderer, that an abused wife can find true love in a second marriage, that talented members of the theatrical and literary world lead headline-producing lives.

Late in the afternoon of November 25, 1869, Albert Deane Richardson, a 36-year-old journalist who had covered Civil War battles for Horace Greeley's *New York Tribune*, walked into the *Tribune* offices in New York's Printing House Square. He went to the first-floor counting room to see if one of its pigeonholes held a letter from his fiancee, an actress and writer named Abby Sage, who was visiting Massachusetts. As Richardson neared the mail desk, a figure rose from the shadows, pointed a pistol at him from five feet away, fired, and ran.

Shot in the stomach, Richardson climbed four flights to the paper's editorial offices. A doctor administered morphine and friends escorted him to the Astor House hotel, two blocks down Park Row.

Not the First Time

Richardson knew his assailant well. He was a 50-year-old lawyer and unsuccessful entrepreneur named Daniel McFarland from whom, only weeks earlier, Abby Sage had obtained a divorce after several years of suffering his drunken abuse. Two and a half years earlier, in 1867, not long after Sage had first become acquainted with Richardson, McFarland had ambushed the journalist, shooting him in the thigh as he escorted the actress home after her theater performance. Richardson had not pressed charges.

Jailed, McFarland denied remembering the shooting but showed no remorse over it. At the Astor House, doctors tried to make the victim comfortable. Facing the inevitable, Abby Sage called on her friend, the prominent preacher Henry Ward Beecher, to perform a death-bedside wedding ceremony. *Tribune* editor Greeley was a witness. On December 2, Richardson died in the arms of his bride. On December 8, McFarland was indicted for murder.

The shooting, and then the wedding, had dominated the front pages of New York's many newspapers. As the trial opened on Monday, April 4, 1870, reporters, stenographers, and spectators fought for space. Defense lawyers Elbridge T. Gerry, John Graham, and Charles Spencer, sensing the emotional pull of the trial of a man for murdering the alleged seducer of his wife, arranged for 10-year-old Percy McFarland to be seen running happily to his father when the defendant was brought into the courtroom, then permitted the boy to sit beside him during the trial.

Prosecutors Noah Davis and Samuel Garvin presented a straightforward case. Dan Frohman, an 18-year-old clerk in the *Tribune* office, described how he was getting Richardson's mail when McFarland, who had been hanging around the office for some 15 minutes, abruptly shot him.

The Libertine's Letter

Defense lawyer Graham's opening depicted McFarland as "a man overtaken by sorrow and calamity brought on by the unholy, reckless, and lawless passion of a bold, bad libertine, a wife-seducer and child-robber sent into eternity by a husband and father wronged when a great sea turned away his reason." The jury—all 12 of them husbands and fathers—listened intently.

Now McFarland's attorneys presented an "intercepted letter" written by Richardson to "Darling Abby" shortly after her marriage broke up—but before the divorce. Interspersed with frequent "darlings," it included such titillating expressions as "I want you always, a hundred times a day my arms seem to stretch outward toward you. I never seek my pillow without wanting to fold you to my heart for a goodnight kiss. . . ." The letter ended with the pencilled notation, "Burn this—will you not?" Spectators gasped. Newspapers printed the letter verbatim.

How had it been intercepted? Richardson had addressed the letter to *Mrs.* McFarland at the *Tribune* office in care of its publisher, in whose home she was staying while separated from her husband. But a *Tribune* mail clerk, seeing *Mr.* McFarland drop in, had handed him the letter.

Insanity Defense

The defense set out to prove McFarland's insanity. A daughter of his first cousin described her own father's 18 months of "fits of crying and melancholy" followed by attempted suicide and, ultimately, commitment in an asylum. An attorney colleague recalled McFarland as "not in his right mind."

Altogether, more than 40 defense witnesses testified with similar observations on the frantic, nervous, and obsessive aspects of McFarland's mental condition. And then Mary Mason, landlady of a boarding house where Richardson had had a front room while the McFarland family occupied the same floor to the rear, testified, "I saw Mr. Richardson and Mrs. McFarland going in and out a great deal together, often when Mr. McFarland was away." A domestic servant and a 16-year-old waiter added similar recollections, with the waiter concluding, "You ask if I have seen Mr. Richardson take 'liberties' with Mrs. McFarland. Yes, I have. I've seen them shake hands together many times." The courtroom exploded with laughter.

The defense interrogated Dr. William A. Hammond, a well-known professor of neuro-surgery, on tests he had recently conducted on McFarland. "I can observe," he said, "many phenomena that he could not feign. There can be no doubt that his state was such as to render him entirely irresponsible for his acts."

The prosecution's first rebuttal witness was famed editor Horace Greeley, whose *Tribune* had rebuked McFarland. He failed to add condemning testimony but, when cross-examined about letters of recommendation he had written on McFarland's behalf, remarked caustically, "Those letters were as true as such letters usually are."

Tribune publisher Samuel Sinclair, in whose home Abby stayed after separating from McFarland in 1867, gave stronger evidence, citing McFarland's drunken brutality toward his wife. And the editor of a competitive paper recalled how McFarland—apparently hoping to embarrass the *Tribune*—offered to sell him, for $100, his wife's personal letters.

In its fifth week, the trial drew ever-larger crowds. They brought basket lunches. Those unseated framed the courtroom, shoulder to shoulder along its walls. They heard more rebuttal witnesses testify on the defendant's drunken and abusive behavior and on Abby Sage's decision to leave him.

". . . In the Day of Vengeance"

Defense attorney Graham's summation took two full days. He cited trials in which aggrieved husbands had been acquitted of murdering their wives' lovers. He alluded to implications of the philosophy of free love—a topic then current in popular magazines—raised by the trial's circumstantial evidence. He quoted the Bible (Proverbs, Chapter VI):

> Whoso committeth adultery with a woman lacketh understanding; he that doeth it destoyeth his own soul. A wound and dishonor shall he get; and his reproach shall not be wiped away. For jealousy is the rage of a man; therefore he will not spare in the day of vengeance.

Prosecutor Garvin's brief summation included appealing questions: "Gentlemen of the jury, did it occur to you that it might be a fact in this case, whether proved or unproved, that Albert Richardson and Mrs. McFarland were entirely innocent of those charges? I put it to you as sensible men, would Albert Richardson have sought to marry Mrs. McFarland, would he have aided her in getting a divorce to marry her, if he had seduced her?"

The jury deliberated for one hour and 55 minutes before pronouncing the defendant "Not guilty."

McFarland moved to Leadville, Colorado, where he was last seen living among laborers in a boarding house in 1880.

Abby Sage Richardson became a successful author and playwright well known in New York society and literary circles. In 1890, she again dominated headlines when she and theatrical producer Daniel Frohman (the very same Dan Frohman who had witnessed the murder two decades earlier) lost a court case when they were enjoined from producing her theatrical adaptation of Mark Twain's novel *The Prince and the Pauper.* The contender proved that Twain had previously authorized him to adapt it.

Abby Richardson died in 1900.

—Bernard Ryan, Jr.

Suggestions for Further Reading

Cooper, George. *Lost Love: A True Story of Passion, Murder, and Justice in Old New York.* New York: Pantheon, 1994.

Stern, Madeleine B. "Trial by Gotham 1870, The Career of Abby Sage Richardson." *N.Y. History* (July 1947): 271–87.

South Carolina Ku Klux Klan Trials: 1871–72

Defendants: Robert Hayes Mitchell, John W. Mitchell, Thomas B. Whitesides, John S. Millar (Miller), Edward T. Avery **Crimes Charged:** Conspiracy to prevent blacks from voting; conspiracy to oppress, threaten, and intimidate blacks who had exercised their right to vote in 1870
Chief Defense Lawyers: Reverdy Johnson, Henry Stanbery, James F. Hart, C. D. Melton, W. B. Wilson and F. W. McMaster **Chief Prosecutors:** Daniel H. Chamberlain, David T. Corbin **Judges:** Hugh L. Bond, George S. Bryan
Place: Columbia, South Carolina **Date of Trial:** December 1871–January 1872 **Verdicts:** Guilty **Sentences:** Robert Hayes Mitchell: 18 months imprisonment and a $100 fine; John W. Mitchell: 5 years imprisonment and a $1,000 fine; Whitesides: 12 months imprisonment and a $100 fine; Millar: 3 months imprisonment and a $20 fine; Avery: fled before sentencing and later pardoned by President Ulysses S. Grant

SIGNIFICANCE

With the arrest and later trials of several Ku Klux Klan members in the South, particularly South Carolina, the federal government attempted to demonstrate the lengths it would go to in order to preserve the Fourteenth and Fifteenth Amendments to the Constitution.

Six bored Confederate veterans founded the original Ku Klux Klan (KKK) as a social club on December 24, 1865, in Pulaski, Tennessee. The organization existed less than 10 years, but for decades it was glorified as the instrument by which northern carpetbaggers and Radical Republicans were driven out of the South, illiterate and "savage" blacks were put down, and whites were restored to their "rightful place" in southern society. This myth reached its height in the early twentieth century with the 1905 publication of Thomas Dixon's novel *The Clansmen*, and the release 10 years later of D. W. Griffith's movie *The Birth of a Nation;* its truth is a fundamental tenet to every modern Klansman.

In reality, the original KKK was a brutal terrorist movement that lynched and shot hundreds and beat, whipped, raped, and mutilated thousands more. While most of its victims were black, other targets included northern whites who moved south after the Civil War, southern whites who supported the federal government's Reconstruction policy, and anyone who violated what the Klan considered the proper social order. A reign of terror existed throughout much of the former Confederacy, and in many places the state and local authorities could do nothing to stop it.

Ku Klux Klan attacking black family inside their home. (drawing by Frank Bellew, *Harper's Weekly*)

The South Carolina Klan

The Klan was particularly active in South Carolina. For various reasons, it began to decline there in late 1868, but it was revived after the Republicans, supported by the state's black majority, won the October 1870 election. The terrorism was worst in the northern part of South Carolina, especially in Spartansburg, Union, and York counties. For example, in Spartansburg County between the election and July 1871, four people were killed and over 200 were beaten, whipped, wounded by gunfire, or had their ears cut off by Klan members.

Until 1870, the crimes committed by the KKK and its members were violations of state and local, but not federal, law. Then, on March 30, 1870, the Fifteenth Amendment to the Constitution, which granted blacks the right to vote, was ratified after a long and bitter national debate. Equally important, it gave the federal government the power to protect that right with appropriate legislation. On May 31, 1870, the Enforcement Act was passed by Congress and signed by President Ulysses S. Grant. The law dealt mostly with the bribery and intimidation of voters, but it also made it a federal offense for two or more persons to conspire to deprive someone of any right of citizenship or to punish that person for exercising those rights.

The Ku Klux Klan Act

Initially, it was hoped that the mere existence of the Enforcement Act would deter further actions by the Klan and little was done to enforce the new law. However, the strategy did not work. In March 1871, conditions in South Carolina were bad enough that Governor Robert Scott asked for federal troops to help suppress KKK activities in his state. In response, Congress passed and President Grant signed on April 20, 1871, the Ku Klux Klan Act.

Because there were so many Klansmen and since many of the local police in the South were members of the KKK or sympathetic to its cause, the Ku Klux Klan Act allowed the president to use the army to apprehend violators of this new law. The legislation also gave the president, until 1872, the power to suspend the writ of *habeas corpus.* The latter provision was important because, if *habeas corpus* was suspended, then the authorities could make mass arrests without having to bring each defendant immediately before a court to face charges. Such a tool was vital in some southern counties where there were too many Klansmen to promptly bring them all to trial. Furthermore, because of the large number of suspects, the suspension of *habeas corpus* allowed the prosecutors to keep evidence (including the identities of Klansmen yet to be arrested) secret until all the defendants were in custody.

In July 1871, the U.S. Justice Department sent instructions to its officers in the South to begin prosecutions under the Ku Klux Klan Act. Those defendants whose crimes were committed before the passage of the law would be prosecuted under the Enforcement Act. Arrests and trials began in Mississippi and North Carolina, but by this time the Klan in South Carolina was out of control. On October 12, President Grant issued a proclamation ordering the Klansmen there to disperse and surrender their weapons. Nothing happened, so on October 17 Grant suspended *habeas corpus* in nine South Carolina counties and sent in troops to help the local U.S. marshal make the arrests.

By the end of the year, hundreds of Klansmen in South Carolina were arrested while even more fled the state; some ran as far away as Canada. Others voluntarily surrendered, gave depositions, and were released. In York County alone, 195 were taken into custody, about 200 evaded arrest, and at least 500 turned themselves in. Another 200 arrests were made in Union County and hundreds more were apprehended in Spartansburg and nearby Chester County. Indeed, the numbers were so great that the legal system could not handle them all. As a result, only the most serious offenders were detained and prosecuted while the rest were released on bail after making sworn confessions. The arrests continued for two years, but most of them were made before December 31, 1871. Fortunately, very little violence accompanied the arrests.

The Trials Begin

Of the original 220 Klansmen who were indicted, only five were prosecuted. 53 others pleaded guilty and the cases against the rest were postponed. The five who went to trial were all charged with violating the Enforcement Act. Four of the defendants, Robert Mitchell, John Mitchell, Thomas Whitesides, and John Millar [or Miller; court transcripts alternate between the spellings], were charged with conspiracy to prevent "male citizens of the United States of African descent" from voting in the upcoming 1872 election. In addition, Robert Mitchell was accused of conspiracy to oppress, threaten, and intimidate a black man because he had voted in the 1870 election. John Mitchell and Thomas Whitesides, were also charged with three counts of conspiracy to prevent a black man from voting in 1872 and to oppress, threaten, and intimidate him because he voted in 1870. The fifth defendant, Dr. Edward T. Avery, was charged with conspiracy to prevent three blacks from voting in 1872 and with conspiracy to oppress, threaten, and intimidate the three because they had voted in 1870.

The initial trials were held before the U.S. Circuit Court in Columbia. Approximately $10,000 (over $100,000 today) was raised by public donations to hire Reverdy Johnson and Henry Stanbery, both former U.S. attorney generals, to assist the local defense lawyers. The prosecutors were U.S. attorney David T. Corbin and South Carolina's attorney general (and future governor) Daniel H. Chamberlain. (Both Corbin and Chamberlain were northerners who had moved to South Carolina after the Civil War.) The trials were presided by U.S. Circuit Court judge Hugh Bond, a former Maryland lawyer and state judge who sat on the recent Klan trials in North Carolina, and U.S. District Court judge George Bryan, a native of South Carolina who had been pro-Union during the Civil War.

At all four trials (Whitesides and John Mitchell were tried together), former slaves constituted the majority of the jurors. (At Robert Mitchell's and Millar's trials, nine of the 12 jurors were black; at the others, 11 of the 12.) In addition, the few whites on the juries were all Republicans and, thus, hostile to the Klan. No former Confederate soldiers (who would probably be Klansmen or supporters of the KKK) sat in judgment of the defendants because federal law prohibited Confederate veterans from sitting on federal juries.

Before the trials began, defense lawyers Reverdy Johnson and Henry Stanbery spent almost two weeks to quash nine of the 11 counts in an indictment against Allen Crosby and others. (Crosby and seven of his codefendants later pleaded guilty to the remaining charges.) Johnson and Stanbery also participated in Mitchell's defense while local counsel alone represented the other four defendants. However, the evidence presented during Mitchell's trial of the Klan's cruelty was so overwhelming that at one point Johnson, while maintaining his client's innocence, felt compelled in the courtroom to attack the activities of the KKK.

The four trials each lasted between two days and a week. In the end, Robert Mitchell was convicted of one of the two charges against him. John Mitchell and Thomas Whitesides were convicted of two of the four counts they faced. Millar and Avery were also convicted. Because Robert Mitchell, Whitesides, and Millar had minor roles in the Klan's activities, they received minor sentences. In contrast, John Mitchell was a prominent Klansman and, although he pleaded for mercy, he was sentenced to five years in prison and fined $1,000. Dr. Avery, however, was never sentenced; free on bail, he realized halfway through his trial that he was going to be convicted and fled. (The trial continued in his absence.) Of the 53 defendants who pleaded guilty, penalties ranged from three months to five years imprisonment with fines varying from $10 to $1,000. Except for those who were underage—they were sent to the Detroit House of Corrections—everyone who received sentences of a year or more was incarcerated at the federal penitentiary in Albany, New York; the rest served their time in various southern prisons and jails.

More convictions of Klansmen were obtained in South Carolina in 1872, but the number (37) was much smaller than those in 1871. Besides South Carolina, arrests and trials for violations of the Enforcement and the Ku Klux Klan Acts occurred all throughout the South in 1871 and 1872. However, only in South Carolina was habeas corpus suspended and in no other state were there as many prosecutions. Indeed, outside Mississippi, North Carolina, and Tennessee, the number of arrests and trials elsewhere was small.

It is impossible to measure the effect of the Ku Klux Klan trials. After the 1871 prosecutions in South Carolina, Klan terrorism in the state and elsewhere dramatically dropped. As a result, the number of arrests for violating the Enforcement and the Ku Klux Klan Acts rapidly declined. However, violence against southern blacks by whites in general did not substantially decline.

—Mark Thorburn

Suggestions for Further Reading

Randel, William Peirce. *The Ku Klux Klan: A Century of Infamy.* New York: Chilton Books, 1965.

Reynolds, John A. *Reconstruction in South Carolina, 1865-1877.* Columbia, S.C.: State Company, 1905. Reprint, New York: Negro Universities Press, 1969.

Shapiro, Herbert. "The Ku Klux Klan during Reconstruction: The South Carolina Episode." *The Journal of Negro History* 49, no.1. (January 1964): 34–55.

Simkins, Francis B., and Robert H. Woody. *South Carolina during Reconstruction.* Chapel Hill, N.C.: University of North Carolina Press, 1932. Reprint, Gloucester, Mass.: P. Smith, 1966.

Swinney, Everette. "Enforcing the Fifteenth Amendment, 1870-1877." *Journal of Southern History* 28, no.2. (May 1962): 202–18.

Williamson, Joel. *After Slavery: The Negro in South Carolina during Reconstruction, 1861-1877.* Chapel Hill, N.C.: University of North Carolina Press, 1965.

Boss Tweed Trials: 1873

Defendant: William Marcy Tweed **Crimes Charged:** 55 criminal offenses relating to embezzlement of public funds **Chief Defense Lawyers:** David Dudley Field, John Graham, and Elihu Root **Chief Prosecutors:** Wheeler H. Peckham, Benjamin K. Phelps, and Lyman Tremain **Judge:** Noah Davis **Place:** New York, New York **Dates of Trials:** January 7–November 19, 1873 **Verdict:** Guilty **Sentence:** 1 year in prison and a $250 fine

SIGNIFICANCE

After decades of committing blatant embezzlement of New York City municipal funds with the connivance of Tammany Hall and public officials, Boss Tweed's power was broken. Tweed's fall from power marked the beginning of a new demand by the public and by the press for efficient and honest urban administration.

Descended from hard-working Scottish immigrants, William Marcy Tweed was born in 1823 in New York City. He was a brawling bully from his early youth, heavyset and strong, and as a boy he enjoyed beating the other children in his neighborhood. As an adult he weighed nearly 300 pounds. Tweed bullied and fought his way to a position of leadership among New York's criminal elements, notably the "Forty Thieves" gang. In the 1851 elections Tweed used threats and intimidation of the voters in his precinct to force his way onto New York City's Board of Aldermen.

Tweed was an alderman for two years, and he used the position as a stepping stone for his political career. He served on the Board of Education, and even finagled his election to the U.S. House of Representatives. In 1857, Tweed was elected to New York City's Board of Supervisors, which ran the city's municipal government and controlled its finances. The position was ideal for the greedy Tweed, who promptly installed his cronies as "assistants" and raised the level of city corruption to new heights.

Tweed and his gang were called the Tweed Ring, and they stole enormous sums from the city treasury by falsifying municipal accounts and by creating false or grossly exaggerated expense records. Anyone who opposed them was beaten or killed. In the 1860s, Tweed extended his power to include control over the city's courts. Tweed had George G. Barnard appointed chief judge, although Barnard had practically no legal experience and his only qualification for the post was his allegiance to Tweed. Other judges were on Tweed's payroll as well, including the father of future Supreme Court Justice Benjamin Cardozo.

Tweed's control of the city was buttressed by the support of the Tammany Hall political organization. To control the elections, Tammany Hall sold citizenship documents to practically any immigrant who promised to vote for the Tweed slate. Since New York was teeming with millions of new immigrants, most of whom had fled poverty and were desperate to stay in America, Tweed and Tammany Hall not only were able to control the elections but made hundreds of thousands of dollars as well.

Cartoonist Thomas Nast recalled growing up in fear of the random beatings meted out by Tweed's gang. In the above cartoon he shows relief that justice has been served. (*Harper's Weekly*)

Reformers Fight Back

By the early 1870s, reform politicians determined to end urban corruption had risen to power. New York State Governor Samuel Tilden and state Attorney General Charles Fairchild went after Tweed. They were supported by influential elements of the New York City press, led by political commentator and cartoonist Thomas Nast of the *New York Times*. Nast had grown up in Tweed's neighborhood, and as a child lived with the fear of Tweed's random beatings. Nast's personal vendetta against Tweed took the form of scathing cartoons depicting Tweed as a fat and corrupt Tammany boss. Other papers, such as *Harper's Weekly*, joined the *Times* in exposing Tweed's abuse of power and in calling for his prosecution.

Nast's *Times* and the other papers successfully stirred New Yorkers out of their apathy toward Tweed. On September 4, 1871, an enormous crowd went to hear various influential reformers speak out against Tweed. Bolstered by the crowd's enthusiasm for their cause, the reformers, led by Tilden and Fairchild, sought an injunction against Tweed and his Ring preventing them from using any more public funds. Probably because Tilden promised him protection, Judge Barnard turned against Tweed and granted the injunction on September 7.

Once Tweed was prevented from plundering the city treasury, his organization began to fall apart. On October 27, 1871, Tilden had Tweed arrested and charged with 55 criminal offenses relating to embezzlement of public funds.

Because each alleged offense involved several counts, or multiple incidents, Tweed was actually prosecuted for several hundred crimes. Tweed's lawyers were David Dudley Field, John Graham and Elihu Root. The chief prosecutors were Wheeler H. Peckham, Benjamin K. Phelps and Lyman Tremain. On January 7, 1873, the trial began before Judge Noah Davis.

The proceedings began badly for the prosecution when their poor choice of witnesses caused a mistrial. Tweed bragged that no jury could ever convict him and took a vacation in California. Tweed's second trial began November 5, 1873. This time, the prosecution conducted its case more carefully, and after only a minimal amount of evidence was presented the jury found Tweed guilty on November 19,1873.

Tweed Fights Verdict

Of the several hundred counts contained within the 55 charges against Tweed, the jury found him guilty of 102 crimes. Each crime was punishable by a year in prison and a nominal $250 fine, and so the prosecutors sought a conviction totaling 102 years and a fine of $25,500. On Tweed's behalf, Graham pleaded for mercy:

> Your honor, we are taught, from the time we enter this world, to ask for mercy; and those prayers which we put up in our own behalf must teach us to render deeds of mercy to. . . .

Graham, either genuinely upset or putting on a superb act, could not continue and broke down in tears. Prosecutor Tremain retorted:

> I cannot but feel, and I am sure my associates feel with me, indeed, all must feel, how terrible is the position of this man, who has been so high and who has fallen so low. He is now drinking the bitter waters of humiliation. The spell is broken.

Tremain turned to Judge Davis, and reminded him of the notoriety of the case:

> The law has placed in your hands the responsibility of the matter. The case is one of international interest and attracts the attention of the whole world. We now leave to you the question of what shall be meted out to the prisoner as an impartial and just penalty.

Judge Davis sentenced Tweed to 12 years in prison and a $12,750 fine. Tweed's attorneys appealed the verdict to the New York Court of Appeals, which ruled that despite the multiple offenses Tweed could not be sentenced for more than the punishment applicable to just one crime. Therefore, Tweed served just one year in prison, paid his $250 fine, and on January 15, 1875, was released from prison.

However, Tilden had anticipated Tweed's release. Tilden had Tweed arrested again, this time to recover the millions Tweed stole from the treasury. Unable to make the $3,000,000 bail, Tweed sat in prison awaiting his next trial. Although greatly diminished, Tweed's influence was still strong enough to enable him to circumvent most of the restrictions of his confinement. The prison warden allowed him to take carriage drives throughout the city, and dine at Tweed's own home if he wished. On December 4, 1875, Tweed took advantage of the warden's laxity and never returned from one of his afternoon drives.

Tweed stayed in various hideouts in Staten Island and New Jersey until he was able to obtain a boat to take him to Florida. From Florida he fled to Cuba and from there on to Spain, which was then a notorious haven for refugees. The Spanish authorities, however, would not tolerate Tweed's presence, and arrested him when he arrived in Vigo, Spain. Spain turned Tweed over to the United States and the naval vessel U.S.S. *Franklin* brought Tweed back to New York.

Tweed returned to prison, having now committed the additional offense of attempted escape. He confessed to the charges against him, and what was left of the Tweed Ring was either arrested or, if they returned their share of the stolen money, allowed to fade into obscurity. Of the tens of millions of dollars embezzled over the decades, however, the city recovered only a fraction. The rest had been frittered away in high living by Tweed and his cronies, spent in maintaining the Tammany Hall organization, or lost to the gangs and criminals affiliated with the Ring.

In 1871, when Tweed was still firmly in power and the public and press had just begun to challenge him, a reporter confronted Tweed and asked him about the charges against him. Tweed answered arrogantly, "Well, what are you going to do about it?" Thanks to the efforts of a new breed of reform politicians, supported by the demands of the public and the press for efficient and honest urban administration, Tweed found out just what could be done about it. Tweed's power was forever broken, and he died in prison on April 12, 1878.

—*Stephen G. Christianson*

Suggestions for Further Reading

Bales, William Alan. *Tiger in the Streets.* New York: Dodd, Mead & Co., 1962.

Clinton, Henry Lauren. *Celebrated Trials.* New York: Harper & Brothers, 1897.

Gustaitis, Joseph. "'Boss' Tweed: Colossus of Corruption?" *American History Illustrated* (November 1988): 34–35.

Lynch, Denis Tilden. *Boss Tweed: The Story of a Grim Generation.* New York: Boni and Liveright, 1927.

Mandelbaum, Seymour J. *Boss Tweed's New York.* Chicago: I.R. Dee, 1990.

U.S. v. Susan B. Anthony: 1873

Defendant: Susan B. Anthony **Crime Charged:** Unlawful Voting
Chief Defense Lawyers: Henry R. Selden and John Van Voorhis
Chief Prosecutor: Richard Crowley **Judge:** Ward Hunt
Place: Canandaigua, New York **Dates of Trial:** June 17–18, 1873
Verdict: Guilty

SIGNIFICANCE
This was one of the first in a series of decisions—including two rendered by the Supreme Court—which found that Section 1 of the Fourteenth Amendment to the U.S. Constitution did not expand or protect women's rights, an interpretation which remained unchanged for almost 100 years.

Several cases in the 1870s, including *U.S. v. Susan B. Anthony*, grew out of women's attempts to gain full rights of citizenship through the judicial system. Had this strategy worked, women would have been spared what followed: a 60-year-long, state-by-state legislative campaign for suffrage and 100 years in which the Fourteenth Amendment's equal protection clause was not applied to sex discrimination cases.

In July 1868, exactly 20 years after the Seneca Falls Convention and American women's first public demand for suffrage, the Fourteenth Amendment was adopted. Section 2, intended to encourage states to grant suffrage to African-American men, angered women's rights leaders because it introduced the word "male" into the Constitution and, some thought, called into question the citizenship of females. Francis Minor, an attorney and husband of Virginia Minor, the Woman Suffrage Association of Missouri's president, thought women were looking at the wrong clause. Section 1, he pointed out in 1869, declared:

> All persons born or naturalized in the United States, and subject to the jurisdiction thereof, are citizens of the United States and of the State wherein they reside. No State shall make or enforce any law which shall abridge the privileges or immunities of citizens of the United States.

Minor wrote that this clause *confirmed* the citizenship of women and concluded, "provisions of the several State Constitutions that exclude women from the franchise on account of sex, are violative alike of the spirit and letter of the Federal Constitution."

Susan B. Anthony and Elizabeth Cady Stanton published Minor's analysis in their newspaper, the *Revolution*, and urged women to go to the polls. In 1871 and 1872, in at least 10 states, women did so. Most were turned away, but a few actually managed to vote.

"I Have Been & Gone & Done it!"

One of those who voted in 1872 was Susan B. Anthony. Before registering in Rochester, New York, she had consulted Judge Henry R. Selden, who agreed that Section 1 of the Fourteenth Amendment should entitle women to suffrage; she carried his written opinion with her and threatened to sue the registrars if they failed to take her oath. They complied. Anthony and 14 female companions were registered and, on November 5, they voted. On November 28, Susan B. Anthony, the other 14 women, and the inspectors who had registered them were arrested.

All parties were offered release upon payment of $500 bail; Anthony alone refused to pay. Henry Selden, acting as her attorney, applied for a writ of *habeas corpus*, and Anthony was temporarily released. A U.S. district judge denied the writ and reset her bail at $1,000 on January 21, 1873. Anthony refused to pay, but Selden—who would later explain that he "could not see a lady I respected put in jail"—paid the bail. Anthony was released and immediately lost her right to appeal to the Supreme Court on the basis of the writ of *habeas corpus*.

Stumping Before the Trial

Anthony tried to present her side of the story to prospective jurors before the scheduled May 13 trial began. She gave the same speech in all 29 postal districts of her county:

> "Friends and Fellow-Citizens, I stand before you under indictment for the alleged crime of having voted at the last presidential election, without having a lawful right to vote. . . . We no longer petition legislature or Congress to give of the right to vote, but appeal to women everywhere to exercise their too long neglected 'citizen's right'. . . . we throw to the wind the old dogma that governments can give rights. The Declaration of Independence, the United States Constitution the constitutions of the several states . . . propose to *protect* the people in the exercise of their God-given rights. Not one of them pretends to bestow rights. . . . One half of the people of this Nation today are utterly powerless to blot from the statute books an unjust law, or to write a new and just one. The women, dissatisfied as they are with this form of government, that enforces taxation without representation—that compels them to obey laws to which they have never given their consent—that imprisons and hangs them without a trial by a jury of their peers—that robs them, in marriage of the custody of their own persons, wages, and children—are this half of the people left wholly at the mercy of the other half."

Because Anthony had "prejudiced any possible jury," her trial was moved out of her own Monroe County to Canandaigua, a town in Ontario County,

New York, and rescheduled for June 17. By June 16, Anthony had spoken in every Ontario village.

Trial Begins June 17

The trial opened before Judge Ward Hunt on June 17, 1873. U.S. District Attorney Richard Crowley presented the government's case: "Miss Susan B. Anthony . . . upon the 5th day of November, 1872, . . . voted . . . At that time she was a woman."

Beverly W. Jones, one of the inspectors under indictment for registering Anthony, testified that he had indeed registered her and that he had received ballots from her on November 5.

Susan B. Anthony's response to Judge Hunt's fine: "May it please your honor, I will never pay a dollar of your unjust penalty. . . ." (Courtesy, Library of Congress)

Crowley introduced the poll list bearing the name of Susan B. Anthony as proof that the woman voted, and the government rested its case.

Henry Selden then tried to call Anthony to the stand. Crowley objected: "She is not competent as a witness in her own behalf." (Women were not permitted to testify in federal court in the 19th century.)

The judge "so held" that Anthony could not testify.

Selden then took the stand and testified that he concurred with Anthony's reading of the Fourteenth Amendment and that he had advised her to cast her ballot. Selden argued: "The only alleged ground of illegality of the defendant's vote is that she is a woman. If the same act has been done by her brother under the same circumstances, the act would have been not only innocent, but honorable and laudable; but having been done by a woman it is said to be a crime. The crime, therefore, consists not in the act done, but in the simple fact that the person doing it was a woman and not a man."

At the conclusion of argument, Judge Hunt read a statement—prepared before he had heard testimony—to the "Gentlemen of the Jury":

> The right of voting, or the privilege of voting, is a right or privilege arising under the Constitution of the State, and not of the United States . . . If the State of New York should provide that no person should vote until he had reached the age of thirty-one years, or after he had reached the age of fifty, or that no person having gray hair, or who had not the use of all his limbs, should be entitled to vote, I do not see how it could be held to be a violation of any right derived or held under the Constitution of the United States.

Judge Hunt directed the jury to deliver a guilty verdict.

Selden objected, saying, "it is for the jury [to decide]."

Hunt addressed the jury again: "I have decided as a question of law . . . that under the Fourteenth Amendment, which Miss Anthony claims protects her, she was not protected in a right to vote. . . . I therefore direct you to find a verdict of guilty."

Hunt then asked the clerk to record the jury's verdict. The next day, Selden presented a motion and arguments for a new trial, which Hunt denied. Hunt then asked Anthony to stand. "The sentence of the Court is that you pay a fine of $100.00 and the costs of prosecution."

Anthony replied: "May it please your honor, I will never pay a dollar of your unjust penalty. . . . 'Resistance to tyranny is obedience to God.' "

Hunt released her, saying, "Madam, the Court will not order to stand committed until the fine is paid."

Anthony never paid the fine.

Supreme Court Reviews Women and the Fourteenth Amendment

In 1873, the Supreme Court heard the case of Myra Bradwell, who claimed that her Fourteenth Amendment rights were abridged by Illinois' law prohibiting women from the practice of law. The Court found that her rights had not been violated since "the right of females to pursue any lawful employment for a livelihood [the practice of law included]" was not "one of the privileges and immunities of women as citizens." Justice Samuel F. Miller, writing for the majority, explained: "The paramount destiny and mission of woman are to fulfill the noble and benign offices of wife and mother. This is the law of the Creator. And the rules of civil society must be adapted to the general constitution of things."

In its decision on *Minor v. Happersett,* the Supreme Court's unanimous opinion was that the right of suffrage was not one of the privileges and immunities of citizenship, and women—although citizens of the United States—could be denied the vote by their respective states.

The first successful Fourteenth Amendment challenge to a sex-biased law was brought by Sally Reed in 1971. Reed's son died intestate (having made no valid will), and the Idaho court automatically appointed Reed's estranged husband Cecil as administrator of the estate, because of his sex, and denied Reed's own petition, because of hers. More than 100 years after the adoption of the Fourteenth Amendment, Chief Justice Warren E. Burger delivered the following opinion for the court: "We have concluded that the arbitrary preference established in favor of males by the Idaho Code cannot stand in the face of the Fourteenth Amendment's command that no State deny the equal protection of the laws to any person within its jurisdiction."

—*Kathryn Cullen-DuPont*

Suggestions for Further Reading

Barry, Kathleen. *Susan B. Anthony: A Biography.* New York: New York University Press, 1988.

Flexner, Eleanor. *Century of Struggle.* Cambridge, Mass.: Belknap Press of Harvard University Press, 1959, revised 1975.

Frost, Elizabeth and Kathryn Cullen-DuPont. *Women's Suffrage in America: An Eyewitness History.* New York: Facts On File, 1992.

Harper, Ida Husted. *Life and Work of Susan B. Anthony.* 1898. Reprint. Salem, N.H.: Ayer Co., 1983.

Stanton, Elizabeth Cady, Susan B. Anthony, and Matilda Joslyn Gage. *History of Woman Suffrage,* Vol. II. 1882. Reprint. Salem, N.H.: Ayer Co., 1985.

Tilton v. Beecher: 1875

Plaintiff: Theodore Tilton **Defendant:** Henry Ward Beecher
Plaintiff Claim: That Beecher had committed adultery with Tilton's wife
Chief Defense Lawyers: William M. Evarts, John L. Hill, John K. Porter, Thomas G. Shearman, and Benjamin F. Tracy
Chief Lawyers for Plaintiff: W. Fullerton, Samuel D. Morris, and Roger A. Pryor **Judge:** Neilson (historical records do not indicate first name)
Place: Brooklyn, New York **Dates of Trial:** January 4–July 1, 1875
Decision: Verdict for Beecher

SIGNIFICANCE

This was one of the most celebrated and emblematic cases of the Victorian era. Despite its notoriety and Beecher's public stature, the woman he allegedly committed adultery with never testified. This was due to the common-law rule of interspousal witness immunity: Because her husband was the plaintiff, she could not testify. This case aptly illustrates the burden this old rule placed on the judicial system's effort to discover the truth.

Reverend Henry Ward Beecher had a long and prestigious career as one of 19th-century America's foremost preachers. Not only was he popular with the faithful at his Plymouth Congregational Church in Brooklyn, New York, he was also well-known for his advocacy of social reform. Beecher spoke out on behalf of abolition before the Civil War freed the slaves, in favor of women's suffrage long before women got the right to vote, and expressed his belief in Charles Darwin's theory of natural selection decades before evolution gained popular acceptance.

Beecher often used a local newspaper called the *New York Independent* as a forum to express his views. The *Independent* was operated by Congregational ministers sympathetic to Beecher's views, and his sermons and letters were routinely published. Beecher's influence over the paper was such that, when in 1861 the *Independent* needed a new editor, he was able to arrange the appointment of his young protege Theodore Tilton. Tilton was a member of the Plymouth Church congregation and had become Beecher's friend. Although in theory Beecher himself became the chief editor of the *Independent* and Tilton was only his assistant, Tilton in fact ran the paper.

Beecher and Tilton remained friends through the 1860s. Beecher regularly visited Tilton, his wife Elizabeth and their family at home. In the late 1860s, however, Tilton's editorials in the *Independent* began to take a very radical turn. He began to espouse the doctrine of "free love," which challenged the institution of marriage and traditional morality. Further, beginning in 1868, Elizabeth Tilton began to see Beecher regularly and privately for what Beecher later claimed was religious guidance and consolation regarding Tilton's unorthodox beliefs.

In July of 1870, however, Elizabeth Tilton went to her husband with an entirely different story. She claimed that Beecher had made "improper advances" to her and implied that Beecher had tried to seduce her, but she didn't expressly admit to adultery. For some reason, Tilton waited nearly four years until June of 1874 to make his wife's claims public. When he did, New York and the entire nation were shocked. Tilton had long since been removed as editor of the *Independent*, and Beecher now saw to it that Tilton was expelled from the Plymouth Church.

Plymouth Church Clears Beecher

When the scandal became public, Beecher asked for an investigation to clear his name. He turned to the membership of the Plymouth Church, and asked its most distinguished members to form an investigating committee. This committee investigated the scandal beginning on June 27, 1874 and issued its report on August 27. The committee's investigation was reputed to be thorough but naturally somewhat suspect since Beecher was their preacher. The committee reported:

> The Committee have given the evidence their most useful consideration, and find therefore that in 1861 Mr. Beecher became editor and Mr. Tilton assistant editor of the *Independent*, and that during this relation they became warm and intimate friends. On or about 1863 Mr. Tilton began to urge Mr. Beecher to visit his [Tilton's] house, and he became more intimately acquainted with Tilton's family. . . .
>
> The friendly relations existing between Mr. Beecher and Mrs. Tilton were always well known and understood, and met with Mr. Tilton's cordial approval. . . .
>
> [Tilton's] social views [around 1870] underwent a radical change in the direction of free love. This marked change in the religious and social views of Mr. Tilton was a source of great grief and sorrow to Mrs. Tilton. Mrs. Tilton seemed to be a very religious woman, amounting almost to enthusiasm, and when this change occurred in her husband she naturally sought her pastor for counsel and sympathy. . . . It now appears that during these years Mrs. Tilton became strongly attached to Mr. Beecher and in July, 1870, confessed to her husband an overshadowing affection for her Pastor.

The committee found Beecher innocent, and issued a ringing endorsement of his character:

> This man has been living in the clear light of noonday, before his people and before all men, a life of great Christian usefulness and incessant work. None have known him but to admire and love him. . . . Upon a review of all the evidence, made with an earnest desire to find the truth, and to advise what truth and justice shall require, we feel bound to state that, in our judgment, the evidence relied on by the accuser utterly fails to sustain the charges made.

Tilton was not satisfied with the committee's findings, however, and filed a lawsuit against Beecher. Beecher's lawyers were William M. Evarts, John L. Hill, John K. Porter, Thomas G. Shearman, and Benjamin F. Tracy. Tilton's lawyers were ex-Judge W. Fullerton, Samuel D. Morris, and Roger A. Pryor. The judge was Judge Neilson. The trial began January 4, 1875 and was to titillate the public for nearly six long months.

Mrs. Tilton Never Testifies

Although Tilton and Beecher both testified during the trial, Elizabeth Tilton never took the witness stand. This was because of the common-law principle of interspousal immunity. When Tilton's attorneys attempted to put Tilton on the witness stand, Evarts objected on Beecher's behalf that the same interspousal immunity rule prevented him from testifying as well:

> Neither in a civil action nor in a criminal prosecution are they [spouses] permitted to give any evidence which, in its future effects, may incriminate each other, and this rule is so inviolable that no consent of the other party may authorize the breach of it.

This rule, accurately expressed by Evarts, meant that spouses couldn't testify for or against each other in court for fear that, if the testifying spouse committed perjury or revealed something adverse under cross-examination, the marriage would be hurt and possibly result in divorce. Marriage was sacred to the common law, which held that "two souls are joined as one."

Although Elizabeth Tilton couldn't testify, Judge Neilson allowed Tilton to take the stand but stated that Tilton couldn't testify concerning any "confidential communications" with his wife. This was an accepted exception to the interspousal testimony rule, but it meant that the courtroom testimony about the alleged adultery took place in very elliptical terms. Further, much of Tilton's testimony suggested that there had been no adultery. An example is the following cross-examination of Tilton by Evarts:

> Question: Now, up to the time of [Mrs. Tilton's alleged confession] had you observed in the demeanor of Mr. Beecher toward your wife, or of your wife toward Mr. Beecher, any variance from that ordinary relation which you had been familiar with?
>
> Answer: No sir; one or two little incidents happened a number of years before that, which Mrs. Tilton explained away, and which left no impression.

Beecher's testimony was equally unimpressive. He contradicted himself and his supporting witnesses many times and repeatedly claimed that he couldn't remember the specifics of certain events. The trial dragged on for nearly six months, as Beecher's attorneys brought in nearly 100 supporting witnesses. These witnesses' testimony was often repetitive, and frequently consisted merely of vouching for Beecher's character.

The jury deliberated for several days, and on July 1 reported to Judge Neilson that it couldn't reach a verdict. Nine jurors believed that Beecher was innocent, the other three that he was guilty. There was no retrial. Beecher was vindicated, and Judge Neilson even expressed his belief in Beecher's innocence when he spoke eight years later at a party given by the Brooklyn Academy of Music to celebrate Beecher's 70th birthday:

> By the integrity of his life and the purity of his character he has vanquished misrepresentation and abuse.

Beecher never quite regained his previous stature as a spokesman on social issues, however, because of the scandal.

In addition to its notoriety, *Tilton v. Beecher* demonstrated the severe limitations of the interspousal immunity rule concerning testimony. The woman Beecher allegedly committed adultery with never testified, because her husband was the plaintiff. The judicial system was thus unable to get at the complete truth. Although Beecher may well have been innocent, there is no way to determine what additional facts would have been brought out by Elizabeth Tilton's testimony. In the 20th century, courts and legislatures began to recognize the problems that the rule imposed on the judicial system, and today it has been virtually abolished.

—Stephen G. Christianson

Suggestions for Further Reading

Abbott, Lyman. *Henry Ward Beecher.* New York: Chelsea House, 1980.

Kohn, George C. *Encyclopedia of American Scandal.* New York: Facts On File, 1989.

Marshall, Charles F. *The True History of the Brooklyn Scandal.* Philadelphia: National Publishing Co., 1874.

Ryan, Halford Ross. *Henry Ward Beecher: Peripatetic Preacher.* Westport, Conn.: Greenwood Press, 1990.

Shaplen, Robert. *Free Love and Heavenly Sinners.* New York: Alfred A. Knopf, 1954.

Waller, Altina L. *Reverend Beecher and Mrs. Tilton: Sex and Class in Victorian America.* Amherst: University of Massachusetts Press, 1982.

U.S. v. Cruikshank: 1875

Defendants: William J. Cruikshank and others **Crimes Charged:** 16 violations of federal law relating to the defendants' involvement in lynching two black men, including violating the victims' "right and privilege peaceably to assemble together." **Chief Defense Lawyers:** E. John Ellis, David Dudley Field, Reverdy Johnson, R.H. Marr, Philip Phillips, and W.R. Whitaker **Chief Prosecutors:** J.R. Beckwith, Edward Pierrepont, and Samuel F. Phillips **Judge:** William B. Woods **Place:** New Orleans, Louisiana **Date of Trial:** 1874 April Term **Verdict:** Guilty, overturned by U.S. Supreme Court **Sentence:** None.

SIGNIFICANCE

The Supreme Court in *Cruikshank* severely limited the ability of the federal government to protect the civil rights of newly freed African-Americans. The federal government would not achieve the power to effectively protect civil rights until well into the 20th century.

In many ways, the Civil War began as a simple struggle between North and South over whether the Union would survive. Abolishing slavery became its primary purpose only after nearly two years of combat. President Abraham Lincoln was initially hesitant about freeing the slaves, and many leading Northerners, such as General George McClellan, were openly against abolition. After Lincoln finally decided to side with the abolitionists and issued the Emancipation Proclamation, however, the Civil War became almost a crusade against slavery for the people of the North. Renewed popular enthusiasm for the war, plus the addition of black regiments to Union forces, contributed to victory for the North in 1865.

African-Americans were finally freed, but their hold on liberty was precarious. The former slaves were uneducated, poor, and dependent on white landowners for their living. Many left the land for the industrial cities of the North, but most stayed home because they had no skills other than as agricultural laborers. During the early years of Reconstruction, the South was under military occupation and ex-slaves in the states of the former Confederacy were protected from their former masters. Further, it seemed as if the abolitionists had succeeded in obtaining permanent and meaningful legal recognition of African-Americans' civil rights through a series of amendments to the Constitution.

The Thirteenth Amendment, forbidding slavery, was ratified in 1865. The Fourteenth Amendment, providing for equal protection and due process under the law, was ratified in 1868. The Fifteenth Amendment, protecting the right to vote, was ratified in 1870. The Fourteenth Amendment is the most extensive of these three amendments, and based on it, Congress enacted legislation May 31, 1870 that made it a felony if two or more people conspired to deprive anyone of his federal civil rights.

Southern Racism Makes a Comeback

Despite the new legal protection for ex-slaves, as Southern states were re-admitted to the Union and the occupation forces went home, the old ways returned in new guises. Landowners no longer owned slaves, but the practice of sharecropping effectively kept blacks tied to the land and subservient to whites. Southern states passed "Jim Crow" laws enforcing the separation of blacks from whites in public accommodations. What states couldn't do in public, Southern whites did in private. The Ku Klux Klan developed as an instrument of terror to enforce white supremacy. Hard-won black liberties began to slip away.

As Congress' act of 1870 demonstrated, however, the North would not give up without a fight. Three years later, matters came to a head. On April 13, 1873, a Southern mob in Grant Parish, Louisiana numbering nearly 100 people lynched two African-American men, Levi Nelson and Alexander Tillman. Apparently Nelson and Tillman had tried to vote in a local election against the wishes of white residents. Approximately 80 people in the lynch mob were indicted for violations of federal law and 17 were eventually brought to trial, including one William J. Cruikshank. The U.S. attorney in charge, J.R. Beckwith, charged each of them with 16 violations of the 1870 law. The most important charge was violating the victims' "right and privilege peaceably to assemble together."

Cruikshank and the others, however, were not charged with murder. Nelson and Tillman's murder was a Louisiana state offense, not a violation of the federal law, and the Louisiana authorities didn't prosecute. The defendants were brought to trial in New Orleans before a judge of the federal Circuit Court for the District of Louisiana, William B. Woods, E. John Ellis, R.H. Marr, and W.R. Whitaker represented the defendants at the trial, which took place during the Circuit Court's 1874 April Term.

Little is known about the actual trial, as the real action was yet to come. Cruikshank and the others were found guilty. The defense lawyers promptly appealed for a stay to Joseph P. Bradley, an associate justice of the U.S. Supreme Court. In that day and age, individual justices of the Supreme Court were charged with hearing appeals in various parts of the country before the appeals went to the full Court in Washington, D.C. The District of Louisiana had been assigned to Bradley.

Justice Bradley granted the defense's motion to stay the guilty verdicts, and Cruikshank's case was sent to the Supreme Court for a final decision. David Dudley Field, Reverdy Johnson, and Philip Phillips joined the defense team, while Attorney-General Edward Pierrepont and Solicitor-General Samuel F. Phillips personally assisted the prosecution as both sides prepared for their arguments before the Court.

At the Court's 1874 October Term, the prosecution argued that the 1870 act and the Fourteenth Amendment gave the government the power to try and convict offenders like Cruikshank. The defense argued that the Fourteenth Amendment gave the federal government authority to act only against state government violations of civil rights, but not against one citizen's violation of another's civil rights, like Cruikshank's violation of Nelson and Tillman's rights. The defense's argument, that Congress could legislate against only "state action," would have the effect of leaving the federal government powerless to prosecute lynch mobs and groups such as the KKK. African-Americans would be protected only by their state courts against white violence, which in the South, of course, meant no protection at all.

Justice Joseph Bradley granted the defense's motion to stay the guilty verdicts, paving the way for a Supreme Court decision in *Cruikshank*. (Courtesy, Library of Congress)

Supreme Court Delivers a Crushing Blow

After hearing both sides' arguments, the Court took a year to render its decision. Chief Justice Morrison R. Waite wrote the Court's ruling, issued in the 1875 October Term. Waite's opinion would stymie the federal government's ability to protect African-American civil rights for 90 years.

Waite began by reiterating the dual nature of American government:

> We have in our political system a government of the United States and a government of each of the several States. Each one of these governments is distinct from the others, and each has citizens of its own who owe it allegiance, and whose rights, within its jurisdiction, it must protect. The same person may be at the same time a citizen of the United States and a citizen of a State, but his rights of citizenship under one of these governments will be different from those he has under the other.

Waite then stated that the 16 violations of the 1870 act charged against Cruikshank and the others were really simple state conspiracy charges. The federal prosecution was thus unconstitutional. Even the most important charge, violating the victims' "right and privilege peaceably to assemble together," was really a violation of state rights. If the victims had assembled to "petition for a redress of grievances," or some other right specifically granted by the Constitution, then perhaps a federal prosecution would be permissible. Waite refused, however, to give the federal government jurisdiction over any civil rights violation not specifically covered by the Constitution:

> This [case] is nothing else than [an allegation of] a conspiracy to falsely imprison or murder citizens of the United States, being within the territorial jurisdiction of the State of Louisiana. . . . Sovereignty, for this purpose, rests alone with the State. It is no more the duty or within the power of the United States to punish for a conspiracy to falsely imprison or murder within a State, than it would be to punish for false imprisonment or murder itself.

Cruikshank and the others would thus go free. Through Waite, the Supreme Court had firmly endorsed the defendants' "state action" argument:

> The Fourteenth Amendment prohibits a State from depriving any person of life, liberty, or property, without due process of law; but this adds nothing to the rights of one citizen as against another.

Because the Court had essentially told people to go to their state governments and courts for protection, African-American civil liberties underwent a long eclipse, particularly in the South, from which they would not recover until the 1960s. The Court had turned a blind eye to the fact that in the South, state governments were *de facto* supporters of "private" racism such as the Ku Klux Klan and the lynch mobs. For African-Americans, state protection was no protection at all.

In the 1960s, the federal government enacted new civil rights laws and moved aggressively to enforce them. This time, in dozens of cases the Court consistently upheld the constitutionality of federal measures. The Court's change in attitude was due to the political upheavals of the time and the new majority of liberal justices. Obstacles such as the "state action" requirement of the Fourteenth Amendment were substantially reduced. Further, the Court allowed the federal government broad civil rights enforcement powers under other sections of the Constitution as well, such as the federal authority to regulate any conduct that even remotely affects interstate commerce. Cases like *Cruikshank*, however, had prevented the federal government from protecting civil rights 90 years earlier.

—Stephen G. Christianson

Suggestions for Further Reading

Burns, James MacGregor. *A People's Charter: the Pursuit of Rights in America.* New York: Alfred A. Knopf, 1991.

Emerson, Thomas Irwin. *Political and Civil Rights in the United States: A Collection of Legal and Related Materials.* Boston: Little, Brown & Co., 1967.

Foner, Eric. "The New View of Reconstruction." *American Heritage* (October 1983): 10–16.

Franklin, John Hope. "Mirror for Americans: a Century of Reconstruction History." *The American Historical Review* (February 1980): 1–14.

Neely, Mark E. *The Fate of Liberty: Abraham Lincoln and Civil Liberties*. New York: Oxford University Press, 1991.

Nieman, Donald G. *Promises to Keep: African-Americans and the Constitutional Order, 1776 to the Present.* New York: Oxford University Press, 1991.

Mary Todd Lincoln Insanity Trial: 1875

Defendant: Mary Todd Lincoln **Petitioner:** Robert Todd Lincoln
Relief Sought: Declaration that Mary Todd Lincoln was insane and the appointment of a conservator to handle her estate
Chief Defense Lawyers: Isaac Newton Arnold
Chief Attorney for Petitioner: Benjamin F. Ayers; Leonard T. Swett handled all of the pretrial preparation **Judge:** Marion R. M. Wallace
Place: Chicago, Illinois **Date of Trial:** May 19, 1875 **Verdict:** Mary Todd Lincoln was adjudged insane (Robert Todd Lincoln was appointed the conservator of her estate a month later)

SIGNIFICANCE

In a bizarre trial, the former first lady of the United States was found insane by a jury and committed.

While vacationing in Florida on March 12, 1875, Abraham Lincoln's widow, Mary Todd Lincoln, was suddenly overwhelmed with the belief that her sole surviving child, Robert, was dying. That night, she sent a telegram to Robert's law partner, Edward Isham:

> My Belief is my son is ill . . . telegraph me at once without a moments delay —on Receipt of this I start for Chicago when your message is received.

Despite assurances that her son was fine, Mary Lincoln boarded a train the next day to take her back to Robert in Chicago. While these events may have only been the actions of an overly concerned mother, they marked a turning point in Mary Lincoln's life. She had long been a burden and an embarrassment to her son, but now he started to question her sanity. In May, Robert Todd Lincoln went to court to commit his mother to an asylum.

A Long Line of Tragedies

Mary Todd and Abraham Lincoln were married in 1842. Wedded for 22 years before the president's assassination, they had four sons. Tragically, three of their sons died young. Mary Lincoln was particularly affected when her third child, 12-year-old William ("Willie"), died in 1862 from typhoid fever. She was never the same again. For months, the mere mention of Willie's name would cause a sudden and violent outburst of tears and she never reentered the room where he died. Once in love with the receptions regularly held at the Executive Mansion, the first lady did not resume any social activities at the White House for over a year, and she wore black mourning clothes the rest of her life. Convinced that her son's death was a punishment from God for her being "so wrapped up in the world," Mary Lincoln consulted mediums who had messages from her dead son, held séances in the Red Room of the White House, and once told her sister that Willie visited her at night. Furthermore, Mary's spending, which constantly swung from miserly to lavish ever since her husband was sworn into office, became even more irrational.

Abraham Lincoln's murder in 1865 plunged Mary further into grief. Her share in the president's estate, combined with an annual pension granted by Congress, made the former first lady rich, but she had an increasingly great fear of poverty. She begged for money from her husband's friends and, in 1867, went to New York City under an alias to sell her old clothes. Mary Lincoln also continued to meet with spiritualists. Finally, she developed such an obsession for privacy that when she went to Florida in November 1874 for an extended visit, she pulled down all the shades in her suite, kept her boardinghouse room dark, and, believing that gaslight was a tool of the devil, used only candles to brighten her quarters.

When Mary Lincoln met her son in Chicago on March 15, 1875, she claimed that someone on the train had tried to poison her. That night, she restlessly wandered about in her nightdress until Robert had her sleep in his room. Soon thereafter, Robert hired Pinkerton detectives to follow his mother. The agents saw the former first lady leave her hotel suite once or twice every day on spending sprees that included $450 for three watches and $600 for lace curtains. Mary told the hotel manager that someone was speaking to her through the walls of her room, and she insisted that part of Chicago was afire. Robert also found out that, since 1873, his mother had been under a doctor's care for "nervous derangement and fever in her head." According to the physician, Mary Lincoln believed that somebody was removing wires from her eyes. She also supposedly attributed her headaches to an Indian spirit who occasionally lifted her scalp and replaced it. Finally, the doctor said that, in March 1874, the former first lady reported that her late husband had told her that she was going to die the following September (when she would reach the same age that President Lincoln was when he was shot).

Robert Lincoln Begins Insanity Proceedings

In April 1875, Robert Lincoln began to consult with physicians and lawyers. The attorney he hired was Leonard Swett, an old friend of his father's, a noted trial advocate, and an expert on the insanity defense. Swett, in turn, called upon a number of doctors who were distinguished in the field of mental health. They all met on May 16. Based only upon the statements of Mary's physician and those of Robert Lincoln, the doctors unanimously concluded that the former first lady was insane and needed to be institutionalized.

During the next two days, Robert learned from Swett that his mother was talking about leaving Chicago. On May 18, Lincoln's detectives observed his mother with $56,000 in government securities sewn into the pockets of her petticoat. Swett urged immediate action and Robert agreed. Papers were drawn up, witnesses were gathered, and on May 19 Swett and two uniformed officers arrived at Mary Lincoln's room with a writ for her arrest.

Unaware that her son had signed a petition to have her declared insane, Mary Lincoln objected to being taken into custody. After an hour of attempted persuasion, Swett pointed to the policemen and warned that:

> . . . unless she yielded to me I either had to seize her forcibly myself or turn her over to the officers, who might handcuff her if necessary and certainly would take her to court.

Mary Lincoln was put into a carriage and taken directly to the Cook County Courthouse in Chicago where, through a side door, she was immediately escorted into a courtroom where her son, a judge, a jury, and 17 witnesses waited.

A Civil Jury Hears the Case

Under Illinois law in 1875, the former first lady was entitled to a civil hearing where she could hear the charges, have an attorney, and defend herself before a jury. Indeed, Illinois offered at that time more legal protection to alleged lunatics than any other state. Most required only a document signed by two physicians, a formal request from a member of the defendant's family, and a court-issued certificate of lunacy before a person was involuntarily committed. In some jurisdictions, women and children had even less protection than that. Today, most states still do not allow for either a jury or for the accused to have a lawyer.

For three hours, 12 witnesses, including Robert, testified to the former first lady's bizarre actions and statements. Five doctors, none of whom ever examined Mary Lincoln, told the jury that based entirely upon statements made to them by Robert before the trial, the defendant was insane. Furthermore, the former first lady's lawyer was ex-congressman Arnold, an old friend of the Lincoln family who had been selected to act as Mary's attorney by Swett. At the beginning of the proceeding, Arnold had second thoughts about his role and was angrily told by Swett:

> That means you will put into her head, that she can get some mischievous lawyer to make us trouble; go and defend her, and do your duty.

Arnold stayed on, but he did not cross-examine the witnesses nor call any (including Mary Lincoln) to testify on his client's behalf. As a result, it took only minutes for the jury to find Mary Lincoln insane. The former first lady was indefinitely committed to a private sanitarium known as the Bellevue Place in Batavia, Illinois, and, one month later, Robert was appointed the conservator of her estate.

Mary Lincoln was a model patient at Bellevue and, thus, was never subjected to any physical restraints or drugs. Still, the institution's superintendent reported that he could give "no encouragement that Mrs. Lincoln would ever be well." With her mail censored, the former first lady sought help by smuggling letters out to various influential figures. One of those letters went to Myra Bradwell, one of the first female lawyers in the United States and the wife of a local judge. The Bradwells knew Mrs. Lincoln since they were neighbors in 1867, and they believed that while Mary was eccentric and did not follow the dictates of the male-dominated Victorian society, she was not insane.

Myra Bradwell came up with a plan whereby the former first lady could leave Bellevue and live with Mary's sister and brother-in-law, Elizabeth Todd Edwards and Ninian Edwards. Without first consulting Robert Lincoln, the Edwardses agreed. Robert was furious and took steps to prevent his mother's release, but when Judge Bradwell threatened to sue the sanitarium, Mary was released into her relatives' custody.

Another Jury Decides Differently

Mary Lincoln, however, had to wait for the restoration of her money and property. Robert Lincoln still believed that his mother was insane and even tried to have her returned to Bellevue, but this time the Bradwells and Edwardses would be in court to testify on Mary's behalf so he did not pursue this option for very long. However, while Mary no longer needed institutionalization, she would never, in her son's opinion, be able to handle her own financial affairs. Over time, an informal agreement was reached whereby an informal conservatorship or trust would be established for the rest of Mary Lincoln's life with someone other than Robert acting as the conservator or trustee.

On June 15, 1876, Ninian Edwards submitted on Mary Lincoln's behalf a petition to the Cook County Court to terminate Robert's conservatorship over her estate. Robert had already agreed not to oppose the move. After the petition was read and a jury was selected, Edwards was sworn in, and he testified that the former first lady "is a proper person to take charge of her own affairs." To the surprise of everyone, the jury quickly decided "the said Mary Lincoln is restored to reason and is capable to manage and control her estate."

Nobody expected Mary to be declared sane. Robert Lincoln blamed Edwards for describing his mother as a fit person without qualifying it with a statement that she was not rational when handling her financial affairs. Defending himself against Robert's charge, Edwards (himself a lawyer) blamed the jury, saying that they "were not called upon to try the question of her sanity" and, thus, decided a legal question that was not before them. In reality, both neglected to take a close look at the law. The governing statute provided "for the restoration of property . . . when the insane person is restored to reason." In essence, the conservatorship could not be terminated without Mary first being judged legally sane.

Much to the former first lady's delight, the headlines on June 16 read: "A HAPPY DENOUEMENT: MRS. ABRAHAM LINCOLN RESTORED TO HER REASON AND FREEDOM." A few months later, Mary Todd

Lincoln left the United States and resided in France until 1880, when she returned to the Edwards residence. She died at their home two years later. To his dying day, Robert remained convinced that his mother was incorrigibly insane.

—*Mark Thorburn*

Suggestions for Further Reading

Baker, Jean H. *Mary Todd Lincoln: A Biography.* New York: W. W. Norton and Company, 1987.

Croy, Homer. *The Trial of Mrs. Abraham Lincoln.* New York: Duell, Sloan and Pearce, 1962.

Neely, Jr., Mark E., and R. Gerald McMurtry. *The Insanity Files: The Case of Mary Todd Lincoln.* Carbondale and Edwardsville, Ill.: Southern Illinois University Press, 1986.

Rhodes, James A., and Dean Jauchius. *The Trial of Mary Todd Lincoln.* Indianapolis: Bobbs-Merrill, 1959.

John "Jack" McCall Trials: 1876

Defendant: John ("Jack") McCall **Crime Charged:** Murder
Chief Defense Lawyers: First Trial: "Judge" Miller; Second Trial: Oliver Shannon and William Henry Harrison Beadle **Chief Prosecutors:** First Trial: "Colonel" George May; Second Trial: William Pound **Judges:** First Trial: William L. Kuykendall; Second Trial: Peter C. Shannon **Place:** First Trial: Deadwood, Dakota Territory (now South Dakota); Second Trial: Yankton, Dakota Territory **Dates of Trials:** First Trial: August 3, 1876; Second Trial: December 4–6, 1876 **Verdict:** First Trial: Not guilty; Second Trial: Guilty
Sentence: Death by hanging

SIGNIFICANCE

Lawman, army scout, and gambler, Wild Bill Hickok's accuracy and speed with handguns, as well as his long hair and striking good looks, made him a national figure and the subject of several dime novels while he was still in his early 30s. But death found Hickok on August 2, 1876, when he was shot in the back of the head in Deadwood, Dakota Territory (now South Dakota) by John "Jack" McCall.

Wild Bill Hickok brought law and order to notoriously lawless communities. Unassuming, never boastful, he was frequently challenged by gunfighters who felt they could take him. Many died when they tested Hickok's skill. It was a trying life, and Hickok sought to settle down.

A Western Boomtown

In 1876, Hickok went to Deadwood in the Dakota Territory to find financial success and a way to a more quiet life. He had married earlier that year and needed a better way to earn a living than by playing cards as he had done since leaving Buffalo Bill's Wild West Show in 1874. So, when gold was discovered in the Black Hills of Dakota, Hickok went off to strike it rich so he could return home and retire or, at least, enter a less dangerous profession.

Like thousands of others, Hickok headed towards Deadwood, a one-street mining town whose population sprang from nothing to over 15,000 in less than a year. But Deadwood was also an outlaw hangout where, like many places before,

Hickok's fame preceded him. As a result, many of the community's seedier types were afraid that Hickok was really there to establish law and order.

Hickok did not find gold, so he returned to gambling. At about noon one day, he entered Carl Mann's No. 10 Saloon and joined a card game. Three hours later, a small, shifty 25-year-old named "Jack" McCall entered the room. While Hickok studied his hand, McCall quickly moved down the bar until he was a few feet behind Hickok's chair. Then, pulling out a gun, McCall shouted, "Damn you, take that!" and fired. Hickok died instantly. He was only 39.

"Black" Jack McCall, the man who shot Wild Bill Hickok. (Courtesy, National Archives)

The First Trial

Preparations began immediately for McCall's trial. Deadwood did not have any formal government, so that evening the local businessmen elected three lawyers (all of whom had left their practices elsewhere to find gold) to serve as judge, prosecuting attorney, and defense counsel. A sheriff and clerk were also appointed, and procedures were established for the selection of the jury. The trial was set for nine o'clock the next morning at McDaniel's Theater. To prevent a lynching, 25 men guarded McCall during the night and the judge insisted that the sheriff and clerk, as well as the lawyers and all the leading businessmen of the community, be "present with their revolvers when the court convened."

McCall pleaded "not guilty" and, after the jury was picked, the prosecution called four witnesses who either saw the actual shooting or were in the saloon when the shot was fired. In turn, the defense called a number of witnesses who all swore to McCall's good character. Finally, McCall himself testified:

> Well, men, I have but few words to say. Wild Bill killed my brother, and I killed him. Wild Bill threatened to kill me if I crossed his path. I am not sorry for what I have done. I would do the same thing over again.

That was enough for the jury to acquit McCall. The entire proceeding took only 12 hours.

The verdict was not well received by many people in Deadwood. There were rumors of bribes and the prosecuting attorney, Colonel George May, vowed to seek justice elsewhere. McCall stayed in town for a while, but left when one of Hickok's close friends, California Joe, arrived. It was also noted by many that while McCall had only $43 on the day he was tried, he was seen soon thereafter with a large amount of cash and a gold watch and chain.

A Federal Trial for McCall

McCall went to Wyoming, first to Cheyenne and then to Laramie, before his arrest on August 29 by a deputy U.S. marshal who was accompanied by May. Although McCall had already been tried, the proceeding in Deadwood was not legal because the town and its inhabitants were inside an Indian reservation established by the federal government and, thus, had no right to be there. Therefore, McCall's acquittal was not valid and would not prevent another court from retrying him for Hickok's murder.

McCall was first held in Laramie to attend a preliminary hearing and to await a formal request to have him extradited to Yankton (in present-day South Dakota) for trial. While in the Laramie jail, McCall claimed in a newspaper interview that not only had Hickok killed his brother, but also that, the day before the shooting in Deadwood, Hickok had cheated McCall in a poker game and laughed at him when they quarreled.

Once in Yankton, McCall was formally indicted for murder on October 18, 1876, and, again, he pleaded "not guilty." To give the marshal's deputies time to find McCall's defense witnesses, the trial was adjourned for six weeks.

On November 9, McCall and his cellmate attempted to escape. They overpowered one guard, but were foiled when a U.S. marshal and an assistant arrived on the scene. McCall then offered to turn state's evidence and alleged that he had been hired by John Varnes to murder Hickok. According to McCall, there was once a "difficulty" between Varnes and Hickok in Denver and the resulting ill feelings were heightened when Hickok, a short time before his death, stepped in with his gun to end an argument between Varnes and another man. A posse immediately headed to Deadwood to find Varnes, but he was gone.

The marshal's office was also unable to find any of McCall's defense witnesses. When the court reconvened on December 1, McCall's new lawyers asked for a continuance until April so these witnesses could be found, but the motion was denied. The actual trial began on December 4.

Again, eyewitnesses were called to the stand. One, the owner of the saloon, confirmed that McCall had lost a poker game to Hickok. However, once McCall realized that he did not have the funds to cover his losses, Hickok offered him money (which McCall refused) to buy supper. Another person claimed to have seen McCall sneak up behind Hickok in the No. 10 Saloon a day or two before the shooting and pull his gun two-thirds out of the holster before a companion led him away. (No explanation was given as to why Hickok was not warned at the time or later told about this incident.)

No witnesses were called on McCall's behalf, and McCall did not testify. However, when cross-examining the prosecution's witnesses, McCall's lawyers tried to insinuate that McCall was drunk and, thus, not responsible for his actions. After all the witnesses were called, some technical motions were made challenging the propriety of the copy of the indictment that was handed to McCall's lawyers at the beginning of the trial. Other motions were also made arguing that a retrial should be granted because the court improperly applied federal law, instead of territorial law, during the trial. (Since the murder occurred on an Indian reservation, Hickok's murder was, under the laws of the time, a federal crime.) These motions were all denied.

The Jury Quickly Reaches a Verdict

On December 6, the jurors retired at about seven in the evening to consider their decision. They returned a little over three hours later with the verdict of "guilty." On January 3, 1877, before a packed courtroom, McCall was sentenced to death.

Even before sentence was pronounced, McCall's lawyers appealed the case to the Supreme Court of the Dakota Territory, but it was denied on January 20, 1877. A petition was then sent to President Ulysses S. Grant for a pardon or a commutation of McCall's sentence to life imprisonment. This, too, was unsuccessful and McCall was hanged on the morning of March 1, 1877.

A few days before McCall's execution, a letter was received by the U.S. marshal in Yankton from Mary McCall of Louisville, Kentucky, inquiring if the condemned prisoner were her brother.

> I saw in the morning papers a piece about the sentence of the murderer of Wild Bill, Jack McCall. There was a young man of the name John McCall left here about six years ago, who has not been heard from for the last three years. He has a father, mother, and three sisters living here in Louisville, who are very uneasy about him since they heard about the murder of Wild Bill. If you can send us any information about him, we would be very thankful to you.

When shown the letter, McCall confirmed that it was from his sister. The letter contained no mention of any brother. Furthermore, a week before his death, McCall had promised the newspaper in Yankton to write about his side of the events leading up to the murder. The article was to be published after McCall's hanging, but the night before the execution, McCall destroyed what he had written. Whatever the real reason was that he shot Hickok, McCall took it to his grave.

—*Mark Thorburn*

Suggestions for Further Reading

Rosa, Joseph G. *Alias Jack McCall.* Kansas City, Mo.: Kansas City Posse of the Westerners, 1967.

——. "Alias Jack McCall: A Pardon or Death?" *The Kansas City Westerners' Trial Guide* 12, no. 2 (June 1967).

——. *They Called Him Wild Bill: The Life and Adventures of James Butler Hickok.* 2nd ed., rev. and enl. Norman, Okla.: University of Oklahoma Press, 1974.

Martinez v. Del Valle: 1877

Plaintiff: Eugenie Martinez **Defendant:** Juan Del Valle
Plaintiff Claim: That Del Valle broke his promise to marry the plaintiff
Chief Defense Lawyer: Joseph H. Choate
Chief Lawyer for Plaintiff: William H. Beach **Judge:** Donohue (historical records do not indicate first name) **Place:** New York, New York
Date of Trial: 1877 January Term **Decision:** Jury verdict in favor of the plaintiff for damages of $50

SIGNIFICANCE

The famous lawyer Joseph Choate represented Juan Del Valle, and his handling of Eugenie Martinez on the witness stand has been hailed as a model of the art of cross-examination.

Juan Del Valle was a wealthy businessman from Cuba who had established himself in New York City. He had divorced his first wife and was well into middle age when he met a dark-haired Spanish beauty in her early 20s named Eugenie Martinez. On January 14, 1875, Martinez slipped while walking on an icy sidewalk and sprained her ankle. Del Valle happened to be nearby, and he helped her up and took her home.

According to Martinez, Del Valle visited her the next day to see how she was recovering. Del Valle became her regular suitor and, after only three weeks of courtship, allegedly promised to marry Martinez but reneged after an "engagement" of several months. Martinez sued Del Valle for $50,000 in damages for breach of promise of marriage.

It was rumored that Del Valle offered Martinez $20,000 to settle out of court and avoid a scandal, but she refused. Martinez was represented by William H. Beach, and Del Valle was represented by Joseph H. Choate. With Judge Donohue presiding, the case was tried in the New York City Court's 1877 January Term. Because Del Valle was a rich man and Martinez's family was poor, the press labeled Martinez a "golddigger" and the case attracted considerable publicity.

Choate was a famous lawyer, known for his verbal skills and scathing comments. From start to finish he stole the show. Choate encouraged the public's low opinion of Martinez when he referred to her case:

Never did a privateer upon the *Spanish Main* give chase to and board a homeward bound [ship] with more avidity and vigor than this family proposed to board this rich Cuban and make a capture of him.

Choate Cross-Examines Martinez

Beach's principal witness was Martinez herself, and he had her relate the entire story to the jury. A key element of Martinez's case was her claim that, when Del Valle proposed to her three weeks after they met, he took her to a jewelry shop and bought her a ring as a token of his sincerity. Del Valle claimed he bought Martinez the ring the day after they met, and not as a promise of marriage but merely out of affection for a young lady in distress that he had helped. As proof that Del Valle's version of the story was the true one, Choate had arranged for the jeweler to be available to testify that the ring was purchased on January 15. First, however, Choate would let Martinez perjure herself under oath.

Choate began by allowing Martinez to claim that, because of her sprained ankle, she didn't leave her house for five days after her fall.

Question: How long was it before you got entirely over it so as to be able to go out of doors?

Answer: Well, I went out the fifth day.

Question: And not before?

Answer: And not before.

Question: So that because of the injuries that you sustained, you were confined to the house for five days?

Answer: I was.

Next, Choate got Martinez to commit herself to her claim that she went to the jewelry store with Del Valle three weeks after they met.

Question: Some considerable number of weeks, you say, intervened between your first acquaintance [with Del Valle] and . . . the giving of the ring?

Answer: About three weeks as nearly as I can fix the time.

Choate now had Martinez on record as testifying that she did not leave her house for five days following her January 14 fall and that Del Valle bought her the ring three weeks after they met. Choate continued to cross-examine Martinez at length on some other issues to raise skepticism in the minds of the jurors about her story, so that once he revealed her lies her credibility would be completely destroyed. For example, Choate questioned Martinez about her claim that Del Valle's courtship included many long, intimate meals at a popular restaurant called Solari's.

Question: How long were these [meetings] at Solari's: these meetings when you went there and had a private room generally?

Answer: They varied in length. Sometimes we arrived there at 2:00 and remained until 4:00, sometimes we arrived there a little earlier.

Question: About a couple of hours?

Answer: Two or three hours.

Question: What were you doing all that time?

Answer: We were eating.

Question: What, not eating all the time?

Answer: Eating all the time.

Question: Two hours eating! Well, you must have grown fat during that period!

Answer: Well, perhaps you eat much quicker than I do.

After Martinez's cross-examination, Choate put the jeweler on the witness stand. The jeweler testified that Martinez and Del Valle were in his shop on January 15, the day after the fall. Further, the jeweler had made an entry in his account books showing that the purchase was made on the 15th.

The jeweler's testimony proved that Eugenie Martinez had lied about being unable to leave her house for five days and about the purchase date of the ring. Her credibility was further shaken by Choate's expert cross-examination, which brought every weakness and hard-to-believe aspect of her story to light. If it hadn't been for Choate's skill, the jury might have taken the obvious signs of Del Valle's affection for Martinez as evidence of a promise of marriage regardless of when the ring was bought. Instead, while the jury returned a verdict in Martinez's favor, it gave her only $50 in damages, far short of the $20,000 Juan Del Valle had been willing to pay to avoid a scandal.

—Stephen G. Christianson

Suggestions for Further Reading

Choate, Joseph Hodges. *The Choate Story Book.* New York: Cameron, Blake & Co., 1903.

Strong, Theron George. *Joseph H. Choate: New Englander, New Yorker, Lawyer, Ambassador.* New York: Dodd, Mead and Co., 1917.

Wellman, Francis Lewis. *The Art of Cross-Examination.* New York: Collier Books, 1986.

Andrew Geddes Court-Martial: 1879

Defendant: Andrew Geddes **Crimes Charged:** Libel, seduction, attempted abduction **Chief Defense Lawyer:** George W. Paschal **Chief Prosecutor:** John Clous **Judges:** Officers from the army's Texas Division **Place:** San Antonio, Texas **Date of Trial:** June 14–August 21, 1879 **Verdict:** Guilty of all charges except abduction **Sentence:** Three years in prison and dishonorable discharge; Geddes conviction was overturned by President Rutherford B. Hayes

SIGNIFICANCE

This case demonstrated the extreme discomfort of Victorian society in accepting the possibility of incest, and the difficulties inherent in proving it.

In April 1879, a letter arrived in San Antonio, Texas, addressed to General E. O. C. Ord, commander of the Department of Texas. It contained a sworn statement from Captain Andrew Geddes of the Twenty-fifth U.S. Infantry accusing another officer, Lieutenant Louis H. Orleman, of having an incestuous relationship with his 18-year-old daughter Lillie. Both men were stationed at Fort Stockton in a remote section of west Texas. Geddes told Ord that he was forced to reveal this shocking state of affairs because he had learned that Orleman planned to file charges against him. In order to defend himself, Geddes claimed, he had to expose the relationship of "criminal intimacy" that he had discovered between the 38-year-old Orleman and his daughter.

Geddes's story was a grim one. On March 2, 1879, he said, "I heard from the adjoining quarters . . . a voice which I recognized to be that of Miss Lillie Orleman, saying, 'Papa, please don't. I'll call Major Geddes, if you don't quit' and . . . in a most piteous and pleading tone, 'Oh Papa, for God's sake don't. Major Geddes is Officer of the Day and will hear us.' I went to the window of said room and looked in, and there saw Lt. Orleman in bed with his said daughter, having criminal intercourse with her."

Geddes, Not Orleman, Is Court-Martialed

The next day, wrote Geddes, Lillie told him that her father "had been having sexual intercourse with her for the past five years . . . and that he had placed a loaded revolver to her head, threatening that he would blow out her brains if she did not consent to his horrible desires. Miss Orleman begged me repeatedly and implored me on bended knee to save her and take her from this terrible life of shame." Afterwards, Geddes told Orleman that he knew of his relationship with Lillie and was prepared to take her away "either to her home in Austin, or to my wife." Geddes concluded by saying he was not alone in suspicions of Orleman, and he claimed to have other witnesses who had seen Orleman behave improperly toward his daughter.

Ord, who had complete discretion over how to proceed with the case, chose not to prosecute Orleman, but instead to court-martial Geddes on Orleman's charge that Geddes had libeled him with a false accusation of incest as part of a plot to seduce and abduct Lillie Orleman. Geddes was charged with two counts of conduct unbecoming an officer and a gentleman. According to the first charge, Geddes, "a married man, did by persuasion, advice, threats and other means, endeavor to corrupt Miss Lillie Orleman to his own illicit purposes." The second charge claimed that Geddes willfully and falsely accused "Lt. Orleman of the heinous crime of incestuous intercourse with the said Orleman's daughter . . . and by threatening to make the same public attempt to force and coerce said Lt. Orleman into giving his consent to the departure of his daughter."

Geddes pled not guilty to all charges. The trial would last for the exceptionally long time of three months. The prosecutor's immediate task was to impeach Geddes's character and portray him as a libertine and a liar. The prosecutor introduced evidence that Geddes had been court-martialed once before on charges of attempting to cash one month's pay in two different places. He had been found guilty, but the judge advocate general recommended leniency in light of his otherwise spotless record. It also quickly came out that Geddes, who lived apart from his wife (whom he had been compelled to marry in a shotgun wedding) was a notorious womanizer who had had several affairs, including one with his commanding officer's wife, who bore him a child.

Lillie Orleman was the prosecutor's first witness. She traced the development of her relationship with Geddes from their meeting at a post dance where he "squeezed her hand meaningfully," and she told of his many visits to her quarters while her father was away and his attempts to take liberties with her. Yet, she confessed, she continued meeting him, claiming that she believed, "Captain Geddes to be a gentleman. I inferred from all his actions that he would get a divorce and make me his wife." She testified that the night Geddes allegedly discovered the incest, she had gone to bed at nine and slept through the night. She also said she had closed the bedroom windows and drawn the curtains, making it impossible for Geddes to see in the window. She also testified that she and her father had had a disagreement earlier in the evening, and that her father had come into the bedroom and told her to stop seeing Geddes or he would turn her out of the house. She then claimed that Geddes told her the next day that "your father is not treating you right." She said she had thought that he referred to Orleman's reprimand over her meetings with Geddes, and she agreed her father treated her "cruelly and meanly, which is really not so. I told him that to enlist his sympathy in order to take me home."

She then testified that Geddes told her father that he would not expose him if Orleman let Lillie leave with him on the evening stage. She firmly denied that any incest had taken place.

Conflicting "Expert" Testimony

The prosecution's most valuable witness was Dr. M. K. Taylor, who examined Lillie to determine whether or not she was a virgin. He testified that in his opinion "she had never had sexual intercourse." The defense called its own expert witnesses to refute Taylor's conclusion, but as they had not been permitted to examine Lillie, their testimony was largely ineffective. The prosecution meant to prove that if there had been no sex there could have been no incest, and that therefore Geddes was guilty as charged.

Geddes took the stand on August 4, and he told the same story that he had written in his letter to Ord. He denied making any improper overtures to Lillie, or visiting her except on one occasion, and he portrayed himself as her rescuer. He told how he had grown suspicious of Orleman when he had seen him fondle his daughter's breast in an ambulance on the way to Fort Davis. Another witness, Joseph Friedlander, testified that Orleman had reached under her clothes, taken hold of her leg, and told a smutty story on the same trip.

The defense called several witnesses to corroborate Geddes's testimony. Michael Houston, the driver of a stage in which Lillie and Louis Orleman had traveled alone, told a story remarkably similar to Geddes's of what he had overheard while driving the stage. He said that Orleman had accused his daughter of having sexual relations with Geddes and other officers as well as with Orleman. Another witness, Corporal George A. Hartford, testified that in 1877 he too had witnessed an intimate scene between father and daughter.

When the defense tried to call Lillie as a rebuttal witness she was pronounced too ill to testify. Her illness was attributed to the strain of her previous testimony. On August 21 the court announced its verdict of guilty on all counts, except abduction. Geddes was sentenced to three years in prison and a dishonorable discharge. The sentence was reviewed by the judge advocate general, William M. Dunn, who submitted his review to the secretary of war and President Rutherford B. Hayes. Dunn concluded that the verdict was a miscarriage of justice and recommended overturning the conviction and the sentence. The president concurred, and Geddes was returned to his unit.

This was not the end of Geddes's difficulties. William T. Sherman, general of the army, intervened to have Geddes investigated and retried. An extensive investigation concluded that Geddes was a notorious womanizer, but that prosecuting him for any related infractions would be damaging to the reputations of other officers and their wives. Ultimately, in 1880, Geddes was court-martialed for the third time, found guilty of drunkenness on duty, and dismissed from the army. This time the Judge Advocate General's office allowed the sentence to stand.

—Carol Willcox Melton

Suggestions for Further Reading

Barnett, Louise. *Ungentlemanly Acts: The Army's Notorious Incest Trial.* New York: Hill and Wang, 2000.

Cresap, Bernard. *Appomattox Warrior: The Story of General E. O. C. Ord.* New York: A. S. Barnes, 1981.

Williams, Clayton W. *Texas' Last Frontier: Fort Stockton and the Trans-Pecos 1861–1895.* College Station, Tex.: Texas A & M University Press, 1982.

Reynolds v. U.S.: 1879

Defendant: George Reynolds **Crime Charged:** Bigamy
Chief Defense Lawyers: George W. Biddle and Ben Sheeks
Chief Prosecutor: William Carey **Judge:** Alexander White
Place: Salt Lake City, Utah **Dates of Trial:** October 30–December 10, 1875 **Verdict:** Guilty **Sentence:** Two years imprisonment and a $500 fine

SIGNIFICANCE

The Mormons, who settled Utah, permitted members of their religion to practice polygamy. In *Reynolds,* the Supreme Court held that federal legislation banning polygamy was constitutional and did not violate the Mormons' First Amendment right to free exercise of their religion. The *Reynolds* case still remains the leading Supreme Court decision that the First Amendment does not protect polygamy.

After a somewhat checkered history and a long trek westward, in the mid-19th century the followers of a religious prophet named Joseph Smith settled the western lands that became the state of Utah. Their religion was called the Church of Jesus Christ of Latter-Day Saints, but most people called them the Mormons. They held a variety of novel beliefs, ranging from their conviction that Jesus Christ visited the American Indians to a prohibition against caffeine drinks such as coffee and tea. Their most controversial belief, however, was that a man could have more than one wife.

Most of the United States knew about the Mormon practice of polygamy since 1852. Most Americans were traditional Christians and believed in monogamy, or having only one spouse. Until the Mormons arrived, however, there were no federal laws against bigamy (legal term for marrying a second spouse while still married to a first spouse) or polygamy (practice of having several spouses). The government left the Mormons alone for many years, but in 1862 President Abraham Lincoln signed the Morrill Anti-Bigamy Act into law. The Morrill Act outlawed polygamy throughout the United States in general and in Utah in particular. The government did not do much to enforce the law, however, because it was preoccupied with the Civil War.

Congress Strengthens Anti-Bigamy Law

After the Civil War, Congress regained interest in the question of Mormon polygamy. Congress strengthened the Morrill Act by passing the Poland Law in 1874. The Poland Law increased the powers of the federal judiciary within the territory of Utah. Because federal judges were federally appointed, they were more likely to be non-Mormons and thus more aggressive about enforcing the law.

Mormon leader Brigham Young and George Q. Cannon, territorial delegate to Congress and advisor to Young, decided to challenge the federal government in court. They were confident that if the government tried any Mormons for bigamy, the United States Supreme Court would throw out the convictions,based on the First Amendment right to free exercise of their religion. Therefore, they planned to arrange for a "test case" to be brought to court. Young and Cannon chose Young's personal secretary, a devout Mormon and practicing polygamist, George Reynolds.

Young and Cannon were successful: the government indicted Reynolds for bigamy in October 1874. Reynolds had to be re-tried, however, due to jury-selection problems. The government indicted Reynolds again in October 1875. The judge was territorial Supreme Court Chief Justice Alexander White, and the prosecutor was William Carey. George W. Biddle and Ben Sheeks represented Reynolds.

The government charged that Reynolds was currently married to both Mary Ann Tuddenham and Amelia Jane Schofield. The prosecution had little difficulty in proving that Reynolds lived with both women, despite some trouble in serving Schofield with her subpoena. The following dialogue is an excerpt from the prosecution's questioning of Arthur Pratt, a deputy marshal sent to serve a subpoena on Schofield:

> Question: State to the court what efforts you have made to serve it.
>
> Answer: I went to the residence of Mr. Reynolds, and a lady was there, his first wife, and she told me that this woman was not there; that that was the only home that she had, but that she hadn't been there for two or three weeks. I went again this morning, and she was not there.
>
> Question: Do you know anything about her home, where she resides?
>
> Answer: I know where I found her before.
>
> Question: Where?
>
> Answer: At the same place.

Following more evidence of Reynolds' two marriages, which the defense had no chance of refuting, Judge White gave instructions to the jury. White's instructions smashed Reynolds' defense that by virtue of the First Amendment he was innocent because of his Mormon religious beliefs:

> [If you find that Reynolds] deliberately married a second time, having a first wife living, the want of consciousness of evil intent, the want of understanding on his part that he was committing crime, did not excuse him, but the law inexorably, in such cases, implies criminal intent. . . .

The jury found Reynolds guilty on December 10, 1875. On July 6, 1876, the territorial Supreme Court affirmed his sentence. Reynolds appealed to the U.S. Supreme Court. On November 14 and 15, 1878, Biddle and Sheeks argued to the Supreme Court that it must overturn Reynolds' conviction on the basis of the First Amendment.

The Supreme Court Destroys Mormons' Hopes

On January 6, 1879, the Supreme Court upheld the trial court's decision. The Supreme Court said that the First Amendment did not protect polygamy, and based its decision on historic American cultural values:

> Polygamy has always been odious among the northern and western nations of Europe, and, until the establishment of the Mormon Church, was almost exclusively a feature of the life of Asiatic and of African people. At common law, the second marriage was always void, and from the earliest history of England polygamy has been treated as an offence against society. . . . In the face of all this evidence, it is impossible to believe that the constitutional guaranty of religious freedom was intended to prohibit legislation in respect to this most important feature of social life. Marriage, while from its very nature a sacred obligation, is nevertheless, in most civilized nations, a civil contract, and usually regulated by law.

Therefore, the Supreme Court upheld Reynolds' sentence of two years imprisonment and a $500 fine. The Supreme Court's decision rocked the Mormons, who initially vowed to defy the Court but later seemed to accept the inevitable. In 1890, Mormon leader Wilford Woodruff issued a document called the Manifesto, which terminated "any marriages forbidden by the law of the land." After 1890, most Mormons abandoned polygamy.

The *Reynolds* case is still the leading Supreme Court decision that the First Amendment does not protect polygamy. In 1984, a U.S. District Court considered the case of Utah policeman Royston Potter, who was fired for bigamy. District Court Judge Sherman Christensen rejected Potter's First Amendment defense, and the U.S. 10th Circuit Court of Appeals upheld Christensen's ruling. In October of 1985 the Supreme Court refused to hear Potter's appeal. By refusing to consider cases like Potter's, the Supreme Court has effectively decided to keep *Reynolds* as the law of the land.

Many legal scholars have criticized the Supreme Court for not modifying or overturning *Reynolds*. It has been over 100 years since 1879, and in many subsequent cases the Supreme Court has greatly expanded the First Amendment's legal protection for free exercise of religion. Further, in the 1960s and early 1970s the Supreme Court increased the Constitution's protection for the civil rights of women, minorities and other persons whose equality under the law had never been a part of the old common law cited in *Reynolds*. Logically, therefore, one could expect the Supreme Court to reconsider its position on the constitutionality of polygamy. To date, however, the Supreme Court has not reversed its decision.

—Stephen G. Christianson

Suggestions for Further Reading

Cannon, George Quayle. *A Review of the Decision of the Supreme Court of the United States, in the Case of Geo. Reynolds vs. the United States.* Salt Lake City, Utah: Deseret News Printing, 1879.

Casey, Kathryn. "An American Harem." *Ladies Home Journal.* (February 1990): 116–121.

Embry, Jessie L. *Mormon Polygamous Families: Life in the Principle.* Salt Lake City, Utah: University of Utah Press, 1987.

Firmage, Edwin Brown. *Zion in the Courts: A Legal History of the Church of Jesus Christ of Latter-day Saints, 1830–1900.* Urbana: University of Illinois Press, 1988.

Foster, Lawrence. *Religion and Sexuality: The Shakers, the Mormons, and the Oneida Community.* Urbana: University of Illinois Press, 1984.

Wagoner, Richard S. *Mormon Polygamy: A History.* Salt Lake City, Utah: Signature Books, 1989.

Wyatt Earp Trial: 1881

Defendants: Wyatt Earp, Virgil Earp, Morgan Earp, John "Doc" Holliday
Crime Charged: Murder **Chief Defense Lawyer:** Thomas Fitch
Chief Prosecutor: Lyttleton Price **Judge:** Wells Spicer **Place:** Tombstone, Arizona **Date of Trial:** October 31–November 29, 1881 **Verdict:** Not guilty

SIGNIFICANCE

The month-long trial—actually a preliminary hearing—made possible an American legend. Nearly every American, and millions in foreign lands, knows about Wyatt Earp, the heroic marshal who brought law and order to a score of Kansas cow towns before wiping out a gang of savage rustlers in the shootout at the O.K. Corral in Tombstone, Arizona. Unfortunately, there is little truth in the legend. If this hearing were conducted under different circumstances, Earp would be remembered as just another shady, if not totally criminal, frontier gunslinger.

In Tombstone, Arizona, a mining town, "cowboy" was synonymous with "rustler." There were a lot of rustlers in surrounding Cochise County, and most of the cattlemen, if not actually thieves, were the rustlers' customers. Tombstone citizens, most of them Union sympathizers during the Civil War, blamed the "cowboys," largely Confederate sympathizers, for every crime. Tombstone citizens had been discussing a vigilance committee to rid the county of undesirables, meaning all the cowboys. The proposed leader of the committee was Wyatt Earp.

Earp was by his own account a hero who had tamed many cow towns in Kansas. Actually, he was a former horse thief and buffalo hunter who had been fired from the Wichita police force for corruption and literally run out of town. He came to Dodge City and got a job on its four-man police force. In Dodge, he spent most of his time gambling with cowboys flush with back pay from the cattle drives. When the cattle boom there ended, he and his brothers moved west to gamble with the silver miners. Earp told everyone about his gunfighting skills and secured a faro dealership in return for protecting the staff of Tombstone's Oriental Saloon soon after he arrived in 1876.

Wyatt and Morgan Earp worked for the Wells Fargo Stage Coach company, but Wyatt wanted to be sheriff of Cochise County. So, although Wyatt was the hero of the "law and order" faction in Tombstone, the Earps also tried to stay on good terms with the cowboys. That may be why, when a prominent rustler, Curly Bill Brocius, shot and killed City Marshal Fred White, Virgil Earp, deputy city marshal, swore it was an accident. It was a most improbable accident: for it to happen, White would have had to be reaching for a cocked revolver pointing at his chest. Coincidentally, White's "accidental" death made Virgil acting city marshal.

The incumbent sheriff, Johnny Behan, was Wyatt Earp's rival in love as well as politics. Wyatt had begun squiring around Behan's mistress, Josie Marcus, an actress and department store heiress. Earp kept his own common-law wife, Mattie, confined to their home.

Wyatt Earp, known for his participation in the shootout at O.K. Corral, Tombstone, Arizona. (Archive Photos)

A Mysterious Stage Coach Robbery

On March 15, 1881, several masked men attempted to hold up a stagecoach leaving Tombstone. The driver and a passenger were killed. Behan's posse included Wyatt and Morgan Earp and their friend, Doc Holliday. Some people said the hunters were hunting themselves. Doc Holliday had been seen shortly after the robbery, riding furiously away from the scene. Further, Holliday was a close friend of Bill Leonard, one of three men identified by Luther King, who held the outlaws' horses. King did not identify Holliday, but as the ferocious little dentist was in the posse, he may not have thought that wise. Later, Big Nose Kate Elder, Holliday's mistress, told the sheriff that Doc had killed both of the holdup victims. When she sobered up, she recanted.

The holdup triggered a deterioration of relations between the cowboys and Wyatt Earp's clique. Leonard and the two others identified by King, Harry Head and Jim Crane, were all known rustlers. But with an election coming up, Earp did not want to sever his ties with the cowboy faction. He went to Ike Clanton and Frank McLaury, members of the faction, with a proposition.

"I told them that I wanted the glory of capturing Leonard, Head and Crane," Earp testified later. "And if I could do it, it would help make the race for sheriff at the next election. I told them . . . I would give them all of the reward and would never let anyone know where I got the information."

Ike Clanton agreed, Virgil Earp later testified. Clanton agreed even though it would mean the death of his friends, testifying that Earp told him he had to kill the robbers.

"He said his business was such that he could not afford to capture them. He would have to kill them or else leave the county." According to Clanton, Wyatt and Morgan Earp were inside men in the robbery, while Holliday was one of the gunmen.

As it turned out, Leonard, Head, and Crane were all killed by other people shortly after Clanton agreed to help Wyatt.

Wyatt Earp went to Ike Clanton with another proposition. He suggested that Clanton and his friends stage a fake coach robbery. The Earp brothers and Holliday would come on the scene and scare away the "robbers." Nobody would be hurt, and Wyatt Earp would have added luster for his political campaign. Clanton was far from sure that nobody would be hurt. He refused. After Clanton's rejection of Earp's second proposition, hostility between the two men and their close associates increased tremendously.

Trouble Brewing

On October 25, Ike Clanton and teenaged Tom McLaury came to Tombstone in a wagon. As the law required, both men checked their guns at a saloon designated as a check point. McLaury came to do business. Clanton came to drink. He was thoroughly potted when he saw Doc Holliday and Morgan Earp in a lunchroom. Holliday challenged him to fight. Clanton said he had checked his guns on entering town. He went outside; Wyatt and Morgan Earp joined Holliday in taunting him. Clanton stumbled off to drink some more. In the morning, Clanton, drunk out of his mind, picked up his guns, saying he was leaving town. He didn't leave. He went staggering through the streets, uttering threats against Holliday and the Earps. Virgil and Morgan Earp sneaked up behind him, bashed him on the head, took his guns and arrested him for carrying weapons.

A little later, Wyatt Earp saw Tom McLaury.

"Are you heeled or not?" Earp asked the teenager.

McLaury said he had no gun. Earp slapped his face, then hit him on the head with his revolver. McLaury went down. When he got up, Earp knocked him down again with the gun.

Billy Clanton and Frank McLaury arrived early in the afternoon to meet their brothers. They had come to help Tom McLaury get Ike Clanton into the wagon: they knew what Ike could be like after a night of drinking. Billy and Frank each had a revolver in a holster and a rifle in a saddle scabbard on his horse. As soon as they got Ike squared away, they'd be leaving, so they saw no need to check their weapons. When the four cowboys met, Sheriff Behan tried to take their guns. Ike Clanton and Tom McLaury said they had no guns. Tom's were still checked, and Ike's had been confiscated. Behan searched them to make sure. Billy Clanton and Frank McLaury were carrying guns openly, but they said they were just about to leave town.

Shootout

Then Behan saw the Earps and Holliday. He knew the situation was about to explode. He stopped arguing with the cowboys. He ran up to Virgil and asked for time to disarm Billy Clanton and Frank McLaury. The Earps pushed past him.

When the cowboys and the "Earp Gang" were within a few feet of each other, shooting began. When it was over, Frank McLaury, Tom McLaury, and Billy Clanton were dead. Virgil Earp and Morgan Earp were seriously wounded, and Doc Holliday was slightly wounded. Wyatt Earp and Ike Clanton were unhurt.

The Hearing

A coroner's jury decided that the McLaurys and Billy Clanton had been killed by the Earps and Holliday, but it didn't assign blame. Ike Clanton swore the Earps and Holliday committed murder, so Behan arrested them. Virgil Earp was suspended as city marshal. Justice of the Peace Wells Spicer, a friend of Wyatt Earp, held a preliminary hearing to determine if the men should be tried.

Dozens of witnesses testified. Johnny Behan, who had observed the fight from an alley, testified that someone in the Earp party had fired first, hitting Billy Clanton just as Clanton was yelling, "Don't shoot me! I don't want to fight." He said Tom McLaury opened his coat and said he wasn't armed. Ike Clanton, also unarmed, ran into Fly's photographic studio after Holliday missed him with the shotgun, then ran out through Fly's back door and sought refuge in a Mexican dance hall.

Several witnesses who had no axe to grind corroborated Behan's testimony. Martha King was shopping when she heard one of the Earp party say, "Let them have it." She said Doc Holliday, whom she knew, replied, "All right." Then the shooting began. B. H. Fellehy said he overheard Virgil Earp tell Behan, "Those men have been making threats; I will not arrest them but will kill them on sight."

According to witnesses, Doc Holliday killed the unarmed Tom McLaury instantly with his shotgun, then missed Ike Clanton. At the same time, Morgan Earp shot Billy Clanton. Wyatt Earp then shot Frank McLaury, who staggered into the street and tried to get the rifle hanging on his horse. Billy Clanton, lying wounded, shot Virgil Earp in the leg. McLaury's horse ran away, so the cowboy drew his revolver. Morgan Earp shot him again, just as McLaury shot Holliday, now using a revolver instead of the shotgun. Billy Clanton then shot Morgan Earp in the shoulder, right before both Morgan and Wyatt Earp shot him again.

The defense presented a number of witnesses, but none who said the cowboys fired first. H. F. Sills said he saw four or five men, two of them armed, who said they were going to kill "the whole party of the Earps." Sills, a stranger in town, had to ask a bystander who the "Earps" were. Spicer allowed Wyatt Earp to read a prepared statement and did not allow cross-examination.

On November 29, Spicer found the Earp party not guilty. His opinion ignored most of the incriminating evidence. The fact that Ike Clanton, who had threatened the Earps, was not hurt, Spicer considered a "great fact, most prominent in the matter," showing that the "Earp Gang" was not bent on revenge.

Clanton was not injured, of course, because he could run fast and Doc Holliday was not as good with a shotgun as he was with a six-shooter. Spicer failed to note that the two armed cowboys had not used their rifles. If they had intended to murder "the whole party of the Earps," they could have mowed down their opponents before they got within pistol range.

Aftermath

On December 28, hidden gunmen tried to assassinate Virgil Earp. They didn't succeed, but they crippled the ex-marshal for life. Wyatt Earp gathered a posse of hard-cases and shot up Charlestown, a Cochise County town a short distance from Tombstone on the San Pedro River. Charlestown, rather than unfriendly Tombstone, was where the cowboys met to drink. On March 18, 1882, someone killed Morgan Earp by shooting him in the back as he was playing billiards.

Wyatt and his posse went out again and killed two men, one in Pima County. Pima County's sheriff swore out a murder warrant for Wyatt Earp. Earp disappeared. He reappeared in Trinidad, Colorado, where his friend, Bat Masterson, was city marshal.

Eventually, everyone forgot about the murders in Arizona. Wyatt Earp traveled all over the West, from Alaska to California, where he married Josie Marcus. (The deserted Mattie Earp had become a prostitute and later committed suicide.) Wyatt, who died in 1929, outlived most of his contemporaries and found writers who eagerly swallowed his tall tales.

An American legend was born.

—*William Weir*

Suggestions for Further Reading

Constable, George, ed. *The Gunfighters.* Time-Life Old West Series. New York: Time-Life Books, 1974.

Cunningham, Eugene. *Triggernometry.* Caldwell, Idaho: Caxton Printers, 1989.

Drago, Harry Sinclair. *Wild, Woolly & Wicked.* New York: Bramhall House, 1960.

Horan, James D. *The Authentic Wild West: the Gunfighters.* New York: Crown Publishing, 1977.

Horan, James D. *The Authentic Wild West: The Lawmen.* New York: Crown Publishing, 1980.

Marks, Paula Mitchell. *And Die in the West.* New York: Simon & Schuster, 1989.

Weir, William. *Written with Lead.* Hamden, Conn.: Archon Books, 1992.

Henry Flipper Court-Martial: 1881

Defendant: Henry Flipper **Crimes:** Embezzlement and conduct unbecoming an officer **Chief Defense Lawyer:** Merritt Barber **Chief Prosecutor:** John W. Clous, Judge Advocate **Presiding Officer:** G. Pennypacker **Court:** J. F. Wade, G. W. Schofield, W. E. Waters, William Fletcher, W. N. Tisdall, R.G. Heiner, E.S. Ewing, W.V. Richards **Place:** Fort Davis, Texas
Date of Trial: September 15; November 1–December 13, 1881
Verdict: Not guilty of embezzlement; guilty of conduct unbecoming an officer
Sentence: Dishonorable discharge from the army, with loss of all benefits

SIGNIFICANCE

This court-martial deserves to be known if only because it drove out of the army the first African American to graduate from West Point and thus the first to be a regular army officer. Beyond that, many historians believe the case grew out of racial prejudice and that the sentence was disproportionately harsh.

In the years following the Civil War, despite the Thirteenth and Fourteenth Amendments to the Constitution, the United States remained a largely segregated society. West Point at least deserves some credit for accepting its first African-American cadet, James Webster Smith, in 1870, even though his time there was filled with continual "pain and strain" and he never graduated. (He failed a course in his fourth year and was dismissed.) Two more African Americans were admitted, but both failed courses and dropped out. Finally in 1873, the fourth African American and the first to graduate was admitted, Henry Ossian Flipper, born a slave in Georgia in 1856.

A Different Kind of Trial

The hazing rituals and other traditions of West Point were challenging enough for even the most socially connected white cadets. Henry Flipper had to endure four years of almost total social isolation and verbal insults, but he stayed the course and graduated with his class in 1877. As the first and only black regular army officer, he was posted to the Tenth Cavalry, a cavalry unit, all of whose personnel except officers were blacks (known by the Indians as "Buffalo Soldiers"). While fighting the Apaches, Flipper and his unit were assigned to

Fort Davis, a frontier post in west Texas. Throughout this time, all his superiors and fellow officers were white, and most of them made no secret of their dislike for having a black officer among them.

In December 1880, Flipper was put in charge of the commissary, responsible for buying and selling food for the fort's personnel and their families. In 1881, Flipper's sloppy bookkeeping, careless security, and a naive willingness to extend credit to various soldiers and civilians led to the discovery that he was short some $2,400 in funds. Although friends made up the shortfall, it was too late, and on August 12, 1881, Flipper was arrested.

The Court-Martial

The court-martial convened at Fort Davis on September 15, 1881, but was suspended until November 1 to allow Flipper time to obtain counsel. Flipper was formally charged with embezzling a total of $3,791.77—most of which he had repaid by that time—and also with conduct unbecoming an officer. As always since he had become part of the army, Flipper found himself confronting an all-white world, but his attorney, Capt. Merritt Barber, mounted a solid defense. On the charge of embezzlement, he argued that under the governing military law, it had to be proven that the individual charged engaged in "intentional, wrongful, and willful conversion of public money to his own use and benefit." This, Barber noted, the prosecution had utterly failed to demonstrate and that at most Flipper was guilty of poor bookkeeping and records maintenance. To support the claim that Flipper had from the beginning planned to repay the missing sum, he argued that Flipper was expecting a check for $2,500 from a New York publisher, the royalties for his book about his time at West Point. One can only imagine the effect this must have had on a panel of white officers: a 25-year-old African American earning royalties from a book describing his mistreatment at the hands of his fellow cadets and officers!

The second charge, conduct unbecoming an officer, involved such actions as writing a false check (in an attempt to cover some of the missing funds), lying to his superior officer, and signing false reports. In fact, Flipper had done all of these, but his defense attorney argued that there were extenuating circumstances: the so-called false check? Flipper had never tried to use it in any transaction—he had only displayed it to his superior. If Flipper lied to this same superior, it was only because this man had not given him the expected guidance and support; therefore, argued Barber—turning conventional reasoning inside out—Flipper had employed minor untruths in a misguided attempt to maintain his image of a West Point officer. As for the false reports, the lawyer argued that behind this charge was the premise that he had embezzled the money for his own purposes—and there was no evidence of that.

On the broader issue of what constituted "conduct unbecoming an officer," the defense attorney referred to two fairly recent court-martials where officers had been charged with this offense. In both cases, the officers were let off on the ground that their actions had not been "prejudicial to good order and military discipline." Captain Barber argued that the same could be said of

Flipper's actions. In his summation, Barber went even further, employing the flowery rhetoric typical of the day:

> May we not therefore ask this court to take into consideration, the unequal battle my client has to wage, poor, naked, and practically alone, with scarce an eye of sympathy or a word to cheer, against all the resources of zealous numbers, official testimony, official position, experience and skill, charged with all the ammunition which the government could furnish from Washington to Texas, and may we not trust that this court will throw around him the mantle of its charity, if any errors are found, giving him the benefit of every doubt . . . and giving him your confidence that the charity you extend to him so generously will be as generously redeemed by his future record in the service.

What was most revealing here, as well as through the entire trial, is that there is no explicit reference to Flipper's being an African American. In any case, realizing they had no evidence to convict Flipper of embezzlement, the court returned a verdict of not guilty on that charge, but they did find him guilty of conduct unbecoming an officer. The sentence was that he be dismissed from the service.

At that time, an officer could not be dismissed as a result of a court-martial until after the sentence had been reviewed by the president of the United States. Flipper's case passed up to the president through the normal channels of review, and the judge advocate general of the U.S. Army, David G. Swain, did in fact recommend that the guilty verdict be "mitigated to a lesser degree of punishment." President Chester Alan Arthur, however, simply approved the original judgment and sentence, and Flipper was dishonorably discharged from the army in 1882.

Lieutenant Henry Flipper, the first African American to graduate from West Point. (Courtesy, National Archives)

Flipper's Later Fate

Flipper took up a career as the first professional African-American civil and mining engineer, eventually attaining several federal appointments and becoming a recognized authority on Mexican and South American law. From the outset and throughout his life, Flipper tried every possible means to get the judgment overturned, but he died in 1940 without succeeding. In 1976, however, thanks greatly to the efforts of the eighth African American to graduate from West Point, Minton Francis (Class of 1944), and Ray McColl, a white Georgia schoolteacher, an army administrative board upgraded Flipper's discharge to "Honorable" and dated it June 30, 1882. But according to the Justice Department,

Flipper remained on record as a convicted felon. The only way to change that was to get a court to retry the case and overturn the finding of guilt—or to get a presidential pardon. In 1994, a West Point graduate (Class of 1966) and lawyer, Thomas Carhart, while working at Princeton on his Ph.D. dissertation about the first African Americans at West Point, decided to take up Flipper's case. After Carhart enlisted the support of others in the legal community, the case was subjected to a close analysis. Among other points, Carhart showed that white officers convicted of more serious crimes had not been dishonorably discharged. Finally, on February 19, 1999, President Bill Clinton signed the first posthumous presidential pardon in American history. Henry Flipper's name was finally cleared.

—*John S. Bowman*

Suggestions for Further Reading

Carhart, Thomas M. III. *African American West Pointers During the Nineteenth Century.* Ph.D. diss., Princeton University, 1998.

"Court Martial Proceedings of Henry O. Flipper, File QQ2952, Record Group 153." Washington, D.C.: National Archives.

Flipper, Henry Ossian. *The Colored Cadet at West Point.* New York: Homer Lee & Co., 1878.

——. *Negro Frontiersman.* El Paso Tex.: Western College Press, 1963.

Charles Guiteau Trial: 1881

Defendant: Charles J. Guiteau **Crime Charged:** Assassinating President James A. Garfield **Chief Defense Lawyers:** Leigh Robinson and George Scoville **Chief Prosecutors:** George Corkhill, Walter Davidge, John K. Porter, Elihu Root, and E.B. Smith **Judge:** Walter Cox **Place:** Washington, D.C. **Dates of Trial:** November 14, 1881–January 13, 1882 **Verdict:** Guilty **Sentence:** Death by hanging

SIGNIFICANCE

Charles Guiteau's trial was one of the first murder trials in which the defendant's claim of insanity was subjected to the modern legal test: namely, whether or not Guiteau understood that his actions were wrong.

Less than 20 years after Abraham Lincoln was shot by John Wilkes Booth, the United States would see another president assassinated. James A. Garfield, a Union major general, had a distinguished military career, on which he capitalized even before the war ended by getting elected to the House of Representatives in 1863. Garfield was a successful politician, becoming the House Republican leader in 1876. Garfield was known for his opposition to President Ulysses S. Grant, a Republican whose scandal-ridden administration and flawed policies had alienated many of his fellow party members such as Garfield. In 1880, Garfield was the Republican candidate for president and won the election.

Unfortunately for Garfield, his presidency had attracted the obsessive interest of one Charles Guiteau. Guiteau claimed to be a lawyer and specialized in taking small-claims court cases for an unheard-of 75 percent contingency fee. Guiteau's legal career never amounted to much, and he was frequently on the run from creditors seeking payment on overdue bills. He also toyed with various political causes, joining the Oneida Community and other experimental religious communities springing up in the 1860s and 1870s. Guiteau tired of the communal life and moved to Washington, D.C., where he joined the Garfield election campaign as a lowly staff member.

Imaginary Insult Prompts Revenge

Guiteau never had any position of importance in the Garfield campaign except in his own mind. Guiteau's behavior had always been erratic, and it is possible that he contracted venereal diseases that further aggravated his mental problems. He was inspired to write a speech, which he hoped that Garfield would use in a debate with the Democratic presidential candidate, W.S. Hancock. Garfield never even read the speech, much less used it in the debate, but Guiteau was convinced that Garfield won the election thanks to his speech. Guiteau demanded to be appointed ambassador to France, and he even personally accosted Secretary of State James G. Blaine several times. Blaine tried to put Guiteau off politely, but be eventually lost patience and, on their final encounter, pushed Guiteau away and told him never to bother him again.

Bitter with resentment, Guiteau decided to take revenge against Garfield. Guiteau trailed Garfield throughout the month of June 1881, waiting for the right opportunity. On July 2, Guiteau got his chance. The Washington newspapers had reported Garfield's plans to go on a trip with his family, and Guiteau waited for the president at the train station, from where he was to leave. In the station's lobby, Guiteau came from behind Garfield and shot the president in the back. Station police rushed to arrest Guiteau, who offered no resistance. Meanwhile, Garfield was taken away for medical attention.

Guiteau's shot didn't kill Garfield outright. The president survived only to be diagnosed as having a fatal wound. The bullet had grazed Garfield's spine and lodged in his stomach, where it came to rest in such a position that blood continued to circulate but the bullet could not be removed without killing Garfield. The doctors therefore didn't operate, and they could do nothing for Garfield except try to make him comfortable until the inevitable happened. Garfield was a strong man, and he lived for almost three months until September 19, 1881. The American public was outraged by the murder, and one of the soldiers that guarded Guiteau's prison even tried unsuccessfully to shoot him before trial.

Was Guiteau Insane?

Once Garfield was dead, the government could finally try Charles Guiteau for murder. The trial opened November 14, 1881, in the District of Columbia. The judge was Walter Cox. Guiteau's lawyers were Leigh Robinson and George Scoville, although Guiteau would insist on trying to represent himself during the trial. U.S. Attorney General Wayne MacVeagh, determined to secure a conviction, named five lawyers to the prosecution team: George Corkhill, Walter Davidge, John K. Porter, Elihu Root, and E.B. Smith. Corkhill, who was also the District of Columbia's district attorney, summed up the prosecution's opinion of Guiteau's insanity defense in a pre-trial press statement that also mirrored public opinion on the issue:

> He's no more insane than I am. . . . There's nothing of the madman about Guiteau: he's a cool calculating blackguard, a polished ruffian, who has

> gradually prepared himself to pose in this way before the world . . . he was a dead-beat, pure and simple. . . . Finally he got tired of the monotony of dead-beating. He wanted excitement of some other kind and notoriety, and he's got it.

Unfortunately for his attorneys, Guiteau not only fought their attempt to assert an insanity defense, but insisted on asserting some bizarre legal defenses of his own. For example, he wrote a plea to Judge Cox arguing that the cause of Garfield's death was the doctors' failure to properly treat the bullet wound and therefore Guiteau was not guilty of murder. Of course, Guiteau's argument had no legal support. Any chance of acquitting Guiteau rested with his attorneys' efforts to prove that he was insane.

An angry Guiteau being restrained during his sensational trial for the killing of President Garfield. (*Harper's Weekly*)

There is still some debate over what constitutes legal insanity, but most authorities generally agree that the basic test is whether the defendant knew that his actions were wrong. At the time of the Guiteau trial, however, the prevailing test of legal insanity was whether defendant knew that his actions were criminal. Therefore, even though someone like Guiteau might be considered insane because he didn't think it was wrong to shoot the president, he could be convicted if the judge determined that he understood that the law made it illegal to shoot people. By the 1880s, courts were beginning to apply the less harsh "was it wrong" test, which also gave the jury rather than the judge the task of determining insanity.

Influenced by this trend in the law, Judge Cox allowed both sides to argue their case directly to the jury, and intervened only occasionally. Despite strong evidence of his insanity, Guiteau insisted he was sane, so his attorneys simply let him ramble on and hoped that the jury drew the right conclusion. For example, they let Guiteau explain that he shot Garfield not only out of revenge, but also because God had told him that Garfield was ruining the Republican Party and must be killed to save the country from the Democrats. Guiteau testified that God had promised to protect him if he shot Garfield:

> I want to say right here in reference to protection, that the Deity himself will protect me; that He has used all these soldiers, and these experts, and this honorable court, and these counsel, to serve Him and protect me. That is my theory about protection. The Lord is no fool, and when He has got anything to do He uses the best means He can to carry out His purposes.

Judge Cox and the prosecutors agreed that Guiteau's sanity or insanity had to be measured by whether he knew his actions were wrong, but they were also determined not to let Guiteau escape the hangman. Cox instructed the jury that any minimal amount of understanding on Guiteau's part would be enough to support a guilty verdict:

> When you come . . . to consider . . . such a crime as we have here, murder most foul and unnatural, the law requires a very slight degree of intelligence indeed.

The way was thus paved for the prosecutors, led by Davidge, to make an emotional appeal to the jurors in their closing argument for Guiteau's conviction:

> A man may not have intelligence enough to be made responsible, even for a less crime; but it is hard, it is very hard to conceive of the individual with any degree of intelligence at all, incapable of comprehending that the head of a great constitutional republic is not to be shot down like a dog.

The defense was paralyzed, and their efforts to portray Guiteau as not guilty by reason of insanity were brushed aside. Davidge asserted that Guiteau's erratic behavior could be explained by his overweening ego:

> Such is the indescribable egotism of this man that he put himself on the same plane as the Savior of mankind and the prophets. There you have the explanation of his applying for the mission at Paris. For this man, in his indescribable egotism, seems to have thought all along that there was nothing in the world too high for him.

On January 13, 1882, the jury rendered its verdict. They found Charles Guiteau guilty of the murder of President Garfield. Guiteau leaped to his feet and screamed at the jurors, "You are all low, consummate jackasses." Guards took Guiteau back to his cell to await execution. On June 30, 1882, Guiteau went to the scaffold, ranting about the Almighty as he went to his death at the end of a rope. Guiteau had been given the benefit of a new and more liberal legal definition of insanity, but like many criminal defendants to come, he found out that public opinion influences judges and juries alike.

—Stephen G. Christianson

Suggestions for Further Reading

Gray, John Purdue. *The United States v. Charles J. Guiteau. Review of the Trial.* Utica, N.Y.: Unknown Publisher, 1882.

Ogilvie, John Stuart. *The Life and Death of James A. Garfield From the Tow Path to the White House.* Cincinnati, Ohio: Cincinnati Publishing Co., 1881.

Porter, John Kilham. *Guiteau Trial.* New York: J. Polhemus, 1882.

Rosenberg, Charles E. *The Trial of the Assassin Guiteau: Psychiatry and Law in the Gilded Age.* Chicago: University of Chicago Press, 1968.

The United States v. Charles J. Guiteau. New York: Arno Press, 1973.

Jennie Cramer Murder Trial: 1882

Defendants: Blanche Douglass, James Malley Jr., Walter Malley
Crime Charged: Murder **Chief Defense Lawyers:** Samuel F. Jones, Levi N. Blydenburgh, William C. Case, Timothy J. Fox (both Malleys); Louis C. Cassidy (James Malley); Edwin C. Dow, William B. Stoddard (Douglass)
Chief Prosecutors: Tilton E. Doolittle, Charles Bush **Judge:** Miles T. Granger **Place:** New Haven, Connecticut **Date of Trial:** April 25–June 30, 1882 **Verdict:** Not guilty

SIGNIFICANCE

Possible witness bribery and an overly specific grand jury indictment helped wealthy defendants elude responsibility for one of Victorian New England's most notorious crimes.

At daybreak on Saturday morning, August 6, 1881, a fisherman found the lifeless body of a young woman floating by the West Haven, Connecticut, shoreline. She was Jennie Cramer, the twenty-year-old daughter of a German immigrant and his wife, who lived in nearby New Haven. Cramer's death shocked the city, for she was well known for her beauty and high spirits, especially among local young men.

One of her most persistent admirers was James Malley Jr., nephew of wealthy dry goods store owner Edward Malley. James Malley had called on Cramer at her father's cigar shop and sent her messages from his uncle's store, where he worked as a clerk. Cramer seemed uninterested in Malley's attentions, but she accepted several of his invitations to go walking or have dinner. The pair was always accompanied by James Malley's cousin Walter—Edward Malley's son—and a woman named Blanche Douglass, whom Walter had met in New York.

Despite her popularity with local bachelors, Jennie Cramer's moral character was considered to be spotless. Consequently, her mother was frantic when Cramer did not return home on the night of Wednesday, August 3. When she turned up on Thursday morning, Blanche Douglass accompanied her. Douglass assured Mrs. Cramer that she and Jennie had spent the night at a rooming house called the Elliott House, where no gentlemen were allowed, but Mrs. Cramer surmised that Douglass was no lady.

"Don't you know that you are disgracing yourself and disgracing your parents by staying out overnight?" Mrs. Cramer cried. "If you carry on like that we must find a place for you to stay when your little sister comes home. We can't have you here!" Mrs. Cramer left the room sobbing. When she regained her composure, Jennie was gone. Mrs. Cramer was terrified by the possibility that Jennie had taken her banishment threat seriously. Guilt-ridden, Mrs. Cramer visited James Malley at his uncle's store that afternoon and accused him of introducing her daughter to bad company. Malley replied that Blanche Douglass was a perfect lady and that the two young women had spent Wednesday night at the Elliott House. Nevertheless, he promised to bring Jennie home or contact the Cramers if he saw her. On Friday, the Cramers received a note from Malley stating that neither he nor Douglass were aware of Jennie's whereabouts. Saturday morning, the Cramers learned that Jennie was dead.

An Inquest's Second Thoughts

Because West Haven lacked a city government, investigating the death fell to a six-man coroner's jury. Bruises on the body nearly led to a conclusion that Cramer had drowned, but an official autopsy was conducted when one juror expressed second thoughts. The autopsy revealed that Cramer had not drowned. Hardly any water was found in her lungs and there was evidence that she had been raped within 48 hours of her death.

When the inquest sought clues about Cramer's last hours, Douglass and "the Malley boys" were called to testify. Douglass now said that she and Cramer had spent Wednesday night at the Malley mansion, where they had been singing and drinking wine alone with James and Walter. When Douglass felt ill, she convinced a reluctant Cramer to remain with her at the mansion all night. In the morning she accompanied Cramer home and witnessed the quarrel with Mrs. Cramer. Douglass swore that she last saw Cramer passing on a streetcar about noon on Thursday.

James Malley testified that he last saw Cramer when the two women left the mansion Thursday morning. Asked about his whereabouts on Friday night, he said that he was at home and that his entire family would swear to it. "My father came to me after the newspaper reports were concluded and asked me where I was Friday night," he replied, peculiarly modifying his answer. "No, he came to me and said, 'It's a lucky thing for you that you were home Friday night.' " Walter Malley echoed his cousin's testimony, adding that he thought that Cramer had gone to her brother's home in New York, accompanied by Douglass.

Other witnesses, however, swore to have seen Cramer with one or more of the trio on Thursday or Friday. It was also learned that Blanche Douglass was a New York prostitute, not Walter Malley's fiancé, as newspapers had reported. Detectives arrested her in a bordello and returned her to West Haven, where she was charged with perjury. Walter and James were arrested shortly thereafter.

According to the inquest autopsy, Cramer's body tissues indicated that she had ingested a fatal dose of over three grains of arsenic hours before her death. Verdicts were returned on September 3, holding James Malley "criminally responsible" and Walter Malley and Blanche Douglass "morally responsible" for the death of Jennie Cramer by "poison and violence."

The case was immediately referred to West Haven's local court, where numerous witnesses placed Cramer with the defendants at times conflicting with their stories. The West Haven trial seemed to dispose of one report that Cramer had been on a carousel at the town's Savin Rock amusement district, accompanied by a man with a black mustache. Margaret Kane produced her mustachioed companion and claimed to be the woman on the flying horses that Friday night. Kane said that a dizzy spell prompted her to say, "My God, I'm paralyzed!" a comment attributed by others to Jennie Cramer.

James Malley's sisters and a servant testified that he had been at home on Friday night, but the defense could not overcome suspicions that the defendants were lying. The case was referred to New Haven's Superior Court for a full trial. Meanwhile, the case became an international sensation and the Malley family's reputation declined. James' and Walter's haughty attitude did not win them public sympathy, nor did Edward Malley's dismissal of the tragedy with the blithe comment, "Boys will be boys." Amid rumors of bribery, prosecutors seethed over increasing memory lapses suffered by witnesses. A dime pamphlet bearing Cramer's portrait on the cover and containing the testimony leading to the arrests enjoyed a second printing, thanks to the Malley family's efforts to buy up every available copy at local bookshops.

The Elm City Tragedy

On January 17, 1882, multiple charges against all three defendants were consolidated by New Haven's grand jury into a single count of first-degree murder. Cramer's body was exhumed to address arguments that she, like many Victorian girls, habitually ate arsenic to improve her complexion. An examination found little of the substance in her bones, discounting the defense's claims.

When the case finally went to trial on April 25, 1882, prosecutor Tilton Doolittle charged that Walter had brought Douglass to New Haven for the purpose of helping James to "ruin" Cramer. The conspiracy succeeded and Cramer had been poisoned with liquid arsenic for fear that the crime would be discovered.

Despite confusion over dates and times, the defendants' version of Cramer's and their own whereabouts were opposed by a parade of prosecution witnesses, many of whom had testified in the earlier proceedings. A woman who lived opposite Elliott House repeated that she had seen Cramer there alone on Wednesday night and together with the Malleys and Douglass on Thursday. A New Haven waiter testified that he had served Walter, Douglass, and Cramer at 10 P.M. on Wednesday, casting doubt on the story of the party at the Malley mansion. A drugstore clerk recalled serving Cramer and Douglass sodas on

Thursday night. A married couple disputed Margaret Kane's story, insisting that it was Cramer who claimed to be stricken on the carousel. The defense offered a sole witness, a doctor who disagreed with medical reports that Cramer had been raped. He also proposed that she had drowned and that the arsenic in her system was the result of habitual use.

In final arguments, one defense attorney theorized that Cramer had committed suicide. Another emphasized the Malleys' alibis, belittled the prosecution's scientific evidence, and said that too little attention had been given to the possibility of a drowning. Douglass's attorney argued that even if Cramer had died of arsenic poisoning, the state had introduced no evidence that the defendants administered it to her. Yet it was the grand jury's decision to charge the defendants only with murder that doomed the prosecution's quest for justice. On June 30, 1882, Judge Miles Granger instructed jurors that they were only to decide if the defendants had murdered Jenny Cramer with arsenic—the accused were not on trial for rape or for telling lies.

The jury acquitted the defendants in less than an hour. Douglass, James, and Walter were freed, but charges that the Malleys had bought their freedom dogged the family for decades. Despite Walter Malley's outspoken desire to discover the real killers, the Cramer case remains unsolved.

—*Tom Smith*

Suggestions for Further Reading

"Jennie Cramer's Death." *New York Times* (June 28, 1882): 1.

McConnell, Virginia A. *Arsenic Under The Elms: Murder In Victorian New Haven.* Westport, Conn.: Praeger Publishing, 1999.

——. *The Beautiful Victim of The Elm City Tragedy.* 2nd ed. New York: M.J. Ivers & Co., 1881.

"The Malleys Acquitted." *New York Times* (July 1, 1882): 5.

Sharon/Hill Divorce and Terry/Field Affair: 1883–1885 & 1887–1890

Sharon v. Hill (Federal Court Appeal) **Plaintiff:** William Sharon (later substituted by Frederick Sharon) **Defendant:** Sarah Althea Hill **Plaintiff Claim:** To cancel and annul the marriage contract between William Sharon and Sarah Althea Hill and to declare the contract a forgery **Chief Lawyers for Plaintiff:** William M. Stewart, Oliver P. Evans **Chief Lawyers for Defendant:** George W. Tyler, W. B. Tyler, David S. Terry **Judges:** Matthew P. Deady, Lorenzo Sawyer **Place:** San Francisco, California **Date of Decision:** December 26, 1885 **Decision:** Marriage contract between William Sharon and Sarah Althea Hill is a forgery and invalid **Cunningham v. Neagle (Supreme Court Appeal in Shooting of David Terry)** **Appellant:** Thomas Cunningham **Appellee:** David Neagle **Chief Lawyers for Appellant:** G. A. Johnson, Zacharias Montgomery **Chief Lawyers for Appellee:** William Henry Harrison Miller, Joseph H. Choate, James C. Carter **Judges:** Samuel F. Miller, Joseph P. Bradley, John M. Harlan, Horace Gray, Samuel Blatchford, Lucius Q. C. Lamar, Melville W. Fuller, David J. Brewer (Stephen F. Field abstained) **Place:** Washington, D.C. **Date of Decision:** April 14, 1890 **Decision:** Neagle was acting within the scope of his duties when he shot David Terry and, therefore, committed no crime

SIGNIFICANCE

When Sarah Althea Hill met U.S. senator William Sharon in 1880, their meeting triggered a series of events that, during the next decade, led to a torrid love affair, Hill's marriage to a notorious knife-carrying judge, the arrest of a U.S. Supreme Court justice for murder, and a series of court cases that included no less than 12 California and federal appellate court decisions.

Sarah Althea Hill met U.S. Senator William Sharon in San Francisco in 1880. She was a 27-year-old (some say 32) beauty from Missouri whose father was a prominent attorney and whose mother was the daughter of a wealthy lumber dealer. Orphaned at a young age, Althea (she preferred her middle name) was raised by her maternal grandfather, educated in a convent, and gained a reputation as a flirt. In turn, Senator Sharon was a 60-year-old multimillionaire and widower whose favorite pastimes included spending time in and out of bed with young women.

A Secret Marriage

Soon after Hill and Sharon met, the senator asked Hill to let him "love her" and offered $500 a month (equal to over $5,000 today) for the privilege. She refused, so Sharon doubled the amount. Hill said no again. Then, according to Hill, Sharon declared that what he really wanted was to marry her. Hill was agreeable to that, but the senator wanted to keep the marriage a secret for two years lest a pregnant woman he once dallied with find out and try to ruin his chances for reelection. The solution was a marriage contract that would, under California law at that time, legally bind Hill and Sharon together in matrimony if they subsequently lived together as man and wife.

Their liaison lasted for about one year, but then the senator tired of his bride and had her evicted from the hotel suite he provided. He also gave her $7,500 for which she signed a receipt indicating that the amount was "payment in full" for "services" rendered.

For the next two years, Hill consulted with fortune-tellers and used various potions and magic powders to win her man back. They briefly reconciled in 1882, but Hill eventually realized that nothing was working and, on September 8, 1883, she had the senator arrested for adultery with another woman. Sharon vehemently denied the allegations, said that he never signed the alleged marriage contract, and claimed that Hill was only trying to blackmail him.

The affair created an immediate sensation, with the public eagerly awaiting every word. After settlement negotiations failed, Sharon filed an action in federal court on October 3 to have the marriage contract declared a forgery. In response, on November 1, Hill filed suit with the California courts seeking a divorce and a division of community property acquired (mostly by Sharon) since the date the contract was signed.

A Long String of Trials Begins

The divorce trial began on March 10, 1884. Shortly afterward, Hill's attorney, George Tyler, hired David Terry as a "special counsel" to assist with the case.

Terry was one of the most colorful individuals in American history. The young Texas lawyer came to California during the 1849 Gold Rush and, eight years later, became the chief justice of the state's supreme court. Within a short time, he was almost hanged by the famous San Francisco Vigilance Committee, had shot a U.S. senator in a duel, and returned to Texas to become a Confederate brigadier general during the Civil War. By 1871, Terry was back in California, where he prospered as an attorney. He also had a volatile temper and was known to frequently carry a bowie knife underneath his vest whenever he entered a courtroom.

The divorce dragged on for several months and the public was enamored with all the titillating details. Sharon testified that the $500 a month he offered Hill was his standard proposal to all of his mistresses. Likewise, Hill admitted that she once hid her friend Nellie in Sharon's bedroom while she and the senator were having sex in the hope that Nellie would overhear Sharon refer to Hill as his "wife."

On Christmas Eve 1884, Judge Jeremiah Sullivan of the California Superior Court granted "Sarah A. Sharon" a divorce, one-half of the community property, $2,500 a month in alimony, and $55,000 in attorneys' fees. That same day, Terry's wife of over 30 years died after a long illness.

Senator Sharon immediately appealed Judge Sullivan's decision and pressed on with his federal forgery lawsuit. Despite objections from Hill's attorneys, the federal court appointed an examiner in early 1885 to hear testimony and collect evidence on the authenticity of the marriage contract. The process lasted six months and it took its toll on Hill. She began to act irrationally, shouted epithets and accusations at virtually everyone in the courtroom, and once pulled a gun on one of Sharon's attorneys. Hill was disarmed, but her actions were brought to the court's attention. On August 5, 1885, Stephen Field, an associate justice of the U.S. Supreme Court, ordered that Hill be disarmed whenever she entered the courtroom. (At this time, Supreme Court judges heard major federal court cases whenever the Court was not in session. In this instance, Field was helping Circuit Court judge Lorenzo Sawyer and District Court judge Matthew Deady, who were presiding over Senator Sharon's lawsuit.)

Although he did not know Hill, Justice Field was a personal and political enemy of David Terry ever since the two sat together on the California Supreme Court nearly 30 years before. Furthermore, it was commonly believed that Terry played a major role behind the 1884 California Democratic State Convention's repudiation of Field that destroyed the judge's candidacy that year for the White House.

Senator Sharon Dies, But the Trials Continue

The examiner's work was completed in August 1885, and his 1,723-page report was sent to Judges Sawyer and Deady. (By this time, Field had returned to Washington, D.C.) Further arguments were made directly to the justices and a decision was to be issued on November 15, but Senator Sharon died on that very day. Ill and in great pain, the senator one week before his death left instructions that the representatives of his estate were to continue the legal battle against Hill.

When the court finally convened on December 26, Sawyer and Deady declared that the marriage contract was a forgery. They also ordered Hill to surrender the document and prohibited her from ever alleging that it was valid and from using it to support any claim (such as her demand for alimony). The court's decision further included this astounding insight as to how the judges weighed the conflicting testimony and evidence from Sharon and Hill:

> . . . the sin of incontinence in a man is compatible with the virtue of veracity, while in the case of a woman, common opinion is otherwise. . . .
>
> . . . it must also be remembered that the plaintiff is a person of long standing and commanding position in this community, of large fortune and manifold business and social relations, and is therefore so far, and by all that these imply, specially bound to speak the truth. . . . On the other hand, the defendant is a comparatively obscure and unimportant person, without property or position in the world. . . . And by this nothing more is meant than that, while a poor and obscure person may be naturally and at heart as truthful as a rich and prominent one, and even more so, nevertheless, other things being equal, property and position are in themselves some certain guaranty of truth in their possessor, for the reason, if none other, that he is thereby rendered more liable and vulnerable to attack on account of any public moral delinquency, and has more to lose if found or thought guilty thereof than one wholly wanting in these particulars.

Twelve days after Sawyer and Deady issued their decision, Terry and Althea Hill were married. It is not known when their romance began, but the union was controversial and it destroyed Terry's standing in California's social circles. When Terry realized this, he became very defensive of his bride. "They shall not brand my wife a strumpet," he repeatedly said.

For two years, the Terrys lived a happy life. The couple believed that the federal court order was not legally binding in light of Sharon's death, so it was neither appealed nor obeyed. In the meantime, Sharon's children continued the appeal of Judge Sullivan's divorce decree. On January 31, 1888, the California Supreme Court, in a 4-3 vote, reaffirmed Sullivan's decisions regarding the marriage and divorce, but reduced the alimony to $500 a month and eliminated the attorneys' fees. (The three dissenting judges concluded that there was no valid marriage to begin with.)

As a consequence of the supreme court's decision, Sharon's family did three things. First, they filed a petition for a retrial of the divorce. When Judge Sullivan denied that petition, they appealed again to the California Supreme Court. Second, the family started to spend enormous amounts to elect some new supreme court judges to ensure a more favorable decision from that bench. Third, they filed a petition in federal court, known as a bill of revivor, to make Sawyer's and Deady's earlier ruling final. Terry filed an objection to that petition and the matter was again before the federal courts.

Pandemonium in the Courthouse

On September 3, 1888, the U.S. Circuit Court for Northern California issued its decision regarding the Sharon family's bill of revivor. Both of the Terrys were present in the courtroom. Neither of them expected a favorable ruling, but when Justice Stephen Field started to personally denounce Althea Terry while reading the court's decision, she stood up and accused the justice of taking a bribe. "Marshall, remove that woman from the courtroom," commanded Field. U.S. Marshall J. C. Franks attempted to do just that and received a slap from Althea. The marshal then grabbed Mrs. Terry's arm, at which point her husband, an adherent of the old southern honor code, roared, "No God damn man shall touch my wife" and knocked Franks to the floor. In the pandemonium that followed, Terry pulled out his bowie knife before several deputies threw him to the floor and put a gun to his head to quiet him down.

The Terrys were both cited for contempt of court and sent to jail; Althea for one month and her husband for six. Justice Field also ordered the local U.S. attorney to prosecute the couple for assault and other charges. David Terry filed a petition to revoke the sentences, but Field denied it. Terry then appealed to the U.S. Supreme Court, but that too was a lost cause. Field even made sure that Terry was not released from the jailhouse a few days early for good behavior.

Events started to really sour for the Terrys. While in jail or shortly afterward, the pregnant Althea suffered a miscarriage. Also, the Terrys were both indicted by a federal grand jury on criminal charges arising out of the incident before Justice Field. Then in May 1889, the U.S. Supreme Court refused to review the order invalidating Althea Terry's marriage contract with Senator Sharon. Finally, in July, with three of the four judges who earlier ruled in Althea's favor now off the bench, the California Supreme Court reversed itself and unanimously held that, because Althea Terry and Sharon had kept their "marriage" a secret, they were never legally married.

Both while imprisoned and after his release, David Terry made several threats to horsewhip Field and slap his face. In the culture of the west that still existed, these comments were an implied challenge to a duel. The newspapers widely printed these comments and the Justice Department in Washington, D.C. discussed them at length. Eventually, Justice Field was assigned a number of secret bodyguards, including David Neagle, one of the deputy marshals who had disarmed Terry the previous September.

A Fateful Train Ride

On August 14, 1889, the Terrys were on a train from Fresno to San Francisco. Unknown to them, Neagle and Field were also on board. At Lathrop, the train stopped long enough that its passengers could have breakfast at a local restaurant. Neagle and Field went in to eat, followed a few minutes later by the Terrys. Althea spotted Field and immediately returned to the train. The restaurant's owner then advised Terry of Field's presence. It is uncertain as to what happened next. According to Field and Neagle, Terry approached Field, violently slapped him across the face two times, and then appeared to be reaching for his famous bowie knife when Neagle jumped to his feet and shot Terry twice. An eyewitness, however, said that Terry did not strike Field, but merely tapped Field on the side of the face to get his attention before Neagle rose and shot Terry. In either case, Terry was dead when he hit the floor. No weapon was found on Terry's body.

As a crowd gathered, Field simply stated that "I am a justice of the Supreme Court of the United States. My name is Judge Field. Judge Terry threatened my life and attacked me and the deputy marshal has shot him." Field and Neagle returned to the train and were on board as it left Lathrop.

Both Field and Neagle were arrested for murder, but Field was quickly released after posting a $5,000 bond. Within a week, political pressure led to the dismissal of the charges against the justice, but the local authorities intended to prosecute his bodyguard. Neagle applied to the federal courts for help. When the U.S. Circuit Court in San Francisco heard the matter, Field was in the courtroom mingling with the witnesses. He was also frequently seen with the presiding judge, Lorenzo Sawyer, whenever the court recessed for lunch or for the night. On September 16, 1889, after a lengthy comment on Terry's "life-long habit of carrying arms," "his angry, murderous threats," "his demoniac looks," and "his stealthy assault upon Justice Field from behind," Sawyer ordered Neagle's release on the grounds that he shot Terry in the line of duty.

Stephen Johnson Field, U.S. Supreme Court justice arrested for murder and later released. (Courtesy, Library of Congress)

Thomas Cunningham, the sheriff of San Joaquin County, California, appealed Sawyer's decision to the U.S. Supreme Court. (Lathrop, where Terry was shot, is in San Joaquin County and it was in Cunningham's jail where Neagle was held after his arrest.) G. A. Johnson, the attorney general of California, was one of the attorneys who presented Cunningham's case. Among those opposing Johnson were the Attorney General of the United States, William Henry Harrison Miller, and Joseph Choate, the country's most famous lawyer and a friend of Justice Field.

Cunningham's entire appeal centered on whether Neagle acted in pursuance of the law when he shot Terry. In 1889, there was no federal statute authorizing security for judges and Neagle's appointment as Field's bodyguard was based solely on a letter from Miller to U.S. marshal J. C. Franks instructing Franks to take steps to protect the judge. The argument was made that this letter alone could not keep Neagle from being indicted for murder. However, on April 14, 1890, in a split six-two decision (with Justice Field abstaining), the Supreme Court held that "any duty of the marshal to be derived from the general scope of his duties under the laws of the United States is 'a law' with the meaning of the phrase." Therefore, since it was within the general scope of Franks' duties to protect Justice Field, then Neagle, as Franks' appointee, was acting "in pursuance of a law of the United States" when he killed Terry. Field's bodyguard was now a free man.

There was one final chapter in the story. Althea Terry still faced federal criminal charges arising from the September 1888 incident before Justice Field. The case went to trial in November 1890, but it ended in a hung jury. Her mind started to go, however, and on March 2, 1892, she was found insane by a state court and committed to an asylum, where she died 45 years later.

—*Mark Thorburn*

Suggestions for Further Reading

Buchanan, A. Russell. *David S. Terry of California: Dueling Judge.* San Marino, Calif.: Huntington Library, 1956.

Lewis, Oscar, and Carroll D. Hall. *Bonanza Inn.* New York: A. A. Knopf, 1939.

Lipsky, Eleazar. *The Devil's Daughter.* New York and Des Moines, Iowa: Meredith Press, 1969.

MacCracken, Brooks W. "Althea and the Judges." *American Heritage* (June 1967): 60–3, 75–9.

Swisher, Carl B. *Stephen J. Field: Craftsman of the Law.* Rev. ed. Chicago: University of Chicago Press, 1969.

Yick Wo v. Hopkins: 1886

Appellant: Yick Wo **Defendant:** Sheriff Peter Hopkins, San Francisco, California **Appellant Claim:** That San Francisco was enforcing an ordinance in an unlawfully discriminatory manner against the defendant and other Chinese persons **Chief Defense Lawyers:** Alfred Clarke and H. G. Sieberst **Chief Lawyers for Appellant:** Hall McAllister, D.L. Smoot, and L.H. Van Schaick **Justices:** Samuel Blatchford, Joseph P. Bradley, Stephen J. Field, Horace Gray, John Marshall Harlan, Stanley Matthews, Samuel F. Miller, Morrison Waite, and William B. Woods **Place:** Washington, D.C. **Date of Decision:** May 10, 1886 **Decision:** That Yick Wo's conviction for violating the ordinance was unconstitutional

SIGNIFICANCE

In *Yick Wo,* the Supreme Court proclaimed that even if a law was nondiscriminatory, enforcing the law in a discriminatory manner was unconstitutional.

On May 26, 1880, the City of San Francisco, California enacted an ordinance requiring all commercial laundries to be in brick or stone buildings. Wooden buildings were permissible, but only with the Board of Supervisors' approval. The ordinance made no distinction between laundries run by Chinese immigrants and those run by whites. However, the ordinance was enforced in a blatantly racist manner. The board rubber-stamped its approval of white petitions to run laundries in wooden buildings, but denied every one of the nearly 200 Chinese petitions.

Sheriff Peter Hopkins enforced the ordinance, arresting Yick Wo and over 150 other Chinese persons who continued to run laundries in wooden buildings without board approval. Yick Wo was convicted and ordered to pay a fine of $10 or spend 10 days in jail. The California Supreme Court upheld his conviction, and he appealed to the U.S. Supreme Court for an order preventing San Francisco in the person of Sheriff Hopkins from carrying out the sentence. Hopkins was represented by Alfred Clarke and H.G. Sieberst and Yick Wo was represented by Hall McAllister, D.L. Smoot and L. H. Van Schaick. The Supreme Court heard both sides' arguments on April 14, 1886 and issued its decision on May 10, 1886.

The Court reversed Yick Wo's conviction, holding that the ordinance was being unfairly administered:

> Though the law itself be fair on its face and impartial in appearance, yet, if it is applied and administered by public authority with an evil eye and an unequal hand, so as practically to make unjust and illegal discriminations between persons in similar circumstances, material to their rights, the denial of equal justice is still within the prohibition of the Constitution. . . .

And while this consent of the supervisors is withheld from [Yick Wo] and from two hundred others who have also petitioned, all of whom happen to be Chinese subjects, eighty others, not Chinese subjects, are permitted to carry on the same business under similar conditions. The fact of this discrimination is admitted. No reason for it is shown, and the conclusion cannot be resisted, that no reason for it exists except hostility to the race and nationality to which the petitioners belong.

The significance of the *Yick Wo* decision is that, even if a law is nondiscriminatory, enforcing the law in a discriminatory manner is unconstitutional.

—*Stephen G. Christianson*

Suggestions for Further Reading

Nelson, William Edward. *The Fourteenth Amendment: From Political Principle to Judicial Doctrine.* Cambridge, Mass.: Harvard University Press, 1988.

Pole, J. R. *The Pursuit of Equality in American History.* Berkeley: University of California Press, 1978.

Haymarket Trial: 1886

Defendants: George Engel, Samuel Fielden, Adolph Fischer, Louis Lingg, Oscar Neebe, Albert Parsons, Michael Schwab, and August Spies
Crime Charged: Murder **Chief Defense Lawyers:** William P. Black, William A. Foster, Moses Salomon, and Sigismund Zeisler **Chief Prosecutor:** Julius S. Grinnell **Judge:** Joseph E. Gary **Place:** Chicago, Illinois
Dates of Trial: June 21–August 20, 1886 **Verdict:** Guilty
Sentence: Death by hanging for all but Neebe, who was sentenced to prison for 15 years

SIGNIFICANCE

The Haymarket Riot was one of the most famous confrontations between the growing labor movement and the conservative forces of industry and government. Eight police officers were killed in a bomb explosion during the Haymarket affair. The resulting public backlash against the labor movement was a serious setback for the unions and their efforts to improve industrial working conditions.

After the Civil War, the United States experienced a period of unparalleled industrial growth that lasted for decades. It was a time when men became famous building new industries and businesses, establishing great corporate empires in the process. Among them were John D. Rockefeller's Standard Oil, which dominated the new petroleum industry; Andrew Carnegie's Carnegie Steel (later U.S. Steel), which revolutionized open-hearth steel technology and became the industry leader; and Marshall Field, named for its founder, which changed retailing from a multitude of mom-and-pop operations into an industry dominated by a handful of giants. However, the wealthy few who controlled this industrial development and its riches did not share their gains with the workers who made their terrific success possible.

By the 1880s, America's rapid industrialization had not yet produced any significant change in the legal relationship between workers and employers. Under the common law, inherited from England, any worker or laborer was free to negotiate individually with his employer concerning his wages, working hours and conditions, and other benefits. This may have been fine for the medieval English guilds whose practices shaped this aspect of the common law, but it was hopelessly out of touch with the realities of the modern industrial workplace. By the 1880s, American business was dominated by companies that employed large numbers of workers in factories, stores, mills, and other workplaces.

An individual worker's right to "negotiate" his wages was thus meaningless. Immigrants from abroad and American migration from the farms to the cities swelled the labor force available to industrial employers. Any worker who complained about his or her wages, sought better hours, or wanted benefits such as sick leave or compensation for on-the-job injuries could be easily replaced.

Police, U.S. military soldiers and firefighters attempting to control the chaos brought on by the Haymarket riots. (Courtesy, Library of Congress)

The only way for workers to improve their lives was to band together, "to unionize," so that one organization representing the combined workforce could compel management to make concessions. Naturally, companies resisted, and relations between the budding union movement and management became strained and often violent. Because unionists saw the government as an ally of big business in oppressing workers, many unionists were attracted to the political ideology of anarchism, which sought to do away with government.

Chicago: Hotbed of Radicalism

Little more than a village when it was founded in the 1830s, by the 1880s, Chicago was one of America's industrial hubs. Jobs brought immigrants from central and eastern Europe to the city. Many of these same immigrants, dissatisfied with their lot, joined the labor movement and embraced anarchism. One of the most vocal members of the labor movement was August Spies, the editor of a German-language newspaper who was deeply involved in the union and anarchist movements.

In 1886, the efforts of unions in general, and Spies in particular, were focused on the struggle to enforce an eight-hour workday. Most businesses insisted on a 10-hour workday, and even longer shifts were common. Labor demanded that management reduce the workday to eight hours, while keeping the daily wage the same. On the great holiday of labor, May 1, or May Day, unions staged nationwide demonstrations in favor of the eight-hour workday. Two days later, on May 3, Spies spoke before the striking workers of the McCormick farm machinery works. Fights broke out between the strikers and the "scab" workers hired to replace them. The police intervened, firing into the crowd of strikers, killing two and wounding many.

Spies promptly publicized the incident in his newspaper, and called for a rally against police brutality at Chicago's Haymarket Square the next day. At first, the meeting proceeded peacefully. Chicago's Mayor, Carter Harrison, showed up briefly so that he would be seen by working-class voters. After Spies spoke and Harrison had left, however, the situation rapidly deteriorated. Two of Spies' fellow anarchists, Samuel Fielden and Albert Parsons, spoke to the gathered workers and lashed out at business, government, and the Chicago police.

Intending to end the meeting and disperse the crowd, Chicago police Captain John Bonfield, who was present with nearly 200 men, ordered his officers to advance toward the crowd. Suddenly, someone in the crowd threw a bomb made of dynamite at the police. The powerful explosion killed eight policemen and wounded 67 others. Furious, the police retaliated. They fired into the crowd, killing or wounding dozens of people.

Police Arrest Eight Anarchists

Both the police and labor had been responsible for loss of life since the May Day rallies. After the Haymarket bomb explosion, however, public reaction was overwhelmingly against the unions. A major Chicago newspaper ran the headline, "NOW IT IS BLOOD!" and yellow journalism fanned public fears of anarchist-, socialist-, and communist-inspired union violence. Despite widespread searches and raids of working-class neighborhoods, however, the police never found the bomber.

Prosecutor Julius S. Grinnell, the Illinois state's attorney charged with finding Haymarket culprits, needed people to prosecute. When the police started to arrest known anarchists in the labor movement, beginning with Samuel Fielden, Michael Schwab, and August Spies the day after the riot, Grinnell supported the arrests. Encouraged by Grinnell, the police arrested five more labor anarchists: George Engel, Adolph Fischer, Louis Lingg, Oscar Neebe, and Albert Parsons. On May 27, 1886, all eight men were charged with murder.

Because of the public outcry, at first the defendants had trouble finding attorneys to represent them. Although Chicago's Central Labor Union arranged for their attorneys, Moses Salomon, and Sigismund Zeisler, to represent the defendants, neither man was an experienced criminal lawyer. Eventually, however, the experienced lawyers William P. Black and William A. Foster joined the defense team. Judge Joseph E. Gary was assigned to preside over the case, which opened June 21, 1886.

Jury selection occupied the first three weeks of the trial. A total of 981 potential jurors were questioned until 12 were finally selected. There have been accusations that Judge Gary used his influence to ensure the jury favored the prosecution. Since none of the jurors worked in a factory, they were not expected to be sympathetic to the union cause, which was really on trial.

Prosecutor Grinnell's tactic was to try to prove that the defendants had conspired not only to attack the police during the Haymarket rally, but also had conspired to create anarchy by overthrowing all government authority. Grinnell's courtroom rhetoric was as expansive as his accusations:

> For the first time in the history of our country are people on trial for endeavoring to make anarchy the rule, and in that attempt for ruthlessly and awfully destroying human life. I hope that while the youngest of us lives this in memory will be the last and only time in our country when such a trial will take place.

Grinnell brought forward several witnesses, all of whom gave poor testimony. They could only testify that the defendants at various times had made inflammatory, pro-anarchist, pro-union statements. Damning as this testimony was to some sectors of the public, it did not prove conspiracy, much less murder. Zeisler for the defense attempted to expose the weakness of the prosecution's evidence:

> It is not only necessary to establish that the defendants were parties to a conspiracy, but it is also necessary to show that somebody who was a party to that conspiracy had committed an act in pursuance of that conspiracy. Besides, it is essential that the State should identify the principal. . . . If the principal is not identified, then no one could be held as accessory.

Judge Gary ruled, however, that if the jury believed the defendants were guilty *beyond a reasonable doubt* of conspiracy to attack the police or overthrow the government, then the jury could also find the defendants guilty of murder. Also, the jury merely had to find *beyond a reasonable doubt* that the defendants arranged for someone to throw the bomb. According to Judge Gary's instructions to the jury, it did not matter that no one had found the bomb thrower.

Judge Gary's interpretation of the law was the final blow. On August 20, 1886, the jury pronounced its verdict. The jury found all eight defendants guilty and gave each the death penalty, except for Neebe, who was sentenced to 15 years in jail. The public and press applauded, and most papers carried glowing accounts of Grinnell's successful prosecution. Despite the efforts of amnesty groups, assisted by a young but soon-to-be-famous lawyer named Clarence Darrow, on September 14, 1887, the Illinois Supreme Court upheld the death sentence. A final appeal to the U. S. Supreme Court was also unsuccessful: on

November 2, 1887, the Supreme Court held that because no principle of federal law was involved, it could not rule on the case.

The convicted men had thus exhausted all their conventional legal avenues of appeal. Lingg committed suicide before his scheduled execution. On November 11, 1887, Engel, Fischer, Parsons, and Spies were hung. Fielden, Neebe, and Schwab sat in jail, Neebe serving out his sentence and the others awaiting execution. Luckily for the condemned men, their stay in prison lasted for years. In the interim, the liberal politician John Peter Altgeld was elected governor of Illinois. On June 26, 1893, Altgeld pardoned Fielden, Neebe, and Schwab. The three left prison as free men.

The Haymarket Riot began with a political confrontation and ended with another political confrontation. Altgeld's pardon made him a political pariah, and in the next gubernatorial election he was soundly defeated. Nevertheless, Altgeld's pardon helped to legitimize labor's claim that the trial had been unfair from start to finish and that Judge Gary had been biased.

—*Stephen G. Christianson*

Suggestions for Further Reading

Avrich, Paul. *The Haymarket Tragedy.* Princeton, N.J.: Princeton University Press, 1984.

David, Henry. *The History of the Haymarket Affair.* NewYork:Russell & Russell, 1958.

Foner, Philip S. *The Autobiographies of the Haymarket Martyrs.* New York: Anchor Foundation, 1978.

Ginger, Ray. *Altgeld's America.* Chicago: Quadrangle Books, 1958.

Haymarket Remembered Project Staff. *Mob Action Against the State: The Haymarket Remembered . . . an Anarchist Convention.* Seattle: Left Bank Books, 1987.

Nelson, Bruce C. *Beyond the Martyrs: A Social History of Chicago's Anarchists, 1870–1900.* New Brunswick, N.J.: Rutgers University Press, 1988.

Roediger, David and Franklin Rosemont, eds. *Haymarket Scrapbook: A Centennial Anthology.* Chicago: C.H. Kerr, 1986.

Vosburg v. Putney: 1890

Plaintiff: Andrew Vosburg **Defendant:** George Putney
Plaintiff Claim: That defendant kicked plaintiff and otherwise ill-treated him, thereby making plaintiff ill, causing great pain and mental anguish, and leaving him permanently crippled **Chief Defense Lawyers:** Milton Griswold, Theron Haight **Chief Lawyers for Plaintiff:** Ernst Merton, Timothy Edward Ryan **Judge:** Andrew Scott Sloan **Place:** Waukesha, Wisconsin
Date of Trial: January 15–17, 1890 **Verdict:** Defendant was liable for injury to plaintiff **Award:** $2,800 plus court costs

SIGNIFICANCE

This seemingly petty trial in an obscure courtroom, little known to most Americans even in its own day, is one of the classic landmark cases in American legal history—and therefore well known to all law students. Its importance lies not only in its implications for the branch of civil law known as tort—specifically, the laws that deal with the recovery of payments for unintended and unforeseeable harm—but also for other issues raised by the series of legal battles that ensued.

By 1889, the village of Waukesha, Wisconsin, just outside Milwaukee, had become known as the "Saratoga of the West" after the curative powers of its local spring water were discovered. While life in Waukesha was more bustling than its location suggested thanks to the wealthy visitors who flocked to its spas, it was an unlikely setting for a spate of litigation that would result in legal doctrine still scrutinized by law students today. The personal injury lawsuit—so often demonized in the shape of the hospital-chasing lawyer today—might have been foreign to the Waukesha litigants. However, the personal drama that unfolded in the Vosburg trials suggests that something in the American experience was ripe for the growth of this area of the law.

It was for work that Seth Vosburg, father of three, located his family to Waukesha, and shortly after their arrival he took on a teamster's job with Barker Lumber Company. His eldest son, Andrew, was enrolled in the highly regarded Union School, the oldest permanent school in the village. Andrew had suffered successive childhood illnesses and in January 1889 had injured his leg in a sledding accident. Despite his physical weakness, Andrew was expected to complete his chores and contribute to the livelihood of his family.

Also enrolled at the Union School was George Putney, son of a prosperous Waukesha family. George had already tried to bully Andrew out of possession of a schoolbook when an incident between the two boys would earn them a place in America's legal canon.

A Kick Rebounds

On February 20, 1889, after the noon recess had ended and the school bell rang, the seventh-grade class at the Union School took their seats. George, just shy of 12, and Andrew, now fifteen, sat across an aisle from one another and, just before the class was to begin, George swung his leg across the aisle and with his foot touched Andrew's injured leg below the knee. Whether George was standing or sitting, and whether he tapped Andrew lightly or kicked him, will never be known for sure. In any case, Andrew said nothing at the moment. It was not until some minutes later that Andrew burst into tears and had to be let out of the classroom.

By the time he left for home that day, Andrew was limping, and the next day he was in too much pain to remain at school. A few days later, after the condition of Andrew's leg had worsened and he was bedridden with fever, Dr. Joshua Bacon was called. Following a house call, Dr. Bacon called in Dr. Solon Marks from Milwaukee and Dr. Hugo Philler from Waukesha to consult. Dr. Philler became one of Andrew's primary care physicians.

By March 8, Drs. Bacon and Philler agreed that Andrew required surgery, which they performed while Andrew was etherized. On March 15, a second operation was performed, this time with the assistance of Dr. Benjamin Jacob. After cutting into the leg, the doctors expected to scrape the bone. Instead, they found the bone had decayed so drastically that to do so would have crumbled it. Only the pleading of Andrew's father, Seth, saved Andrew from amputation during this second operation.

It appeared that Andrew would be crippled for life. Having lost the labor of their eldest son and too poor to cover the mounting medical expenses, the Vosburgs retained Timothy Ryan and Ernst Merton, local law partners. The Putneys had in fact offered to reimburse the Vosburgs for the medical bills but Seth Vosburg felt that the sum was insufficient. Who first proposed it was never made known, but the Vosburgs decided to bring both a criminal suit and a civil action against George Putney.

"A Peculiar Suit"

Prior to the first trial for the civil suit, George Putney was brought up on the criminal charge of misdemeanor assault. In small towns in those days, minor criminal cases did not require full-scale trials but were heard by justices of the peace and quickly disposed of. On October 22, 1889, the boy was arrested, tried, and convicted by a justice of the peace, Alonzo Tyler. He was ordered to pay a fine of $10, but an appeal was filed immediately (although it appears that young

Putney actually spent one night in the local jail). Represented by Theron Haight, Putney's conviction was overturned on appeal, apparently on account of George's young age.

Meanwhile, a civil action had been filed on behalf of Andrew Vosburg against the now 12-year-old Putney. *Andrew Vosburg v. George Putney* came to trial on January 15, 1890, in the Waukesha County Court House, before Judge Andrew Sloan. The case had already received considerable attention in the Waukesha newspaper, and the story was now newsworthy as far away as Milwaukee. Most likely, too, the relative prominence and wealth of the Putney family further highlighted the dramatic story line in the dispute between young George and the unfortunate Andrew Vosburg.

Andrew Vosburg and his seventh-grade teacher were the first called to testify. The teacher, however, was not of much help as she seemed unwilling to say she had witnessed the actual kick. Andrew's attorneys sought to rest their case on the liability rule of "trespass" on Andrew's person, seeing no need to establish any malicious intent on George's part. The defense, however, suggested that intent mattered, and asked George whether he intended to hurt Andrew. George claimed that the reason he tapped Andrew on the shin was that, "I wanted his attention, wanted to get him to look around." Judge Sloan seemed satisfied that the plaintiff had not made a claim of intent on George's part to do injury, and reduced the case to one of causation.

By this time it was well known to all concerned that Andrew's right leg had been injured prior to the incident in a sledding accident. Vosburg's lawyers had to establish, then, that Andrew's current crippled state was not merely the result of his earlier injury and that the kick by George was not simply responsible for speeding the course of an inevitable illness in Andrew's leg. In other words, they had to establish that even a minor tap by George could have triggered the crippling disease, and that it was the kick, in fact, that left Andrew lame.

Vosburg's case relied heavily on expert testimony from Drs. Bacon and Philler, who testified that they believed George's kick to have been the "exciting" cause of Andrew's illness. While they conceded that it took only a light tap to injure the bone, they insisted that it was the trauma of the "kick" that led to his ultimate disability. These doctors, early adherents to germ theory, argued that while germs were present in Andrew's leg prior to the kick, they required some exciting cause to grow.

The case was closed on January 16, after two days of testimony. The defense wanted to instruct the jury in a manner that would require them to take into account the ordinary nature of the incident between these two schoolboys. This suggested that without any intent to do harm, George should not be held liable for the unforeseen injuries resulting from an innocent tap. They also wanted to instruct the jury that germs would have grown with or without George's kick. Judge Sloan rejected the defense counsel's instructions, and instead used an analogy for the jury: "If in reaching over to the clerk, in passing a book or paper, I hit this ink stand and knock that over and strike him on the head and produce a serious injury, it would be an unavoidable accident; but if I shove it over knowingly, consciously, then the law comes in and says I am liable for all the necessary, natural consequences of the act." Since there was no question that George had acted knowingly and consciously, the question for the jury was simply whether the kick was the cause of Andrew's condition.

After deliberating all night, the jury found for the plaintiff and awarded damages in the amount of $2,800. To modern ears accustomed to multimillion-dollar awards, this judgment sounds almost ludicrous. Although the sum was about four times Seth Vosburg's annual wages, it could not have been that big a strain on the Putney family. One might assume that this ended the matter.

Litigation Continues

Instead, the Putneys saw it as a matter of principle and so the verdict in the original trial of Andrew Vosburg versus George Putney was only the beginning of what turned into years of litigation between the two families. First, the Putneys appealed the decision in the original trial. Their appeal was heard before the Supreme Court of Wisconsin on October 20, 1890, and in a decision issued by Justice Harlow Orton on November 5, 1890, the verdict was reversed on error and remanded for a retrial. After all of the wrangling by both sides over the issue of intent, the reversal was premised on a technicality over the admissibility of evidence.

The case was then retried before Judge Sloan on November 14, 1890. The cast of characters and the issues were much the same, but the tone in the courtroom was considerably more contentious. This time the Putneys placed family members and friends on the stand to testify that Andrew had been limping long before the day of the incident. The Vosburgs disputed this and also the Putneys' claim that Mrs. Vosburg had specifically told them that Andrew had not suffered from the kicking incident. Despite the Putneys' vigorously mounted defense, the jury again came back with a verdict for the plaintiff, and awarded damages in the amount of $2,500.

The Putneys again appealed, and the case was argued before the Wisconsin Supreme Court on October 26, 1891. Extremely complex arguments regarding theories of negligence and the Vosburgs' contributory negligence—for not dealing with Andrew's medical problems properly—were raised by the Putneys' lawyers. The Vosburgs' attorneys instead stressed that the rule of law was well established: An individual who committed a wrongful act was liable for all direct injury resulting from the act, even when the injury was unforeseeable. The Putneys' lawyer also introduced a new argument, claiming that upholding the verdict "will render every schoolboy in Wisconsin guilty of assault and battery a dozen times a day."

Despite the ingenious arguments by both sides, the verdict in the second trial was reversed on a technicality, just as the first had been. The decision, written by Justice William Penn Lyon, did not dispute the liability rule promoted by the Vosburgs. Rather, the trial judge had failed to sustain an objection to a question posed to Dr. Philler during his testimony, and the error warranted reversal of the judgment.

Meanwhile, Seth Vosburg had also taken young George Putney to court in a separate civil suit to recover the expenses incurred by his family and the anticipated costs of Andrew's future problems. The jury found for the father and awarded him $1,200, and this judgment was upheld on appeal. But after one criminal trial, three civil trials, and four appeals, it appears that all parties ran out of steam. In fact, it has never been clear just how much if any money was exchanged between the Vosburgs or the Putneys; because of the court costs assigned in the various trials and appeals, one expert has calculated that the Vosburgs actually ended up owing the Putneys some $770! As for Andrew Vosburg, although he wore a laced leather brace on his injured leg that somewhat limited his activities, he led a quite normal life, dying at age 64. The case, which appeals court Judge Orton had called "very strange and extraordinary," still challenges law students to untangle its complexities and their implications on the practice of law.

—*Michael Bowman*

Suggestions for Further Reading

Henderson, James A., Jr. "Why Vosburg Comes First." *Wisconsin Law Review* (1992): 853ff.

Rabin, Robert. "The Historical Development of the Fault Principle: A Reinterpretation." *Georgia Law Review* (1981): 925 ff.

Zile, Zigurds L. "Vosburg v. Putney: A Centennial Story." *Wisconsin Law Review* (1992): 877 ff.

Dr. Mary Amanda Dixon Jones Trials: 1890 & 1892

Defendants: Mary Amanda Dixon Jones, Charles Dixon Jones
Crimes Charged: Manslaughter, medical malpractice
Chief Defense Lawyer: Richard S. Newcombe **Chief Prosecutor:** James A. Ridgway **Judge:** Willard Bartlett **Place:** Brooklyn, New York
Date of Trial: February 17, 1890–February 23, 1890 **Verdict:** Mary Amanda Dixon Jones: not guilty; Charles Dixon Jones: directed acquittal
Libel case Jones v. *Brooklyn Eagle*, February–March 1892
Defendant: *Brooklyn Eagle* **Plaintiff:** Mary Amanda Dixon Jones
Plaintiff Claim: $150,000 **Chief Defense Lawyer (for *Eagle*):** Mr. Dykman
Chief Lawyer for Plaintiff: Charles A. Jackson **Judge:** Willard Bartlett
Place: Brooklyn, New York **Date of Trial:** February 1–March 12, 1892

SIGNIFICANCE

The trials of Dr. Mary Amanda Dixon Jones focused attention on the state of surgical practice, the role of women in medicine and the professions more generally, issues of class and status, and the power of the popular press to focus public concern on scandals.

Dr. Mary Amanda Dixon Jones had established the first women's hospital in Brooklyn, New York, when it was still a separate city, proud of its reputation as a family-oriented, churchgoing pure city in contrast to crime-ridden New York. Middle-class women in Brooklyn participated actively in charitable activities and were avid readers of newspapers.

In 1889, the daily *Brooklyn Eagle* launched a series of articles denouncing the medical practice of Dr. Dixon Jones, claiming her malpractice amounted to manslaughter in several cases. Further, the articles claimed that she conducted experiments on helpless women, unnecessarily removing organs for her own scientific study. The paper charged her with secretly concealing deaths at her hospital, mismanaging funds at the hospital, and mishandling surgical practice so badly that many of her patients were rendered incapable of having children, were disfigured, or died as a result.

The sensational series of articles soon led a competing newspaper, the *Citizen*, to publish a set of countercharges. That newspaper claimed the *Eagle* simply sought to discredit a decent woman and a leading physician in order to increase circulation and to create scandal where none existed.

The newspaper crusade evoked many themes current in the popular mind of the 1880s and 1890s in the United States. Medical practice and surgery was evolving, but public faith in medicine was shaky. Women entered medical practice in fairly large numbers in the late nineteenth century, leading to very mixed feelings. On the one hand, the profession appeared to coincide with the popular concept that the female gender was particularly suited to the care-giving nature of medicine. On the other hand, some male doctors and many members of the public regarded female doctors with suspicion. Women in traditionally male roles had to behave with circumspection, maintaining a ladylike demeanor.

Mary Amanda Dixon Jones did not quite conform to that stereotype, with an often abrasive and imperious manner. Furthermore, even her supporters agreed that she did not always communicate well with patients, often failing to explain risks associated with certain procedures.

Able Doctor or "Difficult Woman"?

Born in 1828 on the Eastern Shore of Maryland to the family of a Methodist minister, Mary Dixon Jones graduated from Wesleyan Female College in Wilmington Delaware, in 1845. She stayed on there and taught physiology and literature for two years and then moved to the Baltimore Female College, and then became principal of a girls' seminary in southern Maryland. She began reading medicine under two doctors, a standard method of medical education in that era. In 1854, she married a lawyer, John Quincy Adams Jones, and the couple lived briefly in Illinois and Wisconsin.

In 1862, Dixon Jones formally studied medicine in New York City, receiving a degree from the Hygeio Therapeutic Medical College. After the Civil War, she settled in Brooklyn and established a small medical practice. In 1872, at the age of 44, Dixon Jones entered Women's Medical College of Pennsylvania in Philadelphia for a three-year term of study, with special training in surgery. Returning to Brooklyn, she reopened her medical practice and founded the hospital that soon became the center of the newspaper exposé.

The Manslaughter Case

In the face of increasing public outcry over the newspaper series, the district attorney brought charges of manslaughter against Dixon Jones and her son, Charles Dixon Jones, in February 1890. She was charged with two manslaughter counts and eight malpractice suits. However, the trial centered around only one of the manslaughter cases, based on an episode reported in the *Eagle.*

In that case, a woman patient, Ida Hunt, had died after being removed to her home following an operation to remove her diseased ovaries. Her parents, husband and the newspaper claimed that Mrs. Hunt had not desired the operation, and when it was bungled, Dixon Jones prematurely sent her home. The carriage ride home led to her death the next day. In defense, Dixon Jones provided expert witnesses who testified to her medical reputation and education, to the standards of medicine at the time, and to the fact that Mrs. Hunt suffered a diseased set of ovaries from a venereal infection caught from her husband. Further witnesses testified that Mrs. Hunt and her husband both insisted on her removal from the hospital. So if her short stay and trip home contributed to her death, the decision was not the doctor's but the patient's.

The judge directed the jury to acquit Charles Dixon Jones for lack of evidence early in the trial. The jury returned a not guilty verdict on Mary Dixon Jones. Although Mary Dixon Jones and her husband had lived separately for many years, he attended her manslaughter trial, and then died of heart failure shortly after the verdict was announced.

The Libel Suit

Despite her acquittal, the publicity and the trial had resulted in a decline in Dixon Jones' medical practice, and she decided to bring a libel suit for $150,000 in damages against the *Eagle.* In light of her earlier acquittal on the manslaughter charges, many observers, including the editors of the *Citizen,* expected the *Eagle* to settle out of court. However, the publishers of the *Eagle* refused to make an offer, and Dr. Dixon Jones refused to drop the libel charge.

The libel case was heard over a period of six weeks in a dreary and freezing courtroom in downtown Brooklyn in February and March 1892. Public attendance at the trial and steady newspaper coverage made the trial a *cause celebre.* The defense introduced 118 witnesses to confirm the charges that had appeared in the *Eagle.* By presenting witness after witness who showed that the general thrust of the newspaper's charges had been well-founded, the defense attorneys hoped to convince the 12-man jury that the evidence mitigated any errors in the newspaper charges. That defense would allow the jury to find for a reduced or nominal financial award.

When attorneys for Dixon Jones presented her case, over 69,000 words of printed material was read into the record, a document the size of a short novel, containing the alleged libelous material. Her attorneys again brought expert witnesses who testified to her skill and reputation as a physician. However, when Dixon Jones took the stand, her own testimony worked against her. Her short temper and disregard for the judge's instructions on how to answer questions appeared to confirm to jurors that she was not the motherly, caring doctor that her lawyers had suggested. Quite the opposite—she appeared calm and unmoved by horrendous testimony of the agonies of former patients. Her apparent arrogance and hostility only strengthened the case of the newspaper's attorneys that she was a "difficult woman," and her manner appeared to work against her with the all-male jury.

After 37 hours of deliberation, the jury rendered a verdict for the newspaper. Although she had been exonerated of the manslaughter charges in her 1890 trial, the effect of the 1892 libel trial was to suggest that the general thrust of the newspaper's charges against her had substance. Her medical practice was destroyed. She retired and moved to New York City with her son, Charles.

Dr. Dixon Jones continued to write, and in 1894, she became an associate editor of the *Women's Medical Journal.* She died in 1908, at the age of 80.

—*Rodney Carlisle*

Suggestion for Further Reading

Regina Morantz-Sanchez. *Conduct Unbecoming a Woman: Medicine on Trial in Turn of the Century Brooklyn.* New York: Oxford University Press, 1999.

The New Orleans "Mafia" Trial: 1891

Defendants: Antonio Bagnetto, James Caruso, John Caruso, Loretto Comitz, Rocco Geraci, Bastian Incardona, Joseph P. Macheca, Antonio Marchesi, Gasperi Marchesi, Charles Matranga, Pietro Monasterio, Pietro Natali, Charles Patorno, Charles Pietzo, Emmanuelle Polizzi, Frank Romero, Antonio Scaffidi, Salvatore Sunzeri, and Charles Traina **Crimes Charged:** Shooting with intent to murder, lying in wait to murder **Chief Defense Lawyers:** Lionel Adams, Charles Butler, John Q. Flynn, Arthur Gastinel, A.D. Henriques, Thomas J. Semmes, and Charles Theard **Chief Prosecutors:** W.L. Evans, Charles H. Luzenberg, and James C. Walker **Judge:** Joshua G. Baker **Place:** New Orleans, Louisiana **Dates of Trial:** February 16–March 13, 1891 **Verdicts:** Scaffidi, Polizzi, and Monasterio: mistrials; Macheca, Matranga, Bagnetto, Incardona, and Antonio and Gasperi Marchesi: not guilty; Natali, Pietzo, Patorno, Sunzeri, and John and James Caruso: charges dismissed

SIGNIFICANCE

The acquittals and mistrial verdicts provoked the worst mass lynching in U.S. history and made the word "Mafia" part of the American vernacular.

On the misty night of October 15, 1890, New Orleans, Louisiana, Police Superintendent David Hennessy was fatally shot in an ambush a block from his home. The dying man's whispers would cause the most controversial trial ever held in New Orleans courts and provoke the most notorious international political incident of the Gilded Age. They would also make "Mafia" a household word in America for the very first time.

Who Killed the Chief?

In May 1890, stevedores of the Matranga & Locasio fruit importing company were ambushed at midnight on their way home from the New Orleans docks. Information was rarely volunteered by crime victims in the Italian immigrant community and, at first, this shooting was no different. However, after first denying that they had recognized their attackers, the stevedores fingered six men. The accused included members of the Provenzano family, who had lost the fruit-unloading work to Matranga & Locasio.

When the "midnight vendetta" trial came to court "Chief" Hennessy's men were strangely absent from the prosecution's case. In fact, most police witnesses were called by the inept defense lawyers. Two Provenzano brothers and the other four defendants were convicted and sentenced to life in prison. Yet Judge Joshua Baker ordered a retrial when affidavits surfaced from witnesses who heard the wounded stevedores say at the ambush scene that they had no idea who had shot them. Baker also ruled that "disinterested" testimony by police officers proved that two of the accused were elsewhere when the shooting occurred.

Popular interest in the "midnight vendetta" faded, but those watching the case closely believed that Chief Hennessy himself would take the stand on the Provenzanos' behalf in late October. When he was gunned down a few days before the retrial date, many people assumed that he had been silenced by the Matrangas. Little attention was given to the fact that the coming trial was no secret, giving anyone with a grudge against the chief a perfect opportunity to throw the blame on the city's Italians and Italian-Americans.

At the crime scene and at the hospital Hennessy gasped that "dagoes" had shot him. Friends repeatedly asked him to identify or describe his attackers, but he lived until the next morning without doing so. The dying man was taken at his word. Mass arrests, forced searches, and beatings shook the immigrant community.

Nineteen men were ultimately charged with planning or executing Hennessy's murder. Charles Matranga and Joseph P. Macheca were well-to-do fruit importers. James and John Caruso belonged to Matranga's dock crew, as did Rocco Geraci and Bastian Incardona, two of the men ambushed the previous spring. Most of the accused were poor men whose arrests were based on circumstantial evidence or outright hysteria. Pietro Monasterio, a shoemaker, was clubbed and arrested because Hennessy's killers had fired from a gateway beside his shack. Pietro Natali was arrested at the railway station "on suspicion" because his suit fit him badly.

To reduce the number of pretrial challenges, two successive trials were planned. The first nine defendants were Macheca, Matranga, Monasterio, Incardona, Antonio Scaffidi, Antonio Bagnetto, Emmanuelle Polizzi, Antonio Marchesi, and Marchesi's 14-year-old son, Gasperi. With the exception of Charles Patorno, who hired his own counsel, the accused were collectively represented by Adams & Henriques, the same law firm the district attorney's office had allowed to help prosecute the Provenzanos in the "midnight vendetta" shooting.

Absent Conspiracy, Missing Witnesses

Lionel Adams was a brilliant former New Orleans district attorney. Ironically, he had once successfully defended David Hennessy on the charge of killing the chief of detectives when Hennessy was a young cop. Ten years later, Adams was hired by the men accused of murdering Hennessy.

Adams tangled the state's case with challenges throughout the winter of 1890. He successfully had all 19 murder indictments thrown out by charging that an unauthorized stenographer was allowed into the grand-jury room during the questioning of witnesses. New indictments were quickly drawn, but Adams immediately submitted a motion to quash them, too. He argued that the grand jury was biased because it contained two members of a "Committee of Fifty" appointed by the mayor to investigate the Hennessy killing. Adams unsuccessfully subpoenaed the mayor and the entire Committee of Fifty, as well as their confidential minutes and affidavits. Officials interviewed 780 "talesmen," or potential jurors before an acceptable jury was found. Prosecutors were expected to present a clear case when testimony began February 28. Things went less smoothly in the courtroom. None of the State's witnesses could agree on whether the streetlight at the scene was burning brightly or nearly extinct when the shooting began in the misty darkness.

Laborer Zachary Foster swore that Scaffidi, Polizzi, Monasterio, and Antonio Marchesi were "like the ones" he saw shooting at Hennessy. The chief's neighbors agreed that the gun battle was brief, but a young bartender named John Daure claimed to have run four blocks in time to see Scaffidi, Bagnetto, and Antonio Marchesi firing. House painter M.L. Peeler said he saw the shooting from an upstairs gallery. Peeler identified Scaffidi, but testimony suggested painter was drunk at the time. A police officer claimed to have recognized Emmanuelle Polizzi by the back of his head from over a block away.

The courtroom tension was too much for the man newspapers called "Manuel Politz." Polizzi became hysterical, causing attorney Charles Theard to quit the case. Judge Baker replaced Theard with John Q. Flynn, who applied himself to the case more diligently than his predecessor. Four days later, however, Polizzi tried to dive through the sheriff's office window. The press theorized that Polizzi had confessed and was deathly afraid of the other defendants.

District Attorney Charles Luzenberg claimed he would prove a conspiracy in which Chief Hennessy was killed for meddling in the Matranga-Provenzano feud. Joseph Macheca was accused of renting the shack where Monasterio lived, thus arranging an ambush to be carried out by hired assassins. Witnesses of varying degrees of reliability identified Scaffidi, Monasterio, Polizzi, Bagnetto, and the elder Marches as the shooters. Yet spectators waiting for details of the alleged plot were disappointed.

In the months after Hennessy's murder, newspapers remained well stocked with stories about cruel Sicilian brigands, the Committee of Fifty's mandate to "root out foreign murder societies," and unsolved killings in the immigrant community. Violence once vaguely blamed on "stiletto societies" and "the practice of the vendetta" was now attributed to "the Mafia," a single shadowy organization devoted to murder and extortion. Much of the information the press used to accuse the Matrangas of leading a New Orleans Mafia came from their enemies, the Provenzanos, who had unsuccessfully attributed a series of extortion letters to Charles Matranga during their own trial.

Expectations of a plot being proven were high in such a climate. Yet no actual evidence of the Mafia conspiracy sketched by the daily press—or any conspiracy at all, for that matter—was offered by the prosecution during the trial.

The defense insinuated that prosecution witnesses were more interested in city-appropriated reward money than in telling the truth. Lionel Adams produced alibis—called "the felon's defense" by cynics—for all of the accused. The defense also pointed out the absence of two expected witnesses. Hennessy had been walking home with a former cop named Billy O'Connor, from whom he parted just before the shooting. Private security guard J.C. Roe was on duty at Hennessy's house that night and had been superficially wounded by the gunfire. Neither O'Connor nor Roe was called by the state. The defense claimed that their testimony would have destroyed the credibility of prosecution witnesses like John Daure.

When final arguments ended after two weeks of testimony, Judge Baker ordered the jury to find Charles Matranga and Bastian Incardona innocent. The state had introduced no evidence against them.

The First, the Best, and Even the Most Law-Abiding

The March 13 verdicts shocked the city. Monasterio, Bagnetto, and Scaffidi got mistrials on the murder charge. The other six defendants were acquitted. All nine were returned to the Orleans Parish prison, expecting the redundant "lying in wait" charge to be dismissed the next day. On the morning of March 14, however, an armed committee headed by two politically prominent New Orleans attorneys and a newspaper editor led a mob of over 6,000 people to the prison and smashed their way in. Macheca, Scaffidi, Monasterio, and Antonio Marchesi were shot to death. So were Geraci, Romero, Traina, Comitz, and James Caruso, none of whom had been tried. Polizzi was dragged out to the street, where a crowd hung him from a lamp post and emptied pistols into him. Bagnetto's broken body was strung up from a tree.

The surviving defendants were soon released by District Attorney Luzenberg, who denied the existence of Polizzi's "confession." A Grand Jury cleared the lynch mob's leaders, saying that "the first, the best and even the most law-abiding" citizens of New Orleans were driven to act because justice had been subverted by jury bribers, a jab at Adams & Henriques' slippery detective associate, Dominick O'Malley.

The Hennessy case jurors denied being bribed. The acquittals, they said, resulted from impatience in the jury room, the absence of Billy O'Connor and Officer Roe, and other holes in the state's case. Two men later got short prison terms for making suggestive comments to potential jurors, but no link between the defense and the chosen jury was unearthed.

Several of the lynched men were Italian subjects. A war scare swept America as the enraged Italian government broke off diplomatic relations. Two years later, the U.S. government paid Italy a $25,000 indemnity, and diplomacy was restored. Yet a national pattern of indiscriminately blaming violent crime in Italian-American communities on a single entity known as the Mafia had been set, helping to fuel anti-immigration sentiment. The anti-Italian insult "Who killa d' Chief?" lived on in New Orleans for decades. To this day, no one has proven who killed Chief David Hennessy.

—*Thomas C. Smith*

Suggestions for Further Reading

Asbury, Herbert J. *The French Quarter.* New York: Alfred A. Knopf, 1936.

Coxe, John E. "The New Orleans Mafia Incident," *Louisiana Historical Quarterly,* Vol. 20 (1937) 1067–1110.

Gambino, Richard. *Vendetta: A true story of the worst lynching in America, the mass-murder of Italian-Americans in New Orleans in 1891, the vicious motivation behind it, and the tragic repercussions that linger to this day.* Garden City, N.Y.: Doubleday, & Co. 1977.

Karlin, J. Alexander. "New Orleans Lynchings in 1891 and the American Press," *Louisiana Historical Quarterly,* Vol. 24 (1941): 187–204.

Kendall, John S. "Who Killa de Chief?" *Louisiana Historical Quarterly,* Vol. 22 (1939): 492–530.

"The Mafia and What Led to the Lynching," *Harper's Weekly,* Vol. 35 (March 28, 1891): 602–612.

Saxon, Lyle, et al. *Gumbo Ya-Ya.* Boston: Houghton Mifflin, 1945.

Charles Kincaid Trial: 1891

Defendant: Charles Euston Kincaid **Crime Charged:** Murder
Chief Defense Lawyers: Charles H. Grosvenor, C. Maurice Smith, Jeremiah M. Wilson. Daniel W. Voorhees assisted with pretrial matters
Chief Prosecutors: Charles C. Cole, Howard C. Clagett **Judge:** Andrew C. Bradley. Judges Edward F. Bingham, Alexander B. Hagner, and Martin V. Montgomery presided over various pretrial hearings **Place:** Washington, D.C. **Date of Trial:** March 23–April 8, 1891 **Verdict:** Not Guilty

SIGNIFICANCE

This trial resulted from the bitter feud between a former congressman and a reporter that eventually led to the first fatal shooting of a current or former congressman inside the nation's Capitol.

Both Congressman William P. Taulbee of Kentucky and news reporter Charles E. Kincaid were rising stars in 1887. The 36-year-old son of a state senator, Taulbee was an attorney and an ordained Methodist minister. First elected to Congress in 1884, he was already a respected member of the House of Representatives and was called the "Mountain Orator" because of his tall, lean build and his ability to sway listeners. Kincaid, age 32, was also from the Blue Grass State. Originally a lawyer, he was elected the municipal judge of Lawrenceburg in 1879 and edited a weekly newspaper before going to Washington, D.C. in 1885 as Senator John Williams's private secretary. Kincaid later became the Washington correspondent for a number of prominent newspapers, including the Louisville *Courier-Journal* and the Louisville *Times*. However, in December 1887, bad blood arose between him and Taulbee.

An Extramarital Affair Exposed

The trouble began when Kincaid published an article exposing Taulbee's extramarital affair with a young woman who worked at the U.S. Patent Office. As described within the modesty of the times, the pair was found "in a compromising way," they held "sweet communion for half an hour before going to plebeian Monday lunch," and the two "were rather warmer than they were proper." The story first appeared in the Washington papers and was reprinted in the Louisville press and the New York *Morning Journal.* As a result, Taulbee's personal and professional life was destroyed. His wife of 17 years left him, and the congressman didn't even bother to seek reelection; instead, he remained in Washington, D.C., to practice law.

Taulbee blamed all of his problems on Kincaid and his hatred steadily grew. The two frequently crossed paths and, each time, there was a confrontation where Taulbee got the better of Kincaid. Taulbee was six feet two inches tall, strong, and in great physical condition. In contrast, Kincaid was short and in terrible health. Born with an eye defect (astigmatism) that narrowed his vision, the correspondent also had a tumor on one eyelid and since 1885 he nearly died twice from attacks of typhoid from which he never fully recovered. He also had liver and digestive problems that his doctors said were due to stress. The reporter tried his best to avoid his tormentor, but it was Kincaid's job to be at the Capitol to interview politicians, lobbyists, and other newsmakers, and Taulbee was frequently there to chat with old friends and acquaintances. Sometimes, the ex-representative even lay in wait to intercept his victim.

For example, Taulbee once tossed Kincaid across a hallway. On other occasions, the former congressman dashed the correspondent against an iron railing and jammed Kincaid against the door of a streetcar. When the two were in an elevator, Taulbee slammed his heel down on the reporter's foot and held it there while his victim screamed in pain. The ex-representative once cornered Kincaid and said, "I ought to cut your throat." The reporter also received warnings from friends and politicians that Taulbee threatened to kill him and had gone to the Capitol's Press Gallery in search of his prey. Every time he met the former congressman, Kincaid did not have the physical strength to resist and he offered apologies in the hope that the attacks would lessen. But it was to no avail. In February 1890, tragedy struck.

A Shooting at the Capitol

At about 12 noon, Kincaid went to the Capitol to conduct an interview. While waiting in the corridor, Taulbee appeared. "I have no time to talk with you. I don't want any trouble with you," said the reporter, but he was shouted at, grabbed by the shoulder, and his ear was violently pulled. "I am a small man and unarmed," maintained Kincaid, but Taulbee replied in a malicious tone, "You had better be armed, or go and arm yourself." Two hours later, the two met again on the steps to the Capitol's basement restaurant. A shot rang out and a bullet hit Taulbee in the face near the eye. Kincaid made no attempt to escape and said, "I did it." Arrested, the reporter was later set free on bail pending any change in the former congressman's condition.

Taulbee was first taken to his residence and then to Providence Hospital. Initially, the wound was not considered fatal, but the doctors were unable to locate the bullet and their patient's condition worsened. He died on March 11. Kincaid again voluntarily surrendered and was taken into custody, but was shortly released due to his frail health and allowed to return to Kentucky to recuperate. While awaiting trial, newspaper editorials in that state proclaimed their support for Kincaid and a group of prominent lawyers began to prepare his defense.

Kincaid's chief lawyer was U.S. senator Daniel Voorhees of Indiana. His other attorneys were C. Maurice Smith, a prominent Washington advocate, Jeremiah Wilson, a former Indiana judge and congressman, and Charles Grosvenor, a three-term member of the House of Representatives from Ohio who was retiring in March 1891. Because Congress was in session and Voorhees and Grosvenor were still busy with the nation's affairs, the court granted a continuance until after the legislature adjourned on March 3, 1891. That March, another motion to delay the trial was made because Voorhees had suffered a rheumatic attack and would not be available before mid-June. That motion, however, was denied on the grounds that Kincaid could still be well represented by his three remaining lawyers.

The trial began on March 23, 1891, in Washington, D.C. U.S. attorney Charles C. Cole led the prosecution's team. President Benjamin Harrison had appointed him to his post only three weeks before. This was Cole's first major case in his new role.

Kincaid Pleads Self-Defense

Because of the publicity, most of the people who were on the panel of potential jurors had already formed an opinion as to Kincaid's guilt or innocence. As a result, only four of the panel's 26 members were accepted by both the defense and prosecution, and another 50 individuals had to be summoned and interviewed before a jury of 12 was finally picked. During the next two weeks, those 12 would hear the testimony of nearly 60 witnesses, some of whom came from as far away as Massachusetts and Louisiana to attend the trial.

Kincaid's lawyers argued that their client acted in self-defense. After Taulbee assaulted and threatened him, the reporter went home upset and frightened, but decided to return to the Capitol to keep an appointment. Before leaving his room, however, Kincaid picked up his revolver for protection. At the Capitol, he met with some other reporters, begged them not to print anything about his latest encounter with Taulbee (some of the earlier incidents apparently were picked up by the press), and then headed down the steps to the basement restaurant for lunch. Kincaid did not realize, however, that Taulbee and another man (Samuel Donaldson) were standing near the bottom of the steps. Once Taulbee saw Kincaid, the former congressman raised his left hand and started to approach. "You're going to kill me," said Kincaid as he backed away. "Stand back." But as the reporter drew his gun, Taulbee merely said, "I'll show you" and continued to march towards Kincaid as his intended victim retreated to the landing on the steps. Once Taulbee was almost within arm's reach, Kincaid was convinced that it was the ex-politician's life or his own, so he fired.

During the trial, eight current and former members of Congress, as well as a number of newspapermen, testified about Taulbee's numerous threats against Kincaid. One said that Taulbee frequently remarked that he ought to kill

Kincaid because Kincaid had ruined his and his family's reputation. Another indicated that Taulbee threatened to kick Kincaid's head off if the correspondent ever came within 10 feet of him. A third quoted Taulbee as saying, "He [Kincaid] ought to be killed. By God, I'll kill him." Many of these witnesses warned Kincaid about the threats and this, according to the defense lawyers, contributed to their client's fears for his life.

Prosecution Calls Shooting Revenge

The prosecution, however, claimed that Kincaid sought out Taulbee with the intention of killing him in revenge for the assault he suffered earlier that day. Samuel Donaldson, a friend of Taulbee's and, aside from Kincaid, the only surviving witness to the shooting, testified that the correspondent waited for Taulbee as he and Taulbee walked down the stairway. Before the former congressman knew that Kincaid was there, the reporter called out, "Taulbee, you can see me now," and fired.

The prosecution also argued that, even if the shooting occurred as Kincaid alleged, the correspondent still had a duty to flee before firing his gun. According to Cole, shooting Taulbee in self-defense was an option only if Kincaid had been backed into a corner and had nowhere that he could safely run to; otherwise, the killing would at least be manslaughter. (Of course, Kincaid's lawyers countered that no such duty existed.)

There was also a "dying declaration" supposedly made by Taulbee to his brother three days before his death. "I did not know Kincaid was near and did not know who it was who shot me until I was told." The defense, however, hammered away at both Donaldson's testimony and the statements recorded by Taulbee's brother, pointing out inconsistencies and raising doubts about their truthfulness.

On April 8, 1891, after only a few hours of deliberation, the jury returned with a verdict of "not guilty." A few days later, Kincaid returned to Kentucky with his sister and nephew. He would later serve on the Kentucky Railroad Commission and as an American diplomat. In 1896, Kincaid returned to the newspaper business and became a reporter with the Cincinnati *Enquirer*. However, his health remained poor and he died in 1906 at the young age of 51. Despite his accomplishments, Charles Kincaid was still best known, at the time of his death, as the man who shot Congressman William Taulbee.

—*Mark Thorburn*

Suggestions for Further Reading

Klotter, James C. "Sex, Scandal, and Suffrage in the Gilded Age." *The Historian: A Journal of History* 42, no.2 (February 1980): 225–43.

Ross, Shelley. *Fall from Grace: Sex, Scandal, and Corruption in American Politics from 1702 to the Present.* New York: Ballantine Books, 1988.

Robert Buchanan Trial: 1893

Defendant: Robert Buchanan **Crime Charged:** Murder
Chief Defense Lawyers: Charles W. Brooks, William J. O'Sullivan
Chief Prosecutors: De Lance Nicoll, James Osborne, Francis Wellman
Judge: E. C. Smyth **Place:** New York, New York **Date of Trial:** March 20–April 26, 1893 **Verdict:** Guilty **Sentence:** Death

SIGNIFICANCE

This was one of the earliest trials to be fought almost exclusively on forensic science testimony.

In May 1892 a New York reporter, Ike White, heard rumors surrounding the sudden death of a brothel keeper named Anna Buchanan. According to the death certificate the madam had succumbed to a stroke, but friends of the dead woman were convinced that she had been poisoned by her husband, Dr. Robert Buchanan, so that he might acquire her $50,000 fortune. White did some digging and uncovered a journalistic gem: just three weeks after Anna's death, Buchanan had remarried his first wife, Helen, in Nova Scotia. Further investigation revealed Buchanan to be a debauchee, who most nights could be found in New York's bordellos, drinking and carousing till the early hours, a lifestyle that made serious inroads into his bank balance, hence the rumors about Anna's death.

Further fanning the flames of suspicion were remarks allegedly made by Buchanan two years earlier during the trial of Carlyle Harris, a New York medical student charged with wife-murder. At first her death, too, had been attributed to a stroke, but pinpointing of the pupils had led investigators to detect a morphine overdose. Harris was convicted and sentenced to death. Buchanan had followed proceedings with great interest, frequently referring to the accused as a "bungling fool" and a "stupid amateur," and boasting that he knew how to avoid the telltale pinpoint pupils.

In receipt of these and other revelations, White started a noisy campaign in the *New York World*, demanding the exhumation of Anna's body. He got his wish. Sure enough, analysis of the organs confirmed the presence of morphine, and Buchanan was charged with murder.

When the trial, presided over by Recorder Smyth, opened on March 20, 1893, it was soon clear that this case would be fought in the test-tube. Courts were just beginning to pay close attention to scientific testimony and in Professor Rudolph Witthaus, the prosecution had one of the nation's foremost toxicologists. Witthaus, who had analyzed the dead woman's organs, told the court how, using the Pellagri test, he discovered that "the body contained 1/10th of a grain of morphine in the remains," which he estimated was the residue of a fatal dose of 5 or 6 grains.

Heartened by this testimony, chief prosecuting counsel Francis Wellman asked the witness if he knew any means whereby it was possible to disguise the pinpoint pupils so characteristic of morphine poisoning. Witthaus referred to his original report: "Treatment of the eyes with atropine might very well eliminate the narrowing of the pupils which otherwise follows morphine poisoning."

Grisly Demonstration

In order to drive home this point the prosecution chose to conduct a gruesome experiment. A cat was brought into court and injected with morphine; then drops of atropine, an alkaloid derived from belladonna, were placed in the poor creature's eyes. It was cruel but effective, as jury members were able to see for themselves how the dying cat's pupils were dilated, just as Witthaus had said.

Wellman now reminded the jury how, earlier, they had heard from the nurse who had attended Anna in her final hours, and who recalled seeing Buchanan bending over his stricken wife, dropping some medicine in her eyes. Needless to say, such an action now assumed a more sinister association.

At this point it appeared as though the state had an open-and-shut case against Buchanan, but Buchanan's chief lawyer, William O'Sullivan, was an ex-doctor turned attorney, and he had spent six months before the trial studying medical literature on morphine and the methods for demonstrating its presence. He rose and greeted Witthaus with a deceptive smile. There then followed a series of seemingly innocuous questions about the various tests that Witthaus had employed: the ferric chloride test, the Huseman test, the Fröhde test, and above all the Pellagri test. O'Sullivan asked casually, "The jury has been told that the so-called Pellagri test is especially important for demonstrating the presence of morphine. Can you confirm this?"

Witthaus agreed that it was, although he stressed the need for a number of tests to provide corroboration.

"Very good," said O'Sullivan. Now, his understanding of the Pellagri test was that if morphine was present, an unmistakable glowing purple color would appear, which soon changed to cherry red. "Is this correct?"

"Yes," replied Witthaus.

O'Sullivan asked if it was possible for an alkaloid produced by a decaying cadaver to produce a similar reaction.

"So far," said Witthaus, "this has not been observed anywhere in the world."

Whereupon O'Sullivan called Professor Victor C. Vaughan to the witness stand. While the jury sat transfixed, Vaughan set up an impressive array of tubes and bottles. Then O'Sullivan asked Vaughan if the Pellagri test was a sure indicator of the presence of morphine.

"No," said Vaughan. "There can be no such certainty."

"Then the Pellagri test can produce deceptive errors?"

"Yes it can," replied Vaughan, who then proceeded to subject a piece of pancreas that had been decaying for several weeks to the same tests that Witthaus had used. In a second tube was a preparation of morphine. Working quickly and sloppily, in a manner that flouted all the standard laboratory procedures for accuracy, Vaughan magically managed to obtain the distinctive purple and then cherry red reaction from the pancreas as well as the morphine. There was an uproar in court. Delighted reporters rushed for the exits to phone this latest sensation to their newspapers.

Witthaus looked on in amazement, unable to believe that O'Sullivan was able to get away with such shoddy science; but strident prosecution objections came too late to lessen the impact that Vaughan's "experiments" had clearly had on the jury.

Throughout, the defendant had been a mute observer of all these shenanigans, almost unnoticed, and he remained that way when acquittal seemed certain. But it wasn't to be. Like others in the New York legal community, O'Sullivan felt that during the Harris trial, the defendant's decision not to testify had militated heavily against him, and he had no inclination to repeat that mistake.

What he did get was a catastrophe. Buchanan's whining manner and self-obsessed answers only became more exaggerated under cross-examination, as Wellman trapped him in so many lies and contradictions that any doubt created by the scientific dispute was entirely canceled out. Buchanan limped from the stand in tatters. Even so, it says much for the contentious nature of the scientific evidence that when the jury retired on April 25, they still needed over 28 hours to find him guilty of murder.

After Buchanan was sentenced to death by Recorder Smyth, his lawyers launched an appeal based on the tainted scientific evidence. This time Witthaus was ready for them. He had taken his courtroom humiliation badly, and set out to reestablish his reputation by proving that Vaughan's methodology had been flawed. Eventually he tracked the source of the error to impurities in the chemicals used by the other scientist.

Buchanan's appeal failed, and on July 2, 1895, just like Carlyle Harris two years beforehand, he made that short, lonely walk to the electric chair at Sing Sing.

—Colin Evans

Suggestions for Further Reading

Smith, Edward H. *Famous American Poison Mysteries.* London: Hurst & Blackett, 1927.

Thorwald, Jurgen. *The Century of the Detective.* New York: Harcourt, Brace & World, 1964.

Vaughan, Victor C. *A Doctor's Memories.* Minneapolis: Bobbs-Merrill, 1926.

Lizzie Borden Trial: 1893

Defendant: Lizzie Borden **Crime Charged:** Murder
Chief Defense Lawyers: Andrew Jennings and George D. Robinson
Chief Prosecutors: Hosea Knowlton and William H. Moody **Judges:** Caleb Blodget, Justin Dewey, and Albert Mason **Place:** Fall River, Massachusetts
Dates of Trial: June 5–20, 1893 **Verdict:** Not guilty

SIGNIFICANCE

On the basis of circumstantial evidence, prosecutors accused Lizzie Borden of murdering her father and stepmother. In an attempt to circumvent its lack of direct evidence, the prosecution appealed to popular stereotypes about the slyness and cleverness of women. Lizzie nonetheless was acquitted. The acquittal was significant in that it represented the triumph of the rule of law over common prejudice.

Born in 1860 and never married, Lizzie Borden lived in quiet obscurity in the small town of Fall River, Massachusetts, until August 4, 1892. On that day an ax-murderer killed her father, Andrew J. Borden, and her stepmother, Abby Durfee Gray Borden. The police arrested Lizzie for the crime, and her trial made her a figure of national notoriety.

Lizzie's birth mother, Sarah M. Borden, died when Lizzie was a small child. Lizzie lived in her parents' house together with the family maid, her uncle, and her older sister, Emma Borden, who was, like Lizzie, a spinster. The Bordens' family life was quite ordinary and unremarkable until the morning of August 4, 1892, when a neighbor looked out of her window and noticed Lizzie, visibly upset, clinging to the screen door that opened onto the Bordens' yard. When the neighbor, Adelaide Churchill, asked Lizzie what the problem was, she replied, "Oh, Mrs. Churchill, do come over. Someone has killed father."

Churchill immediately notified the police. When a policeman, followed by a doctor, arrived at the Borden house, they found Andrew Borden's body in the family living room. Someone had come upon him, apparently while he was napping, and brutally and repeatedly attacked him with an ax. Although blood splattered the furniture, there were no signs that he had fought with an intruder. Churchill and another neighbor, Alice Russell, had accompanied the policeman and doctor into the Borden house. Churchill went upstairs with the maid to look for Abby Borden. They found her in a guest room, murdered in the same terrible fashion. Like Andrew, Abby's morning routine had been unremarkable and there was no sign of resistance to an intruder. Apparently Abby had been making the bed at the time of her murder.

Lizzie Charged with Murder

The police began an investigation and questioned Lizzie on the events of the morning of the murder. Whether out of shock or deliberate evasiveness, her answers were rambling and inconsistent. The police asked her where she had been at the time of the murders, and she answered at different times with different versions. Lizzie at various times told the police that she had been getting a piece of fishing gear from the family barn, or that she had been in the yard, or that she had been picking pears.

Turn-of-the-century-police questioning tactics, particularly those used on a murder suspect, were often less than sensitive to the effect of trauma upon a suspect's answers. It is difficult to determine, therefore, whether Fall River Mayor John Coughlin was justified in ordering the police to arrest Lizzie on the basis of their investigation and her inconsistent answers. The local coroner conducted a formal inquest, and Lizzie's answers were just as confused.

The police charged Lizzie with the murder of her father and stepmother. They suspected that Lizzie's motive was either a deep-rooted resentment related to her natural mother's death, or a desire to collect her father's sizable fortune. The police did not, however, attempt to implicate Lizzie's older sister Emma in the murders. Logically, Emma could have had the same motives as Lizzie and have committed the murders herself. With this question hanging in the air, the state of Massachusetts opened Lizzie Borden's trial on June 5, 1893.

Judges Caleb Blodget, Justin Dewey, and Albert Mason presided over the trial. The prosecutors were Hosea Knowlton and William H. Moody. Knowlton was the more experienced attorney, but because he was feeling ill he had brought Moody along as co-counsel. Lizzie's defense lawyers were Andrew Jennings and George D. Robinson. Robinson was a particularly distinguished lawyer, having once been the governor of Massachusetts.

Moody opened the prosecution's case by describing the facts to the jury and preparing them to accept the idea that a woman could have committed such horrible crimes:

> Upon the fourth day of August of the last year an old man and woman, husband and wife, each without a known enemy in the world, in their own home, upon a frequented street in the most populous city in this County under the light of day and in the midst of its activities, were, first one, then, after an interval of an hour, another, severally killed by unlawful human agency. Today a woman of good social position, of hitherto unquestioned character, a member of a Christian church and active in good works, the own daughter of one of the victims, is at the bar of this Court, accused by the Grand Jury of this County of these crimes.

The prosecution's case rested in large part on circumstantial evidence. For example, Moody made a point of emphasizing that Emma Borden had seen

Lizzie burning a dress after the murders. Implying that Lizzie had burnt the bloodstained dress she wore while murdering her parents, Moody said to the jury:

> Now, gentlemen, it will appear that about the two rooms in which the homicides were committed there was blood spattering in various directions, so that it would make it probable that one or more spatters of blood would be upon the person or upon the clothing of the assailant.

The prosecution went on to present four axes and hatchets found in the Borden house. None of these implements had any bloodstains on them, however.

Andrew Jennings, who had been the Borden family's attorney for many years, opened Lizzie's defense with a direct attack on the prosecutors' reliance on circumstantial evidence:

> They have either got to produce the weapon which did the deed . . . or else they have got to account in some reasonable way for its disappearance. . . . There are two kinds of evidence: direct evidence and circumstantial evidence. Direct evidence is the testimony of persons who have seen, heard or felt the thing or things about which they are testifying. . . . [T]here is not one particle of direct evidence in this case, from beginning to end, against Lizzie Andrew Borden. There is not a spot of blood: there is not a weapon connected with her.

Jennings and Robinson went on to challenge the prosecution's assertion that Lizzie's dress-burning was an implication of guilt. They brought Emma Borden to the witness stand and were able to elicit testimony, favorable to Lizzie, that the dress had in fact been very old, faded and stained and thus was legitimately destroyed. After nearly two days, the defense concluded its case.

Attorneys Wrap Up

Robinson made the closing argument for the defense. Of course, he could not dispute that a particularly heinous crime had occurred:

> One of the most dastardly and diabolical of crimes that was ever committed in Massachusetts was perpetrated in August, 1892, in the city of Fall River, . . . the terror of those scenes no language can portray.

Robinson went on, however, to stress how close Lizzie and Andrew Borden had been. Many years ago, Lizzie gave her father a ring to symbolize her love for and fidelity to him. Robinson used this fact to emphasize how unlikely it would be that Lizzie would murder her father:

> Here was a man that wore nothing in the way of ornament, of jewelry but one ring, and that ring was Lizzie's. It had been put on many years ago when Lizzie was a little girl and the old man wore it and it lies buried with him in the cemetery. He liked Lizzie, did he not? He loved her as a child: and the ring that stands as the pledge of plighted faith and love, that typifies and symbolizes the dearest relation that is ever created in life, that ring was the bond of union between the father and the daughter.

When the prosecutors' turn came to make their closing argument, Knowlton and Moody knew that their principal weakness was their heavy reliance on circumstantial evidence. They deliberately appealed to the all-male jury to decide the case on the basis of prevailing attitudes toward women:

> If they lack in strength and coarseness and vigor, they make up for it in cunning, in dispatch, in celerity, in ferocity. If their loves are stronger and more enduring than those of men, on the other hand, their hates are more undying, more unyielding, more persistent.

In the hope that the jurors would accept at face value this assessment of the female psyche, prosecutor Knowlton went on to dismiss the prosecutors' failure to find any bloodstained clothing belonging to Lizzie:

> How could she have avoided the spattering of her dress with blood if she was the author of these crimes? . . . I cannot answer it. You cannot answer it. You are neither murderers nor women. You have neither the craft of the assassin nor the cunning and deftness of the sex. . . . You are merciful men. The wells of mercy, I hope, are not dried up in any of us. But this is not the time nor the place for the exercise of it!

The end of the prosecutors' closing argument marked the end of the trial. All that remained were the judges' final instructions to the jury. Before the judges adjourned the court, however, they gave Lizzie the opportunity to make a statement to the jury. Under Massachusetts law, she had not been required to testify at the trial. Thus, the following words were the first that the jury had heard from Lizzie: "I am innocent. I leave it to my counsel to speak for me."

If she were convicted, the state of Massachusetts would execute her in a newly invented machine, popularly known as the electric chair.

Judges' Instructions Favor Lizzie

Judge Dewey spoke for the three judges when he gave the jury their instructions concerning the law and evidence in the case. First, he reiterated the defense's point that the prosecutors had relied on circumstantial evidence. Second, he dismissed her inconsistent statements to the police after the murders as being normal under the circumstances. Having thus effectively challenged the basis of the prosecution's case, Judge Dewey went on to remind the jury members of their duty to Lizzie:

> If the evidence falls short of providing such conviction in your minds, although it may raise a suspicion of guilt, or even a strong probability of guilt, it would be your plain duty to return a verdict of not guilty. . . . [S]eeking only the truth, you will lift this case above the range of passion and prejudice and excited feeling, into the clear atmosphere of reason and law.

On June 20, 1893, the jury left the courtroom to deliberate. Perhaps Judge Dewey's instructions had swayed the jury, or perhaps the jury was truly convinced of her innocence. In either event, after little more than an hour of deliberation the jury returned to the courtroom with its verdict. It found Lizzie Borden not guilty of the murder charges.

After two long weeks of what was one of the nation's most widely publicized trials, Lizzie left the courtroom a free woman. To this day, historians have speculated that she had been covering up for sister Emma. It is possible that Emma committed the murders, or hired someone to enter the Borden house and murder her parents. There were conflicting accounts, not fully explored by the prosecutors or Lizzie's attorneys, that a hired assassin had been seen fleeing Fall River. Other accounts about visits that Emma had made to a nearby town, visits that could have related to the murders, were also left unexplored.

Her trial over, Lizzie left the old Borden residence and moved into a new house. Collecting her inheritance from her father's estate, Lizzie could live a comfortable life. She invested this money wisely, and became a prominent local benefactor of worthwhile charities, particularly animal shelters. By all accounts, she led a respectable life for nearly 35 years until her death in 1927. The infamy of her trial, however, has outlived her death.

Despite her acquittal, to this day Lizzie is still popularly regarded as one of America's most famous murderesses. In fact, her acquittal was really a triumph for women, because the jury refused to bend the rules of law that protect defendants when the prosecution played upon popular stereotypes about the "sly sex."

—*Stephen G. Christianson*

Suggestions for Further Reading

Brown, Arnold R. *Lizzie Borden.* Nashville, Tenn.: Rutledge Hill Press, 1991.

Hunter, Evan. *Lizzie.* New York: Arbor House, 1984.

Lincoln, Victoria. *A Private Disgrace.* New York: G.P. Putnam's Sons, 1967.

Porter, Edwin H. *The Fall River Tragedy.* Portland, Maine: King Philip Pub. Co., 1985.

Radin, Edward D. *Lizzie Borden.* New York: Simon & Schuster, 1961.

Satterthwait, Walter. *Miss Lizzie.* New York: St. Martin's Press, 1989.

Spiering, Frank. *Lizzie.* New York: Random House, 1984.

Sullivan, Robert. *Goodbye Lizzie Borden.* Brattleboro, VT: Greene Press, 1974.

William Breckinridge Breach of Promise Trial: 1894

Plaintiff: Madeline V. Pollard **Defendant:** William Campbell Preston Breckinridge **Plaintiff Claim:** Breach of promise
Chief Lawyers for Plaintiff: Jeremiah M. Wilson, Calderon Carlisle, William G. Johnson. E. P. Farrell assisted with pre-trial matters
Chief Defense Lawyers: Benjamin Butterworth, Philip B. Thompson, Jr., W. A. McKenny, John H. Stoll, John T. Shelby, William G. Mattingly. Enoch Totten, Desha Breckinridge, Charles H. Stoll assisted with pretrial matters
Judge: Andrew C. Bradley **Place:** Washington, D.C. **Date of Trial:** March 8–April 14, 1894 **Verdict:** For Plaintiff **Award:** $15,000

SIGNIFICANCE

In 1893, it seemed William Campbell Preston Breckinridge of Kentucky was destined for great things. The five-term Democratic congressman's grandfather was an Attorney general, his cousin was a vice president, and several other relatives were senators, representatives, and governors. There was talk of higher office and the congressman dreamed of the White House. But Breckinridge's career and reputation rapidly collapsed once Madeline Pollard sued him for breach of promise.

When Madeline Pollard first met Congressman William Breckinridge on April 1, 1884 while riding a train, she was a 17-year-old student at Wesleyan College in Cincinnati, Ohio, one of the most prestigious girls' schools in the country. Pollard was on her way home to Frankfort, Kentucky, to visit a sick sister. At that same time, the 47-year-old Breckinridge was heading to Lexington, some 30 miles away from Frankfort, where he lived and maintained a law practice.

A Relationship Blossoms

An orphan and not remarkably attractive, Pollard was so quiet and unobtrusive at school that one of her classmates described her as "mouse-like." Therefore, she was probably in awe when Breckinridge introduced himself and struck up a conversation. Three months later, Pollard wrote to the congressman for advice on how to handle a debt incurred to pay her tuition. In response, Breckinridge went to Wesleyan on August 3 to consult with Pollard on the matter. There he asked for a more "confidential" discussion away from the eyes and ears of protective chaperones, and they left the campus that hot summer night in a closed carriage. Breckinridge then convinced Pollard to meet him in Lexington. Two days later, after he had dinner with his wife, the couple met at a secret location and he seduced her.

At the congressman's suggestion, Pollard transferred to the Sayre Institute in Lexington so she could be closer to him. During the next three years, Breckinridge paid her tuition and board at Sayre and the two met at least 50 times. Pollard quickly became pregnant, giving birth to a child in a foundling asylum in Ohio on May 29, 1885. Two years later, she was pregnant again and gave birth on February 3, 1888. (The second child died two months later.) Pollard knew that Breckinridge was a married man with children, but she thought nothing of it; she was in love and "his slightest wish was law to me then." Pollard even gave up her two babies "because he asked me. He said that if I kept them it would be traced to him and they would be known as his children. A woman can't do more than that."

A Promise Broken

Breckinridge moved the pregnant Pollard to Washington, D.C., in September 1887. There, the congressman got her a job with the Department of Agriculture and the pair continued to meet three or four times a week. After his second wife died in July 1892, the two met even more often and Breckinridge promised marriage. Pollard became pregnant a third time, but the congressman was going to acknowledge this child; the couple even considered names for the baby. They were supposed to be wed on May 31, 1893, but on April 29 Breckinridge secretly married his cousin. (According to the congressman, this was done so his new wife could gain the affections of his children before they learned about the wedding.) Before Pollard learned about the marriage, she and the congressman postponed their nuptials until December (long after their child's anticipated birth) so no one would know that Breckinridge was the baby's father. But a few weeks later, Pollard found out about Breckinridge's secret marriage. Then, on May 24, she suffered a miscarriage. Finally realizing that she had been conned all along, Pollard sued for $50,000 (equal to more than $500,000 today) for breach of promise.

A Trial Watched by the Nation

The trial began on March 8, 1894, and it lasted 28 days. Circuit Judge Andrew Bradley, a member of the church that Breckinridge attended in Washington, presided over the trial as a jury of 12 men heard the testimony and considered the evidence. (In 1894, women were not allowed on juries.) Jeremiah Wilson, a former Indiana congressman and state judge who now practiced law in the District of Columbia, led Pollard's legal team. Breckinridge's defense lawyers were under the command of Benjamin Butterworth, a former Republican representative from Ohio, and included Breckinridge's son, Desha, Breckinridge's law partner, John Shelby, and former congressman Philip Thompson, Jr.

For over one month, the country enjoyed the scandalous headlines that came from the courtroom. Upholding the morals of the time, Judge Bradley once refused to allow women in the audience lest they hear some lurid testimony. At one point, a fist fight broke out among the lawyers and Breckinridge's attorneys had to swear to Bradley that they did not bring concealed weapons into the courtroom.

Dressed in black and accompanied by a nun, Madeline Pollard made an impressive witness; the defense was unable to crack her story, and she even fainted when she testified about the death of her second child. Breckinridge's attorneys hoped to attack Pollard's reputation to show that she was someone an influential congressman would not associate with, but much of their evidence was inadmissible hearsay and, in the words of Judge Bradley, "too filthy and obscene" to hear anyway. Furthermore, their tactics only earned Pollard more sympathy. Halfway through the trial, Breckinridge and his lawyers changed their strategy and started to depict Pollard as a wanton woman who pursued the congressman as much as he pursued her.

"I was a man of passion. She was a woman of passion," Breckinridge testified. "There was no seduction, no seduction on either side. It was simply a case of human passion."

Defense Portrays Pollard as a Harlot

According to the congressman, Pollard schemed to trap him from the very beginning. She was not underage when they met, but an experienced woman between 20 and 22 years old. She approached him on the train. They went on an unchaperoned carriage ride, but it was at her suggestion and he paid her 10 dollars for it. Pollard came to Lexington shortly after they met, but she followed Breckinridge on her own initiative, just as she followed him to Washington three years later. The congressman paid Pollard's tuition and board at the Sayre Institute from 1885 to 1887, but he did not see her at all during that time. He got Pollard a government job, introduced her to acquaintances as his fiancée and as his daughter. After his second wife's death, he visited her up to seven times a day, but he had to; at various times, she threatened to ruin him, to kill him, or to kill herself if he broke off their affair. Most astonishingly, the congressman denied all knowledge of Pollard's first two children.

In their closing remarks, Breckinridge's attorneys described Pollard as a "self-acknowledged prostitute," but it did no good. The jury took only one hour and 23 minutes to consider their verdict. They ruled in Pollard's favor and awarded her $15,000 (three times the annual salary in 1894 of a congressman). Breckinridge filed a motion for a new trial and later appealed, but both were denied.

A Career in Ruin

The congressman went back to Kentucky to run for reelection, but he was in trouble. In his home state and across the nation, newspapers, civic organizations, and religious groups denounced him. Breckinridge was called a "rapist," a "lust fiend," and a "wild beast in search of prey." But most importantly, the trial galvanized the suffrage movement in Kentucky. As one local paper reported, "Women who never took the slightest interest in politics in their lives have become active politicians." Thousands of ladies attended protest meetings, and resolutions were adopted calling for the congressman's defeat. Businesses that supported Breckinridge were boycotted and parents sent letters to newspapers warning the congressman's young supporters that they could no longer date their daughters.

Breckinridge pleaded for forgiveness. "I have sinned and I repent in sackcloth and ashes." And he still had many friends and supporters. Pollard predicted that the congressman would be reelected and she was nearly right; when the ballots were counted, he lost by only 255 votes out of 19,000 cast. Breckinridge never held public office again.

—*Mark Thorburn*

Suggestions for Further Reading

Klotter, James C. *The Breckinridges of Kentucky, 1760-1981.* Lexington, Ky.: University Press of Kentucky, 1986.

——. "Sex, Scandal, and Suffrage in the Gilded Age." *The Historian: A Journal of History* 42, no.2 (February 1980): 225–43.

Lexington, Fayette. *The Celebrated Case of Col. W. C. P. Breckinridge and Madeline Pollard.* Chicago: Current Events Publishing, 1894.

Parker, Agnes. *The Real Madeline Pollard: A Diary of Ten Weeks' Association with the Plaintiff in the Famous Breckinridge-Pollard Suit.* New York: G. W. Dillingham, 1894.

Ross, Shelley. *Fall from Grace: Sex, Scandal, and Corruption in American Politics from 1702 to the Present.* New York: Ballantine Books, 1988.

In Re Debs: 1895

Defendant: Eugene V. Debs **Crimes Charged:** Contempt of court and conspiracy **Chief Defense Lawyers:** Clarence Darrow, S. Gregory, and Lyman Trumbull **Chief Prosecutors:** John C. Black, T. M. Milchrist, and Edwin Walker **Judges:** Peter Grosscup and William A. Woods **Place:** Chicago, Illinois **Dates of Trial:** January 26–February 12, 1895 **Verdict:** Guilty of contempt, no verdict on conspiracy **Sentence:** 6 Months imprisonment for contempt of court (a pretrial conviction)

SIGNIFICANCE

In one of the most egregious cases of the courts siding with industry against labor, a federal judge issued an injunction ordering the American Railway Union to stop a strike against the Pullman Company and sentenced the strike's leader, Eugene Debs, to six months in jail for violating the injunction. The government then put Debs on trial for conspiracy but dropped the case in mid-trial. The Supreme Court upheld Debs' sentence for contempt of court in a major confirmation of federal judges' power to enforce their orders.

In the late 19th century, as heavy industry grew and railroads spread across the country, commercial centers like Chicago and other cities mushroomed. With this industrial growth, however, came growing abuses. Ownership of industry was concentrated in a handful of wealthy men, while the factory workers and others who made industrialization possible were not protected by the government. Companies were able to get away with paying workers low wages for long hours. Further, most companies did not give workers benefits such as sick leave or disability pay. To make matters worse, there were many "company towns" where workers rented their houses and bought food from stores all owned by the very company that employed them.

The city of Chicago, where the famous Haymarket Riot occurred, was home to one of the most flagrant abusers of industrial power. George M. Pullman's Pullman Palace Car Company manufactured the world-famous railroad cars. The company operated its own company town just outside of Chicago. Not surprisingly, it was named Pullman, Illinois.

The company charged workers higher than average rents to live in company-owned housing while paying substandard hourly wages. Further, in 1893 the company responded to an economic depression by cutting wages 25 percent. In the winter of 1893, conditions were grim in Pullman, Illinois.

The "Debs Rebellion"

Eugene Debs was born in 1855 to a blue-collar Midwestern family. He began his career as a lowly railroad worker. However, he soon discovered that his real gift was in politics, and he rose quickly in the budding union movement. By 1893 Debs was president of the American Railway Union. Although the ARU was primarily a railroad-track workers union, in the spring of 1894 many Pullman employees joined. On May 11, 1894, the smoldering discontent in Pullman ignited and all 3,300 workers went on strike. Although it is likely that the strike was a spontaneous local event not called by the ARU, Debs quickly went to Pullman and assumed leadership of the strike. Because the ARU represented workers in nearly every railroad system in the United States, and the railroads threw their support behind Pullman, the strike soon became a nationwide railway work stoppage. The resulting paralysis of the American rail network was dubbed the "Debs Rebellion."

Eugene Debs, leader of the strikers from the American Railway Union. (Courtesy, Library of Congress)

President Grover Cleveland was alarmed by the strike and sided with Pullman and the railroads. His attorney general, Richard Olney, went to federal judges Peter Grosscup and William A. Woods to ask for a court order stopping the strike. Ironically, one of Olney's arguments in asking for the injunction was that the ARU strike violated the Sherman Antitrust Act of 1890. The Sherman Act was intended to break up large corporate monopolies and gave federal judges broad powers to issue orders stopping actions they deemed harmful to interstate commerce. At Olney's suggestion, Grosscup and Woods twisted the act's meaning and on July 2, 1894 used their power to order Debs and the other ARU leaders to abandon the strike. The order even made answering a telegram from the strikers a violation of the terms of the injunction.

Furious, Debs and the ARU leadership resolved to ignore the injunction. Because violating a court order constitutes contempt of court, Judge Woods had Debs hauled into court and sentenced him to six months in jail. Contempt of court is the traditional means by which judges enforce their authority, requiring no trial or jury. The government also charged Debs with conspiracy to block the federal mail: the ARU's nationwide railroad work stoppage had halted a Rock Island Railroad train carrying mail for the post office. In the meantime, the federal government's actions were not limited to the legal system. President Cleveland sent federal troops to Chicago to crush the strike.

Debs Tried for Conspiracy

Unlike the contempt charge, the government had to try Debs for conspiracy before a jury. The ARU retained the famous lawyer Clarence Darrow, who was assisted by S. Gregory and former Illinois Supreme Court Judge Lyman Trumbull. The prosecutors were John C. Black, T. M. Milchrist, and Edwin Walker.

When the trial opened January 26, 1895, from the start Darrow made it clear to the jury that the issue at trial was not Debs' guilt but the government's desire to crush the union movement. Referring to an executive committee of the railroads called the General Managers' Association, Darrow said:

> This is an historic case which will count much for liberty or against liberty. . . . Conspiracy, from the days of tyranny in England down to the day the General Managers' Association used it as a club, has been the favorite weapon of every tyrant. It is an effort to punish the crime of thought.

Darrow cleverly decided to subpoena George Pullman and the members of the General Managers' Association to testify at the trial. While the real opposition to the "Debs Rebellion" was being served with legal process, the prosecutors grilled Debs. They hoped to provoke him into a socialist tirade against American industry and thus alienate the jury. Prosecutor Walker asked Debs how he defined the word "strike." Debs, however, merely responded in a detached manner:

> A strike is a stoppage of work at a given time by men acting in concert in order to redress some real or imaginary grievance.
>
> Walker: Mr. Debs, will you define the meaning of the word "scab"?
>
> A scab in labor unions means the same as a traitor to his country. It means a man who betrays his fellow men by taking their places when they go on strike for a principle. It does not apply to non-union men who refuse to quit work.

After Debs' testimony, events took a surprising turn. Judge Grosscup, probably influenced by George Pullman and the General Managers' Association, who were reluctant to testify in open court, stated on the day after Debs's testimony that:

> Owing to the sickness of a juror and the certificate of his physician that he will not be able to get out for two or three days, I think it will be necessary to adjourn the further taking of testimony in this case.

Grosscup then adjourned the case. In a remarkable turn of events, the trial never reconvened. In effect, the government dropped the conspiracy charge. It has never been conclusively determined whether this decision was the result of Pullman's influence or the weakness of the government's case.

Darrow and Debs' other lawyers appealed the still-valid contempt conviction. However, on May 27, 1895, the U.S. Supreme Court rejected their pleas and refused to overturn Woods' decision. Debs served his six-month sentence in Illinois' Woodstock Prison with other ARU leaders jailed for contempt. *In Re Debs* has been cited many times since to demonstrate the sweeping powers of federal judges to punish those who violate court orders.

Debs' Political Career Continued

Although his strike was crushed, Debs left prison with his political reputation intact. He became the leading spokesman for the American left, and was the presidential candidate for the American Socialist Party in every election (except 1916) from 1900 to 1920. He lost every election.

When the United States entered World War I, Debs was outraged. He criticized President Woodrow Wilson in the harshest terms, and in *U.S. v. Debs* was charged with treason. For the most part, the charges against Debs were the result of his support of the International Workers of the World, known as the "Wobblies." This time, however, a court found Debs guilty. Debs' appeals to the Supreme Court were unsuccessful. While in prison, Debs ran for the fifth and final time as the Socialist Party's candidate for president. Again, he was unsuccessful in his bid to become the nation's chief executive.

Stung by Debs' criticism, President Wilson refused to pardon him. Among Debs' choicer comments about Wilson were such gems as:

> No man in public life in American history ever retired so thoroughly discredited, so scathingly rebuked, so overwhelmingly impeached and repudiated as Woodrow Wilson.

Warren G. Harding, who won the 1920 presidential election, was more charitable. Harding pardoned Debs in December 1921 and even invited him to the White House on Christmas Day. But Debs found that the Socialist Party had lost its political force. He spent his final years with his wife in quiet retirement and died in 1926.

—Stephen G. Christianson

Suggestions for Further Reading

Coleman, McAlister. *Eugene V. Debs, a Man Unafraid.* New York: Greenberg, 1930.

Ginger, Ray. *The Bending Cross.* New Brunswick, N.J.: Rutgers University Press, 1949.

McHugh, Clare. "Why Has Socialism Never Caught on in the U.S.?" *Scholastic Update* (September 1986): 12.

Noble, Iris. *Labor's Advocate.* New York: Julian Messner, 1966.

Selvin, David F. *Eugene Debs.* New York: Lothrop, Lee & Shepard, 1966.

Theo Durrant Trial: 1895

Defendant: William Henry Theodore Durrant **Crime Charged:** Murder
Chief Defense Lawyers: Eugene N. Deuprey and John H. Dickinson
Chief Prosecutors: W.H. Anderson, William S. Barnes, W.F. Fitzgerald, and Edgar D. Peixotto **Judge:** D.J. Murphy **Place:** San Francisco, California
Dates of Trial: April 15–November 1, 1895 **Verdict:** Guilty
Sentence: Death by hanging

SIGNIFICANCE

"Theo" Durrant was tried, convicted, and executed for murdering two girls despite the fact that the prosecution never proved any motive for the murders.

William Henry Theodore Durrant, known as "Theo," was probably the last person the people of San Francisco, California, would have suspected as being capable of the "Crime of the Century," as San Francisco newspapers described the murders Durrant committed in the Emanuel Baptist Church in 1895.

Durrant was a 21-year-old medical student at the Cooper Medical College. He also belonged to the Emanuel Baptist Church, where he taught Sunday school, assisted with church services, and helped out with various repair jobs in his spare time. He was liked and well respected in the community. In April of 1895, however, he revealed a different side to his personality.

On the afternoon of April 3, Durrant took his fiancée, a high-school girl named Blanche Lamont, into the church. The church was empty, and Durrant grabbed Blanche and proceeded to strangle her to death. He then dragged her corpse to the church belfry where he committed necrophilia with the body. Afterwards he left the church, leaving Lamont's body in the belfry.

That evening, Lamont's parents contacted the police and reported that their daughter was missing. The police went to Durrant's house and questioned him. He feigned ignorance and suggested that Lamont had been kidnapped by one of the white slavery gangs then common in San Francisco. While the police investigated this possibility, Durrant murdered another girl.

On Good Friday, April 12, Durrant lured young Minnie Williams into the Church late at night. He raped and killed her, then dismembered her body in the church library. Durrant made no effort to clean up the bloodstained library or dispose of Williams' body, and once he was finished, he simply left. Some members of the congregation entered the church the next morning and discovered the scene of butchery. They summoned the police, who searched the Church and discovered Lamont's body in the belfry as well. The police promptly arrested Durrant and began the inquests that were the prelude to Durrant's trial on April 15.

Durrant Tried for Murder

The case attracted considerable publicity, with the San Francisco newspapers trumpeting that it was the "Crime of the Century." The prosecutors were W.H. Anderson, William S. Barnes, W.F. Fitzgerald and Edgar D. Peixotto. Durrant was represented by Eugene N. Deuprey and John H. Dickinson. Presiding was Judge D.J. Murphy.

The evidence against Durrant was overwhelming, except for the motive behind the murders. Why did Durrant kill the two girls? There was no inheritance that he stood to collect, no personal possessions worth stealing. In fact, there were no rational reasons for the murders. Durrant's lawyers relied on the lack of motive as their primary defense during the trial. In response, Peixotto stated for the prosecution that:

> The brilliant counsel for the defendant in his opening statement challenged the prosecution to answer the questions where Blanche Lamont was murdered, when she was murdered, by whom she was murdered, and what the motive was. We are now ready to answer these questions. . . . "What was the motive?"; unbridled passion, that same motive that has ruled and governed the world, made nations totter and decay, brought men from the highest pinnacles in life down to brutish beasts; that same motive that has filled our histories with black pages; that gave to the Roman Empire such characters as Nero, Tiberius and Caracalla.

In other words, Durrant's only motive was an inexplicable impulse to vent his sexual urges through murder. A modern court would have little difficulty accepting this, but in a 19th-century murder prosecution, the lack of a rational motive was still something of a novelty. The defense retorted that Durrant's good character and outstanding reputation in the community made it implausible that he could have acted out of such a twisted motive. It was not a terribly strong argument, but the defense had little else to go with. There was always the hope that the prosecution could be prevented from meeting its burden of proving Durrant's guilt beyond a reasonable doubt.

Dickinson presented the defense's argument to the jury:

> Now, gentlemen, in leaving this case with you, I ask you to consider carefully the good character of the defendant, which stands before you today unimpeached except by the suspicions which this testimony has thrown upon it. His character has been good these many years and there is not a particle of evidence that his character was not at all times uniformly good. His conduct has been entirely natural throughout this entire trial and since the day of his

arrest. What motive could he have had for doing such an act? What motive had he for wrecking his home and his life and his future?

By the fall of 1895, the Durrant trial was the sensation of the West Coast. The courtroom was filled to capacity with spectators every day. Despite the gruesome crimes Durrant was accused of committing, many of these spectators were young women attracted by Durrant's dark good looks. When the attorneys for the prosecution and the defense had rested their cases, Judge Murphy read his instructions to the jury. In particular, he instructed them on the law concerning proof of motive for murder:

> Motive for the killing is an important essential fact in the trial for murder . . . If upon a review of the whole evidence, no motive is apparent or can be fairly imputed to the accused in the commission of the crime charged against him, then this is a circumstance in favor of innocence, and should be so considered by you. The motive may not be apparent in many cases of homicide; there may be no motive discernible, except what arises at or near the time of the commission of the act, and yet the killing is not without a motive. . . . With regard to the grounds from which motive may be inferred, the law has never limited them; therefore it is immaterial whether the motive be hatred, wealth, or *the gratification of desires or passions.*

Judge Murphy offered the jury an illustration, to which they could compare the Durrant case:

> To illustrate this principle: If a man, being of sane mind, and in the absence of a sudden impulse, without any quarrel or word of explanation or warning, should draw his pistol, and take aim and deliberately fire its contents into the breast of another, and death should immediately follow such shooting, and upon his arrest, and ever after, he should refuse to give any explanation or excuse for his criminal act; upon the trial of such a man under such circumstances, it is certainly clear that the prosecution would not be called upon to prove by affirmative testimony what motive, or that any motive, impelled the accused to commit homicide, for the reason that the law will presume that he acted from motive, and that his actions were prompted by reason and was the result of causes acting upon his mind, and deemed sufficient by him to inspire his action.

Therefore, in a restrained manner befitting contemporary morality, Judge Murphy had told the jury that if they believed that Durrant committed the murders to satisfy some twisted sexual urge, then that would constitute a sufficient motive. On November 1, 1895, the jury returned a verdict of guilty against Durrant. Under California law, Durrant faced the death penalty.

Durrant sat in prison for more than a year following the trial while Deuprey and Dickinson filed a series of appeals challenging the verdict. On March 3, 1897, the Supreme Court of California upheld the verdict and denied the defense's appeals. Justice Frederick William Henshaw spoke for California's highest court when he said that the trial court had acted properly:

> Appellant further urges that the evidence fails to disclose any motive for the crime; that proof of motive is essential to support a conviction; and that, therefore, the judgment must be reversed. If by this is meant that proof of a particular motive must be as clear and cogent as proof of the crime, the

> proposition finds no support in either reason or authority. To the act of every rational human being pre-exists a motive. In every criminal case proof of the moving cause is permissible, and oftentimes is valuable; but it is never essential. . . . *Proof of motive is never indispensable to a conviction.*

In essence, the court was telling judges and juries that they were not required to speculate as to the cause of irrational crimes such as Durrant's:

> The wellsprings of human conduct are infinite, and infinitely obscure. An act may owe its performance to complex and multitudinous promptings. Who:
>
> Knows each cord its various tone,
>
> Each spring its various bias?

After some further delays, Durrant's execution was set for January 7, 1898. He asked to say some final words, but he was hung from the scaffold before he had the chance.

Durrant's execution put an end to the story of the Crime of the Century. In a sense, it also put an end to a certain amount of judicial innocence concerning proof of motive in a murder case. It was recognized that some people of apparently good character with no prior history of violence can commit bizarre, brutal crimes for no rational reason. Although motive was still a relevant issue, the prosecution's inability to explain such behavior would not stand in the way of the guilty party's punishment.

—Stephen G. Christianson

Suggestions for Further Reading

Churchill, Allen. *A Pictorial History of American Crime, 1849–1929.* New York: Holt, Rinehart and Winston, 1964.

Durrant, William Henry Theodore. *Report of the Trial of William Henry Theodore Durrant, Indicted for the Murder of Blanche Lamont.* Detroit: The Collector Publishing Co., 1899.

Jackson, Joseph Henry. *San Francisco Murders.* New York: Duell, Sloan and Pearce, 1947.

Leach, Harold. *The Crime of a Century.* San Francisco: Yosemite Publishing Co., 1895.

Scott, Harold Richard. *The Concise Encyclopedia of Crime and Criminals.* London: A. Deutsch, 1961.

Maria Barbella Trials: 1895–96

Defendant: Maria Barbella **Crime Charged:** Murder
Chief Defense Lawyers: First trial: Amos Evans, Henry Sedgewick; Second trial: Frederick B. House, Emanuel Friend **Chief Prosecutors:** John F. McIntyre, Alfred Lauterbach **Judges:** First trial: John W. Goff; Second trial: H.A. Gildersleeve **Place:** New York, New York **Dates of Trials:** First trial: July 11–15, 1895; Second trial: November 17–December 10, 1896
Verdict: First trial: Guilty; Second trial: Not guilty **Sentence:** First trial: Death by electrocution

SIGNIFICANCE

Maria Barbella was the first woman in the United States condemned to die in the electric chair.

On July 18, 1895, Maria Barbella became the first woman in the United States sentenced to be executed in a new invention called the electric chair. Efforts to save the young Italian immigrant from the deadly, unreliable contraption focused on whether or not she deserved to have been convicted in the first place.

Three months earlier on New York City's lower east side, Barbella had tried to reason with the man she loved and with whom she lived, Domenico Cataldo. Cataldo had forcibly taken the young woman's virginity, but despite assurances that he planned to marry her, he showed no intention of honoring his promises. On April 26, he was more interested in playing cards than in discussing matrimony when Barbella stood behind him in a saloon, pleading quietly. Before the astonished patrons, Cataldo suddenly lurched toward the door, his neck bleeding from a mortal wound inflicted by a straight razor in Barbella's hand.

Premeditation at Issue

Prosecutors accused Barbella of murdering Cataldo for ruining her reputation and to gain access to $825 in his bank account. This theory assumed a premeditated plan, so Barbella was charged with the capital offense of first-degree murder. When her trial began on July 11, the defense presented a different view of Barbella's behavior. They accused Cataldo of being a cad with a distasteful record of seducing young women. When Barbella pleaded with him to marry her, his reply was derisive laughter and the retort, "Only pigs marry!" Driven into a rage by his words, she had killed him. Since the rage provoked a spontaneous act, there was no premeditation. The defense asked that their client be charged with second-degree murder, which was not a capital offense, but Judge John Goff denied the motion.

When Barbella took the stand in her own defense, she testified in Italian. In spite of the imperfect translation heard by jurors, it became clear that Cataldo had drugged and seduced her. With her reputation ruined, she had gone to live with him. Shortly thereafter he announced that he was returning to Italy without her. The prosecution relentlessly asked Barbella why she had stayed with a man possessing such reprehensible morals. She replied that she loved him. Barbella continued to insist that she wanted to marry Cataldo, not murder him, and that she had no memory of the attack. Barbella's mother testified that she too had begged Cataldo to marry the girl and restore her honor. Cataldo, said Mrs. Barbella, had laughed and demanded two hundred dollars before he would do such a thing.

Such testimony elicited growing public sympathy, particularly from women. Their feelings were not shared by Judge Goff when he charged the jury on July 15. Goff said that the defendant should expect no compassion from the court simply because she was a woman. If Barbella had planned to kill Cataldo, said Judge Goff, such premeditation made her guilty of first-degree murder. The judge offered his own view of her intent. "It is, in my opinion, futile to claim before any sensible men, constituting a jury, that she intended to use that razor at the time for some purpose not disclosed, that is, for some harmless purpose; and after she took that razor, she secreted it, and followed Cataldo to the saloon. That required thought. It is for you to say whether that was an act of deliberation."

Death Sentence Sparks Protests

The jury took less than an hour to find Barbella guilty. On July 18, Judge Goff sentenced her to be taken to Sing Sing state penitentiary and executed. News of the sentence transformed the case into a national sensation. Philanthropist missionary Rebecca Foster and an expatriate American, the Countess di Brazzá, hired new lawyers for Barbella and organized a petition drive. Thousands of signatures poured into New York governor Levi Morton's office, asking him to pardon the immigrant woman or, at least, commute her death sentence. The execution was effectively halted when an appeal was filed on her behalf.

Frederick House, Barbella's new lawyer, requested a new trial before New York's state court of appeals. House argued that the state had offered no evidence of any premeditation. House accused Judge Goff of multiple errors, such as excluding testimony critical of Cataldo's character and misleading the jury about the facts of the case. House said that the judge erred in charging that only Barbella's acts could be used to weigh her mental condition. Most significantly, House characterized Goff's jury charge as a direct instruction to return a guilty verdict.

On April 21, 1896, the court of appeals agreed. Barbella was granted a new trial on grounds that the defense had not been allowed to use all the evidence at their disposal. The lengthy appellate decision ruled that Judge Goff's charge to the jury was riddled with serious errors and reflected a troubling lack of impartiality from the bench.

When the retrial began on November 17 before a new judge, H. A. Gildersleeve, the defense made a concerted effort to establish that the Barbella family had a history of mental instability and alcoholism. Numerous Italian witnesses who knew the families of Barbella's parents were called. It became clear that her ancestors and all of her siblings had suffered from seizures, some of them fatal. In testimony that was not allowed during the first trial, Barbella's parents testified that Maria had once tried to commit suicide by leaping from a roof and remembered nothing after she was restrained. Her mother was also allowed to recount the abuse Maria had suffered at Cataldo's hands.

The defendant apparently shared her family's mental problems. "Sometimes I feel a machine in my head and the pain is so great I cannot stand it," she said. The defense benefited from her new ability to speak English, which she learned at Sing Sing with the help of the warden and his wife. She stated that she had planned to drown herself if Cataldo rebuffed her final request for marriage. She had taken the razor to hasten her own death after jumping into the river. Despite hours of grueling cross-examination by prosecutors, she insisted that she loved Cataldo and had no memory of what had happened following his comment about "pigs," apart from a red flash and an overwhelming heat in her head.

The defense also introduced the fact that Cataldo was carrying a knife when he was killed, which was confirmed by police reports. Character witnesses included Julia Sage, the wife of Sing Sing's warden, who had come to know the immigrant woman well. Mrs. Sage testified that in her judgment Barbella was incapable of committing a premeditated murder.

During nine days of medical testimony, doctors testifying for the defense presented a scenario in which Barbella had killed Cataldo during a brief fit of epilepsy, triggered by the shock of his "pigs marry" dismissal. The prosecution's experts contended that Barbella was in full control of her faculties. Yet defense attorney House concluded his final argument by steering the burden of proof toward the prosecution. "The only truth here is that Maria Barbella suffers from epilepsy. Distressed at Domenico's insults and unaware of her own illness, she killed a man whom, at any rate, the city will not miss."

As swiftly as the earlier jury had found her guilty, Barbella was found not guilty on December 10. She was freed immediately. Instead of facing the electric chair, she used another recent invention, the telephone, to call Mrs. Sage and the Countess di Brazzá with the news.

—Tom Smith

Suggestions for Further Reading

"Marie Barbella Acquitted." *New York Times* (December 11, 1896): 9.

"Marie Barbella's Story." *New York Time* (December 5, 1896): 9.

Pucci, Idana. *The Trials of Maria Barbella* New York: Four Walls Eight Windows, 1996.

"Recorder Goff's Errors." *New York Times* (April 22, 1896): 9.

"To Save Maria Barbella." *New York Times* (April 8, 1896): 10.

Plessy v. Ferguson: 1896

Appellant: Homer A. Plessy **Respondent:** New Orleans Criminal District Court Judge J.H. Ferguson **Appellant's Claim:** That Louisiana's law requiring blacks to ride in separate railroad cars violated Plessy's right to equal protection under the law **Chief Defense Lawyer:** M.J. Cunningham **Chief Lawyers for Appellant:** F.D. McKenney and S.F. Phillips **Justices:** Supreme Court Justices David J. Brewer, Henry B. Brown, Stephen J. Field, Melville W. Fuller, Horace Gray, John Marshall Harlan, Rufus W. Peckham, George Shiras and Edward D. White **Place:** Washington, D.C. **Date of Decision:** May 18, 1896 **Decision:** That laws providing for "separate but equal" treatment of blacks and whites were constitutional

SIGNIFICANCE

The Supreme Court's decision effectively sanctioned discriminatory state legislation. *Plessy* was not fully overruled until the 1950s and 1960s, beginning with *Brown v. Board of Education* in 1954.

In the years following the Supreme Court's 1875 decision in *U.S. v. Cruikshank* (see separate entry), which limited the federal government's ability to protect blacks' civil rights, many states in the South and elsewhere enacted laws discriminating against blacks. These laws ranged from restrictions on voting, such as literacy tests and the poll tax, to requirements that blacks and whites attend separate schools and use separate public facilities.

On June 7, 1892, Homer A. Plessy bought a train ticket for travel from New Orleans to Covington, Louisiana. Plessy's ancestry was one-eighth black and the rest white, but under Louisiana law he was considered to be black and was required to ride in the blacks-only railroad car. Plessy sat in the whites-only railroad car, refused to move, and was promptly arrested and thrown into the New Orleans jail.

Judge John H. Ferguson of the District Court of Orleans parish presided over Plessy's trial for the crime of having refused to leave the whites-only car, and Plessy was found guilty. Plessy's conviction was upheld by the Louisiana Supreme Court, and Plessy appealed to the U.S. Supreme Court for an order forbidding Louisiana in the person of Judge Ferguson from carrying out the conviction.

Ferguson was represented by Louisiana Attorney General M.J. Cunningham and Plessy by F.D. McKenney and S.F. Phillips. On April 13, 1896, Plessy's lawyers argued before the Supreme Court in Washington, D.C., that Louisiana had violated Plessy's Fourteenth Amendment right to equal protection under the law. Attorney General Cunningham argued that the law merely made a distinction between blacks and whites, but didn't necessarily treat blacks as inferiors, since theoretically the law provided for "separate but equal" railroad car accommodations.

John Marshall Harlan, the only dissenting justice, argued that, "Our Constitution is color-blind, and neither knows nor tolerates classes among citizens." (Courtesy, Library of Congress)

On May 18, 1896, the Court issued its decision. It upheld the Louisiana law:

> A statute which implies merely a legal distinction between the white and colored races—a distinction which is founded in the color of the two races, and which must always exist so long as white men are distinguished from the other race by color—has no tendency to destroy the legal equality of the two races.

Therefore, the Court affirmed Plessy's sentence, namely a $25 fine or 20 days in jail. Further, the Court endorsed the "separate but equal" doctrine, ignoring the fact that blacks had practically no power to make sure that their "separate" facilities were "equal" to those of whites. In the years to come, black railroad cars, schools and other facilities were rarely as good as those of whites. Only Justice John Marshall Harlan dissented from the Court's decision. Harlan's dissent was an uncannily accurate prediction of Plessy's effect:

> Our Constitution is color-blind, and neither knows nor tolerates classes among citizens. . . . In my opinion, the judgment this day rendered will, in time, prove to be quite as pernicious as the decision made by this tribunal in the Dred Scott case. . . . The present decision, it may well be apprehended, will not only stimulate aggressions, more or less brutal and irritating, upon the admitted rights of colored citizens, but will encourage the belief that it is possible, by means of state enactments, to defeat the beneficient purposes which the people of the United States had in view when they adopted the recent amendments of the Constitution.

It was not until the 1950s and the 1960s that the Supreme Court began to reverse *Plessy.* In the landmark 1954 case of *Brown v. Board of Education,* the Court held that separate black and white schools were unconstitutional, and later cases abolished the separate but equal doctrine in other areas affecting civil rights as well.

—*Stephen G. Christianson*

Suggestions for Further Reading

Jackson, Donald W. *Even the Children of Strangers: Equality Under the U.S. Constitution.* Lawrence: University Press of Kansas, 1992.

Kull, Andrew. *The Color-Blind Constitution.* Cambridge, Mass.: Harvard University Press, 1992.

Olsen, Otto H. *The Thin Disguise: Turning Point in Negro History.* New York: Humanities Press, 1967.

Roland Molineux Trials: 1899

Defendant: Roland Burnham Molineux **Crime Charged:** Murder
Chief Defense Lawyers: First trial: George Gordon Battle and Bartow Weeks; Second trial: Frank C. Black **Chief Prosecutor:** James W. Osborne, both trials **Judge:** First trial: John Goff; Second trial: John Lambert
Place: New York, New York **Dates of Trials:** First trial: November 14, 1899–February 11, 1900; Second trial: October 1902 **Verdicts:** First trial: Guilty, overturned on appeal; Second trial: Not guilty **Sentence:** First trial: Death by electrocution, overturned on appeal

SIGNIFICANCE

Roland Molineux's acquittal was the result of the New York courts enforcing more stringent limitations on the admissibility of evidence in criminal cases, which provided increased protection for the rights of defendants.

Roland Molineux was born into a distinguished family which had become rich in the chemical dye business. Molineux's father had been a Union general in the Civil War, and Molineux was raised in the upper crust of New York society. Molineux was a handsome, muscular man who had developed a reputation as a playboy and as a snob by the time he was 30.

Molineux was extremely vain about his athletic prowess, and he belonged to the Knickerbocker Athletic Club, whose membership came exclusively from wealthy and old-line New York families. He was such a snob that he repeatedly went to the club's management to demand that people he considered socially inferior be expelled. In 1898 he also began to compete with one Henry Barnet for the affections of a young and beautiful woman named Blanche Cheeseborough.

In November, Barnet received a package in the mail containing some over-the-counter stomach medicine produced by a well-known drug company. He assumed that it was a free sample, but when he took some, he became violently sick and later died. Less than two weeks after Barnet's death, Molineux married Blanche Cheeseborough. Despite the suspicious circumstances, there were no charges against Molineux. Then, in December 1898, Molineux had a confrontation with Harry Cornish, the Knickerbocker Athletic Club's athletic director. Cornish beat Molineux in a weight-lifting competition, and in a fit of pique, Molineux demanded that the club expel Cornish. The management refused.

In late December, Cornish received a bottle containing a popular liquid headache medicine. He gave it to his aunt, Katharine Adams, who took some on December 28 and died after a bout of violent convulsions. This time, the authorities and the club performed a thorough investigation and discovered that the bottle contained cyanide, which had killed Adams. The police uncovered some letters to various drug companies, written by the murderer to obtain medicines and poisons, which bore Barnet's and Cornish's forged signatures. The handwriting was very similar to Molineux's, and so the police charged Molineux with murder.

Molineux is Tried for Adams' Murder

The state accused Molineux of murdering Katharine Adams but was silent with respect to Henry Barnet. The trial began November 14, 1899, with Judge John Goff presiding. The prosecutor was James W. Osborne and Molineux's lawyers were George Gordon Battle and Bartow Weeks. Osborne brought in more than a dozen expert witnesses to prove that the handwriting on the letters was Molineux's. Judge Goff repeatedly denied the defense's objections concerning the credibility of the prosecution's experts and throughout the trial clearly demonstrated his bias against Molineux. Therefore, Battle and Weeks had to restrain themselves in the hope that Osborne and Goff would commit legal blunders that could be used to overturn the verdict on appeal. After Osborne finished presenting the prosecution's case, Battle and Weeks told Judge Goff that the defense would rest without presenting its side of the case or any witnesses, stating simply that:

> We believe that the prosecution has failed to establish its charge and we rest the defense upon the People's case.

The trial then proceeded directly to the attorneys' closing arguments to the jury. Osborne's statements contained the mistake that the defense had hoped for, namely improper references to evidence concerning Barnet's death:

> You must remember that this defendant was married on November 29, 1898. You must remember that Barnet died on November 10, 1898. . . . You must remember that the defendant testified at the inquest that he had been trying to marry this woman from a time running back to January 1898. . . . The plain, cold facts are that this defendant had been trying to marry this woman and that this woman had refused him until Barnet was cold in his grave.

Osborne blatantly implored the jury to draw a connection between the deaths of Barnet and Adams:

> There have been times in this case when I began to think of poor old Mrs. Adams, stricken down, stricken down without an opportunity to make her peace with her God, stricken down while she was in the performance of her family duty, leaving alone and unprotected her daughter and her son; stricken down in the most cruel and the most brutal manner. . . . Sometimes it seems to me in the nighttime that I can almost hear the voice of Mrs. Adams, calling to me. . . . And then Barnet, Barnet, in the vigor of his youth

and manhood, stricken down in that same manner. . . . And will a jury of my countrymen quail before the honest and just verdict? I think not.

On February 11, 1900, the jury returned a verdict of guilty. Judge Goff sentenced Molineux to die in the electric chair. Battle and Weeks, however, appealed to the New York Court of Appeals in Buffalo. Although it took the Court of Appeals over a year and a half, during which time Molineux stayed in Sing Sing Prison, the court finally heard Molineux's case in June 1901. Molineux's lawyers argued that Osborne's reference to Barnet's death was improper, since Molineux had only been charged with Adams' death. On October 15, 1901, the court's seven judges unanimously ruled that Molineux's conviction had to be reversed and a new trial held.

Because the Court of Appeals had also criticized Judge Goff for being biased during the trial, Judge John Lambert presided over Molineux's second trial. It was a speedy retrial, and took only a couple of days during October of 1902. James Osborne was once again the prosecutor, but this time former Governor Frank Black led the defense team.

Lambert was more sympathetic than Goff to the defense's criticism of Osborne's handwriting experts. Further, many of the prosecution's experts, witnesses and other evidence were no longer available because nearly three years had elapsed since Adams' death. The jury this time returned a verdict of not guilty.

Roland Molineux had written a book while in Sing Sing, called *The Room With the Little Door,* which enjoyed some success. After his acquittal, Molineux lived off his income as a writer and what remained of his family fortune once the lawyers' fees were paid. Molineux did some writing for a couple of newspapers and even worked with a popular playwright. He and Blanche Cheeseborough got a divorce, and although he married again, Molineux's life never returned to normal. In 1913, Molineux suffered a nervous breakdown and was committed to an insane asylum, where he died in 1917.

Molineux owed his freedom to the New York Court of Appeals' having enforced more stringent limitations on the admissibility of evidence in criminal cases. These limitations, which provided increased protection for the rights of defendants, were part of a trend among state courts at the turn of the century. This increased concern for the rights of the accused would eventually come to fruition in Supreme Court decisions of the 1950s and 1960s that expanded the scope of Constitutional protections in criminal trials.

—*Stephen G. Christianson*

Suggestions for Further Reading

Carey, Arthur A. *Memoirs of a Murder Man.* Garden City, N.Y.: Doubleday, Doran & Co., 1939.

Crouse, Russel. *Murder Won't Out.* Garden City, N.Y.: Doubleday, Doran & Co., 1932.

LeBrun, George Petit. *It's Time to Tell.* New York: William Morrow & Co., 1962.

Pearson, Edmund Lester. *Instigation of the Devil.* New York: Charles Scribner's Sons, 1930.

Pejsa, Jane. *The Molineux Affair.* Minneapolis: Kenwood, 1986.

Leon Czolgosz Trial: 1901

Defendant: Leon F. Czolgosz **Crime Charged:** Assassinating President William McKinley **Chief Defense Lawyers:** Loran L. Lewis and Robert C. Titus **Chief Prosecutor:** Thomas Penny **Judge:** Truman C. White **Place:** Buffalo, New York **Dates of Trial:** September 23–24, 1901 **Verdict:** Guilty **Sentence:** Death by electrocution

SIGNIFICANCE

Leon Czolgosz, an avowed anarchist, was tried and sentenced to death for his sensational assassination of President McKinley. The trial was remarkably short. Because the court said that the law presumed Czolgosz was sane, despite important evidence to the contrary, the jury may well have convicted Czolgosz for his extremely unpopular political beliefs.

Leon Czolgosz was one of eight children in a poor Michigan family. Czolgosz worked in various menial jobs from childhood, and he eventually moved to Cleveland and worked in a factory. In his late 20s, Czolgosz became fascinated with anarchism. At the time, anarchism had a certain popularity amongst radical working-class circles, but most Americans viewed it with an abhorrence.

After an Italian anarchist killed the King of Italy, Czolgosz became obsessed with assassinating President William McKinley to strike a blow for the cause. In August 1901, he went to Buffalo, New York for the Pan-American Exposition, which McKinley was planning to attend. Because McKinley was very popular, there were large crowds at the Exposition to see the President. On September 6, Czolgosz made his way through the crowds to where McKinley was greeting the public and shaking hands. Czolgosz successfully made his way past the President's security men, and pulled out a concealed pistol. He shot McKinley twice before the stunned spectators could subdue him.

One shot gave McKinley only a flesh wound, but the other pierced his midsection and tore through his stomach. Despite the best efforts of his doctors, McKinley developed complications and died September 14, 1901.

Czolgosz's Trial is Swift

The public was outraged and demanded speedy justice. Czolgosz's trial began September 23, 1901, little more than a week after President McKinley died. The trial took place in Buffalo before Judge Truman C. White, and the prosecutor was Thomas Penny. Finding attorneys to represent Czolgosz was difficult; no one wanted to be associated with such a hated defendant. After some prodding by the president of the local bar association, Loran L. Lewis and Robert C. Titus agreed to be Czolgosz's counsel.

The anti-anarchist sentiment during this period is evident in this somewhat overzealous cartoon of admitted anarchist and assassin Leon Czolgosz. (*Harper's Weekly*)

Lewis and Titus had had practically no time to prepare a defense, and to make matters worse, Czolgosz obstinately refused to talk to them. Lewis could only argue that anyone who would kill the president in the face of an almost certain death penalty must be insane:

> Every human being . . . has a strong desire to live. Death is a spectre that we all dislike to meet, and here this defendant, . . . we find him going into this building, in the presence of these hundreds of people, and committing an act which, if he was sane, must cause his death.

The prosecutor, however, brought out Czolgosz's anarchist affiliations and called upon the jury to heed the popular demand for a quick trial and execution:

> We have shown you that he had gone to these anarchistic or socialistic meetings and that there had been embedded in his diseased heart the seeds of this awful crime. . . . What evidence is there in this case that the man is not sane? Under the presumption of the law that he is sane . . . how brief ought to be your meditation, how brief ought to be your consultation about the responsibility and criminality of this individual?

The prosecutor had argued to the jury that the law presumed Czolgosz was sane unless he could prove otherwise. Since the defense had been able to enter practically no evidence of any kind, there could be only one verdict. At Penny's request, Judge White closed the trial with instructions to the jury that supported the prosecutor's argument:

> The law in this case presumes that the defendant was sane. . . . The burden of showing insanity is upon the person who alleges it.

Even if the jury believed the defense's claim that no sane man would have killed the president in such a public and blatant manner, there was still the legal definition of insanity to be overcome. Under New York law, Czolgosz was legally insane only if he was unable to understand that what he was doing was wrong on the day he shot McKinley. This legal definition was called the "test of responsibility," and was the gist of Judge White's instruction to the jury on legal insanity:

> In other words, if he was laboring under such a defect of reason as not to know the nature and quality of the act he was doing or that it was wrong, it is your duty, gentlemen of the jury, to acquit him in this case.

Judge White's instruction was the final blow to the defense. Any chance that remained of acquitting Czolgosz on the basis of insanity was gone, since the defense had no evidence to offer that he couldn't understand the wrongness of his actions. On September 24, only one day after it began, the trial ended. After a token deliberation, the jury returned its verdict that Czolgosz was not insane and that he was guilty of murder in the first degree.

Czolgosz went to the electric chair on October 29, 1901. His final statement showed no regret:

> I killed the President because he was the enemy of the good people, the good working people. I am not sorry for my crime. . . .

Czolgosz's last words, like all his other statements, contained no reason for his hatred of McKinley other than an unsupported belief that the president was an enemy of the people. Czolgosz's irrationality strongly suggested insanity, but the issue was brushed aside due to the speed of his trial and the strength of popular feeling against him in particular and anarchists in general.

—*Stephen G. Christianson*

Suggestions for Further Reading

Briggs, L. Vernon. *The Manner of Man that Kills.* New York: Da Capo Press, 1983.

Glad, Paul W. *McKinley, Bryan and the People.* Chicago: T.R. Dee, 1991.

Johns, A. Wesley. *The Man Who Shot McKinley.* South Brunswick, N.J.: A.S. Barnes, 1970.

Leech, Margaret. *In the Days of McKinley.* Norwalk, Conn.: Easton Press, 1986.

Restak, Richard. "Assassin." *Science Digest,* (December 1981): 78–84.

Gregorio Cortez Appeals: 1902–04

Appellant: Gregorio Cortez **Crime Charged:** Murder
Chief Defense Lawyers: R.B. Abernathy, with Samuel Belden Jr. (1902) and J.R. Wooten (1904) **Chief Prosecutors:** J.V. Vandenburg, Robert A. John (1902); Howard Martin, S.L. Green, S.H. Hopkins (1904) **Judges:** W.L. Davidson, John N. Henderson, M.M. Brooks **Place:** Austin, Texas
Dates of Decisions: January 15, 1902; June 24, 1902; June 15, 1904
Verdicts: In favor of appellant (both 1902 cases); guilty verdict affirmed (1904) **Sentence:** Cases dismissed (1902); life imprisonment (1904)

SIGNIFICANCE

Gregorio Cortez's trials stemmed from an act of self-defense that made him a well-known Mexican-American folk hero.

On June 12, 1901, Gregorio Cortez and his brother Romaldo heard a surrey roll into the farmyard they shared in Kenedy, Texas. Their visitors were Karnes County Sheriff W. T. Morris and deputy D. P. Choate, who were investigating a horse theft. The Cortez brothers were innocent of any crime, but the language barrier between the farmers and the lawmen resulted in tragedy. Gregorio Cortez's misunderstood answers to the sheriff's questions erupted into gunfire that left Morris dying, Romaldo wounded, and Gregorio leading pursuers on a 10-day chase that became one of the great legends of the border country.

Gregorio Cortez first fled north on foot toward Ottine, stopping at a ranch owned by friends, the Roblero family. Acting on a tip, a posse stormed the Roblero house. Sheriffs Robert Glover and Henry Schnabel were killed in the resulting gunfight. Cortez then rode south, eluding his pursuers in the rough scrub. The exhausted fugitive was finally captured near Laredo on June 22. Because of the furor over Morris's death in Karnes County, he was jailed in San Antonio.

Cortez was charged and tried separately for murdering the three sheriffs. His trials were rarities in an era when any Mexican American accused of killing a Texas law officer stood little chance of living long enough to appear in court. When he was tried in Gonzales for killing Schnabel, a deadlocked jury reduced the charge to second-degree murder before agreeing on a conviction. While he was in the Gonzales jail, a mob tried unsuccessfully to lynch him. He was transported to Karnes City, where he was convicted and sentenced to death for murdering Morris. A third trial in Columbus ended with a life sentence for killing Glover.

Appeals Challenge Convictions

Efforts to win Cortez's freedom attracted support on both sides of the border. Well-organized appeals by the law firm of Atkinson & Abernathy earned Cortez's first reprieve on January 15, 1902, when the Texas Court of Criminal Appeals overturned his conviction in the Schnabel case. The appellate court ruled that the trial court should have waited to hear testimony from a state witness who had been unavailable due to illness. The missing witness was a deputy who had accompanied Sheriff Glover as he approached Cortez on the eastern side of the Roblero house. The appellate court noted that Cortez could not possibly have killed Schnabel, who was shot at close range beside a barn on the opposite side of the house.

There were other irregularities. A state witness whose command of Spanish was so weak that he could not distinguish between the words for "house" and "barn" had taken an alleged confession. The court also ruled that the jury should have scrutinized more closely an alleged voluntary statement elicited by three armed sheriffs who attempted to get Cortez drunk in his cell.

The court declined to weigh part of the appeal that may have explained Schnabel's death. The defense learned that the posse had been drinking whiskey while riding to the Roblero ranch and that surviving deputies later discussed whether they had been drunkenly shooting at each other. There was conflicting testimony over who started the gunfight. The defense held that the posse had attacked without warning. The appeals court did not settle these issues. It did, however, fault the trial court for not instructing jurors that Cortez could be found innocent if he had lawfully fired in self-defense while resisting an illegal arrest. This was a possibility, for Sheriff Glover had not obtained a warrant. With so many errors in the Schnabel case, the state's prosecution of Cortez collapsed.

Six months later, the appellate court examined Cortez's conviction for killing Sheriff Morris. Prosecutors characterized Morris's warrantless haste to arrest Cortez as an act any man "who knows the character and habits of treacherous Mexicans" would have performed. They denied that any prejudice existed in Karnes City to have merited a change of trial venue. The appeals court disagreed, noting that no Karnes County lawyer would take Cortez's case and that dozens of influential citizens had contributed to an arrest fund that assumed his guilt.

The court acknowledged that the mare over which Morris had mistakenly attempted the arrest was Cortez's legal property, but added that this was beside the point. Morris had erred by not identifying himself as a law officer, compounding the mistake by simply announcing to Cortez that he was under arrest without informing him why. The court ruled that Morris had sufficient time to obtain a warrant, implying that no valid evidence had ever existed to justify such an authorization. Therefore, the attempted arrest was illegal.

Deputy Choate and Cortez's wife offered conflicting testimony over which man drew his gun first. The appeals court found this issue less relevant than the fact that the trial court did not instruct jurors that any case involving a deadly act of self-defense explicitly merited a manslaughter charge, not murder. For this and because of the prejudiced proceedings against him in Karnes County, Cortez's conviction was overturned on June 24, 1902.

Yet the decision did not end the Morris case. If Cortez's gunshots were a response to the sheriff wounding his brother and then shooting at him during an illegal arrest, Cortez had committed no offense under Texas law. This, the ruling said, was an issue to be decided in any subsequent manslaughter trial, not by an appellate court. State prosecutors immediately re-indicted Cortez, but the theory that he had acted in self-defense in the face of an unauthorized arrest endured. He was eventually acquitted in Corpus Christi on April 30, 1904.

Convictions Upheld in Glover Shooting

Cortez still remained in jail for killing Sheriff Glover at the Roblero ranch. When his attorneys returned yet again to the state court, his luck ran out. The court found that Glover's intention to arrest Cortez without pausing to seek a warrant was lawful and prudent because of the sheriff's knowledge of the Morris killing. Allowing deputy Choate to testify about the Morris incident in the Glover trial was accepted as unpredjudicial and pertinent to the posse's motive. A statement Cortez made in jail when he was told that the Robleros were blaming the killing on him was ruled admissible as a confession.

The court dismissed most of the remaining defense challenges to the trial court's decisions and upheld Cortez's life sentence on June 15, 1904. Ironically, the ruling implied that the appeal might have been successful had it been based on the fact that the Glover incident resulted from Sheriff Morris's unlawful arrest attempt. Because the defense had chosen to appeal the sentence on other grounds, however, the court was precluded from judging the matter in this way. Cortez began to serve his sentence at Huntsville penitentiary.

Clemency requests for Cortez continued and were even supported by his jailers. On July 14, 1913, Cortez accepted a conditional pardon from Governor Oscar B. Colquitt and was released. He never apologized for defending himself and his family. His courage and legendary flight were celebrated in a popular border song, "El Corrido de Gregorio Cortez," which was sung for decades on both sides of the Rio Grande. His story was also told in a 1983 film, *The Ballad of Gregorio Cortez.*

—*Tom Smith*

Suggestions for Further Reading

Paredes, Américo. *With a Pistol in His Hand.* Austin: University of Texas Press, 1958.

The Texas Criminal Reports, Cases Argued and Adjudged in the Court of Criminal Appeals of the State of Texas: Vol. 43, Reported by John P. White. Austin: Gammel-Statesman Publishing Co., 1903. Vol. 44, Reported by John P. White. Austin: Gammel-Statesman Publishing Co., 1904. Vol. 47, Reported by Rudolph Kleberg. Chicago: T. H. Flood and Co., 1908.

Albert Patrick Trial: 1902

Defendant: Albert T. Patrick **Crime Charged:** Murder
Chief Defense Lawyer: Albert T. Patrick **Chief Prosecutor:** William Travers Jerome **Judge:** John William Goff **Place:** New York, New York
Dates of Trial: January 22–March 26, 1902 **Verdict:** Guilty
Sentence: Death by electrocution, later commuted to life imprisonment, and ultimately pardoned by the governor of New York

SIGNIFICANCE

The Albert Patrick trial illustrated the often uncertain nature of medical evidence in proving a murder. Although the jury found Patrick guilty, lingering doubts about the evidence eventually caused the governor of New York to pardon him.

Albert T. Patrick was the sort of man who gives lawyers a bad name. A native of Texas, where he went to law school and then practiced law for several years, Patrick moved to New York in 1892 to escape disbarment proceedings initiated by a federal judge who was outraged by Patrick's conduct in a particular case. Once in New York, Patrick continued his shady ways. Although nothing was ever proven, there were suspicious circumstances surrounding the death of a wealthy fertilizer magnate who had sued Patrick for restitution of $5,500—a respectable sum in those days—and surrounding the death of Patrick's wife in 1896.

In 1896, Patrick also became involved in the affairs of William Marsh Rice, a multimillionaire and philanthropist. Rice was born in 1816 in Springfield, Massachusetts, and moved to Texas in the 1830s when it was still the raw frontier. Rice built a fortune in oil, retailing, and real estate, and his empire extended into Louisiana and Oklahoma as well. In his old age, Rice had returned to the East Coast to live with his second wife in Rice's Dunellen, New Jersey mansion. Rice's wife died in July 1896, and in her will left a considerable amount of her estate to her family and relatives. Under Texas law, her estate consisted of half of all property acquired by Rice during their marriage, which amounted to millions of dollars. Her will conflicted with Rice's desire to leave virtually all of his estate to the William M. Rice Institute for the Advancement of Literature, Science and Art in Houston, Texas. Rice, having a Madison Avenue apartment, asserted that he was a New York resident and therefore not subject to Texas law. When he started legal actions against the executor of his wife's estate, O.T. Holt, Holt went to Patrick for help.

William Marsh Rice Murdered

Holt retained Patrick to obtain evidence from anyone who had ever known Rice that could be used to prove that Rice was legally still a Texan. During his investigations, Patrick met Rice's personal valet and secretary, Charles F. Jones. Patrick and Jones thought up an ambitious scheme to murder Rice, plunder his estate by cashing forged checks on his New York bank accounts, and get at the rest of Rice's assets through a forged will naming Patrick and Jones as beneficiaries. Patrick himself drafted the fake will, also deliberately inserting generous legacies to Rice's relatives at the expense of the institute in the hope that the relatives would not challenge the will.

On the night of September 23, 1900, Jones covered the sleeping Rice's face with chloroform-soaked towels. The old man died without a struggle. Patrick and Jones were unable to carry through their scheme, however. Rice's Texas lawyer demanded an autopsy and came to New York to begin an investigation. When Patrick tried to cash the forged checks at Rice's bank, the bank officials became suspicious and notified the authorities. Patrick and Jones were soon arrested for Rice's murder. After unsuccessfully trying to commit suicide, Jones confessed and agreed to testify against Patrick in return for leniency.

Patrick Tried and Convicted

Albert Patrick's trial began on January 22, 1902. Patrick defended himself. The prosecutor was District Attorney William Travers Jerome and the judge was John William Goff. The central issue of the trial was proving the *corpus delicti*, namely that a murder had occurred. Although the doctors who had performed the autopsy generally agreed that Rice had been killed by chloroform poisoning, there was enough scientific uncertainty, given Rice's advanced age, that Patrick was able to keep the trial stalled for over two months. For example, take Patrick's questioning of Dr. Edward W. Lee:

> Patrick: Doctor, assuming that a patient is eighty-four years of age, that prior to death he had dropsy of the lower limbs for several months from the knees down, and that the post-mortem findings revealed . . . the lungs congested slightly . . . the kidneys firm [with] a number of small cysts, and that on the day preceding his death the patient was troubled with his urine, and had to urinate frequently, . . . what would you say would be the cause of death?
>
> Lee: Congestion of the lungs and diseased kidneys [which could be caused by chloroform or by tuberculosis, pneumonia or kidney disease]

On March 26, 1902, the jury returned a guilty verdict against Patrick. Goff sentenced Patrick to death by electrocution. Luckily for Patrick, however, one of his sisters had married a wealthy man, John T. Milliken, who was convinced of Patrick's innocence. Milliken financed a team of lawyers to handle Patrick's appeals, which tied up the courts for years. In 1906, Governor Frank Higgins commuted Patrick's sentence to life imprisonment. Patrick continued to fight for total freedom, however. For the next six years, Patrick and the Milliken-financed team of lawyers pursued every avenue of appeal, including, according to accounts in the press, under-the-table payments to state legislators and officials.

On November 28, 1912, Governor John A. Dix pardoned Patrick. Dix claimed that "there has always been an air of mystery about the case." Dix's pardon was widely criticized, but there was nothing that could be done about it, especially as Dix was about to leave office anyway. Patrick left New York, never to return, and died in Tulsa, Oklahoma, in 1940. Although the Patrick case amply illustrated the fact that medical evidence is often inconclusive in proving a murder, it also demonstrated that money makes a difference in the American system of justice.

—*Stephen G. Christianson*

Suggestions for Further Reading

LeBrun, George Petit. *It's Time to Tell.* New York: William Morrow & Co., 1962.

Medico-Legal Society. *Medico-Legal Questions Arising in the Case of People v. Patrick.* New York: Unknown Publisher, 1905.

Nash, Jay Robert. *Murder, America: Homicide in the United States from the Revolution to the Present.* New York: Simon & Schuster, 1980.

Pearson, Edmund Lester. *Five Murders.* Garden City, N.Y.: Doubleday, Doran & Co., 1928.

Symons, Julian. *A Pictorial History of Crime.* New York: Crown Publishers, 1966.

Captain William Van Schaick Trial: 1906

Defendant: William Van Schaick **Crime Charged:** Criminal negligence and misconduct **Chief Defense Lawyers:** Terence J. McManus and William M.K. Olcott **Chief Prosecutors:** Ernest E. Baldwin and Henry I. Burnett **Judge:** Edward B. Thomas **Place:** New York, New York **Dates of Trial:** January 10–27, 1906 **Verdict:** Guilty **Sentence:** 10 years in prison pardoned after serving 4 years

SIGNIFICANCE

Captain Van William Schaick was found guilty, but his corporate employer and its board of directors, who bore at least as much responsibility for the tragic death of over 900 people, went scot-free. This trial and other trials of the period, such as the Triangle Shirtwaist fire trial (see separate entry), illustrate the extreme reluctance that the legal system has had in recognizing that corporations should be held accountable for their actions.

William Van Schaick was the captain of a steamboat, called the *General Slocum,* which for years traveled the waters of the bay and harbor of New York City. Captain Van Schaick was an experienced seaman, having been a sailor for decades, and was a trusted employee of the Knickerbocker Steamboat Company, which owned the *General Slocum.*

On June 15, 1904, the *General Slocum* was traveling New York's East River. Only six weeks previously, the *General Slocum* had passed federal inspection and gotten a renewal of its sailing permit. For reasons that never became entirely clear, a fire developed on board. The fire spread quickly, and the hundreds of passengers began to panic. They rushed to the lifeboats and life preservers, only to find that the boats were lashed to the ship with wires and couldn't be freed. The life preservers, made of cork, were so old and shoddy that they crumbled in the passengers' hands. The ship's crew couldn't put out the fire because the pumps were old and the hoses leaked. Desperate to escape the flames, over a thousand people jumped overboard and hundreds drowned because they couldn't reach the shore.

The *General Slocum* disaster shocked New York and dominated the local press for weeks as bodies were fished from the East River. The final death tally was nearly 900 people. The day after the disaster, Secretary of Commerce and

Labor George B. Cortelyou ordered a federal inquiry, to be headed by George Uhler, supervising inspector general of the Steamboat Inspection Service, and James A. Dumont and Thomas H. Barrett of the local New York Board of Steamboat Inspections. Meanwhile, Bronx Coroner Joseph Berry ordered an inquest, which was to be the precursor to a criminal trial.

Only Van Schaick is Tried

On June 20, 1904, the inquest began. There were eight days of testimony by Captain Van Schaick, the crew of the General Slocum, surviving passengers and officers and directors of the Knickerbocker Steamboat Company. Although it was Captain Van Schaick's duty to run the ship, the company should have paid for the necessary repairs to, and upkeep of, the safety equipment. Company President Frank A. Barnaby denied that the condition of the *General Slocum* had been allowed to deteriorate, but the receipts for repairs that Barnaby presented were highly suspect.

A dramatic photograph of the *General Slocum* sinking. (*Harper's Weekly*)

Questions: You know of your own knowledge that these bills are for *Slocum* apparatus?

Barnaby: I do.

Question: You are sure all these were for the *General Slocum?*

Barnaby: Yes.

Question: If this is the case, how is it I find in some of these bills the name *Grand Republic* [another company steamboat] scratched out or taken out with acid and the name *Slocum* inserted?

Barnaby: I suppose some book-keeper must have done that.

On June 28, 1904, the coroner's inquest jury found Captain Van Schaick and the officers and directors of the company guilty of manslaughter in the form of criminal negligence for not having fulfilled their collective duty to see that the ship had the proper safety equipment. Only Captain Van Schaick, however, was brought to trial.

The trial began on January 10, 1906, before Judge Edward B. Thomas. Captain Van Schaick was defended by Terence J. McManus and William M.K. Olcott. The prosecutors were Ernest E. Baldwin and U.S. District Attorney Henry I. Burnett. On January 27, 1906, the jury found Van Schaick guilty of the charges of criminal negligence and misconduct. Thomas told Captain Van Schaick, "You are no ordinary criminal; I must make an example of you," and sentenced him to the maximum penalty under the law, 10 years in prison.

On February 12, 1908, Captain Van Schaick's appeal was denied. He went to New York's infamous Sing Sing prison to serve his sentence, not a pleasant prospect for a man over 70 years old. His wife, Grace Mary Van Schaick, worked for his release and got over 200,000 signatures on a petition for his pardon. President Theodore Roosevelt twice refused to pardon Captain Van Schaick, but the next president, William Howard Taft, was more receptive. On Christmas Day of 1911, Taft pardoned Captain Van Schaick, who had already served nearly four years of his sentence. After leaving Sing Sing, he retired to live on a farm in Fulton County, New York until he died at the age of 90 on December 8, 1927.

Captain Van Schaick may have been partially responsible for the *General Slocum* disaster, but there was surely no justice in letting the company, its officers and directors escape punishment for their misconduct as well. The Captain Van Schaick trial and other trials, such as the one following the Triangle Shirtwaist fire (see separate entry), illustrate the extreme reluctance that the legal system had in that period in recognizing that corporations should be held accountable for their actions.

—*Stephen G. Christianson*

Suggestions for Further Reading

Hanson, John Wesley. *New York's Awful Excursion Boat Horror, Told By Survivors and Rescuers.* Chicago: Unknown Publisher, 1904.

Northrop, Henry Davenport. *New York's Awful Steamboat Horror.* Philadelphia: National Publishing Company, 1904.

Ogilvie, John Stuart. *History of the General Slocum Disaster.* New York: J.S. Ogilvie Publishing Company, 1904.

Rust, Claude. *The Burning of the General Slocum.* New York: Elsevier/Nelson Books, 1981.

Werstein, Irving. *The General Slocum Incident: Story of an Ill-Fated Ship.* New York: John Day Co., 1965.

Chester Gillette Trial: 1906

Defendant: Chester Ellsworth Gillette **Crime Charged:** Murder
Chief Defense Lawyers: Albert M. Mills and Charles D. Thomas
Chief Prosecutor: George W. Ward **Judge:** Irving R. Devendorf
Place: Herkimer, New York **Dates of Trial:** November 12–December 4, 1906 **Verdict:** Guilty **Sentence:** Death by electrocution

SIGNIFICANCE

The sordid murder of a secretary by her social-climbing boss received its share of press attention at the time but would be long since forgotten had it not provided Theodore Dreiser with the inspiration, the characters and the plot of arguably the greatest novel of the literary movement known as "naturalism": *An American Tragedy.*

Chester Ellsworth Gillette was born in 1884 to a well-to-do Christian family. His youth gave no inclination that he would become one of the most famous murderers of his time. As a child, Gillette did missionary work for the Salvation Army. He went to prestigious Oberlin College, which was well-known for its divinity school and missionary work in China. After Oberlin, Gillette went to work for a wealthy uncle who owned a dress factory in Cortland, a town located in upstate New York not far from Syracuse.

Gillette rose steadily in his uncle's business and soon became the factory manager. The local business community accepted Gillette as an up-and-coming young man. Gillette developed social ambitions as well. He was good looking and charming, and he mingled easily with the local gentry. Soon Gillette was a regular at the parties and other functions of Cortland society.

Still in his early 20s, Gillette had high hopes of marrying a girl from one of the town's wealthy families. There was an obstacle to Gillette's plans, however. Grace Brown, nicknamed "Billie," had left her parents' farm in South Otselic, New York, for Cortland and a clerical job at Gillette's factory. Gillette had an affair with her, and in 1906 she became pregnant. If he were to marry Brown, it would ruin Gillette's ambitions as a social climber.

One of the characteristics of the criminal mentality is that when faced with a difficult personal situation, a criminal will go beyond the boundaries of normal behavior and use violence to resolve the problem. Gillette was such a man. In

July 1906, he went on vacation, taking Brown with him to a hotel on the shores of Big Moose Lake outside the little town of Herkimer, New York, roughly 60 miles from Cortland. Grace Brown never returned from this vacation.

Tragedy at Big Moose Lake

On the morning of July 11, Gillette took Brown out in a rowboat. As was reconstructed later, Gillette rowed Brown around the lake for a while, then when they were out of sight, he hit her with a tennis racquet and threw her into the lake. Whether the blows killed her instantly or she died of drowning was never made clear. At any rate, after returning to shore, Gillette buried the racquet along the shore and left for another hotel. Gillette checked in at the nearby Arrowhead Inn and later asked the desk clerk whether there had been a drowning reported at Big Moose Lake. When Brown's body was found in the lake shortly thereafter, the police quickly tracked down Gillette.

Gillette claimed that Brown committed suicide by jumping in the water after he started to talk with her about the baby. However, Gillette's behavior didn't betray grief or sorrow. Further, someone discovered the tennis racquet Gillette had buried, broken as if from striking hard blows. The police arrested Gillette, charged him with Brown's murder, and kept him in the Herkimer County jail pending his trial. The press, always eager for a juicy society scandal, made him famous. From his cell, Gillette sold pictures of himself and used the proceeds to have hotel caterers deliver meals to his cell.

On November 12, 1906, Gillette's trial began. The prosecutor was District Attorney George W. Ward, with Judge Irving R. Devendorf presiding. Gillette's defense lawyers were Albert M. Mills and Charles D. Thomas.

Chester Gillette: Murderer or Coward?

Mills and Thomas knew that the evidence of Gillette's guilt was highly persuasive. He had been on the boat with Brown, left the scene under highly suspicious circumstances, and had the stigma of having gotten Brown pregnant but having not married her. However, they believed they could make a reasonable defense, based on Gillette's story that the boat had capsized after Brown jumped in the lake. According to Gillette, after the boat tipped over, he fell into the water. He came up but could not find Brown. Could it be that he had panicked and fled? This would indicate poor judgment, in that day tantamount to cowardice. But poor judgment and cowardice are not murder.

Thomas made the defense's pitch to the jury:

> Now gentlemen, there are such things as moral cowards. There are men so constituted that in the presence of a great calamity they must loose themselves, and this boy, in my opinion, in that condition, wandered to the Arrowhead and registered under his own name. He didn't try to run away. He didn't try to conceal himself at all.

Thomas then called Gillette to the stand, and asked him about the critical events immediately following what Gillette said was Brown's decision to kill herself. The following is an excerpt from Thomas' questioning of his client:

> Gillette: Then she said, 'Well, I will end it here,' and she, well, jumped into the lake; stepped up onto the boat, kind of threw herself in.
>
> Thomas: What did you do?
>
> Gillette: I tried to reach her, I leaned back in the seat in the other end, the bow seat, I guess. I tried to reach her and, well, I was not quick enough. I went into the lake, too. The boat tipped over as I started to get up. The boat went right over then. Of course, I went into the lake.
>
> Thomas: Go on and describe what you did.
>
> Gillette: Then I came up. I halloed, grabbed hold of the boat. Then, as soon as I could get the water out of my eyes and see, I got hold of the boat or got to the boat.
>
> Thomas: Did you see her?
>
> Gillette: No, I stayed there at the boat but a minute or two. It seemed like a long time, anyway, and I didn't see her. Then I swam to shore.

District Attorney Ward, knowing the thinness of the defense's argument, pressed home his attack. Not only could the defense not explain the tennis racquet, but Ward had five doctors to testify that Brow's autopsy showed evidence of blows to the body. Further, Gillette later seemed to change his story, suggesting that the boat had tipped over first and Brown had hit her head against the side before sinking beneath the lake. This sounded like an attempt to explain away the results of the autopsy. Ward said of the defense:

> When the learned counsel made this address to you in a despairing effort to withdraw from the clutches of the law a man whom he knows and whom I know and whom you all know that this evidence condemns beyond all question, when he stands up here and says that five of these doctors, men who enter your houses day after day and have your lives and the lives of your families in their hands, are perjurers and wanton liars, it ought not to be necessary to make an argument against such a statement as that.

Ward Finishes his Closing Argument

But why had Gillette been so inept in covering his tracks? If Gillette had planned Brown's murder, why hadn't he disposed of the tennis racquet better or otherwise killed her in a less suspicious manner? After all, it had taken practically no time for the police to arrest Gillette. Ward pointed out that the arrogance of murderers is often beyond the pale of ordinary human reason:

> He is bloodthirsty and brutal. He is a blunderer. He does not reason on the lines that any one of us do. He reasons on different lines. Everything looks red before him. There is nothing but one object that he is going to grasp, and that is his personal safety, his personal well-being, the possibility of an arrest. He sees nothing else. He cares for nothing else. He casts all these things behind him and says "I can do this slyly. I can get the girl on the bottom of the lake. I can do it secretly. I can do it carefully. I stand well in Cortland. I

go to church. They think I am a paragon of virtue, a decent man, when in reality I am a ravisher. What I do in secret will be unknown. I can take her out there and leave her body in the lake. . . ."

On December 4, 1906, after deliberating for only a couple of hours, the jury announced its verdict: guilty. Judge Devendorf prepared to sentence Gillette to death, as prescribed by New York law. But before he pronounced sentence, the judge asked Gillette if he had anything to say. Gillette replied:

> I have. I desire to state that I am innocent of this crime and therefore ought not to be punished. I think that is all.

Judge Devendorf then sentenced Gillette to die in the electric chair. Following Gillette's trial and sentence, his execution was delayed while Mills and Thomas appealed. They based their appeals on a lengthy list of objections that they had made at trial and a trial record that was more than 3,000 thousand pages long. On February 18, 1908, the New York Court of Appeals rejected Mills' and Thomas' arguments. Chief Judge Frank A. Hiscock's opinion was terse and unequivocal:

> No controversy throws the shadow of doubt or speculation over the primary fact that about 6 o'clock in the afternoon of July 11, 1906, while she was with the defendant, Grace Brown met an unnatural death and her body sank to the bottom of Big Moose Lake.

With the legal appeals finally at an end, Gillette went to the electric chair on March 30, 1908.

Gillette's story lingered in the memory of a young muckraking novelist. In *An American Tragedy,* a novel whose plot and principal characters were closely modeled on the events and figures in the case, Theodore Dreiser resurrected Gillette as the embodiment and culmination of the money-grubbing and social climbing that Dreiser believed had corrupted the nation's moral values. The novel's critical and commercial success ensured that the sordid murderer became one of the archetypal and tragic villains in American literature.

—*Stephen G. Christianson*

Suggestions for Further Reading

Brandon, Craig. *Murder in the Adirondacks.* Utica, N.Y.: North Country Books, 1986.

Brown, Grace. *Grace Brown's Love Letters.* Herkimer, N.Y.: Citizen Pub. Co., 1906.

Brownell, Joseph W. *Adirondack Tragedy.* Interlaken, N.Y.: Heart of the Lakes Publishing, 1986.

Dreiser, Theodore. *An American Tragedy.* New York: Boni & Liveright, 1925.

Abraham Ruef Trials: 1906–08

Defendants: Abraham Ruef and Eugene E. Schmitz
Crimes Charged: Bribery and extortion **Chief Defense Lawyer:** Henry Ach
Chief Prosecutors: Francis J. Heney, Hiram Johnson, and William Langdon
Judges: Frank Dunne, Maurice T. Dooling, and William P. Lawlor
Place: San Francisco, California **Dates of Trials:** 1906–08
Verdicts: Ruef: Mistrial, mistrial, guilty; Schmitz: Guilty (later reversed on appeal) **SIGNIFICANCE** The Abraham Ruef trials revealed the rise and pervasiveness of graft and the power of political bosses in modern industrial America, and the growth of the Progressive movement that challenged such forces.

In 1901, San Francisco's reformist mayor, James D. Phelan, angered many labor groups when he authorized the use of force to break a citywide strike. In response, a powerful coalition supposedly representing the labor movement formed the Union Labor Party (ULP) and helped get Eugene E. Schmitz, head of the Musicians' Union, elected as the new mayor. But in reality, the new party did not represent any of the city's large labor interests or unions. Instead the ULP and Schmitz were the creatures of Abraham Ruef, a well-connected, little-known local lawyer. Within a few years, Ruef would use the ULP and the officials that it helped elect to become San Francisco's undisputed political boss.

Following Schmitz's 1901 election, Ruef began collecting "retainers" from "clients" who wanted contracts with the city or who wished to gain protection for their illegal businesses of gambling, prostitution, and the like. As time went by and Ruef managed to place more and more cronies in the city government, especially the all-important Board of Supervisors, his "fees" grew to astronomical proportions. In one transaction with a streetcar company, Ruef charged $200,000; in the wake of the great San Francisco earthquake and fire of April 1906, Ruef paved the way for the grant of a telephone monopoly for a "fee" of $125,000. Since the politicians he helped to elect owed him their allegiance and he shared his "fees" with them, "seeing Ruef," as the phrase went, was soon the only way to conduct business—legitimate or shady—with the city.

Reformers Begin To Battle Ruef

But Ruef had also made political enemies along the way, people who wanted to put an end to graft, clean up the city government, and put Ruef behind bars. Chief among them were Fremont Older, managing editor of the San Francisco *Bulletin*; the former mayor, James Phelan; and Rudolph Spreckels, a sugar tycoon whom Ruef had once crossed, who now offered to underwrite the cost of Ruef's prosecution. With the cooperation of President Theodore Roosevelt, these men brought in the incorruptible federal prosecutor Francis J. Heney to take on Ruef. Heney, in turn, hired the great detective William J. Burns to help him.

William Langdon, the city's honest district attorney, quickly appointed Heney as a special prosecutor. Just as quickly, Ruef got Mayor Schmitz to fire Langdon and to appoint Ruef in his place, but a judge blocked the maneuver as illegal. A few months after the massive earthquake, with the city still in ruins, Heney filed bribery charges against Schmitz and Ruef in connection with the licensing of several "French restaurants"—in reality, brothels. After pleading not guilty to the charges Ruef jumped bail and went into hiding. However, Detective Burns and court officers soon found him and brought him back to court to face trial.

By now the reformers had decided to go after not only the politicians and bosses, but also the businessmen who had bribed them. After all, one can't be bought off without someone doing the buying. Among these were many prominent and popular San Franciscans, and the reformers began to lose public support. Heney offered Ruef a plea bargain in exchange for information about those who had bribed him. Ruef eventually agreed to the plea bargain, but then refused to give Heney any names. Heney retracted the offer and instead charged Ruef with several more counts of bribery and extortion, which caused a public outcry.

At this point, things took a violent turn. Fremont Older, the *Bulletin's* editor and Ruef's strongest critic, was kidnapped and later released; a prosecution witness's house was blown up; the officer who had discovered Ruef's hideout was found dead floating in San Francisco Bay. During the trial a former convict whom Heney had rejected as a juror, walked up to the prosecutor in the courtroom and shot him in the face, although Heney survived the attack. While he recovered, a young prosecutor named Hiram Johnson filled in for Heney; this was the start of a career that would take Johnson to the governor's office and ultimately to the U.S. Senate.

Ruef Is Convicted

In the end, none of the havoc saved Ruef, whom a jury finally convicted in 1908. He was sentenced to 14 years imprisonment in San Quentin, and finally, after exhausting his appeals, began serving his sentence. Of all of the bosses and corrupt politicians who had controlled the city since 1901, he was the only man to go to prison for his deeds. Mayor Schmitz was also convicted of bribery and extortion, but an appellate court overturned the verdict.

In August 1915, after serving fewer than five years of his term, Ruef was granted parole. During the course of his career he had taken at least half a million dollars in bribes. However, by the time he died in 1936 he had become bankrupt.

Ruef's case is one of the more dramatic stories of the rise of urban graft, the influence of political cronyism, and the battle of labor and party bosses with the emerging forces of the Progressive movement. Rarely in American history has a private citizen so tightly controlled a city's political machinery, and rarely has his downfall been so notorious and complete.

—*Buckner F. Melton, Jr.*

Suggestions for Further Reading

Bean, Walton. Boss. *Ruef's San Francisco: The Story of the Union Labor Party, Big Business, and the Graft Prosecution.* Berkeley: University of California Press, 1967.

Older, Fremont. *My Own Story.* Oakland, Calif.: The Post-Enquirer Publishing Co., 1925.

Thomas, Lately. *A Debonair Scoundrel: An Episode in the Moral History of San Francisco.* New York: Holt, Rinehart and Winston, 1962.

Harry Thaw Trials: 1907–08

Defendant: Harry Kendall Thaw **Crime Charged:** Murder
Chief Defense Lawyers: First trial: Delphin M. Delmas, John B. Gleason, Clifford Hartridge, Hugh McPike, and George Peabody; Second trial: Martin W. Littleton, Daniel O'Reilly, and Russell Peabody **Chief Prosecutor:** William Travers Jerome **Judge:** First trial: James Fitzgerald; Second trial: Victor J. Dowling **Place:** New York, New York **Dates of Trials:** First trial: January 23–April 12, 1907; Second trial: January 6–February 1, 1908
Verdict: First trial: None, jury deadlocked; Second trial: Not guilty by reason of insanity

SIGNIFICANCE

Harry Thaw married the glamorous showgirl Evelyn Nesbit, who had previously been the mistress of the famous architect Stanford White. Thaw shot White during a public performance in Madison Square Garden and was subsequently tried for murder. Thaw's attorneys took the insanity defense to murder to new extremes, successfully arguing that Thaw suffered from "dementia Americana," a condition supposedly unique to American men that caused Thaw to develop an uncontrollable desire to kill White after he learned of White's previous affair with Nesbit.

Harry Thaw was born in 1872 into a family of wealthy Pennsylvania industrialists. His father made a fortune estimated at $40 million in the Pittsburgh coke business and had also invested heavily in the Pennsylvania Railroad. Thaw's mother spoiled him as a youth and indulged him throughout his life—with tragic consequences.

As a young man, Thaw went to Harvard University for his higher education, but he was expelled because he spent all of his time playing poker. Over his father's objections, Thaw's mother provided him with a substantial allowance and paid off massive gambling debts that Thaw incurred after moving to New York City. Thaw also had a taste for pleasures more decadent than gambling, such as frequent visits to a whorehouse. Although Thaw had several incidents with the police, his mother and his family's money always secured his release.

Evelyn Nesbit Comes to New York

Evelyn Nesbit's background was much more modest than Thaw's but became equally as sordid sexually. Nesbit's parents in Pittsburgh were poor and could never provide for their daughter's education. Nesbit was beautiful, however, and from an early age she also showed some skill as a singer and dancer. Nesbit's family came to rely on the money she earned as a model and in the theater. Within a short time, Nesbit's career soared and she became a "Floradora girl," joining a prestigious all-girl chorus.

During a performance of the Floradora chorus, Nesbit attracted the attention of architect Stanford White. White had made a fortune designing the homes of New York's society set and had designed several famous buildings, including Madison Square Garden. White kept a private suite of rooms for himself in the Garden's tower. The apartment was decorated with oriental furnishings, and featured a red velvet swing hung from the ceiling. White's wealth enabled him to bring young showgirls to his apartment and have them use the swing while he looked underneath their long dresses. Showered with gifts and presents, Evelyn Nesbit soon became White's mistress, and their affair lasted for three years. As Nesbit later testified at trial, White's behavior was not limited to voyeurism; he ultimately got Nesbit intoxicated and raped her when she passed out.

Nesbit left White early in 1905 for Harry Thaw, who like White had seen Nesbit on stage and for some time had been pursuing her at every opportunity. Whether out of love or a desire for another wealthy benefactor, Nesbit married Thaw April 4, 1905. Thaw took Nesbit to Europe for their honeymoon and reportedly began to whip and beat her. Thaw became obsessed with Nesbit's previous relationship with White and forced her to repeat intimate details of their affair. Thaw's obsession became a conviction that he had to avenge Nesbit's disgrace and rid the world of a human monster.

On June 25, 1906, Thaw acted on his obsessions. At Madison Square Garden, where the Thaws were attending the public performance of a new musical, Thaw spotted White. With no thought in his mind but murder, Thaw charged up to White's table and pulled out a pistol; he shot White several times while hundreds of people at the musical watched in horror. Thaw made no attempt to resist arrest, and he was promptly seized by policemen who rushed to the Garden.

Thaw is Tried for Murder

Upon learning of his arrest, Thaw's mother rushed to his defense. Publicly declaring that she would spend the family's $40-million fortune to set Thaw free, she paid to have her son represented by one of the most formidable lawyers of the age, Delphin Delmas. Delmas, an attorney short in stature but tall in reputation before the California courts, was known as the "Napoleon of the Western bar." Delmas brought four other attorneys with him to assist in Thaw's defense when the trial opened January 23, 1907: John B. Gleason, Clifford Hartridge, Hugh McPike, and George Peabody. Gleason would speak occasionally during the trial, but Delmas conducted the bulk of Thaw's defense.

The prosecutor was William Travers Jerome, New York's district attorney, who had once served as a judge and reportedly had ambitions to become governor one day. Jerome knew that the Thaw trial would be closely followed by the press and the public, for as the *New York Times* reported, "the Thaw trial is being reported to the ends of the civilized globe" due to:

> The eminence of the victim, the wealth of the prisoner, the dramatic circumstance of the crime, and the light it sheds not only on Broadway life, but on the doings of the fast set in every capital. . . .

Thaw and his mother not only wanted to save Thaw from the electric chair, which was the penalty for murder, but prevent him from spending the rest of his life in an insane asylum. Therefore, from the beginning of the trial, Delmas conducted the defense with the aim of proving that Thaw was and always had been sane except for that evening of June 25, 1906, when he temporarily went insane and shot White. Delmas exploited Nesbit's beauty to appeal to the jury's emotions. He called Evelyn Nesbit to the stand, and asked her to describe the events of the night on which White raped her:

> Mr. White asked me to come to see the back room and he went through some curtains, and the back room was a bedroom, and I sat down at the table, a tiny little table. There was a bottle of champagne, a small bottle and one glass. Mr. White picked up the bottle and poured the glass full of champagne. . . . Then he came to me and told me to finish my champagne, which I did, and I don't know whether it was a minute after or two minutes after, but a pounding began in my ears, then the whole room seemed to go around. Everything got very flat. . . . Then, I woke up, all my clothes were pulled off of me, and I was in bed. I sat up in the bed, and started to scream.

Prosecutor Jerome, who had produced a score of eyewitnesses testifying that Thaw shot White at point-blank range, watched in frustration while Delmas, in effect, put White's treatment of Nesbit on trial. Delmas then introduced the defense's argument of temporary insanity by asking Nesbit about Thaw's reaction upon learning of the rape incident. Delmas and Nesbit both carefully avoided the subject of Thaw's penchant for sadistic sex:

> He would get up and walk up and down the room a minute and then come and sit down and say, "Oh, God! Oh, God!" and bite his nails like that and keep sobbing.

Nesbit's acting experience complemented Delmas' legal ability: the jury was masterfully presented with the picture of a young, pretty and innocent girl relating the story of her outrage to her husband, who then flies into a murderous fury. In his closing argument, Delmas hammered the argument home to the jury:

> And if Thaw is insane, it is with a species of insanity known from the Canadian border to the Gulf. If you expert gentlemen ask me to give it a name, I suggest that you label it Dementia Americana. It is that species of insanity that inspires of every American to believe his home is sacred. It is that species of insanity that persuades an American that whoever violates the sanctity of his home or the purity of his wife or daughter has forfeited the protection of the laws of this state or any other state.

Judge James Fitzgerald reminded the jury that they could only find Thaw not guilty by reason of insanity if Thaw could not understand at the time of the murder that his actions were wrong. Jerome urged the jury to resist Delmas' appeal to their emotions:

> Will you acquit a cold-blooded, deliberate, cowardly murderer because his lying wife has a pretty girl's face?

On April 12, 1907, the jury reported to Judge Fitzgerald that it could not reach a verdict and was deadlocked: seven jurors finding Thaw guilty of first degree murder, five jurors finding Thaw not guilty by reason of insanity. Judge Fitzgerald adjourned the court, pending a retrial of Thaw.

Harry Thaw's "dementia Americana" was cited as his motive for murdering architect Stanford White. (AP/Wide World Photos)

Thaw is Tried Again and Found Insane

Thaw's second trial began January 6, 1908. Although Jerome was still the prosecutor, Thaw had a new team of defense lawyers: Martin W. Littleton, Daniel O'Reilly, and Russell Peabody. Further, Judge Victor J. Dowling had replaced Judge Fitzgerald. Essentially the same witnesses, including Nesbit, testified as in the first trial. Neither Jerome nor the defense, however, fought as hard as they did in the first trial over the issue of temporary insanity. Perhaps both sides had decided that they would be content with a verdict of not guilty by reason of insanity, which would put Thaw in a mental institution but prevent his execution. Accordingly, this time the jury on February 1, 1908, after a trial of less than four weeks, found Thaw not guilty by reason of insanity.

After the jury's verdict, Judge Dowling sent Thaw to the Asylum for the Criminally Insane at Matteawan, New York. Thaw's trials had taken the insanity defense to a murder charge to new heights, particularly with Delmas' "dementia Americana" argument in the first trial. This defense stratagem had first been used successfully to acquit Congressman Daniel Sickles of the murder of his wife's lover back in 1859. Further, the sensationalism surrounding Nesbit and her testimony eventually led to the famous movie, "The Girl in the Red Velvet Swing."

Thaw divorced Nesbit in 1915, and spent the rest of his life in and out of insane asylums and the courts. He escaped from Matteawan and fled to Canada, but he was soon extradited by Canadian authorities back to New York. Briefly freed from the asylums by the battery of lawyers still retained by his mother,

Thaw was arrested in 1917 for kidnapping and whipping 19-year-old Frederick Gump nearly to death. Mother Thaw arranged for her son to be sent to a Pennsylvania insane asylum, where he stayed until 1924. After 1924, Thaw was periodically in the news in connection with various wild parties or lawsuits by showgirls alleging that Thaw had beaten and whipped them. Thaw died February 22, 1947, at the age of 76, having lived until his last days off his inheritance from his mother.

—Stephen G. Christianson

Suggestions for Further Reading

Abramson, Phyllis L. *Sob Sister Journalism.* Westport, Conn.: Greenwood Press, 1990.

"Beauty as Evidence." *Life* (June 1981): 10–13.

Hodge, Clifford M. "The Benefactor at Dorr's Pond." *Yankee* (December 1986): 154.

Langford, Gerald. *The Murder of Stanford White.* London: V. Gollancz, 1963.

Mooney, Michael M. *Evelyn Nesbit and Stanford White: Love and Death in the Gilded Age.* New York: William Morrow & Co., 1976.

Thaw, Harry K. *The Traitor.* Philadelphia: Dorrance Publishing Co., 1926.

United States v. Shipp, et al.: 1907–09

Defendants: Joseph F. Shipp, Matthew Galloway, Jeremiah Gibson, Nick Nolan, William Mayes, Henry Padgett, Alf Handman, Bart Justice, Luther Williams **Crime Charged:** Criminal contempt of court
Chief Defense Lawyer: Judson Harmon **Chief Prosecutors:** Terry Sanford, Charles Bonaparte **Judges:** Melville W. Fuller, John Marshall Harlan, David J. Brewer, Edward D. White, Rufus W. Peckham, Joseph McKenna, Oliver Wendell Holmes, William R. Day, William H. Moody; James D. Maher was appointed by the Court to oversee initial arguments **Places:** Initial Arguments: Chattanooga, Tennessee; Closing Arguments: Washington, D.C. **Dates of Trial:** February 12–June 29, 1907; March 1909 **Verdicts:** Shipp, Gibson, Nolan, Mayes, Padgett and Williams: Guilty; Galloway, Handman, and Justice: Not Guilty **Sentences:** Shipp, Williams, Nolan: 90 days imprisonment; Gibson, Padgett, Mayes: 60 days imprisonment

SIGNIFICANCE

In the long history of the U.S. Supreme Court, this was the first—and only—criminal trial tried by the Court.

On a dark January evening in 1906, a 21-year-old woman named Nevada Taylor left her bookkeeping job in downtown Chattanooga, Tennessee. She boarded an electric trolley for her ride home. Stepping off the trolley, Taylor began the short walk to her home, a cottage in Forest Hills Cemetery where her father was the groundskeeper. As she approached the cemetery gate, she felt her throat grabbed from behind and a voice say, "If you scream, I will kill you." Taylor was raped and left unconscious.

An Arrest is Made

When Nevada Taylor regained consciousness, she walked home and told her father, William Taylor, what had happened. Her father called for Sheriff Joseph F. Shipp. When Shipp arrived at the Taylor house he asked Nevada Taylor what she could remember of the attack. She couldn't recall much. Shipp asked, "Was the man white or Negro?" Taylor answered at first that she did not get a good look at the attacker, but then added that she thought he was black.

An investigation of the crime scene turned up a black leather strap that perfectly matched red streaks around Taylor's neck. Will Hixon, a man who worked at a medicine company near the cemetery, reported that he had seen a black man "twirling a leather strap around his finger" shortly before 6 P.M. on the evening of the rape. Hixon called Shipp later to say that he had just seen that same man walking north toward town with a tall black man. Finding the tall black man alone, Shipp learned that his companion—and now prime suspect—was a drifter and sometimes carpenter named Ed Johnson. Within hours, Shipp spotted Johnson riding on the back of an ice wagon. Johnson was seized, handcuffed, brought to jail, and identified by Hixon as the man he had seen with the strap.

A Near Lynching and a Trial

Word of Johnson's arrest spread quickly. A large crowd gathered at the front of Hamilton County Jail, where they thought Johnson was being held. Men with sledgehammers smashed at the hinges on the heavy front door of the jail, but the men were not able to get in. In fact, Johnson had been sent to Nashville earlier that evening.

On January 27, Nevada Taylor traveled to Nashville and identified Ed Johnson as her attacker. However, it was a less than certain identification. That same day, a grand jury was convened and an indictment was returned within two hours. Through it all, Johnson maintained that he was innocent.

The trial of Ed Johnson opened on February 6, 1906. Three local attorneys, including Lewis Shepherd, one of Chattanooga's most prominent defense attorneys, defended him. The first witness for the prosecution was Nevada Taylor. Prosecutor Matt Whitaker asked Taylor if the man who attacked her was in the courtroom.

"I believe he is the man," said Taylor, pointing to Ed Johnson.

Will Hixon also testified and told the jurors that he saw Johnson "with a strap in his hand near the scene of the crime." The state also called Sheriff Joseph Shipp, who recounted the investigation for the jury.

The defense opened their case with Ed Johnson taking the stand. Johnson denied raping Taylor and said he spent the evening of January 23 working as a pool room porter at the Last Chance Saloon between 4:30 P.M. and 10 P.M.The defense then called 13 witnesses to the stand who swore they saw Johnson at the Last Chance Saloon around the time that the rape occurred. The defense also called several witnesses to the stand who attacked the credibility of Will Hixon.

The most dramatic event of the Johnson trial occurred on its last day. At the request of jurors, Nevada Taylor was recalled to the stand. Juror J. L. Wrenn stood and asked Taylor, "Miss Taylor, can you state positively that this Negro is the one who assaulted you?" Taylor answered, "I will not swear he is the man, but I believe he is the Negro who assaulted me." Wrenn, still not satisfied, asked again: "In God's name, Miss Taylor, tell us positively—is that the guilty Negro? Can you say it? Can you swear it?" With tears streaming down her face, Taylor replied, "Listen to me. I would not take the life of an innocent man. But before God, I believe this is the guilty Negro." At that point another juror rose and lunged in the direction of Johnson. As fellow jurors restrained him, he shouted out, "If I could get at him, I'd tear his heart out right now."

A Guilty Verdict and Lynching

On February 9, 1906, the jury returned a guilty verdict. In a surprising move, Johnson's defense attorneys decided against an appeal. Two of Johnson's attorneys, W. G. M. Thomas and Robert Cameron, concluded that an appeal would be futile. Lewis Shepherd disagreed, but was outvoted. That same day, Johnson was sentenced to hang on March 13, 1906.

Soon after the sentence, Johnson told his father that he did not want to die and that he wanted to appeal the verdict. Johnson's father hired Noah Parden, Chattanooga's most highly respected African-American attorney, to lead the appeal. After both the Tennessee Supreme Court and a federal district court upheld the verdict, Parden brought the case to the U.S. Supreme Court. On the morning of March 17, 1906, Parden and attorney Emanuel Hewlett presented Johnson's case to Supreme Court justice John Marshall Harlan. The justice listened to their arguments and nodded without giving them a word of encouragement.

In the hours after his meeting with Parden, Harlan read the transcript of the federal court appeal and became convinced Johnson's case raised serious constitutional issues. At Harlan's request, a majority of justices gathered on Sunday morning at the home of Chief Justice Melville Fuller to hear his plea for intervention. After debating the issue for an hour, the justices agreed upon their unprecedented action of staying the execution and granting Johnson's appeal. Harlan ordered telegrams sent to all the parties involved, including Sheriff Shipp, informing them of the Supreme Court's action.

The news that the Supreme Court had stayed Johnson's scheduled execution did not sit well with many in Chattanooga. About 8 P.M. on March 19 a group of men carrying guns descended on the Hamilton County Jail where Johnson was being held. Only a single guard, jailer Jeremiah Gibson, was on duty. Sheriff Shipp had given his other deputies the night off. The mob entered the jail and began their search for Johnson. Soon the mob made their way up the spiral staircase to the third floor where Johnson was being held. It was not until 10:35 that the last bolt on the heavy outer door gave way to the pounding of the mob. The men tied Johnson's hands with rope and dragged him from the cell. The crowd made its way to the Walnut Street Bridge that spanned the Tennessee River, where Johnson was lynched. A leader of the mob pinned a sheet of paper to Johnson's body. The note read: "To Justice Harlan. Come and get your nigger now."

Word of Johnson's lynching soon reached the justices of the Supreme Court. The justices expressed their outrage to the press. President Theodore

Roosevelt promptly ordered a federal preliminary investigation, with the understanding that the findings could be used by the U.S. Supreme Court should it choose to bring criminal contempt charges against members of the lynch mob.

On May 28, 1906, the U.S. Justice Department filed papers accusing 27 men of conspiring to lynch and murder Ed Johnson, including Sheriff Shipp, Deputy Matthew Galloway, and jailer Jeremiah Gibson. Eventually, charges would be dropped against most of the 27 men, but in addition to Shipp, Galloway, and Gibson, six members of the lynch mob—Nick Nolan, William Mayes, Henry Padgett, Alf Handman, Bart Justice and Luther Williams—were charged with criminal contempt.

A Long Road to Justice

Before the Court would allow evidence to be taken in the Shipp case, it needed to resolve the question of jurisdiction: Did the Court have the power to try Shipp and the others for criminal contempt? The Supreme Court heard oral arguments on the jurisdictional issue on December 4, 1906. Solicitor General Henry Hoyt argued that the Court did have jurisdiction. Hoyt contended that Johnson's right to be heard on his application for *habeas corpus* was protected by the Constitution and that the Court acted appropriately in staying his execution. Judson Harmon, a Cincinnati lawyer representing Sheriff Shipp, countered by arguing that none of Johnson's federally protected rights had been violated and that therefore the Court improperly granted its stay. On Christmas Eve, the Court, in a unanimous decision written by Oliver Wendell Holmes, ruled that it had the jurisdiction to try Shipp and the others.

On February 12, 1907, *United States v. Shipp et al.* opened in the United States Custom House in Chattanooga. (The Court decided that witnesses could more easily be gathered there than in Washington.) Having neither the time nor inclination to travel to Tennessee to hear weeks of testimony, the justices appointed James D. Maher, deputy clerk of the Supreme Court, to preside at the trial and prepare an evidentiary record which they could review.

Assistant Attorney General Terry Sanford presented the prosecution's case. His first witness was J. L. Chivington, a reporter for the *Chattanooga Times,* who had witnessed Johnson's lynching. Chivington testified that "there were normally six or seven deputies on guard every night" at the jail—except the night of March 19. Edward Chaddick, manager of the Western Union telegram office, testified that he had hand-delivered to Sheriff Shipp a telegram from the United States Supreme Court on the afternoon of the lynching.

A key witness for the prosecution was John Stonecipher, a Georgia contractor who had talked with some leaders of the mob at a saloon just hours before the lynching. According to Stonecipher, a man named Frank Ward said to him as he stood on a curb waiting for a car to go home, "We want you to help us lynch that damn nigger tonight." Stonecipher replied, "I believe Sheriff Shipp would shoot the red-hot stuff out of you." "No," answered Ward, "it is all agreed. There won't be a sheriff or deputy there."

In all, the government produced 31 witnesses over five days. Maher then recessed the trial until June. On Saturday, June 15, the defense began to present its case. Friends, relatives, and coworkers took the stand to offer alibis or attest to the high moral character of the defendants. Some of the defendants testified, but only one, Luther Williams, admitted being present at the lynching. He claimed to have been only a spectator.

Sheriff Shipp was the last witness called by the defense. He testified: "I never conspired with any living man, my deputies or anyone else; and I had no knowledge, not the slightest, that there would be any effort on my part or anybody to interfere with Johnson." Shipp claimed to have "run most of the way and walked rapidly the balance of the way" to the jail as soon as he learned that a lynching was in progress. At the jail, Shipp told the court, "I was seized from behind by several men." They "stood over me with a guard." On cross-examination, Shipp claimed not to have recognized any of the mob members at the jail, even though he was held there—without blindfolds—for 30 minutes.

On June 29, 1907, the defense rested. It wasn't until March of 1909 that the trial moved to the Supreme Court in Washington, where both sides presented closing arguments. U.S. Attorney General Charles Bonaparte told the Court that he believed the issues involved in the Shipp case to be so important that he decided to deliver the final argument himself. In his six-hour summation, Bonaparte reviewed the evidence of the trial and made the case for a guilty verdict. Judson Harmon presented the closing argument for Sheriff Shipp the following day. Harmon conceded that his client did not, in retrospect, handle the situation properly. But certainly, Harmon argued, "Captain Shipp cannot be convicted of contempt by this Court simply because, in the performance of his duties, he exercised bad judgment." After listening to brief arguments from lawyers for the other defendants, the Court adjourned to consider its verdict.

On May 24, 1909, the Supreme Court met to announce its decision. In his quiet voice, Chief Justice Fuller read his opinion. Fuller said that Sheriff Shipp "resented the necessary order of this court as an alien intrusion" and believed it to be "responsible for the lynching." The Court concluded: "Shipp not only made the work of the mob easy, but in effect aided and abetted it."

Shipp was found guilty of criminal contempt. The Court also declared jailer Jeremiah Gibson and four members of the lynch mob—Nick Nolan, William Mayes, Henry Padgett, and Luther Williams—guilty. Evidence was found insufficient to convict Deputy Matthew Galloway, Alf Handman, and Bart Justice. Justices Holmes, Harlan, Brewer, and Day joined Chief Justice Fuller's decision. Three dissenting justices voted to acquit all defendants.

Shipp, Williams, and Nolan were sentenced to 90 days imprisonment, while Gibson, Padgett, and Mayes were sentenced to 60 days.

On January 30, 1910, after completing his three-month sentence, Sheriff Shipp returned to Chattanooga, where he received a hero's welcome. As he stepped off the train from Washington, A crowd of more than 10,000 people singing "Dixie" greeted him.

—Doug Linder

Suggestions for Further Reading

Curriden, Mark, and Leroy Phillips, Jr. *Contempt of Court: The Turn-of-the-Century Lynching that Launched a Hundred Years of Federalism.* New York: Faber & Faber, 1999.

Fiss, Owen. *History of the Supreme Court of the United States,* Vol. 8. New York: Macmillan, 1993.

William "Big Bill" Haywood Trial: 1907

Defendant: William Dudley Haywood **Crime Charged:** Conspiracy to commit murder **Chief Defense Lawyers:** Clarence Darrow, Fred Miller, John Nugent, Edmund Richardson, and Edgar Wilson
Chief Prosecutors: William E. Borah, James H. Hawley, Charles Koelsche, and Owen M. Van Duyn **Judge:** Fremont Wood **Place:** Boise, Idaho
Dates of Trial: May 9–July 28, 1907 **Verdict:** Not guilty

SIGNIFICANCE

The government used the courts and the military in a blatant attempt to discredit and destroy the left-wing labor movement during a time of civil unrest. William Haywood's acquittal was widely applauded as a victory for organized labor and a defeat for big business.

Born in 1869, William Dudley Haywood, popularly known as "Big Bill," grew up in the rough-and-tumble world of the old Wild West, where the discovery of vast deposits of valuable metals had led to the exploitation of natural resources by the big mining companies. Conditions in the mines were poor: miners performed back-breaking labor for long hours and low pay in dark, cramped, and poorly ventilated mines. During the rise of organized labor in the late 19th century, union organizers found miners a ready audience for their message of labor activism.

Haywood rose through the Western labor movement and became an executive officer of the Western Federation of Miners. He was one of organized labor's recognized radicals. Haywood belonged to the Socialist Party and actively supported the anarchist International Workers of the World, or "Wobblies." Further, Haywood publicly endorsed strikes and violence to further the workers' cause. Haywood's radicalism made him the enemy of big business and the federal government.

The Coeur d'Alene Strike

Idaho's Coeur d'Alene region is the site of some of the world's richest mineral deposits. Haywood's Western Federation of Miners led a general miners' strike against all the mining companies in the area. By 1898, when Frank

R. Steunenberg was re-elected governor of Idaho, the strike had become a full-blown struggle between labor and management. The miners fought Pinkerton guards hired by the companies and "scabs," or replacement workers, sent by the companies to break the strike. When a bomb explosion killed two men, Steunenberg feared the strike would degenerate into open warfare and begged Washington for help.

In response, President William McKinley sent federal troops to Idaho, crushing the strike. In the process, the legal rights of the strikers were trampled and hundreds of men were held without bail in stockades nicknamed "bull pens." Steunenberg, who had been considered a pro-labor politician when first elected, now was a marked man. Years later, on December 30, 1905, when his term as governor had expired, Steunenberg was killed by a bomb blast in the front yard of his house in Caldwell, Idaho.

Two days later, January 1, 1906, the police arrested Harry Orchard in Caldwell for Steunenberg's murder. Orchard confessed, telling the police that Haywood and Charles H. Moyer, another executive officer of the Western Federation, paid him to kill Steunenberg. After a controversial extradition from Colorado, Haywood, Moyer, and another union member named George Pettibone were sent to Boise, Idaho, to stand trial.

The famous criminal lawyer Clarence Darrow went to Boise to defend Haywood, assisted by Fred Miller, John Nugent, Edmund Richardson, and Edgar Wilson. On the bench was Judge Fremont Wood. The prosecution team was comprised of William E. Borah, James H. Hawley, Charles Koelsche, and Owen M. Van Duyn. Haywood's trial for conspiracy to commit murder began May 9, 1907.

Haywood's Fate Rests on Orchard's Credibility

The prosecution's star witness was Harry Orchard, the confessed assassin. Orchard had a long criminal career, however, and readily admitted that he lied many times in the past "whenever it suited my purpose." Nevertheless, Orchard stuck with his story that Haywood and Moyer wanted him to murder Steunenberg. Darrow suspected that the mining companies were Orchard's real masters and said so to the jury:

> The mine owners of Colorado and Idaho are pulling the wires to make you dance like puppets. They gathered these officers of the Western Federation of Miners and sent them here to be tried and hanged.

When the prosecutors called Haywood to take the stand, Haywood denied hiring Orchard to kill Frank Steunenberg. He admitted that he hated the former governor, but no more or less than could be expected from a union radical. Responding to the prosecution's question, Haywood said:

> I felt toward him much as I did toward you and others who were responsible for martial law and the bull pen in the Coeur d'Alene.

Darrow questioned more than 80 character witnesses who knew Orchard well and who testified that he could not be trusted to tell the truth. Most of this testimony was redundant, however, since Orchard had already admitted to a history of chronic lying. Darrow went on to declare that the real issue was big business' effort to crucify Haywood and the unions. Addressing the jury, Darrow said:

> Gentlemen, it is not for him alone that I speak. I speak for the poor, for the weak, for the weary, for that long line of men who, in darkness and despair, have borne the labors of the human race. The eyes of the world are upon you, upon you twelve men of Idaho tonight. . . . If you kill him your act will be applauded by many. If you should decree Bill Haywood's death, in the railroad offices of our great cities men will applaud your names. If you decree his death, amongst the spiders of Wall Street will go up paeans of praise for these twelve good men and true.

Because the jury was composed of Idaho farmers, Darrow deliberately appealed to their working-class roots. His lengthy closing argument made it sound as if all farmers and miners were brothers united against their corporate oppressors.

Prosecutor William Borah tried to get the jury to focus on the real issue, namely whether Haywood was a party to Steunenberg's murder as Orchard had claimed:

> [T]hat bleak winter night with the blood of my dear friend marking the white earth, I saw Idaho dishonored and disgraced. I saw murder, no, a thousand times worse, I saw anarchy unfold its red menace. . . . This trial has no other purpose or implication than conviction and punishment of the assassins of Governor Steunenberg.

Not only did Borah try to keep the jury's focus on the heinous crime of murder-by-hire, but Borah saw Darrow's political appeal to the jury as a two-edged sword and effectively wielded it against him. Borah knew that the unpopular aspect of the union movement was its connection with anarchists, Wobblies, and others trying to overthrow the government. Knowing that Haywood's connection with these elements was well publicized, Borah played on the threat of social revolution to traditional values:

> We see anarchy, that pale, restless, hungry demon from the crypts of hell, fighting for a foothold in Idaho! Should we compromise with it? Or should we crush it? . . . I only want what you want, the gates to our homes, the yard gate whose inward swing tells of the returning husband and father, shielded and guarded by the courage and manhood of Idaho juries!

Haywood Goes Free

By the end of the trial, the jury had seen one of Clarence Darrow's great performances and equally respectable oratory from the prosecution. Judge Wood, however, said very little until the time came for him to give his instructions to the jury. Unexpectedly, Wood's instructions came down heavily on William Haywood's side. Wood reminded the jury that while they might not be convinced of Haywood's innocence, under the law they must find him not guilty unless the prosecutors had proven his guilt beyond a reasonable doubt. Further, in effect, Wood's instructions to the jury attacked the prosecution's inability to bring forward other evidence in support of Orchard's accusations:

> Gentlemen, under the statutes of this state, a person cannot be convicted of a crime upon testimony of an accomplice, unless such accomplice is corroborated by other evidence.

Whether it was the result of Darrow's eloquence or Judge Wood's instructions, on July 28, 1907, the jury finished its deliberations and, before a packed courtroom, returned a verdict of not guilty.

After leaving Boise and the Steunenberg murder trial behind him, Haywood returned to his radical affiliations, keeping up his support for the Wobblies. When World War I broke out, public opinion and the government turned against the Wobblies and other leftists, who were then considered unpatriotic for promoting the cause of world labor instead of American victory. The Wobblies not only circulated posters and pamphlets denouncing the war, but maintained contacts with the communists who had seized power in the former Russian Empire.

In 1918, the government again brought Haywood to trial, this time for treason. Haywood's luck had run out. The jury found him guilty and he was sentenced to 20 years imprisonment. While out on bail, Haywood fled the United States for the Soviet Union, where the communist regime granted him asylum. Haywood lived in the Soviet Union for the rest of his life, and after his death in 1928 the Soviets honored him with a burial in the Kremlin.

Despite Haywood's colorful postscript, his earlier acquittal was an important victory for organized labor. The government brought the full weight of the courts and the military to bear against labor but was unable to taint it with the blood of Steunenberg's murder. Because the government was supported by the mining companies, Haywood's acquittal was also seen as a defeat for big business.

—*Stephen G. Christianson*

Suggestions for Further Reading

Archer, Jules. *Strikes, Bombs & Bullets.* New York: Julian Messner, 1972.

Carlson, Peter. *Roughneck.* New York: W.W. Norton & Co., 1983.

Conlin, Joseph Robert. *Big Bill Haywood and the Radical Union Movement.* Syracuse, N.Y.: Syracuse University Press, 1969.

Dubofsky, Melvyn. *"Big Bill" Haywood.* New York: St. Martin's Press, 1987.

Haywood, William. *Bill Haywood's Book.* Westport, Conn.: Greenwood Press, 1983.

Anne Bradley Trial: 1907

Defendant: Anne Maddison Bradley **Crime Charged:** Murder
Chief Defense Lawyers: Orlando W. Powers, George P. Hoover, Robert W. Wells **Chief Prosecutors:** Daniel W. Baker, Charles H. Turner
Judge: Wendell Philips Stafford **Place:** Washington, D.C.
Date of Trial: November 13–December 3, 1907 **Verdict:** Not guilty

SIGNIFICANCE

Was Anne Bradley insane when she shot former U.S. senator Arthur Brown, or did she shoot him in a fit of jealous rage? That was what a jury had to decide in this scandalous early twentieth century trial.

Arthur Brown was born in Michigan in 1843. After college, he was a successful attorney in Kalamazoo before moving to Salt Lake City, Utah in 1879. There, he again practiced law and became prominent in the local Republican Party. Elected one of Utah's first two U.S. senators when the territory achieved statehood in 1896, he served for 13 months and unsuccessfully sought reelection in 1902.

Brown wedded twice. His first marriage ended in the late 1870s when his affair with Isabel Cameron became public knowledge. Cameron later followed Brown to Salt Lake City and became his second wife. The senator had a child by each spouse.

A Woman Ahead of the Times

Anne Bradley (nee Maddison) was 30 years Brown's junior. Born in Missouri, her family moved to Salt Lake City in 1890. For three years she worked as an assistant to her uncle who was the superintendent of the city's Water Works Department. Anne Maddison married Clarence Bradley in 1893, and the couple had two children.

Anne Bradley was active in the social and literary affairs of Salt Lake City. Unlike most women of her time, Bradley was also active in politics. In 1902, she was elected to a two-year term as the secretary of the state Republican committee. Afterward, Bradley received her party's nomination for city auditor, but lost the election. (At this time, Utah was one of the few states to allow women to vote and hold public office.)

Bradley was introduced to Brown by her uncle in 1890, and they became close friends. In 1898, Bradley separated from her husband. That's when the senator began his protestations of affection. Despite Bradley's initial objections, the two became lovers. In February 1900 a son was born, and he was christened "Arthur Brown" in the senator's presence.

Brown and Bradley Arrested for Adultery

Brown frequently promised to divorce his wife and marry Bradley. In 1902 he separated from Isabel, began divorce proceedings, and gave Bradley an engagement ring. Isabel Brown, however, had other ideas. In 1902, she hired a private detective to follow the pair and later had her spouse and Bradley arrested for adultery. In 1903, Brown reconciled a couple of times with his wife, but continued his affair with Bradley and made more promises to marry her. That was also the year when a confrontation occurred between the women at a hotel whereby Isabel Brown grabbed Bradley by the throat, threw her down, and screamed, "Let me alone, I will kill her" before they were pulled apart. Shortly afterward, the senator gave Bradley a revolver to use as protection from his wife. (Ironically, it was the same gun that later killed him.)

Before they were tried for adultery, Bradley told Brown that she would plead "Guilty" unless the senator publicly acknowledged his paternity of their son. Brown countered that he could not lest he faced prison. He begged Bradley not to testify against him. He also promised to divorce his wife and wed Bradley within 12 months. Bradley carried out her threat, but was never fined nor sentenced to jail. But neither did she testify against her lover. The senator pleaded "not guilty" and was acquitted. In November 1903, the couple's second son was born, but Brown remained married to his wife.

On August 22, 1905, Mrs. Brown died of cancer. That very night, Brown called Bradley and told her to "go ahead and get your divorce and we will make this matter right." Bradley quickly did as she was told, but now the former senator kept putting off the wedding date. In the meantime, their third child was born in March 1906, but the baby lived for only a few days. The two were finally to be married on June 2, but when the day arrived, Brown was "ill" and the only thing the couple exchanged was a telephone call. As Bradley would later testify, the strain was now taking its toll and she was severely depressed and suicidal. "I just cried. I hoped I would die and I felt at times as if I should kill myself."

Still, Bradley continued to try to convince Brown to marry her. She became pregnant again and, on October 26, 1906, told the senator about her condition. By the end of November, however, Bradley was starting to have doubts about Brown's true intentions and confronted him. What she got was mixed messages. At times, Brown was distant, sad, and said that he could do nothing for her. On other occasions, he renewed his pledges of love and promised to wed her.

Shortly after Thanksgiving, Brown left Salt Lake City to plead a case before the U.S. Supreme Court. Bradley knew of his plans, but not the specific date of his departure. On December 1, after learning that he had left without saying good-bye, Bradley suffered a miscarriage. She could neither eat nor sleep. She was depressed and again thinking of suicide. After the senator went to Washington, Bradley found out that he left behind at his office money for her to buy a train ticket to anywhere she wanted. Bradley decided on Los Angeles and left on December 3, but she only got as far as Ogden, Utah. Believing that Brown would not keep his promise to marry her once he was away from "the local influence," she impulsively changed her ticket for one to Washington, D.C. Unaccompanied, the five-day trip was hard on Bradley. She was still very ill and the travel made her condition worse.

The Final Showdown

Bradley arrived in Washington on Saturday morning, December 8. She immediately went to the Hotel Raleigh, asked about Brown, and then took a room for herself. A maid let her into the senator's room. Bradley did not know yet what she was going to do when Brown arrived. While waiting, she saw a letter on the table and read it. It was from Annie Adams, a famous actress, and it gave Bradley the impression that Adams and Brown were soon to be married.

Brown and the 58-year-old entertainer had known each other for about 20 years. Bradley knew they were once an item, but thought their affair had ended long ago. Extremely upset, Bradley aimlessly walked the streets of Washington for hours and frequently returned to the hotel. Then, lying in her room, she heard the senator's footsteps. Bradley went to his door and knocked.

"Come in," said Brown and when he saw Bradley, he asked, "What are you doing here?" Bradley replied, "I have come to ask you to keep your promise to me." Exactly what happened next is unknown. After her arrest, Bradley claimed that "he said he wouldn't keep his promises, so I shot him." However, once told by her lawyers that Brown had completely disowned her and their children in a new will written four months earlier, Bradley said that she didn't remember what happened in the senator's room. And it is possible that the shooting was an accident. There were powder burns on Brown's hand. The bullet that hit the senator entered his stomach and went downward into his body. Finally, letters were found by the police in Bradley's room which her attorneys interpreted as suicide notes. This all led Bradley's lawyers to believe that after Brown said he would not marry her, Bradley drew out the pistol to kill herself, but as the senator rushed to take the weapon away from her, they struggled and Brown pulled the trigger and shot himself.

The senator was rushed to the hospital and operated on, but the bullet was tightly lodged in his pelvic bone and could not be removed. He lingered a few days, but died on December 13. Following an inquest, Bradley was held for murder.

Bradley spent nearly a year in jail awaiting her trial. During that time, her health deteriorated even more. At one point, she had surgery for "a badly lacerated cervix." By the time her trial began, her physical condition was so poor that some thought she had contracted tuberculosis.

Defense: Temporary Insanity

Bradley's original attorneys had no luck in getting from Bradley any of the information needed to prepare her defense. Instead, constantly sitting with Brown's picture in her hands and wrapped up in her own thoughts, all that she would say was that the senator refused to talk to her and, as he started to put on his overcoat and leave the room, she shot him. Eventually, Orlando Powers, a former Utah judge and one of the most prominent Democrats in the state, with the assistance of two young Washington attorneys, George Hoover and Roberts Wells, took over Bradley's defense. As Powers would later recall:

> I reached Washington and went to see her [Bradley]. The first two visits resulted in nothing, so reluctant was she to have Brown's side of their relations laid bare. One afternoon in the midst of her protestations, I drew from my pocket a copy of the former Senator's will, completely disowning Mrs. Bradley's boys. I worked up to the passage in the will as strongly as I could and then read it over to her. Her eyes blazed and with a sob that sent her reeling to her cot, she said, 'Judge Powers, I will tell you all.'

At the trial, the prosecution argued that Bradley traveled to Washington to try one more time to get Brown to marry her or to publicly acknowledge their children and to kill the senator if he refused. The government's lawyers included U.S. attorney Daniel W. Baker and his assistant, former congressman Charles Turner.

While some evidence was submitted that the shooting was an accident, Bradley's defense was primarily one of temporary insanity. However, her attorneys were hampered by lack of funds. Bradley and her family had little money, and her lawyers donated most of their time. The three psychiatrists who testified on her behalf did so without any compensation. Furthermore, most of Bradley's witnesses were back in Salt Lake City and while the law allowed for some of them to be brought to Washington at government expense, just how many was up to the judge. Therefore, because Judge Wendell P. Stafford (at U.S. attorney Baker's urging) decided that only five would be sent for, many of Bradley's other witnesses had to pay their own way, and some could not afford the trip to attend the trial. In contrast, the prosecution was not limited as to the number of witnesses it could afford to bring, and the two physicians who testified that Bradley was sane when she shot the senator were well paid for their time.

At the trial, all the details of Bradley's and Brown's affair came out, including the fact that Bradley had three illegal abortions that were performed by the senator himself. Many witnesses testified about how Brown treated Bradley and about Bradley's increasingly irrational behavior as the senator continually refused to marry her or acknowledge their children. Brown's former law partner, Judge Henry Henderson, said that he dissolved their partnership because of the way Brown treated women. U.S. Senator George Sutherland of Utah, whom Bradley had known since 1895, testified that he interviewed

Bradley shortly after her arrest and concluded that she was not in her right mind. Evidence was presented that two of her aunts were insane and that she had an uncle who was "full of violent hallucinations." Finally, three physicians testified that, due to the effects on her nervous system of the frequent pregnancies and abortions, Bradley was insane when she fired the gun at Brown.

Under District of Columbia law at that time, the jury could have found Bradley not guilty by reason of insanity. If they had, then a sanity proceeding would have immediately commenced after her trial. Instead, at one in the morning on December 3, 1907, after deliberating for almost nine hours, the jury in Bradley's trial took its third vote and found her not guilty of murdering the former senator from Utah.

After her release from jail, Bradley returned to Salt Lake City. An attempt was made to break the senator's will so her sons could inherit part of his estate, but it was unsuccessful. Bradley held a series of jobs over the years and, from 1921 until her death in 1950 at the age of 77, she operated an antique store named "My Shop." She never remarried.

—*Mark Thorburn*

Suggestions for Further Reading

Ross, Shelley. *Fall from Grace: Sex, Scandal, and Corruption in American Politics from 1702 to the Present.* New York: Ballantine Books, 1988.

Thatcher, Linda. "The 'Gentile Polygamist': Arthur Brown, Ex-Senator from Utah." *Utah Historical Quarterly* 52, no.3 (Summer 1984): 231–45.

Dr. Hyde Trial: 1910

Defendant: Dr. Bennett Clarke Hyde **Crime Charged:** Murder
Chief Defense Lawyers: R.R. Brewster, M. Cleary, and Frank Walsh
Chief Prosecutors: M. Atkinson, Virgil Conkling, Elliott W. Major, and James A. Reed **Judge:** Ralph S. Latshaw **Place:** Kansas City, Missouri
Dates of Trial: April 16–May 16, 1910 **Verdict:** None. There were three attempts at retrial after a conviction in the first trial was overturned, but no verdict was ever sustained against Dr. Hyde.

SIGNIFICANCE

The Dr. Bennett Clark Hyde trial was a monument to the power of money in the criminal justice system. Hyde's wealthy wife hired the best attorneys available to defend him, and despite the overwhelming evidence of his guilt, he was never convicted.

Bennett Clarke Hyde was born in 1872 in Cowper, Missouri, the son of a Baptist minister, and grew up in Lexington, Missouri. He went to medical school in Kansas City, and stayed in that city to practice medicine after graduation.

From the very start, Hyde's medical career was tainted with scandal. When Hyde was working for his alma mater as an anatomy instructor, two men were arrested for grave robbing, and they confessed that they had been working for Hyde. Charges were filed against Hyde, but were dropped in March 1899. In 1905, Hyde became the Kansas City police surgeon, but he was fired in 1907 for alleged mistreatment of a patient.

On June 21, 1905, Hyde married Frances Swope in a secret marriage that connected him with the richest family in Missouri. Hyde's wife was the niece of Thomas Hunton Swope, who was born in 1829 in Kentucky and moved to Kansas City in 1860. Swope made a fortune in Kansas City real estate, and was now known as Colonel Swope. By 1909 Colonel Swope was 80 years old, and although he was a lifelong bachelor with no children of his own, he was devoted to his many nephews and nieces, several of whom lived with him in his Kansas City mansion.

In September 1909, Colonel Swope suffered a minor injury, and Hyde came to the Swope mansion to take care of him. On October 2, Hyde gave

Colonel Swope a pill, which made him violently ill, and he died on October 3. Hyde said that the cause of death was "apoplexy," but the nurse was suspicious. Hyde stayed in the Swope mansion, supposedly to look after the other residents, but a mysterious epidemic of illnesses suddenly swept through the estate over the next few months. Nine people came down with typhoid fever, and Chrisman Swope died after being treated by Hyde. By now there were five nurses in the Swope mansion, and they became afraid that Hyde was trying to kill off the entire Swope clan to collect the family fortune. The nurses went to the authorities. After autopsies on the bodies of Colonel Swope and Chrisman Swope revealed traces of strychnine and cyanide poison, Hyde was indicted for murder on February 15, 1910.

Hyde Escapes Justice

Hyde's trial began on April 16, 1910, with Judge Ralph S. Latshaw presiding. Hyde's defense lawyers were R.R. Brewster, M. Cleary, and Frank Walsh. The prosecutors were M. Atkinson, Virgil Conkling, Elliott W. Major, and James A. Reed.

The State of Missouri had an overwhelming case against Hyde and presented numerous expert witnesses who testified as to the medical evidence of poisoning. The testimony of a Dr. Hektoen was typical:

> Question: State to the jury what in your opinion that man [Colonel Swope] was suffering from and died from?
>
> Hektoen: In my opinion, death resulted from some convulsive and paralyzing poison or combination of poisons.

On May 16, 1910, the jury found Hyde guilty of murder. Latshaw on July 5, 1910, sentenced Hyde to life imprisonment. Hyde, however, had a secret weapon: his wife Frances, who refused to listen to any suggestion that her husband was guilty. Hyde publicly stated, "This case is not closed. My wife Frances will not forsake me. Yes, Frances will know what to do."

Indeed, Frances Hyde knew what to do. She financed Hyde's defense team, which launched an aggressive appeal. On April 11, 1911, the Supreme Court of Missouri reversed Hyde's conviction and remanded the case for a retrial. Hyde's second trial ended in a mistrial, ostensibly because one juror became sick towards the conclusion of the case. There were rumors, however, that the juror was bribed by agents of Mrs. Hyde.

A third trial was commenced, but the jury could not agree on a verdict. Once again, there were unsubstantiated allegations that Frances Hyde had used her share of the Swope family's millions to bribe certain jurors. Further, there were more rumors that Mrs. Hyde was financing a smear campaign against the surviving Swope family, who hated her for her efforts to absolve Hyde.

In January 1917, Hyde was put on trial for the fourth and last time. After three trials and more than seven years after the alleged murders, the fourth trial was abruptly terminated when Hyde's lawyers correctly pointed out that, under Missouri law, Hyde could not be tried more than three times for the same criminal charges. Hyde was a free man, but he never practiced medicine again, preferring to live off his wife's money instead. Frances Hyde never recanted her faith in her husband's innocence. However, it is worth noting that more than 10 years after Hyde's acquittal, she abruptly left him and took up her own household when he offered to prepare a special remedy for her upset stomach.

Despite the lengthy proceedings and the weight of evidence against him, Hyde was never convicted. Under the law, he must therefore be deemed innocent of the Swope murders, but no law can prevent the obvious conclusion that his loyal wife's money had an impact on the outcome. Not all criminal defendants are equal under the law. Sometimes justice lifts her blindfold when the defendant waves a sufficiently large billfold.

—*Stephen G. Christianson*

Suggestions for Further Reading

Duke, Thomas Samuel. *Celebrated Criminal Cases of America.* San Francisco: James H. Barry Co., 1910.

Nash, Jay Robert. *Almanac of World Crime.* New York: Bonanza Books, 1986.

—— *Murder Among the Mighty: Celebrity Slayings That Shocked America.* New York: Delacorte Press, 1983.

McNamara Brothers Trial: 1911

Defendants: James B. McNamara and John J. McNamara
Crimes Charged: Murder, for James; dynamiting the Llewellyn Iron Works, for John **Chief Defense Lawyers:** Clarence Darrow, LeCompte Davis, Job Harriman, Cyrus McNutt, and Joseph Scott **Chief Prosecutors:** W. Joseph Ford and John D. Fredericks **Judge:** Walter Bordwell **Place:** Los Angeles, California **Date of Trial:** December 1, 1911 **Verdict:** Guilty
Sentences: Life imprisonment for James B. McNamara and 15 years imprisonment for John J. McNamara

SIGNIFICANCE

The McNamara brothers trial, which ended just as it began with confessions of guilt by the McNamaras, set the cause of organized labor on the West Coast back by decades. It also nearly ruined the career of Clarence Darrow, one of America's leading criminal defense lawyers.

At the turn of the 20th century, the issue of labor relations divided America. The unions were fighting to organize the industrial work force and for legitimacy in the face of entrenched corporate and government opposition. Both sides frequently resorted to violence to advance their interests.

Two brothers, James B. McNamara and John J. McNamara, were active in the International Association of Bridge and Structural Iron Workers, headquartered in Indianapolis, Indiana. Both men were in their late 20s. The union represented workers in the construction industry, and was particularly active on the West Coast. Harrison Gray Otis, publisher of the *Los Angeles Times,* was the Union's arch enemy. Otis used his newspaper as a public platform for his tirades against the unions and to promote the interests of the pro-management Merchants and Manufacturers Association. On the morning of October 1, 1910, a bomb exploded in the *Los Angeles Times* building, killing 20 people and causing considerable damage to the building. Shortly thereafter, there was another bombing at the Llewellyn Iron Works in Los Angeles.

The bombings drew immediate, nationwide attention. Private detectives hired by the mayor of Los Angeles found evidence that incriminated the McNamaras. In April 1911, the detectives forcibly brought the McNamaras from Indianapolis to Los Angeles for trial by means that were legally questionable at best. Unions and labor sympathizers across the country put together a $250,000 defense fund and hired the famous criminal defense lawyer Clarence Darrow to represent the McNamaras. The pro-McNamara forces claimed that escaping gas, not a bomb, had destroyed the *Times* building. More extremist labor sympathizers charged that Otis himself had arranged the explosion.

Darrow was assisted by LeCompte Davis, Job Harriman, Cyrus McNutt, and Joseph Scott. Harriman was, in fact, the Socialist candidate for mayor in the upcoming city elections, and he joined the defense team for publicity's sake. The prosecutors were W. Joseph Ford and District Attorney John D. Fredericks, and the judge was Walter Bordwell. The trial began on December 1, 1911.

The trial lasted for one short but memorable day. When Bordwell called the case of *People v. James B. McNamara,* Davis rose to his feet and said:

> Your Honor, the defendant is in court. . . . We have concluded to withdraw the plea of not guilty, and have the defendant enter in this case a plea of guilty. A like course we intend to pursue with reference to J.J. McNamara.

Before a stunned courtroom audience, James McNamara stood and pleaded guilty to the charge of murder for bombing the *Times* building. John McNamara then confessed to dynamiting the Llewellyn Iron Works. On December 5, 1911, Bordwell sentenced James to life imprisonment and John to 15 years imprisonment.

Darrow Tried for Bribing Jurors

Darrow had suffered a humiliating defeat by being unable to rescue his clients in the face of the evidence against them. Worse was yet to come, however.

One of the people on Darrow's payroll was Bert Franklin, a former investigator for the U.S. Marshal's office. District Attorney Fredericks had learned that Franklin was trying to bribe jurors to acquit the McNamaras and had approached at least two jurors, namely Robert Bain and George Lockwood. Fredericks arranged a "sting" operation, and on November 28, 1911, three days before the McNamara trial, arrested Franklin in the act of handing money to Lockwood. In January 1912, Franklin pleaded guilty to charges of jury tampering, and on January 29, he testified that Darrow had known and approved of the bribery efforts.

Fredericks arrested Darrow and put him on trial before Judge George Howard Hutton on May 15, 1912. Fredericks was assisted by W. Joseph Ford and Arthur Keetch, while Darrow's defense attorneys were Horace Appel, Harry Dehm, Jerry Giesler and Earl Rogers. When organized labor turned its back on Darrow's request for financial assistance, Darrow had to pay all the legal costs of the 13-week trial out of his own pocket. Darrow denied the charges, and on August 14 and 15, 1912, gave an impassioned closing speech to the jurors, in which he claimed that:

> I am not on trial for having sought to bribe a man named Lockwood. I am on trial because I have been a lover of the poor, a friend of the oppressed, because I have stood by Labor for all these years.

On August 15, 1912, the jury returned a verdict of not guilty after deliberating for less than an hour. Fredericks, Otis and the anti-union forces hadn't given up, however.

The MacNamara brothers confession of guilt in the bombing of the *Los Angeles Times* building set back the cause of organized labor on the West Coast. (*Harper's Weekly*)

In October 1912, 50 members of the McNamaras' International Association of Bridge and Structural Iron Workers, primarily senior officers including the union's president, were put on trial in Indianapolis for illegally transporting dynamite. Thirty-nine of the defendants were eventually found guilty. In November 1912, Darrow was put on trial for a second time, this time for an alleged bribery attempt involving juror Robert Bain.

The jury couldn't reach a unanimous decision, although eight of the 12 jurors thought Darrow was guilty, and therefore Darrow was found not guilty a second time. The prosecutors continued to pursue Darrow, although somewhat halfheartedly after two trials, but decided to drop plans for a third trial in December 1913. Darrow returned to his practice in Chicago, and after several years of difficulty was able to revive his reputation as a great criminal defense lawyer. When Darrow died on March 13, 1938, few people remembered his disgrace at the McNamara trials.

Nevertheless, the McNamara case represented a serious defeat for Clarence Darrow. It also represented a serious defeat for organized labor on the West Coast and elsewhere in America, discredited as it was by the tactics of self-confessed bombers and murderers. It took decades for the unions to recover the public trust and their former political influence.

—Stephen G. Christianson

Suggestions for Further Reading

Burns, William J. *The Masked War*. New York: Arno Press, 1969.

"Clarence Darrow: the Lawyer Who Made the Case for Lost Causes." *Life* (Fall 1990): 86–87.

Jensen, Richard J. *Clarence Darrow: the Creation of an American Myth*. New York: Greenwood Press, 1992.

Livingston, John Charles. *Clarence Darrow: the Mind of a Sentimental Rebel*. New York: Garland, 1988.

Robinson, W.W. *Bombs and Bribery*. Los Angeles: Dawson's Book Shop, 1969.

Triangle Shirtwaist Fire Trial: 1911

Defendants: Triangle Shirtwaist Company partners Max Blanck and Isaac Harris **Crime Charged:** Manslaughter **Chief Defense Lawyer:** Max D. Steuer **Chief Prosecutors:** Charles S. Bostwick and J. Robert Rubin **Judge:** Thomas C.T. Crain **Place:** New York, New York **Dates of Trial:** December 4–27, 1911 **Verdict:** Not guilty

SIGNIFICANCE

Despite Max Blanck's and Isaac Harris' acquittal, the death of 146 young workers in a sweatshop fire focused public attention on the problem of poor workplace safety conditions and led to the passage of legislation providing for stricter regulations and tougher enforcement.

As American industry grew through the 1800s and into the early 20th century, the number of persons employed as factory workers or in other industrial occupations soared into the millions. Always eager for the cheapest possible labor, big business had no qualms about hiring women and children to perform tasks that required minimal strength, because companies could pay them lower wages than male workers commanded. Lower wages meant bigger profits, and so did spending as little as possible on safety precautions. For example, most factories had few, if any, safeguards to prevent accidental fires, such as sprinkler systems, proper ventilation, or adequate emergency exits. There were no federal safety laws, and while there were some state laws, enforcement was spotty at best.

In 1911, an incident occurred that dramatically illustrated the need for industrial safety reform. The Triangle Shirtwaist Company, which manufactured articles of women's clothing, operated several factories or "sweatshops" in New York City. Two partners, Max Blanck and Isaac Harris, owned Triangle. As was common in the garment industry, Triangle employed mostly young women, who were usually barely in their teens, to perform the fabric cutting, stitching, and sewing that went into making the finished product. The women worked side-by-side at their cutting tables and sewing machines in cramped, dirty rooms. Further, Triangle supervisors routinely locked the door to the workplace from the outside to ensure that the employees never left their stations. Triangle factories were occasionally inspected by the lax city authorities, who took no actions to improve safety.

146 Triangle Employees Die

One of the Triangle factories was located in the ninth story of a building overlooking New York City's Washington Place. A stairway led down to Washington Place. On another side of the ninth floor, the factory overlooked Greene Street. A stairway led down to the street, and also up to the roof. On March 25, 1911, a fire began on the eighth floor and came up through the Greene Street stairwell into Triangle's ninth floor, where the employees were busy at work. As smoke and fire filled the shop from the Greene Street side, the frightened women ran to the Washington Place exit, only to discover that the door was locked. They were trapped inside a burning building.

Bodies from the Triangle Shirtwaist Company fire. (Courtesy, Library of Congress)

Although firemen rushed to the scene, they were too late to prevent scores of the women from being burnt alive. Driven by panic, many women jumped out the windows, only to fall to their death nine stories below. The impact of their bodies from such a height tore through the firemen's safety nets, and smashed holes in the pavement below. A total of 146 Triangle employees died.

The tragedy drew national attention, and the public demanded action against the parties responsible. On April 11 Max Blanck and Isaac Harris were charged with manslaughter. Blanck and Harris were represented by Max D. Steuer, one of the most celebrated and skillful lawyers of the period. The prosecutors were Assistant District Attorneys Charles S. Bostwick and J. Robert Rubin. The judge was Thomas C.T. Crain, and the trial began on December 4, 1911.

The trial took over three weeks, and 155 witnesses testified. one of the most gripping descriptions of what had happened came from Kate Alterman, a Triangle employee who survived the fire. First, she described how, amidst the chaos, she saw one Margaret Schwartz die in the flames because no one could open the Washington Place stairway door:

> I saw Bernstein, the manager's brother, trying to open the door but he couldn't. He left; and Margaret was there, too, and she tried to open the door and she could not. I pushed her on a side. I tried to open the door, and I couldn't. . . . And then she [Margaret] screamed at the top of her voice, "Open the door! Fire! I am lost, there is fire!"

Horrified, Alterman watched the fire consume Schwartz. Alterman then described how she survived a mad dash through the fire raging through the Greene Street stairway:

> And then I turned my coat on the wrong side and put it on my head with the fur to my face, the lining on the outside, and I got hold of a bunch of dresses and covered the top of my head. I just got ready to go and somebody came and began to chase me back, pulling my dress back, and I kicked her with my foot and she disappeared.
>
> I tried to make my escape. I had a pocketbook with me, and that pocketbook began to burn. I pressed it to my heart to extinguish the fire, and I made my escape right through the flames: the whole door was a flame right to the roof.

Once she was on the roof, firemen eventually rescued Alterman. Despite Alterman's dramatic testimony and that of other witnesses, however, the trial turned upon the question of whether Blanck and Harris knew that the Washington Place door was locked. Judge Crain read his instructions to the jury on this point:

> You must be satisfied from the evidence, among other things, before you can find these defendants guilty of the crime of manslaughter in its first degree not merely that the door was locked, if it was locked, but that it was locked during the period mentioned under circumstances bringing knowledge of that fact to these defendants.
>
> But it is not sufficient that the evidence should establish that the door was locked, if it was locked, during such a period; nor yet that the defendants knew that it was locked during such a period, if it was locked . . . Was the door locked? If so, was it locked under circumstances importing knowledge on the part of these defendants that it was locked? If so, and Margaret Schwartz died because she was unable to pass through, would she have lived if the door had not been locked and she had obtained access to the Washington Place stairs and had either remained in the stairwell or gone down to the street or another floor?

Blanck and Harris go Free

On December 27, 1911, the jury announced its verdict. It pronounced Blanck and Harris not guilty. Although the prosecution's evidence was compelling,, it was not enough to overcome the judge's instructions. As one juror stated:

I believed that the door was locked at the time of the fire. But we couldn't find them guilty unless we believed they knew the door was locked.

With the support of District Attorney Charles S. Whitman, the prosecutors moved for another trial. Judge Samuel Seabury presided over the retrial. Despite public outrage against the first trial's acquittal, on March 12, 1912, Judge Seabury ordered the retrial dismissed on the grounds that the defendants were being tried for the same offense. Based upon the principle of double jeopardy, Judge Seabury proclaimed:

A union march in memory of the victims of the Triangle Shirtwaist fire. (Courtesy, Library of Congress)

The court has neither the right nor the power to proceed with the present trial. These men are to be tried for the same offense again and under our constitution and laws, this cannot be done. I charge you, gentlemen of the jury, to find a verdict for the defendants.

Blanck and Harris left the courtroom free men. The impact of the Triangle fire, however, was not lost. New York City soon had a Bureau of Fire Prevention, which implemented stricter safety regulations and saw to their enforcement. Other cities and states followed suit in the years and decades to come. The federal government finally acted to ensure workplace safety during the administration of Franklin D. Roosevelt, and FDR's measures were the predecessor to such protective agencies as the Occupational Safety and Health Administration.

Today, there are extensive federal and state safety regulations to protect workers from the sort of dangers that resulted in the Triangle fire.

—*Stephen G. Christianson*

Suggestions for Further Reading

Crute, Sheree. "The Insurance Scandal Behind the Triangle Shirtwaist Fire." *MS.* (April 1983): 81–82.

Stein, Leon. *The Triangle Fire.* Philadelphia: J.B. Lippincott, 1962.

"A Sweatshop Worker Remembers." *MS* (April 1983): 83.

Floyd Allen Trial: 1912

Defendant: Floyd Allen **Crime Charged:** Murder
Chief Defense Lawyer: J.C. Buxton **Chief Prosecutors:** J.C. Wysor and W.S. Poage **Judge:** Walter Staples **Place:** Wytheville, Virginia
Dates of Trial: April 30–May 18, 1912 **Verdict:** Guilty **Sentence:** Death by electrocution

SIGNIFICANCE

The Floyd Allen affair represents one of the rare incidents in American history when a criminal defendant attempted to avoid justice by assassinating the trial judge.

Carroll County, Virginia, is a rural county, located in the Blue Ridge Mountains and far from any major city. The Allens were the county's leading family, owning a great deal of land and dominating local politics. They ran Carroll County as their private chiefdom. In the early 1900s, the patriarch of the Allen clan was Floyd Allen.

In 1911, two of Allen's nephews, Sidna Allen and Wesley Edwards, were involved in a scuffle with some Allen opponents outside a schoolhouse where Baptist services were being held. The local prosecutor in nearby Hillsville, Commonwealth's Attorney William M. Foster, was also an Allen adversary, and he promptly charged Sidna Allen and Edwards with disturbing public worship. Foster's men arrested Sidna Allen and Edwards after tracking them down in Mount Airy, North Carolina and brought them back to Carroll County for justice. On the way back to Hillsville, Floyd Allen and his henchmen set upon the lawmen and freed their kin. Foster then charged Allen with assaulting officers of the law and had Allen arrested.

A jury found Allen guilty, and on March 14, 1912, Allen went to his sentencing hearing before Judge Thornton L. Massie in the Hillsville courthouse. Massie sentenced Allen to one year in prison. There were, however, nearly 20 Allen men among the spectators in the courtroom. Allen rose to his feet and calmly said, "Gentlemen, I ain't goin'." That was the cue. The Allen men (Floyd included) pulled out their concealed pistols and began firing. Five people were killed: Judge Massie, Commonwealth's Attorney Foster, Sheriff Lew F. Webb, a member of the jury named Augustus C. Fowler, and a witness named Betty Ayers. Floyd Allen was wounded when the deputies and guards returned fire, and he was quickly arrested. The rest of the Allens fled, and it took a manhunt of several months to round them all up.

Virginia Tries Floyd Allen for Murder

Allen's murder trial began on April 30, 1912, in Wytheville, Virginia before Judge Walter Staples. His defense lawyer was J.C. Buxton, and the prosecutors were W.S. Poage and J.C. Wysor. The other Allens were tried separately. There were scores of witnesses who had actually seen Allen fire shots in the Hillsville courthouse, and so there was no plausible defense to the charges. On May 18, 1912, the jury found Allen guilty of murder, and he was sentenced to death by electrocution.

Of the many other Allens involved in the courthouse shooting who were also tried for murder, several bear mentioning. Allen's son, Claude Allen, went to trial on May 20, 1912. It took three trials, however, before a jury could agree on a verdict. On July 17, 1912, Claude Allen was found guilty of murder and also sentenced to death. Friel Allen, who had cooperated with the authorities during the manhunt, was sentenced to 18 years in prison after his trial in August 1912, despite the fact that the authorities had promised him a sentence of only five years. Sidna Allen was tried in November 1912 and sentenced to 35 years in prison, but on April 29, 1926, Virginia Governor Harry F. Byrd pardoned him.

On March 28, 1913, Floyd and Claude Allen, father and son, were electrocuted in Richmond, Virginia, within 11 minutes of each other. The Allens were one of the few people in American history who tried to escape justice by assassinating the trial judge and the prosecutor. As Judge Staples said in his sentencing order:

> You, Floyd Allen, were in custody of the law: When ordered to jail, you uttered your defiance of its authority, such a defiance as was never before heard in Virginia court.

—*Stephen G. Christianson*

Suggestions for Further Reading

Gardner, Rufus L. *The Courthouse Tragedy*. Hillsville, Va.: Unknown Publisher, 1962.

Parker, George Martin Nathaniel. *The Mountain Massacre*. Bluefield, WV: Country Life, 1930.

Charles Becker Trials: 1912–14

Defendant: Charles Becker **Crime Charged:** Murder
Chief Defense Lawyers: First trial: John F. McIntyre, Lloyd B. Stryker, and George W. Whiteside; Second trial: W. Bourke Cockran, John Johnstone, and Martin Manton **Chief Prosecutors:** First trial: Frank Moss and Charles S. Whitman; Second trial: Charles S. Whitman **Judges:** First trial: John W. Goff; Second trial: Samuel Seabury **Place:** New York, New York
Dates of Trials: October 7–30, 1912, May 2–22, 1914 **Verdicts:** Guilty, both trials **Sentence:** Death by electrocution

SIGNIFICANCE

The sordid career of New York police Lieutenant Charles Becker included graft, extortion, and ultimately the murder of his former gambling hall partner. Becker's brazen operation of a personal crime syndicate from within the police department provided novelist Stephen Crane with the inspiration for his work *Maggie: A Girl of the Streets.* Becker's trial also inspired the public and the press to give more attention to big-city corruption.

Charles Becker was born in 1869 into a family of German immigrants who had taken up residence in New York City. When Becker grew into manhood in the early 1890s, New York was teeming with immigrants and a new industrial prosperity. It was also a city rife with corruption. The Tammany Hall political machine and the crime bosses openly ran New York together and had a long tradition of sharing the wealth from prostitution, gambling, extortion, and other flourishing vices. Although there were many honest policemen, plenty of officers were willing to fatten their wallets by cooperating with the crooked politicians and the bosses. Unlike the lowly cop on the beat who looks the other way every now and then, however, Becker became actively involved in the New York crime world.

Becker was a tall man weighing well over 200 pounds, all of it muscle. He was violent but also intelligent. While the thugs that he controlled took in more and more protection money from pimps and gambling houses, Becker also obtained promotion after promotion in the police department. In 1911, police Commissioner Rhinelander Waldo promoted Becker again, not only making him a lieutenant and Waldo's aide, but also the officer in charge of a special squad charged with cracking down on crime.

Becker Runs Crime Ring from within Police Department

Putting Becker in charge of such a squad was the height of irony, and Becker lost no time in turning the squad into his personal mobile hit squad. Soon, every pimp and gambler on Broadway and in Manhattan knew that failure to pay Becker the cut he demanded meant swift and sure retaliation in the form of a raid by Becker's squad. From outside the police department, Becker also recruited the cream of New York's thugs to work for him, such as "Gyp the Blood," "Dago Frank," "Whitey" Lewis, "Lefty Louie," bald "Billiard Ball" Jack Rose, Sam Schepps, Harry Vallon, "Bridgey" Webber, and "Big Jack" Zelig.

Funeral procession for Herman "Beansie" Rosenthal. (Courtesy, Library of Congress)

Becker's criminal enterprises included dealings with Herman Rosenthal, nicknamed "Beansie," a well-known gambler. For a while, Becker and Rosenthal jointly ran and shared the profits from a gambling house, but a dispute arose between them over who was entitled to what percentage. Becker's squad raided and shut down Rosenthal's operation. In retaliation, Rosenthal went to New York's new and squeaky-clean district attorney, Charles S. Whitman, and told him everything he knew about Becker's criminal operations. Whitman surprised all of New York by attacking the powerful Becker head-on, summoning a grand jury for the purpose of bringing criminal charges against Becker.

Furious, Becker ordered his thugs to kill Rosenthal, brazenly promising them police protection. On July 21, 1911, several of Becker's men, led by Jack

Rose, approached Rosenthal outside the Cafe Metropole and shot him to death. Undaunted by the murder of his star witness, Whitman was able to trace the getaway car to Rose and promptly arrested him. At first, Rose refused to talk, but when Becker failed to come to his rescue, Rose cracked and told Whitman everything about Becker ordering Rosenthal's murder. Whitman mobilized his forces and smashed Becker's ring, arresting Becker and his associates for Rosenthal's murder.

Tried Before New York's Hanging Judge

On October 7, 1912, Becker's trial opened, with Judge John W. Goff presiding. Like Whitman, Judge Goff had no tolerance for corruption and had earned a reputation for being one of the toughest judges to sit on the New York bench. Whitman and his assistant prosecutor, Frank Moss, therefore had the advantage over Becker's defense attorneys, John F. McIntyre, Lloyd B. Stryker, and George W. Whiteside. The prosecution lost no time in bringing Rose to the stand and asking him what Becker had said with respect to Rosenthal. Rose replied:

> Becker said to me: "There is only one thing to do with a fellow like Rosenthal—just stop him so that he will not bother anybody any more for all time." I said: "What do you mean?" He said: "Well, there is a fellow that ought to be put off the earth." "Why," I says, "I agree with you. He is no account." He said: "Well, no use saying he is no account, and all of that, but the idea is now to do something to him." I says: "What do you mean?" and he said: "There is a fellow I would like to have croaked."

Rose went on to relate how Becker gave the order to murder Rosenthal:

> And Becker said: "I don't want him beat up. I could do that myself. I could have a warrant for any gambling house that he frequents and make a raid on that place and beat him up for resisting arrest or anything else. No beating up will fix that fellow, a dog in the eyes of myself, you, and everybody else. Nothing for that man but taken off this earth. Have him murdered, cut his throat, dynamited, or anything."

McIntyre, Becker's lead counsel, was frustrated in his efforts to cross-examine Rose and the other prosecution witnesses by Judge Goff. Goff repeatedly cut McIntyre's questioning short and denied his motions for more time. In their private conferences during breaks in the trial, Becker railed at McIntyre for his seeming ineffectiveness, but McIntyre's strategy was to lay the groundwork for a successful appeal. Goff obliged him, giving final instructions to the jury that went overboard in their bias against Becker:

> If it be true that Becker instructed Rose to kill Rosenthal, I instruct you that Becker constituted Rose his agent and instrument in the carrying out of the design; whatever Rose did, Becker in the eyes of the law did. . . .
>
> It is apparent from this testimony that the main witnesses against the defendant Becker are what are called accomplices. There is no doubt that Rose, Webber, and Vallon are accomplices.

The jury found Becker guilty on October 30, 1912. As McIntyre predicted, the Court of Appeals overturned the conviction and ordered a new trial, ruling that Goff committed "gross misconduct" and that Whitman's witnesses were "dangerous and degenerate."

Tried Again

Becker's second trial began May 2, 1914. This time, the judge was Samuel Seabury. McIntyre was tired of representing Becker, and Becker had a new defense team: W. Bourke Cockran, John Johnstone, and Martin Manton. Whitman continued as prosecutor, but without Frank Moss' assistance.

Whitman changed his strategy in the second trial, relying less on Rose and Becker's other thugs and more on James Marshall, a young black man who had been on Becker's payroll as an informant and who had been present when Becker ordered Rose and the others to kill Rosenthal. Unlike the other witnesses, Marshall had not participated in the actual murder and thus Whitman reasoned that if Becker was convicted again, the Court of Appeals would be less likely to criticize the prosecution. Further, Judge Seabury was more scrupulous than Goff in his instructions to the jury. In his closing argument for the defense, Manton tried to convince the jury that Marshall couldn't be trusted because he used to be an informer and because he was black:

> Remember this, gentlemen of the jury, the men who accuse Lieutenant Becker would be on trial for murder had they not accused Lieutenant Becker. And the only corroboration of their desperate testimony comes from a little coloured boy whose only motive is that he was paid, fed, clothed and housed by the district attorney; a little coloured boy who was once a police informer, a man who betrays others for pay.

The jury was not swayed, however, and on May 22, 1914, found Charles Becker guilty again. Seabury sentenced Becker to die in the electric chair. This time the conviction was upheld, although Becker's appeals postponed his execution for over a year. During that time, Whitman became a celebrity for his much-publicized victory. He capitalized on his popularity by running for governor and winning the election on November 3, 1914. Ironically, when Becker's appeals ended, he begged for a pardon from the one man who could give it, now-Governor Whitman. Becker's wife Helen even went to Whitman personally, but to no avail. On July 30, 1915, Becker was executed in the Sing Sing prison electric chair.

Becker's long criminal career included an incident when he beat a young prostitute who had been reluctant to pay protection money he demanded. Stephen Crane witnessed Becker's assault on the defenseless woman and was inspired to write his famous novel *Maggie: A Girl of the Streets.* Becker's trial and execution would also live on due to its publicity and the attention it focused on urban corruption and the efforts of people such as Whitman to combat it.

—Stephen G. Christianson

Suggestions for Further Reading

Crane, Stephen. *Maggie: A Girl of the Streets*. London: Cassell, 1966.

Delmar, Vina. *The Becker Scandal: A Time Remembered*. New York: Harcourt, Brace & World, 1968.

Logan, Andy. *Against the Evidence: the Becker-Rosenthal Affair*. New York: McCall, 1970.

Root, Jonathan. *One Night in July: the True Story of the Rosenthal-Becker Murder Case*. New York: Coward-McCann, 1961.

——. *The Life and Bad Times of Charlie Becker: The True Story of a Famous American Murder Trial*. London: Secker & Warburg, 1962.

Mother Jones Court-Martial: 1913

Defendants: Mary Harris "Mother" Jones, W.H. Adkins (alias Bunk Adkins), Charles Batley, Tip Belcher, C.H. Boswell, Clyde E. Bowe, William Brandridge, John W. Brown, Leonard Clark, H.V. Craise, Ernest Creigo, Harrison Ellis, Grady Everett, Charles Gillispie, Ed. Gray, Boyd Holley (alias Boyd Adkins), W.H.H. Huffman, Frazier Jarrett, John Jones, Charles Kenney, Sanford Kirk, Charles Lanham, A.D. Lavender, G.W. Lavender, George W. McCoy, Tom Miskel, Carl Morgan, Cal J. Newman, Bert Nutter, Ernest O'Dell, John O'Dell, Robert Parrish, G.F. Parsons, W.H. Patrick, Paul Paulsen, Will Perdue, W. Lawrence Perry, Oscar Petry, Jim Pike, William Price, Joe Prince, John Seachrist, John Siketo, Emory J. Sowards, Cleve Vickers, E.B. Vickers, Charles Wright, Steve Yager, and J.D. Zeller (alias Dutch Zeller)
Crimes Charged: Conspiracy to inflict bodily injury, murder, conspiracy to destroy personal property, conspiracy to inflict bodily injury, accessory to crime after the fact, unlawfully carrying weapons
Chief Defense Lawyers: Albert M. Belcher, Harold W. Houston, Adam B. Littlepage, M.F. Matheny; court-appointed attorneys: Edward B. Carskadon, Charles R. Morgan **Prosecutor:** George Selden Wallace, Judge Advocate
Judges: Clarence F. Jolliffe, Captain Boughner (first name unrecorded), Samuel L. Walker **Place:** Pratt, West Virginia **Date of Trial:** March 7–14, 1913 **Verdicts:** Officially unrecorded, but deduced from contemporary newspaper accounts: Mother Jones, Boswell, Brown, Creigo, Kenney, A.D. Lavender, G.W. Lavender, Miskel, Parsons, Seachrist, Cleve Vickers and E.B. Vickers: guilty; all others: not guilty **Sentences:** Up to 20 years' imprisonment (commuted to time served)

SIGNIFICANCE

This trial of an 83-year-old labor agitator who had become known as "the Miners' Angel" caused such tumult that the United States Senate investigated labor conditions in the coal fields of West Virginia. Historians of labor relations consider the trial a major event in the movement, from the mid-nineteenth to mid-twentieth century, to protect laborers against low wages, long hours, and dangerous working conditions.

Born in 1830 in Ireland, Mary Harris was brought to America at the age of five. She graduated from teacher' school at 17, taught in Michigan, moved on to dress-making in Chicago, and then returned to teaching in Memphis, Tennessee.

Yellow Fever and Chicago Fire

There in 1861 she married iron molder George E. Jones, a worker dedicated to the union viewpoint. In six years, the couple produced four children, but in 1867, within one week, yellow fever killed all four and then their father. Widow Jones returned to dressmaking in Chicago.

For three days in October 1871, the Great Chicago Fire ravaged the city. Mary Harris Jones's home and shop became rubble. Shortly thereafter she joined the Knights of Labor, an organization determined to unite workers in a single cooperative system.

Mary "Mother" Jones, 83-year-old labor agitator.

Working as a seamstress for Chicago's well-to-do, Jones pondered her late husband's convictions, the goals of the Knights of Labor, the hungry wretches shivering in one-room shantytown "houses," and those oblivious to it all—her wealthy employers. Soon she was recruiting new Knights.

In 1877, the fourth year of a grueling depression, railroad workers struck over reduced wages. Marching on picket lines in Pittsburgh, Jones watched 6,000 workers defy strike-breaking troops, dispatched by the governor. After the soldiers killed 26 of their comrades, the strikers destroyed 105 locomotives and 79 railroad buildings before President Rutherford B. Hayes sent in federal troops. Mary Jones became convinced that, while workers could exercise power, private industry commanded the federal troops.

"Mother" of All American Workers

Soon known as Mother Jones—for she considered all American workers her family—Mary traveled and spoke constantly, living in shantytowns and tent villages. In fact, she lived, she said, "wherever there is a fight."

By 1890, Mother Jones was helping organize the United Mine Workers of America (UMW). The year 1902 saw her leading Pennsylvania coalminers' wives who wielded mops and brooms to drive away strikebreakers. When the

Industrial Workers of the World (IWW) was founded in 1905, she was the only woman among the 27 signers of its manifesto. By 1911 she was a paid organizer for the UMW.

"I Warn This Little Governor"

In July 1912, the UMW struck against the Paint Creek Mining Company near Charleston, West Virginia. Advising a crowd of 1,000 workers that the governor could—if he would—ban the armed guards who protected company premises, Mother Jones described him as a "goddamned dirty coward." She said, "I warn this little governor that unless he rids Paint Creek of these mine-guard thugs, there is going to be one hell of a lot of bloodletting in these hills."

By September, Governor William E. Glasscock, seeing 2,000 workers supporting the strikers, ordered in 1,200 National Guardsmen to establish martial law. The strike continued into February. On Monday the 10th, 50-armed strikers attacked 25 mine guards—watchmen, office workers, and nonunion volunteers—along a ridge above the town of Mucklow. At a machine-gun post, guards Fred Bobbitt and W. R. Vance were killed and three others wounded before National Guard soldiers arrived. The militia arrested 48 strikers but no nonstrikers.

On Wednesday, county prosecutor T. C. Townsend ordered police to arrest Mother Jones and release her only to the military authorities at Pratt, West Virginia. There she and the 48 were charged with murder and conspiracy to commit murder in the Mucklow deaths and injuries.

Under martial law, the trial was a court-martial. Opening on March 7, 1913, the prosecution described how the defendants had murdered Bobbitt and Vance and feloniously wounded John Crockett, Thomas Nesbitt, and R. L. Taylor in their conspiracy to steal a machine gun, and had then conspired as accessories after the fact to help the murderers escape.

Judge Advocate George S. Wallace, the prosecutor, first tried to name defendants John W. Brown, George F. Parsons, and Charles H. Boswell (editor of the Socialist newspaper *Labor Argus*) as leaders of the strikers. Cross-examination revealed that witnesses identifying them were themselves defendants who had been promised release for testifying for the prosecution.

Posed As a Miner for Five Months

A surprise prosecution witness, detective Frank Smith of the J. W. Burns agency, testified that he had posed as a miner for five months, holding a union card and noting which defendants were armed. Other witnesses, including National Guardsmen, identified defendants but could not say they saw them firing guns. And, to prove that the 83-year-old Mother Jones had incited the strikers, the prosecutor placed in evidence some 100 pages of speeches she had delivered during the preceding August and September.

The court-martial was suspended for 24 hours while defense attorneys Albert M. Belcher and Harold W. Houston obtained an order from circuit-court judge Samuel D. Littlepage ending the court-martial. They argued that the U.S. Constitution placed civil authority above the military and that the state constitution protected civilians from military trials. Recently elected Governor Henry D. Hatfield intervened, insisting that either the judge withdraw his order or he would withdraw the troops. The judge backed down.

The prosecutor now introduced witnesses who had heard Mother Jones's speeches. They refused to describe them as inflammatory. The strongest testimony, from a company clerk, simply said Jones advised the miners not to hand over their guns to local authorities.

Defense witnesses were few. Two militiamen affirmed the orderliness of defendants they guarded. One witness swore that defendant Cal Newman spent February 10 not fighting but arranging to put a boar to a sow.

Like Roosevelt, Wilson, and Bryan

Closing, defense attorney M. F. Matheny compared the Mother Jones' speeches to the "inflammatory" speeches of Teddy Roosevelt, Woodrow Wilson, and William Jennings Bryan. Calling the case industrial warfare, he said, "West Virginia cannot afford to take one side of these contending armies and cast them in prison, deny them their rights, and disarm them and leave the other people in control."

Prosecutor Wallace's concluding remarks summed up the testimony of nine witnesses who had heard Mother Jones speak—including her warning that if any miner were imprisoned "we would tear up the state." The defense neglected to point out that all the crimes alleged had occurred before she made this threat.

The military commission presented sealed findings to Governor Hatfield. Details of the verdicts were not disclosed, but within a week 25 defendants were released as not guilty and 19 more were given freedom conditional on good behavior. The others were moved to civilian jails for further disposition that remains unrecorded.

Mother Jones was imprisoned until May 7, when Governor Hatfield released her. Shortly, she watched from the Senate gallery as a resolution established an investigation of conditions in West Virginia coalfields by the Senate Committee on Education and Labor.

Some 20 years later, while serving as a U.S. senator, Hatfield disclosed that the verdict would have sent miners and Mother Jones to prison for many years. "I did not confirm the findings of the military court," he said, "in the case of Mother Jones nor any of the other cases."

Mother Jones worked for striking coal miners for another 10 years. During a yearlong Colorado strike, she was arrested and imprisoned twice more. Following the killing of 20 strikers and their families at Ludlow, Colorado, in April 1914, she prevailed on the House Mines and Mining Committee and President

Woodrow Wilson to establish a grievance committee. Later she participated in strikes of streetcar workers and garment workers in New York City and of steel workers in Pittsburgh.

Mother Jones died seven months after her 100th birthday. At her request, she was buried in the United Miners Cemetery in the coalfields of southern Illinois.

—*Bernard Ryan, Jr.*

Suggestions for Further Reading

Atkinson, Linda S. *Mother Jones: The Most Dangerous Woman in America.* New York: Crown, 1978.

Fetherling, Dale. *Mother Jones: The Miner's Angel, A Portrait.* Carbondale: Southern Illinois University Press, 1974.

Foner, Philip S., ed. *Mother Jones Speaks: Collected Writings and Speeches.* New York: Monad Press, 1983.

Guttridge, Leonard F. *Great Coalfield War.* Boston: Houghton, Mifflin, 1972.

Jones, Mary Harris. *Autobiography of Mother Jones.* Edited by Mary Field Parton. 1925. Reprint, Chicago: Charles H. Kerr & Co. for the Illinois Labor History Society, 1972.

Long, Priscilla. *Mother Jones, Woman Organizer, and Her Relations with Miners' Wives, Working Women, and the Suffrage Movement.* Cambridge, Mass.: Red Sun Press, 1976.

Steel, Edward M., ed. *The Correspondence of Mother Jones.* Pittsburgh: University of Pittsburgh Press, 1985.

——. *The Court-Martial of Mother Jones.* Lexington: University Press of Kentucky, 1995.

——. *The Speeches and Writings of Mother Jones.* Pittsburgh: University of Pittsburgh Press, 1988.

Leo Frank Trial: 1913

Defendant: Leo Max Frank **Crime Charged:** Murder
Chief Defense Lawyers: Reuben Arnold, Herbert Haas, Stiles Hopkins, and Luther Z. Rosser **Chief Prosecutors:** Hugh Dorsey, Frank Arthur Hooper, and Edward A. Stephens **Judge:** Leonard Strickland Roan **Place:** Atlanta, Georgia **Dates of Trial:** July 28–September 26, 1913 **Verdict:** Guilty **Sentence:** Death by hanging, commuted by Georgia Governor John Slaton to life imprisonment (After his commutation, Frank died at the hands of an angry lynch mob.)

SIGNIFICANCE

The Leo Frank trial was a national scandal, which exposed the double standard of Southern justice: one for whites and one for minorities such as Frank, who was Jewish. Not only was Frank hung by a lynch mob after his death sentence was commuted, but the Ku Klux Klan experienced a period of renewed growth for years afterward due to the racist feelings brought on by the trial.

Leo Max Frank was born in Paris, Texas, in 1884. His family moved to Brooklyn, New York while he was still a baby. Frank's family was Jewish, and he was raised in New York City's extensive Jewish community. Frank was a quiet, shy man, but he had exceptional mechanical aptitude and he graduated from Cornell University with an engineering degree. After working for brief periods with several companies, Frank went to work for his uncle, Moses Frank, who was the principal owner of the National Pencil Company. The National Pencil Company had a factory in Atlanta, Georgia, and in 1907 Frank was appointed the superintendent and moved to Atlanta.

It probably never occurred to Frank that, since he was moving to the South, racism might be a problem. Atlanta's Jewish community was small by New York standards but nevertheless significant and had deep roots in the city's history. In 1911, Frank married Lucile Selig, whose family was also Jewish and well-off. Frank spent most of his time supervising the pencil factory, avoided politics and racial issues, and was honored by the Jewish community as one of Atlanta's most promising young businessmen. By 1913 Frank was one of Atlanta's leading citizens and was enjoying a successful career.

Little Mary Phagan Murdered

As was common at the time, Frank's factory employed women and children, who were capable of performing the light labor necessary to manufacture pencils and who could be paid lower wages than men. One such worker was Mary Phagan, a blond 13-year-old girl who lived in nearby Marietta. She was one of several workers caught in a temporary layoff, and on April 26, 1913, she came to collect her final wages from Frank. Frank paid her and thought no more of the matter after she left. Shortly before he left for the day, Frank had another encounter with a former employee, this time with John Gantt, who asked if he could retrieve some shoes he had left in his locker. Frank allowed Gantt to get his shoes, but Frank's nervous personality made him afraid of Gantt, who had a reputation as a drunkard and who Frank had fired for stealing.

That night, Frank called the night watchman, a black man named Newt Lee, several times to ask if there was any trouble. Frank probably feared some sort of action by Gantt, but there was none. In the early hours of the morning, however, Lee discovered the bound and brutalized corpse of Mary Phagan in the basement. Someone had raped and killed her after she collected her pay that day. Afraid that he would be blamed for the crime, Lee went straight to the police and reported the crime. His honesty did him no good: After the police arrived at the factory and investigated the scene of the crime, they threw Lee in jail anyway, to be held without charges for months.

The police then went to Frank's house, took him to the scene of the crime for questioning, and then to the police station for several days of further interrogation. Meanwhile, the murder had become a local sensation, and the Atlanta newspapers were filled with lurid headlines describing the details of the crime and calling for justice. Hugh Mason Dorsey, the chief prosecutor for that portion of Atlanta, had political ambitions and seized on the meek, Jewish Frank as an easy target. On April 29, 1913, Frank was formally arrested for the murder of Mary Phagan.

Frank's lawyers were Reuben Arnold, Herbert Haas, Stiles Hopkins, and Luther Z. Rosser. In addition to Dorsey, the prosecutors were Frank Arthur Hooper and Edward A. Stephens. The judge was Leonard Strickland Roan, and the trial began on July 28, 1913.

Prosecutors Emphasize Frank's Nervousness

Newt Lee, still in prison "under suspicion," was one of the first prosecution witnesses. Frank's telephone calls to Lee on the night of the murder came back to haunt him, because the prosecutors made it look as if Frank was checking to see if the body had been discovered that Saturday night. Lee Testified:

> Mr. Frank phoned me [the first time] that night about an hour after he left, it was sometime after seven o'clock. He says, "How is everything?" and I says, "Everything is all right so far as I know," and he says, "Goodbye." No, he

did not ask anything about Gantt. Yes, that is the first time he ever phoned to me on a Saturday night.

The prosecutors then turned Frank's nervous disposition to their advantage, and using the testimony of the police officers who had taken Frank to the scene of the crime on the morning of Sunday, April 27, to create suspicion in the mind of the jury. First, officer John N. Starnes testified:

> I reached the factory between five and six o'clock on April 27th. I called up the superintendent, Leo Frank, and asked him to come right away. He said he hadn't had any breakfast. He asked where the night watchman was. I told him to come, and if he would come, I would send an automobile for him. I didn't tell him what had happened, and he didn't ask me.
>
> When Frank arrived at the factory, a few minutes later, he appeared to be nervous, he was in a trembling condition. Lee was composed at the factory, he never tried to get away.

Another officer, one who had gone to pick up Frank at Frank's home, confirmed Starnes' testimony:

> Mrs. Frank came to the door; she had on a bathrobe. I stated that I would like to see Mr. Frank and about that time Mr. Frank stepped out from behind a curtain. Frank's voice was hoarse and trembling and nervous and excited. He looked to me like he was pale. He seemed nervous in handling his collar; he could not get his tie tied, and talked very rapid in asking what had happened. He kept insisting on a cup of coffee.
>
> When we got into the automobile, Mr. Frank wanted to know what had happened at the factory, and I asked him if he knew Mary Phagan, and told him she had been found dead in the basement. Mr. Frank said he did not know any girl by the name of Mary Phagan, that he knew very few of the employees.

The implication from this testimony was that Frank's nervousness was the result of a guilty conscience. Next, the prosecutors tried to prove that Frank had deliberately planned to get Mary Phagan to come to the factory that weekend. For example, a factory employee named Helen Ferguson testified that she had been Mary Phagan's friend and had in the past picked up Phagan's pay for her, but on the day before the murder, Frank suddenly refused to let Ferguson pick up Phagan's final pay:

> [I went to] Mr. Frank Friday, April 25, about seven o'clock in the evening and asked for Mary Phagan's money. Mr. Frank said, "I can't let you have it," and before he said anything else I turned around and walked out. I had gotten Mary's money before.

Prosecution Clinches their Case

The prosecutors saved their best witness for last: Jim Conley, a large black man who was the factory janitor. Despite some very suspicious circumstances that tended to implicate Conley as the actual murderer, the prosecutors put him on the stand. It has even been written that Dorsey deliberately chose to prosecute a "Yankee Jew" rather than a "nigger" for purposes of sensationalism, regardless of Frank's innocence. The gist of Conley's lengthy testimony was that he had been at the factory on the day of the murder and that Frank had confessed to the murder:

> Mr. Frank was standing up there at the top of the steps and shivering and trembling and rubbing his hands like this. He had a little rope in his hands and a long wide piece of cord. His eyes were large and they looked right funny. He looked funny out of his eyes. His face was red. . . . After I got up to the top of the steps, he asked me, "Did you see [Mary Phagan] who passed here just a while ago?" I told him . . . she hasn't come back down, and he says, "Well, that one you say didn't come back down, she come into my office awhile ago and wanted to know something about her work in my office and I went back there to see if the little girl's work had come, and I wanted to be with the little girl, and she refused me, and I struck her and I guess I struck her too hard and she fell and hit her head against something, and I don't know how bad she got hurt. . . ."

The defense lawyers cross-examined Conley for several days but were unable to impeach his testimony. The defense lawyers also had to contend with the presence of spectators in the courtroom who constantly made catcalls and racist comments—such as "Hang the Jew!"—while the defense attempted to make its case. Although Judge Roan had once been defense lawyer Rosser's partner in private practice, he made no serious effort to curb these distractions.

At the conclusion of the defense's case, Frank himself took the stand. For nearly half a day he spoke, and unequivocally denied murdering Phagan. He explained his apparent nervousness as the natural result of being dragged out of his home so early on a Sunday morning and being confronted with such a gruesome crime:

> Now, gentlemen, I have heard a great deal, and have you, in this trial, about nervousness, about how nervous I was that morning. Gentlemen, I was nervous, I was completely unstrung, I will admit it; imagine, awakened out of my sound sleep, and a morning run down in the cool of the morning in an automobile driven at top speed, without any food or breakfast, rushing into a dark passageway, coming into a darkened room, and then suddenly an electric light flashed on, and to see that sight that was presented by that poor little child; why, it was a sight that was enough to drive a man to distraction; that was a sight that would have made a stone melt.

Further, Frank bluntly called Conley a liar:

> The statement of the Negro Conley is a tissue of lies from first to last. I know nothing whatever of the cause of the death of Mary Phagan and Conley's statement . . . that I had anything to do with her or to do with him that day, is a monstrous lie.

Frank Convicted, Commuted, and Lynched

On September 26, 1913, after one of the longest trials in Georgia history, the jury found Leo Frank guilty of the murder of Mary Phagan. Judge Roan sentenced Frank to be executed by hanging on October 10, but the execution was stayed by the defense lawyers' appeals. On February 17, 1914, the Georgia

Supreme Court upheld Frank's conviction, although two judges dissented. The defense lawyers, however, did not give up. They pursued evidence that Conley had committed the murder: Witnesses had seen Conley washing his bloody clothing at the factory after the murder, Conley's girlfriend gave testimony concerning Conley's perverted sexual tendencies, and Conley's own lawyer told Judge Roan that Conley had confessed to the murder to him.

Despite the evidence of Conley's guilt and therefore Frank's innocence, Judge Roan refused to overturn the verdict and the Georgia Supreme Court again affirmed on October 14, 1914. On December 9, 1914, Frank's execution was rescheduled for January 22, 1915, but it was again stayed, this time by the defense lawyers' *habeas corpus* petition (release from unlawful confinement) to the U.S. Supreme Court. On April 19, 1915, the Court denied the petition, despite the strong dissents of Justices Oliver Wendell Holmes and Charles Evans Hughes.

Leo Frank was lynched for the murder of Mary Phagan. (Bettmann/Corbis)

Frank's last chance was an appeal to the governor of Georgia, John Slaton, for commutation of his sentence. This appeal began with a hearing on May 31, 1915, before the Georgia Prison Commission. On June 9, 1915, the Commission voted 2–1 against recommending commutation to the governor. Slaton, however, was an independent man, and had on several occasions used his power to grant clemency when in his opinion justice demanded it, regardless of the unpopularity of his decision. On June 21, 1915, Slaton commuted Frank's sentence to life imprisonment, citing the widespread national criticism of Georgia justice and the many doubts raised over the evidence against Frank.

> This case has been marked by doubt. The trial judge doubted. Two judges of the Court of Georgia doubted. Two judges of the Supreme Court of the United States doubted. One of the three Prison Commissioners doubted.

As he probably foresaw, Slaton's decision was instantly unpopular in Georgia. There were demonstrations in Atlanta and in Marietta, Phagan's home town, and sporadic acts of vandalism against Jewish homes and stores. On August 16, 1915, a vigilante group drove from Marietta to the Milledgeville Prison Farm outside Macon, Georgia. They overpowered the skeleton crew of prison guards and took Frank from his cell. The vigilantes drove back to Marietta, a seven-hour trip, with Frank. Once back in Marietta, a lynch mob of local citizens gathered and watched as Frank was hung from a tree limb on the morning of August 17, 1915. The racist hatred stirred up by the Frank trial did not end with Frank's lynching. For decades, the "vindication" of Mary Phagan was a rallying cry for the resurgent Ku Klux Klan.

In 1982, an old black man named Alonzo Mann, who had worked at Frank's pencil factory as a child, publicly declared that he had seen Jim Conley drag Mary Phagan's corpse to the basement but had kept silent because Conley had threatened to kill him. On March 11, 1986, the Georgia State Board of Pardons and Paroles posthumously pardoned Frank.

—*Stephen G. Christianson*

Suggestions for Further Reading

Dinnerstein, Leonard. *The Leo Frank Case.* Athens, Ga.: University of Georgia Press, 1987.

Liebman, James S. "Lesson Unlearned." *The Nation* (August 1991): 217.

Lindemann, Albert S. *The Jew Accused: Three Anti-Semitic Affairs (Dreyfus, Beilis, Frank), 1894–1915.* New York: Cambridge University Press, 1991.

MacLean, Nancy. "The Leo Frank Case Reconsidered: Gender and Sexual Politics in the Making of Reactionary Populism." *The Journal of American History* (December 1991): 917–948.

Oney, Steve. "The Lynching of Leo Frank: Two Years Ago, and Seventy Years Too Late, a Witness Came Forward to Prove That Frank's Only Crime was Being a Stranger in the Old South." *Esquire* (September 1985): 90–98.

Phagan, Mary. *The Murder of Little Mary Phagan.* Far Hills, N.J.: New Horizon Press, 1987.

Hans Schmidt Trials: 1913 & 1914

Defendant: Hans Schmidt **Crime Charged:** Murder
Chief Defense Lawyers: W. M. K. Olcott, Alphonse G. Koelble, Terence J. McManus **Chief Prosecutors:** James A. Delehanty, Deacon Murphy
Judge: First trial: Warren W. Foster; Second trial: Vernon M. Davis
Place: New York, New York **Dates of Trials:** First trial: December 7–30, 1913; Second trial: January 19–February 5, 1914 **Verdict:** First trial: jury deadlocked; Second trial: guilty **Sentence:** Death

SIGNIFICANCE

The question of sanity has always been a vexatious issue in the American courtroom. Here it would decide whether the defendant—a priest—would live or die.

On September 5, 1913, two youths walking along the New Jersey shoreline of the Hudson River stumbled across a package containing the headless trunk of a woman, severed at the waist. The next day, some three miles downriver at Weehawken, a second package was found, a pillowcase monogrammed with the letter "A", and containing the lower torso of the same woman, wrapped in a newspaper dated August 31. Despite the fact that both packages had washed ashore in New Jersey, jurisdiction passed to the New York Police Department. This decision was made because both parcels had been weighted down with a large chunk of schist, a grayish-green rock rarely found in New Jersey but very common in Manhattan, leading to the strong presumption that the crime had taken place in New York.

A preliminary examination of the body suggested a woman aged under 30, approximately 5 feet 4 inches in height and weighing between 120 and 130 pounds, and that she had been in the water a few days at most. An autopsy later revealed that the woman had given birth prematurely not long before she died.

Skilled detective work, tracing the manufacturer of the highly distinctive pillowcase, then studying that company's order books, led officers to a Manhattan apartment. The landlord said that the apartment had been rented two weeks earlier by someone called Hans Schmidt, ostensibly for a young female relative.

When officers let themselves into the apartment, they spotted bloodstains on the wallpaper and floor; stains that someone had struggled hard to remove, judging from the new scrubbing brush and six cakes of soap that lay by the sink. Inside a trunk they found a foot-long butcher's knife and a large handsaw, both recently cleaned. Another trunk held several small handkerchiefs, all amateurishly embroidered with the same letter "A" as on the pillowcase. A bundle of letters addressed to one Anna Aumuller led to St. Boniface's Church, on 42nd Street, where the 21-year-old German immigrant had worked as a servant in the rectory, until being discharged for misconduct. Mention of Schmidt's name brought another lead—St. Joseph's Church, 405 West 105th Street.

Father Hans Schmidt, aged 32 and German-born, almost fainted when police officers came to interview him. Just minutes later, racked by remorse, he unburdened his soul with a bizarre tale of having gone through a form of marriage with Aumuller—a ceremony conducted by himself for obvious reasons—only to then kill her, excusing himself on the grounds that "I loved her. Sacrifices should be consummated in blood."

Insanity Plea

That Schmidt killed Anna Aumuller was not in doubt when his trial began on December 7, 1913, but his defense team, lead by W. M. K. Olcott, was emphatic that their client had been consumed by a "blood lust" and, therefore, was not responsible for his actions. As support for this view they produced Dr. Arnold Leo, who had treated Schmidt and Aumuller some months before the tragedy.

Leo told the court that at their first meeting Schmidt had initially claimed to be a music teacher, but later admitted that he was a priest. "Schmidt told me that he was very much in love with the girl, and that he intended to give up the priesthood and marry her." Leo described how during one of his professional visits to see Schmidt at the rectory, the priest unaccountably became "wildly excited," then sprang across the room and grabbed a zither. After playing the instrument for a few minutes he stopped, sat down and began to talk calmly.

So far as the prosecution, which knew a great deal about the defendant's shady background, was concerned, Schmidt was a scheming con man, entirely responsible for his actions. The arresting officer, Inspector Joseph A. Faurot, testified that at first Schmidt had denied knowing Anna Aumuller, but had yielded when Faurot said, "Come now, tell us the whole truth about this thing."

According to Faurot, Schmidt admitted purchasing the knife and handsaw on August 31, then creeping into Aumuller's bedroom on night of September 2, while she lay sleeping, and slashing her throat. Quizzed about the obvious signs of experience in the dissection, Schmidt admitted that he had been a medical student before being ordained.

Assistant District Attorney James A. Delehanty wanted the jury to know more about what Faurot had discovered about Schmidt's background. Faurot detailed the extraordinary career of a priest who often posed as a doctor, in which capacity he had performed illegal abortions, a man who turned his hand to counterfeiting, someone who had aroused concern at several churches across America, and yet who had miraculously avoided censure.

Clearly Schmidt was peculiar, but was he mad? It would be up to the jury to decide.

Deadlocked

After 34 hours of often acrimonious deliberation the jury came back on December 30, and announced themselves hopelessly deadlocked at 10–2 for conviction. Jury foreman William Ottinger, visibly exhausted, told Judge Foster, "Your Honor, we have voted many times, and we stood the same on the first ballot as the last," leaving the judge no option but to declare a mistrial.

One of the holdout jurors, William McAuliffe, afterwards claimed, "The other ten were willing to acquit the defendant on the grounds of insanity, except that they were afraid that he would go to Matteawan and get out like Thaw. So they thought the only thing to do was send him to the electric chair."

When defense lawyer Alphonse Koelble suggested that the jury be allowed to bring in a verdict of guilty to second-degree murder, Delehanty bitterly rejected the idea and declared that the state would try Schmidt again.

This trial began on January 19, 1914, and was essentially a carbon copy of the first, except that in his charge to the jury Justice Davis made a plea for some cold, hard logic:

> If you are satisfied that the defendant purchased the knife and saw with which he cut up the body, thinking of using them as he did, and if you are satisfied that in the middle of the night he went to the flat, took off his coat and cut her throat, and then cut up her body, what conclusion do you come to? Use your common sense . . . your experience with men. Bear in mind, it isn't every form of mental unsoundness that excuses a crime.[See Harry Thaw Trials]

The jury took this admonition to heart and, on February 5, 1914, after just two hours' deliberation, they convicted Schmidt of first-degree murder.

One week later the disgraced priest was sentenced to death, and after a lengthy appeal process he was executed on February 18, 1916.

The issues of mental competence raised in these trials resonate to the present day, as juries continue to wrestle with the conundrum of deciding whether someone is mad or bad.

—Colin Evans

Suggestions for Further Reading

Lunde, Donald T. *Murder and Madness.* New York: Simon & Schuster, 1976.

New York Times. See Aumuller, Anna, in the *New York Times Index*, September 15, 1913–February 13, 1914.

Joe Hill Trial: 1914

Defendant: Joe Hill **Crime Charged:** Murder
Chief Defense Lawyers: Soren X. Christensen, Orrin N. Hilton, E.D. McDougall, and F.B. Scott **Chief Prosecutor:** E.O. Leatherwood
Judge: Morris L. Ritchie **Place:** Salt Lake City, Utah **Dates of Trial:** June 17–28, 1914 **Verdict:** Guilty **Sentence:** Execution by firing squad

SIGNIFICANCE

The trial of Joe Hill launched the legend of Joe Hill, a lyrical spokesman for the Industrial Workers of the World. His conviction and execution made him a martyr symbolizing, in the eyes of many union workers, all the injustice of American society.

The Industrial Workers of the World (IWW, better known as the Wobblies), organized in 1905, sent its messages to laboring people through song. Its *Little Red Song Book,* which set new words to popular, often religious, tunes, enjoyed print runs of 50,000. Before World War I, the Wobblies directed or participated in 150 strikes, some as large as a 10-week holdout by 25,000 textile workers in Lawrence, Massachusetts. Songs were an important element in Wobbly tactics, for they brought a sense of solidarity to heterogeneous groups of workers.

The song book's 1911 edition introduced a writer named Joe Hill and a song—"The Preacher and the Slave"—that became one of his most famous. To the tune of "In the Sweet Bye and Bye," it sang:

> You will eat, bye and bye,
> In that glorious land above the sky;
> Work and pray, live on hay,
> You'll get pie in the sky when you die.

Hill, a native of Sweden, was soon a popular hero. He meandered across the country, playing piano, banjo, guitar, and violin in hobo jungles, migrant workers' camps, and city slums. Each edition of the songbook introduced several of his new Joe Hill songs.

Hill was staying with friends in Salt Lake City, Utah, on Saturday, January 10, 1914, when he went out for the evening. Toward midnight, he knocked at the door of Dr. Frank M. McHugh, who dressed a bullet wound that pierced

Hill's chest. Hill told the doctor, "I got into a stew with a friend who thought I had insulted his wife."

The same night, police investigated a shooting at a grocery store. Proprietor John G. Morrison and his elder son were found dead. His younger son, Merlin, 13, reported seeing two men come in carrying pistols. They shouted, "We have got you now!" and fired, then ran.

Morrison was a former policeman who had lived in constant dread of those he had previously arrested. Twice he had shot and wounded men who attacked him.

Police found Morrison's pistol, discharged. A witness reported seeing two men run from the store, one holding his hands to his chest.

After Dr. McHugh dressed Hill's wound, he read of the murders and called the police. Since Hill had been wounded the same night as the murders and he would say only that his shooting occurred during a fight over a woman, he was arrested.

Circumstantial Evidence but no Motive

As the trial opened on June 17, 1914, prosecutor E.O. Leatherwood admitted that the state had only circumstantial evidence. Thirteen-year-old Merlin Morrison could not positively identify Hill as his father's murderer.

Press interest intensified as Wobbly lawyers Orrin Hilton and Soren Christensen took over the defense. They complained that Hill would rather face death than reveal his exact whereabouts and the identity of those he was with on the night of the murder. They challenged the prosecutor to prove a motive for his killing Morrison, or even for shouting "We have got you now!" before shooting. They tried to prove that Hill was wounded by a steel bullet, while Morrison's gun fired lead.

On June 28, the jury returned a guilty verdict, and Hill was sentenced to die. Attorney Hilton appealed, citing the prosecution's failure to identify Hill as the murderer, the lack of motive, the court's disallowing testimony on previous attempts on Morrison's life, errors in the admission of expert testimony (a newsman had been accepted as a gun expert), and several critical errors by the judge. The appeal was denied.

Hill's attorneys decided that an appeal to the U.S. Supreme Court was useless because the case involved no federal considerations. While rallies were held and funds were raised nationwide, execution was set for October 1. Hill's attorneys asked the Utah Board of Pardons to commute his sentence to life imprisonment. Petitions, telegrams, and letters mounted. Hill refused an offer of freedom if he would reveal, with corroboration, where he was during the Morrison murder. The execution date was set repeatedly as the Swedish minister to the United States, American Federation Labor President Samuel Gompers, and the highly respected Helen Keller all appealed to President Woodrow Wilson, who in turn, appealed to Utah governor William Spry. But Spry refused clemency unless Hill satisfactorily explained how he was wounded.

Hours before his execution, Hill wired IWW General Secretary Bill Haywood, "I will die like a true-blue rebel. Don't waste any time in mourning—organize."

At 10:00 P.M., Hill handed a guard his last poem, titled "My Last Will":

. . . let the merry breezes blow
My dust to where some flowers grow.
Perhaps some fading flower then
Would come to life and bloom again.
This is my Last and Final Will.
Good luck to All of you
—Joe Hill

The next morning, November 19, a firing squad shot Joe Hill through the heart. Thousands attended his funeral in Salt Lake City, then another in Chicago. Cremation followed. Joe Hill's ashes, distributed in small packets, were scattered worldwide.

The song, "I Dreamed I Saw Joe Hill Last Night," soon appeared, with its verse,

The copper bosses killed you, Joe,
"They shot you, Joe," says I.
"Takes more than guns to kill a man,"
Says Joe, "I didn't die."
Says Joe, "I didn't die."

In the years following, such noted authors as Upton Sinclair, Carl Sandburg, John Dos Passos, Eugene O'Neill, and Wallace Stegner, as well as folk singers Pete Seeger and Woody Guthrie and millions of workers, have all dreamed they saw Joe Hill last night.

The last of Joe Hill's ashes were scattered in Washington, D.C., in November 1988.

—Bernard Ryan, Jr.

Suggestions for Further Reading

Hampton, Wayne. *Guerrilla Minstrels: John Lennon, Joe Hill, Woody Guthrie, and Bob Dylan*. Knoxville: University of Tennessee Press, 1986.

Smith, Gibbs M. *Labor Martyr Joe Hill.* New York: Grosset & Dunlap, 1969.

Snow, Richard F. "American Characters: Joe Hill," *American Heritage* (October 1976): 79.

Stegner, Wallace. *The Preacher and the Slave.* Boston: Houghton Mifflin, 1950.

"Wobbly," *The New Yorker* (December 19, 1988): 28.

Tom Mooney Trial: 1917

Defendant: Thomas J. Mooney **Crime Charged:** Murder
Chief Defense Lawyers: W. Bourke Cockran and Maxwell McNutt
Chief Prosecutors: Edward A. Cunha and Charles Fickert **Judge:** Franklin A. Griffin **Place:** San Francisco, California **Dates of Trial:** January 3–February 9, 1917 **Verdict:** Guilty **Sentence:** Death by hanging, later commuted, then pardoned

SIGNIFICANCE

Tom Mooney's case demonstrated how America's phobia about radicals from before World War I and through the 1920s and '30s corrupted its sense of justice and even its common sense. While the improper conviction of Mooney—based on perjury, suppression and fabrication of evidence, and subornation of perjury—was established within a year after the trial, political maneuvering kept him in prison until 1939. This failure of the legal system to acknowledge that a conviction based on perjured testimony justified a new trial is demonstrated that an unpopular defendant could be denied due process in the state of California.

On "Preparedness Day," July 22, 1916, a bomb killed 10 spectators and injured 40 others during a military parade in San Francisco. Opposition to the parade had been planned and announced by radical labor leaders and anarchists who thought the march promoted militarism, and who were against American entry into the World War then raging in Europe. The bombing looked like anarchists' work.

Within hours of the bombing, District Attorney Charles Fickert was visited by Martin Swanson, a private detective employed by the Pacific Gas and Electric Company (PG&E). Swanson suspected that the insurgent responsible for the parade bombing was 34-year-old Tom Mooney, a union organizer who had drifted through at least a dozen jobs across the country as an ironworker and had earned a reputation as "a comer" with officers of his union, the International Molders. Mooney had even drifted twice to Europe, where he was strongly attracted to socialism. Back in the United States, he had been an active orator and fund-raiser in the 1908 presidential campaign of Socialist Eugene V. Debs, who liked Mooney's forceful persistence and made him his "official party literature agent."

One of "The Blasters'

Swanson knew Mooney had been acquitted of possessing dynamite in a strike against PG&E. Swanson also implicated Warren K. Billings, another labor activist who had been convicted of transporting dynamite.

Billings, Mooney, his wife Rena and their friend Israel Weinberg, a taxi driver, were arrested immediately without warrants. Rena Mooney and Weinberg were charged with complicity; Billings and Mooney with murder.

Billings was tried first, convicted, and sentenced to life imprisonment—mainly on the testimony of John McDonald, who said he had seen Billings and Tom Mooney at the scene just before the bomb went off.

On January 3, 1917, opening the Mooney trial for the prosecution, Prosecutor Edward Cunha reviewed Mooney's earlier association with an organization called "The Blasters." Their stated goal was an uprising of California's workers, who would seize property and destroy the government. Their revolution called for violence, even the assassination of the president. For a week, Cunha presented circumstantial evidence, most of which had been seen or heard in the Billings trial.

A Surprise Witness—and a Jitney

Then Cunha came up with a surprise witness: one Frank C. Oxman, an Oregon cattleman who traveled frequently to California and Kansas, buying and selling cattle. He testified that he had arrived in San Francisco on the morning of the parade and was watching it when he saw a jitney containing five people turn from Market Street onto Stewart. As it stopped, men he identified as Mooney and Billings jumped out, put a suitcase on the sidewalk, and hopped back in the car. Oxman declared under oath that Weinberg was at the wheel, and Rena Mooney was visible in the car. Dramatically pulling a yellow envelope from his pocket, Oxman stunned the courtroom by announcing he had had the presence of mind to jot down the jitney's license number. It was Weinberg's.

The Mooney defense team, led by W. Bourke Cockran, was flustered by Oxman's sudden appearance. The defense did not ask for a recess while it could check on his credibility. It also failed to exploit the inconsistencies in the testimony of Oxman and McDonald, who had testified to seeing the defendants on foot, not in a car. It did not put on the stand any of the 18 policemen stationed along Market Street during the parade, any one of whom could have testified that they had orders to keep cars off Market Street that afternoon and that only two, with official passes, had trespassed on the parade route—neither one of which was Weinberg's jitney.

The Clock in the Photos

In his defense, Tom Mooney said he and Rena Mooney had watched the parade from atop the Eilers Music Company Building at 975 Market Street, 1.15

miles from the site of the bombing. To prove this, Cockran introduced three photographs taken from the roof by an Eilers employee. Enlargements made in the presence of two detectives revealed the time on a street clock down on Market: eight minutes, five minutes, and two minutes before the bomb went off. In each photo, Tom and Rena Mooney could be seen in the foreground, on the rooftop. In addition, 12 witnesses swore that Tom Mooney had been there throughout the parade.

The defense tried to show that Mooney was being framed. Weinberg testified that private detective Swanson had earlier tried to bribe him. Cockran asked for a directed acquittal, but Judge Franklin A. Griffin ruled that was up to the jury.

The district attorney himself, Charles Fickert, summarized for the prosecution and asked for the death penalty. His stirring words urged the jury to be fearless:

> For, with conscience satisfied with the discharge of duty, no consequence can harm you. There is no evil that we cannot face or fly from but the consciousness of duty disregarded. A sense of duty pursues us ever. It is omnipresent like the deity . . .

The D.A. went on for another minute or two in this vein, an inspiration to juryman and spectator alike. But on the front page of the *Bulletin* that evening, two reporters revealed that the same inspiration had been uttered, word for word, by Daniel Webster at a murder trial in 1830.

Defense attorney Maxwell McNutt's summation to the jury charged that Martin Swanson had devised a frame-up—an idea that prosecutor Cunha labeled absurd. Judge Griffin advised jury members they were entitled to question the trustworthiness of the prosecution if they viewed the arrest of the defendants without warrants as a violation of their rights, and he invited them to weigh the credibility of the witnesses as well.

In 6 and one-half hours, the jury found Tom Mooney guilty of first-degree murder and recommended the death penalty.

Letters to an Old Friend

Within two months, an old friend of Frank Oxman named Ed Rigall tried to sell the prosecutors several letters that Oxman had written him soon after the bombing, inviting him to San Francisco to swear that he had been with Oxman at the parade. It turned out that Oxman had arrived in the city four hours after the bombing and later, upon learning that the reward for information leading to the conviction of the perpetrator had climbed to $15,350, had had another friend inform Cunha that he, Oxman, was available as a witness.

Mooney's defense team got hold of the letters and published them. Subsequently the juries in Weinberg's and Rena Mooney's trials for complicity in the bomb murders found them each not guilty. Oxman was tried for subornation of perjury and acquitted. Meanwhile, Mooney sat on death row in San Quentin prison. In March 1918, the California Supreme Court upheld his conviction. Execution was set for August 23. President Woodrow Wilson appealed to the California governor, William D. Stephens. Demonstrations on Mooney's behalf were being held around the world. William Randolph Hearst, reversing the support his papers had given District Attorney Fickert, announced that Mooney should not be put to death. "Mooney Day" was celebrated nationwide in July, with speeches by top labor leaders and liberals, and the governor approved a reprieve. In November, Judge Griffin proposed a pardon and retrial. Two weeks before the scheduled hanging, the governor commuted Mooney's sentence to life imprisonment.

During the 22 years Tom Mooney unjustly spent in prison, numerous demonstrations were held on his behalf. (Courtesy, National Archives)

For 20 more years, attempts were made to free Mooney through legal channels. But California had an outdated system for review of convictions, and the courts declared there was no procedure that could give him a new trial based on the evident perjury. Every governor during these two decades refused to take the political risk involved in freeing the radical. From his prison cell, Mooney himself interfered with his lawyers, passing up at least one chance to ask for parole.

In 1939, Democratic Governor C. L. Olson, five days after his inauguration, gave Mooney an unconditional pardon. San Francisco then saw another Market Street parade—a victory procession with Tom and Rena Mooney, with the mayor, and prominent labor leaders at the head.

Mooney lived only three more years. For most of that time, he was bedridden with illnesses contracted in prison.

—Bernard Ryan, Jr.

Suggestions for Further Reading

Frost, Richard H. *The Mooney Case.* Stanford, Calif.: Stanford University Press, 1968.

Gentry, Curt. *Frame-up: The Incredible Case of Tom Mooney and Warren Billings.* New York: W.W. Norton & Co., 1967.

Sifakis, Carl. *The Encyclopedia of American Crime.* New York: Facts On File, 1982.

The Trials of Alice Paul and Other National Woman's Party Members: 1917

Defendants: Gertrude Crocker, Gladys Greiner, Alice Paul, and Dr. Caroline Spencer **Crime Charged:** Obstructing a sidewalk
Chief Defense Lawyer: Dudley Field Malone **Chief Prosecutor:** Hart (first name unavailable) **Judge:** Alexander Mullowney **Date:** October 22, 1917
Verdicts: Guilty **Sentences:** Alice Paul and Caroline Spencer: 7 months in prison; Gertrude Crocker and Gladys Grenier: $5.00 fine or 30 days in prison

SIGNIFICANCE

In 1917 and 1918, almost 500 suffragists were arrested during their picketing of the White House; 168, including National Woman's Party Chairperson Alice Paul, were tried, convicted, and imprisoned for terms of up to seven months, ostensibly for blocking traffic on a sidewalk. The women believed they were actually imprisoned for their political beliefs and became the first U.S. citizens to claim that their government held them as political prisoners.

Women first organized to demand suffrage in 1848, at what became known as the Seneca Falls Convention. In 1917, despite 69 years of active campaigning, women were still without the vote. Members of Alice Paul's National Woman's Party decided to try a new tactic, and on January 10 they began picketing President Woodrow Wilson and the White House.

Prior to the United States' entrance into World War I, the women received no attention from the government. Shortly after the declaration of war, however, Alice Paul was warned by the chief of police for the District of Columbia that picketers would now have to be arrested. Paul replied that her lawyers had "assured us all along that picketing was legal," and she maintained that it was "certainly . . . as legal in June as in January." The first two picketers were nonetheless arrested on June 22, 1917. They were charged with obstructing a sidewalk but released and never tried, as were 27 other women within the next four days. This process failed to put an end to the picketing, and on June 27 six women stood trial for obstructing traffic. They were found guilty and fined $25.00. Because they refused to pay their fine, they were sentenced to three days in jail.

The picketing continued. On July 14, 16 women were arrested, including Florence Bayard Hilles, the daughter of a former American ambassador to Great Britain, and Allison Turnbull Hopkins, the wife of President Wilson's New Jersey campaign coordinator. They stood trial the same day before district court Judge Alexander Mullowney.

Mullowney had earlier consulted the U.S. Attorney about the possibility of trying the women under the Espionage Act of 1917. Passed in June, it outlawed,

Alice Paul and Lucy Burns picketing the White House with others for the National Woman's Party. (Courtesy, Library of Congress)

among other things, the making of untrue statements which interfered with the conduct of war. The women's banners, Mullowney said, contained "words . . . [that] are treasonous and seditious." As it turned out, however, the women's banners contained what they considered ironic quotations of President Wilson's own speeches, such as a line from his War Message Speech of April 2: "WE SHALL FIGHT FOR THE THINGS WHICH WE HAVE ALWAYS HELD NEAREST OUR HEARTS—FOR DEMOCRACY, FOR THE RIGHT OF THOSE WHO SUBMIT TO AUTHORITY TO HAVE A VOICE IN THEIR OWN GOVERNMENTS." Since the president's own words could not feasibly be brought up under the Espionage Act, and because—as Paul had earlier insisted—picketing was perfectly legal in the United States, the women were charged with the by-now expected "crime" of obstructing traffic. All 16 women were sentenced to 60 days in the Occoquan Workhouse.

A Wilson appointee and friend, Dudley Field Malone, collector of the Port of New York, happened to witness the women's trial. Outraged at its conclusion, he took a taxi to the White House and gave Wilson his resignation, stating that he planned to offer his legal services to the suffragists. Wilson refused to accept Malone's resignation. On July 20, the President pardoned all the suffragists imprisoned at Occoquan.

Picketing continued unabated, and arrests resumed in August. Dudley Field Malone offered his resignation again on September 7, this time forwarding copies of his letter to all the leading newspapers as well as to President Wilson, writing, "I think it is high time that men in this generation, at some cost to themselves, stood up to battle for the national enfranchisement of American women." This time, Malone's resignation was accepted.

On October 4, Alice Paul herself was arrested along with 10 other women. In court October 8, the women refused to be sworn or to recognize the legitimacy of the court. Paul said: "We do not consider ourselves subject to this Court since, as an unenfranchised class, we have nothing to do with the making of the laws which have put us in this position." Although the charge was not dismissed, the women were released without sentence.

Alice Paul was arrested again on October 20, this time in the company of Dr. Caroline Spencer, Gladys Greiner, and Gertrude Crocker. The four were tried on October 22 before Judge Mullowney.

Police Sergeant Lee testified: "I made my way through the crowd that was surrounding them, and told the ladies they were violating the law by standing at the gates, and would not they please move on."

When Assistant District Attorney Hart asked Lee about the women's response, he replied: "They did not [move on], and they did not answer either . . . [I] placed them under arrest."

Paul and Spencer, who had been carrying banners, were sentenced to seven months imprisonment. Greiner and Crocker, given the choice between $5.00 fines or 30 days imprisonment, elected to go to jail.

Lucy Burns, one of the first women arrested and released on June 22, had been arrested again in September and convicted; in Occoquan Workhouse before Paul's imprisonment, Burns organized the other incarcerated suffragists to request political prisoner status. Their petition was smuggled to the commissioners of the District of Columbia. Each of the signers was immediately placed in solitary confinement. At the end of October, Paul arrived at Occoquan with the recently sentenced Rose Winslow, and the two announced a hunger strike to "secure for [their] fellow comrades treatment accorded political prisoners in every civilized country but our own."

Paul, Winslow, and others who joined the hunger strike were force-fed. Paul was held in solitary confinement and then transferred to a psychiatric hospital, where her windows were boarded over. Dudley Field Malone, finally managed to have her released to a regular hospital on a writ of *habeas corpus*.

On November 27 and 28, 1917, all of the imprisoned suffragists were released without condition or explanation. On March 4, 1918, the District of Columbia Court of Appeals ruled on an appeal filed earlier by Malone. Each one of the suffragists had been "illegally arrested, illegally convicted, and illegally imprisoned."

The Nineteenth Amendment, enfranchising women, was adopted on August 26, 1920.

—*Kathryn Cullen-DuPont*

Suggestions for Further Reading

Frost, Elizabeth and Kathryn Cullen-DuPont. *Women's Suffrage in America: An Eyewitness History.* New York: Facts On File, 1992.

Irwin, Inez Hayes. *The Story of Alice Paul and the National Woman's Party.* Fairfax, VA: Denlinger's Publishers, 1964.

Lunardini, Christine A. *From Equal Suffrage to Equal Rights: Alice Paul and the National Woman's Party, 1910–1928.* New York: New York University Press, 1986.

Paul, Alice. *Conversations with Alice Paul: Woman Suffrage and the Equal Rights Amendment.* An Interview conducted by Amelia Fry. Berkeley, Calif.: Bancroft Library, Regional Oral History Office, University of California, c. 1976.

Stevens, Doris. *Jailed For Freedom.* 1920, reprint. Salem, New Hampshire: Ayer Co., 1990.

Schenck v. U.S. Appeal: 1919

Appellant & Defendant: Charles T. Schenck **Appellee & Plaintiff:** The United States of America **Appellant Claim:** Not guilty, as convicted, of conspiracy to violate the Espionage Act of 1917
Chief Defense Lawyer: John Lord O'Brian
Chief Lawyers for Appellant: Henry J. Gibbons and Henry John Nelson
Justices: Louis D. Brandeis, John H. Clarke, William R. Day, Oliver Wendell Holmes, Charles Evans Hughes, Joseph McKenna, James C. McReynolds, Willis Van Devanter, and Edward D. White, Chief Justice **Place:** Washington, D.C. **Date of Decision:** March 3, 1919 **Decision:** Guilty verdict unanimously affirmed

SIGNIFICANCE

This case marked the first time the Supreme Court ruled directly on the extent to which the U.S. government may limit speech. It produced, in the affirmative opinion written by Justice Oliver Wendell Holmes, two of that fabled jurist's most memorable and oft-quoted statements on the law.

On June 15, 1917, just after the United States entered the World War, Congress passed the Espionage Act, which made it a federal crime to obstruct the country's war effort. The act closely followed the Conscription Act of May 18, which enabled the government to draft men for military service.

At the Socialist Party headquarters in Philadelphia, Pennsylvania, the executive committee quickly passed a resolution authorizing the printing of 15,000 leaflets, to be sent through the mails and otherwise distributed to men who had been drafted. The leaflets recited the first section of the Thirteenth Amendment to the U.S. Constitution, which states:

> Neither slavery nor involuntary servitude, except as a punishment for crime whereof the party shall have been duly convicted, shall exist within the United States or any place subject to their jurisdiction.

Advising the reader that a conscript is little better than a convict, the leaflets described conscription as despotism in its worst form and as a monstrous wrong against humanity in the interest of Wall Street's chosen few. "Do not submit to intimidation," said the leaflets, urging readers to petition for repeal of the Conscription Act.

"Largely Instrumental in Sending the Circulars About"

As general secretary of the Socialist party, Charles T. Schenck was in charge of the Philadelphia headquarters from which the leaflets were sent.

Schenck was soon arrested and indicted for sedition in conspiring to cause insubordination in the armed forces and obstruction of recruitment and enlistment. No evidence was presented to prove that he had corrupted even one draftee. Rather, the publication of the pamphlets was itself considered proof enough of his guilt.

In this significant First Amendment case, the 1919 Court unanimously affirmed that Schenck was guilty of violating the Espionage Act of 1917. (Courtesy, Library of Congress)

The defense presented a simple argument: Schenck had exercised the right guaranteed him by the First Amendment—the right to speak freely on a public issue.

Found guilty, Schenck appealed through the district courts and to the Supreme Court, steadfastly insisting on his right to freedom of speech.

Schenck's defense argued that there was not enough evidence to prove that he himself was concerned with sending out the pamphlets. Reviewing the testimony, Holmes pointed out that Schenck was the general secretary of the Socialist Party and was in charge of the headquarters from which the pamphlets were sent to men who had been called and accepted for military service. The general secretary's report of August 20, 1917, Holmes noted, said, "Obtained new leaflets from printer and started work addressing envelopes." Holmes also pointed out that "there was a resolve that Comrade Schenck be allowed $125 for sending leaflets through the mail."

"No reasonable man," concluded Holmes, "could doubt that the defendant Schenck was largely instrumental in sending the circulars about."

Justice Holmes wrote the opinion that was shared unanimously by the court. Noting that no case had been made for the leaflets having actually caused any insurrection, he commented:

> Of course the document would not have been sent unless it had been intended to have some effect, and we do not see what effect it could be expected to have upon persons subject to the draft except to influence them to obstruct the carrying of it out.

Holmes agreed with the defense that the leaflets were entitled to First Amendment protection, but only in peacetime—not in wartime.

> We admit that in many places and in ordinary times the defendants in saying all that was said in the circular would have been within their constitutional rights. But the character of every act depends upon the circumstances in which it is done. The most stringent protection of free speech would not protect a man in falsely shouting fire in a theater and causing a panic.

It may be noted in passing that Holmes never said the theater was crowded; posterity has consistently and mistakenly ascribed that adjective to the quotation. Next came the justice's second memorable phrase:

> The question in every case is whether the words used are used in such circumstances and are of such a nature as to create a clear and present danger that they will bring about the substantive evils that Congress has a right to prevent.

The "clear and present danger," said Holmes, is a question of "proximity and degree."

> When a nation is at war many things that might be said in time of peace are such a hindrance to its effort that their utterance will not be endured so long as men fight and that no court could regard them as protected by any constitutional right.

Finally, the justice observed, it made no difference that Schenck and his compatriots had failed to obstruct recruitment. "The statute," he said, "punishes conspiracies to obstruct as well as actual obstruction."

> If the act [speaking or circulating a paper], its tendency and the intent with which it is done are the same, we perceive no ground for saying that success alone warrants making the act a crime.

With that, the judgments of the lower courts were affirmed. Charles T. Schenck, who had been sentenced to 10 years' imprisonment on each of the three counts of the indictment, but with the three terms to be served concurrently, was sent to federal prison.

The Schenck case, in establishing the "clear and present danger" criterion, marked a turning point in First Amendment thinking by the court. Until then, Chief Justice Edward White and other judges had permitted the government to suppress any speech that displayed a "dangerous tendency." Within months, moreover, Holmes refined his views on the First Amendment when seven of his colleagues found a "clear and present danger" in the *Abrams v. United States* case. A Russian-born American named Jacob Abrams had been found guilty of violating the Espionage Act when he scattered leaflets protesting the sending of American troops into Russia after the Revolution of 1917. Holmes' dissent objected that Abrams had been condemned not for what he did but for what he believed. The justice insisted that the First Amendment guaranteed one's right to freedom of *opinion,* if not (as in the Schenck case during wartime) of *action.* One may assume that Holmes would have continued to insist on the guarantee of this right during the dark days of McCarthyism and the House Un-American Activities Committee.

In 1927, Holmes again dissented when the court upheld the conviction of Socialist Benjamin Gitlow under a New York state law for advocating criminal anarchy. Holmes found that Gitlow's publications, which advocated overthrowing the government, were protected by the Fourteenth Amendment's due process clause against interference by the state. The justice saw "no present danger of an attempt to overthrow the Government by force" in Gitlow's papers.

—*Bernard Ryan, Jr.*

Suggestions for Further Reading

Bowen, Catherine Drinker. *Yankee from Olympus: Justice Holmes and His Family.* Boston: Little, Brown and Co., 1943.

Burton, David H. *Oliver Wendell Holmes, Jr.* Boston: Twayne Publishers, Div. of G. K. Hall & Co., 1980.

Commager, Henry Steele, and Milton Cantor. *Documents of American History.* Englewood Cliffs, N.J.: Prentice Hall, 1988.

Friedman, Leon and Fred L. Israel, eds. *The Justices of the United States Supreme Court 1789–1969: Their Lives and Major Opinions.* New York: Chelsea House, 1969.

Novick, Sheldon M. *Honorable Justice: The Life of Oliver Wendell Holmes.* Boston: Little, Brown and Co., 1989.

Schnayerson, Robert. *The Illustrated History of the Supreme Court of the United States.* New York: Harry N. Abrams, 1986.

Witt, Elder, ed. *The Supreme Court and Individual Rights.* Washington: Congressional Quarterly, 1980.

Benjamin Gitlow Trials: 1920–25

Defendant: Benjamin Gitlow **Crime Charged:** Criminal Anarchy
Chief Defense Lawyers: Trial Court: Clarence Darrow; U.S. Supreme Court: Walter H. Pollak, Walter Nelles **Chief Prosecutors:** Trial Court: Alexander I. Rorke; U.S. Supreme Court: John Caldwell Meyers, W. J. Wetherbee, Claude T. Dawes **Judges:** Trial Court: Bartow S. Weeks; U.S. Supreme Court: Chief Justice William Howard Taft, Willis Van Devanter, James McReynolds, Edward T. Sanford, George Sutherland, Pierce Butler, Harland Fiske Stone, Louis Brandeis, Oliver Wendell Holmes **Places:** Trial Court: New York, New York; U.S. Supreme Court: Washington, D.C. **Dates of Trials:** Trial Court: January 30–February 5, 1920; Supreme Court decision: June 8, 1925
Verdict: Guilty **Sentence:** Five to ten years in prison

SIGNIFICANCE

Benjamin Gitlow was charged in 1919 with "criminal anarchy" by the state of New York. His offense: publishing the *Left Wing Manifesto,* a call for revolution. He was convicted and sentenced to five to ten years in prison. The verdict was upheld by the New York Court of Appeals and affirmed by the U.S. Supreme Court. The case is significant not because the Supreme Court upheld Gitlow's right to publish what he did. It did not. The Court held that the states' police power allowed New York to prosecute utterances that were blatantly inimical to the general welfare. But for the first time, it held that the Fourteenth Amendment's due process clause protected personal rights, like freedom of speech, as well as property rights, from infringement by the states.

When World War I ended, the Communist revolution in Russia was in full swing. Communist uprisings were occurring in Germany, Hungary, Finland, and other countries. In the United States, there was a "red scare." In November 1919, New York police rounded up leaders of the left wing of the disintegrating American Socialist Party. One was Benjamin Gitlow, a former state representative and publisher of a left-wing Socialist newspaper (he was later to become a co-founder of the Communist Labor Party). He was charged with criminal anarchy for publishing *The Left Wing Manifesto,* which called for "mass strikes of the American proletariat," to overthrow the government.

Darrow for the Defense

Realizing the strength of the anti-Red hysteria, the Socialists knew they needed a powerful trial lawyer. They persuaded Clarence Darrow to take the case. Darrow was not optimistic.

"I know you are innocent, but they have the country steamed up," Darrow told Gitlow. "Everybody is against the Reds."

Gitlow later wrote that Darrow "seemed not a little frightened when I told him I intended to stand by every Communist principle and to defend my position regardless of the consequences."

Darrow said that in that case, there was no use in Gitlow taking the stand. Gitlow agreed, but demanded to be allowed to address the jury in his own way.

"Well, I suppose a revolutionist must have his say in court even if it kills him," Darrow said.

Benjamin Gitlow, convicted of "criminal anarchy." (Bettmann/ Corbis)

"I Ask No Clemency"

A special jury had been selected from New York's wealthy and conservative "Silk Stocking District." Gitlow insisted that Darrow defend the right of revolution.

"For a man to be afraid of revolution in America, would be to be ashamed of his own mother," the lawyer told the jury, reminding it of the American Revolution.

Then Gitlow rose to make his own statement. He told the jury he agreed with the principles expressed in the manifesto. "No jails will change my opinion in this respect. I ask no clemency. I realize that as an individual I have a perfect right to my opinions, that I would be false to myself if I tried to evade that which I supported. . . . All I ask of you gentlemen of the jury is to consider the language of the manifesto, to realize that the manifesto stands for a new order in society, a new form of government, that the Communists believe in a new form of society and necessarily in a new form of government and will bend all their efforts in that direction."

His stalwart defense of Communism earned Gitlow an honorary membership in the Moscow Soviet. It also got him a guilty verdict and a sentence of five to ten years in prison.

Gitlow went to Sing Sing, but in April 1922, he was released on bail pending a decision on his appeal to the state court of appeals. The basis of his appeal was that the conviction violated the due process clause of the Fourteenth Amendment.

The Fourteenth Amendment

The Fourteenth Amendment, passed after the Civil War, was intended to prevent the former Confederate states from depriving freed slaves of their rights by making the Bill of Rights apply to states as well as the federal government. In 1833, in *Baron v. Baltimore,* the Supreme Court had ruled that the Bill of Rights did not apply to the states. Without the amendment, everyone knew there would be no freedom for ex-slaves. But in 1873, seven years after the passage of the amendment, the Supreme Court effectively nullified it. In the *Slaughterhouse Cases,* it held that there were two forms of citizenship—U.S. citizenship and state citizenship. The amendment guaranteed the rights of all persons as U.S. citizens, but had nothing to do with what rights they enjoyed as state citizens.

In 1897, in *Allgeyer v. Louisiana,* the Court ruled that the Fourteenth Amendment protected "liberty of contract" by corporations from interference by state governments. It did not hold, however, that the amendment prevented states from interfering with the personal liberties, like freedom of speech, guaranteed by the Bill of Rights.

On July 12, 1922, the appellate division of the court of appeals upheld Gitlow's conviction. He went back to Sing Sing, where the inmates nicknamed him Mr. In And Out. In December, Mr. In And Out was out again, released on bail when the U.S. Supreme Court agreed to hear his appeal. The case was argued before the Court twice in 1923.

Unnoticed Landmark

On June 8, 1925, the Supreme Court issued its decision. Gitlow's conviction was affirmed by a 7–2 vote. The two dissenters, Louis Brandeis and Oliver Wendell Holmes, had long been called "the dangerous twosome" by conservatives.

"*Gitlow v. New York* is one of the landmark cases in constitutional law," says Leo Pfeffer, a lawyer generally regarded as one of the nation's leading authorities on the Bill of Rights. "Its importance has been obscured by the fact that the actual holding was to affirm the conviction of a radical who had exercised freedom of speech; but this was merely incidental."

"For the first time," Pfeffer wrote in *This Honorable Court,* "the Court proceeded on the assumption that liberty in the due process clause included liberty of expression."

After reviewing Gitlow's case, Justice Edward T. Sanford, writing the majority decision, wrote, "For present purposes we may and do assume that freedom of speech and of the press—which are protected by the First Amendment from abridgement by Congress—are among the fundamental personal rights and 'liberties' protected by the due process clause of the Fourteenth Amendment from impairment by the States.''

So, offhandedly, without fanfare, without notice in the press, the Court made one of the great advances in American civil liberties. Gitlow's conviction was upheld, but it was followed by a series of other cases involving people convicted of essentially the same crime that were reversed.

For the moment, Mr. In And Out had to go back in. But on December 11, 1925, New York governor Alfred E. Smith pardoned the stubborn radical.

Gitlow v. Stalin

Gitlow continued agitating, but in 1929, when in Moscow as a delegate to the Comintern, he defied Josef Stalin to his face. He told Stalin that plans developed in Moscow would not work in America. He was expelled from the Comintern and then from the U.S. Communist Party. For a while, he worked with some dissident Communist groups, but by the late thirties, he had become bitterly anti-Communist. He testified before many congressional committees and wrote and lectured extensively against Communism. He died in 1965.

For all his activity, though, his greatest legacy comes from the case he fought all the way up to the Supreme Court—and lost at every stage.

—*William Weir*

Suggestions for Further Reading

Gitlow, Benjamin. *I Confess: The Truth About American Communism.* New York: E. P. Dutton, 1940.

Irons, Peter. *A People's History of the Supreme Court.* New York: Viking, 1999.

Murray, Robert K. *Red Scare: A Study in National Hysteria, 1919-1920.* New York: McGraw-Hill, 1955.

Pfeffer, Leo. *This Honorable Court: A Complete Account of a Unique American Institution—The Supreme Court.* Boston: Beacon Press, 1965.

John S. Williams and Clyde Manning Trials: 1921

Defendants: John S. Williams and Clyde Manning **Crime Charged:** Murder **Defense Attorneys:** Williams: Greene F. Johnson, W. H. Key, and C. C. King; Manning: E. Marvin Underwood, A. D. Meadows **Prosecuting Attorneys:** A. M. Brand, William M. Howard, Graham Wright **Judge:** John B. Hutcheson **Place:** Covington, Georgia **Dates of Trials:** April 5–9, 1921 (Williams); May 30–1, 1921 (Manning) **Verdicts:** Williams: guilty; Manning: guilty **Sentences:** Williams: life imprisonment; Manning: life imprisonment

SIGNIFICANCE

Technically, the Emancipation Proclamation and the Thirteenth Amendment to the Constitution freed over four million black slaves. In a sense, slavery in the United States did not end in 1865, but merely took other forms. For example, there was the system of "peonage" whereby blacks were held in servitude until they worked off their debts. This use of "peons" thrived throughout the South for over five decades and it did not start to decline until the brutal murder of 11 men in 1921.

After the Civil War, southern states adopted a series of laws known as the "Black Codes." These statutes required the former slaves to have jobs; unemployment meant arrest and imprisonment for vagrancy or loitering. A local farmer, who would be entitled to his labor until the sum was worked off, paid the black's fine after he as jailed. The peons lived on their employer's farm and worked long hours at hard labor while receiving extremely low or nonexistent wages. Few ever earned enough to pay off what they owed; for most, peonage equaled a lifetime of hardship and toil. Harsh punishment, including severe beatings, whippings, and even death, were common if the workers did not perform up to their employers' expectations or if they committed some real or imagined act of disobedience. Often, the workers were so scared of the farmers that they assisted in, or actually carried out, the tortures and murders lest the same fate befall them. If a black ran away, he was hunted down and returned to whatever punishment awaited him.

Peonage Outlawed, But Flourishes for 50 Years

In 1867, Congress outlawed peonage in an effort to curb the problem; violators were subject to a $10,000 fine and 10 years imprisonment. Some states also prohibited the practice. However, the police and courts usually turned a blind eye to what was going on. Many local law enforcement officials even arrested blacks on false charges to maintain a supply of manpower for the local farmers and actively helped to keep the workers on the farm.

One of those who took advantage of the situation was John S. Williams. In 1921, the 54-year-old father of 12 was the owner of a 2,000-acre plantation in Jasper County, Georgia, approximately 40 miles southeast of Atlanta. With three of his adult sons, he ran his spread by using peons.

Williams managed his farm like a brutal dictator. One man made only 35 cents during an entire year and there is no record of any peon paying off his debt to Williams. At night, the hands were crowded into bunkhouses whose windows were nailed shut, shutters boarded from the outside, and doors locked and secured with a chain. But worst of all was the physical treatment the men received.

Beatings and whippings were handed out daily for such offenses as picking less cotton than the other field hands and being unable to do physical tasks because of on-the-job injuries. On Sundays, the Williams family took their tracking dogs out for practice by forcing a black to run through the woods for the hounds to chase. And there was murder. Before 1921, there were at least four, and possibly as many as 10, killings for such offenses as trying to escape from the plantation and not rolling wire up a hill the way the family liked.

For years, stories circulated in Jasper County about conditions at the Williams place, but nothing was done to discourage or stop John or his sons. The Williams family was rich, powerful, respected, and intimidating. They were not alone in using peons and no one wanted to be seen as being on the side of the blacks. Besides, the occasional killing of a peon was considered nothing more by the southern white society than as a minor business expense (you could always get another peon cheap) and no white southerner had been convicted of murdering a black for over 40 years. But all of that changed in early 1921.

Murdering the "Evidence" of Peonage

In November 1920, a peon named Gus Chapman successfully escaped from the Williams' farm and, a few weeks later, made his way to the Atlanta offices of the Bureau of Investigation (as the FBI was then called). Peonage was not high on the Bureau's list of priorities, but at least it might take the complaints seriously and investigate. While looking into other federal matters in the area, two federal agents visited the Williams plantation on February 18, 1921. They interviewed the black farmhands and Williams. Most of the blacks said nothing, but the agents caught one, Clyde Manning, in a lie about an earlier escape attempt by Chapman. Still, they left only vaguely suspicious and not very eager to pursue the matter further. Williams, however, heard rumors that some local farmers might soon be charged with peonage and he concluded that the agents' visit meant that he was a target. Therefore, Williams decided to get rid of the evidence.

The 26-year-old Manning was the Williams's farm boss. Uneducated and illiterate, he came to the Williams farm with his family at about age 13 or 14 when his father was ambushed and murdered by unknown assailants. Also working and living on the Williams' farm were Manning's mother, siblings, wife, and children and Manning knew that to protest even the smallest of Williams's orders would put his family's lives at stake. Furthermore, he had no idea of where he could escape to or where to turn for help; Manning knew the local police would be of no assistance, and he had virtually no knowledge of anything beyond Jasper County. Indeed, when two peons escaped the Williams place and had gone beyond Jasper County before they were captured and returned, Manning referred to them as having "been out of the United States."

On the morning of February 19, Williams walked out to Manning's shanty and told him of his plans to kill the peons who worked on the farm: "Clyde, it won't do for those boys to get up yonder and swear against us. They will ruin us. You have got to get rid of all the stockade niggers."

After a long pause, Manning responded: "Mr. Johnny, you telling me you want me to do away with them boys?"

"Yes, we'll have to do away with them."

After another long pause, Manning quietly said: "I don't want to do it. I hate to do it."

"Well, by God, if you don't want to do it, that's all right. But it's your neck or theirs. If you think more of their necks than you do of your own neck, it's your neck then."

Over the next week, nine of the Williams farmhands were killed. Sometimes, Manning committed the murders; other times, he was assisted by Charlie Chisolm, another of the Williams peons, or the crime was done by Chisolm in Manning's presence. Every time, Williams was there, selecting the victims and telling Manning and Chisolm what to do. Some of the men were killed with axes or pickaxes; others were thrown off bridges into the Yellow River while chained and weighted down with rocks. The murders then stopped, but a week later, Williams decided that Chisolm had to go and he and Manning threw him over a bridge as well. A few days later, Williams shot an eleventh man with a shotgun and had Manning help him dispose of the body.

Manning himself might have become the twelfth victim if the bodies of three men who were tossed into the Yellow River had not been found on March 16. At about the same time, Eberhardt Crawford, one of Williams's black neighbors, went to the Bureau of Investigation's Atlanta office and told of how Williams recently accused him of talking to the authorities and later returned with a carload of white men and shot up Crawford's house.

The bureau suspected that the killings were connected with its earlier investigation of Williams, but murder is a local matter. Federal agents took

Crawford with them and went to Georgia's Governor Hugh Dorsey. (Dorsey was then actively denouncing lynching and other forms of persecution against the blacks and was considered to have a possibly sympathetic ear.) The governor listened. He then persuaded the judge and prosecuting attorney in Newton County (on whose side of the Yellow River the bodies were found) to issue warrants for the arrest of a number of witnesses and suspects, including Williams and Manning. At first, Manning said nothing, but after hours of constant questioning he began to talk.

Southern Peonage Draws National Attention

Williams and Manning were both indicted in Newton County for three counts of murder. They were to be tried separately. They would also go to trial for one murder at a time; that way, if found innocent on one charge, they could then be tried on another.

Williams went to trial first. In the meantime, the "death farm" killings drew national attention. The extent of Williams's crimes shocked even southern society and forced southerners to openly admit that peonage existed. Editorials tried to set Georgia apart from the rest of the former Confederacy, and southern political and religious leaders declared that the trials should mark the beginning of an improvement of how blacks were treated.

Described by the *Atlanta Constitution* as "Georgia's greatest murder trial," Williams's trial began on April 5, 1921. Williams's attorneys protested that they didn't have enough time to prepare an adequate defense, but their objections were overruled. Because of the unusual circumstances of the case, the state provided two lawyers to assist the local prosecutor. Manning was the main witness against Williams. In his own defense, Williams claimed that he knew nothing about the killings and that Manning was a dangerous character. The defense also tried to imply that the charges were a conspiracy by Governor Dorsey, the Bureau of Investigation, and wealthy urban liberals from Atlanta to stir up the blacks in Jasper County.

Williams wasn't too concerned about his fate. After all, the 12 members of his jury were all white, and Williams did not believe that they would convict a white man of anything on the word of a black. Therefore, his "temporary" confinement and trial were a small price to pay for disposing of the evidence that would have led to a peonage conviction. However, after several hours of deliberation, the jury returned with a verdict of "guilty." Indeed, it later became known that the jurors were quick to agree on Williams's guilt and that they spent most of their time trying to decide whether he should hang. On the jury's recommendation, Williams was sent to prison for life.

Manning's trial began on May 30. The proceeding was unusual for a southern trial of a black in the 1920s in that a serious attempt was made by Manning's lawyers to prove he was innocent. The state, which relied upon Manning's testimony in Williams' trial, now called him a "mean Negro" who committed the murders to avoid prosecution for peonage. The defense countered that Manning feared for his and his family's lives and was forced to commit the murders by Williams. As in the Williams trial, the jury was all white. The entire proceeding lasted only two days, and it took the jury a mere 40 minutes to find Manning guilty. Still, in light of the attitudes at the time in the South, the defense was successful because this jury, too, recommended life imprisonment instead of death.

Manning died in prison of tuberculosis in 1927. Williams was killed four years later in an accident at the state penitentiary in Milledgeville, Georgia. During the 1920s, encouraged by Williams' conviction, a number of state and federal prosecutors successfully tried peonage cases in Georgia and the rest of the South.

—*Mark Thorburn*

Suggestions for Further Reading

Daniel, Pete. *The Shadow of Slavery: Peonage in the South, 1901–1969.* Urbana, Ill.: University of Illinois Press, 1972.

Freeman, Gregory. A. *Lay This Body Down: The 1921 Murders of Eleven Plantation Slaves.* Chicago: Chicago Review Press and Lawrence Hill Books, 1999.

Grant, Donald L. *The Way It Was in the South: The Black Experience in Georgia.* Secaucus, N.J.: Carol Publishing Group, 1993.

Sacco–Vanzetti Trial: 1921

Defendants: Nicola Sacco and Bartolomeo Vanzetti
Crime Charged: Murder **Chief Defense Lawyers:** William J. Callahan, Herbert B. Ehrmann, James M. Graham, Arthur Dehon Hill, Jeremiah J. McAnarney, Thomas F. McAnarney, Fred H. Moore, Michael Angelo Musmanno, William G. Thompson, and John P. Vahey
Chief Prosecutors: Frederick Gunn Katzmann, Donald P. Ramsey, and Harold P. Williams **Judge:** Webster Thayer **Place:** Dedham, Massachusetts
Dates of Trial: May 31–July 14, 1921 **Verdict:** Guilty **Sentences:** Death

SIGNIFICANCE

The Sacco–Vanzetti case began as a simple trial for murder. It ended as an international cause in which the world believed that Massachusetts had executed two innocent men because they held radical views. A study of the trial and its aftermath provides a superb lesson in how myths are made.

On the afternoon of April 15, 1920, as a shoe manufacturer's paymaster, Frederick Parmenter, and his guard, Alessandro Berardelli, carried the $15,777 cash payroll in South Braintree, Massachusetts, they were killed by two men armed with pistols. Seizing the money, the men jumped into a car containing several other men and sped away. Eyewitnesses thought the murderers looked like Italians.

At the time, police were investigating an attempted holdup on the preceding Christmas Eve by a gang of Italians with a car in nearby Bridgewater. Police Chief Michael E. Stewart suspected one Mike Boda, whose car was now awaiting repairs in Simon Johnson's garage. Stewart told Johnson to call the police when anyone came to get Boda's car.

A Car to Move Red Literature

Stewart also was busy rounding up alien communists following raids by the U.S. Departments of Labor and Justice. Many were being deported. In May, a radical held on the 14th floor of the New York City offices of the Department of Justice was found dead on the sidewalk below. His friends, including Mike

Boda, decided they had better hide a large quantity of Red literature. To move it, they needed Boda's car.

Boda and three others appeared at Johnson's garage. Mrs. Johnson called the police. Johnson refused to hand over the car because it had no up-to-date license plates. Boda and one man departed on a motorcycle. The other two boarded a street car. Arrested aboard the car minutes later were Nicola Sacco and Bartolomeo Vanzetti. Sacco carried a .32-caliber pistol loaded with nine bullets, and 23 additional bullets in his pocket. Vanzetti had a fully loaded .38-caliber revolver and four 12-gauge shotgun shells. Also found on Sacco was a notice, in Italian, of a forthcoming meeting at which Vanzetti was to speak on "the struggle for existence." The two men were active anarchists.

Bartolomeo Vanzetti and Nicola Sacco. (Courtesy, Library of Congress)

Grilled by District Attorney Frederick Gunn Katzmann, Sacco said he had bought the gun two years earlier for $16 or $17 and had bought a new box of cartridges. Vanzetti said his gun cost $18 or $19 four or five years earlier. Neither gun was licensed.

Vanzetti's shotgun shells put him under suspicion for the failed holdup on Christmas Eve, when a 12-gauge shotgun was fired. His alibi was that, as a fish peddler, he spent a busy Christmas Eve selling eels for traditional Italian dinners that night. At his trial, several witnesses identified him as the man with the shotgun. He did not take the stand to refute them and was convicted and sentenced to 12 to 15 years. Sacco, meantime, had a solid alibi: He had been on the job in a shoe factory when the attempted robbery occurred. But he was held for trial in the South Braintree murders, for on April 15 he had taken the day off.

Defense Committee Organized

Anarchist friends organized the Sacco–Vanzetti Defense Committee. For three months, it collected money. Then the committee hired Fred H. Moore, a long-haired radical labor lawyer from California. Moore, experienced in handling underdog cases for Elizabeth Gurley Flynn, founder of the Workers' Defense Union, and for the International Workers of the World (The "I.W.W."), saw the Sacco–Vanzetti case as a cause. "In saving them," he said, "we strengthen our muscles, develop our forces preparatory to the day when we save ourselves."

Moore spent a busy year writing, traveling, and organizing volunteers. The United Mine Workers, the Amalgamated Clothing Workers, the American Federation of Teamsters, and the American Civil Liberties Union were among the many organizations that responded. Pamphlets were printed in batches of 50,000. Publicity releases flooded the mail weekly to 500 newspapers. The murder charge was depicted as "a mere device to get them [Sacco and Vanzetti] out of the way."

Outdated Bullets and a Cap

Opening May 31, 1921, the trial revealed that Sacco had lied about his gun. It was several years old, and his box of "new" cartridges contained a mixture of old bullets that were all obsolete. The bullet that killed Berardelli was so outdated that the state's expert witness could locate none like it with which to test Sacco's gun—except the equally obsolete bullets from Sacco's pocket.

Vanzetti, too, had lied. Although he had said he paid $18 or $19 for it, the jury learned that his was a $5 gun, that Vanzetti had said he bought a new box of cartridges and threw it away when six remained and he put them in the revolver, but that it held only five and those in the gun were not all the same make. And it learned that Vanzetti's nickel-plated pistol was identical to that of the murdered guard, whose gun could not be found after the crime.

Then there was the cap found beside the dead guard. It was not his. Sacco's employer testified that it looked like a cap that Sacco regularly wore. When the prosecutor asked Sacco to put the cap on, the defendant, pulling it down over his ears in trying to prove it was too big, threw the courtroom into giggling hysterics—but the state also put into evidence a cap of exactly the same size, found in Sacco's home. "Some one of you who wears a seven and one-eighth," said Katzmann to the jury, "try them both on. If they are not identically the same size, then so find, so find, gentlemen."

Trial for Murder, Nothing Else

Before the trial opened, Judge Webster Thayer had told counsel on both sides that he saw no reason to bring up the issue of radicalism. It was not mentioned during the prosecution's entire presentation. But on the 29th day, Vanzetti himself, under direct examination by his attorney Jeremiah J. McAnarney, was explaining why the four men sought Boda's car: "We were going to take the automobile for to carry books and newspapers," he said. Why hadn't he told the police that when he was arrested? "Because there was the deportation and the reaction was more vivid than now and more mad than now." In a word, his defense was that he lied out of fear of deportation as a radical.

Under Massachusetts law, since the defense had brought it up, the door was now open for prosecutor Katzmann to cross-examine Vanzetti about all his radical activities. But the jury heard no such questions. "Neither is Radicalism being tried here," the prosecutor told them. "This is a charge of murder and it is nothing else."

Next, Sacco explained that he, too, lied when he was arrested because he feared deportation on a radical charge. And he explained another lie. Upon arrest, he had said that he was at work all day April 15. But now his boss testified that Sacco had taken that day off to see the Italian consul in Boston about a passport for a trip to Italy. The consular clerk testified that Sacco was in his office at about 2:00 P.M. April 15, but the alibi was weak: Sacco had been turned down immediately because the passport photo he offered was too large. While the jury was being told that Sacco spent an entire day in Boston (several witnesses for the defense testified to having seen him there in the morning, at lunch, and in the afternoon), his business at the consulate had consumed only 10 minutes. Then Sacco noticed a spectator in the courtroom whom he had seen on the late afternoon train home. Sworn as a witness, the man could not remember seeing Sacco but was confident he had been on the train Sacco described.

As with Vanzetti, prosecutor Katzmann refrained from any line of questioning that might have led the jury to consider Sacco a dangerous radical.

Bullets Convince Jury

At three o'clock, July 14, the jury retired. It immediately voted 10–2 for conviction. "Then," said one juror afterward:

> [W]e started discussing things, reviewed the very important evidence about the bullets, and everybody had a chance to speak his piece. There was never any argument, though. We just were convinced Sacco and Vanzetti had done what the prosecution had charged them with.

Asked later what evidence impressed him most, another juror said:

> The bullets, of course. That testimony and evidence on it sticks in your mind. You can't depend on the witnesses. But the bullets, there was no getting around that evidence.

The guilty verdict brought violent reactions around the world. American consulates and embassies in Europe and South America were flooded with letters of protest. The *Communist International* urged all communists, socialists, anarchists, and trade unionists to join in rescuing Sacco and Vanzetti. Demonstrations were mounted in France, Italy, Switzerland, Belgium, Spain, Portugal, and Scandinavia. It took 10,000 police and 18,000 troops to hold back the crowd besieging the American embassy in Paris. Bombs exploded in that embassy and around the world. One destroyed the home of one of the jurors. Judge Thayer's house was put under guard.

Vehement Appeals Follow

Over the next six years, the furor raged. Motion after motion for a new trial was denied. So-called experts examined the pistols, took them apart, wrongly reassembled them. Elizabeth Gurley Flynn raised $25,000 in two days to pay the advance legal fee of Harvard Law School lecturer and Massachusetts insider William G. Thompson, who replaced Moore, the radical outsider. Imprisoned criminals volunteered confessions.

By 1926, with "Sacco–Vanzetti" a worldwide battle cry, the Massachusetts Supreme Judicial Court, the state's highest, rejected an appeal. The International Labor Defense (ILD) (later to defend the Scottsboro Boys, [See separate entry]), set up by the communists, received only some $6,000 of millions raised in the names of Sacco and Vanzetti. Harvard Law professor Felix Frankfurter (later to serve on the U.S. Supreme Court), in an *Atlantic Monthly* article, attacked the jury, witnesses, verdict, and judiciary. The state's supreme court, having already rejected Thompson's appeal, now upheld the judge: He had committed, it declared, no errors of law or abuses of discretion.

The execution of two men who held radical views provoked outrage throughout the world. (Courtesy, Library of Congress)

Lowell Committee Reviews Case

In June 1927, on Thompson's urging, Massachusetts Governor Alvan T. Fuller, who was considering an appeal for clemency, appointed an Advisory Committee headed by Harvard president Abbott Lawrence Lowell to review the entire case. After two months, and after himself interviewing 102 witnesses in addition to those from the trial, he agreed with the Lowell Committee's conclusion: Sacco and Vanzetti had a fair trial and were guilty.

Worldwide protests grew more violent. A London demonstration injured 40 people. Paris, Berlin, Warsaw, Buenos Aires, and countless other cities saw riots. Now picketers before the State House in Boston, including novelists John Dos Passos and Katherine Anne Porter, humorist Dorothy Parker, and poet Edna St. Vincent Millay, were arrested. All Boston public buildings were garrisoned by the police, who for the first time in memory permitted no meetings on Boston Common. Columnist Heywood Broun found his column suspended by the New York *World* for his violent comments on Lowell.

By now, Judge Thayer had denied a half-dozen motions for a new trial, the state superior court had denied another, and the state supreme judicial court had turned down four appeals. Several petitions for a writ of *habeas corpus*, for extensions of time, and for stay of execution were denied by the Circuit Court of Appeals for the First Circuit of the United States and by U.S. Supreme Court justices Oliver Wendell Holmes and Harlan F. Stone.

Sacco and Vanzetti were executed August 23, 1927. In 1977, their names were "cleared" when Massachusetts Governor Michael S. Dukakis signed a special proclamation.

—Bernard Ryan, Jr.

Suggestions for Further Reading

Ehrmann, Herbert B. *The Case That Will Not Die.* Boston: Little, Brown & Co., 1969.

Frankfurter, Felix. *The Case of Sacco and Vanzetti.* Boston: Little, Brown & Co., 1927.

Montgomery, Robert H. *Sacco–Vanzetti: The Murder and the Myth.* New York: Devin-Adair, 1960.

Porter, Katherine Anne. *The Never-Ending Wrong.* Boston: Little, Brown & Co., 1977.

Russell, Francis. *Sacco & Vanzetti: The Case Resolved.* New York: Harper & Row, 1986.

Sifakis, Carl. *The Encyclopedia of American Crime.* New York: Facts On File, 1972.

Sinclair, Upton. *Boston: A Documentary Novel.* Cambridge, Mass.: Robert Bentley, 1978.

Tragedy in Dedham. New York: McGraw-Hill, 1962.

"Why I Changed My Mind about the Sacco–Vanzetti Case," *American Heritage* (June-July 1986): 106.

"Black Sox" Trial: 1921

Defendants: Edward Victor "Eddie" Cicotte, Oscar Emil "Happy" Felsch, Arnold "Chick" Gandil, Joseph Jefferson Wofford, "Shoeless Joe" Jackson, Frederick William "Fred" McMullin, Charles August "Swede" Risberg, George Daniel "Buck" Weaver, Claude Preston "Lefty" Williams, David Zelser, and Carl Zork **Crimes Charged:** Statutory conspiracy and common-law conspiracy to fix the outcome of the 1919 World Series
Chief Defense Lawyers: Michael Ahern, Henry A. Berger, A. Morgan Frumberg, Max Lusker, Thomas D. Nash, Thomas J. O'Brien, and Benedictine J. Short **Chief Prosecutors:** George E. Gorman, Edward Prindeville, and John F. Tyrrell **Judge:** Hugo N. Friend **Place:** Chicago, Illinois
Dates of Trial: July 18–August 3, 1921 **Verdict:** Not guilty

SIGNIFICANCE

The first American trial involving national sports figures—heroes to many after the horrors of WWI—ended an ineffective three-person National Baseball Commission. It also saw the arrival of Kenesaw Mountain Landis to the new office of Baseball Commissioner. The day after the acquittal verdict, Landis ruled that the eight players who had been tried were banned from playing professional baseball for life.

In 1918, the baseball season ended on Labor Day to show baseball's support of the nation's World War effort. The next year, apparently to make up for lost time, the World Series was increased from the best of seven to the best of nine games. The National League's Cincinnati Reds went to bat against the American League's Chicago White Sox that September.

Cicotte Hits First Batter

In the first inning of game one, White Sox pitcher Eddie Cicotte faced leadoff batter Maurice Rath. Famed for his pinpoint control, Cicotte had won 29 games with a 1.82 ERA (earned run average) in the regular season. Only Walter Johnson was considered a better pitcher. Cicotte hit Rath smack between the shoulder blades, and by the end of the fourth inning he had given up seven hits and six runs. The Reds won, 9 to 1.

In game two, Chicago's "Lefty" Williams, who had a 23-11 record in a league-leading 40 starts, uncharacteristically walked six and struck out only one. The Sox lost, 4 to 2.

Dickie Kerr won game three for Chicago with a three-hit shutout. Cicotte lost game four in another three-hit shutout, and the Reds took game five with the series' third successive three-hit shutout. Game six saw Williams give up three hits and a walk in a four-run sixth inning that also brought a remarkably unusual throwing error by center fielder "Happy" Felsch. The Reds won again, 5 to 0.

Kerr and Cicotte won games six and seven for the Sox. But Williams, pitching game eight, was pulled in the first inning after yielding two singles and two doubles with only one out. "Shoeless Joe" Jackson—who, with a lifetime average of .356 was considered a hitter second only to Ty Cobb—homered and doubled to no avail. The Reds won, 10 to 5, to take the series, 5 to 3.

Rumors began to spread about the reasons for Chicago's loss. Sportswriters asked how come Cicotte, an ace at dusting batters, hit leadoff man Rath and blew that opening game? How could Williams, a 23-game winner, lose all 3 of his series' games? Could it be true that White Sox owner Charlie Comiskey paid his players so little they would stoop to accepting bribes? Comiskey was a known tightwad who charged his players 25 cents for cleaning their uniforms. Hence, they were called the "Black Sox" because, refusing to pay, they played in dirty outfits.

"Say It Ain't So, Joe"

In September 1920, a grand jury began investigating allegations by a professional boxer, William Maharg, that he and former White Sox pitcher Bill Burns had been go-betweens for White Sox players who fixed games for gamblers. Summoned before the grand jury, Cicotte, Felsch, Jackson, and Williams admitted taking bribes for throwing the World Series. Comiskey suspended seven players (in addition to "Chick" Gandil, who was alleged to have made the deal with the gamblers and who was already suspended in a salary dispute).

To fans, the heartbreaker was the accusation against Jackson, who not only batted .351 in the regular 1919 season but, in the World Series loss, hit for .375 and achieved a perfect 1.000 fielding average. He had been endeared to fans as "Shoeless Joe" since 1908 when, playing for Greenville, South Carolina, he played one game in his stocking feet when a new pair of spikes gave him blisters. After the confessions, writer Charley Owens of the *Chicago Daily News* penned a lump-in-the-throat tribute headlined, "Say it ain't so, Joe." The phrase became legend when it was erroneously attributed to a child outside the trial's courthouse.

The suspended players at this point went back on their confessions and now demanded to have their day in court. New indictments were brought, and extradition proceedings failed to round up several named "fixers," including former featherweight boxing champion Abe Attell, former White Sox player Hal Chase, White Sox 1919 utility man "Fred" McMullen, and gamblers Rachel Brown and John J. "Sport" Sullivan.

As the trial opened on July 18, 1921, with Judge Hugo N. Friend presiding, Sox pitcher Bill Burns, who had turned state's evidence, testified that the indicted players had agreed to make the series "a made-to-order one" for famed big-time gambler Arnold Rothstein of New York (who wasn't indicted), Attell, Maharg, and indicted gamblers David Zelser and Carl Zork. Burns quoted Cicotte as saying, "I will throw the first game if I have to throw the ball clear out of the Cincinnati park."

Chicago White Sox baseball team, among them are players involved in the Black Sox Scandal of 1919. (Courtesy, National Baseball Library & Archive)

Burns said he met with the players and told them the gamblers would pay $20,000 as they lost each of five games. He also said Jackson was not present when he had talked with the players.

A Double, Double Cross

After the White Sox lost the first game, said Burns, Attell failed to provide the first $20,000. Still unpaid after the second game and suspecting a double cross, the players accepted a sop of $10,000 just before the third game began, but played that one to win—and did. Thus the gamblers, betting heavily on Cincinnati, lost all they had won on the first two games.

July 22 brought the news to the courtroom that immunity waivers signed by Cicotte, Jackson, and Weaver—proving that rewards had not been promised to the defendants for their confessions—had disappeared. Gone also were the confessions themselves and other documentary evidence supporting the indictments. (American League president Ban Johnson publicly charged Arnold Rothstein with paying $10,000 for the confessions and, not finding his name mentioned, giving them to a New York newspaper editor who then offered them for sale.)

Judge Charles A. McDonald, who had directed the grand jury inquiry, testified that Cicotte had told him that after throwing the first game he had found $10,000 under his hotel pillow. Then, said the judge, Cicotte's conscience began to bother him and he decided not to throw another game—but he did not return the money.

As the prosecution and the defense rested, Judge Friend told the jury the state had to prove that it was the intent of the ballplayers and gamblers not merely to throw the games but to defraud the public and others as well. After deliberating for two hours and 47 minutes, the jury took only one ballot to vote not guilty. With hats sailing into the air, the several hundred people jamming the courtroom shouted "Hooray for the clean Sox!" Bailiffs pounded for order and then, seeing the judge's smile, joined in the whistling and cheering.

Kenesaw Mountain Landis, recently appointed to the new office of Baseball Commissioner to clean up the game in the wake of the scandal, was not amused. He imposed a lifetime ban from professional baseball on the eight indicted, and acquitted, players. "Regardless of the verdict of juries," he proclaimed, "no player that throws a ball game, no player that undertakes or promises to throw a ball game, no player that sits in a conference with a bunch of crooked players and gamblers where the ways and means of throwing games are planned and discussed and does not promptly tell his club about it, will ever play professional baseball. . . . Baseball is entirely competent to protect itself against crooks, both inside and outside the game."

—Bernard Ryan, Jr.

Suggestions for Further Reading

Asinoff, Eliot. *Eight Men Out: The Black Sox and the 1919 World Series.* New York: Henry Holt, 1963.

Burns, Ken, and Geoffrey C. Ward. *Baseball.* New York: Knopf, 1994.

Gropman, Donald. *Say It Ain't So, Joe!—The True Story of Shoeless Joe Jackson.* Boston: Little, Brown, 1979.

Luhrs, Victor. *The Great Baseball Mystery—The 1919 World Series.* South Brunswick, N.J.: A.S. Barnes, 1966.

Thompson, Joe. *Growing Up with "Shoeless Joe."* Laurel Fork, Va.: JTI Publishing, 1997.

"Fatty" Arbuckle Trials: 1921–22

Defendant: Roscoe Conkling "Fatty" Arbuckle
Crime Charged: Manslaughter **Chief Defense Lawyer:** Gavin McNab
Chief Prosecutor: Matthew Brady **Judge:** Harold Louderback **Place:** San Francisco, California **Dates of Trials:** November 14–December 4, 1921; January 11–February 3, 1922; March 13–April 12, 1922 **Verdicts:** First and second trials: Jury deadlocked; Third trial: Not guilty

SIGNIFICANCE

The trials of "Fatty" Arbuckle, Hollywood's most popular and highest-paid comedian, for manslaughter not only destroyed the defendant's career, they also focused America's attention on the level of morality in the movie-making kingdom. Coming just when nationwide efforts were under way to censor the film industry, the trial brought the immediate establishment of "the Hays office" and, in 1930, the Motion Picture Production Code—the industry's self-regulatory system.

In five years, "Fatty" Arbuckle had climbed from the vaudeville stage to the $1,000-a-day pinnacle of stardom in silent films. America adored his uproarious antics with the Keystone Kops, his deadly aim with a custard pie, his light-footed, talented dancing. He was the first movie comedian to sign a $3-million contract.

When America learned that Arbuckle had thrown a wild party in a San Francisco hotel at which he—according to a complaint sworn out by one Maude Delmont—had raped and murdered actress Virginia Rappe, it was ready for a lurid trial. The country got not one but three trials, each loaded with juicy details of the alleged sexual rampage committed by the 266-pound Arbuckle. For eight months, the Hearst newspapers fed the country a diet of three-inch headlines. But, as the jury of the third trial recognized by voting acquittal in only five minutes, the sensationalism of the newspapers and the truth were far apart.

Tabloids Conjure up Lurid Details

The indisputable facts were that 26-year-old film actress Virginia Rappe went to Arbuckle's party on Labor Day with her friend Maude Delmont, drank too much, was violently ill with severe abdominal pains for three days, and died on Friday of peritonitis brought on by a ruptured bladder. On Monday, Delmont swore out her complaint. Arbuckle was charged with murder.

The disputable "facts" or allegations were myriad and sordid. They included the charge that the comic had been alone with the actress in a bedroom for an hour during the party, at which time he raped her. "I'm hurt, I'm dying. He did it, Maudie," Rappe was reported to have yelled when Arbuckle left the room.

The doctor who examined Rappe's body just after she died on Friday issued a public statement:

> The post-mortem examination showed a ruptured bladder, the rupture being due to natural causes. There were no marks of violence on the body. There was absolutely no evidence of a criminal assault, no signs that the girl had been attacked in any way.

District Attorney Matthew Brady ignored that statement on Monday as he watched Delmont swear out her murder complaint. The tabloids that morning had already published Brady's statement that "the evidence in my possession shows conclusively that either a rape or an attempt to rape was perpetrated on Miss Rappe by Roscoe Arbuckle. The evidence discloses beyond question that her bladder was ruptured by the weight of the body of Arbuckle either in a rape assault or an attempt to commit rape." Brady's main source was Maude Delmont.

What Brady did not yet know was that on Wednesday, as Virginia Rappe lay in pain in the Arbuckle hotel suite, Delmont had sent a telegram to each of two friends: "WE HAVE ROSCOE ARBUCKLE IN A HOLE HERE. CHANCE TO MAKE SOME MONEY OUT OF HIM." Her official complaint—with its description of how Arbuckle had dragged Virginia Rappe into his bedroom saying, "I've waited five years to get you;" how Rappe had cried for help from behind the locked door and Delmont had banged on the door; how Arbuckle had at last emerged, perspiring from the struggle and she had rushed in to find Rappe naked and bruised and dying—all had been a fabrication. Delmont, the D.A. learned on Monday afternoon, had been locked in a bathroom with one Lowell Sherman for an hour when Arbuckle went to his bedroom for a few minutes and found Rappe vomiting into the toilet in that room's bathroom.

When Brady learned the truth, his extensive statement was already in newspapers around the world. He decided to proceed with the case. But he knew that if he brought Maude Delmont to the witness stand, his prosecution would fall apart. When it came to the trials, he never called on her.

The grand jury attributed the ruptured bladder to "some force which, from the evidence submitted, we believe was applied by Roscoe Arbuckle." Therefore, it charged the comedian with manslaughter. In the police court's committal proceedings, Arbuckle's lawyer established that Virginia Rappe's manager had been not only her lover but Maude Delmont's as well, and announced that the manager and Delmont had planned to extort money from Arbuckle.

"A General Lowering of the Moral Standards"

Meantime, boards of censors, mayors, and film exhibitor associations in countless cities, as well as the states of Missouri, Pennsylvania, and Kansas, banned all Arbuckle movies. The Anti-Saloon League, the Moral Efficiency League, the Women's Vigilant Committee of San Francisco, and club women everywhere agreed. Pastors in pulpits nationwide echoed the words of the minister in Hollywood's Little Church Around the Corner: "The real essence of this Arbuckle matter is a general lowering of the moral standards in this country."

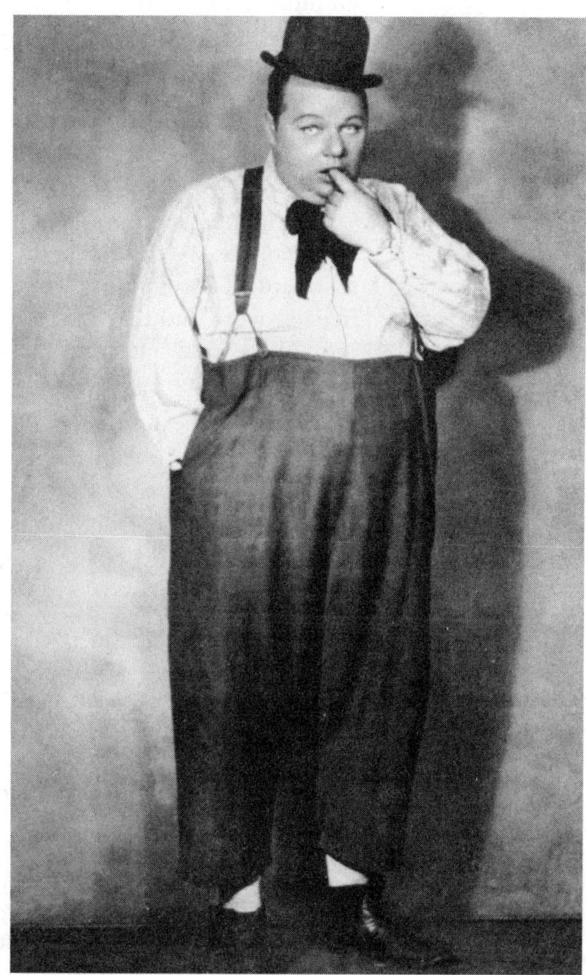

In this atmosphere the police judge weighing committal for trial concluded:

> I do not find any evidence that Mr. Arbuckle either committed or attempted to commit rape. The court has been presented with the merest outline.... The district attorney has presented barely enough facts to justify my holding the defendant on the charge which is here filed against him.
>
> But we are not trying Roscoe Arbuckle alone; we are not trying the screen celebrity who has given joy and pleasure to the entire world; we are actually, gentlemen, in a large sense trying ourselves.
>
> We are trying our present-day morals, our present-day social conditions, our present-day looseness of thought and lack of social balance. The issue here is really and truly larger than the guilt or innocence of this poor, unfortunate man; the issue is universal and grows out of conditions which are a matter of comment and notoriety and apprehension to every true lover and protector of our American institutions.
>
> I have decided to make a holding on the ground of manslaughter.

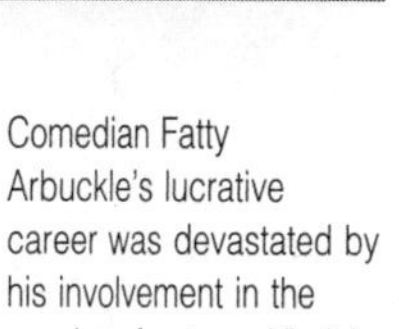

Comedian Fatty Arbuckle's lucrative career was devastated by his involvement in the murder of actress Virginia Rappe. (Archive Photos, Inc.)

The first trial produced 60 witnesses, including 18 doctors. Through defense witnesses, lawyer Gavin McNab revealed Virginia Rappe's moral as well as medical history: As a young teenager, she had had five abortions in three years; at 16, she had borne an illegitimate child; since 1907, she had had a series of bladder inflammations and chronic cystitis; she liked to strip naked when she drank; the doctor who attended her in the several days before she died concluded that she had gonorrhea; when she met Arbuckle for the first time on Monday, she was pregnant and that afternoon had asked him to pay for an abortion; on Wednesday, she had asked her nurse to find an abortionist.

On the stand, "Fatty" Arbuckle was simple, direct, unflustered. He related how he had tried to help the ill actress, spending not more then 10 minutes with her before Maude Delmont dismissed him.

Medical testimony proved that Virginia Rappe's bladder was cystitic—one of the causes of rupture of the bladder.

"Until Hell Freezes Over"

The jury was out for 44 hours before Judge Harold Louderback dismissed it as hopelessly deadlocked. Members later revealed that one juror, Helen Hubbard, had announced at the start that she would vote guilty "until hell freezes over" and that she refused to discuss the evidence, look at the exhibits, or read the trial transcript. All others voted acquittal until the end, when one other joined her.

Hubbard's mother-in-law was the first California Regent of the Daughters of the American Revolution. Her husband, a lawyer, did business with the D.A.'s office. Why defense attorney Gavin McNab let Hubbard, who was clearly biased, get onto the jury remains a mystery.

Four days later, 12 of Hollywood's top leaders, including Samuel Goldwyn, Lewis J. Selznick, and Adolph Zukor, asked William Hays, chairman of the Republican National Committee and President Warren G. Harding's postmaster general, to become the czar of the film industry. His assignment, at $100,000 a year for three years, was "to have the industry accorded the consideration and dignity to which it is justly entitled." The assignment stretched into thirty years, and thus began "the Hays office" and, ultimately, the self-regulation provided by the Motion Picture Production Code.

Arbuckle Tried Again . . . and Yet Again

Trial number two brought even more defense testimony on Virginia Rappe's habit of stripping when she drank. It also discredited some major evidence: the identification of "Fatty" Arbuckle's fingerprints on the hotel bedroom door. But the defense decided not to put Arbuckle through the ordeal of testifying again, and so deprived the second jury of seeing his strongly effective manner on the witness stand. This jury came in deadlocked nine to three for conviction.

The third time around, Gavin McNab put Arbuckle on the stand and left no doubt about his version of the hotel party. He also managed to get in still more detail of Virginia Rappe's lurid past. He reviewed how the district attorney fell for the outlandish charges of Maude Delmont, "the complaining witness who never witnessed."

The jury was out and back in five minutes with its verdict: "We the jury find Roscoe Arbuckle not guilty of manslaughter." The foreman then read a statement that the jurors had spent the five minutes composing:

> Acquittal is not enough for Roscoe Arbuckle. We feel that a great injustice has been done him. We feel also that it was only our plain duty to give him this exoneration, under the evidence, for there was not the slightest proof adduced to connect him in any way with the commission of a crime.
>
> He was manly throughout the case, and told a straightforward story on the witness stand, which we all believed.
>
> The happening at the hotel was an unfortunate affair for which Arbuckle, so the evidence shows, was in no way responsible.
>
> We wish him success.... Roscoe Arbuckle is entirely innocent and free from all blame.

Six days later, Will Hays banned Roscoe Arbuckle from the screen. The decision, however, was not his. The heads of Paramount, Adolph Zukor and Jesse Lasky, knew that Arbuckle had become poison at the box office. If his own company banned him, Hollywood would never forgive them. So they got Hays to ban him. Based on average Arbuckle box-office draw before the trials, Paramount's projected loss was more than $100 million.

Hays lifted the ban eight months later, and "Fatty" Arbuckle started work in January 1923 on a two-reeler, *Handy Andy.* Under constant pressure from reporters, he soon quit and, under an assumed name, turned to directing. Over the next 11 years, he directed, made stage appearances, ran a popular Hollywood nightclub, and paid off debts amounting to nearly $1 million. At last, in 1932, Jack Warner invited Arbuckle to perform in a "talkie." The Hays Office permitted just one, a two-reeler, to see if the public accepted him. It did, and Arbuckle signed for six more. In June 1933, he finished the film, celebrated at dinner, and went to bed. Within minutes, his 46-year-old heart stopped beating.

—Bernard Ryan, Jr.

Suggestions for Further Reading

Olson, James S. *Historical Dictionary of the 1920s.* Westport, Conn.: Greenwood Press, 1988.

Sifakis, Carl. *The Encyclopedia of American Crime.* New York: Facts On File, 1982.

Yallop, David A. *The Day the Laughter Stopped: The True Story of Fatty Arbuckle.* New York: St. Martin's Press, 1976.

Moore et al v. Dempsey Appeal: 1923

Appellants: Frank Moore and 11 others **Defendant:** E.H. Dempsey
Appellants Claim: That a petition for writ of *habeas corpus* was wrongfully dismissed **Chief Defense Lawyers:** Elbert Godwin
Chief Lawyer for Appellant: U.S. Bratton, Scipio A. Jones, and Moorefield Storey **Justices:** Louis D. Brandeis, Pierce Butler, Oliver Wendell Holmes, Joseph McKenna, James C. McReynolds, Edward T. Sanford, George Sutherland, William Howard Taft, and Willis Van Devanter
Place: Washington, D.C. **Date of Decision:** February 19, 1923
Decision: Order dismissing writ reversed; case remanded to district court

SIGNIFICANCE

Twelve African-Americans who had been condemned to death and had nearly been lynched ultimately were freed from imprisonment because the U.S. Supreme Court, led by fabled Justice Oliver Wendell Holmes, found that a threatening mob inflamed by racial prejudice had made the trial, which lasted only 45 minutes, "absolutely void."

On the evening of September 30, 1919, a number of black people gathered in their church in the Hoop Spur neighborhood of the village of Elaine, Arkansas, near the Mississippi River and a few miles south of Helena. Their purpose in meeting was to organize so they could get legal counsel to protect them against extortion that they said was practiced on them by the landowners under the sharecropping system then prevalent in Arkansas. The meeting was attacked and fired upon by a group of white landowners. In the melee that followed, a white man was killed.

The report of the killing stirred greater excitement. Many black men were hunted down. Some were shot. By the morning of October 1, a second white man, named Clinton Lee, had been killed. Twelve black men were arrested for his murder.

A "Committee of Seven" white men was chosen to direct the operation of putting down the "insurrection" and help discover who was guilty in the two killings. Local newspapers published inflammatory articles daily. On October 7, one member of the Committee of Seven made a public statement that the trouble was "a deliberately planned insurrection of the negroes against the whites, directed by an organization known as the 'Progressive Farmers' and 'Household Union of America' established for the purpose of banding negroes together for the killing of white people."

A mob marched to the jail, ready to lynch the 12 prisoners. National Guard troops held them off. Members of the committee promised then that, if the mob would refrain, those found guilty would be executed under the law.

A grand jury was organized. It included a member of the committee and several men who had been in the posse organized to fight the blacks. It heard testimony against the defendants from two black witnesses.

In a trial that lasted 45 minutes on November 3, the courthouse neighborhood was thronged with a threatening crowd. The 12 prisoners were informed that a lawyer had been appointed their counsel. He held no preliminary consultations with them. He challenged no member of the jury, which was all white (blacks were systematically excluded from all juries). He demanded no delay or change of venue. He did not ask for separate trials for each of the accused. Although witnesses for the defense could have been produced, he called none. He did not put the defendants on the witness stand.

The jury took less than five minutes to bring in a verdict of guilty of murder in the first degree. The sentence was death for all.

Studded Straps and Strangling Drugs

The National Association for the Advancement of Colored People (NAACP) entered the case. Its appeal to the Arkansas Supreme Court for a new trial cited the riotous atmosphere in which the case was tried and the appointment of counsel at the start of the trial. It also introduced affidavits of the defendants and of the two black witnesses, who now revealed that they had been rounded up by the Committee of Seven and that, along with some of the prisoners, they had been whipped with straps studded with metal, had had "strangling drugs" forced into their nostrils, and had been made to sit in an electric chair—all until they agreed to testify against the defendants.

The appeal was denied. The NAACP then applied to the Arkansas Chancery Court for a writ of *habeas corpus* on behalf of Frank Moore et al. (one of the defendants by name, and the other 11) against E.H. Dempsey, keeper of the Arkansas State Penitentiary, claiming that the conditions in which the case was tried deprived the defendants of their lives without due process of law.

The chancery court issued the writ and an injunction against the execution of the prisoners, who were scheduled to die two days later. But the Arkansas Supreme Court then held that the chancellor had no jurisdiction. With the executions delayed, however, the NAACP then filed a petition for a writ of *habeas corpus* in the District Court of the United States for the Eastern District of Arkansas. It dismissed the writ.

"The Whole Proceeding is a Mask'

The NAACP went to the Supreme Court of the United States. It cited testimony of two white men who had been members of the sheriff's posse and who swore that Clinton Lee had been killed by members of the posse during the confusion and that the black men had nothing to do with the murder. They also testified that they had personally whipped and drugged the two black witnesses to force from them the testimony they wanted.

One of Oliver Wendell Holmes' most famous comments, "there never was a chance for the petitioners to be acquitted," was made during the *Moore et al v. Dempsey Appeal.* (Courtesy, Library of Congress)

The state of Arkansas argued that the Supreme Court had no jurisdiction to consider the appeal because "mere errors in point of law, however serious, committed by a criminal court in the exercise of its jurisdiction over a case properly subject to its cognizance cannot be reviewed by *habeas corpus.*" Justice Oliver Wendell Holmes, writing the opinion of the court, disagreed. "The ground of the petition for the writ," he said,

> is that the proceedings in the State Court, although a trial in form, were only a form, and that the appellants were hurried to conviction under the pressure of a mob without any regard for their rights and without according to them due process of law.
>
> According to the allegations and affidavits, "there never was a chance for the petitioners to be acquitted"; no juryman could have voted for an acquittal and continued to live in Phillips County and if any prisoner by any chance had been acquitted by a jury he could not have escaped the mob.
>
> If the case is that the whole proceeding is a mask—that counsel, jury and judge were swept to the fatal end by an irresistible wave of public passion, and that the State Courts failed to correct the wrong, neither perfection in the machinery for correction nor the possibility that the trial court and counsel saw no other way of avoiding an immediate outbreak of the mob can prevent this Court from securing to the petitioners their constitutional rights.
>
> It does not seem to us sufficient to allow a Judge of the United States to escape the duty of examining the facts for himself when if true as alleged they make the trial absolutely void. Order reversed. The case to stand for hearing before the District Court.

The Supreme Court's remanding ended the case. The rehearing was never held, for shortly, under order of Governor Thomas C. McRae, the prisoners were released from the Arkansas State Penitentiary.

—*Bernard Ryan, Jr.*

Marcus Mosiah Garvey Trial: 1923

Defendants: Elie Garcia, Marcus Mosiah Garvey, Orlando Thompson, and George Tobias **Crime Charged:** Using the U.S. mail to defraud
Chief Defense Lawyers: Armin Kohn, William C. Mathews, Cornelius W. McDougald, and Vernal Williams (Garvey also represented himself)
Chief Prosecutor: Maxwell S. Mattuck **Judge:** Julian W. Mack
Place: New York, New York **Dates of Trial:** May 18–June 19, 1923
Verdicts: Guilty (Garvey); not guilty (Garcia, Thompson, Tobias)
Sentence: 5 years' imprisonment and $1,000 fine

SIGNIFICANCE

The trial of Marcus Garvey for defrauding his followers destroyed the "Back to Africa" movement. Garvey's conviction resulted more from his unpopular concepts than from the evidence, which was slight.

Marcus Mosiah Garvey, born in Jamaica in 1887, emerged as the leader of black Americans at the end of World War I. He organized the Universal Negro Improvement Association (UNIA), a mass movement of people of African descent larger than any seen before or since. By 1922, its several million members in the United States, the West Indies, Latin America, and Africa were considered a significant threat by the European powers that controlled Africa. Garvey not only pioneered the idea that "Black is beautiful!" He set Africa's liberation from white domination as his goal.

To implement his plan to redeem Africa, Garvey established his own newspaper, *The Negro World.* Preaching the absolute separation of blacks from all forms of white domination, his eloquent speeches and articles promised hope and prosperity to black people. When he proposed a practical step—that the Black Star Steamship Line move passengers and cargo to and from African wharves—stock in the corporation was sold only to blacks. As money poured into UNIA divisions nationwide, the line bought several old freighters, none of which was entirely seaworthy (at least one sank), and paid for costly repairs.

Super Salesman in Fancy Dress

Next, Garvey organized the Negro Factories Corporation, to "build and operate factories in the big industrial cities of the United States, Central America, the West Indies, and Africa to manufacture every marketable commodity."

While Garvey succeeded as a super salesman and no one questioned his honesty and dedication, his shortcomings included a penchant for fancy dress uniforms, an ego that required he be surrounded by yes-men, and an abysmal lack of business skills—all of which made him vulnerable to enemies. By 1921, while the Black Star Line was supposedly negotiating to buy two more ships, the editor of an opposing paper revealed that the Department of Commerce said its Navigation Bureau had no record of either vessel.

Stockholders complained. Postal authorities arrested Garvey and the Black Star Line's treasurer, George Tobias, its secretary, Elie Garcia, and its vice president, Orlando M. Thompson, on charges of using the mails to defraud by selling passages on a nonexistent boat. Headlines screamed, "U.S. AGENTS SEARCH FOR 'MYTH' SHIP" and "GARVEY BUNK EXPOSED."

As the trial opened on May 18, 1923, prosecutor Maxwell S. Mattuck charged:

> While there center around Garvey other associations or corporations having for their object the uplift and advancement of the Negro race, the entire scheme of uplift was used to persuade Negroes for the most part to buy shares of stock in the Black Star Line . . . when the defendants well knew . . . that said shares were not and in all human probability never could be worth $5 each or any other sum of money.

Within two days, Garvey's lawyer, UNIA Counsel General William C. Matthews, advised the defendant to plead guilty on a technical charge and make a deal in closed chambers. Garvey fired Matthews and defended himself, making countless errors in procedure and frequently, as Judge Julian W. Mack condescendingly corrected him, producing gales of courtroom laughter.

"A Loss in Money but . . . a Gain in Soul"

Prosecution witnesses, all ex-Garveyites, testified to the defendants' wide variety of haphazard financial practices. Defense witnesses were bent on proving the value of the movement. "The Black Star Line was a loss in money but it was a gain in soul," one declared. The key prosecution witness, Benny Dancy, said he had bought 53 shares of Black Star stock, but the only evidence of mail fraud he could produce was an empty envelope from the line; he could not remember what came in the envelope.

Legal experts noted that Dancy had not been named in the indictments of the defendants as one of the persons they intended to defraud. No evidence showed when Dancy bought the stock. He did not testify that he actually received the envelope, but only that he recognized it. The envelope was offered in evidence with no other supportive testimony.

Garvey's cross-examination of some witnesses showed that the prosecution had rigged their testimony. One, who testified to working for Black Star as a mail clerk and delivering mail to the College Station post office in 1919, admitted he had not worked for the line then and didn't know where the post office was. Indeed, he conceded that the prosecutor had schooled him on dates and a postal inspector had told him the name of the post office.

Garvey was found guilty. Garcia, Thompson, and Tobias were found not guilty, on the jury's conclusion that they had merely complied with instructions from the head man. Sentenced to five years' imprisonment and a $1,000 fine, Garvey appealed. While the execution of his sentence was stayed, he organized a new shipping line.

His appeal rejected by the U.S. Circuit Court of Appeals, Garvey was immediately imprisoned in Atlanta, Georgia. President Calvin Coolidge rejected his petition for a pardon, but later, after two years and nine months, commuted his sentence to time served. Garvey then worked unsuccessfully to revive the UNIA until his death in London in 1940.

—Bernard Ryan, Jr.

Suggestions for Further Reading

Clarke, John Henrik. *Marcus Garvey and the Union of Africa.* New York: Random House, 1974.

Cronon, Edmund David. *Black Moses.* Madison: University of Wisconsin Press, 1969.

——. *Marcus Garvey.* New York: Prentice Hall, 1973.

Fax, Elton C. *Garvey.* New York: Dodd, Mead, & Co., 1972.

Foner, Eric. *America's Black Past.* New York: Harper & Row, 1970.

Garvey, Amy Jacques. *Garvey and Garveyism.* New York: Collier Books, 1970.

Stein, Judith. *The World of Marcus Garvey.* Baton Rouge: Louisiana State University Press, 1986.

Vincent, Theodore G. *Black Power and the Garvey Movement.* New York: Ramparts, 1971.

Leopold and Loeb Trial: 1924

Defendants: Nathan F. Leopold, Jr., and Richard Loeb
Crimes Charged: Murder and kidnapping
Chief Defense Lawyers: Clarence Darrow, Benjamin Bachrach, and Walter Bachrach **Chief Prosecutors:** Robert E. Crowe, Thomas Marshall, Joseph P. Savage, John Sbarbaro, and Milton Smith **Judge:** John R. Caverly
Place: Chicago, Illinois **Dates of Trial:** July 23–September 10, 1924
Verdict: Guilty **Sentences:** Life imprisonment for murder; 99 years for kidnapping

SIGNIFICANCE

Clarence Darrow, America's foremost criminal lawyer at the time, saved the defendants from execution for their "thrill murders" by changing their pleas from not guilty to guilty. The change took the case away from a jury so it was heard only by the judge, giving Darrow the opportunity to plead successfully for mitigation of punishment—life imprisonment rather than execution. The bizarre nature of the crime and the wealth of the victim and the defendants focused the nation's attention on the courtroom for nearly two months.

In May 1924, 18-year-old "Dickie" Loeb was the youngest graduate of the University of Michigan and already a postgraduate student at the University of Chicago. "Babe" Leopold, at 19 a law student at Chicago, had earned his Phi Beta Kappa key with his Bachelor of Philosophy degree. Each came from a wealthy and well-known Chicago family. Each believed his mental abilities set him apart as a genius superior to other people. Each dwelt in a fantasy world.

The Perfect Murder . . . for its Thrill

Over several years, Leopold and Loeb had developed a homosexual relationship. In the fall of 1923, they devised a plan for the perfect murder, to be committed for the sake of its thrill. The more they detailed their plan, the stronger their compulsion to carry it out became. In March 1924, according to a report later prepared by leading psychiatrists for their defense, "they decided to get any young boy whom they knew to be of a wealthy family, knock him unconscious, take him to a certain culvert, strangle him, dispose of all his clothes, and push the body deep into this funnel-shaped culvert, through which the water flowed, expecting the body to entirely decompose and never be found."

On May 21, 1924, Leopold and Loeb rented a car. With Loeb in the back seat, Leopold drove slowly past the exclusive Harvard Preparatory School. They saw 14-year-old Bobby Franks, like them a son of a millionaire and also a cousin of Loeb, and offered him a ride. Within minutes, Loeb grabbed Franks and bashed his skull four times with a heavy chisel.

After wrapping the boy's body in Leopold's lap robe, the two drove around Chicago until dark. Then they went to the culvert, near the Pennsylvania Railroad tracks and carried out their plan. Next they buried Franks' shoes, belt buckle, jewelry, and the bloodstained lap robe, stopped off for dinner, and burned the lad's clothes in the furnace at Loeb's house. Later, they mailed a special-delivery ransom note to Franks' father and, at Leopold's house, washed the bloodstains from the car and phoned the Franks' home to say that Bobby Franks was safe, and instructions were on the way.

Unable to reach Bobby's father the next morning, they quickly learned why: Newsboys were hawking extras announcing discovery of the boy's body. A railroad workman had noticed a human foot protruding from the culvert. Another worker had found a pair of eyeglasses.

The police soon traced the glasses to Leopold. He admitted recent bird-watching near the culvert. His alibi for his whereabouts on May 21? Bird-watching with Richard Loeb, then a ride around Lincoln Park in his car with Loeb and a couple of girls. But the Leopold chauffeur said he had been repairing Leopold's car all day, and in the evening he had seen the boys washing the floor of a strange car.

Next the police pulled a beat-up Underwood typewriter from Jackson Park Harbor and proved that the ransom note had been written on it. Leopold said he owned a Hammond typewriter, but *Chicago Daily News* reporters checked with his college classmates and learned that when they borrowed "Babe's" typewriter to type their papers, it was an Underwood.

Now came the grilling. Through a day of intensive questioning, both Leopold and Loeb stuck to their story. But the next day, thinking that Leopold had betrayed him, Loeb angrily confessed.

"I Have a Hanging Case"

Now State's Attorney Robert E. Crowe tackled Leopold, surprising him with facts that could have come only from Loeb. Nathan Leopold confessed. Before noon, the confessions of each were read to them, admitting they had killed Bobby Franks for the thrill of it. Said Crowe, "I have a hanging case. The state is ready to go to trial immediately."

Clarence Darrow was already the nation's foremost criminal lawyer. (Tennessee's famous Monkey Trial, which would bring him worldwide fame, was still a year away.) He had saved some 50 accused murderers, many of whom were guilty beyond the shadow of a doubt, from execution. He told the Leopold and Loeb families he would take the case for a $100,000 fee.

Darrow threw his energy, and that of a battery of assistants, into researching the minds of his clients. Since State's Attorney Crowe had already lined up Chicago's best-known psychiatrists to examine the accused, Darrow turned to such national figures as the president of the American Psychiatric Association and the supervisor of the psychiatric clinic at Sing Sing Prison. Prominent psychiatrists Karl Bowman and Harold S. Hulbert developed profiles that revealed the defendants' mental instability and confused personalities. The doctors' extensive report came to several thousand pages and was supplemented by thousands more from the other psychiatrists.

"They Should Be Permanently Isolated from Society"

By July 23, when the trial opened, all America except Clarence Darrow and his team expected Leopold and Loeb to hang. Shocked by the idea that the sons of the rich had nothing better to do than kill younger rich kids for the thrill of it, the country wanted an eye for an eye. Darrow knew that no jury would settle for less. Standing before Chief Justice John R. Caverly, he went right to the point: "We want to state frankly here that no one believes these defendants should be released. We believe they should be permanently isolated from society. After long reflection, we have determined to make a motion for each to withdraw our plea of not guilty and enter pleas of guilty to both indictments."

Flabbergasted, the prosecution realized that Darrow had instantly wiped out the chance of a jury conviction. Now the judge alone would consider the case. Darrow went on. "We ask that the court permit us to offer evidence as to the mental condition of these young men. We wish to offer this evidence in mitigation of punishment."

The prosecution objected violently, but Judge Caverly said he would hear evidence of mitigation. "I want to give you all the leeway I can," he said. "I want to get all the doctors' testimony. There is no jury here, and I'd like to be advised as fully as possible."

"Total Lack of Appropriate Emotional Response"

At that point, Darrow had earned his fee. His job now was to convince the judge that Leopold and Loeb not only did not deserve to be executed but that justice and humanity would be served by reaching a thorough understanding of their peculiar mental states. He introduced psychiatrist witnesses who had found that Richard Loeb was a habitual liar. Since the age of 10, he had fantasized about crimes and imagined himself the "Master Mind" directing others, always outsmarting the world's best detectives; he had cheated at cards, shoplifted, stolen automobiles and liquor, thrown bricks through store windows, and only last November—with Leopold, each carrying loaded revolvers—had burglarized his own fraternity house. "The total lack of appropriate emotional response is one of the most striking features of his present condition," said the Bowman-Hulbert report, noting that Loeb felt no remorse for his actions. "He has gradually projected a world of fantasy over into the world of reality, and at times even confused the two."

Reviewing the reports on Leopold, Darrow noted that the young man had been strongly influenced by a governess who encouraged him to steal, so that she could blackmail him, and who "gave him the wrong conception about sex, about theft, about right or wrong, about selfishness, and about secrecy." To Leopold, said Darrow, "selfishness was the ideal life. Each man was a law unto himself."

Nathan Leopold's main fantasy was a king-and-slave relationship. He preferred to be the slave who could save the life of the king, then refuse the reward of freedom. Richard Loeb was his king. He had been in love with Loeb since they were 15 and 14 years old. "I felt myself less than the dust beneath his feet," Leopold had told the psychiatrists. "I'm jealous of the food and drink he takes because I cannot come as close to him as does his food and drink."

As to the kidnapping and murder, said the report, Leopold "got no pleasure from the crime. With him it was an intellectual affair devoid of any emotion. He had no feeling of guilt or remorse."

For a month, as State's Attorney Crowe's psychiatrists insisted that Leopold and Loeb were entirely sane and normal, Darrow pressed his psychiatrist witnesses to testify that the legal sanity of the defendants was undisputed, but that mental instability was not insanity and was not normal.

Leopold and Loeb were each sentenced to life for the murder of Bobby Franks and 99 years for his kidnapping. (AP/Wide World Photos)

Finally, for 12 hours Clarence Darrow pleaded for mitigation of punishment. He noted that, while the prosecution charged the murderers with kidnapping Bobby Franks to get money to pay off gambling debts, testimony had proved that both boys had ample money and could get more from their extremely wealthy parents at any time.

"They Killed him Because They Were Made that Way"

"Why did they kill little Bobby Franks?" asked Darrow. "They killed him as they might kill a spider or a fly, for the experience. They killed him because they were made that way. Because somewhere in the infinite processes that go to the making up of the boy or the man, something slipped. That happened, and it calls not for hate but for kindness, for charity, for consideration."

Darrow said he was astonished that the prosecution asked the judge for the death sentence. "Your Honor, if a boy of 18 and a boy of 19 should be hanged in violation of the law that places boys in reformatories instead of prisons—then we are turning our faces backward toward the barbarism which once possessed the world. Your Honor stands between the past and the future. You may hang these boys by the neck until they are dead. But you will turn your face toward the past. I am pleading for the future, for a time when hatred and cruelty will not control the hearts of men, when we can learn by reason and judgment and understanding and faith that all life is worth saving, and that mercy is the highest attribute of man."

As Darrow ended his summation, no sound was heard in the courtroom. Tears were streaming down the face of Judge Caverly.

His verdict, two days later, sentenced Leopold and Loeb each to life imprisonment for murder, plus 99 years for kidnapping. "In choosing imprisonment," he said, "the court is moved chiefly by the age of the defendants."

The prisoners were taken to the Illinois State Prison at Joliet. In 1936, Richard Loeb was slashed to death by a fellow prisoner during an argument. After World War II, Governor Adlai Stevenson reduced Nathan Leopold's original sentence, thus making him eligible for parole, in gratitude for his contribution to testing for malaria during the war. Freed in 1958, Leopold was permitted to serve out his parole in Puerto Rico in order to avoid media attention. There he worked in hospitals and church missions, married, earned a master's degree, and taught mathematics. He died in 1971.

Clarence Darrow was forced to dun the Leopold and Loeb families repeatedly. Of the $100,000 fee agreed to, he collected $40,000 before he died in 1938.

—Bernard Ryan, Jr.

Suggestions for Further Reading

Aymar, Brandt, and Edward Sagarin. *A Pictorial History of the World's Great Trials.* New York: Bonanza Books, 1985.

Leopold, Nathan F., Jr. *Life Plus 99 Years.* Garden City, N.Y.: Doubleday & Co., Inc., 1958.

Sifakis, Carl. *The Encyclopedia of American Crime.* New York: Facts On File, 1982.

John Thomas Scopes Trial: 1925 (The "Monkey Trial")

Name of Defendant: John Thomas Scopes **Crime Charged:** Teaching evolution **Chief Defense Lawyers:** Clarence Darrow, Arthur Garfield Hays, and Dudley Field Malone. **Chief Prosecutors:** William Jennings Bryan and A.T. Stewart **Judge:** John T. Raulston **Place:** Dayton, Tennessee **Dates of Trial:** July 10–21, 1925 **Verdict:** Guilty; however, neither side won the case because the decision was reversed on a technicality involving the judge's error in imposing a fine that legally could only be set by the jury **Sentence:** $100 fine

SIGNIFICANCE

The John Thomas Scopes trial checked the influence of Fundamentalism in public education and stripped William Jennings Bryan of his dignity as a key figure in American political history. It also marked the displacement of religious faith and rural values by scientific skepticism and cosmopolitanism as the dominant strains in American thought.

Rarely has the American psyche been so at odds with itself as in the early 1920s. In the cities, Americans were dancing to the opening bars of the Jazz Age, debating Sigmund Freud's theories and swigging bootleg liquor in defiance of Prohibition. In the rural heartland, particularly in the South, believers in old-fashioned values were caught up in a wave of religious revivalism. Preachers damned modern scientific rationalism in all its guises and upheld a strict and literal interpretation of the Bible as the only source of truth. A showdown between modernists and traditionalists to decide which would dominate American culture seemed inevitable. Both sides itched for a decisive battle.

Fundamentalists were particularly galled by the gains modernism had made in public schools, where the teaching of Charles Darwin's theory of evolution by natural selection had supplanted the Biblical story of creation. To them, it seemed their tax dollars were being spent to turn their own children against—even to scoff at—the religion of their parents. Led by William Jennings Bryan, the thrice-defeated presidential candidate of populism, the Fundamentalists tried to drive the Darwinian "heresy" out of the schools by legislative fiat.

In Tennessee a bill sponsored by John Washington Butler was enacted in February 1925, declaring it unlawful for a teacher in any school supported by state funds "to teach any theory that denies the story of the divine creation of man as taught in the Bible, and to teach instead that man has descended from a lower order of animals." Fearful that if the Tennessee law went unchallenged other states would soon pass similar bills, the American Civil Liberties Union (ACLU) immediately announced it would defend any teacher charged with violating the Butler Act.

A few weeks later, in the little town of Dayton, a transplanted New Yorker with Darwinian views got into a debate at the local drugstore soda fountain with two Fundamentalist lawyers. However much they fought over evolution and whether mankind and monkeys were close relatives, they quickly agreed that a trial to test the law would do wonders for Dayton's commerce. The 24-year-old science teacher of the local high school, John Thomas Scopes, was recruited that very afternoon to be the legal guinea pig. Just as quickly, the ACLU confirmed it was prepared to defend Scopes.

Using a state-approved textbook, Scopes taught a lesson on evolutionary theory on April 24 to his Rhea County High School science class. Arrested on May 7, Scopes was quickly indicted by the grand jury, setting the stage for what newspaper headline writers were already calling the "Monkey Trial."

The Circus Comes to Dayton

The legal teams fielded by both sides guaranteed the press attention they and Dayton's business leaders craved. The ACLU dispatched its chief attorney, Arthur Garfield Hays, and his partner, Dudley Field Malone, along with Clarence Darrow. Darrow, who had made his reputation by defending controversial clients, became the chief lawyer for the defense. A militant agnostic, he had long been on a personal crusade against resurgent Fundamentalism, and he saw the Scopes trial as the perfect opportunity to kick the wobbly intellectual props out from under that ideology.

Personifying the Fundamentalist world view, the star of the prosecution team was none other than William Jennings Bryan himself. No one was more holier-than-thou or more effective on the stump in defending old-fashioned rural America's Fundamentalist values than "The Great Commoner," as he liked to be called.

Pro- and anti-evolutionists alike billed the trial as a winner-take-all debate between incompatible ideologies, a forensic armageddon between religion and science, faith and reason, traditional and modern values, the forces of light and the forces of darkness. Scientists and intellectuals were horrified at the prospect of a state barring scientific knowledge from the classroom. Civil libertarians saw the case as a crucial test of academic freedom, which had to be defended regardless of the prevailing religious beliefs of the local population. Fundamentalists proclaimed the case a last-ditch battle to save the souls of their children from atheism.

Big-city editors recognized it as a circus and sent their most waspish reporters and columnists to poke fun at the hayseeds. Dozens of new telegraph lines had to be strung into Dayton to handle their cable traffic. In addition to the lawyers and reporters, the town was overrun with itinerant preachers, commercial hucksters, eccentrics of every stripe, and numerous chimpanzees accompanied by their trainers. Monkey dolls, umbrellas with monkey handles, and dozens of other souvenirs with a monkey motif were put on sale.

Despite the circus-like atmosphere, the trial was no laughing matter for Bryan. Arriving a few days early, he preached to a large audience, "The contest between evolution and Christianity is a duel to the death. . . . If evolution wins in Dayton, Christianity goes."

Evolution on Trial

The trial began Friday, July 10, 1925, with Judge John T. Raulston presiding. More than 900 spectators packed the sweltering courtroom. Because of an error in the original indictment, most of the first morning was spent selecting another grand jury and drawing up a new indictment. With that task done, a trial jury of 10 farmers, a schoolteacher and a clerk was quickly impaneled, and the court adjourned for the weekend.

On the first business day of the trial, the defense tried and failed to quash the indictment on grounds that the law violated both the Fourteenth Amendment to the U.S. Constitution, which states that no one may be deprived of rights without due process of law, and the freedom of religion clause of the First Amendment. Describing the Butler Act to be "as brazen and as bold an attempt to destroy learning as was ever made in the Middle Ages," Darrow predicted there would be a natural progression from the forbidding of the teaching of evolution in public schools to the banning of books and censoring of newspapers.

The opening statement for the prosecution was made the next day by A.T. Stewart, the attorney general of Tennessee, who charged Scopes with contradicting the Biblical story of Creation, thus violating the Butler Act. Responding for the defense, Dudley Malone insisted that for Scopes to be convicted the state had to prove two things: that he had denied the Biblical story of creation and that he had taught instead that man descended from a lower order of animals. Proving both would considerably complicate the prosecution's task. (While Scopes had admitted teaching evolution, there was no evidence he had denied the Bible's version of man's origins.) Malone conceded there was there were some apparent contradictions between the Darwinian and Biblical accounts of creation, but he noted that many people managed to reconcile the two theories. Only the Fundamentalists maintained that science and religion were totally incompatible on the subject.

The prosecution's case was presented briskly. The superintendent of the Rhea County school system testified that Scopes had admitted teaching evolution in a biology class. Stewart then offered a King James Version of the Bible as

The crowded courtroom of the Scopes trial. Clarence Darrow is in the foreground. (Bettmann/Corbis)

evidence of what the Butler Act described as the Biblical account of Creation. The judge accepted this as evidence over the objection of Arthur Garfield Hays, who pointed out that there were several different versions of the Bible.

Scopes' students testified that he had taught that mammals had evolved from one-cell organisms and that humans share the classification "mammal" with monkeys, cats, etc. The owner of the local drugstore where Scopes had purchased the textbook he used to teach evolution acknowledged that the state had authorized sale of the textbook. Darrow and the druggist read aloud portions on Darwin. To counter, Steward read the first two chapters of the Old Testament's Genesis into the record. With that, the prosecution rested.

The next day, Thursday, July 16, the defense started calling its witnesses, beginning with a zoologist from Johns Hopkins University. The prosecution objected, arguing the evidence was inadmissible and irrelevant since the jury did not need to understand evolutionary theory to decide whether Scopes had violated the law in teaching it.

Bryan seized this opportunity to give his major speech of the trial. Clutching the offending textbook in one hand and a palm fan in the other, he belittled the theory of evolution and ridiculed a diagram in the textbook. Bryan charged that Darwinism produced agnostics and atheists, thus weakening moral standards. As evidence of this, he claimed it had inspired the German philosopher Friedrich Nietzsche, whose writings, in turn, had motivated the Chicago "thrill-killers," Nathan Leopold and Richard Loeb. Darrow, who had been the defense attorney in that case, angrily objected, stating that Bryan was misrepresenting Nietzsche's views to prejudice the jury; Judge Raulston overruled him. Bryan closed on a defiant note, assuring his audience that the Bible would survive attacks by scientists trying to reconcile it with evolution. Although some of his quips provoked appreciative laughter from spectators, observers noted that the speech lacked the eloquence and punch of Bryan's best stump performances.

Dudley Malone, presenting the defense's last argument for the admissibility of scientific evidence, charged the Fundamentalists with suppressing new ideas out of fear and claiming they had a monopoly on the truth. Malone proclaimed: "The truth always wins. . . . The truth does not need the forces of Government. The truth does not need Mr. Bryan. The truth is imperishable," Malone declared. "We feel we stand with progress. . . . We feel we stand with fundamental freedom in America. We are not afraid. Where is the fear? We defy it!" Although Malone's speech received more applause than Bryan's, it failed to persuade the judge.

The phrase "descended from a lower order of animals" was clear enough to define evolution under the law, Judge Raulston decided, ruling out the admissibility of scientific testimony.

Enraged by this decision, Arthur Hays requested the judge at least permit the expert statements to be entered into the court record, not to be heard by the jury but to be available to an appeals court. Avoiding cross-examination of its expert witnesses, the defense lawyers submitted their written statements, summaries of which went into the record.

Darrow Deflates Bryan

The trial, which had been moved to the courthouse lawn to accommodate the crowds, seemed to be winding down when defense attorney Hays dropped a bombshell: He called William Jennings Bryan to the stand as an expert on the Bible. This was an unheard-of legal tactic, but, with jaunty overconfidence, Bryan sprang up to accept the dare and the doubtful judge agreed. Darrow, whose skill at trapping witnesses with their own words was legendary, dropped his previously gentle manner when Bryan took the stand. First, he got Bryan to state every word in the Bible was literally true. He then asked how the Old Testament figure Cain got a wife if he, Adam, Eve, and Abel were the only four people on earth at the time, as the Bible said. Next, Clarence Darrow pointed out that the Book of Genesis states that the serpent who tempted Eve in the Garden of Eden was condemned by God to slither on its belly, Darrow then asked Bryan if before that, had the snake walked on its tail? The more Darrow bored in, the more entangled Bryan became in contradictions, and the more foolish he and his cause appeared.

Sweating and shaking, Bryan shocked his own supporters by admitting he didn't think the earth was made in six 24-hour days, as a literal reading of the Bible suggested. This was significant, since literalism was the cornerstone of Fundamentalist doctrine. The personal antagonism between Darrow and Bryan charged the courtroom with electricity. Bryan accused Darrow of insulting the Bible. Darrow responded, "I am examining you on your fool ideas that no Christian on earth believes."

Finally, after an hour and a half, Judge Raulston adjourned the proceedings in a transparent attempt to save Bryan further embarrassment. The next morning Bryan's testimony was described as irrelevant and removed from the record by the judge. The defense immediately rested, denying Bryan any opportunity to erase the previous day's humiliation.

Closing for the defense, Clarence Darrow stole the prosecution's lines by asking the jury to find Scopes guilty so that the case could be appealed. After nine minutes, the jury came back with a guilty verdict. In violation of Tennessee law, which required that the fine be set by the jury, Raulston advised the jury to let him fix the fine, an error that led the court of appeals to reject the original verdict. While the appeals court upheld the constitutionality of the Butler Act, it did not order a retrial for John Thomas Scopes, who by that time had given up teaching.

In a narrow sense, Scopes and the evolutionists lost the battle. But it was soon apparent that they had won the war. No attempt was made to enforce the Butler Act again, although it was not repealed until 1967. Within a few years, efforts to enforce similar laws in other states were also abandoned. The Supreme Court put the issue to rest in 1968, when it held a similar statute in Arkansas unconstitutional because it violated the separation of church and state required by the First Amendment of the Constitution.

But the Scopes trial is remembered not so much for its legal as its social and cultural significance. It marked a watershed in intellectual history; before Scopes, religious faith was the common, if not universal, premise of American thought; after Scopes, scientific skepticism prevailed. Friends and enemies alike viewed William Jennings Bryan's death just a few weeks after the trial ended as tolling the end of an era. A 1955 play and subsequent film based on the events in Dayton, Tennessee, *Inherit the Wind* by Jerome Lawrence and Robert Lee, ensured that the trial would remain among the most remembered courtroom battles in U.S. history.

—*Edward W. Knappman*

Suggestions for Further Reading

Allen, Leslie H., ed. *Bryan And Darrow At Dayton: The Record And Documents Of The "Bible Evolution Trial."* New York: Arthur Lee, 1925.

Coletta, Paolo E. *William Jennings Bryan.* Lincoln: University of Nebraska Press, 1969.

Darrow, Clarence. *The Story Of My Life.* New York: Charles Scribner's Sons, 1932.

De Camp, L. Sprague. *The Great Monkey Trial.* Garden City, N.Y.: Doubleday & Co., 1968.

Ginger, Raymond. *Six Days Or Forever: Tennessee v. John Thomas Scopes.* Boston: Beacon Press, 1958.

Hays, Arthur Garfield. *Let Freedom Ring.* New York: Boni & Liveright, 1928.

Koenig, Louis W. *Bryan: A Political Biography of William Jennings Bryan.* New York: G.P. Putnam's Sons, 1971.

Levine, Lawrence. *Defender of The Faith: William Jennings Bryan: The Last Decade 1915–1925.* New York: Oxford University Press, 1965.

Scopes, John. *Center of The Storm.* New York: Holt, Rinehart & Winston, 1967.

Stone, Irving. *Clarence Darrow For The Defense.* Garden City N.Y.: Doubleday & Co., 1941.

Tierney, Kevin. *Darrow: A Biography.* New York: T.Y. Crowell, 1979.

Tompkins, Jerry. *D-days at Dayton.* Baton Rouge: Louisiana State University Press, 1965.

Weinberg, Arthur, ed. *Attorney For The Damned.* New York: Simon & Schuster, 1957.

Billy Mitchell Court-Martial: 1925

Defendant: Brigadier General William Mitchell
Crime Charged: Insubordination and "conduct of a nature to bring discredit upon the military service" **Chief Defense Lawyers:** Frank G. Plain, Frank Reid, and Colonel Herbert A. White **Chief Prosecutors:** Major Allen W. Gullion, Lieutenant Joseph L. McMullen, and Colonel Sherman Moreland **Judges:** Major General Charles P. Summerall, Chief of the U.S. Army General Staff; Major Generals William S. Graves, Robert L. Howze, Douglas MacArthur, Benjamin A. Poore, and Fred W. Sladen; Brigadier Generals Ewing E. Booth, Albert L. Bowley, George Irwin, Edward K. King, Frank R. McCoy, and Edwin B. Winans; and Colonel Blanton Winship **Place:** Washington, D.C. **Dates of Court-Martial:** October 28–December 17, 1925 **Verdict:** Guilty **Sentence:** Suspension from rank, command, and duty with forfeiture of all pay and allowances for five years

SIGNIFICANCE

The Billy Mitchell court-martial demonstrated not only that a prophet is without honor in his own country but that he is particularly unwelcome in the military. The longest and most controversial court martial in U.S. history, it came to epitomize the difficulty military strategists have in adapting to changing times and technologies. The cost of the country's resultant unpreparedness for World War II lies beyond reckoning.

Nineteen-year-old William Mitchell enlisted in the Army in 1898, at the outbreak of the Spanish-American War. By World War I, he had realized the significance of the airplane, put himself through flying school at his own expense, risen to the rank of colonel, and was chief of Air Service. Seeing the Army using the airplane at first only for observation and, later, to shoot at enemy planes, he was perplexed that strafing and bombing never occurred to the men who ran the war. He proposed to General John J. Pershing that troops be dropped behind German lines by plane and parachute "in order so to surprise the enemy by taking him from the rear that it would give our infantry an opening." Pershing found the idea impossible and absurd.

By the war's end, Mitchell was convinced that "Only an air force can fight an air force." Soon he had trained the first paratrooper, used the airplane for aerial mapping, developed the turbo booster and the variable-pitch propeller, predicted high-altitude flight where the thin atmosphere would permit speeds of 300 to 400 miles per hour, and mounted cannons on planes—ordnance not flown again until, ironically, it was mounted on the B-25 Mitchell bomber (named for Billy Mitchell) for Colonel Jimmy Doolittle's daring bombing of Tokyo early in World War II.

Declaring in 1921 that "the first battles of any future war will be air battles," Mitchell became an outspoken critic of the government's failure to develop the Air Service. When the House Naval Affairs Committee refused to let him demonstrate air power by bombing former German ships that had to be destroyed under the Armistice agreement, he went public, earning so many headlines nationwide with his descriptions of Navy vessels as "sitting ducks" that the House Appropriations Committee approved his plan.

Mitchell's bombers easily sank an old American battleship and a German submarine, cruiser, destroyer, and battleship.

The Joint Board of the Army and Navy promptly announced, "The battleship is still the backbone of the fleet." A colonel from the Engineer Corps was promoted to major general in command of the Air Service. Mitchell exhausted himself appearing before clubs and organizations, prophesying the air power of Germany, Russia, Italy, and Japan. Before a Congressional inquiry, he accused Army and Navy witnesses of "deliberate falsification of facts with intent to deceive the country and Congress."

To counter Mitchell's alarms, the Navy sent the aging dirigible *Shenandoah* on a tour. It crashed. Next a Naval "publicity flight" to Hawaii crashed. Mitchell told reporters:

> My opinion is: Those accidents are the result of the incompetency, the criminal negligence, and the almost treasonable administration of our national defense by the Navy and War Departments.

Court-martial papers were served, charging the general with insubordination and conduct "to the prejudice of good order and military discipline."

For three weeks, defense counsel Frank G. Reid introduced witness after witness to prove that Mitchell, "after exhausting every usual means to safeguard the aerial defense of the United States without result, took the only way possible that would cause a study of the true conditions of the national defense to be made." Major (later General) Carl Spaatz testified on the country's numerical weakness in planes, Major (later General) "Hap" Arnold on the appalling number of deaths from worn-out equipment, former Captain Eddie Rickenbacker on the uselessness of anti-aircraft fire.

Mitchell himself testified:

> The people have placed their trust in the War and Navy Departments, to provide a proper defense for the safety of the nation. It has not been done. I consider this failure to be . . . the criminal offense of treason.

The judges, not one of whom had ever been up in an airplane, debated for three hours, found Billy Mitchell "Guilty on all counts," and sentenced him "to be suspended from rank, command, and duty with the forfeiture of all pay and allowances for five years."

Colonel Billy Mitchell (far right) at his court-martial. (Courtesy, Library of Congress)

A joint resolution of Congress immediately proposed to restore Mitchell's rank and reimburse his expenses. President Calvin Coolidge, as commander-in-chief, upheld the suspension but restored the allowances and granted the general half pay. Mitchell resigned. Congress passed no resolution.

Mitchell settled on a farm in Virginia, raising livestock, writing, speaking, and trying without success to found a University of Aviation.

Billy Mitchell died of pneumonia in 1936. Precisely as he had predicted, on December 7, 1941, the Japanese, without formally declaring war, destroyed Clark Field in the Philippines and the "sitting duck" U.S. Navy fleet at Pearl Harbor by aerial bombardment.

—*Bernard Ryan, Jr.*

Suggestions for Further Reading

Davis, Burke. *The Billy Mitchell Affair.* New York: Random House, 1967.

Encyclopedia Americana, Volume 19. New York: Americana Corp., 1953.
Lardner, Rex. *Ten Heroes of the Twenties.* New York: G.P. Putnam's Sons, 1966.
Mitchell, Ruth. *My Brother Bill.* New York: Harcourt, Brace and Co., 1953.

D.C. Stephenson Trial: 1925

Defendants: Earl Gentry, Earl Klinck, and David Curtis Stephenson **Crime Charged:** Murder **Chief Defense Lawyers:** Floyd Christian, Ira W. Holmes, and "Eph" Inman **Chief Prosecutors:** Charles E. Cox, Ralph Kane, William H. Remy **Judge:** Will M. Sparks **Place:** Noblesville, Indiana **Dates of Trial:** October 28–November 14, 1925 **Verdicts:** Stephenson: guilty; Gentry and Klinck: not guilty **Sentence:** Life imprisonment

SIGNIFICANCE

Specific events often make or break entire movements. The D.C. Stephenson case was such an event. The defendant had been Grand Dragon—and the most influential Northern leader—of the notorious Ku Klux Klan, dedicated to hatred and racial and religious intolerance. The trial and conviction of Stephenson, calling America's attention to the sinister hypocrisy of the organization, marked the high tide of Klan membership, which dropped within three years from 10 million to a few thousand. The case also established that a defendant who committed a criminal assault that caused the victim to commit suicide could be tried on murder charges.

David Curtis Stephenson was a Texan who settled in Indiana in 1920 when he was 29. There he joined the Ku Klux Klan, a fraternal organization that had been created during Reconstruction in the South to "maintain white supremacy." Expanding nationally after World War I, the Klan had broadened its program to include nativism, anti-Catholicism, and anti-Semitism. It grew rapidly in the North.

Stephenson worked tirelessly to expand the Klan in Indiana, recruiting more than 300,000 fanatics in less than two years and becoming Grand Dragon of the Realm of Indiana. Next, under contract from the Klan, he became supreme organizer in 19 other states, was paid $4 out of every $10 initiation fee, and pocketed $4.25 from every $6 robe and hood a Klansman bought.

"I Am the Law in Indiana"

Stephenson was less successful, however, in the in-fighting with his boss, Hiram W. Evans, Imperial Wizard and director of the Klan. After Stephenson's friend Ed Jackson was elected governor in 1924, along with a majority of the state's House of Representatives—all nominated and supported by the Klan—Stephenson repeatedly declared, "I am the law in Indiana." Imperial Wizard Evans decided to subject the Klan's Indiana leader to the K.K.K.'s own program. In addition to its persecution of blacks, Catholics, and Jews, the Klan preached virtue. It regularly tarred and feathered whoremongers and habitual drunkards. Now Evans let out word of Stephenson's hypocrisy: The Grand Dragon was a secret lecher and a drunkard. The Evansville Klavern tried him in secret for his many "immoralities" in several cities and "on trains and boats," found him guilty, and banished him from the Klan.

In January 1925, at a banquet honoring governor-elect Jackson, Stephenson met 28-year-old Madge Oberholtzer, manager of a public-welfare program in the state's Department of Public Instruction, who lived at home in Indianapolis with her parents. They danced together. Soon Stephenson was making dates and calling for her in his chauffeured car. He was, Oberholtzer found, always the perfect gentleman.

On Sunday, March 15, 1925, Oberholtzer came home about 10:00 P.M. from a day with young friends. Stephenson had left an urgent message. When she called back, he said he was leaving for Chicago but needed to see her first and would send an escort to get her. Thinking that Stephenson wanted to discuss some aspect of her work and expecting to return shortly, Oberholtzer left home without her purse or hat.

With a stranger later identified as Earl Gentry, she departed for Stephenson's house. In the morning, her parents, who had gone to bed soon after she went out, realized she had not come home. Distressed, they talked with a lawyer and stopped by Stephenson's house in search for her. Then came a telegram: "We are driving through to Chicago. Will be home on night train. Madge." Mrs. Oberholtzer met the train, but her daughter did not appear.

In a Pullman-Car Drawing Room

On Tuesday morning, a car arrived while Mrs. Oberholtzer was out (a roomer was the only person at home). A man later identified as Earl Klinck carried Madge Oberholtzer, who was moaning, into the house and to her bed upstairs. The man said she had been in an automobile accident, then hurriedly departed. Oberholtzer asked the roomer to call a doctor. He and her mother arrived together, and Oberholtzer, sobbing and groaning, told them how she had been taken to Stephenson's kitchen, where she found him quite drunk and where he, his chauffeur, and Gentry twice forced her (each man holding a revolver) to drain a glass of liquid that immediately made her ill and confused. When she protested that she wanted to go home, Stephenson said, "You can't go home. You are going with me to Chicago. I love you more than any woman I have ever known."

Next they took her to the railroad station and boarded a Pullman car. In a drawing room, with Gentry in the upper berth, "Stephenson [her later declaration stated] took all my clothes off and pushed me into the lower berth. He chewed me all over my body, particularly my neck and face, chewed my tongue, chewed my breasts until they bled, my back, my legs, my ankles, and mutilated me all over."

Next morning, in Hammond, Indiana, the men took Madge to a hotel, where Gentry helped bathe her wounds. Stephenson dictated the telegram and Gentry sent it. When Madge begged for a hat, Stevenson gave her $15 and sent her out with the chauffeur, who had driven to Hammond. Without his seeing her, she managed to buy bichloride-of-mercury tablets and, back at the hotel, to take six, vomiting the rest of the day. By nightfall, she had told the men she had taken the poison. She had also refused Stevenson's demands that she go to a hospital and that she marry him. The men put her in the car and headed back to Indianapolis, Madge vomiting, groaning, and screaming all the way. At Stephenson's house, they carried her to a loft over the garage at midnight, just missing her mother, who was again at Stephenson's door. In the morning, Klinck took her home.

The doctor worked for 10 days to get the poison out of Madge's system. Her wounds and bruises responded to medication—except one, the deep wound in her breast, which was infected. Soon after making a formal statement to her doctor and two lawyers, she died on April 14.

Madge's father, George Oberholtzer, a postal clerk, had already filed a criminal complaint against Stephenson, Gentry, and Klinck, and the grand jury had indicted them for assault and battery with intent to commit a criminal attack, malicious mayhem, kidnaping, and conspiracy to kidnap. The three were free on bail. Now the grand jury charged them with murder. They were arrested and held without bail.

After 11 days of interrogating 400 veniremen to get a jury that had no affiliation with or sympathy for the Klan, the trial began October 18. The prosecution quickly established the facts of Stephenson's Sunday-evening phone call and Madge's going off with Gentry for the fatal trip.

A Secondary Staphylococci Infection

Testimony in two areas established the prosecution's case. One was Madge's sworn declaration, made in the presence of four witnesses (two of them lawyers) when her doctor had told her that she could not expect to recover. The other was testimony by three pathologists that Madge had died from a secondary staphylococci infection, resulting from Stephenson's biting assault on her breast, that imposed itself on an acute nephritis, or kidney infection, caused by the poison. Cross-examination by the defense lawyers failed to shake the pathologists.

The defense itself tried to prove that Madge's infection was the residue of an attack of flu some months earlier, that she and Stephenson had been intimate and the trip with him was voluntary, and that Madge's dying statement was "a dying declaration of suicide and not of homicide, made for the justification of herself, to free herself from fault and place the blame on others."

"She Would have Worn a Hat"

Prosecutor Ralph Kane struck the common-sense human chord during his summation:

> There are some things that you and I know. If Madge Oberholtzer had gone willingly with Stephenson that night she would have done it by prearrangement, and she would have worn a hat. If I understand anything at all about women, when they start on a 250-mile Pullman ride they take along their clothes, their hats, their cosmetics, their lingerie and other things.
>
> Another thing. Do you think she would ever have had big, pug-nosed Gentry in the same compartment if she had been conscious of what was happening? If she was a willing companion, why bring her home looking like she had been in a fight?

In six hours on November 14, the jury found Stephenson guilty of murder in the second degree and recommended life imprisonment. Gentry and Klinck were found not guilty. Stephenson immediately began a series of more than 40 proceedings to try to gain a pardon, a new trial, or release on parole. In each, an entirely different set of lawyers represented him. At last, in 1950, he gained parole but disappeared within five months. When found in November, he had failed to report to his parole officer for three months. Returned to prison, he next made disclosures to newspapers that resulted in his temporary release to produce records he had hidden. His papers resulted in the indictment of Governor Ed Jackson as well as the Republican political boss, George V. Coffin, for violation of Indiana's corrupt practices act by bribing the governor's predecessor to appoint a Klan henchman as a prosecuting attorney. Stephenson's disclosures also brought indictments against the mayor of Indianapolis and six city aldermen for accepting bribes. The governor and Coffin escaped by pleading the statute of limitations, while the mayor spent 30 days in jail and, along with the aldermen, resigned.

Stephenson's house burned soon after he went to prison. Klinck and Gentry were indicted for arson, but the case was dismissed for lack of evidence. Gentry was murdered in 1934 by a jealous rival in a love triangle. Pleading guilty and receiving a life sentence, his murderer said:

> I am not in the least sorry for the act I committed, as I feel I did a good deed for society when I killed Earl Gentry.

—*Bernard Ryan, Jr.*

Suggestions for Further Reading

Busch, Francis X. *Guilty or Not Guilty?* New York: Bobbs-Merrill Co., 1952.

Nash, Jay Robert. *Encyclopedia of World Crime.* Wilmette, Ill.: CrimeBooks, 1991.

Sweet Trials: 1925–26

Defendants: Ossian and Henry Sweet **Crimes Charged:** Conspiracy to commit murder and murder **Chief Defense Lawyers:** Clarence Darrow, Arthur Garfield Hays, and Thomas Chawke **Chief Prosecutors:** Robert M. Toms and Lester S. Moll **Judge:** Frank Murphy **Place:** Detroit, Michigan **Dates of Trials:** First trial: November 1925; second trial: April–May 1926 **Verdicts:** First trial: Mistrial/hung jury; second trial: Not guilty

SIGNIFICANCE

The Sweet trials revealed the growing racial tension in northern and Midwestern cities following World War I, and provided a dress rehearsal for more such episodes during the Civil Rights era 30 years later.

During the First World War, thousands of African-American families moved from the south to the industrial cities of the north, such as Detroit, in search of high-paying, wartime jobs. While they found the employment that they were after, they also learned that they had not escaped the racism that they had experienced in the southern states. Northern white attitudes were hostile to the black newcomers, and northern society and neighborhoods remained closed to them. The few neighborhoods in which these African-Americans settled soon grew overcrowded and filthy.

Dr. Ossian Sweet, a black Detroit physician, moved to the city in 1924, after studying for a time in Vienna and Paris, where he had worked with Marie Curie. Having recently married and fathered a child, he wished to avoid the slums and find decent housing. By 1925, one or two black friends of his had bought homes in white neighborhoods, but they soon left in the face of white hostility. Sweet was determined not to let the same thing happen to him.

In the summer of 1925, Sweet found a house at 2905 Garland Avenue, in a lower-middle-class, white neighborhood. The sellers were a white woman and her light-skinned, black husband. Perhaps this made Sweet think that the neighbors would accept him and his family, but in reality (as events would later show) the neighbors had probably thought the husband was white. At any rate, Sweet moved in with the help of his brothers, Otis and Henry, as well as a few friends. Among his possessions were enough guns and ammunition for the entire group—just in case they were needed—when the Sweet family moved in on September 8.

Menacing Crowd Gathers

The Ku Klux Klan had been very active in the area recently. One result of this was the organization of the neighborhood Waterworks Park Improvement Association, which had formed shortly after Sweet bought the Garland Avenue house, and which was in reality a group designed to keep the neighborhood all white. The day that the Sweets moved in, a white crowd began to gather outside the house. Eventually the mob disbanded, but the following evening a new one formed. Later testimony as to its size varied, but the best evidence suggests that it consisted of a few hundred people. Among them were several police officers, who were there because Sweet had asked for police protection.

The second evening after the Sweets moved in, with Sweet and 10 others inside the house, the crowd grew restless, and some people began throwing stones and breaking windows after the arrival of Otis Sweet and William Davis, a family friend. Others yelled racial epithets. Suddenly gunfire erupted from several windows of the house. Across the street Leon Breiner fell dead, and another man suffered a leg wound. After the gunfire ended, the police burst into the house and arrested everyone inside. Within a few weeks prosecutors sought indictments against the 11 occupants for conspiracy to commit murder.

Darrow for the Defense

The National Association for the Advancement of Colored People (NAACP) soon turned to Clarence Darrow for help. At the time Darrow was perhaps the nation's most celebrated attorney. Darrow, long a champion of the underdog, agreed to take the case. The first trial took place in the Detroit Recorder's Court in November 1925. The judge was the liberal and humanitarian Frank Murphy, who later became an associate justice of the United States Supreme Court. The chief prosecutor was Robert M. Toms, whom Darrow afterward described as "one of the fairest and most humane prosecutors that I ever met."

The facts of the case were unfavorable for the defendants. The crowd had been restless and abusive, yes, but no one had tried to enter Sweet's house forcibly, so under Michigan law, self-defense would not be easy to prove. That the gunfire seemed to come in a volley, as if prearranged, indicated provocation on the part of those inside, rather than self-defense. Breiner had been shot in the back, so he himself could not have been an aggressor.

On the other hand, the prosecutors' case wasn't all that cut and dried, either, and it was mismanaged. Toms called a large number of witnesses, all of them white, to show that the "crowd" was really quite small. However, Darrow's incisive cross-examination revealed that the police had coached some, and perhaps most (if not all), of the witnesses to say this. Darrow also attacked the prosecution for relying upon the theory of conspiracy to commit murder, which the prosecution had to do since it could not prove who in the house had fired the fatal shot, much less show who had fired at all. Darrow once called conspiracy "the favorite weapon of every tyrant . . . an effort to punish the crime of thought."

Darrow, despite the restrictive Michigan definition, used the argument of self-defense to explain what had happened that night. Calling upon Ossian Sweet himself to tell his story, Darrow tried to make this case symbolic of earlier black persecution.

"When I saw that mob," Sweet said, "I realized in a way that I was facing that same mob that had hounded my people through its entire history. I realized my back was against the wall and I was filled with a particular type of fear—the fear of one who knows the history of my race."

After deliberating for three days, the all-white jury announced that it could not reach a verdict, and Murphy declared a mistrial. Five months later, in April 1926, Toms indicted Henry Sweet, who finally admitted to firing a gun, bringing him to trial a second time for murder. Judge Murphy again presided, and both Toms and Darrow used much the same litigation tactics that they had employed in the first trial. This time, Sweet was acquitted, and the following July Toms moved to dismiss the charges against all of the other defendants.

Although Darrow had argued more famous cases, he considered the Sweet trials to be his greatest personal triumph. The issues brought forth in these trials presaged the growing racial tensions throughout the country that would eventually give rise to the Civil Rights movement.

—*Buckner F. Melton, Jr.*

Suggestions for Further Reading

Darrow, Clarence. *The Story of My Life.* New York: Grosset & Dunlap, 1932.

Fine, Sidney. *Frank Murphy.* Ann Arbor, Mich.: University of Michigan Press, 1975.

Tierney, Kevin. *Darrow: A Biography.* New York: Thomas Y. Crowell, 1979.

Weinberg, Arthur and Lila Weinberg. *Clarence Darrow: A Sentimental Rebel.* New York: G.P. Putnam's Sons, 1980.

David Marshall Trial: 1926

Defendant: David L. Marshall **Crime Charged:** Murder
Chief Defense Lawyer: Abraham Wernick **Chief Prosecutor:** Charles E. Fox **Judge:** Harry S. McDevitt **Place:** Philadelphia, Pennsylvania
Date of Trial: March 8–24, 1926 **Verdict:** Guilty: second-degree murder
Sentence: 10–20 years

SIGNIFICANCE

Illicit sex, blackmail, and a savage killing all combined to make this one of the most sensational trials in Pennsylvania's history.

When Anna May Dietrich, a milliner who lived in Philadelphia, failed to return home on the evening of January 19, 1926, anxious relatives contacted the police. Two days later her headless remains, expertly dismembered, were found in the nearby suburb of Media. Another 24 hours and the grisly jigsaw puzzle was complete, when the missing head, wrapped in newspapers, was discovered seven miles away. From the way in which the body had been almost totally drained of blood, detectives suspected they were seeking a killer with medical knowledge.

Investigation of Dietrich's social life revealed a fun-loving, liberated woman in her mid-thirties, fond of dancing and socializing. Nor was she encumbered by the rigid social conventions of the day, as it became known that for several years she had been having an affair with a married chiropractor named David Marshall, who, when interviewed, claimed not to have seen Dietrich in over a week.

Evidence soon surfaced which suggested that Marshall was lying and he was arrested. After several hours of what newspapers termed a "severe grilling," Marshall finally broke. He claimed that Dietrich had committed suicide, using poison she found in his surgery, and that he had cut up her body in order to dispose of it. Still the detectives weren't satisfied and another bout of rigorous questioning brought forth a different version of events, leading to Marshall being charged with murder.

Double Confession

The trial, which opened on March 8, 1926, generated lurid public interest. Prosecutor Charles E. Fox declared that although the crux of his case rested on the two confessions made by Marshall, there was plenty of other damning evidence, as well. First, a chauffeur named E. J. Barry described how the defendant had hired him on the night of January 20, to haul away some parcels from his surgery. As Barry lifted one of the packages its paper wrapping broke and out fell a human leg. Barry just gaped. Frantically, Marshall began thrusting fistfuls of dollars at him, begging him to get rid of the parcel, but Barry would have none of it and later approached the police.

David L. Marshall, flanked by county detectives, O.N. Smith and William Quinn. (AP/Wide World Photos)

When in custody, Marshall had been hustled off to the morgue by Delaware County District Attorney William Taylor. Testifying for the prosecution, Taylor told how he had assembled everyone around the remains of Anna Dietrich:

> I made the others take off their hats, and I turned to Marshall and said: "In the presence of God and this girl's body, didn't you do this?" He smiled at me and put his hand to his mustache and took a cigar out of his pocket and said: "Why, certainly not."

After this, said Taylor, Marshall was returned to the station where he made a statement. Taylor then handed this alleged confession to Fox, who read it aloud to the jury. In it Marshall said: "I cut the body up, but I had nothing to do with her death. She committed suicide. She came into my office and took something—I don't know what it was—and died there."

Listening to this, Marshall squirmed in his chair and had to be prevented by his counsel, Abraham Wernick, from attempting to leave the court.

Worse was to follow. Over heated objections from the defense, Fox was allowed to introduce the second confession, made just hours after the first. In this, Marshall described how Dietrich turned up at his office and tried to blackmail him over their longstanding relationship, demanding money for some items she had just purchased:

> I refused, then a quarrel started. I tried to scare her. The result was that, I guess, I choked her . . . I would like to say this, though . . . I don't want the impression that I deliberately intended to choke her to death, for I didn't.

Which seemed an odd thing to say, in light of the fact that Marshall's next course of action was to cut Dietrich's throat. The court listened spellbound as his account of dissecting the body—a three-hour task—was read out.

Desperate to impeach this second confession, Wernick attacked the new witness, Assistant District Attorney William B. McClenachan, who had been present at its dictation. Grudgingly, McClenachan admitted that the defendant had appeared "all in" when he signed the confession, having been grilled nonstop for almost 14 hours.

It was important for the prosecution to demonstrate that the victim had been fearful of Marshall, and to this end they produced Kenneth Gleason, a fellow commuter on the train used by Anna Dietrich, who had spoken to the woman on the night of her death. According to Gleason, she had produced a photograph of Marshall, then mentioned that she was attending a party the next night with another man. When Gleason said, "I hope you have a nice time at the party," Dietrich appeared edgy. "I don't know," she said ruefully. "Maybe the man I'm going to meet tonight will object to a date with another man."

Throughout the trial Marshall had remained an oddly peripheral character—so many of his words were read aloud by other people—and it remained that way when he gave testimony. Glib and evasive, he insisted that the second confession had been beaten out of him by overzealous investigators, and he reiterated his claim that Anna had swallowed poison, that he had panicked and cut up the body to conceal his illicit relationship with her.

Cigars and Hilarity

To nullify the claim of police brutality, the prosecution produced Rodney W. Shaver, one of the detectives who had interviewed Marshall. He denied emphatically that the defendant had been abused while in custody and raised hoots of laughter with his comment that the defendant "was treated better than we were. He got cigars and we didn't!"

Gradually the trial developed into a fierce battle between the various expert witnesses. For the prosecution, Dr. Clarke Stull, who conducted the autopsy, would not be deflected from his belief that Anna May Dietrich had been strangled, while defense witness Dr. Henry Cattell maintained that there was nothing in the autopsy results inconsistent with Marshall's version of events.

Had Miss Dietrich been strangled, Cattell said, then marks should have been left on her neck; he could find none. Nor did he rule out Marshall's claim that the victim had taken poison.

In rebuttal, the state called Dr. J. Atlee Dean, a chemist and bacteriologist who had examined organ tissue from the dead woman. He testified that there was nothing to suggest any hint of poisoning.

On March 24, after five hours behind locked doors, the jury signaled that their labors were complete by bursting into an impromptu chorus of "Show Me the Way to Go Home." They convicted Marshall of second-degree murder and he was sentenced to a minimum of 10 years imprisonment.

It later emerged that several jurors were initially inclined to convict Marshall of first degree murder, only to be swayed by those who felt that, as an admitted adulteress, Anna Dietrich had in some way contributed to her own demise. Marshall's infidelity was, apparently, overlooked.

—*Colin Evans*

Suggestions for Further Reading

Grex, Leo. *Stranger than Fiction Detection.* London: Robert Hale, 1977.

New York Times. See Dietrich, Anna May, in the *New York Times Index,* January 22–March 25, 1926.

Frances Hall, Henry Stevens, and William Stevens Trial: 1926

Defendants: Frances Stevens Hall, Henry Stevens, and William Stevens **Crime Charged:** Murder **Chief Defense Lawyers:** Clarence E. Case, Robert H. McCarter, and Timothy N. Pfeiffer **Chief Prosecutors:** Francis L. Bergen and Alexander Simpson **Judges:** Frank L. Cleary and Charles W. Parker **Place:** Somerville, New Jersey **Dates of Trial:** November 3–December 3, 1926 **Verdict:** Not guilty

SIGNIFICANCE

This trial came four years after the execution-style murders of two lovers—both adulterers—had produced sensational headlines nationwide. In what mystery writer Rex Stout called "sustained official ineptitude surely never surpassed anywhere," New Jersey authorities were unable for four years to produce an indictment. When they finally did so and the trial resulted in acquittal, *The New York Times* commented, "Jersey Justice can at least acquit the innocent if it cannot always find the guilty." The crime has never been solved.

On Saturday morning, September 16, 1922, a young couple strolling on a lovers' lane on the outskirts of New Brunswick, New Jersey, discovered two bodies. A woman's head lay on a man's right arm, her hand on his knee, a scarf over her throat. The man's business card leaned against his foot. Scattered over the bodies were pieces of paper.

The man was the Reverend Edward W. Hall, rector of the Episcopal Church of St. John the Evangelist. Handsome and popular, he had some 11 years earlier, at the age of 30 married 37-year-old Frances Noel Stevens, daughter of a well-to-do New Brunswick family.

"I Have the Greatest of All Blessings"

It was known almost instantly who the murdered woman was, for it was common knowledge that Reverend Hall was deeply involved with a member of the St. John's choir, Eleanor Mills. Her quiet and unambitious husband James served as sexton of the church. The country was titillated when the newspapers, hot on the trail of a story of torrid love, revealed that the papers scattered over the bodies were love letters such as this:

> There isn't a man who could make me smile as you did today. I know there are girls with more shapely bodies, but I do not care what they have. I have the greatest of all blessings, a noble man, deep, true, and eternal love. My heart is his, my life is his, all I have is his, poor as my body is, scrawny as they say my skin may be, but I am his forever.

The autopsies reported that the minister had been shot once and the 32-year-old choir singer three times—both in the head. Her throat had been slit from ear to ear and her voice box nearly removed.

Middlesex and Somerset county detectives and prosecutors vied for authority, for the bodies had been found almost on the line between the two counties. Soon Middlesex County prosecutor Joseph Stricker charged one Clifford Hayes with the murders. He believed a young man who said Hayes had mistaken the victims for a girlfriend and her father, whom Hayes had threatened. But Hayes was jailed in Somerset County, where its prosecutor was unable to make the mistaken-identity theory explain the slit throat or the love letters. Two days later, Hayes' accuser admitted he had lied.

Meantime, in four weeks, the police and the prosecutors had found no reason to suspect the choir singer's husband, James Mills, whom columnist Damon Runyon later described as "a harmless, dull little fellow." As for Frances Hall, she had spent the evening of the murders with her husband's visiting niece after Reverend Hall had gone out in response to a call from Eleanor Mills. At 2:30 in the morning, Frances Hall had discovered that her husband had not returned. With her brother Willie Stevens, who had been at home the entire evening, she had gone to the church to search for her husband.

The police questioned Frances Hall and her brothers extensively on October 17, even forcing her to don the gray coat she had worn on her middle-of-the-night search and submit to inspection by an unidentified woman who peered at her intently.

By now, countless eager curiosity-seekers, propelled by daily sensational newspaper stories, had traipsed through the lovers' lane property. The weekends brought hundreds of cars, police to handle traffic, and vendors to hawk peanuts, popcorn, and soft drinks.

A Mule-Riding Pig Woman

At the end of October, a 50-year-old widow named Jane Gibson, who raised hogs near the murder site, disclosed that she had mounted a mule on the night of September 14 to follow a suspected thief. In the lovers' lane, she had seen two men and two women silhouetted against the night sky, then heard screams and shots and the shouted name "Henry."

Dubbing her "The Pig Woman," the press thronged Gibson's dilapidated living room. She told them she had always wanted to talk to the police, but they wouldn't listen. When Hayes was arrested, she had forced them to pay attention. It was she who had peered intently at Frances Hall at police headquarters.

The grand jury spent five days hearing 67 witnesses, including The Pig Woman. It took no action.

Three and a half years later, a piano tuner named Arthur S. Riehl filed a petition for annulment of his 10-month marriage. His wife, he said, had withheld from him "knowledge of the doings in the well-known Hall-Mills case." He said his wife, who at the time was a maid in the Hall household, told Mrs. Hall on September 14, 1922,

> . . . that she knew Dr. Hall intended to elope with Mrs. Mills. About ten o'clock that night respondent [Mrs. Riehl], Mrs. Hall, and Willie Stevens were driven to Phillips farm. . . . Respondent told your petitioner that she got five thousand dollars for her part in the matter and for keeping quiet about it. . . . Respondent told your petitioner Willie Stevens was a good shot and that there was always a pistol in the Hall library drawer.

Mrs. Riehl denounced her husband's statement as "a pack of lies." But for the next three weeks, the New York *Daily Mirror,* a new Hearst paper eager to win a circulation war with the established *Daily News,* led the press in demanding the reopening of the Hall-Mills case. At midnight on July 28, Frances Hall was arrested and arraigned. Over the next month, several hearings, each with more than 50 witnesses, produced enough testimony to convince the grand jury to indict not only her but her brothers Willie and Henry Stevens and their cousin, Henry Carpender, for each murder. Special Prosecutor Alexander Simpson asked for a separate trial for Carpender.

The trial turned Somerville's Main Street into what one wag called "a country fair," with dozens of souvenir and refreshment stands. In the courthouse, some 300 reporters pumped their stories into 60 leased wires while 28 special operators handled a 129-position switchboard moved in from the recent Jack Dempsey-Gene Tunney prizefight in Philadelphia. In view of the intense interest, Somerset County Judge Frank L. Cleary invited New Jersey Supreme Court Justice Charles W. Parker, who had presided over some of the hearings, to help him run the trial in the murder of Eleanor Mills.

For the prosecution, a fingerprint expert testified that Reverend Hall's business card bore Willie Stevens' fingerprint, despite the fact that it had been handled by police and reporters and the curious, had developed "flyspecks," and after three years had languished in the possession of the editor of the *Daily Mirror.*

The Pig Woman provided the ultimate drama. Severely ill, she was brought by ambulance to the courthouse, where she lay flat in a bed before judges and jury and told again her story of riding her mule into the night and hearing voices. She said she had heard a woman shout, "Explain those letters." Then, she went on, "I could hear somebody's wind going out, and somebody said, 'Ugh!' " A flashlight shone, and she saw Henry Stevens. Then a woman said, "Oh, Henry," and another screamed "Oh, my; oh, my!" She heard a shot, then three shots, and she rode away.

Defense attorney Clarence Case worked to destroy The Pig Woman's credibility. Known as Mrs. Gibson, she said she was really married to a Mr. Easton—except that she couldn't remember in which church or city she married him, and at the hearings four years earlier, she had denied that marriage. Hadn't she been married in 1890 to a man who divorced her in 1898 for adultery? Had she lived with Harry Ray? Had she known "Stumpy" Gillan? She couldn't remember.

The defense produced witnesses to prove that Henry Stevens spent the night of the murders bluefishing on the Jersey shore. Three fingerprint experts could find no resemblance between the smudge on the card and Willie Stevens' prints. The detective who received the card in 1922 said he had put his initials on it then, but the card in evidence showed no initials.

"A Sort of Genius"

Cross-examining, Simpson asked Willie Stevens if it wasn't "rather fishy" to look for the missing minister in the middle of the night. Willie Stevens said, "I don't see that it is at all fishy." The prosecutor wanted to know how Stevens could prove he had been in his room during the evening of September 14. "If a person sees me go upstairs," said Stevens, "isn't that a conclusion that I was in my room?"

The press hailed Willie Stevens. The deflated prosecutor called him "a sort of genius."

Frances Hall testified that her husband was "absolutely" devoted to her. Her interest in and devotion to Eleanor Mills was demonstrated by the fact that she had taken Mills to the hospital for a kidney operation in January and paid her bills there.

Having heard 87 witnesses for the state and 70 for the defense, the jury deliberated for five hours. It found the three defendants not guilty of the murder of Eleanor Mills. The next morning, Justice Parker granted the New Jersey attorney general's motion for dismissal of all remaining charges against them. All charges against Henry Carpender were then dropped.

Willie Stevens, Henry Carpender, and Frances Hall sued the *Daily Mirror* for libel, each asking for $500,000. Later they sued William Randolph Hearst and the *Evening Journal.* All suits were settled out of court for undisclosed sums.

On the books of the Somerset County prosecutor, the Hall-Mills case continues to be unsolved.

—Bernard Ryan, Jr.

Suggestions for Further Reading

Kunstler, William M. *The Minister and the Choir Singer.* New York: William Morrow & Co., 1964.

Nash, Jay Robert. *Almanac of World Crime.* Garden City, N. Y.: Anchor Press/Doubleday, 1981.

Sifakis, Carl. *The Encyclopedia of American Crime.* New York: Facts On File, 1982.

The Teapot Dome Trials: 1926–30

Defendants: Sherman Burns: trial 3; William J. Burns: trial 3; Henry Mason Day: trial 3; Edward L. Doheny: trials 1 and 8; Albert B. Fall: trials 1, 3, and 7; Harry F. Sinclair: trials 2, 3, and 4; and Robert W. Stewart: trial 6 **Crimes Charged:** Conspiracy to defraud the U.S. government: trials 1 and 4; Contempt of the U.S. Senate: trials 2 and 5; Contempt of court for jury shadowing: trial 3; Perjury: trial 6; Accepting a bribe: trial 7; Giving a bribe: trial 8 **Chief Defense Lawyers:** Frank J. Hogan, George P. Hoover, Wilton J. Lambert, William E. Leahy, Martin W. Littleton, R.W. Ragland, G.T. Stanford, and Mark B. Thompson **Chief Prosecutors:** Neil Burkinshaw, Peyton C. Gordon, Atlee W. Pomerene, Owen J. Roberts, and Leo A. Rover **Judges:** Jennings Bailey, William Hitz, Adolph A. Hoehling, and Frederick L. Siddons **Place:** Washington, D.C. **Dates of Trials:** November 22–December 16, 1926; March 3, 1927; December 5, 1927–February 21, 1928; April 16–21, 1928; May 31–June 14, 1928; November 12–20, 1928; October 7–25, 1929; March 12–22, 1930 **Verdicts:** 1: Not guilty; 2: Guilty; 3: Guilty; 4: Not guilty; 5: Not guilty; 6: Not guilty; 7: Guilty; 8: Not guilty **Sentences:** Three months imprisonment and $500 fine: trial 2; Sinclair, six months, Day, four months, Sherman Burns, $1,000, William Burns, 15 days: trial 3; One year and $100,000: trial 7

SIGNIFICANCE

Teapot Dome in the "roaring twenties" was the largest scandal in the U.S. government since the administration of President Ulysses S. Grant. It became a permanent symbol of corruption in government. It marked the first time in U.S. history that an officer in a president's cabinet was convicted of a felony and served a prison sentence.

Oil for the U.S. Navy mixed with the greed of men in power to produce the Teapot Dome trials. American naval ships had been converted from coal to oil power before World War I. In 1909, President William Howard Taft had reserved public lands containing oil as Naval Petroleum Reserves in case of war. One such area, in Wyoming, was called Teapot Dome.

Civilian use of oil was expanding rapidly. Throughout President Woodrow Wilson's Democratic administration (1913–20), freshly made multimillionaire oil barons tried unsuccessfully to obtain leases from the government to drill the naval reserves, arguing that valuable oil was draining into private fields nearby. Finally, in 1920, Congress gave the Navy secretary broad powers to lease naval reserves, selling oil or exchanging it for supplies or construction the Navy needed.

Shortly, Republican candidate Warren G. Harding was elected president. Assembling his cabinet, Harding appointed his friend Albert Bacon Fall, with whom he had served in the U.S. Senate, as secretary of the interior.

Fall Owed Eight Years' Back Taxes

Fall had been elected as New Mexico's first senator when that state entered the Union in 1912. Born in 1861, he was a self-educated lawyer who had worked as a cowboy and prospector and, with drooping handlebar moustache and constant cigar, looked the part. He even toted a gun in the Senate. But now he owed eight years' taxes on his rundown ranch at Three Rivers, New Mexico, and had recently sold his major interest in the *Albuquerque Journal* to raise cash. Nearly broke, he was ready to quit the Senate. He took the cabinet post without hesitation.

The word "conservation" was not in Fall's vocabulary. He believed the government's lands—particularly the Naval Petroleum Reserves—should be held by private interests. He revised an executive order giving the Navy control over the reserves so that leasing did not require the approval of the Navy secretary. Next he recommended that the Navy take any royalties on oil sold from leased reserves not in cash but in oil certificates, which could be used to pay for construction done for the Navy.

By early 1922, Fall, playing on fear of drainage of the oil fields, was urging the Navy to develop Teapot Dome, build a pipeline to storage tanks on the Atlantic coast, and build storage tanks at Pearl Harbor in the Pacific. As Pacific builder, he proposed oilman Edward L. Doheny, who had prospected with him in 1886, leased profitable oil lands in California (Doheny brought in the first gusher in Los Angeles), and was currently worth $100 million.

Meantime, Harry F. Sinclair, head of the Sinclair Consolidated Oil Corporation, who had oil holdings worth $380 million, invited himself to visit Fall at his ranch. They talked about Sinclair's Mammoth Oil Company (he owned all the stock) obtaining a lease on the entire 9,481-acre Teapot Dome naval reserve.

In Washington, without competitive bidding, Fall signed the lease and locked it in his desk drawer. It gave Mammoth Oil exclusive rights to Teapot Dome oil for 20 years, with the government getting a royalty of 16 to 17 percent of the price per barrel, paid in oil certificates, which were to be used to buy fuel oil and storage tanks from Mammoth.

Word of the contract leaked. Neighbors observed sudden prosperity at Fall's ranch: A race horse and fine cattle arrived; Fall paid $100,000 to buy the ranch next-door and built a $35,000 hydroelectric plant; he also paid taxes owed since 1912.

"Sluice-way for Ninety Percent of the Corruption"

The *Albuquerque Journal* began an expose in February 1922. By April, its publisher was forced to sell the *Journal* to a bank controlled by a Harding crony. Soon Senator Robert M. La Follette of Wisconsin, saying Fall's Interior Department was "the sluice-way for ninety percent of the corruption in government," demanded an investigation. Fall resigned.

Senate Public Lands Committee, which investigated the activities of the Secretary of the Interior, Albert Fall. (Courtesy, Library of Congress)

The Senate started hearings in October 1923, soon after President Harding's sudden death. Edward Doheny testified that Fall had not profited by his Navy contracts. But he had "loaned" Fall $100,000. To show for it, however, he could produce only a note from which the signature had been torn. Secretary of the Navy Edwin Denby admitted that the contract with Mammoth Oil was his responsibility and that, having had no part in its preparation, he had not sought the competitive bids required by law. Harry Sinclair, on the stand, stonewalled so the Senate learned nothing more.

"Everything Points to Sinclair"

Called before the committee, Fall relied on the Fifth Amendment's right to not incriminate himself. President Calvin Coolidge appointed Republican Owen J. Roberts and Democrat Atlee W. Pomerene as special counsel to prosecute the oil cases. "Everything about Fall's sudden wealth points to Sinclair as the source," said Roberts.

Investigation disclosed that Fall, who had earned $12,000 a year in the Senate, had recently spent $140,000 improving his ranch and that $230,500 in Liberty Bonds deposited in his accounts bore the serial numbers of bonds distributed earlier to Sinclair and to Colonel Robert W. Stewart, chairman of the Standard Oil Company of Indiana. Indictments followed.

In 1924, Roberts brought civil suits to cancel the government's leasing contracts with Doheny and Sinclair because they were obtained fraudulently. He won against Doheny, then lost against Sinclair but won on appeal as three U.S. Circuit Court of Appeals judges agreed that:

> A trail of deceit, falsehood, subterfuge, bad faith, and corruption, at times indistinct but nevertheless discernible, runs through the transaction incident to and surrounding the making of this lease.

With the contracts proved fraudulent, Roberts tried Fall and Doheny in November 1926 for criminal conspiracy to defraud the government. Defense lawyer Frank J. Hogan dramatically compared his clients' situation to the Crucifixion and invoked the ghost of President Harding "from his sacred tomb in Marion [Ohio]" as a character witness. Debating all night, the jury acquitted both men.

In March 1927, a one-day trial found Sinclair guilty of contempt of the Senate for refusing to answer committee questions. He was sentenced to three months in jail.

Now Fall and Sinclair were tried for conspiracy to defraud the government with the Teapot Dome lease. Sinclair brazenly put 12 William J. Burns detectives to work shadowing the 12 jurors, one of whom boasted that he expected to make $150,000 to $200,000 for deadlocking the case. Judge Frederick L. Siddons declared a mistrial, then put Sinclair, his export official, Henry Mason Day, and two Burnses (father and son) on trial for criminal contempt. All were found guilty. Sinclair's six-month sentence was the stiffest.

At the fourth trial—Fall and Sinclair for conspiracy to defraud the government—in April 1928, Fall was excused, as his doctors reported him dying. Sinclair admitted giving Liberty Bonds and cash to Fall. The jury confounded the prosecution by acquitting the oil baron.

Trial five, in May, charged Colonel Robert W. Stewart with contempt of the Senate. He had told its committee he did not know where the Liberty Bonds had come from and had not profited from the deal when he helped pass them on to Fall. But he had changed his story when he made a second committee appearance, recounting the bonds' history and revealing his share in the profits. The jury said, "Not guilty."

That trial produced trial six, charging Stewart with perjury as a result of his changed story in his second Senate testimony. The jury acquitted him. Meantime, in June 1929, the U.S. Supreme Court upheld Sinclair's conviction for jury tampering, sending him to prison.

October 1929 brought Fall to trial for accepting a bribe from Doheny. In a wheelchair, frail and gasping, he heard his defense lawyer, Frank Hogan, tell the judge he should be vindicated "before he passes into the Great Beyond." The jury said, "guilty," but recommended mercy. Judge William Hitz sentenced him to one year in jail and a $100,000 fine.

When Judge Hitz held Doheny's trial in March 1930 for giving Fall the bribe, a different jury heard the same basic evidence. But Hogan dramatized Doheny's patriotism in building Navy tanks and the elderly Fall's innocent backing of a longtime friend. The jury said, "Not guilty."

Fall appealed for a year. The District of Columbia Court of Appeals upheld his bribery conviction. The U.S. Supreme Court refused to hear the case. President Herbert Hoover turned down several petitions for a pardon. On July 18, 1931, Fall went by ambulance to prison in Santa Fe, New Mexico—the first cabinet officer ever convicted of a felony and imprisoned. Parole was denied in November, but he was released in May 1932. His $100,000 fine—unpaid—remained as a judgment against him (in case he acquired the money) until he "passed into the Great Beyond" 12 years later at age 83.

As a result of cancellation of the Teapot Dome lease, the Navy recovered more than $12 million from Sinclair. The Doheny cancellation brought back nearly $35 million. The Naval Petroleum Reserves were utilized extensively in World War II and have continued to generate money, through limited exploitation, for the government.

Edward Doheny died at 79 in 1935, Harry Sinclair at age 80 in 1956. Owen J. Roberts, who persisted in the Teapot Dome prosecutions through 6½ years (much of that time without remuneration), was appointed a justice of the U.S. Supreme Court by President Hoover in 1930 and retired in 1945 after a distinguished career. He died at the age of 80 in 1955.

—*Bernard Ryan, Jr.*

Suggestions for Further Reading

Daniels, Jonathan. *The Time Between the Wars: Armistice to Pearl Harbor.* Garden City N.Y.: Doubleday & Co., 1966.

Henry, Laurin L. *Presidential Transitions.* Washington: Brookings Institution, 1960.

Morrison, Samuel Eliot. *The Oxford History of the American People.* New York: Oxford University Press, 1965.

Russell, Francis. *The Shadow of Blooming Grove: Warren G. Harding in His Times.* New York: McGraw-Hill Book Co., 1968.

Werner, M.R., and John Starr. *Teapot Dome.* New York: Viking Press, 1959.

Wish, Harvey. *Contemporary America: The National Scene Since 1900.* New York: Harper & Brothers, 1945.

Ruth Snyder–Judd Gray Trial: 1927

Defendants: Ruth Snyder and Judd Gray **Crime Charged:** Murder
Chief Defense Lawyers: For Ruth Snyder: Edgar F. Hazleton and Dana Wallace; For Judd Gray: Samuel L. Miller and William J. Millard
Chief Prosecutor: Richard E. Newcombe **Judge:** Townsend Scudder
Place: Long Island City, Queens, New York **Dates of Trial:** April 27–May 9, 1927 **Verdict:** Guilty **Sentence:** Death by electrocution

SIGNIFICANCE

In a macabre way, the verdict and sentence in Ruth Snyder's case was a milestone in progress toward equality of the sexes. As a *New York Times* editorial summed it up after Governor Al Smith denied clemency to Ruth Snyder: "Equal suffrage has put women in a new position. If they are equal with men before the law, they must pay the same penalties as men for transgressing it." It was also significant that the two defendants, each of whom had confessed and tried to shift the burden of guilt to the other, were tried together, so that each was cross-examined by the other as well as by the State—a procedure labeled "novel and dangerous" by Ruth Snyder's attorney.

Nine-year-old Lorraine Snyder slept late on Sunday morning, March 20, 1927. She had gone to bed at 1:45 A.M. when she came home with her parents from a bridge party. Long after her usual 7:30 rising time, she was awakened by her mother, whom she found lying on the floor, her feet tied together, and her wrists tied. Her mother said burglars had knocked her out and tied her up, leaving her in the next room. After coming to, she had wriggled into Lorraine's room. Lorraine's father was dead.

The police found Albert Snyder in bed, smelling of chloroform. His head was bludgeoned, and picture wire was tied around his neck. The house had been ransacked. Bureau drawers were empty, their contents strewn everywhere. And Ruth Snyder claimed jewelry was missing. The house had already been robbed three times in the past year.

"It Don't Look Right"

Within two hours, New York City's best detectives were on the job in the Snyders' fashionable home, which 44-year-old Albert Snyder, art director of

Motor Boating magazine, had bought in the Queens suburb for his 32-year-old wife. The cops exhausted Ruth Snyder, questioning her through the day and into the night. When they told her the burglary was a fake, she indignantly replied, "What do you mean? How can you tell?"

"It don't look right," said a detective. "We see lots of burglaries. They aren't done this way."

The police explained. Mrs. Snyder said she had been hit on the head by "a tall man with a dark mustache" and knocked out for five hours, but she had no bruise or bump. Her wrists and ankles had been tied so loosely they bore no marks. Neither doors nor windows had been forced, so any intruder must have been let in. The missing jewelry had been found, under a mattress. Albert Snyder's revolver had been found on his bed, broken open at the breach but not discharged—a clumsy effort, the detectives said, to make it look as if he had resisted. And in the basement they had found a sash weight that was evidently the murder weapon.

"What About Judd Gray?"

The police did not disclose to Ruth Snyder the fact that they had found a small pin with the initials "J.G." on the bedroom floor. In Ruth Snyder's address book was an entry under "G" for the name Judd Gray. The investigators questioned her: "What about Judd Gray?"

Surprised, Ruth Snyder asked, "Has he confessed?" Bluffing, the police replied that he had, prompting Ruth Snyder's confession. For a year and a half, she and Gray had been lovers. Gray, she said, wanted her husband dead. Gray had hidden in the house while they were at the bridge party, then emerged from a closet to bludgeon Albert Snyder after he had fallen asleep. Ruth admitted she had helped to make the arrangements and ransack the house, but she said Gray had wielded the sash weight. The police later found Gray in the Syracuse, New York hotel she named.

When the Syracuse police arrested him, Gray first laughed at the accusation. "Ridiculous," he said. He had ample proof that he had been in Syracuse on Saturday night. But when he realized that Ruth Snyder had confessed, he admitted taking part in the crime. He said, however, that *he* had not wanted to kill Albert Snyder. Gray claimed he had been coerced by his lover, who threatened to tell Gray's wife about their affair.

By Tuesday, the front pages boasted pictures of Gray and Ruth Snyder, along with the full text of both their confessions. But while both had confessed, each said the other had proposed the murder. Queens District Attorney Richard Newcombe therefore obtained their indictment together as co-conspirators.

While Lorraine was in the Elevators

The testimony—and the newspapers that eagerly reported it—brought out the inherent drama of a situation that had culminated in a crime: The older, gloomy, ill-tempered and dull husband whose idea of fun was staying home and making artistic doodads; the lively, young, party-loving, suburban housewife dutifully sewing slipcovers for the furniture and dresses for little Lorraine; the Mr.-Nice-Guy friend, a Sunday-school teacher, family man, traveling salesman for a corset-and-bra manufacturer, and member of the Orange, New Jersey, Lodge of Elks, who took an interest in Ruth and became her lover; the bribed postmen; the coded letters; the afternoon lovers' trysts at the Waldorf-Astoria, while little Lorraine was dispatched to the fun of riding up and down with the elevator operators. It all added up to the inevitable need, said prosecutor Newcombe, to get rid of Albert Snyder so Ruth Snyder and Gray could be together. But Ruth Snyder's motive was twofold: unbeknown to her husband, she had recently increased his life insurance to $100,000 and she was quietly paying the premiums.

Ruth Snyder and Judd Gray confessed to murdering Snyder's husband and proceeded to shift the blame onto each other during this notorious trial. (AP/Wide World Photos)

Then, too, testimony brought out that Ruth Snyder had tried twice to asphyxiate her husband by disconnecting the gas range, had nearly succeeded in killing him with carbon monoxide by closing the garage door while the car was running inside, had poisoned his whiskey so ineptly that he dumped it out and said he must change bootleggers, and had added narcotics to his medicine when he was ill—all without Albert Snyder suspecting her.

An ironic footnote to the case was that the "J.G." pin had been a keepsake of Albert Snyder's from his long-ago engagement to one Jessie Guischard, who died before they could be married.

Judge Townsend Scudder said a jury's task, amid the conflicting stories of the confessors, was to decide who had done what. The judge reminded the jury that Gray testified Ruth Snyder "arranged the joint plan and jointly participated in the actual killing," while she testified that "Gray was determined to take the life of Albert Snyder and that she endeavored to prevent him from so doing and that she was not present at the time Gray struck the blows . . . and she testified she believed she had dissuaded the defendant Gray from his alleged evil purpose. . . ."

"Her Fault is that she has No Heart"

If the jury had much to ponder, so did the public. The tabloids were filled with colorful analyses of the characters of the defendants. The *Mirror* hired a well-known phrenologist (one who studies the conformation of the skull based on the belief that it is indicative of mental faculties and character) to study photos of Ruth Snyder. His conclusion: Her mouth was "as cold, hard, and unsympathetic as a crack in a dried lemon." Natacha Rambova, a reporter best known as Rudolph Valentino's widow, wrote, "There is lacking in her character that real thing, selflessness. She apparently doesn't possess it and never will. Her fault is that she has no heart."

In one hour and 40 minutes, the jury decided to accept Gray's version: He had struck the first blow with the sash weight, Albert Snyder had groaned and turned, and Ruth Snyder had finished him off with blows of her own, after which they together applied the strangling wire and added chloroform-soaked cotton for good measure. Both were found guilty and sentenced to death in the electric chair at Sing Sing prison.

Appeals were filed. One sought a stay of execution on the grounds that Ruth Snyder was a necessary witness in a civil suit to force three insurance companies to pay the benefits of Albert Snyder's life insurance to his daughter Lorraine. Another appeal sought a writ of *habeas corpus* (release from unlawful confinement) for Gray on the grounds that his constitutional rights had been violated by the joint trial rather than a trial of his own. Both appeals were dismissed.

Ruth Snyder went to the electric chair at 11:00 P.M. January 12, 1928. She was the eighth woman put to death for murder in New York State. As the power surged through her body, a *Daily News* photographer in the reporters' pool crossed his legs, thus triggering a forbidden concealed camera to take an unprecedented picture. When Judd Gray was executed six minutes later, no one took a snapshot.

—*Bernard Ryan, Jr.*

Suggestions for Further Reading

Jones, Ann. "She Had to Die." *American Heritage*, (October/November 1980): 20–31.

Sann, Paul. *The Lawless Decade*. New York: Crown Publishers, 1957.

Sifakis, Carl. *The Encyclopedia of American Crime*. New York: Facts On File, 1982.

Buck v. Bell: 1927

Plaintiff: Carrie Buck **Defendant:** Dr. J.H. Bell **Appellant's Claim:** That Virginia's eugenic sterilization law violated Carrie Buck's constitutional rights
Chief Defense Lawyer: Aubrey E. Strode
Chief Lawyer for Appellant: Irving Whitehead **Justices:** Louis D. Brandeis, Pierce Butler, Willis Van Devanter, Oliver Wendell Holmes, James C. McReynolds, Edward T. Sanford, Harlan F. Stone, George Sutherland and William N. Taft **Place:** Washington, D.C. **Date of Decision:** May 2, 1927
Decision: Upheld as constitutional Virginia's compulsory sterilization of young women considered "unfit [to] continue their kind"

SIGNIFICANCE

Virginia's law served as a model for similar laws in 30 states, under which 50,000 U.S. citizens were sterilized without their consent. During the Nuremberg war trials, Nazi lawyers cited *Buck v. Bell* as acceptable precedent for the sterilization of 2 million people in its "Rassenhygiene" (race hygiene) program.

The Supreme Court's decision in *Buck v. Bell* resulted in only one letter of sympathy to the soon-to-be sterilized Carrie Buck and surprisingly little newspaper coverage. Oliver Wendell Holmes, who wrote the decision, had no second thoughts. As he wrote in a letter later that month, "One decision . . . gave me pleasure, establishing the constitutionality of a law permitting the sterilization of imbeciles." The decision had far-reaching and disastrous consequences, however, not only for Carrie Buck—who was not "feebleminded" or retarded—but for many other similarly sterilized individuals and the peoples involved in World War II.

Emma Buck was the widowed mother of three small children, whom she supported through prostitution and with the help of charity until they were removed from her. On April 1, 1920, she was brought before Charlottesville, Virginia Justice of the Peace Charles D. Shackleford; after a cursory interview, Shackleford committed Emma Buck to the Virginia Colony for Epileptics and Feebleminded, in Lynchburg, Virginia.

At the age of three, Emma Buck's daughter Carrie had joined the family of J.T. and Alice Dobbs. Her school records indicate a normal progression through five years, until she was withdrawn from school by the Dobbs so that she could assume more of the family's housework. The Dobbs were completely satisfied until Carrie turned 17. Then, during what Carrie claimed was a rape by the Dobbs' son, she became pregnant.

The Dobbs brought Carrie before Shackleford and asked him to commit her to the Colony for the Epileptic and Feebleminded, as he had her mother. The Dobbs and their family doctor testified that Carrie was feebleminded; a second doctor agreed. That same day, January 24, 1924, Shackleford signed the order committing the second member of the Buck family to the state colony. The Dobbs institutionalized Carrie as soon as her daughter Vivian was born; they then raised the infant as their own.

Carrie Buck Eagle and her husband, William Eagle. (Courtesy, Mrs. A.T. Newberry, Bland, Virginia)

Virginia Approaches its Courts with a "Solution"

Dr. Albert Priddy, the first superintendent of the colony, advocated eugenics—the controlled mating of humans to "improve" the species—as society's best response to the presence of those he called "mental defectives." In the seven years prior to Carrie Buck's arrival, he had sterilized 75 to 100 young women without their consent, claiming that he had operated to cure "pelvic disease." In 1924 the Virginia Assembly adopted a bill permitting the forced sterilization of "feebleminded" or "socially inadequate person[s]." It had been prepared by Aubrey Strode, a state legislator and chief administrator of the Colony for the Epileptic and Feebleminded. Strode had worked from a model sterilization act drafted by American eugenicist Harry H. Laughlin, who considered compulsory sterilization to be "the practical application of those fundamental biological and social principles which determine the racial endowments and the racial health—physical, mental, and spiritual—of future generations."

Carrie Buck as a Test Case

On November 19, 1924, *Buck v. Priddy* was argued before Judge Bennett Gordon in the Circuit Court of Amherst County. Aubrey Strode represented

Dr. Priddy, who had come to have Buck declared feebleminded and suitable for compulsory sterilization. Irving Whitehead, a lifelong friend to Strode and one of the first board members of the colony, represented Buck in a manner that seems to have been halfhearted. Whitehead's fee was paid by the colony.

Anne Harris, a Charlottesville district nurse, was the first witness. She testified that "Emma Buck, Carrie Buck's mother . . . was living in the worst neighborhoods, and that she was not able to, or would not, work and support her children, and that they were on the streets more or less."

Strode asked, "What about the character of her offspring?"

Harris replied, "Well, I don't know anything very definite about the children, except they don't seem to be able to do any more than their mother."

Strode pounced. "Well, that is the crux of the matter. Are they mentally normal children?"

And Harris responded, "No, sir, they are not."

Harris then admitted during Whitehead's cross examination: "I really know very little about Carrie after she left her mother [at age 3]. Before that time she was most too small."

Three teachers testified about Carrie's sister, brother, and cousin, using descriptions such as "dull in her books." There was additional testimony about several of Carrie's other relatives, one of whom was described as "right peculiar." The testimony did not relate to Carrie herself until Caroline Wilhelm—a Red Cross social worker contacted by the Dobbs family during Carrie's pregnancy, took the stand.

Strode asked Wilhelm, "From your experience as a social worker, if Carrie were discharged from the Colony still capable of child-bearing, is she likely to become the parent of deficient offspring?"

Wilhelm replied, "I should judge so. I think a girl of her mentality is more or less at the mercy of other people. . . . Her mother had three illegitimate children, and I should say that Carrie would be very likely to have illegitimate children."

Strode concluded, "So that the only way that she could likely be kept from increasing her own kind would be by either segregation or something that would stop her power to propagate."

Wilhelm next testified about Carrie's daughter, Vivian "It seems difficult to judge probabilities of child as young as that [eight months], but it seems to me not quite a normal baby."

Whitehead, on cross-examination, raised what should have been a pivotal point: "[T]he question of pregnancy is not evidence of feeblemindedness, is it? The fact that, as we say, she made a miss-step [*sic*]—went wrong—is that evidence of feeblemindedness?"

Wilhelm replied, "No, but a feebleminded girl is much more likely to go wrong."

Arthur Estabrook of the Carnegie Institute of Washington testified, discussing his 14 years of genetic research and his studies of "groups of mental defectives." Of his conclusions in *The Jukes in 1915*, a study of one family over four years, he said, "The result of the study was to show that certain definite laws of heredity were being shown by the family, in that the feeblemindedness was being inherited . . . and . . . was the basis of the antisocial conduct, showing up in the criminality and the pauperism."

Spode asked, "From what you know of Carrie Buck, would you say that by the laws of heredity she is a feebleminded person and the probably potential parent of socially inadequate offspring likewise afflicted?"

And Estabrook replied, "I would."

Dr. Priddy testified last. Carrie Buck, he said, "would cease to be a charge on society if sterilized. It would remove one potential source of the incalculable number of descendants who would be feebleminded. She would contribute to the raising of the general mental average and standard [by not reproducing]."

And, finally, Harry H. Laughlin's deposition was read into the court record. Dr. Priddy had written Laughlin, describing Carrie and asking for Laughlin's help in enforcing the sterilization law against her. The information contained in Dr. Priddy's own letter forms the basis of Laughlin's sworn testimony: Carrie, he wrote, has "a mental age of nine years, . . . a record during her life of immorality, prostitution, and untruthfulness; has never been self-sustaining; has one illegitimate child, now about six months old and supposed to be mentally defective. . . . She is . . . a potential parent of socially inadequate or defective offspring." There is no evidence that Carrie Buck was examined by Laughlin.

In February 1925, Judge Gordon upheld the Virginia sterilization law and ordered the sterilization of Carrie Buck. Irving Whitehead appealed to the Virginia Court of Appeals. (The case was now *Buck v. Bell* because Dr. Priddy had died a few weeks earlier and Dr. J.H. Bell had taken his place at the colony.) The appeals court decision upheld the circuit court decision.

Supreme Court Reviews Case

In the brief he submitted to the Supreme Court, Whitehead claimed Fourteenth Amendment protection of a person's "full bodily integrity." He also predicated the "worst kind of tyranny" if there were no "limits of the power of the state (which, in the end, is nothing more than the faction in control of the government) to rid itself of those citizens deemed undesirable." Strode, in contrast, likened compulsory sterilization to compulsory vaccination.

Justice Oliver Wendell Holmes delivered the nearly unanimous opinion on May 2, 1927:

> We have seen more than once that the public welfare may call upon the best citizens for their lives. It would be strange if it could not call upon those who already sap the strength of the state for these such lesser sacrifices, often not felt to be much by those concerned, in order to prevent our being swamped with incompetence. It is better for all the world, if instead of waiting to

> execute offspring for crime, or to let them starve for their imbecility, society can prevent those who are manifestly unfit from continuing their kind. The principle that sustains compulsory vaccination is broad enough to cover cutting the Fallopian tubes.

Only Justice Pierce Butler dissented. Carrie Buck was sterilized by Dr. Bell on October 19, 1927. Shortly thereafter, she was paroled from the Virginia colony. She married twice: William Davis Eagle in 1932 and, after his death, Charlie Detamore. The letters she wrote to the Virginia colony seeking custody of her mother, as well as the recollections of her own minister, neighbors and health care providers, belie the notion that Carrie Buck was "feebleminded" or retarded.

Other Applications Result from *Buck v. Bell*

Laws similar to the Virginia statutes were passed in 30 other states, leading to the forcible sterilization of more than 50,000 people, including Carrie Buck's sister Doris.

Harry L. Laughlin, author of the model sterilization act adapted by Aubrey Strode for Virginia, made his draft available to state and foreign governments, and his model became Germany's Hereditary Health Law in 1933. In appreciation, he was awarded an honorary degree from Heidelberg University in 1936. After World War II, defending the forcible sterilization of 2 million people, lawyers for Nazi war criminals cited this law and pointed out that the U.S. Supreme Court, in *Buck v. Bell,* had declared such laws constitutional.

Buck v. Bell has yet to be reversed by the Supreme Court. In 1973, *Roe v. Wade* guaranteed women the right to make their own decisions concerning abortion during the first two trimesters of pregnancy. The decision, written by Justice Harry Blackmun, balances the interests of the state and the woman and finds in favor of the woman's right of privacy. Nonetheless, citing *Buck v. Bell,* Justice Blackmun specifically denies "the claim . . . that one has an unlimited right to do with one's body as one pleases."

—*Kathryn Cullen-DuPont*

Suggestions for Further Reading

Cushman, Robert F. *Cases in Constitutional Law,* 6th ed. Englewood Cliffs, N.J.: Prentice Hall, 1984.

Smith, J. David and K. Ray Nelson. *The Sterilization of Carrie Buck: Was She Feebleminded or Society's Pawn.* Far Hills, N.J.: New Horizon Press, 1989.

Henry Colin Campbell Trial: 1929

Defendant: Henry Colin Campbell **Crime Charged:** Murder
Chief Defense Lawyer: Francis A. Gordon **Chief Prosecutor:** Abe J. David
Judge: Clarence E. Case **Place:** Elizabeth, New Jersey
Date of Trial: June 9–13, 1929 **Verdict:** Guilty **Sentence:** Death

SIGNIFICANCE

A curious case in which claims of amnesia were used by a killer to demonstrate his mental instability and hopefully keep him off death row.

When the charred remains of a woman—her skull blasted by a bullet—were found beside a highway in Cranford, New Jersey, on February 23, 1929, the crime left local police baffled. For six weeks they struggled to identify the victim, until a routine circular came back from Greenville, Pennsylvania, saying that the corpse sounded very much like a local woman, Mildred Mowry, who had been missing since early February. Investigation revealed some bizarre recent developments in the life of the middle-aged widow. In August 1928, she had apparently married a 60-year-old doctor named Richard Campbell, whom she had met through a matrimonial agency. Just one day after the ceremony, Campbell had convinced Mildred to deposit her life savings of $1,000 in his bank account; then, claiming pressure of work, he took off for California.

Mildred labored to keep in touch by mail, but as the silences between letters grew longer, concern overwhelmed discretion and she set out to track down her errant husband.

And then she disappeared.

Far from being on the West Coast, Campbell had moved no farther than Elizabeth, New Jersey. He was living under his real name of Henry Colin Campbell, with his genuine wife and family, when police came knocking on his door on April 11, 1929, with an arrest warrant for murder. Campbell's claims to be a doctor were as spurious as the marriage he had entered into with Mildred Mowry, and it soon became apparent to the police that not only had they trapped a career criminal, but possibly a serial killer, as well.

Fit to Plead

When the case against Campbell came to court June 9, 1929, the first day was given over to evidence from two alienists, or psychologists, Drs. Gus Payne and Lawrence Collins, both of whom declared that the defendant, although clearly affected by his morphine addiction, was legally fit to stand trial.

This went to the heart of the trial: for at no point did Campbell attempt to deny that he had first shot and then burnt Mildred—the murder weapon, a .38 automatic, was recovered from his home—only that he had no recollection of having done so. Prosecutor Abe J. David ridiculed this as nonsense and read aloud a confession made by Campbell shortly after his arrest, in which he admitted killing Mildred to conceal his bigamous marriage. David also offered into evidence 17 letters written by Campbell to the murdered woman. Together, they formed a heartless catalog of deception and manipulation, a clear blueprint of the way in which Campbell traded on Mildred's loneliness and vulnerability to line his own pockets. And, said David, when the hapless Mildred eventually ran Campbell to ground and confronted him about the situation, he had shot her.

Henry Colin Campbell, at his trial for murdering his bigamous wife. (AP/Wide World Photos)

Guided by defense counsel Francis A. Gordon, Rosalie Campbell, the defendant's genuine wife, fought hard to save her beleaguered husband. In moving terms she described his downward spiral, telling how life had been "wonderful always" at first, but after moving from Chicago to Maryland, "he began to fall. He had headaches and began to lose weight. Then he started taking something for his headaches . . . He took the medicine not very frequently at first, then more frequently."

During the few months prior to the murder, she said, Campbell's nervousness and irritability appeared to be building toward a peak, and for no apparent reason he had begun carrying a gun.

When Campbell took the stand he looked like a man at the end of his tether. Small and shrunken, with yellow skin and straggly white hair, he trembled visibly behind rimless glasses as Gordon led him through his testimony. After repudiating the confession as a police fabrication, he claimed he had visited Mildred on February 21 in order to return the money she had lent him. First, though, he needed to raise funds, and this meant driving Mildred to several banks, none of which would help him. In between stops, he said, he told Mildred of his secret life. She told him that she did not want him to leave his wife and children. Campbell maintained that throughout the journey he kept dosing himself with drugs to "keep my nerve from going to pieces." Then, he said, everything went blank.

"Do you have any recollection of shooting Mrs. Mowry and burning her body?" asked Gordon.

"No, I don't remember doing so."

Scathing Prosecution Attack

Prosecutor David wasn't convinced. As the precursor to a blistering cross-examination, he thrust two application forms for "friendship clubs" in front of the witness. Campbell cringed when he saw them. He had filled them out before meeting Mildred, and in one, under the heading "Disposition," he had answered, "The best ever if well treated," and on both he had described his health as "good." Hardly, sneered David, the responses of a man who was seriously ill. And what about his listed preference—"Widows with no children"—evidence, surely, of someone with an ulterior motive?

Campbell lowered his head and said nothing, utterly defeated.

In closing, David went over Campbell's original confession point by point, saying how it matched in every detail the known circumstances of the crime, and he implored the jury to set aside both sympathy and any scruples they might have against capital punishment. Campbell was a thrice-married rogue, he said, with a string of convictions for fraud and forgery that had led to numerous jail terms. In his opinion, the accused man's wife and three children would be "better off without him."

Justice Clarence E. Case, in his final charge to the jury, went to the question of insanity by saying:

> If the defendant was conscious of the nature of his act he cannot be acquitted. The law does not recognize that form of insanity in which the faculties are so affected as to render a person suffering from it unable to control those urges . . . In medicine a man who steals and cannot control his stealing is called a kleptomaniac, in law he is regarded as a thief and punishable as such. If the accused sets up a defense of insanity the burden of proof lies with him; he must overcome the legal presumption of his sanity.

On June 13, 1929, the jury found Campbell guilty of first degree murder, with no recommendation for mercy, and he was sentenced to death.

In all probability Mildred Mowry was not Campbell's first victim. Just one year earlier, a New York governess named Margaret Brown had suddenly left her job to marry a mysterious "doctor" she had met through a matrimonial agency, taking with her $7,000 in savings. Her body, also shot and burned, was found just 15 miles away from the spot where Mildred Mowry met her death. While the similarities were marked, it proved impossible to fix the blame for that murder on Campbell. Not that it mattered. On April 17, 1930, the philandering "doctor" went on his final date—with the electric chair.

—*Colin Evans*

Suggestions for Further Reading

Crimes and Punishment. Vol. 4. Paulton, England: BPC Publishing, 1974.

New York Times. See Mowry, Mildred, in the *New York Times Index*, April 10–June 19, 1929.

Wilson, Colin and Pitman, Patricia. *Encyclopedia of Murder.* New York: G. B. Putnam's Sons, 1961.

Alexander Pantages Trials: 1929

Defendant: Alexander Pantages **Crime Charged:** Rape
Chief Defense Lawyers: Earl M. Daniels, W. J. Ford, Jerry Giiesler, and W. I. Gilbert **Chief Prosecutors:** Burton Fitts, and Robert P. Stewart
Judge: Charles Fricke **Place:** Los Angeles, California
Dates of Trials: First: October 4–27, 1929; Second: November 3–27, 1931
Verdict: First trial: Guilty; Second trial: Not guilty **Sentence:** First trial: 50 years imprisonment

SIGNIFICANCE

The Alexander Pantages case marked a turning point in California law as the state's Supreme Court ruled on appeal that, where rape was alleged, if the girl was under 18, evidence of her previous sexual activity was admissible to discredit her testimony that she had been criminally attacked. The case also established a national reputation for defense attorney Jerry Giesler, who went on to handle many Hollywood cases.

By 1929, 54-year-old Alexander Pantages, a Greek immigrant who had never learned to read or write any language, had put together a chain of 60 vaudeville-and-movie palaces across the western half of the United States. Those in the know thought him worth $30 million.

On August 9, 17-year-old Eunice Irene Pringle, a well-trained dancer hoping to book her act on the Pantages circuit, appeared at Pantages' Los Angeles, California office, insisting, despite several previous turn-downs, on an interview with "Alexander the Great," as he was known in Hollywood. Reluctantly, he agreed and showed her into his private office on the mezzanine level of his theater.

Shortly, matinee moviegoers saw Eunice Pringle, her clothing disarranged, running into the street, screaming that she had been raped. Within days, a preliminary hearing produced an indictment and the press made Pantages the nation's best-known "wealthy old goat" in a sordid scandal.

Pantages' defense was that the young woman had thrown herself at him like a tigress, tearing at his shirt, suspenders, and trousers, and screaming at him. It had taken all his strength to push the athletic young dancer from his office.

As the trial began, Hollywood law partners W.J. Ford and W.I. Gilbert asked bright junior attorney Jerry Giesler to cross-examine. He led Pringle back and forth through her story several times. Then he asked, "Did your studies in dramatic school include a course in memory training?"

"Yes."

"Were you taught to express your emotions dramatically?"

"Yes."

Giesler's thought, he said later, was that although Miss Pringle had told her pitiful tale several times to the press and to the law, she had scarcely varied a comma each time. . . . "I pointed out that her story seemed rehearsed as only a girl who was studying acting would have rehearsed it."

Schoolgirl versus "Slinky"

Next, Giesler asked Pantages' accuser, "Is that the dress you were wearing the day you say you were attacked?"

"No."

Eunice Pringle was dressed like a 13-year-old schoolgirl: blue dress, Dutch collar and cuffs, black stockings and Mary Jane shoes, small black bag and black gloves, long hair down her back and tied with a bow.

Giesler asked Judge Charles Fricke to order her to dress the next day in the same outfit and makeup she had worn to the Pantages Theatre. The jurors then saw not a schoolgirl but a well-endowed young woman in a revealing and (to use Giesler's word) "slinky" scarlet dress. Now his cross-examination tried to explore earlier acts of unchastity on her part—including a live-in affair with 40-year-old Nick Dunave, a Russian dancer. But the judge sustained the prosecution's objections and cut off the line of questioning.

The jury found "The Great God Pan" guilty. His sentence: 50 years in state prison. On appeal to the California Supreme Court, Giesler filed a three-volume, 1,200-page brief citing hundreds of cases and authorities. It pointed out that the lower court had erred in not permitting testimony on the earlier immoral conduct of the complaining witness. "There were so many new elements in that brief," Giesler later said, "that the final decision established precedent throughout the nation."

The state supreme court granted Pantages a new trial. Admitting evidence of Eunice Pringle's private life and conduct, it marked the first time in which the defense could probe the morals of an underage girl who claimed that she was criminally attacked.

Giesler even implied a conspiracy to frame Pantages. The jury found him not guilty. On her deathbed many years later, Pringle alleged that her boyfriend, Nick Dunave, had received a big payment from Joseph P. Kennedy, who had been determined to gain control over movie distribution.

In recent years, the trend in both federal and state courts has been to rule inadmissible evidence concerning the alleged victim's past sexual behavior in rape cases. Such evidence was barred from federal courts by Congress in 1978 (Rule of Evidence 412).

—*Bernard Ryan, Jr.*

Suggestions for Further Reading

Giesler, Jerry, as told to Pete Martin. *The Jerry Giesler Story*. New York: Simon & Schuster, 1960.

Nash, Jay Robert. *Encyclopedia of World Crime*. Wilmette, Ill.: CrimeBooks, 1990.

The Scottsboro Trials: 1931–37

Defendants: Olin Montgomery, Clarence Norris, Haywood Patterson, Ozie Powell, Willie Roberson, Charles Weems, Eugene Williams, Andy Wright, and Roy Wright **Crime Charged:** Rape **Chief Defense Lawyers:** Joseph Brodsky, George W. Chamlee, Samuel S. Leibowitz, Milo Moody, Stephen R. Roddy, and Clarence Watts **Chief Prosecutors:** H. G. Bailey, Melvin Hutson, Thomas G. Knight, Jr., Thomas Lawson, and Wade Wright **Judges:** Alfred E. Hawkins, James Edwin Horton, Jr., and William Washington Callahan **Places:** Scottsboro, Alabama; Decatur, Alabama **Dates of Trials:** April 6–9, 1931; March 27–April 9, 1933; November 20–December 6, 1933; January 20–24, 1936; July 12–24, 1937 **Verdicts:** All but Roy Wright: Guilty; Roy Wright: Mistrial **Sentences:** Death by electrocution, later reduced

SIGNIFICANCE

No one knows how many cases like Scottsboro occurred in Southern states before this one—with its large number of defendants, their youth, their brief and almost cursory trials and severe sentences—demanded national attention. The trials, and their appeals, gave America lessons in the procedures of Southern courts, the opportunism of American communists, the prejudice in the South, and the hypocrisy among Southern whites.

On a March morning in 1931, seven bedraggled white youths appeared in a railroad station master's office in northern Alabama and announced that, while riding as hobos, they had been thrown off a freight train by a "bunch of Negroes" who picked a fight. The station master phoned ahead and, near Scottsboro, a deputy sheriff deputized every man who owned a gun. When the train stopped, the posse rounded up nine black boys and two white girls—the latter dressed in men's caps and overalls.

While the white girls chatted with townspeople, the deputy sheriff tied the blacks together and quizzed them. Five were from Georgia. At 20, Charlie Weems was the eldest. Clarence Norris was 19, Ozie Powell, 16. Olin Montgomery, 17, looked "sleepy-eyed," for he was blind in one eye and had only 10 percent vision in the other. Willie Roberson, 17, suffering from syphilis and gonorrhea, walked unsteadily with a cane. Four were from Chattanooga, Tennessee. Haywood Patterson and Andy Wright were 19. Eugene Williams was 13. And Wright's brother Roy was 12.

When the deputy sheriff had loaded his prisoners onto an open truck, one of the girls, Ruby Bates, from Huntsville, Alabama, told him that she and her friend Victoria Price had been raped by the nine blacks.

In Scottsboro, the sheriff sent the women off to be examined by two doctors. Meantime, word of the rape charge spread through Jackson County. By nightfall, a mob of several hundred, promising to lynch the prisoners, stood before the little jail. The sheriff, barricaded with 21 deputies, phoned the governor. But by the time 25 National Guardsmen arrived, the mob had cooled down and most people had drifted away.

As the trial began on April 6, 1931, 102 guardsmen held a crowd of several thousand at a distance of 100 feet from the courthouse.

Ready to appoint defense counsel, Judge Alfred E. Hawkins offered the job to any lawyer in the county who would take it. He accepted Chattanooga attorney Stephen R. Roddy, who admitted he didn't know Alabama law, when local attorney Milo Moody offered to help. Roddy, who had a jail record for drunkenness, was already inebriated at 9:00 A.M.

Circuit Solicitor H.G. Bailey tried Weems and Norris first. Victoria Price described how she and Ruby Bates had hopped freight trains to Chattanooga to look for jobs and, finding none, were returning when the black boys, after throwing the whites off the train, turned on them. She described how she was "beaten up" and "bruised up" by rape after rape, then "lost consciousness" and next found herself on her way to the jail in Scottsboro.

Dr. R.R. Bridges testified he saw no evidence of violence when he examined the girls. Victoria Price, he said, "was not lacerated at all. She was not bloody, neither was the other girl." A second doctor agreed that while both girls showed evidence of recent sexual intercourse, the semen found was "non-motile," or inactive, whereas semen is normally viable for 12 to 48 hours.

By Thursday afternoon, all defendants except 12-year-old Roy Wright had been found guilty. Because of his age, the state had asked for life imprisonment for him, but the jury was deadlocked—seven jurors insisted on death. The judge declared a mistrial for Roy Wright and sentenced the eight others to electrocution.

"Legal Lynching . . . Victims of 'Capitalist Justice' "

Liberals and radicals nationwide reacted. The Central Committee of the Communist Party of the United States called the sentences "legal lynching" of "the victims of 'capitalist justice.' " Its International Labor Defense (ILD) wing pushed the National Association for the Advancement of Colored People (NAACP) to cooperate on taking the case to the U.S. Supreme Court. In Harlem, 300,000 blacks and whites marched to the slogan "the Scottsboro Boys Shall Not Die."

The ILD hired prominent Chattanooga attorney George W. Chamlee. Requesting a new trial, he and the ILD's chief lawyer, Joseph Brodsky, produced affidavits from Chattanooga blacks stating that they had seen Victoria Price "embracing Negro men in dances in Negro houses," that Ruby Bates had bragged that she could "take five Negroes in one night," that a boarding-house operator had let Victoria use a room for prostitution, that she turned down a white man one night because it was "Negro night." The local press denounced the statements as slander, but a Huntsville detective confirmed that the girls were prostitutes.

Defendant Haywood Patterson, holding a horseshoe, with defense attorney Samuel Leibowitz. (Courtesy, Library of Congress)

"You Can't Mix Politics with Law"

The motion for a new trial was denied. The defendants switched allegiance constantly from the NAACP to the ILD and back again. Prominent attorney Clarence Darrow declined the NAACP's request that he steer the case through the Supreme Court. "You can't mix politics with law," he said, adding that the cases would have to be won in Alabama, "not in Russia or New York." The NAACP then withdrew its support.

In March, the Alabama Supreme Court upheld the convictions of all except Eugene Williams; as a juvenile, he was granted a new trial.

In November, the U.S. Supreme Court ruled that the seven boys had been denied "due process" under the Fourteenth Amendment when Judge Hawkins treated the appointment of defense counsel so casually.

As the state ordered a new trial, the ILD turned to Samuel Leibowitz, a noted criminal lawyer in New York. He argued successfully for a change of venue to Decatur, Alabama, where townspeople welcomed the reporters, and Western Union brought in extra operators.

Haywood Patterson was tried first. Leibowitz produced several revelations: Ruby Bates recanted, saying she and Price had invented the rape story to avoid arrest for vagrancy (but she damaged her credibility by testifying in smart "New York clothes" bought for her by the ILD during a trip they provided to the big city); the boys had been seized from several points all over the 42-car train; Willie Roberson's painful, raging syphilis made him incapable of sexual activity; Olin Montgomery's blindness was equally limiting; and Victoria Price, who was married, had served time for adultery and fornication.

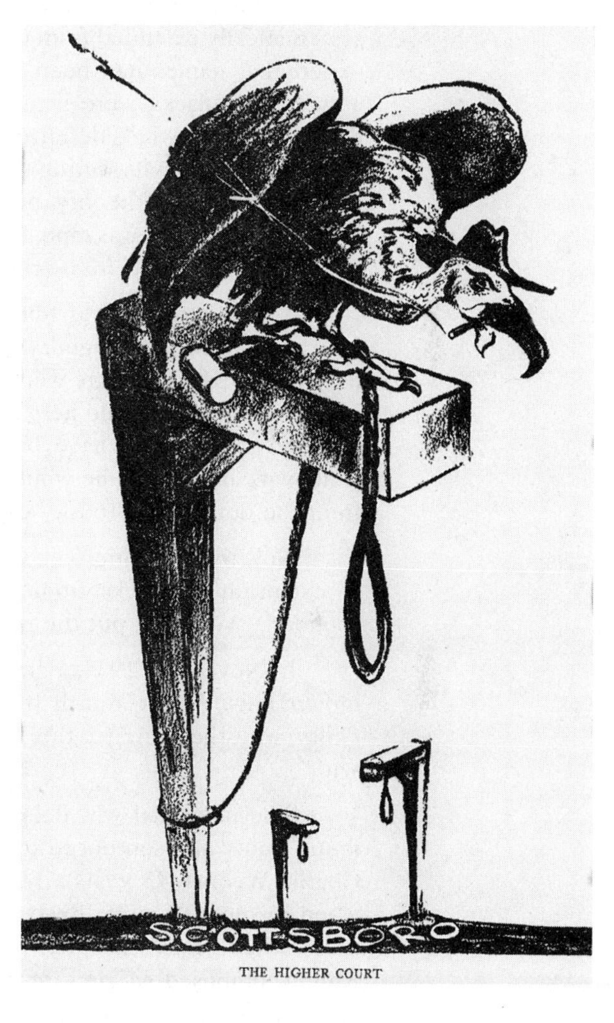

A poignant cartoon from the Scottsboro trials. (Courtesy, Library of Congress)

After Dr. Bridges repeated his testimony that the girls had not been raped, the second doctor—Marvin Lynch—spoke privately with Judge James Edward Horton during a recess. "I told the women they were lying, that they knew they had not been raped," said the doctor, "and they just laughed at me." But, he added, if he testified for the boys, "I'd never be able to go back into Jackson County." The judge, believing the defense would prove Patterson's innocence, said nothing.

Defense attorney Leibowitz himself now lived with National Guard protection against threats of lynching. County Solicitor Wade Wright added to the incendiary atmosphere: "Show them," he told the jury, "that Alabama justice cannot be bought and sold with Jew money from New York."

The jury found Patterson guilty. The sentence: death. When the defense filed a motion for a new trial, Judge Horton reviewed the medical testimony about the women, the lack of physical evidence of sexual activity on the part of the boys, and the unreliable testimony of Victoria Price and Ruby Bates. He set aside the jury's judgment and ordered a new trial. Then, under pressure from Attorney General Thomas Knight and the chief justice, he withdrew from the case.

"No More Picture Snappin' Around Here"

Opening the new trial, Judge William Washington Callahan, 70, dismissed the National Guard. Declaring, "There ain't going to be no more picture snappin' around here," he banned cameras inside or outside the courtroom. He dismissed Leibowitz's motion to quash the indictment because blacks had been systematically excluded from the jury lists—despite testimony by a handwriting expert that names had been fraudulently added to the jury book to make it appear that blacks were listed. He ran a 12-hour day in the courtroom. He destroyed Leibowitz's defense plan by refusing to permit testimony on Victoria Price's sexual activity during the two nights before the train ride. And when he made his charge to the jury, he told them any intercourse between a black man and a white woman was rape, but he omitted—until Leibowitz darted up to the bench and reminded him—the instructions on how to render an acquittal.

Again Patterson was found guilty and the sentence was death. Clarence Norris was next found guilty. But now Leibowitz faced an unexpected challenge: Two ILD lawyers were caught trying to bribe Victoria Price, who had hinted that money could help her change her story. Brodsky told Leibowitz the changed story would have been "good propaganda for the cause." Furious, Leibowitz announced he would withdraw "unless all Communists are removed from the defense." Brodsky capitulated.

Now the U.S. Supreme Court overturned the convictions on the evidence of exclusion of blacks from jury duty. Alabama Governor Bibb Graves responded, "We must put the names of Negroes in jury boxes in every county."

In November 1935, a grand jury of 13 whites and one black brought new indictments. At the fourth trial, in January 1936, Patterson was again found guilty, with the sentence this time 75 years' imprisonment. "I'd rather die," he said.

The next trial was delayed until July 1937. Then Clarence Norris was found guilty and sentenced to death, followed by Andy Wright (99 years) and Charlie Weems (75 years). The rape charge against Ozie Powell was dropped when he pleaded guilty to stabbing a deputy sheriff (during a jail transfer) and received 20 years. Abruptly, prosecutor Thomas Lawson, who had succeeded Knight, proposed *nol pros,* or dropping of charges, for Olin Montgomery, Roy Wright, Willie Roberson, and Eugene Williams. The Scottsboro trials were over.

"All were Guilty or All Should be Freed"

The U.S. Supreme Court refused to review Patterson's conviction. Alabama Governor Bibb Graves listened to a clemency appeal and agreed that "all were guilty or all should be freed." He officially set a date to pardon all four, then reneged. While Graves said he changed his mind after personally interviewing the Scottsboro boys, those close to the governor said he realized public opinion had not changed and simply got cold feet.

Weems was freed in November 1943, Andy Wright and Clarence Norris in January 1944—but Wright and Norris broke parole by moving north and were sent back to prison. Wright was paroled again in 1950. Patterson escaped from prison in 1948 and was arrested in Detroit, but Michigan Governor G. Mennen Williams refused to sign extradition papers; later convicted of manslaughter, Patterson died of cancer in prison in 1952. Norris, the last surviving Scottsboro boy, was pardoned at age 64 by Alabama Governor George C. Wallace in 1976.

Victoria Price worked in a Huntsville cotton mill until it closed in 1938, then moved to nearby Flintsville, Tennessee. Ruby Bates toured briefly as an ILD speaker, then worked in a New York state spinning factory until 1938, when she returned to Huntsville. Both women died in 1961.

—*Bernard Ryan, Jr.*

Suggestions for Further Reading

Carter, Dan T. *Scottsboro: A Tragedy of the American South.* Baton Rouge: Louisiana State University Press, 1969.

Chalmers, Allan Knight. *They Shall Be Free.* Garden City, N.Y.: Doubleday & Co., 1951.

Crenshaw, Files and Kenneth A. Miller. *Scottsboro: The Firebrand of Communism.* Montgomery, Ala.: Brown Printing Co., 1936.

Hays, Arthur Garfield. *Trial by Prejudice.* New York: Covici, Friede Publishers, 1933.

Jordan, J. Glenn. *The Unpublished Inside Story of the Infamous Scottsboro Case.* Huntsville, Ala.: White Printing Co., 1932.

Nash, Jay Robert. *Encyclopedia of World Crime.* Wilmette, Ill.: CrimeBooks, Inc., 1990.

Patterson, Haywood. *Scottsboro Boy.* Garden City, N.Y.: Doubleday & Co., 1950.

Reynolds, Quentin. *Courtroom* (biography of Samuel Liebowitz). New York: Farrar, Straus and Cudahy, 1950.

Al Capone Trial: 1931

Defendant: Alphonse "Scarface Al" Capone **Crime Charged:** Income tax evasion **Chief Defense Lawyers:** Michael J. Ahern and Thomas D. Nash **Chief Prosecutor:** George E. Q. Johnson **Judge:** James H. Wilkerson **Place:** Chicago, Illinois **Dates of Trial:** October 6–24, 1931 **Verdict:** First indictment (tax liability for 1924): Not guilty; second indictment (22 counts): Guilty on five counts (tax liability for 1925, '26, '27, '28, and '29); third indictment (violation of Volstead Act): Indictment not pursued **Sentence:** 11 years' imprisonment, $50,000 in fines, $30,000 in court costs

SIGNIFICANCE

While for 10 years the Chicago police had been unable, if not unwilling, to put the most notorious and murderous of mobsters behind bars, the federal authorities found a way to jail him: through the tax laws. Thus the head of the country's most powerful syndicate providing Americans with bootleg liquor, gambling and prostitution wound up in Alcatraz.

A Brooklyn boy who quit school in the sixth grade after beating up his teacher and getting beaten up by the principal, Al Capone earned the nickname "Scarface Al" as a teenager when his face was severely slashed in a fight. At 21, he moved to Chicago to help his uncle—the city's most powerful brothel keeper—broaden his business to include control of bootlegging. By 1925, at age 26, Capone was running an organization of 1,000 racketeers with a $300,000 weekly payroll.

By eliminating his competition (he ordered 500 deaths, while an estimated 1,000 people died on both sides in his bootleg wars), Capone built a vast network of liquor distributorship, distilleries, breweries, and brothels. To maintain control, he paid off countless politicians and police. At the same time, he made certain all his accomplices were absolutely trustworthy—a key factor in ensuring his safety. So successful was Capone that when a rival gang sent a string of cars filled with machine-gunners to pump a thousand rounds into Capone's headquarters, he remained unscathed.

The St. Valentine's Day Massacre

On St. Valentine's Day, 1929, Capone ordered his men to kill "Bugs" Moran, head of the gang that had machine-gunned the Capone headquarters. Masquerading as police officers, Capone's men massacred seven opponents in a downtown warehouse. The people of Chicago were outraged.

Colonel Frank Knox, publisher of the *Chicago Daily News*, asked newly inaugurated President Herbert Hoover for help. Reportedly, Hoover told Secretary of the Treasury Andrew Mellon, "I want that man in jail."

Federal authorities held jurisdiction over Capone's activities in only two areas: violation of the Volstead Act (i.e., Prohibition) and evasion of income taxes. The problem was proving either case: Capone had never maintained a bank account; he owned no property under his own name; he endorsed no checks; he paid cash for whatever he bought.

Nevertheless, the Internal Revenue Service sent Special Agent Frank J. Wilson to Chicago to analyze Capone's net worth and net expenditures. Over two years, Wilson compiled a list of Capone's purchases, which included custom-made suits, telephone bills, town cars and limousines, a house on Palm Island, Miami, Florida, with two new docks, a boathouse, and an extra garage.

To connect Al Capone with brothels, gambling, and bootlegging, Wilson moved Special Agent Michael F. Malone, who could be taken for an Italian, Jew, or Greek, into Capone's inner circle.

Malone supplied Wilson with inside information. But getting witnesses would not be easy because, as Wilson wrote in a memo:

> . . . all important witnesses were either hostile and ready to give perjured testimony to protect the leaders of their organization or were so filled with fear of the Capone organization . . . that they evaded, lied, left town and did all in their power to prevent the government using them as witnesses. . . . To serve them with subpoenas it was necessary to pick them up on the streets near the Capone headquarters, at Cicero hotels and at nightclubs.

Malone identified a potential witness in the Smoke Shop manager who had quarreled with Capone. Though the manager talked very little, he implied that *Chicago Tribune* reporter Jake Lingle, who knew more about Chicago's gangland than any other reporter, might have information about Capone. Colonel Robert R. McCormick, the publisher, set up a confidential meeting in the Tribune Building. On his way to it, Lingle was murdered.

By 1931, IRS agent Wilson, who had been living with round-the-clock guards after learning that Capone had brought five New York gunmen to Chicago with a contract to kill Wilson, was ready for the grand jury. It returned three indictments: the first for failure to pay 1924 income taxes; the second (with 22 counts) for not paying 1925 through 1929 taxes; the third (based on information compiled by agent Eliot Ness, citing 5,000 specific offenses) for conspiring to violate the Volstead Act. The last was reserved as an ace in the hole.

"Impossible to Bargain with a Federal Court"

If found guilty on every count, Capone would face a maximum sentence of 34 years. His lawyers negotiated with U.S. Attorney George Johnson, who, considering how tough it would be to get key witnesses to testify, agreed to 2½ years in exchange for a guilty plea. With good behavior, the time would be short. But an angry Judge James Wilkerson said, "It is time for somebody to impress upon the defendant that it is utterly impossible to bargain with a Federal court." Capone then pleaded not guilty.

Al Capone and John Stege. (Courtesy, Library of Congress)

Prosecutor Johnson produced witnesses who proved Capone's ownership of the extremely profitable Smoke Shop, which had brought in more than $550,000 in two years and had picked up telegrammed money orders for Capone. A parade of witnesses including decorators, contractors, jewelers, butchers, bakers, brokers who had bought his Palm Beach house and boat for him, and tailors who had sold him pea-green and mustard-brown suits, provided ample evidence of Capone's expenditures.

Capone's defense was gambling losses: He almost never won. The argument was specious, for a taxpayer must have gambling winnings to deduct gambling losses. Defense attorney Michael Ahern, without calling Capone to the stand, concluded, "The evidence in this case shows only one thing against Capone—that he was a spendthrift."

The jury found Al Capone not guilty of tax evasion in 1924, but guilty on the counts for 1925 through 1927, and guilty of failing to file returns for 1928 and 1929. He was found not guilty on 17 remaining counts of tax evasion.

Judge Wilkerson imposed sentences totaling 11 years on the various counts, with fines of $50,000 and court costs of $30,000—the strongest penalties on a tax evader to that date. Capone was put in Cook County Jail, where he had a private cell with shower, freely made phone calls and sent telegrams, and entertained visiting gangsters "Lucky" Luciano and "Dutch" Schultz.

Shortly, however, Capone was moved to Atlanta, Georgia, then to the brand-new maximum-security prison on the island of Alcatraz in San Francisco Bay, California, where he enjoyed not one special privilege. By 1938 he was hospitalized with advanced syphilis. Treatment slowed but could not stop the disease. On his release in 1939, partially paralyzed, he settled in his Miami

Beach home, where his wife and son had been waiting. There, fat and balding and haunted by imaginary killers, he lived until 1947.

—*Bernard Ryan, Jr.*

Suggestions for Further Reading

Kobler, John. *Capone: The Life and World of Al Capone.* New York: G.P. Putnam's Sons, 1971.

Murray, George. *The Legacy of Al Capone.* New York: G.P. Putnam's Sons, 1975.

Olson, James S. *Historical Dictionary of the 1920s.* New York: Greenwood Press, 1988.

Sifakis, Carl. *The Encyclopedia of American Crime.* New York: Facts On File, 1982.

Thomas Massie Trial: 1932

Defendants: Grace Fortescue, Albert O. Jones, Edward J. Lord, and Thomas H. Massie **Crime Charged:** Murder **Chief Defense Lawyers:** Clarence Darrow, George S. Leisure, Lieutenant L.H.C. Johnson, U.S.N., Frank Thompson, and Montgomery Winn **Chief Prosecutors:** John C. Kelley and Barry S. Ulrich **Judge:** Charles S. Davis **Place:** Honolulu, Hawaii **Dates of Trial:** April 4–29, 1932 **Verdict:** Guilty, second-degree murder **Sentences:** 10 years imprisonment at hard labor, commuted to one hour in the dock

SIGNIFICANCE

The Thomas Massie trial provides a footnote to history as the last appearance of world-famous lawyer Clarence Darrow in a headline-making case. It provides a penetrating glimpse into the relationship between U.S. personnel stationed in the Hawaiian Territory before World War II and the island's natives and other "foreigners." And it proves that it is possible for murderers sentenced to 10 years to go free after serving only one hour.

In Honolulu, Hawaii, on September 12, 1931, 31-year-old Navy Lieutenant Thomas H. Massie and his 21-year-old wife, Thalia, attended a Saturday night party. Bored with her husband's boisterous U.S. Naval Academy classmates, Thalia took a stroll outdoors. Missing her toward midnight, Tom phoned home. Thalia answered: "Come home at once. Something terrible has happened."

Tom Massie found his wife hysterical, her face bleeding and bruised. She had been seized on the roadside by several natives, she said, driven to an abandoned animal quarantine station, punched in the jaw when she resisted, raped by five men of mixed race, and abandoned. She had flagged down a car whose driver had taken her home.

Tom Massie called the police. Together they took Thalia Massie to the hospital. Medical examination disclosed that her jaw was broken but did not produce conclusive evidence of rape. After examination and treatment, they went to police headquarters. There Thalia Massie suddenly remembered the license number of the car used by her assailants—a number only one digit different from one described earlier in the hospital's busy emergency room in another incident. Soon the police brought in Horace Ida, who admitted that he and four friends had had an altercation with another woman that night but denied assaulting Thalia Massie. The other four—David Takai, Henry Chang, Joe Kahahawai, and Benny Ahakuelo—were equally adamant. Thalia Massie identified Kahahawai, a well-known prizefighter who had a criminal record, as the assailant who broke her jaw.

Mother-in-Law Takes Charge

A cable from Tom Massie to the mainland brought Thalia Massie's mother, Grace (Mrs. Granville) Fortescue, a domineering woman accustomed to issuing orders from her high position in the social register. She immediately took charge. While Hawaii was abuzz with doubt that Horace Ida and his friends were indeed the assailants, and with equal doubt whether rape had indeed occurred, Fortescue had no doubt. She pushed the Naval commandant, Rear Admiral Yates Stirling, to increase the Navy's already strong pressure on the authorities to prosecute the suspects.

Their trial lasted three weeks. The jury then deliberated for 97 hours but failed to reach agreement. Fortescue demanded that the defendants be held without bail for the new trial. The judge was not empowered to hold them, but he ordered them to report to the courthouse daily.

Impatient and headstrong, Grace Fortescue decided to kidnap Kahahawai and force a confession. When he reported at the courthouse on the morning of January 9, he was intercepted by Navy enlisted man Albert O. Jones, who had a fake summons prepared by Fortescue and told him that "Major Ross" of the Territorial Police wanted him. Jones and enlisted man Edward J. Lord, both of whom were Navy boxers, hustled Kahahawai into a rented car driven by Massie, who was disguised as a chauffeur.

When Kahahawai missed his courthouse appearance, the police suspected the Massies. The rented car was spotted, stopped, and searched. In it were Massie, Fortescue, sailor Lord, and, on the floor of the back seat, the body of Kahahawai, who had been shot with a .32-caliber gun. Sailor Jones, drunk, was shortly found at Fortescue's rented house.

All four were charged with murder and imprisoned aboard the decommissioned U.S.S. *Alton* in Pearl Harbor. All Navy personnel were confined to base. The native population was treated as if the rape of white women were typical behavior. Demonstrations and riots among mainland whites, island natives, and Asians broke out time and again.

Fortescue's friends advised enlisting the best legal mind from the mainland. That meant Clarence Darrow, America's most famous trial lawyer. Now 75, Darrow had been in semiretirement four years. Much of his reputation had been built on his understanding of racial minorities and on his many court fights on behalf of the National Association for the Advancement of Colored People, or NAACP. When Fortescue's friends approached him, he turned them down, writing:

> I learned that one who tried this case could scarcely avoid discussing race conflict. I had so long and decidedly fought for the Negro and all so-called

> "foreigners" that I could not put myself in a position where I might be compelled to take a position, even in a case, at variance with what I had felt and stood for.

Darrow's retirement savings had been severely depleted by the Great Depression. When Grace Fortescue sent word that he would have complete control of defense strategy, he changed his mind. His own friends then charged him with "selling out" to reactionaries. The lurid stories in the American press about Naval officers and socialites who took the law into their own hands had led them to believe that Tom Massie and Grace Fortescue were not the typical underdogs whom Darrow had always defended.

The trial opened on April 4, 1932. For a week, prosecutor John C. Kelley detailed the events that led to Kahahawai's death. He did not try to show who fired the shot that killed the prizefighter, however, as under Hawaiian law all four were considered equally guilty of homicide.

Clarence Darrow came out of semi-retirement to defend Thomas Massie. (Courtesy, Library of Congress)

In the packed courtroom, Darrow launched the defense by putting Massie on the stand to describe the assault on his wife. Kelley objected: Massie's account could be relevant only if the defense planned to prove insanity. That, said Darrow, was the aim. Kelley asked which defendant was insane. Darrow said, "The one who shot the pistol," but he did not identify that one.

As tears flowed throughout the courtroom, Darrow took Tom Massie painfully through the kidnapping to the point where he remembered grilling Kahahawai in Fortescue's house while holding a .32-caliber automatic pistol provided by Jones. Kahahawai, he remembered, admitted after lengthy questioning that he and his friends had raped and beaten Thalia Massie. Then, asked Darrow, "Do you remember what you did?"

"No, sir."

"Do you know what became of the gun?"

"No, I do not, Mr. Darrow."

"Do you know what became of you?"

"No, sir."

Darrow introduced two psychiatrists who testified that, while Massie was now sane, he had been insane at the time of the kidnapping. One described his condition as "chemical insanity" brought on by changes in body chemistry resulting from the strain of the event.

"Is this Your Handwriting?"

Darrow called Thalia Massie. She sobbed through her description of the kidnapping and Jones' telling her of Kahahawai's death. The courtroom was awash in tears. Then, cross-examining, Kelley handed her a sheet of paper—a psychological self-analysis she had made while a student at the University of Hawaii—while asking, "Is this your handwriting?"

Instantly, Thalia Massie was transformed from a pathetic mass of tears to an indignant blaze of fury. "Where did you get this? Don't you know this is a confidential communication between doctor and patient?" She tore the paper into tiny bits. "I refuse to say whether that is my handwriting or not. What right have you to bring this into a public court?" To a burst of applause, she tossed the fragments aside.

"Thank you, Mrs. Massie," said Kelley. "At last you've shown yourself in your true colors."

Said Darrow to reporters afterward, "I've seen some pretty good court scenes but nothing like that one. I was pretty limp when it was all over."

It took the jury nearly 50 hours to find the four defendants guilty of manslaughter. Judge Charles S. Davis sentenced each to 10 years at hard labor. Governor Lawrence Judd then said he would grant executive clemency if the Massies and Fortescue would agree not to press for a retrial of the rape case, for the governor was determined to end the racial disturbances throughout Hawaii caused by the issue. The prosecutors agreed. Darrow got Thalia Massie to agree. The governor commuted the sentences to one hour in the courtroom dock.

Massie's naval career was destroyed by the trial. He died at 44 in 1944, 10 years after he and Thalia Massie were divorced. Thalia Massie died in 1963 after years of depression and several attempted suicides. Her mother had died years earlier.

Clarence Darrow had worked all his life toward reducing tension and conflict between races. While he lost the Massie trial in terms of the jury verdict, he was pleased to have accepted a jury of mixed races and to have avoided racial overtones in the testimony despite his clients' attitudes.

He died in 1938 without ever again handling a headline-making trial.

—*Bernard Ryan, Jr.*

Suggestions for Further Reading

Nash, Jay Robert. *Encyclopedia of World Crime.* Wilmette, Ill.: CrimeBooks, 1991.

Tierney, Kevin. *Darrow: A Biography.* New York: Thomas Y. Crowell, Publishers, 1979.

Weinberg, Arthur and Lila Weinberg. *Clarence Darrow: A Sentimental Rebel.* New York: G.P. Putnam's Sons, 1980.

William Lancaster Trial: 1932

Defendant: William Lancaster **Crime Charged:** Murder
Chief Defense Lawyers: James M. Carson, James H. Lathero
Chief Prosecutors: N. Vernon Hawthorne, Henry M. Jones, H.O. Enwall
Judge: Henry Fulton Atkinson **Place:** Miami, Florida
Date of Trial: August 2–18, 1932 **Verdict:** Not guilty

SIGNIFICANCE

A steamy trial from South Florida that made global headlines, and provided a stark reminder of just how vital courtroom demeanor is to those who matter most—the jury.

February 1932 found Captain William Lancaster, a 34-year-old British pilot, and his Australian lover, Jessie "Chubbie" Miller, down on their luck in Miami, Florida. It was a far cry from the glory days of four years earlier, when the couple had flown from England to Australia in a rickety biplane, making Chubbie Miller one of the most famous female aviators alive.

In a bid to revive their fortunes they invited a young American, Haden Clarke, into their Coral Gables home, with the intention that he would ghost-write Miller's memoirs. While Lancaster was away looking for work in Mexico, Miller and Clarke became lovers. Lancaster reacted badly to news of the affair and scraped together enough money to fly back to Miami. He arrived on April 20, 1932. In the early hours of the following morning, Clarke received a bullet wound to the head and subsequently died.

Initial police inquiries centered on an assumption of suicide, but it soon became clear that Lancaster's story of events that night didn't hold water, and he was charged with murder.

The Miami courthouse was packed with reporters from around the world when the trial opened on August 2, 1932. According to District Attorney Vernon Hawthorne, it was all about jealousy. Lancaster, having trusted Clarke to look after Miller in his absence, had become incensed by the younger man's duplicity. Witnesses would state, said Hawthorne, that Lancaster "paced the floor saying, 'I'll get rid of him.' " Hawthorne told how, after buying a revolver and cartridges, Lancaster flew to Nashville where, "On the last night out from Miami he broke open the box of cartridges and loaded the pistol."

The events of the fateful night were described by Charles Ditsler, an ambulance driver. At 3 A.M., on April 21, he was summoned to the house in response to a shooting, and found Clarke lying on his bed, a huge bullet wound in his head. Beneath the body lay the revolver purchased by Lancaster. Clarke wasn't dead, said Ditsler, but Lancaster kept asking, "Do you think he will talk again?" to which Ditsler had replied, "I doubt it."

British pilot, William Lancaster, and his Australian lover, Jessie "Chubbie" Miller. (Bettmann/Corbis)

Ditsler had spotted two typed suicide notes by the body, both signed in pencil. One was addressed to Chubbie, one to Bill. In each Clarke apologized for his execrable conduct and begged their forgiveness.

Ernest Huston, an attorney, also summoned to the house by Lancaster took up the story. He, too, saw the notes, but had resisted Lancaster's suggestion that they destroy them, saying, "No, they're important."

Forged Letters

Indeed, they were. For by Lancaster's own admission, the notes were forgeries. Asleep in the same room as Clarke, he claimed he had been jolted awake by a gunshot to find Clarke bleeding in bed. Instead of immediately aiding the injured man, he had dashed off the notes in an attempt to convince Miller that he had played no part in this tragedy.

This was a damaging confession, but did it amount to evidence of murder? To illuminate some of the murkier corners in this story, Hawthorne called Chubbie Miller as a court witness, which allowed him the option of cross-examination if necessary

A volley of photographers' flash bulbs greeted Miller as she took the stand. Although she had fallen out of love with Lancaster, she now seemed determined to stand by him in his hour of greatest adversity. This had been made easier for her by a number of damning revelations about Clarke, in particular his admission to her that he was suffering from a venereal disease. Miller lowered her head as she spoke,"[I told him] there would be no marriage until he was cured."

She described her own misery at the situation they had created. "We were lying on the [chaise] longue . . . I said I wished I could put an end to it all. Haden answered that he felt the same." Within two hours he was dead.

As the reporters scribbled gleefully, Miller disclosed ever more intimate details of drunkenness and sexual intrigue at the house. She spared no one, least of all herself. It was a brave act of loyalty at huge personal cost.

Among a welter of confusing testimony from various forensic experts, the testimony of Albert H. Hamilton, a controversial criminologist with a long and checkered history, shone beacon bright. His chief asset was his forthrightness. Shades of gray simply vanished whenever Hamilton took the witness stand. Here, having examined the bullet wound, he issued his verdict: "Absolutely suicide. There is not a scintilla of evidence to support a theory of homicide or murder . . . I found nothing to support anything but suicide. I say this not as an opinion, but actual knowledge."

Confident Defendant

Such ironclad certainty was music to the ears of chief defense lawyer, James Carson, and he was also delighted to have a self-possessed client such as Captain William Lancaster. In contrast to Haden Clarke, whom Carson's skilled advocacy had turned into a bigamous, drug-taking backstabber, Lancaster seemed the very embodiment of British decorum, far too gentlemanly for such coarse pursuits as murder!

He stood up well under Hawthorne's cross-examination, frankly admitting his "unworthy, foolish, and cowardly" actions in forging the suicide notes. No matter how many times Hawthorne trapped him in lies and discrepancies, Lancaster always managed to shade the exchanges in his favor. He had captured the mood of the court and it showed. Several times the gallery burst into spontaneous, boot-stamping applause at his answers, prompting Judge Atkinson on one occasion to pound his gavel and thunder, "This is not a vaudeville show!"

In final speeches, Assistant District Attorney Henry Jones urged the jury not to be gulled by Lancaster's witness stand fluency. "He is a supreme actor, shrew beyond degree. Cold, calculating."

By this time, though, Carson had no doubt he was holding the winning hand. "Where is the State's case?" he asked. "We have been over it step by step, and it is gone. They have utterly and completely failed."

It was left to Hawthorne to have the final word. He begged the jury to set aside any prejudices they may have held about Clarke's unconventional lifestyle and judge the case on its facts. "Do not let sympathy or emotions play a part. Decide simply if Haden Clarke committed suicide or if William Newton Lancaster killed him."

It took them two minutes under five hours to reach a verdict—not guilty.

On August 18, Lancaster walked free from the court to a chorus of wild cheering.

Seven months later he set off on another solo air record-breaking attempt, this time from London to Cape Town in South Africa. On April 13, 1933, his plane vanished over the Sahara. Lancaster's whereabouts remained a mystery until February 12, 1962, when a French Army patrol found his crashed plane and mummified remains in a remote part of Algeria. His diary showed that he survived for over a week in the scorching desert, before dying of thirst, one year to the day after Haden Clarke was shot.

—Colin Evans

Suggestions for Further Reading

Barker, Ralph. *Verdict on a Lost Flyer.* New York: St Martins Press, 1971.

Dorschner, John. "What Goes Up." *Miami Herald,* October, 1, 1989.

Joseph Zangara Trial: 1933

Defendant: Joseph Zangara **Crime Charged:** Murder
Chief Defense Lawyers: James M. McCaskill, Alfred A. Raia, and Lewis Twyman **Chief Prosecutor:** Charles A. Morehead **Judge:** Uly O. Thompson **Place:** Miami, Florida **Date of Trial:** March 9, 1933
Verdict: Guilty **Sentence:** Death by electrocution

SIGNIFICANCE

Joseph Zangara's failed attempt to assassinate U.S. President-elect Franklin D. Roosevelt demonstrated how the frustrations of financial misfortune in the Great Depression could lead to desperate and mindless acts of violence.

Early in 1933, Joseph Zangara, a bricklayer who was out of work, bummed rides from Hackensack, New Jersey, to Florida in hope of finding warm weather and a job. A self-proclaimed anarchist, he carried a revolver, probably as much to protect his diminutive 5-foot frame as to protest the system.

On February 15, Franklin D. Roosevelt arrived in Miami, scheduled to make a major speech at a rally of Democrats. In November, he had won an unprecedented victory over incumbent President Herbert Hoover as the country, hoping for a savior from the economic devastation of the Great Depression, responded to his personal charm and the concern for "the forgotten man" that he had expressed in one campaign speech after another. His inauguration was set for March 4.

Huge crowds turned out to welcome Roosevelt as he rode in an open car in the official motorcade from the railroad station to his hotel. One of his escorts, seated directly behind him and Eleanor Roosevelt, was Anton J. Cermak, the mayor of Chicago, who had helped to deliver FDR's landslide vote.

At one point, the car stopped in the midst of the surging crowd. As he often did because of his relative immobility (the result of his attack of polio, or "infantile paralysis," in 1921), Roosevelt stayed in the car to deliver a short speech. Then the crowd pressed forward, eager to shake his hand. With his usual wide grin and buoyant enthusiasm, he welcomed them.

"Too Many People Starving to Death"

Amidst the tide of people pressing toward the car came Joseph Zangara. Suddenly he was eight feet away, swinging his gun toward the president-elect, shouting, "There are too many people starving to death." As he emptied his revolver, a woman seized his arm. Two shots hit Mayor Cermak. Others scattered widely, wounding four spectators.

The crowd crushed Zangara to the ground, kicking and pounding him. When the police seized him moments later, he was already bloody. Roosevelt, barely glancing at the would-be assassin, turned to help the mayor. "He was the calmest person present," said a witness. Twice, as the car moved from the fray, he had it stopped so he could help make the wounded mayor more comfortable. The whole event was Roosevelt's first national demonstration of his daring lack of fear or concern for his personal safety.

With Mayor Cermak and the wounded spectators in the hospital, Zangara was immediately tried for assault with a deadly weapon, convicted, and sentenced February 21 to 80 years in prison.

On March 6, the mayor died of his wounds. Blaming the murder of Cermak on "that woman who got in the way," Zangara said he was sorry that Cermak had died but that he had fully intended to kill the president-elect.

Dade County Solicitor Charles Morehead, who had been standing by with an indictment for murder ready, brought Zangara to trial on March 9. He pleaded guilty and was condemned to death. A few days before his execution on March 20, he told a newsman he had always hated Roosevelt. "If I got out," he said, "I would kill him at once." He sat down in the electric chair without remorse.

—*Bernard Ryan, Jr.*

Suggestions for Further Reading

Gunther, John. *Roosevelt in Retrospect.* New York: Harper & Brothers, 1950.

Hurd, Charles. *When the New Deal Was Young and Gay.* New York: Hawthorn Books, 1965.

Nash, Jay Robert. *Almanac of World Crime.* Garden City, N. Y.: Anchor Press/Doubleday & Co., 1981.

——. *Encyclopedia of World Crime.* Wilmette, Ill.: CrimeBooks, 1991.

"Roosevelt, Franklin D." *Encyclopedia Americana,* Vol. XXIII. New York: Americana Corp., 1953.

Llewellyn and Edith Banks Trial: 1933

Defendants: Llewellyn and Edith Banks **Crime Charge:** Murder
Chief Defense Lawyers: Thomas J. Enright, William Phipps, Frank J. Lonergan, Charles A. Hardy, Joseph L. Hammersly
Chief Prosecutors: William S. Levens, Ralph P. Moody, George Codding, George W. Neilson **Judge:** George F. Skipworth **Place:** Eugene, Oregon
Date of Trial: May 1–21, 1933 **Verdict:** Llewellyn Banks: Guilty of second-degree murder; Edith Banks: not guilty **Sentence:** Life Imprisonment

SIGNIFICANCE

The Great Depression sprouted many fringe and radical political leaders. Llewellyn Banks was one such person. Banks felt so strongly about his beliefs that it eventually led to murder.

With the onset of the Great Depression, the number of unemployed in the United States increased from 1.5 million in 1929 to 15 million in 1933. Millions more were underemployed, thousands of banks and businesses closed, prices and wages plummeted, savings were lost, and many were forced from their homes into breadlines. Malnutrition was common and, in some parts of the country, starvation began to appear.

During these frightful times, dozens of extremist groups emerged and many people feared that a revolution would occur. Several charismatic demagogues appeared who drew thousands of followers by appealing to various fears and prejudices. U.S. Senator Huey Long of Louisiana was the most famous of these, but there were many others. However, only one ended his days in prison: Llewellyn A. Banks of Medford, Jackson County, Oregon.

A Millionaire Before the Depression

Born in Ohio in 1870, Banks became wealthy growing apples and pears in Oregon's Rogue River Valley. He acquired Medford's *Daily News* newspaper in 1929 and, the next year, ran as an independent for the U.S. Senate. A reputed millionaire before the Depression, he aligned himself with the smaller growers in southern Oregon by supporting their fight against the large packing houses. A distinguished-looking gentleman, Banks was able to galvanize large audiences with a voice described as hypnotic.

When he faced financial ruin during the Depression, Banks went on the offensive against his perceived enemies by publishing editorials that accused local, state, and national leaders of conspiracy and corruption. Banks attacked Wall Street and the Bank of England. Frequently equating patriotism with his version of Protestant Christianity, he called the Jews a "menace to our free American institutions." Banks also praised the formation of the "Khaki Shirts," a violent, anti-Semitic, paramilitary group formed in 1932, and he called upon retired general John J. Pershing to become a dictator to straighten America out.

A friend of Banks was Earl Fehl, a building contractor, real estate speculator, and perennial candidate for public office. Fehl was also the publisher of the *Pacific Record Herald,* a weekly newspaper that consistently assailed Medford's business leaders, lawyers, and politicians. Together, Banks and Fehl had a strong following in Medford's lower income neighborhoods and in the rural areas surrounding the city.

In 1932, Fehl was a candidate for Jackson County judge while Banks/Fehl supporters ran for other offices. The election was a particularly ugly one, with the editor of one opposition newspaper threatened with violence and the offices of another threatened with sabotage. Fehl won the election. Also elected was Gordon Schermerhorn, the Banks/Fehl candidate for sheriff, who narrowly defeated the incumbent, Ralph Jennings.

Banks Supporters Bully County Officials

Things got worse after Fehl and Schermerhorn were sworn in. Government operations came to a halt when Banks/Fehl supporters flooded the courthouse (where the county government offices were located) and harassed those who opposed their leaders. The courthouse steps and the local armory became the sites of pro-Banks/Fehl rallies. Banks started talking about "the hangman's noose" and of using vigilance committees to remove the local district attorney and circuit court judge (both Banks opponents) from office. A county commissioner who opposed Banks and Fehl found a large group of people outside his home one night demanding his resignation. Another commissioner and the former county judge were arrested on bogus charges of mutilating county records. A paramilitary group, consisting mostly of unemployed young men, served as Banks's personal bodyguard and protected the offices of his newspaper. An organization called the Good Government Congress (GGC), which consisted of Banks/Fehl supporters, was formed, and it soon claimed 6000 members throughout the county. Tensions were high, and fears that Banks's and Fehl's followers would turn violent led members of the local American Legion posts to guard the homes of anti-Banks/Fehl officials.

When former sheriff Jennings lost his reelection bid, he immediately demanded a recount. As it proceeded, demonstrations were held denouncing the "plot" to unseat Sheriff Schermerhorn. Then, on February 20, 1933, as a

GGC rally was being held in the courthouse auditorium, about 15 men acting under Banks's and Fehl's orders broke into the courthouse vault and stole three dozen pouches containing ballots from the contested sheriff's election. The next morning, after the break-in was discovered, the Oregon State Police were called in by Governor Julius Meier to investigate. Over the next few days, some ballot pouches were found burned in the courthouse furnace and ballots were found floating in the Rogue River.

Fehl expressed outrage at the break-in and blamed Jennings and his supporters for the crime. However, after extensive questioning of two GGC members who worked at the courthouse, the police had enough evidence to arrest Fehl, Schermerhorn, and several others. On February 27, they were all taken into custody. That evening, GGC members threatened to march on the jail, but the sight of state police armed with submachine guns at the jailhouse prevented anything from happening. However, one anti-Banks/Fehl newspaper editor was cornered on a public street and horsewhipped across the face by a GGC official.

Initially, Banks was not implicated in the break-in, but the investigation continued. Sheriff Schermerhorn's authority to make arrests was revoked by the local circuit court judge and placed into the hands of Medford constable George Prescott. Later, after more evidence was collected, the circuit court ordered Banks arrested for his role in the ballot theft.

Banks Flees to Avoid Arrest

At about 10:15 A.M. on March 16, 1933, Prescott and Sergeant James O'Brien of the Oregon State Police arrived at the Banks residence. By coincidence, Banks lost his newspaper, orchards, and packing house to creditors just the day before. Banks had been warned by supporters of possible assassination attempts, and he had heard that new arrests were going to be made regarding the theft of the ballots. Therefore, Banks decided to flee on March 16 to a remote log cabin and had set out a revolver and hunting rifle in his foyer to take along when he left.

After Prescott and O'Brien knocked on the door, they told Banks's wife, Edith, that they had a warrant for her husband's arrest. Edith Banks opened the door and threw some papers at Prescott and O'Brien which, written by Llewellyn Banks, denied their authority to arrest him. Then, as Edith Banks started to shut the door, Prescott placed his foot inside just enough to prevent her from closing it. Edith stepped aside and Banks appeared with the rifle pointed at Prescott's chest. Banks fired and Prescott fell back, dying almost immediately. Banks then slammed the door as O'Brien retreated to safety. O'Brien called for reinforcements and, within minutes, more officers arrived on the scene. Banks and his wife then surrendered without further resistance.

To forestall any rescue attempt by Banks's supporters, the couple were driven 35 miles to the Grants Pass jail in neighboring Josephine County. By the end of the day, police armed with tear gas and sawed-off shotguns were patrolling the streets of Medford to prevent a feared uprising by the GGC and 23 more arrests were made regarding the courthouse break-in.

The Trial Begins

Banks and his wife were both charged with first-degree (premeditated) murder and faced the death penalty if convicted. Initially, Banks intended to say that a bodyguard, whose name he did not recall, had shot Prescott and escaped during the ensuing confusion. His lawyers eventually convinced him to drop this idea. Instead, their strategy was to focus on Banks's feelings of persecution and the threats from his enemies as part of a temporary insanity defense.

Arguing that the residents of Jackson County were so biased that an impartial jury could not be selected, the defense moved for a change of venue. The motion was granted and the trial was moved 150 miles to the circuit court in Eugene, Oregon. After a jury was chosen, a three-week trial began on May 3, 1933.

According to the prosecution, Llewellyn and Edith Banks killed Prescott with premeditation. "Banks laid in wait for Prescott and took dead aim at him through the partly open door," argued one of the prosecution's attorneys. It was also revealed that, the previous February, Banks and Fehl had urged Sheriff Schermerhorn to arrest Jackson County district attorney George Codding and to hold Codding for ransom or, if necessary, to kill him. When Schermerhorn rejected this plot, Banks met with some GGC members to organize a secret army and to arrange for the storage of weapons in abandoned mines.

In his own defense, Banks took the witness stand and testified about the injustices he suffered at the hands of his opponents. He also spoke of conspiracies, dizzy spells, visions, and of his fears for his own life. According to Banks, when Prescott and O'Brien were at his front door, "I saw what I believed to be a pistol." Convinced that Prescott was trying to break in, Banks shot in self-defense. Other defense witnesses claimed to have heard Prescott threaten Banks's life or to have seen Prescott climb up Banks' front porch with a gun aimed to fire. However, testimony from the prosecution's rebuttal witnesses cast serious doubt on this version of events.

The jury deliberated for 10 hours. On Sunday, May 21, Edith Banks was acquitted, but her husband was found guilty of second-degree (unpremeditated) murder and was sentenced to life imprisonment.

Aftermath of Trial

Banks spent the rest of his years at the Oregon State Penitentiary in Salem. While in prison, Banks appealed his conviction and his supporters petitioned the governor for a pardon, but both were denied. Later on, a state official was arrested for taking a $50,000 bribe to help Banks win an early parole. In 1935, Banks alleged that someone tried to poison him. Prison officials confirmed that a lethal dose of bichloride of mercury was in Banks's hot chocolate, but an investigation concluded that Banks himself had dropped the tablets into his cup. Llewellyn A. Banks died in prison in 1945.

Fehl, Schermerhorn, and others also were imprisoned for their roles in the courthouse break-in and, in 1937, Fehl was declared insane by a court. Many people, shocked by Prescott's murder, quit the GGC, but others managed to keep it alive until the mid-1930s. In 1934, the Medford *Mail Tribune,* an anti-Banks/Fehl newspaper, was awarded the Pulitzer Prize for meritorious public service "for stemming a rising tide of public insurrection which was the growth of a bitter political fight."

—*Mark Thorburn*

Suggestions for Further Reading

LaLande, Jeffrey M. " 'Jackson County in Rebellion': The Turbulent 1930s." In *Land in Common: An Illustrated History of Jackson County, Oregon.* Edited by Joy B. Dunn. Medford, Ore: Mail Tribune, Rogue Federal Credit Union, and the Southern Oregon Historical Society, 1993.

O'Brien, James R. "The Man Who Tried to Be Hitler." *True Detective Mysteries* (February 1940): 41–48, 97–112.

Ulysses Trial: 1933

Defendant: One Book Entitled *Ulysses* by James Joyce
Crime Charged: Obscenity **Chief Defense Lawyers:** Morris L. Ernst and Alexander Lindey **Chief Prosecutors:** Nicholas Atlas, Samuel C. Coleman, and Martin Conboy **Judge:** John M. Woolsey **Place:** New York, New York
Date of Trial: November 25–26, 1933 **Verdict:** The book was ruled not obscene

SIGNIFICANCE

Judge John Woolsey's decision in the *Ulysses* case marked a notable change in the policies of the courts and legislative bodies of the United States toward obscenity. Before this decision, it was universally agreed that: a) laws prohibiting obscenity were not in conflict with the First Amendment of the U.S. Constitution and b) the U.S. Post Office and the U.S. Customs Service held the power to determine obscenity. *Ulysses* became the major turning point in reducing government prohibition of obscenity.

Friends of James Joyce had warned him that *Ulysses* would run into trouble with American postal and customs officials. As early as 1919 and 1920, when the *Little Review* serialized some of the book, the U.S. Post Office confiscated three issues of the magazine and burned them. The publishers were convicted of publishing obscene material, fined $50 each, and nearly sent to prison.

After that decision, several American and British publishers backed off from considering publishing the book in its entirety. Joyce, visiting his friend Sylvia Beach's Parisian bookstore, Shakespeare and Company, despaired of finding a publisher. Beach then asked if Shakespeare and Company might "have the honor" of bringing out the book. Thus *Ulysses* was first published in 1922 in Paris and instantly became an object of smuggling pride and a valuable collector's item when successfully transported past British and American customs agents. By 1928, the U.S. Customs Court officially listed *Ulysses* among obscene books to be kept from the hands and eyes of American readers.

Meantime, such literary figures as T.S. Eliot, Virginia Woolf, and Ezra Pound had acclaimed the Joyce work as already a classic. In Paris, Bennett Cerf, who with Donald S. Klopfer had successfully put the Random House publishing firm on its feet by establishing the Modern Library, told Joyce he would publish the book if its publication could be legalized.

Two Percent for Life

Cerf engaged Morris L. Ernst, America's leading lawyer in obscenity cases. Ernst's fee, contingent on winning the case, was a five percent royalty on the first 10,000 published copies, then two percent for life on all subsequent printings.

Ernst and his associate, Alexander Lindey, carefully planned their strategy. Early in 1932, they had a copy of the book mailed across the sea, expecting Customs to seize it. It arrived untouched.

"So we had a friend bring a copy in," wrote Klopfer many years later, "and we went down to the dock to welcome him! The Customs man saw the book and didn't want to do anything about it, but we insisted and got his superior over, and finally they took the book and wouldn't allow us to bring it into the U.S. because it was both obscene and sacrilegious." That copy was sent by Customs to the U.S. attorney for libel proceedings. One meaning of the word "libel" is "the publication of blasphemous, treasonable, seditious, or obscene writings or pictures."

Ernst then got the U.S. attorney to agree to have the issue tried before a single judge—thus avoiding the potential pitfalls of a jury trial.

Finally, Ernst managed to keep postponing the case until it came before one particular judge: John M. Woolsey. The judge was known to Ernst as a cultivated gentleman who wrote elegant decisions and who loved old books and antique furniture.

The judge further postponed hearing the case to give himself time to read *Ulysses* and other books that had been written about it. But at last, on November 25, in a jam-packed small hearing room that seated fewer than 50 people, the hearing began. One of the prosecuting attorneys turned to Morris Ernst. "The government can't win this case," he said. Ernst asked why. "The only way to win," said the prosecutor, "is to refer to the great number of vulgar four-letter words used by Joyce. But I can't do it." Why not, asked Ernst.

"Because there is a lady in the courtroom."

"But that's my wife," said Ernst. "She's a schoolteacher. She's seen all these words on toilet walls or scribbled on sidewalks by kids who enjoy them because of their being taboo."

The government's case against Joyce's book made two distinct objections. First was the use of four-letter words not mentionable in polite company. Ernst set out to prove that standards of obscenity change, and that by the standards of 1933, Joyce's choice of words did not make the work obscene. To help make his point, Ernst traced the etymologies of a number of four-letter words. Of one particularly abhorrent word, he said, "Your Honor, it's got more honesty than phrases that modern authors use to connote the same experience."

"For example, Mr. Ernst?"

"Oh—"they slept together.' It means the same thing."

"That isn't usually even the truth," said Judge Woolsey.

At that moment, Ernst later remarked, he knew "the case was half won."

The second objection was to the frankness of the unconscious stream of thought that Joyce portrayed in such characters as Molly Bloom. This was (as Ernst later put it) Joyce's "dramatic incisive attempt to record those thoughts and desires which all mortals carry within themselves."

The judge asked Ernst if he had read through Joyce's entire book. "Yes, Judge," he replied. "I tried to read it in 1923 but could not get far into it. Last summer, I had to read it in preparation for this trial. And while lecturing in the Unitarian Church in Nantucket on the bank holiday. . . ."

"What has that to do with my question—have you read it?"

"While talking in that church I recalled after my lecture was finished that while I was thinking only about the banks and the banking laws I was in fact, at that same time, musing about the clock at the back of the church, the old woman in the front row, the tall shutters at the sides. Just as now, Judge, I have thought I was involved only in the defense of the book—I must admit at the same time I was thinking of the gold ring around your tie, the picture of George Washington behind your bench and the fact that your black judicial robe is slipping off your shoulders. This double stream of the mind is the contribution of *Ulysses*."

The judge rapped on the bench. "Now for the first time I appreciate the significance of this book. I have listened to you as intently as I know how. I am disturbed by the dream scenes at the end of the book, and still I must confess, that while listening to you I have been thinking at the same time about the Hepplewhite furniture behind you."

"Judge," said Ernst, "that's the book."

"His Locale was Celtic and his Season Spring"

On December 6, Judge Woolsey delivered his opinion on *United States v. One Book Called Ulysses*:

> I hold that *Ulysses* is a sincere and honest book, and I think that the criticisms of it are entirely disposed by its rationale. . . . The words which are criticized as dirty are old Saxon words known to almost all men, and, I venture, to many women, and are such words as would be naturally and habitually used, I believe, by the types of folk whose life, physical and mental, Joyce is seeking to describe. In respect of the recurrent emergence of the theme of sex in the minds of his characters, it must always be remembered that his locale was Celtic and his season Spring. . . .
>
> I am quite aware that owing to some of its scenes *Ulysses* is a rather strong draught to ask some sensitive, though normal, persons to take. But my considered opinion, after long reflection, is that whilst in many places the effect of *Ulysses* on the reader undoubtedly is somewhat emetic, nowhere does it tend to be an aphrodisiac. *Ulysses* may, therefore, be admitted into the United States.

Ten minutes after the judge completed his statement, Random House had typesetters at work on *Ulysses.*

The government appealed Woolsey's decision to the Circuit Court of Appeals, where Judge Learned Hand and his cousin, Judge Augustus Hand, affirmed the judgment. Judge Martin Manton dissented.

—Bernard Ryan, Jr.

Suggestions for Further Reading

Esterow, Milton. "Perspective: United States of America v. One Book Called *Ulysses.*" *Art News* (September 1990): 189–190.

Moscato, Michael, and Leslie LeBlanc. *The United States of America v. One Book Entitled ULYSSES by James Joyce.* Frederick, MD: University Publications of America, 1984.

Oboler, Eli M. *The Fear of the Word: Censorship and Sex.* Metuchen, N.J.: Scarecrow Press, 1974.

The Obscenity Report (report to the President's Task Force on Pornography and Obscenity). New York: Stein and Day, 1970.

Berrett-Molway Trial: 1934

Defendants: Louis Berrett and Clement F. Molway **Crime Charged:** Murder **Chief Defense Lawyers:** Charles W. Barrett, Charles E. Flynn, John P. Kane, and Frank Tomasello **Chief Prosecutors:** Hugh A. Cregg, Charles E. Green, and John S. Wilson **Judge:** Thomas J. Hammond **Place:** Salem, Massachusetts **Dates of Trial:** February 12–27, 1934 **Verdict:** Not guilty

SIGNIFICANCE

The Berrett-Molway trial is a classic case of mistaken identity. It proved that eight eyewitnesses who had been in close proximity to the "defendants" for two hours could all wrongly identify them, pushing them perilously close to the electric chair. The trial wiped out the jury foreman's firm belief in capital punishment.

Arriving home on Friday, January 5, 1934, Boston taxi driver Louis Berrett, 29, found a stranger in the hallway outside his apartment. The man grabbed him. Suddenly the hall was filled with strangers pointing guns at him and asking who he was. At gunpoint they backed Berrett into his kitchenette. Then one showed a police badge and Berrett recognized him. "I had seen him before," he said later. "A taxicab driver gets to know a lot of cops."

Next, the police wanted to know where Clement F. Molway was. Molway, 22, was a taxi-driver friend of Berrett. The police sought him, they said, in connection with a holdup. "I knew he was a good kid from a respectable family," said Berrett afterward. He told the cops they were crazy, that Molway "was never mixed up in any holdups," and that he would go to police headquarters with them if it would help Molway.

At headquarters, Berrett soon found himself and Molway booked. Next, handcuffed, they were driven to Lynn, Massachusetts, where the chief police inspector asked Berrett for a statement of where he had been from Sunday night to Wednesday night of the preceding week. Only after Berrett had signed a five-page statement that the chief wrote out did the chief tell him there had been a holdup and murder at the Paramount Theatre in Lynn on Tuesday morning. Berrett then insisted on writing a second statement, in his own handwriting, like the first. By the time he was locked in a cell, it was 3:00 A.M. on Saturday.

"Boys, You've Been Picked by Five People"

Morning brought more officials and more questions, while Berrett vainly asked to phone friends and the police laughed at him. Late Saturday afternoon, unwashed, unshaven, unfed, and having slept in their clothes on hard board "beds" in separate cells, Berrett and Molway found themselves in a lineup as strangers inspected them. "A girl picked me out," said Berrett later. "When she placed her hand on my shoulder, I all but passed out. I knew I had never seen her before in my life, but what could I do?"

After the lineup, the chief inspector said, "Boys, you've been picked by five people. We are changing the charge from suspicion of murder to murder."

On Sunday night, the police phoned lawyer Charles W. Barrett on Berrett's behalf, then told Berrett that Molway had cracked and "told everything." Berrett laughed at them and promised to "give them a true statement for Tuesday. When they came down, all excited, I gave them the same statement I had given them before. Gee, they were mad."

As the trial opened on Monday, February 12, the defendants challenged 19 prospective jurors to get a jury composed of laborers, mechanics, and machine operators, including a janitor, a clerk, a truck driver, and a foreman, who was made foreman of the jury. Engineers, businessmen, and professionals were excused.

In the courtroom, Berrett and Molway found themselves shackled together in a green wire cage. In front of them sat a deputy sheriff, his back to the courtroom, staring in the defendants' faces. Defense attorney Charles E. Flynn protested to the court that the prisoners' situation represented "the most prejudicial atmosphere possible" in an attempt "to impress the jury with the guilt of the defendants at the bar." Judge Thomas J. Hammond waited until the second day of the trial to have the deputy sheriff moved to the side of the prisoners' cage.

District Attorney Hugh A. Cregg opened with a description of the crime: how Berrett and Molway, with an unknown third man (named as "John Doe" in the indictment), carrying out a well-planned robbery in mid-morning at the Paramount Theatre, were interrupted by the arrival of the Paramount's bill poster, Charles F. Sumner. When Sumner turned to run, eyewitnesses would testify, he was shot down.

"That Rare Element in Murder Trials"

The state's first witness to identify Berrett and Molway was Michael Ford, a former soldier in the Irish Republican Army, who described how he was cleaning the Paramount lobby when the men came in. "Here," reported the *Boston Globe,* "was that rare element in murder trials, confident eyewitness testimony." After pointing out the defendants in the courtroom, Ford testified that upon arrival they asked for the Paramount's manager and assistant manager. When he said they wouldn't be in for two hours, the two pushed him at gunpoint into the office and warned him to make no noise. Next, they grabbed Harry Condon, an employee who came up from the basement. He broke away. "Molway said, 'Get him,'" testified Ford. "Then I saw Molway raise the gun and fire at Condon." Wounded, Condon was pushed into the office with Ford.

Next, said Ford, the men rounded up eight other Paramount employees who were in the building, tying them to chairs in the office. One was forced to phone the Paramount's manager and, on a ruse, hurry him to the office to open the safe.

"Head Him Off"

Then, testified Ford, Molway asked about two men he saw out in the parking lot. He was told they were bill posters. "We'll leave them there," said Molway. But presently Molway saw bill poster Sumner coming into the lobby. "Head him off," he ordered. Sumner was beaten with a gun butt, said Ford, then shot after he had been felled.

When assistant manager Stephen Bresnahan arrived, he was forced to open the safe. The robbers emptied it, took the manager's wallet (which contained $4), locked the 10 Paramount employees in a cloakroom, and departed.

Seven other eyewitnesses corroborated Ford's identification of Berrett and Molway as the robbers and murderers. One, Leo Donahue, pounded the rail of the witness box with his closed fist as he shouted, "I absolutely identify them as the men who held up the Paramount Theatre."

Prosecution and defense had rested and final arguments in the case were scheduled for Monday when defense attorney Flynn, in Judge Hammond's chambers, informed the court that the defense intended to show that the persons who committed the Lynn murder had committed similar holdups and murders recently in Needham and in Fitchburg, and had been convicted in Needham. The judge said he was not going to try the Needham and Fitchburg cases at this trial. Flynn pointed out that shells found at each site proved that a gun used at Lynn had been used earlier at Fitchburg.

Instead of final arguments, prosecutor Cregg asked the judge to reopen the evidence. Paramount Assistant Manager Bresnahan took the stand.

Question: Mr. Bresnahan, were you in Dedham with me today?

Answer: I was.

Question: There you were shown a defendant connected with the Needham holdup?

Answer: Yes, sir.

Question: You were shown certain statements and pictures?

Answer: Yes, sir.

Question: And as a result of what you were shown, you desire to make a statement to the jury?

> Answer: I do. As a result of the pictures and statements shown me today at Dedham I feel sure that these two defendants were not at the theatre that morning.

Next, janitor Leo Donahue refuted in one minute the eyewitness testimony that, with pounding fists, he had taken nearly a full trial day to tell.

While he had taken all eight eyewitnesses to Dedham, Cregg spared the six others this moment of embarrassment. He moved for a directed verdict of not guilty. The defense made the same motion. The judge made notes for a full minute, then addressed the jury:

> It may surprise you, Mr. Foreman and jury, to learn that you have agreed upon your verdict. I instruct you now that as the names are read by the clerk you will return verdicts of not guilty.

"Not guilty," said each juror in turn. The judge then ordered the defendants released from their cage. As the taxi drivers rushed into the arms of families and friends, prosecutor Cregg released a full confession to the Lynn holdup and murder by one Abraham Faber, along with photographs of two members of his gang who could easily have been mistaken for Louis Berrett and Clement Molway.

—Bernard Ryan, Jr.

Suggestions for Further Reading

The Boston Globe. See Berrett, Louis, in *The Boston Globe* index, January 6–March 3, 1934.

Sifakis, Carl. *Encyclopedia of American Crime.* New York: Facts On File, 1982.

Gloria Vanderbilt Custody Trial: 1934

Defendant: Gertrude Vanderbilt Whitney (Mrs. Harry Payne Whitney)
Appellant: Gloria Morgan Vanderbilt (Mrs. Reginald Vanderbilt)
Appellant Claim: Custody of Gloria Laura Vanderbilt, a minor
Chief Defense Lawyer: Herbert C. Smyth
Chief Lawyer for Appellant: Nathan Burkan **Judge:** John Francis Carew
Place: New York, New York **Dates of Trial:** October 1–November 21, 1934
Decision: Custody awarded to Whitney

SIGNIFICANCE

The claim by her mother that Gloria Morgan Vanderbilt was unfit to have custody because of her debauched lifestyle and cold indifference to her child scandalized both society and the general public. Coming in the depths of the Great Depression, this custody battle within one of the nation's wealthiest families confirmed Americans' worst suspicions about the super-rich, while giving them two months' diversion from their own financial worries.

Gloria Laura Vanderbilt was 1 year old and her mother was 20 when her father, Reginald Vanderbilt, died at 45 in 1925. Cirrhosis of the liver, brought on by countless brandy milk punches, ended Reggie's dissipated life. By then, he had exhausted not only his own body but a $7.5-million fortune inherited at 21 and the income from a $5-million trust fund.

Once all Vanderbilt's creditors and taxes had been paid, his young widow, Gloria Morgan Vanderbilt, ended up with $130,000. But the principal in the $5-million trust fund remained to be shared between his baby daughter and her 21-year-old half-sister. Since the widow was still a minor, the fund was to be administered by New York Surrogate Court Judge James Aloysius Foley.

Shortly, little Gloria's mother petitioned the court for an allowance to cover "monthly expenses necessarily incurred for the maintenance and support of said infant and the maintenance of the home in which said infant resides." The court granted $4,000 per month.

With the allowance, Gloria Morgan Vanderbilt flitted from New York to Paris, London, Cannes, Hollywood, Monte Carlo, Biarritz, and Switzerland. She crossed the Atlantic as often as once a month. In her international set, the pace was led by the Prince of Wales, with whom Gloria's twin sister, Thelma, was having a five-year love affair (it ended when Thelma introduced her friend Wallis Warfield Simpson to the prince, who subsequently gave up the throne of England to marry the divorced Simpson).

Meanwhile, little Gloria was more than overprotected by her grandmother, Laura Kilpatrick Morgan, and by nurse Emma Keislich, who had not missed a day or night with the child since she was hired two weeks after her birth. Together the grandmother and the nurse grew to feel that little Gloria, neglected by a mother who came home intoxicated, toward dawn (if she came at all), was theirs.

"We are Moving Again—Oh what a Life"

For almost a decade, little Gloria sometimes did not see her mother for months on end. At other times, she and nurse Keislich lived in Paris or London with her mother, who was also living with Gottfried Hohenlohe Langenburg, a destitute German prince and a great-grandson of Queen Victoria. Langenburg wanted to marry Gloria Morgan Vanderbilt, but Surrogate Judge Foley had ruled, "No part of the infant's income can be used to finance a second marriage." Little Gloria feared and hated the prince, who never spoke to her. She sent post cards from Europe to her grandmother Morgan declaring that "My mother is so bad to me I wish I could run away to New York to you," that "my mother was in Paris enjoying herself while poor me was unhappy in England [*sic*]," and "We are moving again oh what a life."

In June 1932, little Gloria's tonsils were removed in New York. Sailing yet again for Europe, her mother welcomed the suggestion of her sister-in-law, Gertrude Vanderbilt Whitney, that the 8-year-old recuperate over the summer at the Whitney home in Old Westbury, Long Island. That fall, the Whitney family doctor urged that she continue to live in Old Westbury. Her mother agreed. Surrogate Judge Foley, notified by Gertrude Whitney that her deceased brother's child was now living with her, cut Gloria Morgan Vanderbilt's allowance from $48,000 to $9,000 a year. Suddenly it dawned on the absent mother that, without little Gloria, she was practically a pauper.

Movie theatre magnate A. C. Blumenthal, Gloria's current lover, introduced her to lawyer Nathan Burkan. The attorney discovered that, since she was still a minor when husband Reggie Vanderbilt died, Gloria Vanderbilt had never been appointed guardian of her own child. He petitioned Surrogate Judge Foley to make her sole guardian. But a complainant appeared: Gloria Morgan Vanderbilt's mother, who said her daughter was unfit.

Lawyers and surrogate reached agreement: Little Gloria could live with Aunt Gertrude during the school year, and her mother could see her at any time. In September little Gloria went to New York City to visit with her mother. But when she arrived, Gloria Vanderbilt announced, "Little Gloria is not going back to Mrs. Whitney's."

The next morning, while her Aunt Gertrude, her Aunt Consuelo (sister of her mother) and her mother sipped sherry in the Whitney mansion, little Gloria was slipped out to the car by nurse Keislich and Gertrude Whitney's private maid. When her mother asked presently where her daughter was, Gertrude said, "Little Gloria is halfway to Westbury by now. I'm not going to let you have her."

In Old Westbury, little Gloria found guards posted throughout the house and the nurse or the maid always at her side. But that afternoon, Gertrude Vanderbilt Whitney was served court papers that commanded her to have "the body of Gloria Laura Morgan Vanderbilt by you imprisoned and detained" presented before Judge John F. Carew.

"Trial of the Century"

The opening of the trial in the "Matter of Vanderbilt" October 1, 1934, was jammed with more than 100 reporters, who dubbed it the "trial of the century," and with countless spectators. They heard nurse Keislich testify that she had seen Prince Langenburg and Mrs. Vanderbilt in bed together reading "vile" books. A chauffeur testified about Gloria Morgan Vanderbilt's several lovers. A French maid testified that she had found Lady Milford Haven at Mrs. Vanderbilt's bedside and "kissing her just like a lover." Judge Carew, who later admitted that until then he thought he had heard everything, immediately closed the courtroom to press and public.

Bedlam followed. The tabloids cried "Lesbianism." More refined papers reported Mrs. Vanderbilt's "alleged erotic interest in women." Women demonstrating outside the courthouse with placards declaring a mother's right to her child were perplexed. Meantime, testimony against Aunt Gertrude, an accomplished sculptress and founder of the Whitney Museum of Art, tried to establish her interest in the nude in art as an immoral influence on her niece.

The judge, baffled by more than five weeks of shocking public testimony, at last decided to take little Gloria, attorney Burkan, attorney Smyth, and the court stenographer into his chambers. Over 2½ hours, the stenographer recorded such questions and answers as:

> How would you like to live with your mother down in the country?
>
> No. Never. I always want to live with my aunt.
>
> You lived a long while with your mother?
>
> Yes, but I have hardly seen her. She has never been nice to me.
>
> Don't you think you could learn to love her?
>
> No. She never even kissed me good night.

On November 21, Gertrude Whitney was awarded custody of little Gloria. But the judge's decision stated that Gloria's mother could have her from Saturday morning to Sunday evening each week, for eight hours on Christmas day, and all the month of July. The *New York Journal American* summed it up:

> Rockabye baby
>
> Up on a writ,
>
> Monday to Friday Mother's unfit.
>
> As the week ends she rises in virtue;

Saturdays, Sundays,

Mother won't hurt you.

Little Gloria now spent quiet weekdays in Old Westbury, ignored by her Aunt Gertrude, who lost interest in her immediately after the trial, and without nurse Keislich, whom the judge had dismissed. On Saturday mornings, under guard, she traveled to her mother's suite in the Sherry-Netherland Hotel in Manhattan, where reporters mingled with detectives and curiosity-seekers to block her way and shout questions.

Gloria Morgan Vanderbilt, (right) and Gloria Laura Vanderbilt, (left) in a photograph of them taken after the court's decision to award custody of the child to Mrs. Whitney. (AP/Wide World Photos)

Lawyer Burkan tried to file an appeal to the New York State Court of Appeals. The court declined. Next, he asked the Supreme Court of the United States to review the case, on the grounds that little Gloria's constitutional rights had been violated. It, too, declined.

At 17, Gloria married Pasquale di Cicco, a Hollywood actors' agent. They divorced when, at 21, she came into her nearly $5-million estate. The next day, she married conductor Leopold Stokowski, who was 42 years older than she. The marriage produced two sons and a nervous breakdown for her, and after 10 years they parted, with Vanderbilt winning a custody fight that, ironically, awarded Stokowski permission to see the boys on weekends and for a month in the summer.

In 1956, Vanderbilt married film director Sidney Lumet. After their divorce in 1963, she married writer Wyatt Cooper, who died in 1978. They had two sons. Over the years, she had written poetry before turning to design, creating note cards, linens, china and chic blue jeans. The jeans brought her new wealth—a 3.5-percent royalty on $125 million in sales in 1979 alone—and new fame. In addition, Gloria Laura Morgan Vanderbilt di Cicco Stokowski Lumet Cooper has written two books in a projected five-volume autobiography.

—Bernard Ryan, Jr.

Suggestions for Further Reading

Clemons, Walter. "Poor Little Rich Girl." *Newsweek* (June 16, 1980): 43–44.

Goldsmith, Barbara. *Little Gloria . . . Happy At Last.* New York: Alfred A. Knopf, 1980.

Howard, Margo. "Gloria Vanderbilt." *People Weekly* (June 10, 1985): 122–131.

Langway, Lynn, Diane Weathers, and Lisa Whitman. "Sic Transit Gloria." *Newsweek* (June 16, 1980): 44–45.

Stasz, Clarice. *The Vanderbilt Women.* New York: St. Martin's Press, 1991.

Vanderbilt, Arthur II. *Fortune's Children.* New York: William Morrow & Co., Inc., 1989.

Vanderbilt, Gloria. *Black Knight, White Knight.* New York: Alfred A. Knopf, 1987.

——. *Once Upon A Time.* New York: Alfred A. Knopf, 1985.

Samuel Insull Trial: 1934

Defendants: Samuel Insull, Samuel Insull, Jr., Harold L. Stuart, and 13 others **Crime Charged:** Use of the mails to defraud
Chief Defense Lawyers: Frederick Burnham, James J. Condon, Harry S. Ditchburne, William H. Haight, John J. Healy, Charles E. Lounsbury, J. Fred Reeve, and Floyd E. Thompson **Chief Prosecutors:** Dwight H. Green and Leslie Salter **Judge:** James H. Wilkerson **Place:** Chicago, Illinois
Dates of Trial: October 2–November 24, 1934 **Verdict:** Not guilty

SIGNIFICANCE

Many people consider the Samuel Insull case to be the father of the Federal Securities and Exchange Act. The revelations of the trial produced immediate legislation to regulate the issuance of securities, control stock exchanges, and protect the unwary from holding companies. The trial gives insight into a time when a stock manipulator could build a pyramid of commercial wealth, making as much as a million dollars a week, at the expense of thousands of small investors doomed innocently to ruin.

Samuel Insull was a 21-year-old Englishman in 1881 when inventor Thomas Alva Edison brought him to America as his private secretary. Eleven years later, Insull was Edison's most trusted adviser, with discretion to handle all the inventor's financial matters.

In Schenectady, N.Y., the Edison General Electric Company was losing money. Edison dispatched Insull upstate: "Whatever you do, Sammy, make either a brilliant success of it or a brilliant failure. Just do something." Within a few years after Insull took charge, the company had grown from 200 employees to 6,000. Soon it was the well-established General Electric Company, or GE.

In 1892, Insull became president of Chicago Edison Company. He borrowed $250,000 from Marshall Field and began buying the independent electricity-generating plants that were proliferating in Chicago. By 1907, his Commonwealth Edison Company served the entire city, and investors had put in hundreds of millions of dollars.

Inventor of the "Power Pool"

Meantime, Insull acquired small electric companies in surrounding counties. Eventually his Public Service Company of Northern Illinois served half the state—some 6,000 square miles. Insull built the world's largest generating plants, with long transmission lines, reducing production costs and consumer rates and increasing efficiency and profits. A reliable "power pool," as he called it (it was entirely his idea), supplied the network covering all Chicago and northern and central Illinois.

By the 1920s, Insull had reorganized the near-bankrupt People's Gas Light & Coke Company (its stock rose from $20 to $400 a share). He controlled Chicago's elevated rail lines and its commuter trolleys. His utilities companies operated in 39 of the 48 states. The man was worth more than $100 million. To trusting investors, his name was magic.

In 1907, when Chicago banks refused to handle the unknown Commonwealth Edison Company securities, Insull had found Halsey, Stuart & Company. Over the years, the firm, headed by Harold L. Stuart, had sold more than 2 billion dollars of Insull properties stock.

Threatened with loss of control when the 1926–29 bull market saw new investment trusts buying up shares in his companies, Insull organized Insull Utility Investments, Inc. He and Halsey, Stuart would hold enough securities of the operating companies to keep him in command. The investment company's common stock opened at $30 a share, boomed to $147, then settled at $100.

Next, in September 1929, Insull created another investment company, Corporation Securities Company of Chicago. An offering circular was mailed to potential investors. Despite the "Black Friday" stock-market crash five days later, faith in Insull was so strong that within a year the public had bought $100 million of the new securities.

But the Great Depression steadily overpowered the Insull empire. By 1932, his holding companies were petitioning for bankruptcy. The operating companies—Commonwealth Edison, Peoples Gas, and Public Service of Northern Illinois—survived, with Insull still in charge. In June, however, he resigned, citing ill health and advanced age (he was 73). He and his wife sailed for Europe.

By September, word reached Insull in Paris: His affairs were under investigation. The Insulls moved to Greece, which had no treaty of extradition with the United States.

Accountants announced findings: Investors in Middle West Utilities had lost more than $700 million. Those in Corporation Securities had lost $85 million. Collateral had been "cross loaned" between the Insull companies. Favored creditors had been given preference. Millions in questionable brokerage fees had been taken from assets. Padded payrolls had included Insull's relatives and friends. Immense secret profits had been paid to as many as 1,600 favorites. They had bought 250,000 shares of Insull Utility Investments common stock at $12 before it opened at $30 and zoomed to $147; selling at only the opening price would have produced $4,500,000 in profits.

Arrested in Istanbul

A Cook County grand jury indicted Insull and his brother Martin for embezzlement from the Middle West Utilities Company and Mississippi Valley Utilities Investment Company. A federal grand jury indicted Insull and 16 others, including Samuel, Jr., who had joined his father's business in the 1920s, and Harold L. Stuart, for using the mails to defraud.

Insull disappeared. Congress passed a special bill allowing U.S. authorities to arrest him in any country where it had extraterritorial rights. Found aboard a ship bound for Egypt, he was arrested in Istanbul and returned under heavy guard to America.

Samuel Insull: stock manipulator or scapegoat? (Archive Photos, Inc.)

U.S. Attorney Dwight H. Green's opening at the trial on October 2, 1934, charged that the defendants, through Utility Securities Company, fraudulently schemed to induce investors nationwide to buy the common stock of Corporation Securities Company at inflated prices. He also charged that Insull-controlled companies had maintained a fictitious market for the common stock, thus misleading prospects as to its value. To carry out the scheme, the defendants had used the mails to send circulars to those they intended to defraud.

"The Jewels of the Insull Empire"

Eighty witnesses identified books and records. Another 50 had been solicited and bought stock. As countless company names became blurs in jurors' minds, the big picture grew clear: The government was out to prove that Insull's success had been gained—repeatedly—by having one Insull electric company sell properties to another Insull electric company at a splendid profit, with the second company then selling to a third. The holding companies—the securities of which were proclaimed by a Halsey, Stuart salesman as "the jewels of the Insull empire"—and the investment companies had been created to expand the bubble . . . until the Depression deflated everything.

The specific charge against Samuel Insull and his cronies was that the circular mailed by Halsey, Stuart & Company inviting subscribers to buy stock in Corporation Securities was false and deceptive: The company, it said, would open with $80 million in assets, whereas it actually had only a bank loan of $3.5 million and 304,000 shares of Insull Utility Investments for which it had paid $7 million. And the circular failed to state that most of the stock the company intended to buy was common stock paying only a stock dividend, not cash.

Chief defense lawyer Floyd E. Thompson, a highly respected former Illinois Supreme Court justice, skillfully brought out his client's English training in business, his success with Thomas Edison and GE, the vast saving in the cost of electricity his "power pool" had generated, and his accumulation of utility companies to assure their continuing control and hold off government ownership.

Insull further testified that divisions of stock were in line with prevailing corporate practice, that stock dividends (rather than cash) were common and represented earnings plowed back to increase equity value. As to the offending circular, Insull said its statement of assets was based on completion of financing, entirely in accordance with market practice.

Next, Insull testified on the "buoyant" optimism of the financial community in March 1930, after the crash, and on how the Corporation Securities Company's portfolio depreciated some $45 million in late 1930, then appreciated $86 million in early 1932, when people thought the Depression was over. He and his associates had done nothing unusual in "supporting the market," he said; even the United States did it for government bonds. He himself had borrowed $5 million to bolster Corporation Securities Company, then borrowed a million from GE to reduce the bank loan. But by April 1932 his holding companies had gone into receivership. To avoid bankruptcy, he had given his creditors everything he had. He now owned no property, had no income, and depended on his son for food and shelter.

"We are Trying that Age"

The gist of the Insull defense was that the government had to find someone to blame for the ills the Depression had caused. Samuel Insull, as the magic name in the era of million-dollar risks and losses, was the logical culprit. Thompson summarized:

> Gentlemen, you have had a description here of an age in American history which we hope never will be repeated. We are trying that age. There is no proof here that anyone had any wrongful motive. There is proof that these men believed implicitly in the business venture in which they were engaged, and they poured their own fortunes and their own good names into it.

The jury agreed. It found all of the defendants not guilty.

Insull faced two more trials. In March 1935, a Cook County jury found him not guilty on the charge of embezzlement. In June in federal district court, he and his son and Harold Stuart were found not guilty of illegally transferring property with intent to prefer selected creditors and defeat the purpose of the Bankruptcy Act.

Insull returned to Paris, where he dropped dead on the street at 78. It was reported that his assets then were $1,000; his debts, $14 million.

—*Bernard Ryan, Jr.*

Suggestions for Further Reading

Busch, Francis X. *Guilty or Not Guilty*? New York: Bobbs-Merrill Co., 1952.

Davidson, Carla. "Chicago Transit," *American Heritage* (December 1985) 33–34.

Fleming, Thomas J. "Good-bye to Everything!" *American Heritage* (August 1965) 89.

Fuhrman, Peter. "Do it big, Sammy," *Forbes* (July 13, 1987) 278–280.

Michaels, James W. "History lesson," *Forbes* (December 24, 1990) 38–40.

Phillips, Cabell. *The New York Times Chronicle of American Life from the Crash to the Blitz: 1929–1939.* New York: Macmillan Co., 1969.

Sifakis, Carl. *The Encyclopedia of American Crime.* New York: Facts On File, 1982.

Bruno Richard Hauptmann Trial: 1935

Defendant: Bruno Richard Hauptmann **Crime Charged:** Murder
Chief Defense Lawyer: Edward J. Reilly **Chief Prosecutor:** David T. Wilentz **Judge:** Thomas W. Trenchard **Place:** Flemington, New Jersey
Dates of Trial: January 2–February 13, 1935 **Verdict:** Guilty
Sentence: Death by electrocution

SIGNIFICANCE

The use of scientific crime detection, a conviction entirely on circumstantial evidence, and the circus-like atmosphere created by spectators and the press made the Lindbergh baby kidnapping trial a landmark in American history. Because of the prominence of the father of the murder victim, probably no case has ever attracted greater worldwide attention.

Influential editor and critic H.L. Mencken called Bruno Richard Hauptmann's trial "the biggest story since the Resurrection." The defendant was charged with murdering the 20-month-old son of Charles A. Lindbergh, the man who, in May 1927, had become the greatest hero of modern times by making the first solo trans-Atlantic flight, from New York to Paris. "Wild enthusiasm" understates the acclaim that had greeted Lindbergh wherever he went for five years. He belonged to America.

In 1929, Lindbergh had married Anne Morrow, daughter of the U.S. ambassador to Mexico. Charles Jr. was born June 22, 1930. Hoping to escape from the crowds they drew everywhere they went, the young family moved into a new home in remote Hopewell, New Jersey. There, on the evening of March 1, 1932, the toddler was kidnapped from his nursery. His body was found May 12 in the woods, two miles from the Lindbergh home.

Discovered Through Ransom Money

More than two years later, in September 1934, a man named Bruno Hauptmann used a $10 gold certificate to buy gasoline. Because gold notes were rare (the United States had just gone off the gold standard), the station attendant jotted down Hauptmann's license number and took the $10 bill to a bank, where it was identified as part of the $50,000 ransom paid by Lindbergh. Hauptmann was arrested. The jury would face the accused carpenter, who lived with his wife and son (now almost the same age as the Lindbergh baby when he died) in the rented second floor of a house in the Bronx, a borough of New York City. Hauptmann, who had a record of petty crime in his native Germany, had voyaged to America twice in 1923 as a stowaway. Apprehended and sent back the first time, he was successful on his second try.

Discovered behind boards in Hauptmann's garage was $14,590 in bills from the ransom. A *New York Times* compilation of his assets totaled $49,671. Written on the trim inside his bedroom closet was the address and telephone number of Dr. John F. Condon, a 71-year-old retired Bronx schoolteacher who had turned up as a self-appointed go-between when Lindbergh, not yet aware that his son had been killed, was negotiating with the kidnapper for the delivery of the ransom. Within earshot of Lindbergh, Condon had met the presumed kidnapper in the dark to hand over the money. When Lindbergh would testify, that "is the voice I heard that night," in identifying Hauptmann as the man he had heard when the ransom for his kidnapped baby was handed over, America believed him implicitly.

The Circus Comes to Town

The trial shaped up as one of the great news stories of the century. To cope with the demands of the press, the largest telephone system ever yet put together for a single event was created—adequate to serve a city of 1 million. Thousands of sightseers, 700 reporters, and hundreds of radio and telephone technicians converged upon Flemington, New Jersey. Hucksters sold models of the ladder used by the kidnapper to get into the baby's nursery, locks of "the baby's hair," and photographs of the Lindberghs, supposedly autographed by them.

On Sundays, tourists trooped through the courtroom, posed for photos in the judge's chair, carved initials in his bench, and tried to steal the witness chair. On Sunday, January 6, the invading army of curiosity-seekers was estimated at 60,000. The next weekend, the local Rotary Club took charge of protecting the courthouse from virtual demolition by the souvenir hunters.

Everything Matches

Not only would the state of New Jersey prove that Hauptmann received the money, promised the cigar-smoking 38-year-old Attorney General David T. Wilentz, it would also prove that Hauptmann had kidnapped and murdered the baby and written the ransom notes. Wilentz presented 40 examples of Hauptmann's handwriting and 15 ransom notes that Lindbergh had received. Colonel H. Norman Schwarzkopf, head of the New Jersey State Police (and father of the U.S. Army commanding general in the 1991 Persian Gulf war), testified that Hauptmann had willingly provided handwriting specimens and that the idiosyncratic or Germanic spellings that were found on the specimens and ransom notes were Hauptmann's own and not dictated by the police.

Crowds lined the streets trying to witness the trial of Bruno Richard Hauptmann. (Courtesy, National Archives)

Next, eight different handwriting experts took the stand. Two had testified in more than 50 trials. Another had helped send Al Capone to prison. A third had been a key witness in a suit over the legitimacy of Rudolf Valentino's will. Using blowups, the experts pointed out similarities between words and letters in the ransom notes and in Hauptmann's writing specimens. By the end of their five days of testimony, Wilentz was rejoicing in a triumph of scientific investigation of evidence.

Even more damning than the handwriting evidence was the testimony on the ladder found alongside the Lindbergh driveway. Arthur Koehler, a wood technologist of the U.S. Department of Agriculture, told how he had examined the ladder microscopically to determine its North Carolina pine origin. Then he traced the distinctive marks of its machine planing through mills to conclude that it had been processed in South Carolina, sold to a Bronx lumber company, and purchased by Hauptmann in December 1931. But one ladder rail was unlike the others. It contained four nail holes that matched four holes in beams in Hauptmann's attic, and the saw-tooth marks across the rail's end grain perfectly matched marks where one attic floor board was shorter than others. When the ladder rail was positioned in the open space on the beams, nails dropped easily into place through the board and into the beams.

The Shoebox on the Shelf

At 52, Hauptmann's defense attorney, Edward J. Reilly, had tried hundreds of murder cases. A hard-drinking blusterer and one of New York's most successful trial lawyers, he had been hired to take the case by the *New York Journal,* a Hearst paper, which had made a deal with Mrs. Hauptmann: exclusive rights to her story if the *Journal* helped pay for the lawyer.

To explain how he came to have the ransom money, Hauptmann testified that he had invested in business with Isidor Fisch, who went home to Germany in December 1933, and died there of tuberculosis in March 1934. Fisch, said Hauptmann, left belongings with him—including a shoebox that Hauptmann stored on the top shelf of a kitchen broom closet.

When rain leaked into the closet, Hauptmann found the forgotten shoebox, opened it, and discovered $40,000 in gold certificates. In his garage, he divided the damp money into piles, wrapped it, and hid it. Because Fisch had owed him $7,500, Hauptmann began spending some. He felt it was his.

Reilly called Mrs. Hauptmann to corroborate the Fisch story. Cross-examining her, Wilentz proved that, while she hung her apron every day on a hook higher than the top shelf and kept her grocery coupons in a tin box on that shelf, she could not remember ever seeing a shoebox there. Later, rebuttal witnesses testified that Fisch could not have been at the scene of the crime, and that he had had no money for treatments when he was dying in Germany.

Reilly had boasted that he would introduce eight handwriting experts. He came up with one, whose authority was undermined in cross-examination. Then Reilly brought in a witness who claimed to have seen Fisch in Manhattan on the night of the crime with a woman who carried a 2-year-old blond child, and that the woman was Violet Sharpe, a maid in the Morrow home who had committed suicide after intensive interrogation (all servants in the Morrow and Lindbergh households had been questioned closely). That witness proved to be a professional who had testified for pay in dozens of trials.

Another Reilly defense witness claimed to have seen Fisch coming out of the cemetery where the ransom was passed. Prosecutor Wilentz made the witness admit he had previously been convicted of a crime and that he was with a woman on the night in question. Still another witness, who testified that he saw Fisch with a shoebox, admitted under cross-examination that he had been in and out of mental institutions five times.

Reilly talked freely with reporters. Radio listeners heard him promise that his client would be a free man within days. In one broadcast, he urged anyone with information to get in touch. During a lunch break, as Reilly sipped his third cocktail from a coffee cup, a stranger approached him and said he had information. After questioning him, Reilly, clearly frustrated by his own failure to produce a credible witness, yelled, "You've never been convicted of a crime? You've never been in a lunatic asylum? I can't use you!"

Reilly's troubles continued: To contradict the ladder testimony, he produced a general contractor as an expert on wood. After Wilentz attacked the witness' expertise, the judge allowed him to testify only as a "practical lumberman." Another carpenter said that the ladder rail had *not* been cut from the attic board, then admitted on cross-examination that he had never compared the grains of the two boards.

When the trial ended, no reliable witness had placed Hauptmann at the scene of the crime; nor had his fingerprints been found on the ladder, nor anywhere in the nursery, nor on the ransom notes. But the circumstantial evidence overwhelmed whatever doubts the jurors may have had: He had the ransom money; scientific experts said he had made the ladder—using wood from his attic for one rail; and other experts said he had written the ransom notes.

Governor Gets into the Act

When the jury found Hauptmann guilty of murder in the first degree, the crowds in and outside the courtroom cheered vigorously. The sentence was death. Execution was set for the week of March 18. Over the next year, Hauptmann's attorneys (Anna Hauptmann had fired Reilly) gained postponements by filing appeals.

New Jersey's 40-year-old governor, Harold G. Hoffman, secretly visited Hauptmann in prison, declared that he was not convinced of Hauptmann's guilt, and that the crime could not have been committed alone. In mid-January 1936, when the state's Court of Pardons denied Hauptmann clemency, the governor granted him a 30-day reprieve. The Court of Pardons turned down a second petition for clemency. By law, the governor could not give a second reprieve. On April 3, 1936, at 8:44 P.M., Hauptmann was electrocuted.

For more than half a century, book after book has re-examined and critiqued the evidence and the testimony. More than one author has described the investigation of the kidnapping and murder as incompetent or has declared Hauptmann an innocent, framed man.

In 1982, 82-year-old Anna Hauptmann sued the State of New Jersey, various former police officials, the Hearst newspapers, and David T. Wilentz (himself by then 86) for $100 million in wrongful-death damages. She claimed that newly found documents proved misconduct by the prosecution and manufacture of evidence by government agents. In 1983, the U.S. Supreme Court refused her request that the federal judge considering her case be disqualified, and in 1984 the judge dismissed her claims.

In 1985, 23,000 pages of Hauptmann-case police documents were discovered in the garage of the late Governor Hoffman. Along with 30,000 pages of FBI files not used in the trial, said Anna Hauptmann, they proved "a smorgasbord of fraud" against her husband. Again, she appealed to the Supreme Court; it let stand without comment the rulings that had dismissed her suit. In 1990, New Jersey's new governor, Jim Florio, declined her appeal for a meeting to clear Hauptmann's name.

In October 1991, Mrs. Hauptmann, now 92, called a news conference in Flemington to plead for the case to be reopened. "From the day he was arrested, he was framed, always framed," she said. Among her allegations was that the rail of the ladder taken from the attic had been planted by the state police. The ransom money, she still insisted, was left behind by Isidor Fisch.

—Bernard Ryan, Jr.

Suggestions for Further Reading

Davis, Kenneth S. *The Hero: Charles A. Lindbergh and the American Dream.* Garden City, N. Y.: Doubleday & Co., 1959.

Fisher, Jim. *The Lindbergh Case.* New Brunswick, N.J.: Rutgers University Press, 1987.

Kennedy, Ludovic. *The Airman and the Carpenter.* New York: Viking, 1985.

King, Wayne. "Defiant Widow Seeks to Reopen Lindbergh Case." *The New York Times* (October 5, 1991): 24.

"Lindbergh Kidnapping's Final Victim." *U.S. News & World Report,* (November 4, 1985): 11.

Mosley, Leonard. *Lindbergh: A Biography.* Garden City, N. Y.: Doubleday & Co., 1976.

Rein, Richard K. "Anna Hauptmann Sues a State to Absolve Her Husband of 'The Crime of the Century.'" *People Weekly* (September 6, 1982): 34–35.

Ross, Walter S. *The Last Hero: Charles A. Lindbergh.* New York: Harper & Row, 1964.

Scaduto, Anthony. *Scapegoat: The Lonesome Death of Bruno Richard Hauptmann.* New York: G.P. Putnam's Sons, 1976.

Waller, George. *Kidnap: The Story of the Lindbergh Case.* New York: Dial Press, 1961.

Albert Fish Trial: 1935

Defendant: Albert Fish **Crime Charged:** Murder
Chief Defense Lawyers: James Dempsey, Frank J. Mahony
Chief Prosecutors: Elbert T. Gallagher, Thomas D. Scoble
Judge: Frederick P. Close **Place:** White Plains, New York
Date of Trial: March 11en22, 1935 **Verdict:** Guilty **Sentence:** Death

SIGNIFICANCE

The always-blurred distinctions between medical and criminal insanity became virtually indistinguishable during this trial of one of America's most extraordinary criminals.

On June 3, 1928, an elderly, meek-mannered handyman calling himself "Frank Howard" lured 12-year-old Grace Budd away from her family in New York City, on the pretext of taking her to a party. She was never seen alive again. A huge search initially raised hopes that Grace would be found, but as days, weeks, and then months passed with no news, the Budds resigned themselves to the inevitable.

Like most families in such ghastly circumstances they got on with their lives and tried to put the tragedy behind them. Then, on November 11, 1934, came a bolt from the blue. The letter they received, postmarked in Manhattan, was obscene and rambling, but its gloating account of Grace Budd's death bore ominous hallmarks of authenticity.

Forensic analysis of the monogrammed stationery eventually led detectives to a rooming house on 52nd Street, and a shabbily dressed old man who made no attempt to resist when he was taken into custody on the morning of December 13.

Something had gone horribly wrong in the brain of Albert Fish. To the outside world this 66-year-old house painter displayed an avuncular, even benign warmth, but beneath the surface lurked a demonically disturbed personality. He was a serial pedophile, a cannibal, a fantasist, irredeemably sado/masochistic, and, ultimately, a child killer.

So said Elbert T. Gallagher, the assistant district attorney, when he opened the state's case against Fish on March 11, 1935. Gallagher spared no emotions, either his own or the court's, as he read aloud the infamous letter. In it, the writer described what happened after he had taken Grace to a deserted house in Westchester County. "I first stripped her naked . . . [and] choked her to death, then cut her in small pieces." These were then roasted in an oven. "It took me nine days to eat her entire body," he wrote, before adding what he imagined to be some kind of palliative: "She died a virgin."

Fish had made no attempt to deny that he was either the author of the letter or the person who had killed Grace Budd. But was he legally insane?

Albert Fish, self-proclaimed murderer/cannibalist, with his lawyer, James Demsey. (Bettmann/Corbis)

The M'Naghten Rule

Ever since Daniel M'Naghten, a deranged workman, was acquitted of an 1843 murder in London by reason of insanity, the so-called "M'Naghten Rule" had been the benchmark of sanity in the American courtroom. It reads as follows:

> To establish a defense on the ground of insanity, it must be clearly proved that, at the time of the committing of the act, the party was laboring under such a defect of reason, from disease of the mind, as to not know the nature and quality of the act he was doing, or, if he did know it, that he did not know he was doing what was wrong.

Gallagher was emphatic: "In this case, there is a presumption of sanity. The proof, briefly, will be that this defendant . . . knows the difference between right and wrong . . . and that he is legally sane and should answer for his acts."

For chief defense attorney James Dempsey, it was a question of getting as much of Fish's bizarre personal history before the jury as he dared. His was a life given over to wholesale perversion: self-flagellation with nail-studded paddles; needles plunged beneath his fingernails; unspeakable violence toward countless children; all fanned by delusions of religious mania. In 1930 he had been committed to Bellevue, New York's psychiatric hospital, only for them to discharge him as "fit to live in society."

"Bellevue has a lot to account for here," said Dempsey, reminding the jury that it was up to the prosecution to prove that a man who killed and ate children was sane.

Of the four psychiatrists who testified on behalf of the state, Dr. Charles Lambert was the most forceful in his insistence that Fish was a "psychopathic personality without a psychosis."

Dempsey stared incredulously at the witness. "Assume that this man not only killed this girl but took her flesh to eat it. Will you state that that man could for nine days eat that flesh and still not have a psychosis?"

"Well, there is no accounting for taste, Mr. Dempsey," replied Lambert smoothly.

Few in court were prepared for the stomach-churning testimony of the star defense witness, Dr. Frederic Wertham, an eminent psychiatrist who had examined Fish at length and would later write voluminously about the defendant. Certainly it was too strong for Judge Frederick Close, who at the outset had announced his intention of having "a quiet orderly trial." He ordered the courtroom cleared of women before permitting Wertham to recount extraordinary details gleaned from Fish's memory. So outlandish did they seem, that at first Wertham had wondered if what Fish told him "might be fancies, but I have never seen fancies which showed up on an X-ray." This was an X-ray of Fish which revealed no fewer than 29 needles embedded deep in his scrotal region.

Admits to Cannibalism

Gradually, as Fish began to open up during the interviews, came confirmation of his cannibalism. "He definitely told me," said Wertham, "that he ate the flesh of Grace Budd." And Fish had gone on to explain himself thus: "What I did must have been right, or an angel would have stopped me, just as an angel stopped Abraham in the Bible."

Wertham had no doubt that Fish was clinically unique. "To the best of my knowledge, every sexual abnormality that I have ever heard of, this man has practiced." And his conclusion was unambiguous. "He does not know the character and quality of his acts. He does not know right from wrong. He is insane now and was insane before."

Dempsey attempted to press home this advantage in closing, explaining why his client had remained mute. "I do not believe an insane man should be on the witness stand, testifying. Secondly . . . the story of this man's life is one of unspeakable horror. You wouldn't believe it: he would disgust and nauseate you."

By contrast, Gallagher kept hammering away on the M'Naghten Rule. Fish, quite clearly, knew the difference between right and wrong. "If this defendant were operating under psychosis, how could he tell you all of the details about the killing of this girl?"

This extraordinary trial concluded on March 22, when, after four hours deliberation, the jury decided that Fish was sane and guilty of murder.

Sentence of death was automatic, and on January 16, 1936, the man who, by his own admission had murdered at least a dozen children and abused countless others, was executed at Sing Sing prison.

Nothing provides a clearer insight into Fish's tortured mind than his reaction to the jury's verdict: momentary disappointment, replaced almost instantly by a glow of near elation. "What a thrill that will be, if I have to die in the electric chair," he beamed. "It will be the supreme thrill—the only one I haven't tried." Then his mood shifted again, and he mumbled, "But it wasn't the right verdict. I'm not really sane, you know."

—Colin Evans

Suggestions for Further Reading

Heimer, Mel. *The Cannibal.* New York: Pinnacle Books, 1971.

Wertham, Frederick. *The Show of Violence.* London: Gollancz, 1949.

Wilson, Colin and Pam Pitman. *Encyclopedia of Murder.* New York: Putnam's, 1961.

Vera Stretz Trial: 1936

Defendant: Vera Stretz **Crime Charged:** Murder
Chief Defense Lawyer: Samuel S. Leibowitz **Chief Prosecutor:** Miles O'Brien **Judge:** Cornelius F. Collins **Place:** New York, New York
Dates of Trial: March 20–April 3, 1936 **Verdict:** Not guilty

SIGNIFICANCE

For defense counsel Samuel S. Leibowitz, the Vera Stretz case was the 116th of 139 consecutive trials in which he saved his client from death in the electric chair. Many lawyers believe the case marked his peak as a trial lawyer before he became one of the New York courtroom's most respected judges.

Vera Stretz was 29 years old when she spent some of her $35,000 inheritance from her mother on a cruise aboard the *Vulcania* in December 1934. There she met Dr. Fritz Gebhardt, a German financier who was 42. Chatting in German (her German was better than his English), they became casual friends.

Soon after returning to New York, Stretz and the doctor dated. Witty and gallant, Dr. Gebhardt seemed determined to sweep Vera Stretz off her feet. But he had a wife and two children in Germany. The marriage, he said, had been one in name only for 10 years.

"He told me that he loved me," Stretz later said. "And then he said that he was an unusual person. Ordinary laws applied to ordinary people, but for an unusual person there must be different standards. I was fascinated by him." Stretz found herself so deeply in love that in May she traveled with him to Lake George as Mrs. Gebhardt.

Soon Stretz moved to Gebhardt's building, Beekman Towers, taking an apartment two floors below his. As he traveled often, they exchanged passionate love letters.

By November, Stretz regularly responded to late-night calls from Gebhardt, applying a heating pad to help him through stomach cramps as often as once a week. Early in November, when he returned from a European trip, he said, "I am going away again in December and you are going with me."

Stretz assumed he had decided to end his marriage. "I'd better hurry with the wedding invitations," she said. No, said Gebhardt, he knew now that he was not the type to get married. They would go on as before.

She told him she would not compromise: She wanted a home and a husband. "No one has ever left me before," he announced, "and you are not going to leave me."

Late in the night of November 11, in great stomach pain, Gebhardt called her. She put a coat on over her nightgown, slipped into shoes, and went up the back stairs.

A Revolver and Bloodstains

At 2:30 A.M., shots were heard in Beekman Towers. The police were called. They discovered Vera Stretz sitting on the stairway just below the third floor. In her large handbag they found a .32-caliber revolver, a box of bullets, two spent shells, and a crumpled silk nightgown with fresh wet bloodstains.

"Did you shoot the man upstairs?" they asked.

"Yes, I did," sobbed Stretz. "But please don't ask me why I did it." She said she was on the way to turn herself in.

The police grilled her for hours, but she would say nothing more. Her father, Frank Stretz, sent for Samuel Leibowitz, who had defended the Scottsboro boys (see separate entry) and was known as the best criminal lawyer in the country. The newspapers called Stretz "the icy blonde" because she wouldn't talk. They dug up Gebhardt's background: He had flown in World War I's famed Richtofen Squadron, was a pal of pilot Hermann Goering, held doctorates in both philosophy and political economy, had made half a million dollars in international business deals, but had made the mistake—from Nazi Germany's point of view—of marrying a non-Aryan. He had, however, moved out, leaving her with two children and no divorce.

Vera Stretz Tells what Happened

When the trial began on March 20, 1936, defense attorney Leibowitz probed each juror's knowledge of Friedrich Wilhelm Nietzsche, the German philosopher whose idea of a super-race attracted Adolf Hitler, and who said, "Man shall be trained for war and woman for the recreation of the warrior; all else is folly." Then, with Vera Stretz on the stand for 13 hours, Leibowitz carefully produced testimony on Gebhardt's attitude toward marriage and toward her. When she announced the night of November 11 that she would not continue their relationship, she testified, Gebhardt had thrown her on the bed and raped her.

Next, laughing at her and saying, "If you want to make it the last night, you will have to make it a good one," he demanded that she perform an act of sodomy so foreign to her, and so shameful, that she had been unable to tell the police. Now she recounted it, at the insistence of Judge Cornelius Collins, only through violent, uncontrollable sobbing. Recalling seeing a gun in Gebhardt's chest of drawers when she looked for his heating pad, she seized it. The doctor, crying, "You damned whore, I will kill you," grabbed at the gun, she said. It went off. He fell on the bed, got up, lunged again at her, and she shot again.

Prosecutor Miles O'Brien cross-examined her for four fours. She killed, he insisted, in a hot fever of jealousy because Gebhardt wouldn't give up his wife for her: "She is a tigress when provoked." But he was unable to produce a single contradiction in Stretz's testimony.

Vera Stretz (center) shown with her attorney Samuel Leibowitz (right) leaving court after her arraignment on murder charges for shooting Dr. Fritz Gebhardt. (AP/Wide World Photos)

The judge's charge lasted five hours, defining first-degree murder, second-degree murder, first-degree manslaughter, and reasonable doubt, excusable homicide, and justifiable homicide. "If you believe her story," he finished acidly, "acquit her."

Within three hours, the jury did so. The furious judge went to his chambers without thanking the jury for its services.

The next day, Stretz met the press. "Don't let this ruin your life," said a woman reporter.

"My life is ruined already," said Vera Stretz.

Years later, the defendant in this trial was identified only as one Laura Parr. When and how her name was changed from Vera Stretz remains a secret buried with her ruined life.

—*Bernard Ryan, Jr.*

Suggestions for Further Reading

The *New York Times. See* Stretz, Vera, in The *New York Times Index,* November 12, 1935–April 4, 1936.

Reynolds, Quentin. *Courtroom: The Story of Samuel S. Leibowitz.* New York: Farrar, Straus and Co., 1950.

Charles "Lucky" Luciano Trial: 1936

Defendant: Charles "Lucky" Luciano **Crime Charged:** Compulsory prostitution **Chief Defense Lawyers:** Francis W.H. Adams and George Morton Levy **Chief Prosecutor:** Thomas E. Dewey **Judge:** Philip J. McCook **Dates of Trial:** May 13–June 7, 1936 **Verdict:** Guilty **Sentence:** 30 to 50 years imprisonment

SIGNIFICANCE

The "Lucky" Luciano case is a paradox: It proves that, no matter how much money a crime boss has made or how well his lawyers and henchmen have protected him, he can be convicted and sentenced to long imprisonment. But it also proves that where there's a will, there's a way to gain release, as Luciano ultimately did.

In 1935, Charles "Lucky" Luciano was the nation's number one crime boss. He had run the national crime syndicate—later famous for its disciplinary arm dubbed "Murder, Inc."—since its organization in 1931.

A New York grand jury, briefed on the extent of vice and racketeering, asked for appointment of a special prosecutor. Governor Herbert H. Lehman appointed Thomas E. Dewey, an ambitious former chief assistant U.S. attorney.

Dewey learned that "Lucky" Luciano (so nicknamed because he usually won craps games and had survived a severe beating and throat-slitting) had expanded his operations from extortion from bordellos to complete control over them. He was taking in more than $10 million annually, with 5,000 prostitutes on the nationwide payroll.

Dewey's staff interviewed whores, pimps, loan sharks, and strong-arm men. Word reached Luciano: Many had talked. He disappeared. Dewey proclaimed him "Public Enemy Number One." The grand jury indicted Luciano on 90 counts of compulsory prostitution (later reduced to 62).

Luciano was found in Hot Springs, Arkansas, where organized crime maintained a well-protected sanctuary. He was extradited only after Dewey pictured the Arkansas governor as a protector of gangsters and 20 Arkansas Rangers removed Luciano from the protection of the Hot Springs sheriff.

"I'm Gonna Organize the Cathouses Like the A&P"

The special blue-ribbon jury heard 68 witnesses. Some 40 were prostitutes or madams who had moved up in the ranks. One, Cokey Flo Brown, testified about meetings where Luciano presided. "I'm gonna organize the cathouses like the A&P," he had told her. "We could syndicate the places on a large scale same as a chain store system."

Lucky Luciano accompanied by guards at his hearing for compulsory prostitution, 1936. (AP/Wide World Photos)

Cokey Flo also testified that strong-arm methods had brought madams and pimps into line. "First you got to step on them," she quoted Luciano as saying. "Talking won't do no good. You got to put the screws on."

Against his lawyers' advice, Luciano insisted on taking the witness stand to deny all charges and deny knowing any of the witnesses. For four hours, Dewey pummeled him with questions, proving that he was lying in answer after answer.

Dewey's seven-hour summation described Luciano's testimony as:

> . . . a shocking, disgusting display of sanctimonious perjury—at the end of which I am sure not one of you had a doubt that before you stood not a gambler, not a bookmaker, but the greatest gangster in America.

The jury agreed: guilty on all counts. Judge Philip J. McCook's sentence: 30 to 50 years—the longest ever for compulsory prostitution. On June 18, 1936, Luciano went to New York State's maximum-security prison at Dannemora.

Dewey later admitted that he had been able to convict Luciano only for "a minor racket," while:

> It is my understanding that top-ranking defendants in this case have absorbed control of the narcotics, policy, loan-shark and Italian lottery syndicates, the receipt of stolen goods and certain industrial rackets.

Aided the War Effort

World War II freed Luciano. In 1942, U.S. Navy officers, frustrated by unstable labor conditions and sabotage on the New York waterfront, visited Luciano. He ordered cooperation and gained a private cell. A year later, the Navy, planning the invasion of Sicily, asked him to enlist the help of the island's natives. A deal was struck. After the war, with the Navy citing Luciano's aid in shortening the war in Sicily and Italy and with by then-Governor Dewey's approval, he was paroled to his birthplace in Sicily.

Luciano settled in Naples, barred from Rome by the Italian government. He lived there, except for an illegal sojourn in Cuba (where he ordered the death of his syndicate associate, "Bugsy" Siegel), until he died of a heart attack in 1962.

—*Bernard Ryan, Jr.*

Suggestions for Further Reading

Fox, Stephen. *Blood and Power.* New York: William Morrow & Co., 1989.

Godwin, John. *Murder USA.* New York: Ballantine Books, 1978.

Gosch, Martin A. and Richard Hammer. *The Last Testament of Lucky Luciano.* Boston: Little, Brown and Co., 1974.

Nash, Jay Robert. *Almanac of World Crime.* Garden City, N.Y.: Anchor Press/Doubleday, 1981.

——. *Encyclopedia of World Crime.* Wilmette, Ill.: CrimeBooks, 1990.

Mary Astor Divorce Trial: 1936

Plaintiff: Mary Astor **Defendant:** Franklyn Thorpe
Plaintiff Claims: Custody of child, annulment of marriage, and abrogation of property settlement in earlier divorce **Chief Defense Lawyers:** Joseph Anderson and Michael Narlian **Chief Lawyers for Plaintiff:** Joseph F. Rank and Roland Rich Woolley **Judge:** Goodwin J. Knight **Place:** Los Angeles, California **Dates of Trial:** July 29–August 14, 1936 **Verdict:** Decree granted for plaintiff

SIGNIFICANCE

The Mary Astor case is a classic Hollywood divorce case. It entertained newspaper readers for weeks with charges, countercharges, and denials, and offered wondrous titillation and breathtaking insight into the daring illicit romances of people in show business. The case reads like the scenario of a life-in-Hollywood movie.

In 1936, actress Mary Astor was at the height of a Hollywood career that had begun in 1922 and had seen her move successfully through dozens of silent films in the 20s and into the "talkies." Her 74th film, the screen adaptation of Sinclair Lewis' novel *Dodsworth,* was in production, with Mary playing the "other woman." Over the years, she had appeared on-screen with such fabled names as George Arliss, Douglas Fairbanks, John Barrymore, William Powell, Jean Harlow, Gilbert Rowland, Dorothy Gish, Richard Barthelmess, Myrna Loy, Edward G. Robinson, Richard Dix, Frederic March, Clark Gable, and Paul Muni, in such classics as *The Man Who Played God, Don Q, Son of Zorro, Don Juan, The Lost Squadron,* and *Red Dust.*

Astor's first husband, director Kenneth Hawks, was killed in 1930 when his camera plane collided with another. In 1931, she married her doctor, Franklyn Thorpe. He sued her for divorce in April 1935, charging mental cruelty and incompatibility. Under the divorce settlement, he gained custody of their 3-year-old, Marilyn, and some $60,000 in negotiable properties and real estate. Astor could visit the child at will and have her for six months of the year if she wished.

"He'd Shake Her So Hard Her Teeth Rattled"

By the summer of 1936, Astor brought suit against Thorpe, saying she was coerced into the divorce and charging him with abusing Marilyn—"He'd shake her so hard her teeth rattled and bit her lips,'' she sobbed in court. Astor demanded custody of her daughter, formal annulment of the marriage, and abrogation of the property settlement. To persuade the court he was unfit to have custody of Marilyn, she produced evidence that Thorpe had been married previously but had not told her so, and that he had had four postmarital love affairs.

Thorpe's attorney, Joseph Anderson, said he would dispute Astor's contention that she was coerced. ''We can prove in her own handwriting that this was not the situation at all,'' he announced, ''but that she wilfully abandoned the child for a married man—George Kaufman.''

The Diary Written in Purple

Anderson had fired a shot heard ''round the world. Headline writers outdid each other shouting that renowned playwright and director George S. Kaufman had been named in Mary Astor's diary as her lover. Thorpe had the diary, dating from 1929. According to Anderson, its presentation as evidence would prove what everyone in show business knew: that Kaufman's sexual appetite was as great as his well-known appetite for work. And the diary—written, the press reported, in purple ink—would reveal a scorecard by Mary Astor on the performance in bed of almost every well-known actor in show business.

Mary Astor conferring with her attorney—Roland Rich Woolley (Hearst Newspaper Collection, University of Southern California Library)

Astor's lawyer, Roland Rich Woolley, told the court he wanted the diary produced by the defense as evidence, to prove that it was not such a compilation of titillation. Astor said the book was a forgery leaked to the press.

Sam Goldwyn, Jack Warner, Irving Thalberg, Louis B. Mayer, and Jesse Lasky and their lawyers tried to convince Astor and Woolley that it would be better for the movie industry and for her not to introduce the diary.

Playwright Flees in a Laundry Basket

Judge Goodwin J. Knight examined the diary. Several pages were missing. It was a ''mutilated document,'' not admissible as evidence. Thorpe's attorneys got Judge Knight to issue a subpoena that would force Kaufman to testify in court on his relations with Mary Astor. Irving Thalberg, for whom Kaufman was working, put Kaufman aboard his yacht, sailed him off to Catalina Island, and said the playwright had "disappeared." The judge issued a bench warrant for Kaufman's arrest. Kaufman sneaked back, hid at Moss Hart's home, then was hauled in a large laundry basket aboard a laundry truck to the San Bernardino railroad station, where he boarded a train for New York. After staying in his berth the entire trip, he said, "That's the best way to travel."

Too late, the judge issued a search warrant for Hart's home. "The bench warrant will hang over Kaufman's head always," he declared. "If he can be cited, I'll sentence him to jail."

Thorpe admitted that, before marrying Mary Astor, he had lived in Florida with another woman as man and wife, and that he also had been married earlier.

The judge negotiated with the lawyers. He ordered the diary impounded. (Later, with Mary Astor's permission, it was incinerated.) The judge awarded custody of Marilyn to Mary Astor for nine months of each year—the child could visit Thorpe during summer vacations from school—and nulled the earlier property settlement.

The bench warrant for Kaufman's arrest continued, but six months later the playwright visited the judge and paid a $500 fine, and they shook hands.

Mary Astor's career soared. Before she retired and turned to writing successful novels, she had made 109 movies, including *The Maltese Falcon, Thousands Cheer, Meet Me in St. Louis,* and *Hush, Hush, Sweet Charlotte.* She died at 81 in 1987.

—Bernard Ryan, Jr.

Suggestions for Further Reading

Astor, Mary. *A Life on Film.* New York: Delacorte Press, 1967.

——. *My Story: An Autobiography.* Garden City, N.Y.: Doubleday & Co., 1959.

Meredith, Scott. *George S. Kaufman and His Friends.* Garden City, N.Y.: Doubleday & Co., 1974.

Teichmann, Howard. *George S. Kaufman: An Intimate Portrait.* New York: Atheneum, 1972.

Herndon v. Lowry: 1937

Appellant: Angelo Herndon **Defendant:** James L. Lowry
Appellant Claim: Unlawful arrest **Chief Defense Lawyer:** J. Walter LeCraw
Chief Lawyers for Appellant: Whitney North Seymour, W. A. Sutherland, Elbert P. Tuttle **Justices:** Louis D. Brandeis, Pierce Butler, Benjamin N. Cardozo, Charles Evans Hughes, James C. McReynolds, Owen J. Roberts, Harlan F. Stone, George Sutherland, Willis Van Devanter **Place:** Washington, D.C. **Date of Decision:** April 26, 1937 **Decision:** Court found for appellant, 5–4

SIGNIFICANCE

In a case that raised political and legal issues of racial injustice in the South, the U.S. Supreme Court gave broader protection to revolutionary speech than it had in *Gitlow v. New York,* ruling that a state must be able to show a direct connection between the speech and an actual attempt to overthrow the government.

Angelo Herndon's worldview changed completely one sultry afternoon in June 1930 in Birmingham, Alabama. The slight, bespectacled black 17-year-old from a poor mining family in Ohio, a devout Christian who worked in a nearby coal mine, happened into a meeting of the Birmingham Unemployed Council. The speaker, a white Communist, was denouncing segregation and urging black and white workers to unite and confront racial and economic injustice. Impressed by the man's earnestness, Herndon committed himself to working for the Communist Party and became an organizer as the Depression deepened in the United States.

Herndon Arrested "On Suspicion"

By 1932 Herndon was in Atlanta, Georgia, forming an Unemployed Council there. Atlanta, like many other American cities, faced a political and financial crisis that year, as its public funds for relief ran out. The Fulton County Commission, which distributed money to needy Atlantans, was considering a tax raise. One commissioner, Walter Hendrix, stated that he believed the amount of suffering and starvation in the city had been overstated. When Herndon learned of this statement, he took it as a challenge and arranged a rally of unemployed people at the commission offices for the next day, June 30. Nearly a thousand workers, black and white, appeared at the commission offices. The startled commissioners immediately arranged to provide an emergency appropriation.

The incident worried Atlanta authorities. Suspecting Communist influence, they put a watch on the post office box given as the council's address, and on July 11, when Herndon showed up to collect his mail, two detectives arrested him "on suspicion."

A search of Herndon's lodgings revealed a quantity of Communist material. Herndon made no effort to hide his affiliation. The Communist Party was not illegal in Georgia at that time, but prosecutor John H. Hudson decided to charge the young man with "insurrection"—a combined attempt to overthrow the state government—under a Reconstruction-era law which provided a maximum penalty of death. Hudson reasoned that the Communist Party advocated the overthrow of the existing government, and that therefore a member of the Communist Party was automatically guilty under the statute. He had already invoked this law against six Communists arrested in 1930. As it happened, however, Herndon's case came to trial before theirs, on January 16, 1933.

Herndon Becomes a Political Symbol

From the beginning, the Herndon case was both a legal challenge and a political symbol. His cause was taken up by the International Labor Defense, a Communist-led organization that specialized in defending leftists. The ILD secured two young black Atlanta attorneys, Benjamin J. Davis, Jr., and John H. Geer, as his counsel. They agreed to present a broad political defense that would concentrate on the absence of blacks from Georgia juries, the unequal treatment of black defendants, and the unconstitutionality of the insurrection statute.

The young defendant shared the political view of his case and was eager to become a martyr for his cause. When his time to speak came, he delivered an impassioned 20-minute attack on the "capitalistic class" for fostering racial segregation in the South. His lawyers, Davis and Geer, were more circumspect. They brought up the matter of the exclusion of blacks from Georgia juries at the beginning of trial, but Judge Lee B. Wyatt dismissed that argument. They contended that the Communist Party was legal and that Communist doctrines were available in Georgia libraries. But they failed to raise the issue of constitutionality except in a brief motion at the beginning of the trial—a mistake that was to be costly for Herndon. In his summation, annoyed by the contempt of the judge and the all-white jury, Davis became more political; he charged the prosecution with waving "the bloody flag of racial prejudice" and declared the indictment "a blot on American civilization." Unimpressed, the jury found Herndon guilty of insurrection, recommended mercy, and set his sentence at 18–20 years.

U.S. Supreme Court Hears the Case

With their client in jail, Davis and Geer filed an appeal with the state supreme court, alleging that the insurrection statute was unconstitutional.

Meanwhile, the ILD publicized the case nationally to raise money for Herndon's bail. On May 24, 1934, the Georgia Supreme Court affirmed the verdict, and in September it refused to rehear the case, clearing the way for an appeal to the U.S. Supreme Court.

By the time *Herndon v. Georgia* reached the U.S. Supreme Court in April 1935, several things had changed. Herndon was now free on bail and living in New York City, where he frequently spoke to leftist rallies. His case had attained national recognition and attracted support from white liberals and organizations like the American Civil Liberties Union (ACLU). Most important, he had a new defense team, headed by the outstanding civil liberties lawyer from New York City, Whitney North Seymour. Seymour took the case on the understanding that he would pursue it entirely as a freedom-of-speech issue, without stressing the racial aspects, and the ILD agreed.

Seymour's argument before the Court was that the insurrection statute violated the Fourteenth Amendment, which forbids states from depriving citizens of life, liberty, or property without due process of law. By failing to define "insurrection" in detail, he argued, the statute opened the way for unjust and absurd prosecutions like Herndon's, in which a defendant was charged with a crime for belonging to a legal political party and advocating doctrines which were publicly available in libraries. J. Walter LeCraw, the assistant Fulton County solicitor, appealed to the Court's 1925 decision in *Gitlow v. New York*, in which it had held that a state had the right to restrict speech that had a "dangerous tendency" to undermine its institutions. His main point, however, was that the constitutionality question had been raised too late to be a proper ground for appeal.

On May 20 the conservative majority on the court, in an opinion by Justice George Sutherland, chose to duck the Fourteenth Amendment issue, ruling that the Supreme Court had no jurisdiction because the constitutional question had not been properly raised. Although three liberal justices, Cardozo, Brandeis, and Stone, issued a ringing dissent, the ruling meant Angelo Herndon was headed back to jail.

Determined to raise the constitutional issue, Seymour and his Atlanta associates, W. A. Sutherland and Elbert P. Tuttle, went back to the beginning. When Herndon returned to Atlanta on October 28 to begin serving his sentence, Sutherland and Tuttle served Fulton County sheriff James L. Lowry with a writ of *habeas corpus,* alleging that Herndon's imprisonment was unconstitutional. From there, the case worked its way up through the Georgia system once again, and again the state supreme court reaffirmed the original conviction.

The stage was set for a rehearing before the U.S. Supreme Court February 8, 1937. The parties were the same as in 1935: Seymour for the appellant, LeCraw for the defense, and the same nine justices. The atmosphere had changed, however. In January, the Court had voided the conviction of an Oregon Communist in a case very similar to Herndon's (*De Jonge v. Oregon*), and in *Herndon v. Lowry* it now had to address the Fourteenth Amendment question directly.

The Court divided 5–4. The majority opinion, written by Justice Owen Roberts, on April 26, struck down the insurrection law as an "unwarranted invasion of free speech." The statute, Roberts wrote, was "merely a dragnet which may enmesh anyone who agitates for a change of government." It was the first time a state law had been overruled on those grounds, and the decision heralded a major expansion in federal court protection of free speech.

—Hendrik Booraem V

Suggestions for Further Reading

Herndon, Angelo. *Let Me Live.* New York: Arno Press, 1969.

Martin, Charles H. *The Angelo Herndon Case and Southern Justice.* Baton Rouge: Louisiana State University Press, 1976.

Martin T. Manton Trial: 1939

Appellant & Defendant: Martin T. Manton **Appellee & Plaintiff:** United States **Appellant Claim:** Reversal of conviction for conspiracy to obstruct the administration of justice and to defraud the United States, and dismissal of sentence **Chief Lawyers for Plaintiff:** John T. Cahill, Mathias F. Correa, Frank H. Gordon, Silvio J. Mollo, and Robert L. Werner **Chief Lawyers for Appellant:** William J. Hughes, William E. Leahy, John E. Mack, and E. Donald Wilson **Judges:** Specially constituted federal court: George Sutherland (former justice, U.S. Supreme Court); Harlan F. Stone (justice, U.S. Supreme Court); Charles E. Clark (judge, U.S. Circuit Court of Appeals, Second Circuit) **Place:** New York, New York **Date of Decision:** December 4, 1939 **Decision:** Conviction upheld (Sentence: 2 years imprisonment and $10,000 fine)

SIGNIFICANCE

This unique appeal brought the senior judge of the country's most prominent federal appeals court before his own colleagues. With all but one of the court's judges disqualified because of their previous association with the appellant, a special federal court had to be constituted to hear the appeal. The case, involving a scandal unique in federal court history, established a landmark in the delineation of conspiracy to obstruct justice.

In 1939, Martin T. Manton was the senior circuit judge of the U.S. Circuit Court of Appeals for the Second Circuit, a position second only to the nine members of the U.S. Supreme Court. As a lawyer, Manton had made more than a million dollars before his appointment to the bench in 1916. His fortune, invested in real estate and business, had been severely depleted by the Depression.

With his friend William J. Fallon and several other men, Manton was indicted in April 1939, for conspiring to influence, obstruct and impede justice and to "defraud the United States of its right to have its legal functions exercised free from unlawful impairment."

"Without Regard to the Merits"

The indictment noted that Manton was a stockholder in, or "wholly or substantially owned or controlled" a number of corporations that had cases pending in his court between 1930 and 1939. It charged that Fallon actively proposed to those litigants that his close friendship with Manton could get them favorable action, and that such parties actively sought Fallon's help "in virtue of Manton's office, position, power and influence." Finally, the indictment charged:

> that Manton would accept and receive sums of money as gifts, loans and purported loans in return for such action, and would corruptly act in each of these cases without regard to the merits.

Harlan Stone was part of a specially constituted federal court in the trial of Judge Martin Manton. (Courtesy, Library of Congress)

Manton moved to quash the indictment, claiming it charged not one conspiracy but several separate conspiracies on one count, that it did not state an offense, and that more than one crime was charged in the indictment. The motion was overruled.

The trial soon produced evidence that Manton's downfall resulted from continuing his business activities after appointment to the bench. Many suits that reached his court involved patent-infringement disputes, with the loser doomed to heavy losses. Evidence showed that Manton owned stock in companies that were litigants and in whose favor he decided.

In one case, a patent infringement suit brought by Schick Industries against Dictograph Products Company, one Archie Andrews, the principal stockholder in Dictograph, provided Fallon with $10,000 in cash through an intermediary, who gave a receipt for the money for the purchase of Dictograph stock. Fallon went off to see Manton and returned within the hour to say, "Everything is O.K. You can go and tell Archie Andrews that he is going to get the decision in his favor." The decision was against Schick.

The district court jury found Manton guilty. He received the maximum sentence: two years in federal prison and a $10,000 fine. He appealed. Paradoxically, the appeal had to land in his own court, where all his fellow judges except one disqualified themselves as his close associates. Only Judge Charles E. Clark, who had been appointed to the bench after Manton resigned while under investigation, could hear the appeal. Therefore, a special federal court was constituted. Its judges were former Supreme Court Justice George Sutherland, Supreme Court Justice Harlan F. Stone, and Judge Clark.

"Conspiracy Constitutes the Offense"

Considering Manton's claim that the indictment wrongly set forth a number of distinct conspiracies in a single count, the special court found:

> that the conspiracy constitutes the offense irrespective of the number or variety of objects which the conspiracy seeks to attain, or whether any of the ultimate objects be attained or not.

Manton's contention, it said, "confuses the conspiracy, which was one, with its aims, which were many." The offense was the single continuing agreement among Manton and his cronies to sell judicial action to all willing to pay the price.

Altogether, the court's review found, Fallon had procured some $186,146 for Manton in 28 "distinct overt acts in pursuance of the conspiracy." In conclusion, the court noted that a mass of canceled checks, promissory notes, and other accounts was "so plainly at variance with the claim of Manton's innocence as to make the verdict of the jury unassailable."

Manton requested review by the U.S. Supreme Court. It denied his petition, and he went to federal prison at Lewisburg, Pennsylvania, on March 7, 1940. While eligible for parole after eight months, he served 19 months before he was released on October 13, 1941. He died in 1946.

—*Bernard Ryan, Jr.*

Suggestions for Further Reading

"Ex-Judge Manton of U.S. Bench Here." (obituary) *The New York Times* (November 18, 1946): 23

"Manton Conviction in Sale of Justice Upheld on Appeal." *The New York Times* (December 5, 1939): 1.

The *New York Times. See* Courts, U.S. Federal Inferior, *New York Times Index*, January–December 1939.

Murder, Inc. Trials: 1941

Defendants: Frank "The Dasher" Abbandando, Louis "Lepke" Buchalter, Louis Capone, Martin "Buggsy" Goldstein, Harry "Happy" Malone, Harry "Pittsburgh Phil" Strauss, and Mendy Weiss **Crime Charged:** Murder **Chief Defense Lawyers:** Hyman Barshay, James L. Cuff, William Kleinman, David F. Price, Daniel M. Pryor, and Alfred I. Rosner **Chief Prosecutors:** William O'Dwyer, Solomon A. Klein, and Burton B. Turkus **Judges:** John J. Fitzgerald and Franklin Taylor **Place:** Brooklyn, New York **Dates of Trials:** May 8–22, 1940 (Abbandando, Malone, and Strauss, for Rudnick slaying); September 9–19, 1940 (Strauss and Goldstein, for Feinstein slaying); March 10–April 3, 1941 (Abbandando and Malone, second trial for Rudnick slaying); October 21–November 30, 1941 (Buchalter, Capone, and Weiss for Rosen slaying) **Verdicts:** Guilty **Sentences:** Death by electrocution

SIGNIFICANCE

These trials awakened America to the fact that crime was one of the nation's biggest businesses, so vast that the crime syndicate had established its own enforcement arm—labeled by the press "Murder, Inc." They also helped advance two political careers: Thomas E. Dewey moved from special prosecutor to district attorney to governor of New York and two unsuccessful campaigns as Republican nominee for the presidency of the United States, and Brooklyn District Attorney William O'Dwyer later became mayor of New York City.

Starting in the early 1930s, crime became organized into a national syndicate as local gangs specializing in bootlegging, prostitution, and racketeering began cooperating to produce greater wealth for themselves. Soon such bosses as Charles "Lucky" Luciano, "Dutch" Schultz, and Meyer Lansky, all of whom served on the board of directors of the syndicate, realized they needed to protect their power by eliminating any underlings caught skimming from the revenue chain, trying to seize more power than had been delegated to them, or otherwise getting out of line.

Meyer Lansky had the idea of creating a small, well-organized army of killers. In succession, the bosses put "Bugsy" Siegel, then Albert Anastasia, and finally Louis "Lepke" Buchalter in charge. Buchalter came up with the code words that eventually found their way into the American language: The murder specialists could accept a "contract" (assignment) to "hit" (kill) any "bum" (intended victim) anywhere at a price per hit that ranged from $1,000 to $6,000. Members of the force operated in secrecy and without territorial claims. The rank-and-file mobsters never knew who they were. The killers prided themselves on their ability to do their homework by studying photographs of a bum they did not otherwise know, move unrecognized into a strange city, find the miscreant, hit him by ice pick or knife or bullets (one used whatever was handy, including a fire ax grabbed from a restaurant's wall case), and quietly leave town while the perplexed police looked around among the local bad guys.

"We Only Kill Each Other"

The organization also prided itself on its businesslike outlook: Killers were provided insurance, health, and pension benefits and were kept on salary between hits. They knew that, if they were caught, the best lawyers would defend them and, if they were convicted, their families would find the take-home pay still coming in while they did time in jail. Furthermore, organization philosophy was summed up in the words of "Bugsy" Siegel to a nervous building contractor hired to make alterations in his home: "We only kill each other." Hitting police or prosecutors was strictly forbidden lest it produce intensive crackdowns by law enforcement people.

By 1935, a New York grand jury, alarmed by the path of blood left by the operations of the national crime syndicate, asked for the appointment of a special prosecutor to supersede the district attorney in investigating vice and racketeering. Governor Herbert H. Lehman appointed Thomas E. Dewey, who earlier had earned prominence as chief assistant U.S. attorney for the Southern District of New York. Within two years, Dewey had gained 72 convictions and suffered only one acquittal and had been elected district attorney of New York County (i.e., Manhattan). Meantime, the New York newspapers had invented the corporate title "Murder, Inc." to identify the hit squad that was Dewey's target. The crime syndicate began to worry.

"Dutch" Schultz told the syndicate board it was time to break the "we only kill each other" rule: A contract on Dewey should be put out, he insisted. The board tried to make the irrepressible Schultz understand what a disastrous avalanche of police pressure he was inviting. Schultz marched angrily out of the meeting, shouting, "If you guys are too yellow to go after Dewey, I'll get him myself and I'll get him in a week."

As the door slammed behind Schultz, the board consulted. Anastasia, who was commandant of the killer troop, said, "Okay, I guess the Dutchman goes." That evening, Schultz was cornered in a restaurant washroom by Charles "The Bug" Workman and Mendy Weiss and riddled with bullets.

Word reached Buchalter in 1937 that Dewey was building a case against him. His buddy Anastasia, who had himself proposed killing Dewey soon after

Schultz was eliminated, visited Lucky Luciano in Dannemora Prison (where the syndicate boss had languished since Dewey convicted him on charges of compulsory prostitution in 1936) and got permission to hide Buchalter. For two years, while Dewey offered a $25,000 reward and J. Edgar Hoover promised $5,000 to the FBI agent who turned Buchalter in, he could not be found. Meantime, from his hiding place in Brooklyn, Buchalter became more and more belligerent, dispatching killers to eliminate every potential witness against him.

DETECTIVE DIVISION
CIRCULAR NO. 11
AUGUST 8, 1939

POLICE DEPARTMENT
CITY OF NEW YORK

CLASSIFICATION

$25,000 REWARD

DEAD OR ALIVE

TWENTY-FIVE THOUSAND DOLLARS will be paid by the City of New York for Information leading to the capture of "LEPKE" BUCHALTER, aliases LOUIS BUCHALTER, LOUIS BUCKHOUSE, LOUIS KAWAR, LOUIS KAUVAR, LOUIS COHEN, LOUIS SAFFER, LOUIS BRODSKY.

WANTED FOR CONSPIRACY AND EXTORTION

The Person or Persons who give Information Leading to the Arrest of "LEPKE" will be fully protected, his or her identity will never be revealed. The information will be received in absolute confidence.

RIGHT HAND

LEFT HAND

DESCRIPTION — Age, 42 years; white; Jewish; height, 5 feet, 5½ inches; weight, 170 pounds; build, medium; black hair; brown eyes; complexion dark; married, one son Harold, age about 18 years.

PECULARITIES—Eyes, piercing and shifting; nose, large, somewhat blunt at nostrils; ears, prominent and close to head; mouth, large, slight dimple left side; right-handed; suffering from kidney ailment.

Frequents baseball games.

Is wealthy; has connections with all important mobs in the United States. Involved in racketeering in Unions and Fur Industry, uses Strong-arm methods. Influential.

This Department holds indictment warrant charging Conspiracy and Extortion, issued by the Supreme Court, Extraordinary Special and Trial Terms, New York County.

Kindly search your Prison Records as this man may be serving a Prison sentence for some minor offense.

If located, arrest and hold as a fugitive and advise the THE DETECTIVE DIVISION, POLICE DEPARTMENT, NEW YORK CITY, by wire.

Information may be communicated in Person or by Telephone or Telegraph, Collect to the undersigned, or may be forwarded direct to the DETECTIVE DIVISION, POLICE DEPARTMENT, NEW YORK CITY.

LEWIS J. VALENTINE, Police Commissioner

TELEPHONE: SPring 7-3100, SPring 7-2722, SPring 7-1366 or CAnal 6-2000

Wanted poster for Louis "Lepke" Buchalter, leader of "Murder, Inc." (Courtesy, National Archives)

Surrender to J. Edgar Hoover and Walter Winchell

By 1939, the syndicate board knew Buchalter was a liability. He had to go. But sending him off the way Dutch Schultz was sent would inspire Dewey to even greater determination to wipe out the syndicate. From prison, Luciano masterminded a scheme to make Buchalter think a deal had been made. Trusting his pals, he came out of hiding and surrendered to J. Edgar Hoover himself in a car driven by gossip columnist Walter Winchell, then learned he had been double-crossed: There was no deal. Within a month, he was tried in federal court on a narcotics charge, convicted, and sentenced to 14 years. Next, Dewey convicted him on a charge of extortion, with a 30-years-to-life sentence.

Within a year, one of Buchalter's killers, Abe "Kid Twist" Reles, arrested on a murder charge, decided to talk in exchange for police protection and immunity from prosecution. Soon the syndicate board knew that Reles, who seemed gifted with total recall, had talked for 12 days, filling 25 stenographic notebooks.

With Reles' testimony in May 1940, Brooklyn District Attorney William O'Dwyer (who later served as mayor of New York City, then resigned to become ambassador to Mexico) convicted Frank "The Dasher" Abbandando, Harry "Happy" Malone, and Harry "Pittsburgh Phil" Strauss of the murder of mobster George Rudnick. Sentenced to die, they appealed, citing an error in Judge Franklin Taylor's charge to the jury.

Meantime, O'Dwyer gained a second death sentence for Strauss in September 1940 for killing gangster Irving "Piggy" Feinstein. Convicted with

Strauss was Martin "Buggsy" Goldstein. When the New York State Court of Appeals reversed the first convictions, O'Dwyer let Strauss sit in Sing Sing Prison in March 1941 while he convicted Abbandando and Malone all over again. All three then lost appeal after appeal. Strauss and Goldstein were executed on June 12, 1941, and Abbandando and Malone on February 19, 1942.

O'Dwyer pulled Buchalter out of Federal prison in November 1941 and tried him, with Louis Capone and Mendy Weiss, for the murder of candy-store operator Joseph Rosen, whom they had forced out of business and then hit after he threatened to complain to authorities. Reles' testimony, including vivid descriptions of garrotings and ice pick stabbings, brought the first and only conviction and execution of a member of the syndicate board. (Buchalter was one of the wealthiest Americans ever lawfully executed.)

Reles was next scheduled to testify in the trial of Albert Anastasia for the murder of Teamster official Morris Diamond—another outside-the-mob murder that Luciano had cautioned Anastasia against. But early on the morning of November 12, 1941, the body of Kid Twist Reles was found lying 42 feet below the window of the hotel room where six policemen were supposedly protecting him. Deprived of his star witness, O'Dwyer withdrew the charges against Anastasia.

Buchalter, Capone, and Weiss, having exhausted all possible appeals, died at Sing Sing on March 4, 1944. With the earlier executions of Abbandando, Malone, Strauss, and Goldstein, then, a handful of men paid with their lives for the dozens upon dozens of ruthless killings by perhaps 60, perhaps as many as 100, professional killers on the "Murder, Inc." payroll over some 15 years.

—*Bernard Ryan, Jr.*

Suggestions for Further Reading

Fox, Stephen. *Blood and Power: Organized Crime in Twentieth-Century America.* New York: William Morrow & Co., 1989.

Godwin, John. *Murder USA: The Ways We Kill Each Other.* New York: Ballantine Books, 1978.

Gosch, Martin A. and Richard Hammer. *The Last Testament of Lucky Luciano.* Boston: Little, Brown and Co., 1974.

McClellan, John L. *Crime Without Punishment.* New York: Duell, Sloan and Pearce, 1962.

Messick, Hank. *The Silent Syndicate.* New York: Macmillan Co., 1967.

Nash, Jay Robert. *Almanac of World Crime.* Garden City, N.Y.: Anchor Press/Doubleday, 1981.

——. *Encyclopedia of World Crime.* Wilmette, Ill.: CrimeBooks, 1991.

Turkus, Burton B. and Sid Feder. *Murder, Inc.* New York: Farrar, Straus/Manor Books, 1951.

Sleepy Lagoon Trials: 1942–43

Defendants: Manuel Delgado, Henry Leyvas, John Matuz, Jack Melendez, Angel Padilla, Ysmael Parra, Manuel Reyes, Chepe Ruiz, Robert Telles, Victor Thompson, Henry Ynostroza, Gus Zammora et al. **Crimes Charged:** Murder, assault with a deadly weapon with intent to commit murder, misdemeanor assault **Chief Defense Lawyers:** George E. Shibley, *et al.* **Chief Prosecutors:** John Barnes, Clyde Shoemaker **Judge:** Charles W. Fricke **Place:** Los Angeles, California **Date of Trial:** October 19, 1942–January 12, 1943 **Verdicts:** The defendants listed above were all convicted on all counts. Three others were convicted of assault with a deadly weapon with intent to commit murder, two were convicted of misdemeanor assault, and five were acquitted on all counts. **Sentences:** Leyvas, Ruiz, Telles: life imprisonment for first-degree murder; Delgado, Matuz, Melendez, Padilla, Parra, Reyes, Ruiz, Telles, Thompson, Ynostroza, Zammora: five years to life imprisonment for second-degree murder

SIGNIFICANCE

The Sleepy Lagoon case was one of the major civil rights cases of the 1940s and exacerbated ethnic tensions which culminated in Los Angeles' "Zoot Suit Riots" of 1943.

Late at night on August 1, 1942, eight to ten uninvited young men were ordered to leave a birthday party at the east Los Angeles ranch home of the Delgadillo family. The party crashers ended up half a mile away on a "lover's lane," where they assaulted several young people parked by a reservoir nicknamed "Sleepy Lagoon." The victims of the beating returned to their own neighborhood, collected a large group of friends, and returned to confront their attackers. Finding no one there, they followed the sound of music to the nearby Delgadillo party. What happened when they arrived would never be clear, but a brawl erupted inside and around the Delgadillo house.

Police arrived to find two stabbing victims. They also discovered 22-year-old José Diaz dying nearby on the roadside. Authorities blamed Diaz's death and the fight at the Delgadillo house on a perceived "Mexican youth gang" problem in Los Angeles. Intending to extinguish gang-related crime, police used Diaz's death as a pretext to arrest hundreds of young Mexicans and Mexican-Americans for offenses ranging from weapons possession to minor charges like vagrancy, curfew violation, "unlawful assemblage," or possessing a draft card with an incorrect address.

By the end of the week, between 300 and 600 people had been detained in nightly police sweeps. Police singled out young "zoot suiters," who wore extravagant wide trousers, drape jackets, and flamboyant hats. Twenty-two of the detainees were charged with murder and assault, while two others were indicted as juvenile offenders. They became known as the "Sleepy Lagoon defendants." Prosecutors accused them of being members of a teenaged "gang," which had conspired to crash the Delgadillo party in search of the group that had attacked them earlier. Since José Diaz was allegedly killed during a fight resulting from this conspiracy, the Sleepy Lagoon defendants were held collectively responsible for Diaz's murder.

American participation in World War II played a major role in how the case was viewed. Conservative dailies like the *Los Angeles Times* and *Los Angeles Examiner* railed against "zoot suit hoodlums," but skeptics derided the trial. The *California Eagle,* Los Angeles' African-American weekly, accused the conservative press of manufacturing fake "crime waves" perpetrated by minority young people in order to perpetuate segregation. Each side accused the other of aiding Nazi attempts to sow discord in the United States during wartime. Worried over reports that the Axis powers were using the trial to encourage a fascist "fifth column" in his country, Mexico's consul accused the prosecution and the conservative Los Angeles press of being motivated by racism.

Zoot Suit Riots

Prosecutors withheld clean clothing and haircuts from the Sleepy Lagoon defendants for two months preceding the trial, so that the accused would look like stereotypical "boy gangsters" when they appeared in court. Pressure from civic groups eventually convinced the district attorney to rescind the clothing ban and offer haircuts to the prisoners. When testimony began on October 19, 1942, however, the typecasting continued. One prosecution witness, Lieutenant Edward Duran Ayres of the Los Angeles Sheriff's Office, testified that Mexicans had a racial propensity for violence, rooted in a pre-Columbian disregard for human life exemplified by Aztec sacrifices. More specific prosecution testimony included identifications by guests at the Delgadillo party and statements to police by the defendants, several of whom incriminated each other. On January 12, 1943, all but five of the 22 Sleepy Lagoon defendants were convicted of murder or assault.

The civil rights implications of the case and Judge Charles Fricke's controversial conduct of the trial created wide support for the defendants. Locally, the trial was denounced by community activists, Chicano organizations, and Hollywood celebrities like Orson Welles, Anthony Quinn, and Rita Hayworth. The Sleepy Lagoon Defense Committee, which was formed to obtain a new trial, attracted nationwide support from labor unions, diplomatic groups, and press guilds. By the time the defendants began serving their sentences, the racial atmosphere in Los Angeles was poisonous. In June of 1943, a rumor that gang members had beaten several U.S. Navy sailors on shore leave prompted hundreds of servicemen to rampage through Mexican-American communities in Los Angeles and other southern California cities. Although the rioters' violence was initially directed against anyone wearing a "zoot suit," any young men with brown or black skin were targeted and beaten, often while police watched. Naval authorities could not restrain the attacks, which lasted for over a week and resulted in hundreds of serious injuries. Incredibly, no one was killed in what became known as the "Zoot Suit Riots."

"Tangible and Substantial Evidence is Woefully Lacking"

The Sleepy Lagoon Defense Committee's efforts were successful on October 4, 1944, when the three-judge 2nd District Court of Appeal unanimously reversed all the guilty verdicts. The court rejected the appellants' contention that Diaz might have been killed by a car or a fall, citing autopsy evidence that he had died from a brain hemorrhage brought on by a blow to the head with an instrument. The court ruled that criminality was involved in Diaz's death. Yet they found no evidence in the 6,000-page trial transcript that connected any of the Sleepy Lagoon defendants to Diaz's death. Apart from one defendant tied to a stabbing during the Delgadillo "free for all" only by inconsistent identifications, the judges similarly found no evidence connecting the defendants with armed assaults. The reversal also ruled that testimony in which several of the accused implicated their codefendants should have been stricken as hearsay and noted that police did not dispute that some of the statements were elicited by jailhouse beatings.

The court agreed that the defendants had returned to Sleepy Lagoon intending to have a fist fight with the youths who had attacked them and their friends. The indictments, however, specifically charged them with conspiring to invade the Delgadillo home with weapons, intending to commit murder. As such, the indictments did not apply to the facts of the case.

While the court ruled that "tangible and substantial evidence" was "woefully lacking," it also extensively criticized Judge Fricke's sarcastic and dictatorial conduct of the trial. "Constant bickering and quarreling with counsel by the court was not conducive to the creation of judicial atmosphere," agreed the appellate judges. Judge Fricke had "materially injured" the defendants' right to a fair trial by denigrating the professional ethics of the defense attorneys and berating their conduct "when in most instances, not even a mild rebuke was deserved." Fricke's multiple errors included a decree that lack of space was an acceptable reason for preventing the five defense lawyers from conferring or even sitting with their clients in the courtroom. If a room is too small for proper trial proceedings, said the appeal decision, "it is not the Constitution or the rights guaranteed by it that must yield."

The court, in agreement with California's attorney general and the defense lawyers, dispensed with a customary waiting period before deeming the original verdict excessive. Facing a unanimous appellate decision and lacking any new evidence to justify a new trial, the Los Angeles district attorney declined to prosecute the case a second time. After experiencing one of the most criticized trials in Los Angeles history and a year in San Quentin penitentiary, the Sleepy Lagoon defendants were released and their records were cleared. The trial was the inspiration for Luiz Valdez's acclaimed 1978 play *Zoot Suit* and his 1981 film of the same name.

—*Tom Smith*

Suggestions for Further Reading

"Conviction of 12 Reversed in Sleepy Lagoon Murder." *Los Angeles Times* (October 5, 1944): 1.

Kinloch, John. "Mexicans Face Police Terror Round-Ups; Vile Press Slurs." *California Eagle* (November 5, 1942): 1A, 7B.

Mazón, Mauricio. *The Zoot Suit Riots.* Austin: University of Texas Press, 1984.

Tobar, Hector. "Sleepy Lagoon Victims Laud Their Champion." *Los Angeles Times* (April 20, 1997): B-1.

Errol Flynn Trial: 1943

Defendant: Errol Flynn **Crime Charged:** Statutory Rape
Chief Defense Lawyers: Jerry Geisler and Robert Neeb
Chief Prosecutors: Thomas W. Cochran and John Hopkins **Judge:** Leslie E. Still **Place:** Los Angeles, California **Dates of Trial:** January 11–February 6, 1943 **Verdict:** Not guilty

SIGNIFICANCE

Despite the outcome, the Errol Flynn trial focused national attention on Hollywood's sexual mores, which both titillated and shocked many Americans. The trial also put the phrase "In like Flynn" into the American language.

In 1942, Errol Flynn was at the height of his swashbuckling Hollywood career. In 10 years, the handsome native of Australia had made 26 movies—among them such overnight classics as *Captain Blood, The Adventures of Robin Hood,* and *The Sea Hawk.* Flynn lived a boisterous, daring life that was also devil-may-care. He worked hard, drank hard, loved hard. Women everywhere had fallen for his splendid physique, his cleft chin, and his enticing dimples, and women everywhere were available to him.

At a party in September 1942, Flynn met 17-year-old Betty Hansen, who arrived with a studio messenger and who dreamed of moviedom fame and fortune. By dinnertime, Hansen had thrown up from too much drinking.

The next day, Hansen told her sister that Flynn had taken her upstairs to clean up, then seduced her in a bedroom. A complaint was filed with District Attorney Thomas W. Cochran, who recalled a similar complaint by one Peggy Satterlee after a voyage aboard Flynn's yacht. That charge had been dropped.

Flynn's stand-in stuntman, Buster Wiles, later said Satterlee's father had earlier approached Flynn with a demand for money, or, said Wiles, "he would lie to the police that his underage daughter had sexual relations with Flynn."

Flynn was arrested in October. He hired Hollywood's ace lawyer, Jerry Geisler.

Fans and sensation seekers thronged Flynn's neighborhood, spying through binoculars, prowling over his 11-acre property, mobbing the courthouse at his preliminary hearing, pulling at his buttons and shoes.

Selecting the jury on January 11, 1943, Geisler purposely took nine women, gambling that the females' attraction to the movie star would outweigh concern over the seduction of innocence.

Prosecutor Cochran opened with the Betty Hansen charge. Geisler's cross-examination proved that her testimony was confused and that she was currently awaiting action on a possible felony charge with her boyfriend, the studio messenger.

"J.B." and "S.Q.Q."

Now Cochran had Peggy Satterlee describe her voyage to Catalina. She said Flynn called her "J.B." (short for "jail bait") and "S.Q.Q." (short for "San Quentin quail")—evidence that he knew she was a juvenile. Nevertheless, she testified, he came to her cabin and "got into bed with me and completed an act of sexual intercourse"—an act against which, she admitted, she did not struggle. The next night, she said, he took her to his cabin to look at the moon through the porthole and there repeated the offense. This time, she said, she fought.

In cross-examination, Satterlee admitted to lying frequently about her age, then revealed that she had had extramarital relations with another man before the Flynn episode, and had undergone an abortion.

Taking the stand, Flynn denied the "jail bait" and "San Quentin quail" allegations, as well as entering Satterlee's cabin or taking her to his cabin or taking Betty Hansen upstairs after she threw up at the party or having sexual intercourse with either girl. As he finished, women were crying hysterically. Men were yelling obscenities. The bailiff had to quell a near riot.

The prosecution introduced an astronomer to back up Peggy Satterlee's description of the moon through the porthole. Geisler made him admit that, judging by the boat's course, the moon could not have been seen from Flynn's cabin.

The jury argued until the next day and found Errol Flynn not guilty. Said foreman Ruby Anderson afterward:

> We felt there had been other men in the girls' lives. Frankly, the cards were on the table and we couldn't believe the girls' stories.

Errol Flynn's career continued, totaling some 60 films before he died in 1959.

—Bernard Ryan, Jr.

Suggestions for Further Reading

Conrad, Earl. *Errol Flynn: A Memoir.* New York: Dodd, Mead & Co., 1978.

Flynn, Errol. *My Wicked, Wicked Ways.* New York: G.P. Putnam's Sons, 1959.

Higham, Charles. *Errol Flynn: The Untold Story.* Garden City, N.Y.: Doubleday & Co., 1980.

Thomas, Tony. *Errol Flynn: The Spy Who Never Was*. New York: Citadel Press, 1990.

Wiles, Buster with William Donati. *My Days with Errol Flynn*. Santa Monica, Calif.: Roundtable Publishing, 1988.

Bernard J. Lotka and Tillie Michalski Trials: 1943

Defendants: Bernard Joseph Lotka, Tillie Michalski
Crime Charged: Murder **Chief Defense Lawyers:** Lotka: George A. Codding, O. H. Bengtson; Michalski: Otto J. Frohnmayer
Chief Prosecutors: George W. Neilson, Allison Moulton **Judge:** H. K. Hanna
Place: Medford, Oregon **Date of Trials:** Lotka: May 17–20, 1943 Michalski: May 24–28, 1943 **Verdicts:** Lotka: guilty of second-degree murder; Michalski: not guilty **Sentence:** Life imprisonment

SIGNIFICANCE

These trials of an unmarried couple for the murder of their baby shocked a small Oregon town during World War II.

After the United States entered World War II in 1941, a number of camps were set up across the country where soldiers trained for war. One of these, Camp White, was located on the Agate Desert in Jackson County, Oregon. Some 30,000 men and officers resided in this temporary city of 1,300 buildings that included barracks, theaters, post offices, a radio station, a small prison, and a hospital.

Camp White had a significant impact on the nearby civilian communities.

For example, the largest city in Jackson County, Medford, was seven miles away, had a population of only 11,500, and gladly welcomed the soldiers to visit and spend their money in a variety of ways. However, the men not only brought their cash to Medford, but their personal problems as well. That led, in 1943, to the murder of a nine-week-old child that scandalized the army and the residents of southern Oregon.

The baby's parents, Bernard Joseph Lotka, 23, and Tillie Michalski, 22, were an unmarried couple from Cleveland, Ohio. Lotka was an army sergeant assigned as a surgical technician to the 79th General Hospital in Camp White, where he had been stationed since October 1, 1942. Michalski arrived in Medford shortly thereafter and, on October 5 they rented a cabin at Merrick's Motor Home under the name of Mr. and Mrs. B. Lotka.

Child of a Secret Relationship

Dating since 1939, Lotka and Michalski's relationship was not perfect. In April 1941, Lotka severely beat Michalski and assaulted her mother. Brought before a judge, the young man was released when he promised to marry the girl. (That promise was never kept.) A year later, when word came that Lotka would be drafted, the two "stepped over the line and became intimate." As a result, Michalski was six weeks pregnant when Lotka was inducted into the army on June 12, 1942. Once she learned of her condition, Michalski wrote to Lotka who told her to have an abortion. Her doctor, however, advised against it, so Michalski followed Lotka as he was sent to Denver, Colorado, and then to Camp White.

Things did not improve in Oregon. On Christmas Day 1942, Lotka left Michalski alone at their cabin to have dinner at a local home. In early January of 1943, he returned to Cleveland on a two-week furlough, but refused to allow Michalski, then eight and a half months pregnant, to come along lest their families found out about their living together and Michalski's condition. (None of their parents approved of the relationship.)

On January 25, 1943, the couple's son, William Lotka, was born. The parents were listed on the hospital's records as Sergeant and Mrs. Bernard Lotka.

Lotka still refused to marry Michalski. He also refused to allow the baby to be adopted for fear that his parents would somehow learn that he and Michalski were living together. Lotka never provided the young mother and child with anything. In addition, he wanted to get into the Army Air Corps, but that could happen only if he were single.

Baby's Body Found at Motor Court

On or around April 1, Lotka was accepted into the Air Corps. Then, on the morning of April 2, a gruesome discovery was made. Shortly before 10 A.M., E. P. Merrick, the manager of Merrick's Motor Home, and Raymond Chapman, the motor court's caretaker, noticed that no firewood had recently been used at the young couple's cabin. Their suspicions aroused, they entered and found William's body stuffed in a brown leather overnight bag on the shelf of the bathroom.

The police were called and two officers immediately went to Camp White to interview Lotka. The sergeant made a full confession and accompanied the police back to the motor home to reenact the crime. Based on information from Lotka, Michalski was arrested a short time later at the Union train depot in Portland, Oregon, nearly 300 miles away.

Lotka signed two statements confessing to the murder of his son. Supposedly, he and Michalski had "many times discussed getting rid of the child, and it was agreed between us to do so." Lotka also claimed that he killed the baby because "it was illegitimate and would never have a chance in society." Furthermore, he had no remorse for what he had done. "I don't consider I killed anyone, only my own flesh and blood, and the baby is better off this way."

According to Lotka's confession, he took Michalski on April 1 to the Greyhound station in Medford at about 8:30 P.M. so she could purchase a bus ticket to Portland. From there, she would go by train back to Cleveland. (According to Michalski, she decided on March 28 to return home.) Lotka also stated that, as far as he knew, Michalski thought he was only going to give the baby away. Instead, the sergeant returned to the cabin and smothered William with a blanket. One hour later, Lotka calmly returned to the bus station to see Tillie off. When asked, he told her that he had done nothing to the child.

Lotka further confessed that, after Michalski's bus was gone, he purchased an overnight bag, returned to the cabin, stuffed the baby's body into it, and then returned to Camp White. It was his intention to return the next day to bury the child, but the corpse was found before he could act.

Both Parents Face Death Penalty

Lotka and Michalski were both indicted for first-degree (premeditated) murder. If convicted, they faced the gas chamber. (The state's theory was that Michalski had previous knowledge of Lotka's intentions and was, therefore, an accessory to the crime.) Given court-appointed lawyers, one of Lotka's counselors was George Codding, a former district attorney. Michalski's lawyer was Otto Frohnmayer, a prominent figure in Jackson County's legal community.

The defendants were tried separately. (Shortly after his arrest, the local authorities were told by the military that Lotka was "definitely out of the army" and, thus, subject to the civilian courts.)

Initially, Lotka pleaded not guilty by reason of insanity. Under Oregon's law in 1943, this would have required his lawyers to prove that he was insane beyond a reasonable doubt. However, after specialists examined by him, the plea was substituted with a regular "not guilty" plea.

Lotka's attorneys did everything they could. They attempted to exclude the confessions from evidence on the grounds that Lotka had not been fully advised of his right to a lawyer before he made and signed the statements. They also argued that the confessions were improperly obtained by police promises to keep the scandal "localized" so the defendant's relatives in Cleveland would not find out. (When asked if he wanted any members of his family present at the trial, Lotka's response was that "I don't want to see any of them, and I would like it better if they knew nothing about it.") Thirteen witnesses from Camp White testified to the sergeant's excellent reputation and character. It was to no avail. As Lotka's other lawyer, O. H. Bengston, said to the jury:

> I am absolutely convinced this soldier is innocent and is trying to protect someone else, even though by so doing he may lose his own life. We have had no assistance from the defendant. He refused to take the stand in his own behalf to refute [the] state's evidence against him. He has sat resolutely by as if trying to protect somebody.

The trial lasted four days. After only three and a half hours, the jury found Lotka guilty on Thursday, May 20, of second-degree murder. (There were later rumors that some jurors refused to convict Lotka of first-degree murder because they did not want to apply the death penalty to a soldier. A conviction of second-degree murder, which required the jury to find the defendant guilty of acting deliberately in an unpremeditated manner, carried a mandatory life sentence.)

Father Blames Mother As Surprise Witness

The following Monday, Michalski's trial started. The state argued that she knew Lotka was going to kill the baby when she left for Portland. It also had a written statement signed by Michalski that she had tried, at Lotka's insistence, to smother the child a month before the actual murder, but became frightened and stopped when William turned blue. The alleged confession, which also contained such incriminating statements as, "I'm as much to blame as he is" and "I've gotten him into an awful mess," was submitted into evidence.

Michalski claimed that she was bullied to sign the statement and denied that she knew Lotka planned to kill William and that she ever tried to murder her son. Michalski further stated that, on the night of April 1, she and Lotka had a terrible fight during which he refused to let her take the child back to Cleveland. "If you leave with the baby, Tillie, I'll do something desperate." Furthermore, Lotka told her that he'd "rather see all three of us dead" than let the young mother take their son to her parents.

On the third day of Michalski's trial, a bombshell was dropped in court. Lotka, who said nothing at his own trial, was called by the prosecution as a rebuttal witness. The state did not expect him to talk, but Lotka now claimed that Michalski killed William and that he signed his confessions "to avert suspicion from her." As he said:

> I knew I had a good military and civilian record and thought perhaps I might receive leniency. All I wanted was for Tillie to get away from here, to go home to Cleveland.

When asked why he decided to speak up, Lotka claimed that Michalski's testimony had "blackened my character" and that he owed the truth to the men at Camp White who believed in his innocence.

In his closing argument, Michalski's lawyer, Otto Frohnmayer, told the jury:

> . . . you jurors may well criticize Tillie for abandoning her child in that cabin the night of April 1st, even though she might have had an inkling Lotka planned to smother it to death. But, that does not make her an accessory before the fact in this charge. That does not show she aided, abetted, or influenced the act.

Frohnmayer also attacked the state's theories of who actually committed the murder. (At first, the prosecution argued that Lotka committed the murder, but after his surprise testimony, the state maintained that Michalski did the deed and that the convicted killer was a credible witness.)

The jury considered the evidence for over seven and a half hours. Late Friday night, on May 28, it found Michalski "not guilty." Two days later, after a brief rest at a local hotel, Michalski left Oregon in the company of her mother and sister for her parents' home in Cleveland. And on June 4, Lotka was transported to his new residence at the Oregon State Penitentiary.

—Mark Thorburn

Suggestions for Further Reading

Medford Mail Tribune April 2–June 6, 1943.

Working, Russell. "Alcatraz: Camp White and Jackson County in the 1940s." In *Land in Common: An Illustrated History of Jackson County, Oregon.* Edited by Joy B. Dunn. Medford, Ore.: Mail Tribune, Rogue Federal Credit Union, and the Southern Oregon Historical Society, 1993.

Eddie Slovik Court-Martial: 1944

Defendant: Private Eddie D. Slovik **Crime Charged:** Violation of the 58th Article of War (desertion to avoid hazardous duty)
Chief Defense Lawyer: Captain Edward P. Woods
Chief Prosecutor: Captain John I. Green **Judges:** 1st Lieutenant Bernard Altman, Captain Stanley H. French, Captain Benedict B. Kimmelman, Major Orland F. Leighty, Major Robert D. Montondo, Captain Arthur V. Patterson, Captain Clarence W. Welch, Major Herbert D. White, and Colonel Guy M. Williams. **Place:** Rotgen, Germany **Date of Trial:** November 11, 1944
Verdict: Guilty **Sentence:** Execution

SIGNIFICANCE

Private Eddie Slovik was the only American executed for desertion of military duty from 1864 in the Civil War to the present. His court-martial during World War II stands as an example of the precise application of the letter of the law. It leaves disturbing questions about whether, all things considered, it was a fair trial.

In August 1944, as American forces in World War II fought across France into Germany, replacement troops, fresh off the troopship *Aquitania* and just out of basic infantry training, were moved toward combat. As one truckload of 12 soldiers neared the city of Elbeuf, some 80 miles northwest of Paris, they passed miles of bloody and charred remains of men, horses, guns, trucks, and tanks left behind by fleeing Germans. The Americans expected to join G Company of the 109th Infantry, 28th Division—Pennsylvania's famed National Guard outfit, known since World War I as the Keystone or "Bloody Bucket" division.

Toward midnight, not having found G Company and with shellfire exploding around them, the raw troops were ordered to dig in for the night. Two men, Privates Eddie Slovik and John F. Tankey, holed into side-by-side foxholes as German shells continued to pummel them. In the morning, Slovik and Tankey, saying they could not find their 10 companions or their unit, presented themselves to a Canadian unit in the vicinity and were welcomed.

A "Damn Good Guy"

Tankey wrote a letter to the 109th announcing that both men were lost. They stayed with the Canadian outfit for six weeks, roving back toward Calais as the unit posted notices explaining martial law to the natives. Eddie Slovik, 25 years old, established himself as a "damn good guy," an outstanding forager, and the creator of delicious potato pancakes, a talent grown on his Polish family tree.

Tankey noticed that Slovik quit carrying ammunition in his cartridge belt. Instead, he wadded pieces of paper, collected from the Red Cross, on which he almost constantly wrote letters to his wife in Detroit.

On October 7, Slovik and Tankey reached 109th regimental headquarters at Rocherath and were sent to Company G. No charges were placed against them, for the system of moving up rookie troops had been severely confused by the rapid movement of the outfits they were supposed to find.

"If I Leave Now, Will it be Desertion?"

Eddie Slovik reported to his company commander, Captain Ralph O. Grotte, in a farmhouse on the afternoon of October 8. He was "too scared, too nervous," he said, to serve with a rifle company. Could he serve in a rear area? If not, he said, he would run away. The captain shook his head and assigned him to Platoon 4. Slovik reported to his platoon leader, then went back to the captain. "If I leave now, will it be desertion?" he asked. Captain Grotte said it would. Slovik disappeared.

The next morning, a cook at the Military Government Detachment, 112th Infantry, found Eddie Slovik before him, presenting a slip of green paper with handwriting and saying he had made a confession. The cook turned Slovik over to his lieutenant, who had a military policeman take him back to the 109th, where Lieutenant Colonel Ross C. Henbest read Slovik's confession:

> I Pvt. Eddie D. Slovik #36896415 confess to the Desertion of the United States Army. . . . I came to Albuff as a Replacement. They were shelling the town and we were told to dig in for the night. The following morning . . . I was so scared nerves and trembling that at the time the other Replacements moved out I couldn't move. I stayed in my foxhole till it was quiet. . . . I then walked in town. . . . I turned myself over to the Canadian Provost Corp. After six weeks I was turned over to American M.P. They turned me lose. I told my commanding officer my story. I said that if I had to go out there again I'd run away. He said their was nothing he could do for me so I ran away again AND I'LL RUN AWAY AGAIN IF I HAVE TO GO OUT THERE.

The colonel advised Slovik to take back the confession and destroy it. When Slovik refused, the colonel had him write a disclaimer on the back noting that it "can be held against me and that I made it of my own free will and that I do not have to make it."

"I've Made Up My Mind"

Eddie Slovik was then locked up in the division stockade. Charges were preferred and investigated. Lieutenant Colonel Henry P. Sommer, the division judge advocate, offered Slovik a deal: "If you will go back to your outfit and soldier," he said, "I'll ask the General if he will suspend action on your court-martial. I'll even try to get you a transfer to another regiment where nobody will know what you have done and you can make a clean start."

"I've made up my mind," said Slovik. "I'll take my court-martial."

The colonel was not surprised. He had heard many men prefer to take their court-martials. The fact was that the 28th "Bloody Bucket" Division was facing its most difficult fighting ever. Deep in the Hurtgen Forest, it was being pounded by heavy and terrifying German artillery barrages. Casualties were high, withdrawals were imperative, rookie reinforcements were inexperienced and disorganized, snow was already falling. Men who had marched exuberantly through Paris in August were ready to take dishonorable discharges and serve months or, if need be, years behind bars to escape from the front lines in November. Desertions were becoming commonplace.

The Slovik court-martial was held at 10:00 A.M. on November 11, 1944 (the anniversary of World War I's Armistice Day). Before nine officers of the court seated behind a long table, the prosecutor, Captain John I. Green, stated the charge: desertion to avoid hazardous duty. On the specific charge of desertion at Elbeuf, a single witness testified that after the rookie troops searching for Company G had dug into foxholes a subsequent order had told them to move out, and that he had heard Slovik's voice among the men. On the specific charge of desertion at Rocherath, witnesses were the MP to whom Slovik handed his confession, Captain Grotte, who told of his interview with Slovik, the cook whom Slovik first encountered at Rocherath, and the officer to whom the cook took him.

Slovik's defense counsel, Captain Edward P. Woods, announced that the accused elected to remain silent. Lieutenant Bernard Altman then read him his legal right to be sworn as a witness. Slovik conferred with Woods, then said, "I will remain silent." The defense rested.

On secret written ballots, the nine officers then found Eddie Slovik guilty on the general charge and on each specific charge. All nine then concurred, on secret written ballots, in sentencing the accused:

> To be dishonorably discharged from the service, to forfeit all pay and allowances due or to become due, and to be shot to death with musketry.

The court adjourned at 11:40 A.M.

Under military law, the sentence had to be approved by the division commander, Major General Norman D. "Dutch" Cota, after the division judge advocate prepared a comprehensive review and recommendations. The review produced an FBI check on Slovik. It disclosed that he had a prison record. After serving five years for embezzling small change and merchandise worth $59.60 from a drug store where he worked, and for automobile theft and violation of paroles, he had been paroled in 1942, had married, and had held a good job until he was drafted in 1944. The prison record, the judge advocate told the general, was a reason for not recommending clemency.

Case Reviewed Extensively

The Slovik case was also reviewed by the military justice section of the European theater judge advocate and by the branch office of the judge advocate general, which reported:

> There can be no doubt that he deliberately sought the safety and comparative comfort of the guardhouse. . . . If the death penalty is ever to be imposed for desertion it should be imposed in this case, not as a punitive measure nor as retribution, but to maintain that discipline upon which alone an army can succeed against the enemy.

General Dwight D. Eisenhower, as European theater commander, issued the order confirming the sentence and directing the execution. Eddie Slovik was executed at St. Marie aux Mines in France on January 31, 1945, by a firing squad of 12 enlisted men.

Slovik's widow received no further pay or allowances. His GI insurance was not paid because, she was told, he died under "dishonorable" circumstances. She did not learn until 1953 that her husband had been executed for desertion.

—Bernard Ryan, Jr.

Eddie Slovik and his bride Antoinette on their wedding day. (AP/Wide World Photos)

Suggestions for Further Reading

Huie, William Bradford. *The Execution of Private Slovik.* New York: Dell, 1970.

Kimmelman, Benedict B. "The Example of Private Slovik." *American Heritage* (September/October 1987) 97–104.

Ex Parte Endo Trial: 1944

Appellant and Defendant: Mitsuye Endo **Appellant Claim:** Entitlement to *habeas corpus* **Chief Lawyer for Plaintiff:** Charles Fahey **Chief Lawyer for Appellant:** James C. Purcell **Justices:** Chief Justice Harlan F. Stone; Justices Hugo L. Black, William O. Douglas, Felix Frankfurter, Robert H. Jackson, Frank Murphy, Stanley F. Reed, Owen J. Roberts, and Wiley B. Rutledge **Place:** Washington, D.C. **Date of Decision:** December 18, 1944 **Decision:** Judgment reversed and the cause remanded to district court

SIGNIFICANCE

This Supreme Court decision ended what the American Civil Liberties Union later called "the worst single wholesale violation of civil rights of American citizens in our history."

In February 1942, soon after the Japanese bombed Pearl Harbor in the surprise attack that committed the United States to World War II, President Franklin D. Roosevelt authorized the War Relocation Authority to detain persons of Japanese ancestry living on the West Coast, many of whom were not only American citizens but native-born.

Military commanders were authorized to designate areas from which such persons could be excluded; if they lived within those areas, the military could move them. Lt. General J. L. De Witt, of the Western Defense Command, proclaimed that the entire Pacific Coast of the United States:

> [B]y its geographical location is particularly subject to attack, to attempted invasion by the armed forces of nations with which the United States is now at war, and, in connection therewith, is subject to espionage and acts of sabotage, thereby requiring the adoption of military measures necessary to establish safeguards against such enemy operations.

On those orders, 110,000 Japanese-Americans, 75,000 of whom were U.S. citizens, were removed from their homes. Meantime, Congress enacted legislation that ratified and confirmed the president's order.

Mitsuye Endo, a native-born American whose ancestors were Japanese, was taken from her home in Sacramento, California, to the Tule Lake War Relocation Center at Newell, California. Endo was 22. A Methodist who had never visited Japan and neither spoke nor read Japanese, she worked in the California Department of Motor Vehicles. At Tule, she and the others found they could not leave the center without written permission issued by the War Relocation Authority.

President Franklin Roosevelt authorized the relocation of people of Japanese ancestry after the attack on Pearl Harbor. (Courtesy, National Archives)

Petition and Appeal Stretch Over 21 Months

In July 1942, through lawyer James Purcell, who had worked with Japanese-American lawyers in Sacramento and who was appalled at the treatment the native Americans had received, Endo filed a petition for a writ of *habeas corpus* (relief from unlawful confinement) in the District Court of the United States for the Northern District of California. She asked for her liberty to be restored. One year passed. The petition was denied in July 1943. In August, Endo appealed to the U.S. Circuit Court of Appeals.

Next, Mitsuye Endo was moved to the Central Utah Relocation Center at Topaz, Utah. It took the Circuit Court of Appeals until April 22, 1944, to decide that it needed to apply to the U.S. Supreme Court for instructions on some questions of law. The Supreme Court promptly demanded the entire record of the Endo case, so that it could "proceed to a decision as if the case had been brought to the Supreme Court by appeal." Thus the case became identified as "Ex parte Endo"—ex parte being a legal way of saying that the case came from one side only (most appeals to higher courts have two sides, the appellant's and the appelee's).

Confined Under Armed Guard

The Supreme Court soon learned that Mitsuye Endo:

> is a loyal and law-abiding citizen of the United States, that no charge has been made against her, that she is being unlawfully detained, and that she is confined in the Relocation Center under armed guard and held there against her will.

The court also learned, from one of General De Witt's reports, that:

> Essentially, military necessity required only that the Japanese population be removed from the coastal area and dispersed in the interior. . . . That the evacuation program necessarily and ultimately developed into one of complete Federal supervision was due primarily to the fact that the interior states would not accept an uncontrolled Japanese migration.

The military's argument, noted Justice William O. Douglas in the opinion handed down December 18, 1944, was that "but for such supervision there might have been dangerously disorderly migration of unwanted people to unprepared communities" and that "although community hostility towards the evacuees has diminished, it has not disappeared and the continuing control of the Authority over the relocation process is essential to the success of the evacuation program."

Justice Douglas wrote:

> We are of the view that Mitsuye Endo should be given her liberty. We conclude that, whatever power the War Relocation Authority may have to detain other classes of citizens, it has no authority to subject citizens who are concedeedly loyal to its leave procedure.
>
> Loyalty is a matter of the heart and mind, not of race, creed, or color. He who is loyal is by definition not a spy or a saboteur. When the power to detain is derived from the power to protect the war effort against espionage and sabotage, detention which has no relationship to that objective is unauthorized.
>
> If we assume (as we do) that the original evacuation was justified, its lawful character was derived from the fact that it was an espionage and sabotage measure, not that there was community hostility to this group of American citizens.

"Mitsuye Endo," concluded the Justice, "is entitled to unconditional release by the War Relocation Authority."

By this time, the War Relocation Authority, aware that no military need existed for barring Japanese Americans from the West Coast, had quietly begun permitting selected evacuees to return home. The Supreme Court decision effectively ended the detention program, as the Western Defense Command announced that "those persons of Japanese ancestry whose records have stood the test of Army scrutiny during the past two years" would be released from internment after January 2, 1945.

—Bernard Ryan, Jr.

Suggestions for Further Reading

Armor, John, and Peter Wright. with photographs by Ansel Adams and commentary by John Hersey. *Manzanar.* New York: Times Books division of Random House, 1988.

Burns, James MacGregor. *Roosevelt: The Soldier of Freedom.* New York: Harcourt Brace Jovanovich, 1970.

Irons, Peter. *Justice at War.* New York: Oxford University Press, 1983.

Melendy, H. Brett. *The Oriental Americans.* New York: Twayne Publishers, 1972.

Wilson, Robert A. and Bill Hosokawa. *East to America.* New York: William Morrow & Co., 1980.

Ezra Pound Trial: 1946

Defendant: Ezra Pound **Crime Charged:** Treason
Chief Defense Lawyers: Thurman Arnold, Julien Cornell, and Robert W. Furniss, Jr. **Chief Prosecutors:** Isaiah Matlack, and Oliver Gasch
Judge: Bolitha J. Laws **Place:** Washington, D.C. **Date of Trial:** February 13, 1946 **Verdict:** Unsound mind; indictment dismissed in 1958

SIGNIFICANCE

This case involved a unique combination of elements: the charge of treason, a defendant who was widely known and respected in the literary world, the question of insanity (never fully resolved), and the commitment of such renowned figures as T.S. Eliot, Robert Frost, Ernest Hemingway, and Archibald MacLeish.

Ezra Pound was born in Hailey, Idaho, a town of one street, one hotel, and 47 saloons, in 1885. After unhappy college years, he moved to Europe before World War I. There, while publishing poetry and working as secretary to Irish poet William Butler Yeats, he helped establish such literary giants as T.S. Eliot, Robert Frost, and James Joyce.

In Paris in the 1920s, the expatriate colony found Pound superbly confident of his own talent and outspokenly critical of all people and ideas that earned his disdain. In the 1930s, he settled permanently in Rapallo, Italy, where he continued to work on the long poems he called *Cantos*.

"Europe Calling! Pound Speaking!"

Hitler's war loomed. Pound had strong opinions on world politics. Turned down when he suggested that the Italian Government put out publications that would improve American sympathy for Italian fascism, he proposed short-wave radio aimed at America. By January 1941, his "Europe calling! Pound speaking! Ezra Pound speaking!" was on the air regularly. Paid for his services, he urged America to stay out of the war and concentrated on anti-Semitism as his chief message. "Clever Kikes," he said, were "runnin' ALL our communications system." After Pearl Harbor, he declared (early in 1942):

> America COULD have stayed out of the war . . . IF America had stayed neutral the war would now be over . . . For the United States to be makin' war on Italy

> AND on Europe is just plain damn nonsense . . . And for this state of things Franklin Roosevelt is more than any other one man responsible.

America heard Pound. Attorney General Francis Biddle had him indicted for treason, the only crime that is defined in the U.S. Constitution:

> Treason against the United States shall consist only in levying War against them, or in adhering to their Enemies, giving them Aid and Comfort. No Person shall be convicted of Treason unless on the Testimony of Two Witnesses to the same overt Act, or in Confession in open Court.

Pound was "completely surprised." He wrote Biddle:

> I do not believe that the simple fact of speaking over the radio . . . can in itself constitute treason. I think that must depend on what is said . . .
>
> I obtained the concession to speak over Rome radio with the following proviso: Namely that nothing should be asked of me contrary to my conscience or contrary to my duties as an American citizen . . .
>
> I have not spoken with regard to *this* war, but in protest against a system which creates one war after another . . . I have not spoken to the troops, and have not suggested that the troops should mutiny or revolt . . .

Learning of the indictment, Librarian of Congress Archibald MacLeish asked if it might not "confer the paraphernalia of martyrdom upon a half-cracked and extremely foolish individual."

Treason charges against author Ezra Pound were finally dismissed based on the finding that he was unfit for trial. (Courtesy, New Directions Publishing Corporation)

In Rome, after the Italian Government collapsed, Pound continued on the air under the German occupation. But the day after Italy surrendered, partisans seized him at gunpoint. He was imprisoned in Italy for six months, then flown to America.

"Poor Old Ezra is Quite, Quite Balmy"

Said Ernest Hemingway, "He ought to go to the loony bin, which he rates and you can pick out the parts in his cantos at which he starts to rate it." MacLeish added, "It is pretty clear that poor old Ezra is quite, quite balmy."

Defense counsel Julien Cornell decided that proving clinical insanity might be the surest way to save Pound from execution. Psychiatric examinations by four doctors brought a unanimous report that Pound was not sane enough to stand trial. One said Pound suffered from delusions that he had valuable connections "in a half dozen countries" and should be "an adviser to the state department." Nevertheless, prosecutor Isaiah Matlack asked for a "public insanity hearing" before a jury.

On February 13, 1946, the jury heard that Pound:

> shows a remarkable grandiosity . . . believes he has been designated to save the Constitution of the United States for the people of the United States . . . has a feeling that he has the key to the peace of the world through the writings of Confucius . . . believes that with himself as a leader a group of intellectuals could work for world order . . .

The jury was out for three minutes, then announced that Pound was of "unsound mind." He was immediately confined until he was fit for trial at the St. Elizabeth Federal Hospital for the Insane in Washington. Friends who were confident that he was *not* insane pondered how he could ever be released without facing another trial.

Pound characteristically accepted his situation, reading and writing in his room. Over the next 12 years, applications for bail and petitions of *habeas corpus* were denied. In 1948, he was awarded the prestigious $10,000 Bollingen Prize for Poetry. Congress then ordered the prize's sponsor, the Library of Congress, to give no more awards. A Presidential pardon was proposed in 1954, but was dismissed under the dubious rationale that one cannot be pardoned until after one has been found guilty.

In 1955, MacLeish began trying to get the attorney general to *nol pros,* or quash, the standing indictment for treason. Hemingway, Eliot, and Frost joined the effort. In April 1958, Judge Bolitha Laws, who had presided at the original insanity hearing in 1945, dismissed the indictment, basing his decision on an affidavit of Dr. Winfred Overholser (the superintendent of St. Elizabeth's) that Pound was still unfit for trial.

Ezra Pound was released from St Elizabeth's and promptly sailed for Italy. He died in Venice in 1972.

—Bernard Ryan, Jr.

Suggestions for Further Reading

Ackroyd, Peter. *Ezra Pound and His World.* New York: Charles Scribner's Sons, 1980.

Carpenter, Humphrey. *A Serious Character: The Life of Ezra Pound.* Boston: Houghton Mifflin, 1988.

Heymann, C. David. *Ezra Pound: The Last Rower.* New York: Viking Press, 1976.

Tytell, John. *Ezra Pound: The Solitary Volcano.* New York: Doubleday-Anchor Press, 1987.

Sally Rand Trial: 1946

Defendant: Sally Rand (Helen Gould Beck) **Crime Charged:** Indecent exposure, corrupting the morals of an audience, and conducting an obscene show **Chief Defense Lawyer:** J.W. "Jake" Ehrlich **Chief Prosecutor:** Frank Brown **Judge:** Daniel R. Shoemaker **Place:** San Francisco, California **Dates of Trial:** November 13–14, 1946 **Verdict:** Not guilty

SIGNIFICANCE

The brief trial of Sally Rand demonstrated the importance of reminding a judge of the need to see all evidence in a case with his or her own eyes. The case also provided a lighthearted, if not frivolous, moment in the usually serious calendar of court proceedings.

By 1946, Sally Rand was a nationally known entertainer whose *shtick* was unique: Synchronized to music, she waved six-foot fans while she danced nude behind them. A show-business veteran who had performed in vaudeville, movies, and Broadway chorus lines, she enjoyed an unprecedented reputation. Ever since her appearance in 1933 as a headliner, with a bevy of associated female dancers, in "The City of Paris" extravaganza at the Chicago World's Fair, the name "Sally Rand" and the term "fan dancer" had been synonymous. (Over that summer in Chicago, Illinois, her weekly pay had risen from $125 to $3,000.) Her act had played in clubs nationwide and won particular acclaim in Los Angeles, California, and Las Vegas, Nevada.

Up the Runway . . . to "Clair de Lune"

At the Golden Gate International Exposition on Treasure Island in San Francisco Bay in 1939 and 1940, "Sally Rand's Nude Ranch," featuring Sally and her troupe of females (all wearing nothing but holsters and badges), was a big hit. But one November evening in 1946, while she was appearing at the Club Savoy on O'Farrell Street in San Francisco, six members of that California city's police department watched her dance slowly and, apparently, naked up a dimly lit runway as she maneuvered a giant white fan in rhythm to Claude Debussy's romantic "Clair de Lune." Professing shock at what they viewed as an indecent performance, they arrested her. Section 311 of the Penal Code, they said, barred "indecent exposure, corrupting the morals of an audience, and conducting an obscene show."

Sally immediately called Jake Ehrlich, a leading San Francisco attorney who was well-known as the defender of celebrities and criminals. He had successfully defended singer Billie Holiday and drummer Gene Krupa against drug charges.

Dancer Sally Rand behind her ubiquitous fan. (Hearst Newspaper Collection, University of Southern California Library)

Prosecutor Frank Brown opened the trial by putting police Captain Joseph Walsh on the stand. The captain testified to the onerous duty his six officers had performed in watching Sally Rand disrobe, behind her fans, from full costume to a single tiny flesh-colored triangular patch—an item which, in the excitement of making the arrest, they had failed to seize as evidence. The captain was able, however, to report specific details: The patch had 10 beads sewn at each corner.

"Dealing With the Naked Truth"

Defense attorney Jake Ehrlich pointed out to Judge Daniel R. Shoemaker that nudity was "respected in the highest artistic circles and elsewhere," and reminded the court of the masterpieces of sculptors Praxiteles, Michelangelo, and Rodin. "May I suggest, Your Honor," he said, "that we adjourn until tomorrow morning, at which time my client will perform her specialty for you? Thus instead of second-hand accounts and narrow-minded criticisms, we'll be dealing with the naked truth."

The judge not only agreed but provided, at Ehrlich's request, a court order that would release Sally Rand immediately if she were arrested for the same offense again before the trial was completed. That night, with the Savoy crammed with customers and policemen, Sally Rand danced, was interrupted for arrest, and was revealed (when the lights were ordered turned up) to be wearing long flannel underwear and, instead of a triangular patch, a small card marked "CENSORED. S.F.P.D." So embarrassed they didn't know what else to do, the cops arrested the dancer even though she was fully clothed. She presented her court order for immediate release and went on with her midnight show as usual.

The next morning at the Savoy, a jam-packed crowd of court and newspaper people watched Sally Rand dance through her customary performance. When all returned to the courtroom, Judge Shoemaker said, "Anyone who could find something lewd about the dance as she puts it on has to have a perverted idea of morals." With that, the judge pronounced Sally Rand not guilty on all counts.

Sally Rand then went back to fan dancing.

—*Bernard Ryan, Jr.*

Suggestions for Further Reading

Ehrlich, J.W. *A Life in My Hands.* New York: G.P. Putnam's Sons, 1965.

Nash, Jay Robert. *Encyclopedia of World Crime.* Wilmette, Ill.: CrimeBooks, 1991.

"1933: Fifty Years Ago." *American Heritage* (April/May 1983): 9.

Bill Tilden Trials: 1947 & 1949

Defendant: William Tatem Tilden II **Crime Charged:** Contributing to the delinquency of a minor **Chief Defense Lawyer:** Richard Maddox **Chief Prosecutor:** William Ritzi **Judge:** A. A. Scott **Place:** Los Angeles, California **Dates of Trials:** January 16, 1947; February 10, 1949 **Verdicts:** Guilty **Sentences:** One year in jail each time

SIGNIFICANCE

Bill Tilden was one of the greatest tennis player who ever lived. He consorted with movie stars and kings. But toward the end of his career, he was arrested for having sex with a 14-year-old boy. The conviction destroyed him. Apart from the tragedy of a man who climbed the heights and dropped to the depths, both by his own efforts, the case illustrates the folly of not listening to one's lawyer.

It was 1920 at Wimbledon, and the world championship tennis matches were under way. The U.S. team's hopes for a world championship vanished when Little Bill Johnston, a 5′8″ giant killer, was eliminated. That left Big Bill Tilden to meet the champion, Gerald Patterson of Australia. The University of Pennsylvania tennis team had rejected Tilden while he was a student there. He had improved since then, but he was 27, almost over-the-hill for a player in those days. The year before, Johnston had beaten him in straight sets.

In the Tilden-Patterson match, the Aussie started strong. He won the first set 6–2. The players changed sides and Tilden noticed a friend, actress Peggy Wood. He nodded slightly to signal that all was well, then he swept the next three sets. Tilden liked to give the crowd a good show. He had been playing with Patterson as a cat plays with a mouse. The Manchester Guardian's tennis correspondent wrote that, "the Philadelphian made rather an exhibition of his opponent."

After winning the world championship, Tilden utterly dominated amateur tennis until he turned professional in 1931. In 1950, American sportswriters voted him the most outstanding athlete in the first half of the century. He won over the likes of Babe Ruth, Jack Dempsey, Red Grange, Bobby Jones, and Johnny Weismuller. He received more than twice as many votes as his nearest rival.

An Unlikely Champion

No one who knew Tilden growing up would have picked him as a future super-athlete. He was a sickly child whose mother kept him out of school and tutored him at home. The Tildens had another son, Herbert, six years older. Herbert was a sturdy, handsome and outgoing boy who delighted his handsome, outgoing father. But Tilden Senior left the raising of his skinny younger son strictly to his wife. Linie Tilden constantly lectured little Bill on health, and especially, on the danger of venereal disease. He seldom saw children his own age. As a teenager, he hung around with younger boys and girls. He loved to play big brother, entertaining the other kids with stories and producing plays. He adored his own big brother, Herbert, an intercollegiate doubles champion, who taught him tennis.

Bill Tilden, holding USTA national championship challenge trophy, 1929. (Bettmann/Corbis)

In 1911, while young Bill was at the University of Pennsylvania, his mother had a stroke and died. Four years later, both his father and brother died. Bill Tilden sank into a deep depression.

An older cousin told him to get interested in something, anything, or he'd waste his whole life. He became interested in tennis and began to study the game seriously. He studied opponents, too. He pinpointed their weaknesses and worked out strategies to deal with each. He combined this intellectual approach with superb coordination and the stamina of 10 ordinary men. In four years, he was champion of the world.

Tilden had no doubts about how good he was. He was the best, and he knew it. But as his nephew, William Tatem Tilden III, put it, "he never grew up." He was most comfortable with children and young teens. He coached a long succession of young boy proteges. He was a homosexual, but none of his proteges, all heterosexual, said he ever made any advances on them. In his glory years, people who knew Tilden thought he was asexual.

As champion, Tilden struck people as being unusually straitlaced, although given to frequent tantrums. He wrote hokey short stories extolling good sportsmanship and similarly moralistic plays, all of which flopped. He acted, too, in his own plays and those of recognized playwrights. He adored actors and wanted to be one, but he always overacted. His lifestyle, especially his demeanor on the tennis court, was too dramatic for the stage.

Tilden feuded continually with the United States Lawn Tennis Association over expenses and other matters. In 1931, he decided to become professional.

Out of the Closet

Gradually, his fabulous stamina began to ebb. Opponents with less skill could wear him out. Tennis fans eventually said he was "still the best player in the world for one set." As his game faded, his homosexuality came to the fore. He began to solicit boys—but never his proteges—he met on tours. At first he kept his sexual activities tightly in the closet. He cut off contact with his nephew and namesake because the younger man learned of his sexual orientation.

But as he got older and his game fell off, Tilden's homosexuality became more overt. Colleagues recognized it. As his reputation grew, clubs began to bar Tilden. Other players shunned him. He moved to California, where he still had friends among the movie elite. Charlie Chaplin, Errol Flynn, and other stars flocked around him.

Tilden Arrested

On November 23, 1946, two police officers in Beverly Hills saw a car driving erratically. The driver appeared to be an underage boy. An older man had his arm around him. When the officers pulled the car over, the man hurriedly changed places with the boy. The boy's fly was open. The police arrested Bill Tilden.

Tilden was numb from shock. He signed a confession without even looking at it. When he recovered, he asked for a lawyer. He wanted Jerry Giesler, who had achieved fame by defending Charlie Chaplin and Errol Flynn in suits resulting from their sexual escapades. Giesler wanted no part of him: he defended only heterosexual predators. Tilden finally engaged Richard Maddox, a young former prosecutor.

Maddox had a hard time convincing Tilden that he was in serious trouble. Maddox pointed out that the scandal sheets and rumor mongers would have a field day imagining tennis parties at the Chaplin estate—orgies with the Communist Little Tramp and "In Like" Flynn seducing the little girls while Queer Bill seduced the little boys.

The state's case was weak, the lawyer said. If Tilden repudiated his statement, the only evidence would be the boy's statement. The boy, a precociously dissolute 14-year-old, had been expelled from several schools because of his sexual activities and general delinquency. If Tilden pleaded not guilty, Maddox said, the boy's parents would not want him to testify. And they had said they didn't want Tilden to go to jail.

Tilden refused to plead not guilty. He said he must accept responsibility. "He was hung up on the sportsman thing," Maddox said later.

And Tilden was still convinced that with his celebrity and his famous friends he would get no more than a tongue-lashing and a fine. Dr. J. Paul De River, a psychiatrist who examined Tilden, told the court he was "impulsively weak . . . passive autistic with egocentric traits . . . in need of special psychiatric care." He said, "Any jail sentence would of necessity be limited and would not tend to work as a curative measure, and would probably bring . . . more harm." He concluded, "He is . . . in some ways quite juvenile. . . . This man should be regarded as someone who is mentally ill."

De River believed Tilden suffered from "an endocrine dysfunction so often seen during the evolutionary stage of life when the sex curve is on the decline."

Even District Attorney William Ritzi said later, "The poor man was a sick individual. We realized it then, and we realize it now. It's just that society treats it differently today than in those days."

At the sentencing hearing, Tilden compounded his trouble by lying to the judge. He said he had never been involved in a situation like this before. Judge A. A. Scott, like almost everybody in Beverly Hills, knew better. He sentenced Tilden to a year in jail. Tilden was so stunned Maddox had to lift him to his feet.

De River was right. Jail was no cure. Tilden was released after serving seven and a half months. Less than a year and a half later, he was arrested for groping a 16-year-old hitchhiker. He was sentenced to another year, but he got out after about 10 months. Shortly before he was released, American sportswriters voted him the greatest athlete of the half century.

Few others honored him. Chaplin had gone home to England and was barred from returning. Almost all Tilden's other acquaintances avoided him. Mentally, he was rapidly disintegrating. He stopped bathing and changing his clothes. When he visited Maddox, the lawyer's secretary complained that his odor was unbearable.

Tilden would not concede that he was finished. Sixty years old, sick and out of shape, he persuaded a former pupil to give him money for the trip to Cleveland for the U.S. Professional Tennis Championships. The day before he was to enter one more championship tournament, he dropped dead.

—William Weir

Suggestions for Further Reading

"Big Bill," *Time* (June 15, 1953).

Deford, Frank. *Big Bill Tilden: The Triumphs and the Tragedy.* New York: Simon and Schuster, 1976.

Tilden, William Tatem II. *My Story.* New York: Hellman, Williams, 1948.

Bercovici v. Chaplin: 1947

Plaintiff: Konrad Bercovici **Defendant:** Charles S. Chaplin
Plaintiff Claim: Plagiarism **Chief Defense Lawyer:** Louis Frohlich
Chief Lawyer for Plaintiff: Louis Nizer **Judge:** Harold P. Burke
Place: New York, New York **Dates of Trial:** April 17–May 1, 1947
Verdict: None; suit settled for $95,000 payment by Chaplin

SIGNIFICANCE

This suit against Charlie Chaplin for plagiarism attracted international attention and tarnished the comedian's benign image. Although the plaintiff in the end settled for a modest amount of money by agreeing to a settlement, Chaplin acknowledged, in effect, that he had plagiarized another's film concept.

Silent-film star Charlie Chaplin and screenwriter Konrad Bercovici became close friends in Hollywood early in the 1920s. They continued to see each other during the 30s, when Chaplin was creating his greatest hits, *City Lights*, *Modern Times*, and *The Great Dictator*. The latter, his first sound film, was released in 1940 as Europe was already deep in World War II and the United States faced inevitable participation; the film was a powerful and caustic burlesque of Germany's Adolf Hitler.

In June 1946, a year after the war ended, the Information Control Division of the Allied Control Council, which oversaw the military administration of occupied Germany, permitted a "sneak preview" showing of *The Great Dictator* in Berlin. Replying to questionnaires, the audience said the film should not be shown throughout the nation lest it stimulate revulsion rather than mirth.

"The Little Tramp" Plays to a Full House

News of the showing brought renewed interest in the film in America. Konrad Bercovici announced a particular interest in the 7-year-old film: He was suing his old friend Chaplin for plagiarism, for, he said, he had first suggested in the mid-1930s that the "Little Tramp" play Hitler. He demanded $6,450,000.

The trial began—"before a full house," as the newspapers reported—on April 17, 1947, in U.S. District Court in New York City, with Judge Harold P. Burke presiding. Bercovici's lawyer, the renowned Louis Nizer, told the jury he would prove that Chaplin had contracted with Bercovici to collaborate in the production of a series of pictures, with the plaintiff to receive 15 percent of the gross profits. In 1938, he said, Bercovici had written a satirical scenario based on Hitler and dictatorship, but Chaplin had rejected it for political reasons. *The Great Dictator*, he charged, was based on that scenario.

A parade of witnesses ranging from actor Melvyn Douglas to producer Alexander Korda to Chaplin's ex-wife, actress Paulette Goddard, testified on Chaplin's behalf during the next two weeks.

Plaintiff Claims Oral Agreement

On the witness stand, Bercovici said that he suggested a picture on dictators while visiting Chaplin's Pebble Beach, California home in 1938, and that Chaplin orally agreed to its production but subsequently rejected the idea. Nevertheless, he insisted, *The Great Dictator*, based on his script, appeared two years later.

In a courtroom filled to capacity, the final witness was Chaplin himself. The white-haired, 58-year-old comedian spoke rapidly and clearly to the jury of nine men and three women, gesturing frequently with his head and arms. When Bercovici suggested the idea, he said, he told the writer that he had been thinking it over himself for some time, and had outlined the story he had in mind not only to Bercovici but to Melvyn Douglas and others.

On direct examination, Chaplin identified his scrapbook for 1936. It contained several stories concerning the similarity of Hitler's mustache to the one Charlie wore on the screen. Chaplin's attorney, Louis Frohlich, asked, "Had the idea of impersonating Hitler come to you for the first time from Mr. Bercovici?"

"It had not," replied the witness.

Attorney Nizer introduced Bercovici's script as evidence. Chaplin said he had never seen it before. Nor did he make oral agreements, he said. His practice was to have all contracts in written form.

The next afternoon, May 1, Judge Burke called the attorneys for both sides to his office and asked them how much longer they expected the trial to last. Then he remarked, "I don't suppose you gentlemen ever thought of settling this, did you?"

The two sides, including Chaplin and Bercovici themselves, bargained from late afternoon until 10:00 P.M. The Bercovici side dropped first to $500,000, then to $350,000. Actively negotiating on his own behalf, Chaplin said he would not consider any settlement "in six figures." They finally agreed that Chaplin would pay Bercovici $95,000, including $5,000 for his legal expenses. Bercovici agreed to deliver to Chaplin a release covering any rights he had asserted in *The Great Dictator*. Chaplin also gained worldwide motion-picture rights to two Bercovici scenarios. Judge Burke dismissed the jury.

Five years later, Charlie Chaplin departed from the United States and settled in Switzerland with his young wife, the former Oona O'Neill, and their growing family. He died there in 1977 at the age of 88. It is not known whether he ever again saw his longtime friend Konrad Bercovici.

—Bernard Ryan, Jr.

Suggestions for Further Reading

Chaplin, Charles. *My Autobiography*. New York: Simon & Schuster, 1964.

Chaplin, Charles, Jr. *My Father, Charlie Chaplin*. New York: Random House, 1960.

Epstein, Jerry. *Remembering Charlie*. Garden City, N.Y.: Doubleday & Co., 1989.

Gifford, Denis. *Chaplin*. Garden City, N.Y.: Doubleday & Co., 1960.

Haining, Peter. *The Legend of Charlie Chaplin*. Secaucus, N.J.: Castle, 1982.

McCabe, John. *Charlie Chaplin*. Garden City, N.Y.: Doubleday & Co., 1978.

McCaffrey, Donald W., ed. *Focus on Chaplin*. Englewood Cliffs, N.J.: Prentice Hall, 1971.

Manvell, Roger. *Chaplin*. Boston: Little, Brown & Co., 1974.

Robinson, David. *Chaplin, His Life and Art*. New York: McGraw-Hill, 1985.

——. *Chaplin, the Mirror of Opinion*. Bloomington: Indiana University Press, 1983.

Caryl Chessman Trial: 1948

Defendant: Caryl Whittier Chessman **Crimes Charged:** Kidnapping, sexual perversion, and robbery **Chief Defense Lawyers:** Caryl Chessman and Al Matthews **Chief Prosecutor:** J. Miller Leavy **Judge:** Charles W. Fricke **Place:** Los Angeles, California **Dates of Trial:** April 4–May 21, 1948 **Verdict:** Guilty **Sentence:** Death

SIGNIFICANCE

Caryl Chessman's uniquely documented struggle against capital punishment not only aroused global sympathy for a possibly innocent man, but highlighted the imponderable sluggishness of the U.S. death penalty process.

In January 1948, a 27-year-old career criminal named Caryl Chessman was arrested after a car chase and shootout as a suspect in the armed robbery of a men's clothing store in Los Angeles, California. When police searched the stolen Ford that Chessman was driving, they found a penlight and a .45-caliber automatic pistol, items that made them suspect that Chessman might be the "Red Light Bandit," a man who had been driving up to couples in parked cars, flashing a red light to make them think it was a police car, then robbing the couples and forcing some of the women to perform sexual acts. Despite the fact that Chessman bore little physical resemblance to descriptions of the attacker, several victims identified him. The charge sheet included multiple counts of robbery, two counts of sexual perversion, and—most importantly—three counts of violating Section 209 of the California Penal Code, the so-called "Little Lindbergh Law." This covered kidnapping with intent to commit robbery: if bodily harm could also be proved, Section 209 was punishable by death.

Defends Himself

Even before the trial began April 4, 1948, Chessman, a cocky, street-smart hoodlum with an overinflated opinion of his own cleverness, created headlines by dismissing his lawyers and announcing that he intended to defend himself. It is impossible to overstate the enormity of this tactical blunder. Not only was Chessman on trial for his life, but he was facing Judge Charles W. Fricke, who in the course of his career sentenced more people to death than any other judge in California history. Right from the outset, Fricke made it plain that he regarded

Chessman as an arrogant interloper, and he did everything possible to stymie the defense. When Chessman asked Fricke that he be given a daily transcript of proceedings, Fricke denied the request, something he had never done before in a capital case. Chessman's further complaint that he had not been shown the correct way to make a motion drew an outburst from Fricke: "Mr. Chessman, the court is not engaged in conducting a law school or advising a defendant what court procedure is." (As a matter of fact, so advising the defendant was *exactly* Fricke's duty in the case of a man conducting his own defense.)

Caryl Chessman's fight as his own attorney unarguably contributed to his demise. (Hearst Newspaper Collection, University of Southern California Library)

Neither did Chessman make much headway with the prosecutor, J. Miller Leavy. A 16-year veteran of capital cases, Leavy outmaneuvered his opponent at every turn. Never was this more apparent than during the jury selection process, when Chessman sat silently by and let Leavy impanel an 11-woman, one-man jury, something no experienced defense lawyer would have allowed in a sex case.

The first witness, Regina Johnson, described being taken from her car at gunpoint by a masked assailant to another vehicle where she was forced to commit a sexual act. (It was that distance between the two cars—22 feet—that made this a capital case. Technically, under California law at the time, she had been kidnapped. Those 22 feet meant the difference between a maximum sentence of 15 years for sexual perversion and death in the gas chamber.) "He told me that we would be taken away in a casket, the both of us, unless I did what he wanted." Briefly the attacker's mask had slipped, affording Johnson a glimpse of his face. She positively identified Chessman as the man.

On cross-examination Chessman emphasized discrepancies between Johnson's description of her attacker and himself. The bandit had been of undistinguished build and 5′8″ or 5′9″. Chessman was close to 6′ and almost 200 pounds. Johnson persisted in her identification. Then she went on the offensive. When Chessman asked, "Did this person . . . state what his intentions in taking you back to the other car was [*sic*]?" Johnson responded: "No, *you* didn't tell me until after I had gotten in your car."

"How long were you in the Ford?"

"In the car with *you*?" Johnson needled, sensing Chessman's increasing agitation. It worked. Chessman erupted, demanding of Judge Fricke that Johnson answer the questions as asked. Fricke denied the request, leaving Chessman to stew.

Another victim of the "Red Light Bandit," Mary Alice Meza, was less feisty but equally damaging. Asked by prosecutor Leavy if Chessman was her attacker, Meza replied, "There is no question. It is definitely him. I know what he looks like."

Chessman the witness was no more impressive than Chessman the lawyer. Leavy repeatedly trapped him in confusing and contradictory answers. Once, when taxed on responses made to police, Chessman replied, "Specifically, I don't remember what my answers were, because they were just fabrications."

Controversial Transcript

On May 21, 1948, Chessman was found guilty on all charges, with punishment fixed at death, and held, pending formal sentencing. Then something unusual occurred. The court reporter, Ernest Perry, an elderly man who had been ill during the trial, died from a coronary thrombosis, leaving behind his 1,800 pages of shorthand testimony. Chessman pounced. Under California law, if the court reporter died before transcribing his notes in a civil case, a new trial must be held. On June 25, 1948, Judge Fricke, pointing out that this was a criminal case, not civil, refused Chessman's request for a new trial. Then he sentenced him to death twice.

In September 1948 responsibility for transcribing the shorthand notes was given to Stanley Fraser, who just happened to be the uncle of prosecutor Leavy. (He also received $10,000 for the task, three times the going rate.) Worse than that, Fraser had several times been arrested for drunkenness—once while actually taking dictation in court. Chessman argued that the transcription which Fraser provided was hopelessly biased and inaccurate.

Over the next decade this mutilated transcript formed the bedrock of Chessman's historic struggle against his sentence. He won eight stays of execution, some within hours of the appointed time. He also wrote three books. The first, *Cell 2455, Death Row,* became a best seller and made him an international cause célèbre.

But on May 2, 1960, Chessman's ordeal ended in the San Quentin gas chamber. The circumstances of his execution were remarkably similar to those of Burton Abbott (see separate entry), three years earlier. Just seconds after guards sealed the door, a ninth stay of execution was telephoned through. Like Abbott's, it came too late. Caryl Chessman's fight was over.

No matter which side one takes regarding Chessman's guilt or innocence, few now doubt that his trial was seriously flawed. Had he been properly represented, there is every likelihood that his sentence would have been commuted. But because, in the eyes of those who mattered, he had brought the law into disrepute, he paid the ultimate price. Arrogance undid him. An old legal maxim states that anyone who defends himself has a fool for a client. Never was this more vividly demonstrated than in the trial of Caryl Chessman.

—Colin Evans

Suggestions for Further Reading

Brown, Edmund G. and Dick Adler. *Public Justice, Private Mercy*. New York: Weidenfeld & Nicolson, 1989.

Chessman, Caryl. *Cell 2455, Death Row*. Westport, Conn.: Greenwood Press, 1954.

Machlin, Milton and William Read Woodfield. *Ninth Life*. New York: G.P. Putnam's Sons, 1961.

Parker, Frank J. *Caryl Chessman, The Red Light Bandit*. Chicago: Nelson-Hall, 1975.

Hollywood Ten Trials: 1948–50

Defendants: Alvah Bessie, Herbert Biberman, Lester Cole, Edward Dmytryk, Ring Lardner, Jr., John Howard Lawson, Albert Maltz, Sam Ornitz, Robert Adrian Scott, and Dalton Trumbo **Crime Charged:** Contempt of Congress **Chief Defense Lawyers:** Bartley Crum, Charles J. Katz, Robert W. Kenny, and Martin Popper **Chief Prosecutor:** William Hitz **Judges:** Edward M. Curran, Richmond B. Keech, and David A. Pine **Place:** Washington, D.C. **Dates of Trials:** April 12–19, 1948 (Lawson); May 3–5, 1948 (Trumbo); June 22–29, 1950 (Biberman, Cole, Dmytryk, Lardner, and Scott); June 23–29, 1950 (Bessie, Maltz, and Ornitz) **Verdicts:** Guilty **Sentences:** 1 year imprisonment and $1,000 fine (Bessie, Cole, Lardner, Lawson, Maltz, Ornitz, Scott, and Trumbo); 6 months and $500 fine (Biberman, and Dmytryk)

SIGNIFICANCE

The Hollywood Ten case stands as a landmark in the history of the abuse of civil liberties. As respected author E.B. White commented, "Ten men have been convicted, not of wrong-doing but of wrong thinking; that is news in this country and if I have not misread my history, it is bad news." By setting the stage for the establishment of the blacklist, the case created a precedent for making political belief a test of employability. In refusing to accept the claims of the Ten that the First Amendment entitled them to remain silent, the House Committee for the Investigation of Un-American Activities caused future witnesses to plead the Fifth Amendment privilege against self-incrimination to avoid answering further questioning.

In 1946 writers, producers, actors, and directors in the film industry in Hollywood who had been drawn—as "good liberals"—to the American Communist Party over the preceding decade began to sense that the party was not the liberal organization they had been told it was. The party's policy and direction—in effect during World War II, patriotic cooperation and the renunciation of revolutionary goals—were changing. Party head Earl Browder, the "good liberal" leader, was deposed and replaced by hard-liner William Z. Foster. The new policy, as described by screenwriter Albert Maltz in an essay in *New Masses*, was that "unless art is a weapon like a leaflet, serving immediate political ends, necessities and programs, it is worthless or escapist or vicious."

Hollywood Divided into Two Camps

At the same time in the film capital, several years of labor unrest had been coming to a head. Two major craft unions—the International Alliance of Theatrical Stage Employees and Motion Picture Machine Operators (IATSE) and the Conference of Studio Unions (CSU)—had been rivals in a series of jurisdictional disputes and actions. When the CSU called a strike in 1945 and were supported by Communist Party members and Communist-dominated unions, IATSE leader Roy Brewer viewed it as a concerted attempt by the Communists to take over the motion picture industry. As the strike dragged on for six months, he convinced studio heads of his conspiracy theory.

Meantime, the Hollywood Independent Citizens Committee of the Arts, Sciences and Professions, led by actor (later President) Ronald Reagan, producer Dore Schary, composer Johnny Green, actress Olivia de Havilland, and screenwriter Ernest Pascal, was becoming a militant anti-Communist unit. By 1947, the film capital seemed divided into two camps: anti-Communist and pro-Communist.

Against this background, on Capitol Hill in Washington, D.C., the House Committee for the Investigation of Un-American Activities, which had been concerned with Communist activities since the late 1930s, sent investigators from Washington to interview "key Hollywood figures," all of whom were members of the anti-Communist Motion Picture Alliance for the Preservation of American Ideals. The interviews resulted in public hearings by the House committee, mislabeled HUAC ever afterward.

"Friendly witnesses," all members of the Alliance, testified first. They included producer Jack L. Warner, novelist Ayn Rand, and actors Gary Cooper, Robert Montgomery, Ronald Reagan (then president of the Screen Actors Guild), Robert Taylor, and Adolphe Menjou. Altogether, they depicted a Hollywood virtually at the mercy of militant Communists whose orders came directly from Moscow; they described a climate all but saturated with Red propaganda.

Next, 19 people, identified by the "friendly witnesses" as suspected Communists, were subpoenaed from a list that totaled 79.

All were known as radicals. Most were writers; therefore, to HUAC, they were likely conduits for spreading Communist propaganda via the silver screen. But why these particular individuals were called has never been explained.

The Right to Remain Silent

To support them and explore strategy, the Hollywood community formed the Committee for the First Amendment. Its sponsors included four U.S. senators, author Thomas Mann, and film producer Jerry Wald. The strategy was to take the position that the First Amendment provided not only the right to free speech but the right to remain silent.

HUAC Chairman J. Parnell Thomas called 11 of the 19 subpoenaed witnesses to testify. Supporting them in the hearing room were such stars as

Humphrey Bogart, Lauren Bacall, Danny Kaye, Gene Kelly, Jane Wyatt, John Huston, and Sterling Hayden. The first witness, screenwriter John Howard Lawson, proposed to read a statement, as each of the "friendly" witnesses had been permitted to do and as called for in the usual procedure of congressional committees. Chairman Thomas looked at the first line of the statement—"For a week, this Committee has conducted an illegal and indecent trial of American citizens, whom the Committee has selected to be publicly pilloried and smeared"—and denied Lawson permission to read it. The chairman then demanded an answer to the question, "Are you now, or have you ever been a member of the Communist Party of the United States?"

"The question of Communism is in no way related to the inquiry, which is an attempt," Lawson replied, "to get control of the screen and to invade the basic rights of American citizens in all fields." The chairman responded by having a nine-page single-spaced memo on Lawson's career, prepared by the committee's investigators, read into the record. Lawson was given no opportunity to respond to it. Repeatedly, as the questions and responses became a shouting match, Lawson was asked about Communist membership. Finally, the chairman, pounding his gavel for quiet, ordered the witness removed and cited him for contempt of Congress.

"I Would Hate Myself in the Morning"

In succession, writers Dalton Trumbo, Albert Maltz, Alvah Bessie, Samuel Ornitz, Herbert Biberman, producer Adrian Scott, director Edward Dmytryk, and writers Lester Cole and Ring Lardner, Jr.—all destined to be known, along with Lawson, as "The Hollywood Ten"—were treated to the same questions and the same denial of permission to read their statements. All were cited for contempt of Congress. Lardner, asked repeatedly if he were a Communist, replied at last, "I could answer, but if I did, I would hate myself in the morning."

The 11th witness was Bertolt Brecht. A successful German playwright, he had been in Hollywood for six years, had taken out first citizenship papers and announced his plan to remain permanently. To date, he had but one screen credit. "I was not a member, or am not a member," he told Chairman Thomas, "of any Communist Party." Immediately, Brecht took a plane for Europe and settled in East Germany.

Shortly, a secret conference in New York's Waldorf-Astoria Hotel brought together Hollywood's leading studio heads, including Nicholas Schenck, Joseph Schenck, Walter Wanger, Samuel Goldwyn, Louis B. Mayer, Dore Schary, Spyros Skouras, and many others, as well as Eric Johnston, president of the Motion Picture Association of America. They issued a statement:

> We will forthwith discharge or suspend without compensation those in our employ and we will not re-employ any of the ten until such time as he is acquitted or has purged himself of contempt and declares under oath that he is not a Communist.
>
> On the broader issue of alleged subversive and disloyal elements in Hollywood our members are likewise prepared to take positive action.

> We will not knowingly employ a Communist or a member of any party or group which advocates the overthrow of the Government of the United States by force or by any illegal or unconstitutional methods.

The studio heads also promised not to be "swayed by hysteria or intimidation from any source"—paradoxically, the very causes of their secret meeting and public statement.

The Blacklist is Born

Thus began the blacklist that determined who would or would not be employed not only in Hollywood films but in all of television and radio for the next several years. Institutionalized, the blacklist meant that no artist in show business who had been accused of Communist Party membership, or called to testify, could get work without naming names.

In November 1947, a special session of Congress was called to appropriate funds to resist Communist infiltration in Europe. To that session, Representative Thomas brought his 10 citations for contempt. After a handful of House members had spoken against them, they were passed, 346 to 17.

On April 12, 1948, John Howard Lawson was brought to trial, followed three weeks later by Dalton Trumbo, in U.S. District Court in Washington. In each brief trial, the jury found the defendants guilty of contempt of Congress. Judges Edward M. Curran and David A. Pine suspended their sentences—one year in jail and $1,000 fine—pending appeals. Commenting later on Lawson's and Trumbo's willingness to stand trial, Thurman Arnold, former special assistant to the U.S. attorney general, said:

> To test the constitutional right of any Congressional committee to ask, "Are you now or have you ever been a member of the Communist Party?' it was necessary for these witnesses to do three things:
>
> 1. Phrase their answers as they did.
>
> 2. Accept citations for contempt of Congress.
>
> 3. Stand trial in the Federal courts, and if convicted of contempt appeal to the Supreme Court of the United States.

Supreme Court Refuses to Review

As Lawson's and Trumbo's attorneys filed appeals, the eight others waived their rights to trial by jury, stipulating that they would stand on the records of the jury trials of the first two. However, they reserved the privilege of appealing. All 10 were confident that the Supreme Court would vindicate them. But in the summer of 1949, two liberal justices—Frank Murphy and Wiley Rutledge—died. Their successors, Tom Clark and Sherman Minton, shifted the court majority to the conservative side, and that majority refused to review the convictions of Lawson and Trumbo.

On June 9, 1950, Lawson and Trumbo began their jail terms. The trials of the remaining eight opened on June 22 before Judges Curran and Pine and

Judge Richmond B. Keech. By June 29, all were found guilty. Six received one-year sentences and $1,000 fines. Dmytryk and Biberman, however, for reasons never explained, were fined $500 each and jailed for only six months.

Defense lawyers Robert W. Kenny and Martin W. Popper introduced motions for acquittal, suspension of sentence, and release on bail pending appeal. The judges denied them all. Since the eight had agreed to stand on the records of the jury trials of the first two, and the Supreme Court had denied any review, they were sentenced and jailed at once.

The "Hollywood Ten" before arraignment on contempt of Congress charges. (AP/Wide World Photos)

From their prison cells, all 10 men sued their employers for breach of contract. Negotiating together until well after the last of the Hollywood Ten had been released from prison, the studios finally settled out of court for $259,000, to be shared—but not equally—by all.

Some returned to their professions but had to write in the "black market"—using pseudonyms—for years. Trumbo wrote scripts under other names for 10 years, winning an Oscar for Best Motion Picture Story in 1957 as "Robert Rich." Lardner's blacklisting ended in 1964; he won an Oscar for *M*A*S*H* in 1971. Maltz wrote novels while blacklisted for 20 years. Cole taught screenwriting and reviewed films. Lawson moved from creating plays and films to writing about them and teaching. Bessie wrote novels.

In 1951, Dmytryk appeared before HUAC and recanted, naming 26 as Communists. Over the next 25 years, he directed a film each year. Ornitz wrote a best-selling novel. Scott wrote and produced for television. Biberman formed an independent production company and produced a semidocumentary peopled with FBI informants and right-wing fanatics that won an International Grand Prize.

In 1948, HUAC Chairman J. Parnell Thomas was convicted of conspiracy to defraud the government by taking kickbacks from his staff. By the time two of the Hollywood Ten—Cole and Lardner—were imprisoned in the federal penitentiary at Danbury, Connecticut, in 1950, Thomas was already there serving his sentence.

—*Bernard Ryan, Jr.*

Suggestions for Further Reading

Aaron, Daniel. *Writers on the Left.* New York: Harcourt, Brace & World, 1961.

Belfrage, Cedric. *The American Inquisition.* New York: Bobbs-Merrill Co., 1973.

Bessie, Alvah. *Inquisition in Eden.* New York: Macmillan Co., 1965.

Biberman, Herbert. *Salt of the Earth.* Boston: Beacon Press, 1965.

Cook, Bruce. *Dalton Trumbo.* New York: Charles Scribner's Sons, 1977.

Dick, Bernard F. *Radical Innocence.* Lexington: University Press of Kentucky, 1989.

Donner, Frank J. *The Un-Americans.* New York: Ballantine, 1961.

Goodman, Walter. *The Committee.* New York: Farrar, Straus & Giroux, 1969.

Kahn, Gordon. *Hollywood on Trial.* New York: Boni & Gaer, 1948.

Kanfer, Stefan. *A Journal of the Plague Years.* New York: Atheneum, 1973.

Kempton, Murray. *Part of Our Time.* New York: Simon & Schuster, 1955.

Lardner, Ring, Jr. *The Lardners.* New York: Harper & Row, 1976.

Navasky, Victor S. *Naming Names.* New York: Viking, 1989.

Taylor, Telford. *Grand Inquest.* New York: Simon & Schuster, 1955.

Vaughn, Robert. *Only Victims.* New York: G.P. Putnam's Sons, 1972.

Alger Hiss Trials: 1949–50

Defendant: Alger Hiss **Crime Charged:** Perjury
Chief Defense Lawyers: Robert M. Benjamin, Claude B. Cross, Chester T. Lane, Edward C. McLean, Robert von Mehren, Victor Rabinowitz, Harold Rosenwald, Harol Shapero, and Lloyd Paul Strykr
Chief Prosecutors: Thomas J. Donegan, Myles J. Lane, Thomas F. Murphy, and Clarke S. Ryan **Judges:** First trial: Samuel J. Kaufman; Second trial: Henry W. Goddard **Place:** New York, New York **Dates of Trials:** First trial: May 31–July 8, 1949; Second trial: November 17, 1949–January 21, 1950. **Verdicts:** First trial: Jury deadlocked; Second trial: guilty **Sentence:** 5 years imprisonment

SIGNIFICANCE

For three years, Alger Hiss was the protagonist in a great human drama that made headlines across America. The case polarized the country between 1948 and 1950, becoming a symbol of American policies in the onset of the Cold War. It accelerated the rise of Richard M. Nixon. The debate about Hiss' guilt remains endless, for either he was a traitor or he was the victim of a framing for political advantage at the highest levels of justice.

Alger Hiss was the president of the Carnegie Endowment for International Peace when, on August 3, 1948, reporters told him a senior editor of *Time* magazine named Whittaker Chambers had just appeared before the Committee for the Investigation of Un-American Activities of the House of Representatives (consistently mislabeled HUAC). Chambers had described his 15 years' service as a Soviet agent. In 1939, he said, two years after he had "repudiated Marx's doctrine," he told Assistant Secretary of State Adolph A. Berle, Jr., about Communists in the U.S. government. One, he said, was Alger Hiss, who had been a State Department official and who later organized the U.S. representation at Yalta, as well as the conferences at Dumbarton Oaks and San Francisco, that launched the United Nations.

Hiss telegraphed the committee, asking to appear under oath to say he did not know Chambers.

Hiss Denies Communist Link

In Washington, Hiss told the committee the accusation was "a complete fabrication." His government service would speak for itself. But, said Karl Mundt, acting chairman of the committee, Chambers had testified that when he was breaking with the communists he had tried to persuade Hiss to break, too, and Hiss had "absolutely refused to break."

Hiss denied such an incident, repeated that the name Chambers meant nothing to him, and said he would like to see the man. Chambers was called to an executive session of a sub-committee led by U.S. Representative Richard M. Nixon of California. The witness described intimate details of the Hiss households in Baltimore, Maryland and Washington, D.C. a decade earlier.

Hiss was recalled. Nixon showed him pictures of Chambers. Hiss said they looked like a man he knew as George Crosley, a freelance writer who had interviewed him when he was counsel to a Senate committee. In June 1935, said Hiss, he and his wife Priscilla bought a house and, subletting their apartment to Crosley and his family, threw in their old Ford. But Hiss would not say that Crosley and Chambers were the same person.

In New York the next day, Congressmen Nixon and John McDowell, as a subcommittee, brought Chambers and Hiss face to face. After observing that this man's teeth were considerably improved over Crosley's, and that he looked "very different in girth and in other appearances—hair, forehead, particularly the jowls," Hiss identified Chambers as George Crosley.

Chambers denied ever going under that name, but he said Hiss was the man "who was a member of the Communist Party" at whose apartment he and his wife and child had stayed. Angry, Hiss invited Chambers "to make those same statements out of the presence of this Committee without their being privileged for suit for libel."

Chambers shortly did so on the "Meet the Press" radio program. Hiss filed a $75,000 defamation suit.

At a pretrial hearing, Hiss' attorney, William Marbury, asked Chambers if he could produce documentary proof of his assertion. Chambers went to the Brooklyn home of a nephew and, from behind a dumbwaiter, retrieved a stained manila envelope containing 43 typed copies of State Department reports, five rolls of microfilm, and four memoranda in Hiss' handwriting. He handed the documents, but not the films, to Marbury. He claimed Hiss had given them to him in 1937. Hiss, said Chambers, regularly took such classified papers home for his wife to type, returning the originals to the files the next day while Chambers transmitted the copies to a Soviet agent.

A "Bombshell," a Seaplane, a Pumpkin

Hiss told his lawyer to give the papers to the Department of Justice. The next day, Representative Nixon, who had just sailed on a vacation cruise to Panama, got a cable that a "bombshell" had exploded. He ordered a HUAC investigator to visit Chambers at his Maryland farm. Meantime, a Coast Guard seaplane picked up Nixon.

By the time Nixon was back in Washington amid flashing cameras, Chambers had led investigator Robert E. Stripling into his farm field, opened a hollowed-out pumpkin, and handed over the five rolls of microfilm that had long been hidden in the stained envelope behind the Brooklyn dumbwaiter. Three rolls, still in their aluminum cans, were undeveloped; two, developed, were in oilpaper bags. While the pumpkin held no paper, the microfilms, which contained *pictures* of documents, became known as "The Pumpkin Papers."

By one vote more than a bare majority, the New York Federal Grand Jury indicted Alger Hiss on two counts of perjury: one for denying that he had turned State Department documents over to Chambers, the second for saying he had not seen Chambers after January 1, 1937, for the jury found that he had delivered reports to Chambers in February and March 1938.

As the trial opened on May 31, 1949, prosecutor Thomas F. Murphy told the jury, "If you don't believe Mr. Chambers' story, we have no case under the Federal perjury rule." Chambers repeated the testimony given before HUAC and the grand jury on his work in the Communist underground, his close friendship with the Hisses, his 1938 break with the party.

In cross-examination, Hiss' defense counsel, Lloyd Paul Stryker, lost no time establishing Chambers' shortcomings. The witness admitted committing perjury in 1937 and 1948, using at least seven aliases between 1924 and 1938, lying to the dean of Columbia University while a student, stealing books from many libraries, living with several women (including, while a teenager, a New Orleans prostitute called "One-Eyed Annie"), and writing not only erotic poetry but an anti-religious play that got him expelled from Columbia.

A Typewriter Proves Elusive

For three weeks, the prosecution presented evidence. State Department witnesses identified the typewritten papers as cables from American diplomats around the world in 1938 and said the four memos were in Hiss' handwriting. An FBI typewriter expert testified that letters the Hisses wrote and all but one of the Chambers documents had been typed on the same machine.

The typewriter became a key piece of evidence. The Hisses said they had given it to the sons of their maid when they moved in December 1937—before the documents were typed in January and April 1938. One of the sons, Perry Catlett, testified to receiving the typewriter in December 1936 and taking it to a repair shop on K Street (where he was told it was not worth repairing), but then said, "I don't know the time" when prosecutor Murphy told him the K Street shop had not opened until September 1938.

The FBI searched unsuccessfully for the typewriter, a Woodstock built some 20 years earlier. Believing it world prove their client innocent, Hiss' own lawyers traced and found it, thus enabling a prosecution witness to demonstrate in the courtroom that it was in working order.

Before Alger Hiss took the stand for direct examination, his defense counsel introduced a parade of character witnesses—State Department officials, a former U.S. presidential candidate, a former U.S. solicitor general, a Navy admiral, a district court judge, and two associate justices of the U.S. Supreme Court. All backed Hiss' reputation "for integrity, loyalty, and veracity."

Alger Hiss arriving in the United States with the United Nations charter for delivery to President Truman. (United States Air Force)

On direct, examination, Hiss denied Chambers' charges and said, "I am not and never have been" a member of the Communist Party. He admitted having known one George Crosley between 1934 and 1936. Cross-examining, prosecutor Murphy tried to establish the gift of the Ford car and use of the Hisses' apartment as out-and-out fabrications.

Stryker's last witness was Dr. Carl Binger, a psychiatrist who had been observing Chambers' testimony. "Have you," asked Stryker, "an opinion within the bounds of reasonable certainty as to the mental condition of Whittaker Chambers?"

Murphy objected. Chambers' credibility, he told Judge Stanley H. Kaufman, was the case's central issue. The psychiatrist's answer would usurp the jury's function. The judge agreed.

In summation, Murphy noted that the case must stand not on Chambers' accusations but on the documents and the typewriter. Said Stryker: "The case comes down to this—who is telling the truth?"

The jury deliberated for 14 hours and 45 minutes, remained deadlocked, and was discharged.

Second Jury Reaches Guilty Verdict

The second trial began on November 17, 1949, with Judge Henry W. Goddard presiding. Most of the earlier witnesses repeated their testimony. Defense attorney Claude B. Cross, who had replaced Stryker, called Dr. Binger. Judge Goddard permitted him to testify that "Mr. Chambers is suffering from a condition known as a psychopathic personality, a disorder of character the distinguishing features of which are amoral and antisocial behavior." One important symptom was "chronic, persistent, and repetitive lying and a tendency to make false accusations."

On January 20, 1950, the jury found Hiss guilty on both counts. His sentence was five years on each, to be served concurrently. Before sentencing, Hiss again denied any guilt, promising that "in the future the full facts of how Whittaker Chambers was able to carry out forgery by typewriter will be disclosed."

Hiss was free on bail for more than a year. The Court of Appeals for the Second Circuit affirmed his conviction. The U.S. Supreme Court refused to review the case. On March 22, 1951, Hiss entered the federal penitentiary at Danbury, Connecticut.

While Hiss was in prison, his attorney of record in the appeals, Chester T. Lane, consulted experts who made exhaustive tests in document analysis, in the chemistry of paper, in metallurgy, and in the construction of typewriters. A noted typewriter engineer, working entirely from samples of typing from the machine exhibited at the trial and without seeing the trial typewriter, built another machine. It produced examples so similar that New England's leading document expert swore in an affidavit that no expert could distinguish documents typed on the two machines.

Through serial numbers and records of manufacturing, Lane also found evidence that Priscilla Hiss' typewriter had been in use in her father's real estate office in 1929—before the Woodstock in evidence in the courtroom had been built. The evidence led Lane to the conclusion that the FBI had known at the time of the trial that the typewriter put in evidence was manufactured two years after Priscilla's machine was bought by her father.

Appeal Effort Fail

Lane collected the affidavits resulting from his efforts and, arguing they provided sufficient new evidence to justify a new trial, appeared before Judge Goddard on June 4, 1952. The judge denied Lane's motion for a new trial. Lane appealed to the U.S. Court of Appeals, but the judge's opinion was affirmed. The Hiss attorneys then petitioned the U.S. Supreme Court for a writ of *certiorari,* or review of the lower courts' rulings. The petition was denied.

Alger Hiss served three years and eight months of his five-year sentence. After his release, he wrote a book about the trial, worked as a salesman for a stationery printer, and, after five years, separated (but was never divorced) from Priscilla Hiss. In 1976, the Massachusetts Bar, from which he had been automatically disbarred when convicted, readmitted him and he began work as a legal consultant.

In 1973, during the Watergate hearings, former Presidential Counsel John Dean told how President Nixon said to Charles Colson, "The typewriters are always the key. . . . We built one in the Hiss case."

At the age of 87, in 1992, Hiss asked General Dmitri A. Volkogonov, chairman of the Russian Government's military intelligence archives, to inspect all Soviet files pertaining to him, his case, and Whittaker Chambers. "Not a single document, and a great amount of materials have been studied, substantiates the allegation that Mr. A. Hiss collaborated with the intelligence services of the Soviet Union," the general reported several months later. He said the accusations were "completely groundless." Volkogonov later backed off a bit from this statement, saying that although there was no evidence in the KGB files, he couldn't speak for other Soviet intelligence agencies. He also added that many KGB documents had been destroyed over the years.

Hiss defenders still regarded Volkogonov's earlier statements as vindication of his innocence. However, in 1996, the National Security Agency released hundreds of pages of declassified material including a reference to a Soviet spy who had been working in the United States during World War II. A cable dated March 30, 1945, said the spy's code name was "Ales" and that he was "probably Alger Hiss." But the cable provided no other information to support this statement.

Alger Hiss died in 1996, asserting his innocence to the end.

—Bernard Ryan, Jr. and Ron Formica

Suggestions for Further Reading

Brodie, Fawn M. "I Think Hiss Is Lying." *American Heritage* (August 1981): 4–21.

Buckley, William F. "Well, What Do You Know?" *National Review* (November 19, 1990) 60.

Chambers, Whittaker. *Witness.* New York: Random House, 1952.

Cook, Fred J. *The Unfinished Story of Alger Hiss.* New York: William Morrow Co., 1958.

Cooke, Alistair. *A Generation on Trial.* New York: Alfred A. Knopf, 1950.

de Toledano, Ralph, and Victor Lasky. *Seeds of Treason.* Chicago: Regnery, 1962.

Hiss, Alger. *In the Court of Public Opinion.* New York: Alfred A. Knopf, 1957.

——. *Recollections of a Life.* New York: Seaver Books/Henry Holt, 1988.

Hiss, Tony. "My Father's Honor." *The New Yorker* (November 16, 1992): 100–106.

Jowitt, William Allen. *The Strange Case of Alger Hiss.* New York: Doubleday & Co., 1953.

Levitt, Morton, and Michael Levitt. *A Tissue of Lies Nixon vs. Hiss.* New York: McGraw-Hill, 1979.

Nixon, Richard M. *Six Crises.* New York: Doubleday Co., 1962.

Smith, Chabot. *Alger Hiss: The True Story.* New York: Holt, Rinehart and Winston, 1976.

Tanenhaus, Sam. "The Hiss Case Isn't Over Yet." *New York Times* (October 31, 1992): 21.

Tiger, Edith, ed. *In Re Alger Hiss.* New York: Hill and Wang, 1979.

Tyrell, R.E. "You Must Remember Hiss." *The American Spectator* (January 1991): 10.

Ward, G.C. "Unregretfully, Alger Hiss." *American Heritage* (November 1988): 18.

Weinstein, Allen. *Perjury: The Hiss-Chambers Case.* New York: Alfred A. Knopf, 1978.

Martha Beck Trial: 1949

Defendants: Martha Beck and Raymond Fernandez
Crime Charged: Murder **Chief Defense Lawyers:** John H. Minton and Herbert E. Rosenberg **Chief Prosecutors:** Edward F. Breslin, James W. Gehrig, and Edward Robinson, Jr. **Judge:** Ferdinand Pecora **Place:** New York, New York **Dates of Trial:** June 9–August 18, 1949 **Verdict:** Guilty
Sentence: Death by electrocution

SIGNIFICANCE

This notorious "lonely hearts murders" case, in which the bizarre defendants were tried for just one of some 20 murders committed over only two years, found the defendants pleading insanity. The jury, however, proved that it clearly understood the difference between the abnormal and the insane.

At 26, Martha Beck weighed 300 pounds. She had been married and divorced twice. A registered nurse, she had become superintendent of the Pensacola Crippled Children's Home in Florida. In 1947, answering an advertisement in a true-romance magazine, she spent five dollars to buy, through the mail, a membership in Mother Dinene's Friendly Club for Lonely Hearts.

A romantic letter came from one Raymond Fernandez of New York. She replied. Letters flew. Soon Fernandez stepped off a bus in Pensacola into Beck's arms and the couple began a two-day orgy. He was the Latin lover of her dreams.

After two days, however, Raymond had learned what was to him the most important fact about Beck: she had no money. He headed back to New York, where he wrote a "Dear Martha" letter that told her he just didn't love her after all.

Meantime, the overseers of the Crippled Children's Home fired Beck. She went straight to Fernandez's New York apartment and moved in. She soon discovered the nature of his business: he answered lonely-hearts ads, seduced well-to-do widows and spinsters, fleeced them of their savings, and disappeared. Undaunted, Beck proposed a partnership. She would play the role of his sister, helping to build the confidence of intended victims, but with a more sinister result than Fernandez had practiced. Rather than disappearing themselves, they would make their victims disappear.

Partnership Thrives

Time and again, lonely women naively handed their bankbooks, their jewelry, and ultimately their lives to the charming romantic who answered their lonely-hearts ads and turned up with his helpful "sister." Late in 1948, 66-year-old widow Janet Fay of Albany, New York, welcomed them, following an emotional and hopeful correspondence. By early January, she had turned over $4,000 in savings and cash, as well as jewelry and bonds, to Fernandez. Beck then skillfully packed the widow's possessions into a large trunk stolen from the most recent victim, and the three moved into a rented apartment in Valley Stream on Long Island. There Beck bashed Fay's skull with a hammer.

The murderers rented another house, buried the body in the cellar, covered it with a fresh cement floor, waited four days for the cement to harden, and departed for Grand Rapids, Michigan, and their next victim, who had already swallowed Fernandez's romance-by-mail bait and was on the hook. Soon the brother-sister act was ensconced in the home of Delphine Downing, a 41-year-old widow with a 2-year-old daughter. Wedding plans were made. But Delphine inadvertently came upon Fernandez without his toupee. Disillusioned, she rebelled: "Why, you're bald!" He shot her. Beck drowned the child in the bathtub. In the cellar, Fernandez dug a hole large enough for both bodies and poured fresh concrete.

The cement had not cured before the police, called by suspicious neighbors when they had not seen the mother and daughter for a couple of days, were at the door. Almost simultaneously, Fay's stepdaughter, unable to find her, had alerted New York police, who found the grave under the new cement floor and traced Fernandez and Beck to Michigan and the Downing home. A search of Fernandez revealed a notebook with the names of some 20 missing women.

As the couple confessed both the Fay and Downing murders, America, titillated by the image of the torrid Latin and the super-passionate fat lady, devoured the bizarre story. Spine-chilling news reports depicted the horror not only of the murders but of Martha Beck's tough, take-charge command of the weird operation.

Because New York had the death penalty for murder while Michigan did not, the two were extradited and tried for the murder of Fay.

The Kiss in the Courtroom

Opening June 9, 1949, the trial produced a torrent of sensational testimony as both defendants, apparently eager to prove their lack of sanity, burned the jurors' ears with lengthy streams of obscenity that described the intensity of their love life. What the court stenographers recorded could not be printed even by New York City's most torrid press. But the news reporters could describe how, when called to the witness stand, Martha Beck strode forward in bright green shoes, her massive body swathed in bright silks, a double-strand necklace clinking brightly, and suddenly detoured across the courtroom to Fernandez. Catching his face in her hefty hands, she pulled it toward her, kissing him on the mouth and, as the guards pulled her away, leaving him with a grin of bright red lipstick.

Following prosecutor Edward Breslin's straightforward presentation of the blood-curdling facts, the defense set out to prove insanity. Beck testified to four attempts to commit suicide, said her mind was a blank on the actual killings, and denied trying to shield Fernandez. A psychiatrist declared her mentally unsound and said that, even if she participated in the killing, she had no idea what she was doing. Defense attorney Herbert Rosenberg, contending that Beck had killed Fay in a fit of insanity inspired by jealousy, tried to prove that Fernandez had no part in the crime.

Charging the jury, Judge Ferdinand Pecora, referring to acts of perversion admitted by the defendants, said, "That kind of abnormality does not, in and of itself, constitute the kind of insanity which will excuse a person of a criminal act."

After debating for 12½ hours, the jury convicted Martha Beck and Raymond Fernandez of first-degree murder. The death sentence was mandatory. The New York State Court of Appeals denied the pair a new trial. Governor Thomas E. Dewey turned down a plea for clemency. The U.S. Supreme Court refused to review the case. Fernandez, claiming he received cruel treatment in Sing Sing Prison, was denied a *habeas corpus* order.

On March 8, 1951, the lonely-hearts murderers—Fernandez first, then Beck—died in the electric chair in Sing Sing.

—*Bernard Ryan, Jr.*

Suggestions for Further Reading

Brown, Wenzel. *Introduction to Murder: The Unpublished Facts Behind the Notorious Lonely Hearts Killers, Martha Beck and Raymond Fernandez.* New York: Greenberg, 1952.

Jones, Richard Glyn. *Killer Couples.* Secaucus, N.J.: Lyle Stuart, 1987.

Sifakis, Carl. *The Encyclopedia of American Crime.* New York: Facts On File, 1982.

Wilson, Colin. *A Criminal History of Mankind.* New York: G.P. Putnam's Sons, 1984.

Ruth Ann Steinhagen Trial: 1949

Defendant: Ruth Ann Steinhagen **Crime Charged:** Assault with intent to commit murder **Chief Defense Lawyer:** George Bieber **Chief Prosecutor:** John S. Boyle **Judge:** James J. McDermott **Place:** Chicago, Illinois **Date of Trial:** June 30, 1949 **Verdict:** Not guilty by reason of insanity

SIGNIFICANCE

The near-murder of Eddie Waitkus, star first baseman of the Philadelphia Phillies, was one of the first sensational examples of what came to be called "stalker" crimes. Waitkus, 29, a World War II veteran of the New Guinea campaign, was almost killed by a love-sick teenage girl. After fewer than three years in a mental hospital, the girl, Ruth Ann Steinhagen, was pronounced cured. Waitkus did not want her prosecuted, and she was released. The result contrasts with the results of most other high-profile crimes where prosecutors seem determined that somebody be punished, regardless of the circumstances. And it did establish that a murderous sort of schizophrenia can be cured.

To Eddie Waitkus, a heavy-hitting first baseman recently traded to the Philadelphia Phillies by the Chicago Cubs, this road trip to Chicago was something like a homecoming. When he returned to his hotel, the night of June 14, 1949, he found a note in his room box.

"It is extremely important that I see you as soon as possible," the note read. "We're not acquainted, but I have something of importance to speak to you about. I think it would be to your advantage to let me explain this to you as I am leaving the hotel the day after tomorrow. I realize this is out of the ordinary, but as I say, it is extremely important."

Thinking the note might be from a friend of a friend, Waitkus called the room listed on the note. A young woman answered and asked him to give her a half-hour so she could get dressed. About 11:30, he knocked on the door. A tall, pretty brunette opened the door. She asked him to come in. She was "very businesslike," he remembered, completely deadpan. He walked over to a chair and asked her what she wanted. When he turned around, she was holding a rifle.

"You're not going to bother me any more," she said. Before he could reply, she shot him. With Waitkus lying on the floor with a hole in his chest, the girl laid down her .22 caliber rifle and called the hotel desk.

"I just shot a man," she said.

"I Just Had to Shoot Somebody"

Medics and police arrived. They took Waitkus to the hospital, where doctors gave him a 50-50 chance to live. They took his assailant, Ruth Ann Steinhagen, a 19-year-old typist, to jail. "I just had to shoot somebody," Steinhagen said by way of explanation. Interviewed at the Cook County jail, she told reporters, "I've never been so happy in my life." She said she liked Waitkus "best of anybody in the world," although she had never met him, that she had dreamed of him and prayed for him during the night. She said she had brought a knife and the rifle to her hotel room. She planned to stab Waitkus as soon as he entered and then shoot herself. The baseball player entered the room too briskly for her to use the knife so she shot him. She decided not to shoot herself.

"Near Miraculous" Recovery

Surgeons at the Illinois Masonic Hospital operated on Waitkus to remove clotted blood from his collapsed lung. The next day, they said his recovery was "little short of miraculous." The bullet had passed under his heart and lodged in his back near the spine. Waitkus was able to talk with reporters. He said when he saw the rifle, he thought it was some kind of practical joke. He expected fellow ball players to suddenly appear and tell him they had put the girl up to the scene.

The doctors said he would soon be out of the hospital. They were too optimistic. They had to perform a second operation on his lung. Then the bullet still in his body started an infection and had to be removed in a third operation. Every couple of days the doctors announced that the Phillies star would soon be home. But he stayed inside. He was to attend the Steinhagen arraignment and then go home. He came to court in a wheelchair. Then he went back to the hospital.

On June 30, Ruth Ann Steinhagen was arraigned for assault with intent to commit murder. Judge Matthew P. Hartigan set bail at $50,000. A grand jury indicted Steinhagen. A criminal court adjudged her insane. And Judge James J. McDermott committed her to the state hospital. It all happened in three hours. Her parents, Mr. and Mrs. Walter Steinhagen of Chicago, asked that she be "sent to an institution without delay."

Obsession at First Sight

The Steinhagens said that their daughter's troubles began three years before when she went to a baseball game. "Waitkus was playing for the Cubs then. She seemed to become infatuated and couldn't talk about anything else. She had his pictures everywhere."

They said she had a nervous breakdown in December 1948. "We sent her to a psychiatrist," Mrs. Steinhagen said, "but she just seemed to get worse. She wanted to commit suicide. I was glad when they traded Waitkus to Philadelphia. I thought that would help, but it didn't."

Ruth Steinhagen seemed to enjoy the arraignment and trial. She posed for photographers and chatted gaily with the bailiff. She told a psychiatrist that she shot Waitkus because "I didn't want to be nervous all my life."

Waitkus slowly recovered. He finally left the hospital a month after the shooting. While he was recuperating at home, the Phillies filed a request to the Pennsylvania Workmen's Compensation Board to settle a dispute with an insurance company over benefits paid to Waitkus. The insurance company claimed that Waitkus was "not at work" when he went to Steinhagen's room. The Phillies claimed that Waitkus was under club surveillance while at the hotel and that ball players had a duty not to "high hat" fans. A referee appointed by the board agreed with the Phillies, but the insurance company appealed.

A little more than a year after the shooting, the state hospital reported that Steinhagen had improved remarkably. She was responding to electric shock therapy and medication. On April 17, 1952, Ruth Steinhagen was adjudged sane. Edwin T. Breen, first assistant state's attorney, said Waitkus did not wish to prosecute her. The attempted murder charge was dropped. Steinhagen said she wanted to stay at the state hospital, but as a physical therapist, not an inmate.

The Workmen's Compensation Board reversed the referee's decision on Waitkus's benefits. It said, "it is evident that his visit . . . was a private enterprise in which he voluntarily engaged for personal reasons and not in the course of his employment or in the furtherance of the business of his employer."

—William Weir

Suggestions for Further Reading

New York Times. See Steinhagen, Ruth in the *New York Times Index,* June 16–21, 28–29, 1949; July 1–3, 8, 10, 12, 1949; October 28, 1949; August 8, 1950; September 14, 1950; April 18. 1952; May 16, 1952.

Tokyo Rose Trial: 1949

Defendant: Iva Ikuko Toguri ("Tokyo Rose") **Crime Charged:** Treason **Chief Defense Lawyers:** Wayne M. Collins, George Olshausen, and Theodore Tamba **Chief Prosecutors:** Thomas DeWolfe, Frank J. Hennessy, John Hogan, and James Knapp **Judge:** Michael J. Roche **Place:** San Francisco, California **Dates of Trial:** July 5–September 29, 1949 **Verdict:** Guilty **Sentence:** 10 years in prison and a $10,000 fine

SIGNIFICANCE

The Tokyo Rose trial was one of only seven American treason trials following World War II.

Iva Ikuko Toguri, the woman who would be labeled "Tokyo Rose" and a traitor to the United States, ironically was born on Independence Day, 1916 in Los Angeles, California. Her parents had migrated from Japan to California, and Toguri grew up as an American. In July 1941, now 25 years old, Toguri went to Japan for the first time to visit a sick aunt. Toguri stayed with relatives for several months, attending to her sick aunt, and she was left stranded in Japan when war broke out December 7, 1941, with the bombing of Pearl Harbor.

Toguri was hard-pressed to earn a living in wartime Japan, where food and shelter were both expensive and scarce, and her only skill was her mastery of English. She worked as a typist for several news agencies and foreign legations before getting a job with Radio Tokyo. In November 1943, Toguri was forced to become one of the several female radio announcers for Radio Tokyo. Although Radio Tokyo broadcasts were made from many different locations throughout the Japanese Empire, which at its height covered much of eastern Asia, the female broadcasters were collectively termed "Tokyo Rose" by American GIs. Toguri never used that name, and her broadcasts were limited to playing popular American music, with a smattering of pro-Japanese propaganda written for her by her supervisors.

Toguri Tried for Treason

Toguri was only one of an estimated 10,000 Japanese-Americans trapped in Japan during World War II and forced to cope with the circumstances of war. She, however, was one of the few singled out for punishment by the American authorities. She was arrested in occupied Japan on October 17, 1945, released on October 25, 1946, when the Justice Department expressed doubts on the charge of treason against her, but re-arrested on August 28, 1948, in Tokyo. She was brought back to the United States to stand trial in San Francisco, California.

Tokyo Rose is being escorted in the federal building in San Francisco by U.S. Deputy Marshal Herbert Cole just before the court found her guilty of treason. (AP/Wide World Photos)

In the anti-Japanese climate of post-war California, Toguri had to struggle to find lawyers to represent her, but finally Wayne M. Collins, George Olshausen, and Theodore Tamba agreed to take her case for free. The prosecutors were Thomas DeWolfe, Frank J. Hennessy, John Hogan, and James Knapp. The trial began on July 5, 1949 with Judge Michael J. Roche presiding.

Before an all-white jury, Toguri pleaded innocent to the eight treason charges against her. Despite Roche's bias in favor of the prosecution and the prevailing public sentiment against Toguri, the trial lasted for nearly three months and the jury was deadlocked. When the jury reported that it was unable to reach a verdict, Roche ordered them to continue deliberating until they had made a decision. Nine of the 12 jurors were willing to vote for a guilty verdict, and after some, time the three holdouts were cajoled to capitulate to the majority decision. One of the holdouts who reluctantly acquiesced in the guilty verdict was the jury foreman, John Mann:

> She was such an inoffensive little thing . . . . I think I know how she felt because I felt the same way when I was cut off from everybody. You ask the judge a question and he reprimands you. He definitely tells you you're out of order. The count is nine to three against you. I couldn't help feeling the isolation she must have felt in Japan.

On September 29, 1949, the jury returned a guilty verdict against Iva Ikuko Toguri. She was sentenced to 10 years in prison and a $10,000 fine. After serving just over six years in a federal women's prison in West Virginia, Toguri was released early for good behavior. On January 18, 1977, and after decades of debate over the fairness of her trial, President Gerald Ford pardoned Toguri. Toguri was thus officially exonerated, and her U.S. citizenship was finally restored. Toguri's trial was one of only seven American treason trials following World War II.

—*Stephen G. Christianson*

Suggestions for Further Reading

Arbus, Diane. "The Victimization of Tokyo Rose." *Esquire* (June 1983): 88–89.

Duus, Masayo. *Tokyo Rose, Orphan of the Pacific.* New York: Harper & Row, 1979.

Gunn, Rex B. *They Called Her Tokyo Rose.* Santa Monica, Calif.: Gunn, 1977.

Japanese American Citizens' League. *Iva Toguri (d'Aquino): Victim of a Legend.* San Francisco: National Committee for Iva Toguri, Japanese American Citizens' League, 1976.